A CELEBRATION OF OLIVES

The Olive Farm

The Olive Season

A CELEBRATION OF OLIVES

The Olive Farm

The Olive Season

Carol Drinkwater

LITTLE, BROWN

A *Little, Brown* Book

This omnibus edition first published in Great Britain
by Little, Brown in 2004
A Celebration of Olives Copyright © Carol Drinkwater 2004

Previously published separately:
The Olive Farm first published in Great Britain by Little, Brown in 2001
Published by Abacus in 2001
Reprinted 2001 (seven times), 2002 (twice), 2003 (three times)
Copyright © Carol Drinkwater 2001

The Olive Season first published in Great Britain by Little, Brown in 2003
Published by Abacus in 2003
Reprinted 2003 (three times)
Copyright © Carol Drinkwater 2003

Quotation from The Songlines *by Bruce Chatwin, published by Jonathan
Cape, reprinted by permission of The Random House Group Ltd.*

The moral right of the author has been asserted.

A CIP catalogue record for this book
is available from the British Library.

ISBN 0 316 72803 9

Typeset in Sabon by M Rules
Printed and bound in Great Britain by Clays Ltd, St Ives plc

Little, Brown
An imprint of
Time Warner Book Group UK
Brettenham House
Lancaster Place
London WC2E 7EN

www.twbg.co.uk

THE
Olive
Farm

A c k n o w l e d g e m e n t s

This book would never have existed without Michel. So it is to him that I first say thank you: for his encouragement, generosity and expansive love. Special thanks also to our families and the friends who inhabit these pages.

I am also extremely grateful to my agent and friend, Sophie Hicks, to Maggie Phillips, Hitesh Shah and Grainne Fox, all of whom help smooth the bumps in the running of my professional life, and to old pals Chris Brown and Bridget Anderson, who are always there in hours of need.

My profound gratitude to a great team at Little, Brown in the UK, among them Caroline North for supportive editing and, most especially, to Alan Samson for buying the book and offering me inspirational notes and guidance.

Contents

For Michel, who made me the believer in impossible things.

A girl can't go far without her mother.

For Michel, who lives life through colours richly.
A private story told out loud.
Je t'aime.

'Too much of a good thing can be wonderful.'

Mae West

'Southwards into a sunburnt otherwhere . . .'

W.H. Auden

Preface

The girls stare in dusty dismay.

'Is this the wonderful surprise, Papa?' asks Vanessa.

Michel nods.

Papa had promised them a villa with a swimming pool. Unfortunately, in his enthusiasm, Michel has omitted to mention that the pool is dry as a bone. Worse, not only is the interior cracked, chipping and devoid of one drop of water, but its faded blue walls and a fair portion of the base are overgrown with thickly entwined skeins of ivy.

'I need a swim!' wails Clarisse.

'We'll cut back the ivy tomorrow and fill it on Sunday, I promise.'

I overhear this pledge as I stagger past with armfuls of cardboard boxes laden with ancient and practically useless kitchenware exhumed from the cluttered cupboards of my London flat. Michel's promise, if given casually, is not without good intention, but a doubt whispering in my ear tells me he may live to regret it. Suppose we discover the pool leaks? I choose not to voice this within earshot. In any case, my doubts are probably nothing more than the negativity born of a sleepless night.

We drove through most of the night to avoid the worst of the holiday traffic which throughout yesterday jammed the main arterial roads to standstill. At around 8.30 in the evening we approached the outskirts of Lyon only to discover that the *péage* had become a holiday resort in itself. The delay to pass through it was announced as two hours. So, the French, in true French fashion, were grabbing the opportunity to attack a spot of dinner which, of course, delayed matters further.

It was a colourful and fascinating spectacle. A tailback of vehicles many miles long, peppered with families and pets seated on camping stools alongside their cars (the less organised spread out picnic blankets on the motorway surface), all eating three-course meals and drinking copious amounts of booze. Aside from our general frustration, I found it highly entertaining. Strolling alongside several miles of the queue, I witnessed vehicle-owners offering *dégustations* of their regional wine to fellow travellers, morsels of succulent dishes whipped up at the roadside, wobbling and brightly coloured desserts passed on spoons up and down the traffic line, snippets of advice on the fine-tuning of an otherwise well-known recipe, and, to round it all off, hands of cards accompanied by after-dinner coffee followed, in one or two instances, by a glass of calvados. What a knack the French have for turning any event into an opportunity to relish the finer points of eating.

By the time the jam was unjammed, I observed families who had become the firmest of buddies with other roadside families exchanging addresses in the way some folk do when they've spent a week or two together at the same resort.

Once through the city of Lyon, we kept going, stopping only for a brief nap in a roadside parking area, where poor Michel had to grab some sleep with fat Pamela attached to his ankle by her lead to stop her attempting an escape. And then we pressed on again before dawn, breakfasting outside Fréjus. There, half the local population were already gathered in bars enjoying their first cognac of the day.

Now, having safely arrived, after sixteen hours of such travelling, Pamela, finally released from her confined space, is huffing at my side. Why has this infernal creature taken such a shine to me? 'The dog needs a drink!' I call. No one takes any notice.

'So, we'll have a pool in two days?' Vanessa is always the more punctilious of the two girls.

Michel nods and embraces both daughters, an arm wrapped around each. 'Well, do you like it here? The house and all the grounds? I know it needs a lot of work, but the sun is shining and it's very hot . . .' The final phrase of his sentence melts away in the midday swelter while the girls stare up at him as though he has singlehandedly created a galaxy of suns. After their initial disappointment they seem happy enough, and I am mightily relieved.

I find an outdoor tap alongside the garage and cast about for a saucer or bowl, to give this dribbling mutt some water. I spy a bright yellow, dirt-encrusted plastic utensil – it looks like the cup from a lost Thermos – lying among the weeds at the foot of one of the cedar trees and I hurry to fetch it. Pamela puffs and waddles along beside me. She seems about ready to collapse. I return to the tap.

By now, Michel and the girls are dragging the mattresses, twisted out of all recognition, from the boot of my VW. Two single mattresses for four of us. In this heat. Are we insane?

'Where shall we put these?' he shouts across to me.

'You decide.' I am busy battling with the wretched tap, which is locked rigid. 'Must be a while since anyone used this,' I mutter, but no one is listening to me. Not even Pamela. She is lying on her side in the shade of twelve tall cedars which form a semi-circle round the parking area, where there is cool, loose earth; a beached whale snoring contentedly.

I turn the tap so hard it almost comes away from the wall. A small green lizard darts out from a fissure in the stucco and, sensing unwelcome visitors, slithers off, disappearing into an otherwhere. Perspiration breaks out all over my face. I can feel the flush. I am giddy with the effort and now it is I who needs the drink. Pamela has long since forgotten her thirst.

Eventually the tap begins to shift, making horrendous squeaking noises as it does so. 'A drop of oil,' I tell myself, beginning a mental 'to do' list which is destined to become longer than life. The ancient faucet turns and turns but still no water flows. 'This tap is not functioning properly, or . . .' But there is no one in sight to hear my concern. I decide to try another.

Upstairs, indoors, the villa is cool and insect-infested. The blinding, dry heat outside emphasises the musty and crepuscular damp within. The smell reminds me of compulsory childhood visits to elderly relatives living alone in unaired spaces.

The mosquito netting, curling away from the windows as though it were fighting to get out into the light, creates blocks of shadows and gives a sombre, prison-like feel to the main living room. Shafts of sunlight cut angular patterns on the floor's terracotta tiles, spotlighting the years of gathering dust and mouldering miniature reptile life. Michel is standing with *les filles*, who are looking about them in horror and disgust.

'*C'est dégueulasse, Papa!*' I cannot avoid noticing Vanessa's battle to keep her tears at bay.

'We'll clean it up,' he encourages, with dwindling enthusiasm.

'Before or after we've attacked the pool?' snaps one of them and stomps outside in a sulk.

'*Chérie!*'

'Michel?' I hardly dare begin, knowing this is a rotten moment to impart such drastic news.

'*Oui*? Go after your sister,' he instructs the remaining daughter.

'I've got a sneaking suspicion . . .'

'What?' he looks frazzled, ready to give up. The drive from Paris, in a baking car packed to the gills with luggage and livestock (Pamela) on roads frying with exhaust fumes and August weather, has been interminable. None of us has slept properly. Nerves are frayed. Even the insistent chirring of the cicadas, a sound I usually find romantic and exotic, is enough to make me want to scream.

Suddenly, I see all this not through the eyes of love emboldened, setting sail on an adventure, but from the children's point of view. This is their summer holiday. I am not their mother. They barely know me. It has been a while since they have spent time with their father and the place to which he has brought them belongs (or will do) to him and this other woman, who is not even fluent in their mother tongue. On top of which, the villa is uninhabitable and we have no money left to put it right.

'The girls are disappointed,' he confides. I hear the weariness and regret in his voice as I struggle not to cast myself in the role of the outsider.

'Michel, I know this is not a great moment, but—'

'Perhaps it was a mistake to bring them here. It was our dream, after all.'

Was? I find myself thinking but refrain – just – from voicing it.

'Michel?'

'What?'

'There's no water.'

'What?'

'No water.'

'Well, you haven't turned it on at the mains!' he snaps and, calling after his daughters, he follows them out on to the terrace. I stay where I am, amid the dust motes and shadows. Through tall French windows I watch them: two slender girls gesticulating angrily at their rangy, handsome father while he attempts to quieten and reassure them. I leave them to it and return to the unloading of the car.

When the girls are less upset and Michel is less harassed, he comes looking for me. 'Is the garage locked?'

'I haven't unlocked it,' I reply, engaged in the business of trying to repair the broom. Beneath heavy boxes in the boot, head and handle have been separated.

'The switch for the water is probably in there.'

He disappears into the garage and finds a tap, which he opens, but there is still no water. He wanders off in silence to pour a glass of wine and figure it out. I return inside the house. 'The water must be fed from an external tank which has dried up,' he says when he comes back.

'Fed from where?'

'Not sure. Once I find the tank, I'll be able to tell you. Madame B. said something about a well. I thought she was referring to a secondary source, but perhaps not. Girls all right?'

I nod. 'They've gone investigating.'

'Good. You're not to worry about them. They'll settle. They love it here. Really.'

Our eyes meet fleetingly, looking into one another's. These last couple of days have been hectic and have left no room for us. I am bustling about the living room with the broom, trying to lift at least the top layers of dirt off the earthenware *tommette* tiles, fearing that if I stop Michel will read my hurt. I don't want to discuss it; I know it will pass because it's stupid.

We are all tired and unhinged. But he approaches me and fondles my neck, strokes my hair. I concentrate on the task in hand but the dust just rises and resettles centimetres from where I have swept. I am wasting my time. The whole house needs a damn good scrub with lashings of hot, soapy water.

'*Je t'aime*,' he says. 'Please don't forget that.' Then he hurries away.

How did we get into this? I am thinking.

All my life, I have dreamed of acquiring a crumbling, shabby-chic house overlooking the sea. In my mind's eye, I have pictured a corner of paradise where friends can gather to swim, relax, debate, talk business if they care to, eat fresh fruits picked directly from the garden and great steaming plates of food served from an al fresco kitchen and dished up on to a candlelit table the length of a railway sleeper. A Utopia where liquor and honey flow freely and guests eat heartily, drink gallons of home-produced wine, chill out to the dulcet chords of evergreen jazz and while away star-spangled hours till dawn. I envisage a haven where city manners and constraints can be cast off and where artists, travellers, children, lovers and extended family can intermingle and find contentment. And, in among all of these gregarious and bohemian activities, I slip away unnoticed to a cool stone room of my own, lined head to foot with books, sprawling maps and dictionaries, switch on my computer and settle down peacefully to write.

Yes, it is me and my crazy chimeras who have got us into this.

Still, who has not idled away a wet winter's afternoon or three with such a dream?

A p p a s s i o n a t a

Four months earlier

'Shall we look inside?' suggests Michel, climbing the stairway
to the main entrance, which is situated on the north-west side
of the upper terrace. The estate agent, M. Charpy, confesses
that he does not have a key.

'No key?'

It is only now that he owns up to the fact that he is not actually handling the sale but, he swiftly assures us, if we are
genuinely interested, he will be able to *faire le nécessaire*.

We are in the south of France, gazing at the not-so-distant
Mediterranean, falling in love with an abandoned olive farm.
The property, once stylish and now little better than a ruin, is
for sale with ten acres of land.

Once upon a time, M. Charpy tell us, it was a residence of
haut standing. With it came land as far as the eye could see in
every direction. He swings his arms this way and that. I stare at

him incredulously. He shrugs. 'Well, certainly that valley in front of us, and the woods to the right but, *hélas*' – he shrugs again – 'most of the terrain was sold off.'

'When?'

'Years ago.'

I wonder why, for nothing else has been constructed. The villa still stands alone on its hillside, and the magnificent terraced olive groves Charpy promised us have become a jungle of hungry weeds.

'An olive farm with vineyard and swimming pool,' he insists.

We stare at the pool. It looks like an oversized, discarded sink. Dotted here and there are various blossoming fruit trees and some very fine Italian cedars, but there's no sign of any vineyard. There are, however, two cottages included in the purchase price. The gatekeeper's house, at the very foot of the hill, is firmly locked and shuttered but, even from the outside, it is plain that it needs major restoration. The other cottage, where the gardener or vine-tender would have lived, has been swallowed up by rampant growth. As far as we can tell, for we cannot get within 200 metres of it, all that remains is one jagged, stone wall.

'The villa was built in 1904 and was used as a summer residence by a wealthy Italian family. They christened it "Appassionata".' I smile. Appassionata is a musical term meaning 'with passion'.

'*Les pieds dans l'eau*,' continues Charpy.

Yes, it is ten minutes by car to the sea. From the numerous terraces, the bay of Cannes, where the two Îles de Lérins lie in the water like lizards sleeping in the sun, is within tantalisingly easy reach.

To the rear of the house is a pine forest. Most of the other shrubs and trees are unknown to me; those that are not dead, that is. Michel asks whether it was drought that killed off the little orange grove and the almond tree, now an inverted broomstick of dead twigs in front of a tumbledown garage.

'*Je ne crois pas,*' says M. Charpy. 'They caught cold. Our last winter was harsh. It broke records.' He stares glumly at four bougainvillaea bushes which once straddled the front pillars of the house. Now they are lying across the veranda like drunks in a stupor. '*Aussi,* the place has been empty for four years. Before that, it was rented to a foreign woman who bred dogs. *Evidemment,* she cared nothing for her surroundings.'

The years of neglect, aided by the recent freak weather, have certainly put paid to Appassionata's former glory. Still, I am drawn to it, to its faded elegance. It remains graceful. There is beauty here. And history. Even the gnarled and twisted olive trees look as though they have stood witness on this hillside for a thousand years.

'The *propriétaire* will be glad to get shot of the place. I can arrange a good price.' Charpy's offer is disdainfully made. To his way of thinking, any sum paid for such dereliction would be scandalous.

I close my eyes and picture us in future summers strolling paths we will discover beneath this jungle of vegetation. Michel, at my side, is surveying the façade. The baked vanilla paint flakes to the touch. 'Why don't we try to find a way in?' He disappears on a lap of the house, tapping at windows, rattling doors.

Charpy, ruffled, sets off after him. I hang back, smiling. Michel and I have known each other only a few months but already I have learned that he is not one to be defeated by such a minor detail as the lack of a key.

The land is not fenced. There is no gate, and the boundaries are not staked. There is nothing to secure the property, to keep hunters or trespassers at bay. There are broken windows everywhere.

'Come and look here,' Michel calls from round the back. He,

with his more practised eye, points out the remains of a makeshift vegetable garden.

'Squatters. Been and gone in the not-too-distant past. The locks on all three doors have been forced. It should be relatively easy to get in. Monsieur Charpy, *s'il vous plaît*.'

And so we look on while the preposterously arrogant M. Charpy totters back and forth, thrusting his pristine Armani suit against the solid wood door.

Once inside, we are moving through a sea of cobwebs. Everywhere reeks. A deep, musty stench that takes your breath away. Walls hang with perished wiring. The rooms are high-ceilinged, sonorous spaces. Strips of wallpaper curl to the floor like weeping silhouettes. Tiny, shrivelled reptiles crunch under-foot. Such decay. We tread slowly, pausing, turning this way and that, drinking in the place. Rip away all the curling and rusted mosquito netting fixed across the windows and the rooms would be blissfully light. They are well proportioned, nothing elaborate. Corridors, hidden corners, huge rust-stained baths in cavernous bathrooms. In the main *salon*, there is a generous oak-beamed fireplace. There is an ambience. A *chaleur*.

As our voices and footsteps reverberate, I feel the rumble of lives lived here. Tugging at the netting, pulling it aside, grazing a finger in the process, I gaze out at eloquent views over land and sea, and mountains to the west. Sun-drenched summers by the Mediterranean. Appassionata. Yes. I am seized.

Charpy watches impatiently, fussing at the sleeves and shoul-ders of his jacket, while we open doors, shove at long-forgotten cupboards, run our fingers through layers of dust and disint-egrating insects and flick or turn switches and taps, none of which work. He does not comprehend our enthusiasm. '*Beaucoup de travail*,' he pronounces.

Back outside, the late-morning sun is warm and inviting. I glance at Michel and, without a word spoken, his eyes tell me he sees what I see: a wild yet enticing site. Still, even if we could scrape together the asking price, the funds needed to restore it would make it an act of insanity.

We head for a bar Michel frequents in the old port of Cannes. The *patron* strolls over to greet him. They shake hands. '*Bon festival?*' he asks. Michel nods, and the *patron* nods in response. The conversation seems complete until Michel takes me by the arm and introduces me. My future wife, he says. '*Mais félicitations! Félicitations!*' The *patron* shakes our hands vigorously and offers us a drink on the house. We install ourselves at one of the tables on the street and I feel the heat of the midday sun beating against my face.

Although it is only late April, there are already many foreigners bustling to and fro, laden with shopping bags. Several wave to Michel, calling out the same enquiry as the *patron*. '*Bon festival?*' He nods in reply. Occasionally, he rises to shake someone's hand or, in French fashion, lightly kiss somebody's cheeks. Mostly these fleeting encounters are with executive types in sharply cut blazers, lightweight slacks, soft Italian leather loafers. They talk of business. It is the closing day of the spring television festival which precedes the internationally famous Cannes Film Festival. Both events are dominated by the markets which run alongside them. The world of television, the filming of it rather than the selling of it, seems to me a million miles removed from these markets. I marvel at how Michel can survive in such a milieu, and am reminded again of how much we have yet to learn about one another.

A lithe waiter zips by with our glasses of Côte de Provence rosé. These are accompanied by porcelain saucers filled with olives, slices of deep pink *saucisson* and crisps. He deposits the dishes on our table and departs without a word. We clink glasses and sip our wine, silent, lost in our morning's visit. Both musing upon our find, buried aloft in the pine-scented hills way above this strip with its glitzy hotels.

'I wish we could afford it,' I say eventually.

'I think we should go for it. They want to be shot of the place, so let's make an offer.'

'But how could we ever . . . ?'

Michel pulls out his fountain pen, spreads out his napkin and we start scribbling figures and exchange rates. The ink bleeds into the soft tissue. The answer is clear. It is way beyond our price range. There are Vanessa and Clarisse, Michel's daughters from his previous marriage, to consider.

'But the pound is strong,' I say. 'That will work in our favour. Still, it *is* way more than we can afford.' I glance at the clock on the church tower up in the old town. It is after one. Charpy's *immobilier* office on the Croisette has closed for the weekend. It is just as well. We will have left by Monday. I am returning to London, where it is raining; Michel to Paris. I turn, peer up the lane which leads to the old fish market and tilt my head skywards. Only rounded summits of green hills are visible above the blocks of crab-coloured buildings. I cannot tell which of them harbours Appassionata. I know, though, that life on that olive farm would be a world away from the money-hungry resort of Cannes, just as this television market is a world away from my experiences of film-making.

'Let me talk to Charpy on Monday,' says Michel. 'I have an idea.'

'What?'

'Perhaps they'll sell it in stages.'

'Of course they won't.'

Our *pension* overlooks the old port. I pass the afternoon watching the to-ing and fro-ing of yachts and the ferries plying their course to the islands. Michel has disappeared for a final, post-festival business meeting. He will not return before evening. I am seized by a desire to slip back up into the hills but I know that, alone in the car, I would never find my way. Instead I idle away the afternoon reading and jotting down notes on my memo pad.

I hadn't come to Cannes to look for a house. Michel had been flying down for the festival and had invited me to come and spend the week with him. But, having always been drawn to 'my house by the sea', whenever I am on the coast, whether it be in Finland, Australia, Africa or Devon, I browse the estate agents' windows and visit the occasional property, hungry to discover something unexpected, to walk into a space where I belong. At no other place I have ever visited have I felt this close to belonging. Even so, to buy Appassionata would be an act of madness. Every bean I have ever earned I have spent travelling, crossing borders, roaming the world. I have been intensely restless, hungry to live a hundred lives in one lifetime. I have never settled anywhere. I have no capital to speak of. I am not fluent in the language; schoolgirl French is my limit. And as for farming: my mother's family owns a farm in southern Ireland, where I spent childhood holidays, and I played a country vet's wife in a television series. Hardly an agricultural pedigree. Still, to restore this old olive farm, with views overlooking the sea; to create roots, and with this man . . .

But he is a man I barely know; a man who proposed the day after I met him. A *coup de foudre*, he said. And, yes since we met life has been giddy. We've been spinning like tumbleweed. It may be illogical, but it feels *right*.

I begin to scribble several 'things to do' lists, which is out of character for me. It is simply an attempt to contain my excitement, to comprehend the enormity of the venture. An exercise to draw the possibility of ownership closer to me, to quieten the fever.

Finally, at about six in the evening, as the church bells chime the first of the Sunday masses, which is celebrated on Saturday evening, and I have exhausted all avenues to make-believe ownership, I stroll down the beach to swim. The water is bracing. I am alone in it, which pleases me. I savour the salty taste on my lips. I flip over on my back and scan the waterfront, the coastline which stretches as far as the Cap d'Antibes, and the hills behind. I drink in its foreignness. The cream and salmon tones of the buildings, the softly evocative light that has drawn so many painters here. I notice the observatory on a hill to the right of me for the first time. I begin to put myself in the role of *habitant*. Could I really live here? Yes. Yes! Although millions have done it before, it feels brave and enterprising. I cast myself in the role of intrepid adventurer, one who is making the choices she dreams of instead of merely daydreaming. I feel empowered. I crawl like a racer, leagues out from the shore. Of course, if I were alone, I may not be so eager to take the risk. *We.* I am diving in at the deep end.

On Sunday we drive out of town and head inland, up into the hills, making for the pretty old town of Vence, perched atop a hill at the end of a long, winding road. Michel wants to show me the Chapel of the Rosary, redesigned by Henri Matisse when he was living at Cimiez, an elegant quarter in the hills above Nice, as a commission for the Congregation of Dominican Nuns of Monteils (Aveyron). But when we arrive it is closed. How disappointing. I had expected a discreet mass to be in progress. Monks and incense. We shove our faces through the fencing, eager for views of the garden and building, and Michel directs my eyeline towards a forty-two-foot high iron cross, and then to the chapel roof. The tiles are a brilliant azure blue. So simple, so unlikely and so pure.

And then, drawn like nails to a magnet, we head for the villa.

Without Charpy breathing down our necks, we can explore the site more thoroughly. On the tarmac driveway, I find several dead shells from hunters' rifles and look about, wondering what they were shooting. Rabbits?

'Wild boar,' suggests Michel.

I laugh. 'This close to the coast? No way.'

Once up on the top terrace, we decide against going inside. Charpy forcing the door is one thing, but alone we will not contemplate it. Instead, we press our faces against sticky, cracked panes of glass and peer in through the windows. The sludge-brown shutters are bleached and peeling.

'We'll paint the shutters the colour of Matisse's chapel,' says Michel. Azure blue. Côte d'Azur. The blue coast. I lift my eyes heavenwards. Blue sky. Cobalt blue. Vanilla walls and blue shutters. I try to picture it. A cool yet vibrant combination.

'Yes, let's,' I murmur.

Many of the slats are splintered and broken, forced by the squatters or robbers. 'They will need to be replaced,' I say.

'Everything will need to be replaced. Nothing is intact.'

A curious feature we had not noticed yesterday is a monstrous bread oven which looks like a giant beehive. It has been added to the main chimney breast at upper-terrace level. 'That will have to go!'

'Definitely!'

'We haven't seen inside the garage.'

'I bet it's locked.' It is. Alongside it are two stables whose upper and lower doors hang loose on heavy, rusted hinges. I expect them to smell of hay but they are stacked with misshapen cardboard boxes crammed with disintegrating papers and files. On the ground are a few broken bits of gardening tools and a cracked cup with no handle. A row of dusty dark-green bottles lines the walls. I wonder whose life those objects belonged to. And what became of that person, those people.

A house is so much more than a house. And a house in a foreign country pushes the learning experience that much further.

It expands, promises to expand, the psyche. The inner journey. Michel and I are embarking on this path together. Newly in love, thrilled by one another. The house that M. Charpy saw with us yesterday and the potential farm, the regeneration we are picturing, are two different habitats. We are purchasing a dream, investing in love, in one another. We will nurture it through the pruning of trees and the harvesting of fruit. We will celebrate our union by extending invitations to friends and family worldwide.

We sit out in the afternoon sunshine at the pool's edge, side by side, fingertips touching, and dangle our feet in the vast, empty basin. We walk down the steps, enter, stand inside it, calling loudly, hooting and singing. Our voices echo. We run round the perimeter until we are out of breath. Swallows wheel and swoop high in the sky above us. We close our eyes and listen to the stillness. I have never walked in an empty swimming pool before. With the soles of our shoes we shove thick plaits of ivy out of our path and find puddles of sludgy rainwater seeping into the deepest crevices of the basin. Drowned black insects float among the speckled ivy leaves. The walls are so much taller than us. I press my back against the bleached blue cement and feel as though I have fallen into the very heart – no, we will be the heart – the watery womb of the property. We linger and kiss, our pulses racing. We look deep into one another, smiling, over-whelmed, two tiny excited people in this vast cubic metreage of space. I think of Jules Verne: *Journey to the Centre of the Earth*. I feel as small as Tom Thumb. I am Alice in Wonderland. The adventure, the challenge, has shrunk us, like Alice, in preparation for our journey. We will grow bigger and taller as we inhabit this space, as we reach into it and learn from it; and in the restoration of it, we will dis-cover one another.

I love this place already. I love this man at my side who has tumbled into this crazy dream with me. He seems to want to make it work as much as I do. He appears to be as energised and bowled over by it as I am.

Although we have only known each other a few months I feel safe with Michel. I trust him. He loves abundantly, with risk, and he is tender. I needed that. I was losing faith. After a series of short-lived affairs, one rather public relationship, a life in the public eye, albeit at a modest level, I had become isolated. I was losing myself. I was hurt, and growing brash. Independent, driven and alone.

The sun is moving to the right, preparing to slip away behind the hills. The sky is changing colour, augmenting its palette with tawny oranges, pastel red and soft purples. 'Where is that?' I ask. 'There, where the sun is setting?'

'Mougins.'

We are back on the upper terrace. Michel is smoking a cigarette – I wish he wouldn't – and it is time to go.

'We'll follow the sun to Mougins and have dinner there. It's too soon to return to Cannes.'

Yes, too soon to return to Cannes, its gaudy lights, its meretricious festival nightlife.

We descend the drive slowly, pootling past the olive terraces to the right and left of us. My attention is drawn to flowers on the olive branches, teeny white specks, weeny crocheted blossoms, delicate as finger lace. Delicate as love.

At the entry to the hilltop village of Mougins, where cars are banned, we find an inviting little hotel-restaurant. It has a terrace with extensive views which nosedive into the deep valley and sweep towards the sea. The *patron* points us to his car park across the narrow street.

We take our places on the terrace.

'*Ça, c'est mon parking*,' he pronounces with proprietorial

pride as he delivers our menus with a flourish. 'My very own private parking.' I am mesmerised by his chestnut toupée and gold jewellery, his lean frame and figure-hugging beige trousers. I expect him to break into a dance.

Michel orders us *deux coupes*. Our host nods approvingly and disappears. We notice a hand-painted sign which reads: '*140f la chambre, parking inclus*'. 'It's a good price.' Less than fourteen pounds. 'We must remember this place for our next visit. It's closer to the house, quieter than Cannes, and cheaper.' The *patron* returns with our two glasses of champagne. 'I am the only one, *le seul*, in the village with my own parking,' he continues.

We nod encouragingly, trying not to giggle as he skips away to welcome new arrivals and to direct them with dramatic gestures to his parking. 'Monsieur Parking,' whispers Michel, and so he is christened.

We eat ravenously. Our meal, the 70f set menu, is delicious and excellent value. I begin with warm goat's cheese melting on a toasted baguette and dressed with a wild roquette salad while Michel chooses *une petite omelette au briccio*, omelette with goat's cheese and mint. I follow with *gigot d'agneau*, succulently pink, with *tian de pommes de terre*, a dish of potatoes and tomatoes cooked beneath the lamb. Michel orders *veau aux olives noires à la sauge*, veal casserole with black olives and sage. Monsieur Parking recommends a red Bandol, a wine from the neighbouring Var region, to accompany our food. Michel, although a faithful Bordeaux man, decides we should go for it. It is fuller-bodied than I would have expected but it complements the meal and our mood of discovery. To finish Michel accepts a slither of *brie de Meaux* and then the *tarte au citron et aux amandes*. I forgo the cheese but am tempted by a dessert I have never come across before: lavender crème brûlée. It is heaven, one of the most sensuous foods I have ever eaten.

We set off into the night replete and happy. Monsieur Parking has wooed our stomachs and won our hearts. To my amazement, as we are leaving, he introduces us to his very glamorous wife. She, he announces proudly, is the chef.

On Monday, after several phone calls to and from Brussels where the vendors, M. and Mme B., reside, a deal is struck. We will buy the house and the first half of its *terrain* immediately and sign a *promesse de vente* for the second five acres, to be paid for within four years of the completion date of the purchase of the villa. On top of this, Michel has beaten down the original asking price by almost a quarter. Charpy is not happy with the arrangement and bids us farewell as though we have done nothing but waste his precious weekend.

Now we must leave the south of France. We have stayed on a day longer than we had planned in order to set the purchase of the house in motion. Although we are leaving the sun and the sea and the bustle of Mediterranean life, and, tonight in Paris, I must say *au revoir* to Michel for several weeks, my heart is flying like a kite. A house in a foreign country. More than a house, the restoration of a disused farm, a canvas to paint on, a new life to forge and someone to share it with. In my mind's eye, I can already picture the pouring and bottling of litres of olive oil, lashings of nature's liquid gold.

Back in England, I am barely able to contain my excitement until a friend takes me to lunch and invites me to ponder some well-meant advice. The horrors are listed: French tax laws, property laws, bylaws, the black holes of the Napoleonic system. And should I decide that the whole affair has been an aberration and choose to sell up, am I aware that the French will hold on to my money for five years? I leave the restaurant shocked and weak at the knees. The lunch is followed by an encounter with another longstanding chum who flummoxes me entirely by telling me, for my own good, that this is what

comes of being too secretive. Next, it is my family. They want
to warn me against undue haste. 'Have you considered the pitfalls?' asks my father, and begins to reel off scenarios of
corruption and deception, summing up with: 'You're too
impetuous. You don't want to get landed with a pig in a poke,
now, do you?'

I am still trying to catch my breath when my mother phones,
confiding that while out shopping with my sister in Bond Street,
she broke down and cried. 'I had to been taken into Fenwick's
coffee shop. I couldn't stand up.'

'What's wrong?' I ask, genuinely perturbed.

'You.'

'Me?'

'How could you? We are Irish Catholics!' she wails.

I say nothing. What can I say?

'And he's a foreigner. You've always been the same. You've
got no common sense.'

I replace the receiver. Slumping into uncertainty, I begin to
stew. Yes, I am impetuous, and I probably lack common sense.
I hadn't been aware that I was particularly secretive and I certainly have not troubled to investigate the pitfalls of the French
system. On top of which, we cannot afford the farm. It is an
unachievable fantasy fed by a whirlwind romance which is
probably destined to go the way of all others. I should pull out.
So my frame of mind when Michel telephones from Paris to say
that he has received a call from Brussels is one of mounting hysteria.

'What?' is my amorous greeting.

'Madame is insisting on ten per cent of the selling price up
front, in cash.'

'Absolutely not. It's illegal.'

That kind of request is quite common, I have heard, in
French property transactions. It is known as the 'deposit'. The
buyer pays a percentage of the agreed asking price in cash and

the vendor declares a sale price lower than the property's true total. It helps to alleviate the astronomical *frais* levied against both purchaser and vendor.

'It's black-market money!' I shout. 'She can't do that!'

'I'm afraid it is a generally accepted practice.'

I refuse to discuss it. In fact, I refuse to discuss anything and replace the receiver rather too abruptly. I know though that if we don't agree we will lose the farm. A decision that felt organic a month ago is now driving me over the edge with doubts. Virtually everything I own, including my one and only insurance policy, which will have to be cashed in – much against my accountant's advice – is going to be sunk into this enterprise. What if it all goes wrong? What if everything my friends and family are telling me is true? I am woken by appalling dreams. I pace the nights away, jabbering to myself. Terror is taking hold.

Now, it is high summer. Due to French bureaucratic nightmares, all hope that the sale would be completed before the holidays is receding fast. And while complications of the contract, such as the division of the land, are being wrangled over and ironed out, sterling is falling and our calculations are out the window. Due to the exchange rate, the property has already risen in price by twenty per cent. If things get any worse, we will have to pull out. I am tearing my hair out. Michel keeps his cool. Bastille Day arrives. We motor down through a celebrating France to visit the abandoned property one more time, mainly to appease my steaming financial fears, before making an irrevocable commitment.

Our arrival is greeted by a magnificent tree alongside the top terrace, which is in full and glorious bloom. Exhausted after twelve hours' solid driving, taking it in turns to catnap in the car because we have too little cash for hotels, we cast ourselves like weary shipwrecked sailors on the upstairs terrace adjacent to the majestic tree. Its blossom is the colour of ivory, its petals thickly textured with a fragrance so heady it envelops the whole hillside. Collapsed before the dawning day, my supine body spreadeagled, head on Michel's chest, I know that this perfume is imprinting itself upon me. It will for ever remind me of the south of France, and of being recklessly in love.

As the day unfolds, the scents, the views, the hot, clear weather seduce me once more and I am calmed by Michel and his quiet strength. I see my doubts for what they are; I am stepping off into the unknown, moving out of one life to inhabit another. Fears, real or illogical, and excitements are part of that transition. Misgivings laid to rest, we make for the beach, where we steep our weary limbs in the Med, doze the afternoon away and shower off salt and sand in fresh cold water before going in search of dinner and a bed *chez* Monsieur Parking.

As evening falls and we dine by candlelight on his terrace, a diorama of fireworks explodes across the Mediterranean sky, illuminating the entire bay. Their purpose is the honouring of the French declaration of independence but, in my heart, soothed for the present, I pretend they are for us.

Here, in France, Quatorze Juillet, the anniversary of the storming of the Bastille and its accompanying revolution, is the greatest of all national holidays. For the French, it is their finest hour, whereas in England, on the anniversary of the Gunpowder Plot, we burn a scruffy, ill-clad effigy of Guy Fawkes, the revolutionary who tried to bring down our government. I ask myself if this is not one of the fundamental differences between the French and the English psyches. I have read that revolutionism is 'imprinted upon the spirit' of the French 'by an inward instinct'. Perhaps it is conservatism that is imprinted on the spirit of the British.

Bright and early the next morning, Michel puts through a call to the vendors in Belgium. He confirms that we will pay the cash advance Madame has requested if, in return, she and her husband allow us to move into the villa before the final contracts are signed.

'Ah, you are eager to begin restoration work while the weather is hot and dry, *n'est-ce pas?*'

Yes, well, that would be true – if the cash advance were not about to eat up almost every penny we can lay our hands on. The fact is, Michel has invited Vanessa and Clarisse, his thirteen-year-old twin daughters, to spend their summer with us. He wants them to get to know me a little better and to share with us the thrill of installing ourselves in the villa. They are dying to see the place, he tells me. Besides, we haven't a bean left to take them elsewhere.

Mme B. agrees, *en principe*, but insists that we discuss it all in detail over lunch in Brussels. Before hanging up, she offers Michel the choice of either swift transference of the money to an account in Switzerland in advance of our Brussels rendezvous or bringing the agreed sum in cash with us on the day.

I am ready to hit Monsieur Parking's ceiling. I will not hear of one sou from my one and only insurance policy, plus savings, disappearing into unknown black-market accounts in Switzerland before anything is signed and settled. Why can't we take a cheque for their wretched Swiss account and hand it over to them?

'I suppose she fears it might not be honoured.'

'*Typical!* At that level, no one trusts anybody!'

I rant and fume until I exhaust myself and Michel's laughter and those gentle blue eyes temper my hysteria.

And so it is arranged.

Two weeks later, the beginning of the mass French exodus from north to south – for a nation of individualists, they certainly behave like lemmings when the holiday season is upon them – we pack my little black VW convertible with old mattresses, bedding and a surplus of kitchenware from my flat in London and set off for Brussels.

Our plan is to introduce ourselves to the Belgian owners, create the 'right impression' (i.e., that we are able to afford the place), sign the *promesse de vente*, hand over our hard-earned money in the brown envelopes secreted in Michel's briefcase (unless he can sweet-talk them into holding off this part of the arrangement until later) and, directly after 'business', drive to Paris, where *les filles* await us.

Michel feels that to turn up outside the vendors' home in a car bursting at the seams with old furniture might appear a trifle presumptuous and might prejudice negotiations. So, when we arrive in the city, we deposit the laden vehicle in the underground car park at the Hilton Hotel and make our way on foot to the address we have been given by Madame's secretary. I barely register the city streets, nor our arrival in the wide, leafy avenue which bears the name we have been looking for. My head is whirring with what ifs. What if these people fall upon us and rob us, or try by other less violent means to cheat us out of our money? How can we be sure they are not crooks? Even if we escape such a fate, there are the documents we are about to sign . . .

Almost before I realise it, we are there and are standing – no, frozen outside a pair of imposingly ornate iron gates which rise to the height of an average oak tree. 'Thank heavens we didn't bring the car,' I whisper, clutching Michel's hand. For a good three or four minutes, we regard the exterior of what looks to us like a miniature Versailles.

'Here goes,' he replies, squeezing my hand tighter before ringing the bell.

The gates slide apart and we crunch across gravel and tiles, climb a marble stairway and approach baronial doors. These are opened by a butler in full uniform. Michel, apparently unflustered, gives him our names.

Nodding a dehumanised greeting, the butler tells us in a thick Belgian accent, 'Madame will be with you shortly.' I, with my already imperfect French, have difficulty understanding even that simple sentence. I sigh at the prospect of the impending negotiations. Then, with a polite but indifferent nod, he leads us across a fabulous black and white marble hallway ablaze with sprays of livid-red gladioli and on into a capacious *salon* which he describes as 'Madame's writing room'.

'I'm in the wrong film, wearing the wrong costume,' I mutter as we perch in two ornate, gilt Louis-something chairs.

As soon as the door closes and we are alone, I rise and cross to the floor-to-ceiling windows which look out upon substantial, perfectly manicured gardens. I count half a dozen gardeners digging and planting a criss-cross arrangement of magnificent flowerbeds. An antique Italian marble fountain stands in the centre of a crossroads of gravelled walkways; a *chef d'œuvre* of gushing, crystal-clear water. I gaze contentedly upon this spectacle until the door opens behind me and a terrifying, tightly coiffed, tight-lipped woman wearing a thick coating of orange face powder enters: Mme B. She is accompanied by another, marginally younger middle-aged woman, twitching like a nervous bird, whom she introduces as Yvette Pastor, her private secretary. Mme B. apologises for the absence of her husband who, she explains, is *malade*. She strides briskly into the hall, requesting us to follow. My heart sinks. I picture our carefree summer plans disappearing faster than Belgian chocolates.

We are seated around an oval walnut table large enough to accommodate twenty diners with ease. A magnum of Cristal champagne arrives on a silver platter. A message is sent from Madame via the butler to Monsieur, bidding him, in no uncertain terms, to get up and come downstairs instantly; there are papers to be signed. I resist my desire to protest.

Business commences. I barely comprehend a phrase, and stare in blind panic as six pages of dense legal French are shoved across the table for my perusal: a copy of the binding documents I am about to put my name to.

Some little while later, the door opens and a frail old man appears, trembling and pale. He is dressed in elegant sportswear with heavy expensive jewellery on his delicate-as-parchment, mottled hands and wrists. He apologises profusely for his malady. We shake our heads sympathetically, at a loss for words. He looks as though he might drop to the marble floor at any second. Madame commands the butler to pour Monsieur a flute of champagne. Monsieur declines. Madame insists. *Le pauvre* Monsieur assents and toasts our good health and the prosperity of our future lives at Appassionata. 'You have much work to do in the garden,' he says.

'Foolish to discuss the growth of the land,' she reprimands him. Monsieur demurs, accepts Madame's fountain pen and signs his shaky, illegible autograph.

Then it is my turn. I down the last mouthful from my crystal flute and, with sticky hands and beating heart, obediently scribble my initials, and/or name, wherever Madame points her bejewelled, manicured fingers. I glance at Michel and smile weakly. I am praying to God he knows what he is doing, because I don't, and he is handing over our envelopes.

The formalities completed, Michel rises. He leans to offer a *bisou* to Mme B., who proffers her cheek, clearly enchanted by his charm and thrilled by his astute business acumen. Watching the pair of them negotiate has been rather like watching two fencing champions in combat. Monsieur and I have not uttered a word. In fact, at the very first opportunity, he has offered his apologies and retired back upstairs to his room.

'*Mais non*, you cannot leave now! We must lunch!'

We have already consumed almost a magnum of champagne between the five of us – Yvette, seated throughout on a chair behind Madame, has tippled immoderately on our future happiness – and we have a three-hour drive ahead of us but, without a word between us, Michel and I both sense that to refuse would be deemed a rebuff and might cloud future business relations.

We nod, attempting enthusiasm. '*Pourquoi pas?*'

'*Très bien.* I suggest zee 'ilton.' She excuses herself and orders us to wait out front.

'Well?' I ask Michel in a fraught whisper when Madame has left the room.

'Well what?'

'Did we get the permission or not?'

'*Chérie*, did you not understand what was being said?'

'Not every word,' I admit.

Michel grins. 'We have signed and sealed permission to occupy the villa for the summer – in fact from this moment on until it is officially ours.'

'Really?'

'Yes, well, at a price.'

'*What price?*'

'Sssh, *chérie*, don't yell. If we fail to complete, no matter what the reason, they keep everything.'

'What? Every halfpenny we have given them today?'

'And anything, everything we spend on the place. We can't claim a franc back.'

'Oh, my God! Whatever made you agree to that?'

'*Chérie*, the deadline for completion is next April. So there's nothing to worry about.'

'Next April. That's almost a year. Yes, we'll have bought the place long before then,' I sigh, relieved.

Outside in the gardens, Madame enquires after our car. For a second we are both flummoxed, recalling guiltily my little Golf, packed to the rafters with furniture for 'our' house, awaiting us in the underground car park of 'zee 'ilton'. Michel, sanguine as always in such moments, comes to the rescue. 'We parked a little distance from here, *chère* Madame, for fear of losing our way in the city.'

Madame nods comprehendingly and then examines me from head to foot as though she is measuring me, which is precisely what she is doing. '*C'est bon,*' she decides, commanding a passing gardener to fetch her car from its garage. 'It is a sports car, but you can squeeze in the back. It's not far; you are slim.' Moments later, to our speechless amazement, the garage doors unfold to reveal a gleaming pillar-box-red 500SL Mercedes sports car creeping towards us. I had been expecting something a little more sedate.

'My weakness,' she confesses with the vulnerability of a child. 'You see, I was born very poor.'

We pile into the car, Madame at the wheel, and shoot off like a rocket. During lunch at the Hilton, we learn that she is one of the richest women in Belgium. 'Poor Robert,' she tells us, 'does not care for money or material possessions. All he wants is to potter about in the garden. He adores flowers and plants. It is very difficult for me. I do not know what to do with him. We know each other since we are twelve. We began a business and have worked very hard and now we are so rich, but he prefers to stay in bed. He cannot handle all the responsibilities our money has brought us. I travel everywhere with Yvette, my secretary. Robert does not want to go anywhere other than our summer house. It is *très tragique.*' As I watch her, Mme B. begins to resemble a bloodhound. Her face droops, her eyes look lost and uncomprehending. The terrifying woman we encountered a few hours ago has disappeared. But the mood does not last long. Soon she is beckoning for the bill, which she insists on paying – thank heavens – and then offers to walk us to our car.

Michel and I exchange furtive glances. At this late stage, we cannot possibly own up to the fact that our little buggy is parked not a hundred metres from her Mercedes in the garage right beneath our feet. Instead, we roam around a few back streets, feeling stupid and dishonest, and seeing our ridiculous charade for the time-waster that it is, but still insist that we just cannot recall where we parked.

Eventually Mme B. gives up, hails a cab to deliver her the three streets back to the Hilton and wishes us *bonne chance*. Our parting is good-natured, almost affectionate. 'See you at the *notaire*'s office. I will fax you the address,' she says, 'I look forward to it.' And she flutters her eyes at Michel like Betty Boop.

By the time we arrive in Paris, it is late. Michel's daughters are disgruntled. They have been awaiting the arrival of Papa all afternoon. The girls and I have met only a few times and I am probably more affected by their mood than Michel who, oblivious of any whining, runs to and from the car, cramming in bags anywhere he can lodge them and telling everyone to get a move on or we won't reach the south before the holidays are over. 'What about Pamela?' asks Clarisse.

I turn my head in surprise. Who is Pamela?

Clarisse points to the gate, and there, panting and waddling towards us, is a startlingly obese Alsatian. The addition of Pamela unbalances the carefully constructed equilibrium of my already dangerously overloaded Golf and worse, *elle fait les pets* all the way from Paris to Cannes. And they are lethal. Embracing a new family is one thing but, by the time we reach Aix-en-Provence, I am seriously asking myself whether I can bring myself to love this smelly dog.

W a t e r M u s i c

The Present

The heat is brutal. The search for water and its source occupies Michel's days; Vanessa and I have set about cutting back the ivy in the swimming pool. We have one pair of garden shears between us. This means one of us clips until defeated by aching arms while the other tugs, untangles and gathers up the dead foliage, and then we swap. We seem to have a good rhythm going. She is a hardworking, bright girl and I thoroughly enjoy her company. Neither of the girls speaks English, which forces me to use my rather rusty French. Consequently our conversations don't amount to much – the odd polite exchange or earnest request on my part to know the French word for this or that. From time to time, particularly given the temperature, the arid conditions and the strenuous activity, it proves difficult and we end up working in companionable silence.

Meanwhile, Michel is scaling the hill, up and down, back

and forth, like a two-legged goat, scouring our ten acres of Provençal jungle for water pipes or signs of a well. His legs are latticed with grazes from the brambles and from tripping over hidden rocks, but he remains determined. Mme B. mentioned to him that somewhere on the property there is a natural spring, but for the moment its whereabouts elude him.

'We may have to cut back the entire acreage before we find it!' he announces on one of his stopovers at the villa in search of refreshment to quench his thirst and to wash down the particles of parched foliage that have caught in his throat. 'Where's Clarisse?'

Vanessa and I shake our heads and wipe our sticky brows. 'Don't know, haven't seen her for hours. You need wellingtons and a hip flask, Michel.'

'Mmm.' He shrugs and disappears in his shorts and supermarket espadrilles – fraying already – ascending yet another barely visible track. I read his concern. The installation of an entire water system at this stage would mean we would be obliged to close up the property and abandon it for the foreseeable future. But neither of us have voiced this worry as yet.

Each evening, one or both of us drives to the village and fills several twenty-litre plastic containers with water to serve us for the day ahead. I learn that in France every village and town has its public supply of *eau potable*. It is considered a basic right in this country that no matter how poor a person may be, wherever in the land he finds himself, he has access to free drinking water. *Vive la France*, I laugh when Michel explains this national kindness. I am very grateful to the Republic of France for such foresight because our funds are diminishing rapidly.

Due to the lack of facilities at the villa, we are obliged to install the girls in a hotel. Naturally, we choose the establishment of Monsieur Parking, who offers Michel a generous deal.

Each morning we drive to Mougins to collect Vanessa and Clarisse but before returning to the villa, we breakfast together. They order the *petit déjeuner* included in the price of the room, which is the usual rolls, croissants, *confiture* and *café au lait* (*chocolat* for Vanessa who cannot abide tea or coffee, although she frets constantly about her pretty, svelte figure), while Michel and I settle for a pot of coffee. Stuffing any uneaten rolls into my bag to take with us for our lunch, we linger in the sunshine on Monsieur Parking's terrace. Then, when he and his wife are occupied with the bills of departing guests, one at a time, Michel and I tiptoe up the twisting, narrow stairway to the girls' room and take a much-needed, illicit shower. Hot water never felt this delicious, nor so wicked. By day three, Monsieur's flamboyant bonhomie is beginning to diminish and he is eyeing us with suspicion. I dread to think how he will greet us towards the end of the month.

Michel pays a visit to *la mairie*, the local town hall, requesting plans of Appassionata's water system. But it is August, and there is nobody to search through the files. Everyone is *en vacances*. Even if they were not, he learns, it is unlikely that the information will have been registered. The house is too old, the land has been divided, it is a private residence. Water systems and septic tanks do not have to be listed. We must continue our search unaided. In desperation, he stops at a phone box and puts in a call to Mme B. in Brussels. 'I've found a *bassin* at the top of the hill but the pipes that lead to it disappear into the undergrowth and I can't trace them or get at them. Where is the water coming from to feed that basin?'

Madame has no idea. The property was bought as a gift for one of her two daughters who was passionate about horses, but the inclines and terraces made it impossible for her to breed them there, and she never lived on the property. '*Hélas*, I cannot remember, Monsieur. It was almost fifteen years ago.'

'And the woman who rented it from you, who bred dogs?'

'I have no idea where she is. She left owing us thousands, including the water bills.'

'Ah! So you do have water bills?'

'*Mais, bien sûr!* At least, I think so. She never paid whatever bills were outstanding. Of that I am very certain.'

'It's just that . . . you mentioned a well?'

'Ah, *la source!* Yes, yes, I think there is a well. Perhaps my daughter has kept everything, but she is away until mid-September. Of course, we will try to supply all these details when the sale goes through. Robert and I are off on holiday tomorrow, so *bonne chance*.'

It is early evening. The sun is glinting through the olive trees and laying shadows across the weedy terraces. We are sitting alone on an expansive dust patch, once lawns, alongside the top terrace, in two supermarket deckchairs, sharing a bottle of local *vin de Provence rosé*. Our conversation is about water, of course, and I am discovering how Michel hates to be defeated.

'If squatters lived here and grew vegetables, there has to be mains water. They wouldn't have known about the well. I am going to pay a visit to Lyonnaise Des Eaux, the local water board, in the morning, and pray to God they haven't also shut down for the month of August.'

'They might have done what we are doing,' I suggest, pouring us both another chilled glass.

'What's that?'

'Taken advantage of French hospitality and collected their daily water supply from the village.'

While Michel considers this possibility, I tell him that I have driven the girls back to the hotel and that I have promised we would take them into Cannes later for a pizza. Money shortages or not, they are ready for an evening out. I sense they are growing impatient with our lack of facilities and bored with the slim choice of meals dictated by our temporary cooking arrangements: a couple of old saucepans from London, a 200f barbecue, plastic salad dish, servers, knives and forks bought locally along with paper plates, and some camping thing belonging to Michel which looks like a Bunsen burner but succeeds in boiling water for potatoes and coffee.

'The girls are fine. It's you who wants to get out,' he teases. It is about now that I am recognising a fundamental difference between us. If I, in my old life, my *real* life, am faced with something that does not work, I leave it, move on, buy another. 'No kitchen? Fine, let's eat out,' is my idea of the perfect solution. Michel, on the other hand, has patience and an ability to fix things, to knock up something practical out of what looks to me like nothing more than a useless piece of wire or wood. I concede, 'Perhaps you are right,' and he hoots with laughter when I confess sheepishly that this is the closest I have ever come to camping.

'Still, you're right. The girls will be happier once I get that pool filled.'

He continues to reassure Clarisse and Vanessa that once we have discovered the water source and how to pump it to our water basin, a circular cement tank at the very summit of the hill, and ensured its freefall passage back downhill to the house unimpeded by clogged pipes (every joke I have ever heard about French plumbing is proving to be true); when this series of *petits miracles* has taken place, the very first thing we will do is fill the swimming pool. I turn my head and look back across two terraces to its empty, bleached-out blueness and I fantasise about cool, crystal swimming water. Yes, the days will be more languid then.

'What about the neighbours?' I ask Michel. 'Have you talked to them?'

'Everyone is away. Or at the beach.'

The beach! We haven't visited the beach yet. 'Hang the water problem. Let's go to the beach tomorrow.'

'Too many tourists.' Michel speaks as though we have lived on this hill for a hundred years.

We rise early. I am delighted to have found a man who loves the early mornings as much as I do. Our days begin when the sun peeps through the towering pines and shines down upon us and our dreadful mattress on the floor to light our bronzed faces.

'I'm off to the sea,' I whisper sleepily, throwing on some old clothes and driving to the coast, falling into combat on the way with great orange dustcarts and the first of the day's horn addicts. Down in the town, the air is rich with traffic fumes and freshly baked bread. A solitary hour spent swimming followed by a fresh cold-water shower on the beach and I am perky and raring to go. This is so much better. I can no longer face beginning each day with Monsieur Parking's glower. Michel laughs and tells me I am too sensitive, but judging by the look of sheer apoplexy on Monsieur P.'s face every time we mount the stairs to the girls' room, I feel sure his nights are spent plotting our deaths. Back at the house I grab a coffee before we drive over to collect Vanessa and Clarisse.

Over breakfast, I relate the delights of the beach at 7 a.m., eulogising about the tranquillity, the absence of tourists, who are all still slumbering – not a footprint written on the golden sand – and the sunrise. Ah, the sunrise! It lifts in majestic silence from a secret heaven beyond the hills, bringing warmth and a honey-ripe light which spreads across the water to meet the horizon, colouring the limpid Med a shimmering gold. At the centre of this miracle is me rippling through the salty stillness.

After I have evoked my moments of bliss, Vanessa expresses a fervent desire to come with me. 'Tomorrow,' she begs, '*s'il te plaît, Carol, chère Carol?*'

I sip my coffee to avoid answering. She and her sister would sleep till noon if we left them to it. '*S'il te plaît, Carol.*' She is so solicitous, requesting with pouting and passion. How can I possibly refuse? It is agreed.

After breakfast, back at the villa, the view is a heat haze. It gives an opiate softness to the contours of the surrounding hills. Michel sets off on a visit to the water board while Vanessa and I clear the last of the ivy still clinging like death to the pool's walls and base. When this back-breaking chore has finally been accomplished, we stand back to admire the results of our labours.

'It's so cracked and old,' she pronounces.

'It needs water,' I say brightly, but it does look strangely desolate.

In blistering heat, we haul the mountains of dead vegetation across the terraces and pile it all up ready for burning at some stage later in the year. We won't dare put a match to it for many months to come. In the south of France it is against the law to light fires during the summer months. There is a high risk of bush incidents here. In these temperatures, with our wild acres of growth and acute lack of water, we risk igniting the entire coastline and turning it to charcoal.

I look about for Clarisse. She is nowhere to be seen.

Baguettes for lunch under his arm, Michel returns from the town looking fried and frazzled. It was noisy, dusty, packed with tourists and motor cars, he says, and he encountered a deeply unhelpful female *fonctionnaire* who informed him that the water board is unable to disclose the whereabouts of our water source without a legal document showing proof of purchase of the property or a recent bill, neither of which we have. Nor would they be willing to trace any location details without the name of the last account-holder. The most likely person is the dog lady who ran off without paying any bills. Michel offered Mme B.'s name but the assistant merely shook her head. And then, with furrowed brow, informed him, by the way, that they had received a letter some eighteen months earlier from Mme B., requesting that the water be cut off.

'Why would she have done that?' I ask.

'In France, if the electricity and water are officially switched off, the proprietors are not liable to pay the land and habitation taxes.'

'So now what?'

'I am going back tomorrow with our passports and our *promesse de vente* signed by Monsieur and Madame B. I'll insist that they revert the instruction.'

'*Coo-coo, Papa!*'

'Ah, you finished the pool. Well done.' And with that Michel hurries inside for his camera to take photos of Vanessa, waving and calling, alongside Pamela. They are investigating the deserted pool. At its deepest point it measures three metres and makes even fat Pamela seem minute. I ponder the rushing gallons of water it will require, as well as Michel's tenacity through all of this.

As each day passes, the land around the house grows more like a dustbowl. When the wind is up, it settles everywhere. In our clothes, in the kitchenware, on our skin, as grit around our teeth. Everywhere. Whatever we attempt, it is hot, dusty work but the girls remain cheerful, most of the time, and in their different ways they offer their assistance with the task we have taken on. They are unidentical twins, and I am enjoying getting to know their separate natures. Clarisse, possibly the less practical of the pair spends hours picking wild flowers, her tiny frame lost among the jungle of growth, delivering them in discarded wine bottles or jam jars to our rigged-up, al fresco dining table: a wooden plank supported by bricks, broken tiles and other debris dug out of the garden. Vanessa takes pleasure in the discovery of language and information. She has now owned up to a knowledge of English but adamantly refuses to speak a syllable of it with me. Why? I enquire, but she merely shakes her head and goes away. Is it some deep-rooted resistance to me, I ask myself, or is it that we are in her country and so, in her exacting mind, must speak her language?

Returning from the *boulangerie*, she and I drive by a house named Mas de Soleil. Back at the villa she comes searching for me to borrow my dictionary to look up the meaning of *mas*. I wonder that she is French and hasn't come across the noun before, but then we learn that it is particular to this region, meaning a farmhouse or traditional Provençal house. She suggests we might like to rechristen our villa 'Mas des Oliviers'.

'Do you like this house?' I probe, but she merely stares at me, shrugs and goes off about her own affairs. I'd like to detain her, engage her in conversation, ask her about her life in Paris, but only when we are at work together do I feel her bond with me. Still, whatever the girls' opinions on the purchase of our dilapidated property – and perhaps they have none: after all, they are only thirteen – they appear to remain neutral. I love them for not judging their father for his choices. I have no children of my own; I have never married before. This will be my first go at it and, I suppose, I am as nervous and as inept as anyone in my position. I make mistakes on a daily basis but, so far, nothing that cannot be redeemed. We are living in combustible conditions in broiling heat but we make allowances for that, and for each other. In spite of the frustrations, I believe we are a happy band.

While Michel battles on with the water crisis, Vanessa, Clarisse and I attack the grounds that encircle the house, cutting them back to take stock of what is there. It is a time of discoveries. Empty bottles, slabs of thick ancient floor tiles painted the Tuscan colours of earth. Were they transported here by the original owner of the house whose name, I have learned from the reams of history documented in our *promesse de vente*, was Signor Spinotti? Signor Spinotti, a merchant from Milan, the creator of Appassionata; yes, I like the sound of him and close my eyes to picture him: portly, exuberant, generous.

And there is a pond! Clarisse has unearthed a pond. Michel! Papa! Come and look! Who would have thought it, in this arid paradise? It is kidney-shaped, about two metres long. It has survived, buried beneath jungles of streaky iris and wild lilies and heaven knows what other thick-stemmed weeds, and, astoundingly, has not dried up. But the water is so dank and muddy that we cannot tell how deep it goes.

'Could it be fed from the well, our elusive well?'

Michel kneels and considers its silty blackness. 'It's very still. I doubt it. But who knows?' He rises, reminded of the well, of our lack of water, and turns around in the hot, cloudless day trying to figure out the puzzle.

I stare at the murky bath, thick as treacle, longing to trickle my fingers to and fro in there, to feel the liquidy velvet sensation and watch the drops dribble and drip back into the pond, but I am hesitant. I don't know what might lurk beneath its surface. Something sinister might rise up and bite me. 'Oh my God, look!' The water shivers and stills again.

Michel bends to survey what I am staring at, but can see nothing. Neither can I.

'Something moved. I definitely saw it. I think it was a fish.'

He laughs. 'A frog, perhaps, but not a fish, *chérie*. The house has been empty for years.'

'Well, when we have water, I'll clean it up and then we can have fish.'

'Mmm. When we have water . . .' He glances at his watch. 'I must get going.'

He tracks down M. Charpy, the estate agent, and persuades him to write an accompanying letter of attestation which, along with photocopies of our passports and a copy of the *promesse de vente*, the water board agrees to accept as proof that we are entitled to receive water. Late in the afternoon, Michel motors up the drive, hooting, triumphant with his news. He rushes to the garage, we switch on the mains tap one more time, but there is still no water.

We exchange a silent, rather desperate look. Is this why Mme B. accepted such a drastic reduction in the price? Have we bought a farm without a water supply to sustain it? The pig in a poke my father warned me against? 'What now?' I ask.

'The EDF are coming to switch on the electricity tomorrow. The water supply shouldn't be affected by it, but maybe it is. Let's wait till then, *chérie*. If there's still no water then . . . well, we'll see.'

My quiet morning swims on the beach alongside the Palm Beach Casino have been supplanted by the hectic, crazy itinerary of a family outing à la M. Hulot. Even Pamela accompanies us now. Gone are the languorous laps which acted as my physical meditation, my preparation for facing the hurdles of house renovation on a shoestring. They have been replaced by a car boot full of soggy towels, wet cozzies and leaking shampoo bottles. Not to mention Pamela, who carries another twenty kilos of sand in her damp fur. Now, instead of me swimming and quitting the beach in rejuvenated isolation and returning to the house to collect Michel by eight, by the time the troops are out of bed and rallied and we are on our way down the Boulevard Carnot, it is rush hour and I am grumpy.

'I don't want to do this any more!' I scream. 'These were *my* morning swims!' The lunatic energy in the car recedes into awkward silence. Our outing is funereal and neither of the girls answers when I speak to them. Both have retreated into a serious sulk.

Later, over a cup of reheated coffee – because we have run

out of water and did not have time to refill one of the plastic canisters on our way back up the hill due to the fact that an electrician and a representative from the EDF are arriving at 10.30 – Michel chides me. Lovingly, he tells me that I am not behaving like a member of a family. 'You are not used to it, *chérie*. The girls understand.' And he brushes my nose with a kiss. But obviously they don't. They think me demented, and indeed I am ready to hurl myself in the bracken or sink into the black viscous pond.

While I am elsewhere feeling inadequate, the electricity is connected – a painless affair, certainly compared to the escalating water saga. In the presence of M. Dolfo, the electrician, Michel gives our water tap another try but the pipes do not respond. Not one throaty gurgle.

'I don't suppose you know anything about this?' he asks M. Dolfo, who shakes his head and shrugs.

To keep our spirits up, we celebrate our first step towards mod-con living by dashing out to the largest hypermarket I have ever visited and purchasing a modest little fridge. On our way back, Clarisse points out a series of brightly coloured posters pasted to the lamp-posts all round the village. They are advertising a firework display to be held on the beach in Cannes tonight. She pleads with Michel to take her down to the coast for the evening. He attempts to dissuade her, warning of the thousands who will be there, assuring her that we will see so much more from our own terraces, but she, and now Vanessa, are insistent. So, along with Pamela, who we dare not leave in case the explosions frighten her and she has a heart attack or waddles away in terror never to find her way back, we join the queues of descending traffic and head for the beach which is *teeming* with holidaymakers. Every car park is bursting; there is nowhere closer to Cannes than our own home to leave my VW. By this stage, I am more than ready to dump the car and walk away, but Michel suggests we drive on a kilometre or two out of town, find ourselves a deserted stretch of sand and watch the display from there. This is what we do. The car parked, I wander over to a small stone jetty and sit down. The girls are engaged in a rather earnest conversation with Papa, and I choose to remain at a discreet distance, looking out to sea. In any case, I cannot follow what is being discussed and since my outburst earlier I have been feeling rather like an exposed nerve. Before me the waves are glinting silver in the moonlight. The water lapping at my feet is tranquil and soothing, but it does not reach the confusions churning about inside me. Way along the coast the pyrotechnics have begun. Great globes of blue, white and red – the colours of the French flag – explode into sprays which fall away silently. I am a foreigner here, an outsider. This is not unknown to me. I travel frequently and have often found myself alone in the most outlandish of situations, but this time there is another nuance. I have given every penny I possess (which, granted, is not a whole heap) and thrown in my lot with a man I barely know. Steamed off into the rosy sunset without a clue as to where I am heading. Now we have a farm which we cannot begin to afford, no water, no prospect of any, two girls who are tolerating me . . .

Clarisse's arm presses up against me as she plumps down beside me. She takes me by surprise. '*Tu est très pensive, Carol.* Are you and Papa going to have a baby?' she enquires without preamble.

'I don't know. Maybe. Why, would that trouble you?'

She thinks hard for a minute and then shakes her head. 'No, it's just that Vanessa and I have been talking about it.'

'Have you? What have you been saying?'

She thinks again. I await her response with trepidation.

'It would be better if it were a girl.'

'Why?'

'You both have such a lot of curly hair. It might look silly on a boy.' Innocent as this comment may have been, by God, it heartens me.

Later, as we undress for bed, I ask Michel: 'Were the girls talking to you about us having a baby?'

He looks at me, amused. 'No, why ever would you think that? They were wanting to know about the pool. They think we need advice on how to maintain it.'

'Shouldn't we wait till we have water in it?' I suggest a mite testily.

'I promised them that one treat. I want to keep my promise, if I possibly can, and give them something to look forward to.'

'So that's what you were so deeply engaged in conversation about, the swimming pool?'

He stares at me in surprise, a tired smile on his nut-brown face, and places his shirt on the cardboard box acting as dressing table. 'What's the matter?'

I scramble into bed. A spring needles me in the back and I curse and drag the sheet over my head.

Michel approaches and lifts it from my face. 'Hey, what's up?'

'Nothing. I just hate this mattress and I want a bath.'

The following morning, even without my daily swim, promising amounts of my good humour have returned and I kiss Michel lovingly as he sets off down the hill for the hot, cramped office set alongside the motorway and occupied by Piscines Azuréene (*Construction et filtration – Produits – Accessoires – Contrats d'entretien – Dé pannage – Robots de nettoyage*) to buy a bucket of chlorine tablets and pick up a useful leaflet or two. The woman recommends that, because our pool has been empty for some time, it is imperative we have an expert pay us a visit.

Within the hour, a swimming-pool-blue van screeches up the drive, hooting insistently, and grinds to a halt. I run to take a look.

'Tie up that blasted dog or I'm not staying!' is its driver's way of introducing himself. Poor dear Pamela, who has been snoring happily and quietly enjoying her day, is dragged off to one of the stables where I attach her with a piece of string to one of the iron rings. It is only now that she begins to bark.

Satisfied, out of the van shuffles *l'expert*. He is a burly bloke in very baggy trousers, scuffed shoes, fag clinging to the spittle on his mouth, red mottled eyes, a big, dark, drooping moustache, and he positively reeks of alcohol (it is only a little after 11 a.m.). He takes one look at the pool, throws his arms in the air and scoffs loudly: 'This pool was constructed in the late twenties.'

'Is that a problem?' I snap.

He screws up his face, eyeing me beadily, and then sets off on a slow plod around the pool's perimeter, bending and lifting like an ostrich, appraising it theatrically. 'It is a capacious and sturdy piece of workmanship, *but* it has no filtering system.'

It is fortunate that both girls are elsewhere, because I know that bad news is about to be imparted. And it is. Within three days of it being filled, *même pas* three days, the water – if we ever locate any – will breed galloping algae and turn a brilliant green which, in this heat, would be a serious health hazard. The long and the short of it is that we cannot simply fill it as we had envisaged; we must construct a cleaning system which, when I hear his estimate, sends me tumbling backwards over the terraces.

The girls' disappointment when Michel breaks this to them over lunch is heartbreaking to behold. To say nothing of mine. We return to our land clearing in despondent mood.

In an attempt to cheer us all up, Michel calls us, beckoning us down the hill. '*J'ai une bonne idée!*' he cries.

'No more stupid ideas, please, Papa,' returns Vanessa, refusing even to glance in his direction. 'This whole place is a stupid idea,' she mutters to her sister, and I feel sinewy knots tighten in my stomach.

'A stroke of genius, *mes chéries*,' he coaxes. 'To put the empty pool to use.'

But they will not even turn their heads. I watch him walk away, saddened by his defeat. Then, curiously, he gathers up our old radio-cassette-player, takes it to the swimming pool and descends the steps with it. I am intrigued. 'Look at your father,' I say, but the girls will not relent. When he has satisfied himself that he is standing in the centre of the empty space, he places the machine, a rather clapped-out ghetto-blaster, on the floor and slips a cassette into it. The voice of Sting bounces off the walls, backed by reverberating bass and acoustic guitar, and reaches up the hill to the terraces, where we three girls are at hot, sticky work. Their cross faces break into expressions of delight. We down tools and race towards the music. There we are, covered in earth and bits of scythed weeds which have stuck to our perspiring flesh, alongside Michel, who is clapping to the beat. 'Every problem has a good side,' he laughs, winking blue eyes in my direction, while Pamela growls uncomprehendingly as we dance and hoot like crazed Indian squaws.

Into this bizarre scene arrives a small white Renault van. It is the electrician, M. Dolfo. He looks at us askance, trying not to notice the radio sitting in the centre of a huge empty pool and the fat Alsatian going bananas barking at us. His exaggerated pretence at not seeing us makes us giggle all the more.

M. Dolfo takes Michel aside as though there is no sense to be had anywhere near three such hysterical females and begins a conversation which appears to be serious and highly secretive.

The evening before, over a glass, M. Dolfo tells Michel, he was in conversation with a fellow workman, a plumber and chimney sweep. By chance, he was relating the woes of the new waterless house owners on the hill. *Quelle surprise!* His colleague, who was born and bred in the village and, as a lad, used to hunt on our land, knows the exact whereabouts of our water house. M. Dolfo offers to drop by at the end of the day with the plumber, M. Di Luzio. There is great excitement. I dash to the village to buy beer, boxes and boxes of it, to chill in our new little fridge and offer to our rescuers. However, as the prospect of water at long last has become almost too improbable to count on, I try very hard not to allow optimism to get the better of me. I could never have imagined that the idea of water running from a tap would send me into such paroxysms of joy.

The viscosity in the light created by the day's heat is evaporating. M. Dolfo arrives up the hilly driveway late in the afternoon in his Renault van (which I later discover he cannot reverse) followed by the chugging of an exceedingly old vehicle the size of a small bus. This is M. Di Luzio. The fellow emerges from behind the steering wheel in filthy blue overalls, covered from head to foot in soot. He has been cleaning chimneys, he explains with a roar of laughter, and the whites of his eyes shine as though he were a member of a troupe of black and white minstrels. I immediately take to him and to his thick Provençal accent, which twangs like country music, and offer him a cold beer. This he accepts like a naughty boy, looking this way and that in pantomimic fashion as though he were about to be chased with a rolling pin. He pats his robust stomach, downs the beer in several thirsty gulps and mutters mischievously about disobeying his wife and the strict diet she keeps him on.

Michel recounts to me later how he and the two men set off on foot. They cross the lane bordering our land and disappear into the valley which sits between us and a narrow track winding down to the village and on to the sea. There, in that valley, they come upon a small stone house about the size of a shepherd's cot.

'Your water shed!' declares M. Di Luzio.

Unbeknown to us, this *petit* cabin was built by our splendid

Italian predecessor, Signor Spinotti, in the same year as Appassionata and remains a part of the estate. When it was first constructed, Appassionata's domain included the valley and the hills beyond. Nowadays, this particular parcel of land is owned by a syndicate in Marseille. Still, the small stone house, which has electricity, a water board meter and an electric pump, remains the property of the proprietors of the villa and they have water rights as well as rights of passage. Its thick wooden door is jammed closed, but M. Di Luzio wastes no time in breaking in and, to reassure Michel, he points out the mains pipes situated above ground outside and running alongside a small stream back towards the town.

First, the three men switch on the water. It gushes forth instantly and splashes into the water house, filling up a cement dugout about a metre deep.

'Now we switch on the electric pump,' continues M. Di Luzio, gesturing his colleague, M. Dolfo the electrician, to do the honours.

The pump begins to shimmy like a plump belly dancer.

'From here the water will be pumped to the basin at the top of the hill and from there it will flow back down to the house,' explains M. Dolfo. Michel and the two artisans at his side look on satisfied; then they pull fast the door and make their way back up to the villa for a second, well-deserved cold beer.

M. Di Luzio takes a deep slug from his bottle, squinting towards the hill's brow. Behind him we stand like extras, the crowd in a film, following his gaze, waiting expectantly. A remarkably large black and white butterfly flutters by me. '*Deux heures,*' our new plumber pronounces with the expertise and wisdom of God.

Two hours. The words are repeated like a Chinese whisper as though the miracle were too incredible to articulate out loud. In two hours we will have water!

'*Quelle heure est-il?*' demands Vanessa, needing, as always to be precise. Clarisse shrugs. She has lost her watch somewhere between wild flower-picking and selecting branches for floral arrangements from among the scythed broom Vanessa and I have decimated.

'Half-past six.'

'So, half-past eight then? Yippee!'

Half-past eight comes, and half-past eight goes. The water does not arrive. Every thirty minutes one of us is given the thirst-inducing duty of pounding up the hill in the failing evening light to confirm whether or not the water has begun to arrive. Each of us returns half dead with a shake of the head. *Pas encore.* Five hours later, as we prepare for bed, there is still no sign of it.

The next morning M. Di Luzio returns. Accompanied by Michel, who by now is acquainted with every overgrown square centimetre of this land, he sets off with shears and a scythe to walk the hills and terraces in search of burst pipes and leaks. They find none. So, *en principe*, there is no reason why the water should not be arriving up in the basin. Eventually, a return visit to the stone house reveals that the electric pump which burst into life at the flick of a switch has died. After so many years of idleness, clearly the effort was simply too much for it. We will need a new pump. After a lunchtime consultation with M. Dolfo, we learn that the new pump will cost, including labour, approximately 10,000f. This is bad news. Ten thousand francs is more than we have left, and we have not yet settled our bill with Monsieur Parking. We thank both M. Dolfo and M. Di Luzio for their assistance and tell them we will be in touch again when we next return to the coast. Shaking hands with us, they slip discreetly away. Their disappointment on our behalf is evident.

Friends arrive in a two-car convoy from England bringing with them bits of furniture: two large terracotta pots I purchased in

Crete, which will look splendid either side of the pool steps, as well as other offerings of one sort or another, plus, most importantly, my mail. We cannot hide our dismay at the water fiasco. A salad lunch is made and Michel recounts the ongoing saga over an aperitif while I disappear to our bedroom to go through my stack of letters. Most are junk, a few are from long-distant friends who have heard on the grapevine of my new life – 'sounds divine, darling!' – and who long to come and visit, and one is from my agent. A letter from my agent usually contains one of two things: some occasional forwarded fan mail or a cheque. This one is a slender envelope, so my hopes are high. I open it with trembling fingers, praying that the cheque will not be for some ridiculous sum, like the 47p I received recently from the BBC for a programme sale to some outlandish cable channel in the middle of Botswana. It is notification of a cheque which has been paid directly into my account in London for a series of sales of and repeat fees on *All Creatures Great and Small*. It more than covers the price of the water pump. In fact, it will stretch to the first instalment on the required cleaning system for the pool. Our day – no, our summer – is made.

I run crazily out on to the upper terrace, waving the statement like a flag of victory. The friends and family seated round the table on the level below me cheer and raise their glasses as I deliver the news.

Michel hurtles off in the car to telephone M. Dolfo while the rest of us lay the table for lunch and change the cassette in the swimming pool. Funky music echoes around the hillside. Our water problem is at an end.

Ah, how much in city life we take for granted! Here the simple rituals of getting clean, brushing our teeth, soaping our flesh recklessly, frothing our hair into sudsy turbans of shampoo make us jubilant. Vanessa discovers a leak in one of the pipes from which the water is spraying out as though from a geyser. She jumps about over it and leaps on the muddied earth, splashing and washing, laughing and whooping. Her exuberant cries cut through the hot, still heat, silencing even the cicadas.

'See, the house faces south-west. It looks out over the bay of Cannes, the promontory of Fréjus and the sweeping Golfe de la Napoule, and if we stand on tiptoe or take a ladder and scale the back wall up on to our flat gravelled roof, you can clearly see the two islands sleeping off the coast of Cannes, west of Antibes, known as the Îles de Lérins.'

From our top terrace, after sundown, when the streetlamps light up along the coastal road that snakes around the promontory, it looks as though someone has dropped a priceless diamond necklace, leaving it to glitter across the westerly half of the horizon. Sometimes, the Estérel mountains turn a dusky blue and resemble a Japanese painting. Alongside them, the sunset creates a pink sky which puts me in mind of flamingos flitting across a mirage. Our friends are falling for this ramshackle farm as much as we have. So we are not alone, not so dizzy.

Thanks to the rooms taken by our guests, Monsieur Parking now has a full hotel. He puts up the sign, '*Complet*,' and the small affair of illicit showers is dismissed with a shrug and a glass of wine. We settle our account with him while the girls pack their bags and then we drive them home to be with us at the farm. And what is more, they seem excited at the prospect.

'*Papa! Papa, viens içi!*' It is Clarisse calling. Everyone downs tools and runs to the terrace, where she is standing and waving. Vanessa is at her side. They are now kneeling and staring into our pond. '*Il y a des poissons!*'

I knew it! Ever since that hot, midge-biting afternoon when we first discovered the pond, I have been returning there to try to penetrate the living mystery of its smoked-glass surface.

Clarisse, with her usual fascination for the minutiae of wildlife, has spent the last hour filling jugs of water from the luxury of our water supply – a running tap! – and pouring them into the pond. The fresh water has stirred the silt and life beneath. There, swimming close to the brimming surface of the diluted, bracken-toned water, are three huge fish, each a good foot long.

'*C'est incroyable!*'

The four of us are on all fours like thirsty moggies bent close over the water examining the fish. They are carp, or monstrous goldfish. Then another appears. And another. In all, we count five or six. Possibly even seven – it is difficult to be precise as they dart and dive. But the first three are the largest.

'How have they lived all this time?' I wonder.

'On the plankton, the natural vegetation. Still, it is rather miraculous.'

Indeed it is. Another discovery of Appassionata's life, its resilience. Each day we are thrilled by new wonders.

Out of the blue a rather disagreeable guest turns up, an elderly single gentleman searching for Michel. He is a writer who has come in the hope of selling him a screenplay. How did he find us? we ask ourselves, but can come up with no satisfactory explanation. Fortunately, our living circumstances are so manifestly primitive that we have no need to apologise for the lack of a bed, but politeness and Michel's endless generosity dictate that we invite him to stay for dinner. Our little gathering has now reached eleven. Dinner is cooked on the barbecue. Its preparation is a communal affair and great fun.

We dine beneath the *Magnolia Grandiflora*. From there we have views to the sea and the mountains. Golden lambent light from the antique oil lamp I brought from England illuminates our late-evening gathering. Water trickling into the pool threatens to drown out Billie Holiday's 'Easy Living'. We hardly care.

The flow is itself music to our ears, even if, at this rate, we calculate that the pool will take three weeks to fill. Chris, one of
my oldest friends, suggests that we invest in several hosepipes
and offers to purchase them for us as a housewarming gift. We
drink to that and assure him that he has guaranteed himself a
welcome return visit.

We recount the trials and tribulations of our search for water
to our unexpected new arrival. In response, rather like an
embittered old Cassandra, he predicts: 'Once a water problem,
always a water problem. In my house in Spain . . .' And goes on
to tell with great relish his woeful tales, as though he were wishing us an equal measure of ill luck. The table goes silent and
still; nothing more than water spluttering into the pool, the
distant chirring of sleepless crickets and the strains of 'Good
Morning Heartache' can be heard.

'Still, the problem is solved. Now we have water,' I chip in
cheerily.

'And there is always wine,' rejoins Michel, replenishing
glasses all round.

Later, replete and wined, our numerous guests set off down the
drive heading over the hills to the cosy amiability of Monsieur
Parking and perhaps to a last nightcap together at the bar.
There is much kissing and embracing, much drunken fooling, a
dozen repeated 'goodnights', bonhomie and promises of outings to the beach and to the various flea markets over the
course of the next few days. And then, with the receding hum
of the last of the cars, we are left alone. *En famille*.

For a short while before turning in, we sit together gazing at
the canopy of stars, arms slung loosely round one another: a
man, his two adoring daughters and the new woman. An
actress; another breed of woman, nothing like Maman. Little is
said. I occasionally read perplexity or guilt in the girls' behaviour, particularly today, when a thick letter arrived from

Maman and they snatched it up like small squirrels and carted it off to read it in the privacy of their bedroom. I am aware that to like me might well be seen by them as an act of infidelity to their mother or their parents' past life, but still I sense we are creeping towards one another. Shattered after work-filled days, in the hot sticky evenings, in the silence or the lack of language, mosquitos buzzing like dive bombers, I dare to believe we are slowly growing to accept one another. With an embrace and a hug, we all drift off to bed.

Michel's back is playing up, probably as a result of scaling the hills and the nights spent on the lumpy old mattress. But it doesn't seem to stop him sleeping while I lie awake thinking a million different thoughts, such as how I wish we could afford a proper bed. Still, I am happy. I love the king-hearted man breathing peacefully at my side. I love this old house, although I am beginning to comprehend the enormity of the task we are taking on. But we are not in any hurry. This is our first summer. Officially, the property is not yet ours. That hurdle – oh Lord! – has yet to be faced. For the moment we have achieved electricity and water. With these two precious commodities in place, we can live here, in a basic sort of fashion. Tomorrow, work on the pool-cleaning system will begin. We have the barbecue for summer; add to that plenty of fresh salad from the richly colourful market in Cannes, a choice of fine cheeses, oven-warm bread and many bottles of local wine, and how better fed could we be? When we return at Christmas, Michel says that he will teach me how to cook on the open fire. I reshuffle myself trying to avoid the springs and cuddle up into the arc of his soft back, closing my eyes preparing to dream of our first winter here – log fires, barbecued turkey and outings in search of woodland ceps – when I hear a pitter-pattering above me.

I lift my head into the warm, starry darkness, trying to locate the sound. The roof of this house is flat. Is it a small animal running to and fro? Rats? Then, as the sound grows faster and more furious, I realise that it is rain. The first we have had here. I drag the flimsy summer sheet around me and listen to it falling. Summer rain, after so many parched and waterless days. With it will come a whole host of new perfumes. Drenched nature. We have our own thin stream of water trickling into the pool and, as if to assist it, the heavens have opened. I fall asleep to the cloudbursts drumming fast overhead.

The next morning, the rain has stopped. The ground is damp and earthy-smelling and the air is clear, washed of its heavy, thick heat.

Unusually, I am the first out of bed and creep sleepy-eyed to the kitchen to brew coffee. Imagine my surprise when I suddenly realise that the floor is wet underfoot and cold. I look down to discover three puddles sitting like rainclouds on the *tommette*-tiled kitchen floor. At first, I am ready to blame poor Pamela for having slunk into the kitchen in the dead of night in search of food and piddled there, and then the horror dawns on me. I lift my head ceilingwards and see that in among all the flaking strips of plaster there are three holes. Tiny holes barely bigger than pencils, but they are lethal, for they are letting in rainwater.

'Michel! We have a leaking roof!'

Holiday Boars and Henri

We haven't a centime left to plough into the leaking roof, or the kitchen or the replastering, or the rest of the *projets* that await us. On top of which the house still has to be finally purchased. I wake nightly, soaked in perspiration, haunted by Mme B.'s proviso: 'If anything should go wrong, you lose everything.' We have certainly invested more than we had bargained for at this stage. Still, our first major hurdle, the water, has finally been resolved so, in the company of the girls, Michel and I decide to ignore the rest and take it easy. We allow ourselves to be *en vacances*.

We sleep with the French windows open, ready to greet the next dawn. Our room looks out on to a scruffy rear terrace partially shaded by two fragrantly scented eucalyptus trees and a Portuguese oak, an evergreen whose silvery-hued leaves rather resemble those of the olive tree. This terrace is where we spend time alone. We breakfast here while the girls sleep late: toast, fresh fruit, coffee. Although it is the only terrace that does not look out over the Mediterranean, I love it; tucked away at the back of the house, it feels like ours.

The rising sun filtering through the treetops promises another warm day. While I put the coffee on, Michel drives down the hill a kilometre or so to the village baker who has been up making bread since 3 a.m. There Michel purchases fresh warm baguettes, *pain au chocolat* so light it practically melts at the touch, and, usually, a *sablé*, a large round biscuit flavoured with almonds, which, in spite of my perennial weight-watching, I devour with a greed which would put Pamela to shame.

By now my morning trips to the beach have been abandoned. Instead, I head for the pool, entering by the steps because there is still insufficient water to dive in. The level in the shallow end has now reached my thighs. I tumble in and doggy-paddle to the deeper end, where I can swim a decent width or two. I try not to splash noisily so as not to wake the girls, who sleep till noon, when they throw open their shutters to blinding hot light.

After the frenzy of the past two weeks, a more languorous pace is taking hold and we give ourselves up to it readily. I am beginning work on a novel, my first, having already completed its storyline. Michel has presented it to various networks and raised the finance to produce it as a television series in Australia later in the year.

Michel is never without his camera now. Photography is his passion. There are the obvious 'before-and-after' house snaps for future albums, but mostly he shoots plants, usually flowers. He spends hours gazing through a lens into the stamen of this yellow flower, that wild rose. It is quite staggering how many varieties of flora have survived in among the brambled chaos of this garden and manage somehow or other to find the light, to hold their heads up towards the sun and blossom richly.

I begin to notice the similarities between Clarisse and Michel as I watch father and daughter discussing the intricacies of a bud, the feather-thin line drawings on a leaf, the shape of a frond, even a blade of grass. Together they disappear down unseen tracks for hours on end in their search to uncover ever more layers of nature. They are true children of the earth. In our different ways we all are – we are all four of us Taureans.

In the quietness of a heat-infested afternoon, while they explore and Vanessa, munching crispy apple after crispy apple, sunbathes or studies or washes her long hair, and myriad bees busy themselves collecting honey, I decide to take an inventory. I begin with the trees. For starters, I count fifty-four olive trees growing along the front terraces and on either side of the house. There may be others further up the hill but, at this stage, it is impossible to reach them. I try to recall tales, myths I have read or heard about the olive, surely the most ancient of all trees. The Greeks brought it to Provence, I believe, two or more thousand years ago while trading in the Mediterranean.

I intend to farm ours. The olive is a bitter fruit and cannot be eaten directly from the tree. The four ways I know of to serve it are to press it into oil; bottle it in brine or marinate it to offer with aperitifs or tossed in a salad; cooking with it; or to make it into tapenade, a paste created by a M. Meynier in Marseille towards the end of the nineteenth century. The name comes from *tapéno*, which is the Provençal word for capers. Tapenade is made by pulping the fruit and mixing it with capers and anchovies (best fresh, particularly those from the Camargue). It can be spread on warm toast and served with crisply chilled wine, and is delicious.

But perhaps these wondrously ancient trees have other offerings I have yet to discover. Since being here, I have learned that the timber burns on an open fire better than almost any other wood, and we will find ourselves with plenty of spare timber; every tree needs pruning. They are far too bushy and tall. A

perfectly pruned olive is one through which a swallow can fly
without its wings brushing the branches.

Slowly, I am gleaning such snippets of information. As I
stroll the land, list in hand, I promise myself that the next
time I am in Cannes, I will find a manual on olive farming.
Still, no matter how much I study, we will need to find someone, a hands-on chap, who can take on this highly specialised
skill. Down here, it is a much-respected occupation. At this
stage, I have no idea how to go about this, but I feel confident
that, in the fullness of time, the right man for the job will
come along.

We have four almond trees, the largest of which is at swimming-pool level to the right of the house, beyond the
frost-bitten orange grove. It leans forward at a rather precarious angle and will need cutting back and shoring up before a
mistral rips it from the ground, taking roots and a drystone
wall with it. I should hate to lose it. Its position is perfect for its
powder-pink blossoms to be in full view of all sea-facing terraces. Almonds flower earlier than most fruit trees, so I expect
we will see the first of the blossoms some time in February.
Later, the nuts, once removed from green shells that resemble
soft, furry caterpillars, can be roasted on our open fire.

Our tiny orange grove is a sorry spectacle. All six trees are
dead. Before we close up the house, I will cut them down.

Over to the left, and facing the sea, I can make out two
cherry trees. They are overgrown and need pruning, and will
probably be fruiting around the time of the Cannes Film
Festival. We could munch them instead of popcorn during the
screenings. On the opposite side there is a tall bay tree which,
due to the growth, I cannot get near but I can almost taste the
many soups and roasts to come, all seasoned with rosemary,
olive oil poured from our own pressed crop and freshly picked
bay leaves.

So far, I have counted eight fig trees, one of which must be the largest fruit tree I have ever set eyes on. It reminds me of a prehistoric beast, its trunk is so thick and gnarled. It shades a segment of our steep driveway and hides a very ugly EDF cement pylon which, as soon as funds allow, we will do away with by cabling the electricity underground from lane to house.

Several of the fig's branches reach across the drive and hang down over the pool. Temptation itself. I imagine relaxing in between laps, stretching for a ripe fruit and devouring it while idling in the water. In the past, I have never been particularly fond of fresh figs, but I wonder if living with them will re-educate my tastes. Gorging on freshly picked figs strikes me as hedonistic. It conjures up images of Roman baths with slaves serving bowls laden with overripe fruit. It is a sexual fruit; luscious, rich in seeds with a viscous juice. Standing in the driveway, head tilted upwards, fingers pressed against my panama, gazing into the green vastness of the tree, it occurs to me that it has no flowers. I wonder why. And how it pollinates. So much syrupy fodder, and the poor bees have no reason to visit.

I took off my watch a fortnight ago and have not worn it since. The sun has become my timekeeper. It rises behind us, greets us in the bedroom and breakfasts with us. From there it passes to the cherry tree side of the house and then, noon-high in the sky, makes its arc around the front, over the glinting sea, until it hovers in the west, where it sinks slowly and graciously behind the hills, leaving a sky of bleeding colours.

Now it is high above the Fréjus promontory. Four o'clock: time for tea. I begin a slow meander back up towards the house to face the dratted water-heater in our primitive kitchen, still cogitating on my list and wondering where the others have got to.

Apples; mandarins; lemons; cut down dead orange trunks and plant new trees, pears . . . no, there is a pear. I caught sight

of it on the level below the pool, next to where we are constructing the pool-cleaning system. There is a smattering of
fruits on it, but they are all misshapen and worm-eaten. It needs
treating. And I have always fancied an orchard. My parents
bought a house with an orchard when I was small but we never
lived in it. I was sad; visits there were the only times I ever saw
my father pottering in the garden. And what about a modest
vineyard? Where did Spinotti plant his vines?

So many dreams. But the stuff of dreams is the food of life,
and I marvel at what we have achieved this summer on a shoestring and a bit of graft. Appassionata is slowly coming back to
life. The house is waking up, its essence re-emerging. Shapes,
colours, aspects of light are speaking to us.

Michel and I met on a film in Australia, a country we both
love profoundly. Its colours, its light, its vast expanses spoke to
both of us and, had our lives not been so locked into our
careers here in Europe, this house we are buying might have
been another somewhere on the Australian continent.

It is widely known that the Australian aboriginals go walkabout but what I did not know, until I crossed the world to work
there, was that one of the purposes of their walkabouts is to sing
nature back into existence. I find that such an enchanting image.
To walk a land every so often, as I have been walking our patch
today, and sing the mountains, rivers, streams, caves, animals,
insects, nature in all its diverse magnificence, back into existence. I equate that idea with what we are attempting to achieve
here. Appassionata had been abandoned. She – I see the house as
she, perhaps because the French word *maison* is feminine – she,
Appassionata, had been left to go to ruin. Her fruits had
dropped from the trees and lay rotting. The plants, every bush,
every shrub, were being strangled. The house had lost its voice.
Or, rather, its voice had gone unheard.

In my understanding of the aboriginal walkabout – and I am
not saying that this is its true purpose, merely my interpretation

of it – every mountain, hill, waterfall, ants' nest, pathway has its voice. To stand at any moment in front of the miracle of any particle of nature and to listen, truly listen, is to hear its song. To hear its song is to allow it to sing. That is how I understand 'singing a place back into existence'; how I have defined the ritual of walkabout.

Michel and I are attempting to sing this smallholding in the south of France back into blooming existence. We will try to listen to what it has to offer and to celebrate its uniqueness. Of course, all this is subjective, and anyone eavesdropping on my train of thought might very well accuse me of being *loco*, suffering from a touch of the midday sun. But then, the discoverers of Australia dismissed the aborigines as an ignorant bunch who had nothing to offer.

The others are nowhere to be found. I abandon the idea of tea, which I am not fond of anyway, and drag a gaudily striped deckchair to the top terrace. There I settle to gaze upon the sea. It is a very pleasing sensation to spend hour after hour sitting still, simply watching the play of light on sea and sky. I have not done it for a very long time. Too long. Time passes and I unwind, watching and listening. Even in its silence, the land is furiously busy. Ants, lizards, geckos, cicadas, they are all going about their days, searching for food, fending off the enemy, screeching their mating calls, thriving on or surviving the heat. They are not on holiday.

But then, neither am I, I suddenly remember. In the short term, for a few weeks with Michel and his daughters, yes, but not in the long term. I am moving the rudder, shifting the course of my life. I have not thought of it in this way before, but that is what I am doing. Taking my fate into my own hands, turning dreams into reality. And there is nothing more sacred or precious than that. To choose a direction: but how often do we miss the signposts?

'What have you been up to all afternoon?'

'Oh, hi there. Counting trees.'

Clarisse and Michel are returning. They are dusty and shiny from walking. Clarisse shows me a tiny crayon drawing she has made during the course of the afternoon. It is very impressive and I tell her so. She beams contentedly. '*C'est la lumière*,' she replies modestly, and Michel ruffles her hair.

Yes, there is a quality to the light here which famously seduced so many great painters. Living with it on a daily basis, the subtleties of it begin to draw me in. On certain days its purity is blinding, on others its colours alter as clouds, winds, hours of heat seep into it. Here light is a living experience of a kind I have known only once before, in Australia. It enhances all photos and frames of footage each moment of the day. Sitting still and contemplating it or, like Michel, reproducing it through flowers on film, is a spiritual experience.

The contemplation of Pamela is another matter altogether. I watch her with dismay as she heaves herself from one shady spot to the next, continuously hunting out respite from the broiling sun. She has lived all her life on the outskirts of Paris and I fear that this relentless Riviera heat is going to kill her. 'Her heart will give out,' I predict. The others tease me and mock my sense of the dramatic, but I pay no attention to them and announce one morning at breakfast that I am putting the corpulent creature on a strict diet.

'Carol, why must you be so strict? Drink your coffee and leave *la pauvre* Pamela in peace!' chides Vanessa.

'Is it a rash and foolish interference?' I ask Michel, who is not listening. He is kneeling on the ground, like a mutt himself, staring with concentration at a wall.

'You will live to regret it,' Clarisse warns me.

'Come and look at these little chaps!'

A procession of brown, furry caterpillars linked to one

another in a crocodile diverts our attention. United, the length of them measures more than a metre.

'They look as though they are bound for somewhere.'

Certainly they are moving with purpose and visible speed. Are they being led to a congenial hideaway where, in tranquillity and privacy, they can transform themselves into butterflies? We are all four of us completely absorbed, mesmerised by their singlemindedness. A family of four on all fours, staring at a wall, must make a curious tableau.

In the hours after breakfast on our hidden terrace, where Michel first spotted the caterpillars marching down one of the drystone walls, making their way across the terrace and into the house, they have preoccupied all four of us. They have exited the house now, having crossed the main living room – leaving a clean trail in the dust of the untouched rooms – travelled the length of the top terrace and descended one of the pillars. They are now tramping, at swimming-pool level, off towards the uncut bracken. Will they get lost in the thicket? Or will they see it for the wilderness that it is, turn round and return to us? The distance they have covered since this morning – it is now siesta time, baking hot and I am alone because the others have disappeared for a nap – is considerable. They put me in mind of a small train puffing away, heading for the great unknown. A tractor crossing Russia en route for Siberia. I see they have reached the uncut terrain and, without a moment's hesitation, have disappeared into it. *Bonne chance!*

I am very taken with the butterflies here. They are numerous and of many different colours and species. In a few weeks' time, I will look closely into the eye of each circling butterfly and enquire of it: were you one of our visiting caterpillars who left your autograph in our dust?

I have wound down to a pace which is almost slow motion. I am watching time elapse. It is a delicious exercise which allows me to focus on details to which, in my ordinary life, my real life, I would not give seconds.

The bucket that was used to flush the loos when we had no water is now in the upstairs kitchen. Well, barely a kitchen: it comprises an aluminium sink, part of a unit containing probably the first dishwasher ever built and now non-functional, an electric kettle which must predate the London Electricity Board and a musty, woodworm-riddled cupboard. I have positioned the bucket beneath those three dratted holes, which stare at me every time I go in there; the three one-eyed Cyclops who made thunderbolts. We have been forced to accept that, for this summer at least, this is the most effective solution we can come up with to deal with the leaking roof. Fortunately, since that monumental downpour, not one drop of rain has fallen. Still, it is amazing to me how much time I can fritter away standing beneath three minuscule holes and fixing them with a malevolent gaze.

Wandering through the fusty, scruffy rooms, basking in the cool generated by the metre-deep stone walls which comprise the husk of the house, I step out on to the upper front terrace and am hit by a blanket of heat and sunshine. I subside into a chair and begin to listen. There are small birds here which flit in and out of the bushes. Their song reminds me of the mellifluous bell bird, which I came across in Melbourne last year when I was filming there. I have no idea if they exist on this side of the world. Occasionally, when these birds start to sing, I charge indoors, thinking the phone is ringing – it's my agent! – until I remember that we have no phone!

There is so much I should be doing: attacking the novel I have begun, washing down walls, scraping encrusted dirt out of wooden window frames, worrying about Mme B. and whether this deal will ever go through, or whether I – we – are living out a summer's fantasy which will lead us right into the mouth of financial disaster. But instead I do nothing except sit, listen and contemplate.

Evening comes and I rise languorously to feed Pamela. Her bowl is kept alongside the garage near the stone-walled stables, well away from our kitchen and food supplies. She wolfs down my offering in two gulps and then glowers at me with hatred. I have underestimated the force of Pamela's attachment to food, her *raison d'être*. But I hearten myself with the fact that she is looking slimmer. Until yesterday evening, she has spent every day lying slumped and panting in the shade as though gasping her last, and then, when Michel put out the dustbins at the bottom of the drive, she actually trudged along after him. Thank heavens, she is growing active.

Although our house is named Appassionata, there are no passion flowers to be found in the garden. None that we have unearthed, that is. Perhaps, later, we will discover a plant or two languishing beneath all our unruly growth. In the meantime I drive to a local nursery to purchase one, along with a twenty-kilo sack of *terreau universel*. My eye is caught by a small pomegranate tree, metres of curly tumbling geraniums and dozens of richly coloured roses, not to mention bananas and lemons and palms. Oh, the list is endless, but I must exercise restraint. I love nurseries, *les pépinières* (coincidentally the same noun is used to describe a school for young actors); I love the lushness and the damp, tropical scents, the splash of sharply coloured, exotic blossoms, the regulated coolness, and I love, now more than ever, that steady drizzle of hosepipes discreetly orchestrating the silent, lusty growth. I happily pass the hours I should be spending more usefully on hacking back the sinuous streams of weeds playing truant at the nursery.

On my way home I stop in the village to pick up fresh salad. I park up, cross the street alongside the square, where half a dozen old-hatted men wearing shades and looking like rejects from the Mafia are playing boules, and make for the *crémerie-fromagerie*. Here I buy two *crottins* of goat's cheese and two spit-roasted organic chickens, succulently seasoned with herbs and creamy toasted garlic cloves for our supper on the terrace.

As I am leaving, a farmer arrives. He has aroused my curiosity on several previous occasions because, in the rear of his Citroën van, which looks as though it is held together by elastic bands, he always carries a motley collection of farmyard animals. They honk and screech, but even though he leaves the van's rear door swinging open, they never attempt an escape. I hang back to observe him. Always the same routine: he unloads three wooden boxes stacked with small plastic pots. They are brimming with golden olive oil seasoned with Provençal herbs and, swimming in the centre of each pot, generous nuggets of goat's cheese. These he delivers to the *crémerie-fromagerie*. Then come the hams, usually ten. Substantial cuts, wrapped in light muslin cloth. Each is carefully weighed as it is handed over the counter. The bearded, keen-eyed owner of this modern-day dairy and this living scarecrow of a farmer, whose hair is never combed and whose clothes look like both he and every moth in the south of France have slept in them, conduct their business in front of waiting customers, including the one in the process of being served. Thick wads of cash pass from the till into the pocket of the farmer and off he goes with his jaunty gait, the wellingtons he wears even in the heat of summer slapping against the pavement. Why does he travel about with his animals? The first time I saw him, with two white goats, four ducks, some chickens and assorted honking geese all wedged tightly together, fowl shuffling in and around the goats' legs, I assumed that his passengers were on their way to be slaughtered or sold. But obviously not. They are his road companions and seem perfectly content, squashed up against one another, to travel with him. Has he no wife to take care of them back home? Judging by his appearance, I would guess not. If the pigs had not now become hams, would he also bring them with him? The owner of the *crémerie* is his regular customer, so there must be more pigs back at base, or else how does he continue to supply the *jambon*? Later, I learn that the hams are not his. He transports and sells them for a neighbouring farmer whose property borders his. The arrangement covers the cost of his petrol. His own lean income is earned from the goat's cheese and his travelling circus of fowls. As I suspected, he has no wife.

Back at the house, I deposit the food on the makeshift table in the kitchen downstairs. Alas, in my excitement to get back to the car and unsack the thick, dark earth into which I will plant my tender climber, I forget to shut the door. When I pass by a mere ten minutes later, I find the two bags which had contained the chickens in tatters on the floor. Even the cheese has disappeared. A brief scout around the garden leads me to Pamela, snoring beneath the cypress trees, surrounded by crunched bones and an army of ants who have already begun to pick dry the skeletal remains. Deciding not to whack an animal, particularly one that is not mine, I take myself back down to the village to buy another pair of chickens and two more of the goat's cheese 'droppings'. The young couple who own the *crémerie* stare at me incredulously as I ask for precisely what I bought only half an hour earlier. Unexpected guests, I mutter, feeling too foolish to admit that the dog ate our dinner.

The pale rays of the late-afternoon sun are lengthening. The hysterical chirring of the cicadas' song grows less strident. The day is slipping into dusky stillness. Evening is falling. Vanessa is lighting anti-mosquito candles as well as my oil lamp. Spaced out on the balustraded terrace, they create golden balls of light. Glasses of chilled Bandol rosé to hand, Michel and I ceremoniously plant the climber on a mezzanine terrace close to the front door. A tender young passion flower, our first purchase for the garden; the perfect offering. Clarisse waters it abundantly. Vanessa takes the shot with Michel's camera.

One day soon our first summer will be at an end, but these are the moments that will live on. I will return to them again and again in the safe harbour of memory. Consummate happiness. I stand back, absorbing the image of Michel with his adolescent girls, and wonder silently what the unknown future holds for us.

I was not prepared for this. When it comes to the refuelling of her stomach, a revitalised and cunning beast has been awakened. Docile Pamela, who identifies me as the enemy, the appropriator of her food, has declared war. This morning I find that the dustbins, ours as well as those belonging to the other two houses situated on the easterly quarter of our hill, have been raided. There are open cans, half-chewed sticks of stale baguette, empty food packets, along with the rest of the mish-mash found in any family's dustbin, trailing along the lane. I waste twenty minutes gathering up the rubbish and chucking it all back into our bin. A note from one of the neighbours attached to its lid politely requests that we keep our animal chained if it cannot keep its head out of *les poubelles*. Mortified, I write an apologetic reply to the unknown neighbours, which I slip into their letterbox. It will not happen again, I assure them.

Indeed, the problem will not arise again, for the girls are departing and with them goes fat Pamela. What a hullabaloo! What a chaos of semi-packed bags, broken zips, lost combs, whirring hairdryers, newly acquired swimwear, presents for Maman which are *très fragile*, as well as the calming of a most unsettled dog who, poor unsuspecting beast, will be obliged to travel in a miserable airline cage. Still, the frenzied activity keeps my sadness at bay. And when everything is finally arranged, albeit in a shambolic sort of way, Michel and I drive Clarisse and Vanessa to the airport and see them off. Today is the first wrench. This journey to Nice Airport will be the first of many. From here on, my life will be governed by trips to and fro, by welcome kisses and aching *au revoirs*.

Vanessa, so passionately at odds with her young body and the deepening colours of her adolescent sexuality and Clarisse, softly, lazily, striving for beauty and form. I have grown to love them and I so long for them to feel the same. I hope that these weeks, this glorious summer, have brought us closer. I want them to care for me, not as a surrogate mother, but as a friend, as kin. Nothing is said, no parting emotion declared. Still, shyly, they step forward and hug me awkwardly and then stagger off with their numerous bags, trailing towels and sneakers, through passport control, waving back and blowing kisses to their beloved Papa and maybe one to his new lady.

This departure is the first nudge that the summer holidays are drawing to a close. In another week Michel will also return to Paris. I have no acting job awaiting me, so I have decided to stay on, to get to grips with my novel and because I cannot bear to tear myself away just yet. Michel will fly down to spend the weekends with me.

We spend our final week together at our desks, preparing ourselves, slowly, for what the French call *la rentrée*, the return after the summer break. Michel's desk is a wobbly wooden table picked up at one of the many *brocantes* off Route Nationale 7, near Antibes. He has placed it in the shade beneath the *Magnolia Grandiflora*. I have learned that these trees were originally from the southern states of America, where they were discovered by the French botanist Plumier, who had been commanded by Louis XIV to seek out exotic plants for the royal gardens. The earliest examples were brought to France in the first half of the eighteenth century. They are named after Pierre Magnol (1638–1715), who was director of the botanical gardens in Montpellier.

Unlike Michel, I cannot concentrate in the blanket of heat and prefer to bury myself indoors. I choose one of the rooms which we have not yet touched, save for washing the floors and airing it. I have secretly bagged it for my workspace – I hate the word office – because it is bright but not too sunny. It has windows to the front which overlook the driveway and the angle of cypress trees. If I lean to my left, I can even glimpse the shallow end of the pool, now brimming with clear water. To the rear its French windows open on to the terrace where we breakfast. From there, if I am gazing out, I see roughly hewn stone steps climbing through the pine forest to the brow of the hill and our famous water *bassin*. Here, in this room, I set up a trestle table and store my laptop, reference books, scribbled notes for my story, maps, research literature and all my other papers. After each working session, to keep dust and falling plaster at bay, I wrap everything in a sheet. When Michel has left, I will strip the walls and whitewash them; rid the room of its hideous pink flowery wallpaper. There is a good feeling about this space; I can lose myself in my own world here. And because it has views in both directions, I don't feel claustrophobic. The only disturbance is an occasional rustling sound which I cannot trace or identify. It seems to be coming from a boxed-in pelmet above the front windows, which probably once stored a blind, but whenever I call Michel in to listen, the noise mysteriously ceases.

During an afternoon break from work I take a walk in the valley beyond our land, where I encounter a most extraordinary person who puts me in mind of a minotaur, or Goliath. He introduces himself as our neighbour, Jean-Claude. Oh, dear. He is the one who wrote the note complaining about Pamela. I smile sweetly. We wouldn't want to get on the wrong side of this fellow: he is built like an ox. He has a wiry black beard and black hair tied back in a ponytail, which falls to his nonexistent waist. He is wearing nothing but a pair of bizarrely cut red poplin shorts and calf-length black wellingtons and he carries two empty buckets, one in each hand like a milkmaid. I have barely given our names when he booms at me: 'Which water plan are you on?' I have absolutely no idea, and refrain from admitting that I was not even aware there were choices in these matters.

'Enquire of your husband, please, and let me know.'

This I dutifully promise to do and, satisfied with my reply, he suggests that we stroll over for an *apéro* with him and his wife, Odile, at seven o'clock. I accept. I am curious.

'Bring your water bill with you!' he yells after me as I set off again along the honeysuckle-scented track.

Buried away for another hour or two with my work before our *apéro*, I take time out to look up 'olive' in the Oxford Dictionary and am amazed to learn how many different varieties of olive tree exist.

An evergreen tree, *Olea Europæa*, esp. the cultivated variety *O.Sativa* with narrow entire leaves, green above and hoary beneath, and axillary clusters of small whitish four-cleft flowers; cultivated in the Mediterranean countries and other warm regions for its fruit and the oil thence obtained.

Extended to the whole genus *Olea*; also applied, with qualifying words, to various trees and shrubs allied to common olive, or resembling it in appearance or in furnishing oil.

American Olive, Bastard or Mock Olive, Black Olive, Californian Olive, Chinese Olive, Holly-Leaved Olive, Negro's Olive, Spurge Olive, Sweet-Scented Olive, White Olive, Wild Olive (the wild variety of the common olive).

The fruit or berry of *Olea Sativa* is a small oval drupe and bluish-black when ripe, with a bitter pulp abounding in oil, and hard stone. It is valuable as a source of oil, and also eaten pickled in an unripe state.

The dictionary also suggests that the blacker the olive fruit is on the outside, the more ripe it will be within. I assume that our trees are of the *Olea Sativa* variety but I will need to confirm this. Where can one seek out the White Olive or Holly-Leaved Olive or, indeed, any of the others listed above? If planted, would they survive here on our farm? What fruit, if any, would they produce for us? Personally, I find 'hoary' too cold an adjective to describe that deliciously sensual, mother-of-pearl tone of the underleaf.

At the designated hour for drinks, Michel and I stroll along the lane, hand in hand. Tall cypress trees guard the route like inscrutable centurions while husky-toned insects scratch into the evening calm. Michel is leaving for Paris in the morning and I am feeling blue. Outside the gate of the stately stone house whose sign reads, 'Le Verger', we pull on the bell chain. Inside my bag I have tucked our best bottle of Bordeaux. It is intended as a peace offering; I feel sure this man will have words about our badly behaved dog. Within seconds, a thickset Rottweiler with a head as broad and round as a car tyre hurls himself against the iron gate. Thud, thud. He growls and barks like a hound at the gates of hell. We retreat a step. They say dogs grow to resemble their masters and this creature is as robust and awesome as Jean-Claude himself.

A deep-throated roar sounds from a terrace beyond the swimming pool. Instantly, the dog retreats like a chastised puppy and cowers behind a camper van parked in the driveway. The gates open and we crunch across the gravelled parking area past several rather magnificent agave cacti, one of which has sprouted a gigantic spear with yellow flowers at its tip. The camper where the dog is still lurking is equalled in rustiness only by M. Di Luzio's old van. Jean-Claude appears, still dressed in only his red shorts but minus his wellingtons. He beckons us to the lower level of the house.

The monster dog rises and stalks terrifyingly at our heels.

Fearing for our safety, we glance back every few steps to keep an eye on him.

Jean-Claude, shadowed by a spotty adolescent, welcomes us inside. The young man, introduced to us as his son, Marcel, nods and retreats hurriedly as though even this amount of human contact has all but shrivelled him. We are now standing in a sombre but spacious kitchen decked out in dark, ivy-green wood with rather elaborate metal fittings.

'Three hundred thousand francs,' Jean-Claude announces proudly, appending to this astronomical figure the name of the firm responsible for what I can only describe as a monstrosity. No doubt it is meant to impress, but the name means nothing to me. A woman scurries into the room, cigarette in hand. '*Ma femme, Odile*,' booms Jean-Claude. Odile has hair as long and unkempt as Jean-Claude's, but unlike her husband, she is dressed, in a curious outfit made up of floaty bohemian bits of cloth and masses of expensive if rather ostentatious gold jewellery. She is exceptionally slender and very effusive and it is impossible not to view her as a refugee from the Addams Family.

'*Ah, les jeunes*,' she cries with a throaty laugh, and hurries over to kiss us both numerous times. I am surprised by the greeting because I cannot believe she is a day older than either of us. Jean-Claude tells her that he has been showing us the kitchen. She holds up her hands as though profoundly sorry for having interrupted a scenario of such gravitas.

'Do you have your water bill?'

I tug it from my shoulder bag, along with the wine, and hand it over to him. 'Sorry about the dustbins,' I murmur. Jean-Claude takes the bill, ignoring or not registering the proffered bottle, studies it with a frown and disappears off somewhere to ponder it in solitary silence. Odile takes over the displaying of the kitchen. Lights flick on in the most unlikely places, drawers open, vegetable racks swivel, canned-food cupboards unfold, bits whirr. Every gadget is exposed, does its party piece and slides back automatically to its resting place. We ooh and aah accordingly. Then, from somewhere deep in the belly of the house, we are summoned by Jean-Claude's roar. Odile starts like a nervous squirrel before leading us up a short flight of steps into a very dark, winding corridor and through to the *salon* which, after the kitchen, rather takes us aback. It is an enormous, high-ceilinged room which stretches the entire length of what we are to discover is an eight-bedroomed, three-storey *mas*. Even though it is a warm late-summer evening, a two-bar electric fire is aglow in the centre of a rather magnificent stone chimney hearth. A glance around shows us that the room is sparsely furnished, to say the least. It contains four white plastic garden chairs, a matching table, beneath which lurks the Rottweiler, and, over in a distant corner, a grand piano.

The telephone rings in a neighbouring room. Jean-Claude, barefoot, strides off to answer it. 'Zurich!' he bellows, and Odile scoots to the phone, closing folding doors behind her.

'She never stops working. *Asseyez-vous*,' waves Jean-Claude, using our water bill as a baton. I am beginning to cast him in the role of a rather offbeat wizard: with his crazy hair, unshod feet and the flimsy poplin shorts, all he lacks is a cloak. We pull out two of the plastic chairs and sit down. No one has so far acknowledged the wine, which I have tried on a couple of occasions to hand over, so I place it on the table where waits a plastic-wrapped white sliced loaf – the first I have encountered in France – a bottle of port, another of whisky, an empty ice bucket, four water tumblers and a large pot of some kind of mud-brown pâté. Three knives have also been left there.

'Marcel!' Jean-Claude yells to his son. From above us, rock music, which I had barely registered, is switched off. Footsteps on the landing and then the stairs bring Marcel to join us, clearly against his will. He and Jean-Claude take the other two chairs, though Jean-Claude rises the instant he has sat down, apparently incapable of stillness.

'What do you make of that?' he asks Michel, referring to our bill. He is opening the bottle of port and pours each of us a more than generous shot. Port is not my drink of choice and certainly not a sticky, tepid treble measure of it at seven on a warm summer's evening. Before Michel has been given the opportunity to comment and, thankfully, before we have taken more than a sip of the cloying liquid, Marcel is ordered to take us on a tour of the house. Jean-Claude returns to the water bill while Odile remains locked away beyond the room. The sound of her voice drifts through to us. Whoever has telephoned cannot have spoken a word, for Odile is chattering breathlessly.

Curiosity is bubbling within me. Who, or what, are these weird, exuberant people? Trailing Marcel, we trek from room to room, each as meagrely furnished as the last.

'Have you just moved in as well?' I ask.

'No. Why?'

There are sleeping bags on the floors of each of the eight bedrooms, except for the master bedroom, which boasts stripy yellow and blue curtains, fitted cupboards, swivel lamps, several floor-to-ceiling mirrors and an ornate gilt dressing table. Has to be the firm who built the kitchen.

'Your parents' room?' I say, stating the obvious, more to make conversation than anything else.

'Yes, but they don't sleep here.'

'Why not?'

Do they bed down in coffins? I am asking myself silently. Michel nudges me. My constant desire to ask questions and establish the full facts is an urge he believes I should temper, but the enquiry is out before I have considered its impertinence. Marcel, however, does not seem in the least put out.

'They sleep in the camper van with the dogs,' is his simple explanation.

Even I am silenced by this response. Having trawled the length and breadth of the house, we are returned to the *salon* just as Odile reappears from behind the folding doors. She is followed by a second dog: a Rottweiler puppy who threatens to grow up looking as mean as his mate.

'Whisky,' she begs. Jean-Claude pours her an exceedingly generous shot and refills our tumblers of port, which, given that they have barely been touched, leaves us each cradling about a third of a litre of ruby port. Marcel unwraps the loaf and begins spreading butter on the anaemic-looking slices. '*Santé!*' We lift our glasses to the toast and sip the alcohol. The telephone rings. Marcel goes.

'Amsterdam!' he calls to his mother. Odile lights a cigarette, sighs wearily, grabs the Camel packet and, Scotch in hand, disappears.

'Drink up!' yells a hearty Jean-Claude, which is precisely what I am trying to avoid doing. We have already been here the best part of an hour, it is our last evening of summer and we want to leave. But it is now announced that we will eat when Odile has finished her call. Michel, coming to the rescue, informs father and son that we have food waiting at home. Jean-Claude will not hear of it. Certainly we can return to our meal later, but first we must share the pâté, whose ingredients he has shot and prepared himself. *Sanglier.* I enquire where around these parts he might have come across a wild boar. This little hill may be the last undiscovered corner of rural paradise on the coast of the Alpes-Maritimes but the fact remains that we are still only ten minutes from Cannes. 'There are no wild boar prancing about our garden,' I jest.

'*Mais, si, si*, on the far side of your hill,' he tells me. 'Families of them.'

Jean-Claude does not strike me as a joker, though what it is he does strike me as I really cannot work out. I peer into his face to see if he is kidding me. No hint of humour registers.

'Are there really?' I squeak.

'Of course not, *chérie*,' says Michel.

'Yes, and snakes and scorpions,' Jean-Claude insists.

I slug down half my glass of port in one mouthful. During the time it takes Odile to talk at length to Marseille, Paris and, finally, Geneva, Jean-Claude has forced Marcel to the piano and dragged us over as well. We are now engaged in a most squawkingly embarrassing singalong which eventually includes a radiantly happy Odile. She loves music (music!), she informs us, helping herself to another tumbler of whisky and another packet of cigarettes. '*Le boulot est fini!*' she ululates. Her work is over for the evening.

The white bread and wild-boar pâté are being enjoyed by the dogs, who are up on the chairs, front paws and mouths on the table, licking, slurping and dribbling at a chaotic mess of food (and these people complained about the antics of poor, gentle, if greedy, Pamela!). No one seems to care. By now Michel and I are completely plastered. I can see six Jean-Claudes in the room, all of them bellowing and trumpeting like a herd of elephants on heat. And when a song is finished he roars goodheartedly, slapping the piano, filling the capacious space with his monstrous happiness. In my present state, I find myself entirely uplifted by his infectious energy.

And so we stay on.

By the time we stagger back up our driveway, pitching about without a torch, the sky is a blanket of midnight navy with the moon and brilliant stars a child's cut-outs within it. It is too late to eat, and we are too drunk to cook, so we linger in the grounds for a while, swimming to clear our heads, and then collapse, recumbent alongside one another on a sun-lounger listening to the night spinning and spinning before our drunken eyes.

'What was Odile talking so earnestly to you about? Was it the water bill?' I slur, without turning my head from its stargazing. The movement would send my brain reeling.

'No, neither of them explained that. She was describing her work,' Michel replies.

'Which is?'

'She's a clairvoyant. Clients telephone from all over Europe, pay her by credit card and she gives them a half-hour "reading". Curious.'

'So my picture of Jean-Claude as a wizard was not so far off the mark,' I drawl.

'Jean-Claude? Oh, no. He's an estate agent.'

Hung over, and nursing a raging headache, Michel departs on the early-morning plane for Paris. A strange emptiness descends upon me. The changing of seasons. The first whiffs of autumn in the air. The swallows swooping low, forgathering close to the house, anticipating their journey to Africa. Colours are turning, resetting. Tinctures of yellows and russet are appearing. An exquisite chunk of time is winding down, drawing to its inevitable close. All my life I have found myself ill equipped to cope with such moments of loss, but then I remind myself that this is a temporary shift. We have our lives ahead of us and the house is barely ours. Challenges await us and Michel will be back on Friday. My mood rallies.

I work off some of the loneliness by stripping the wallpaper in my study. The rustling noise is still there, augmented from time to time by the odd squeak. Has a strange creature just been born? My imagination leaps to trailers I have seen for Hollywood horror movies in which small plastic beings begin to move around silently in the cellar of some unsuspecting all-American home. At first they are cute and squeak; then they grow bigger, and by reel six they are threatening world domination. I am tempted to rip the pelmet away from the wall, but fear what I might discover. Best to leave well alone. It is probably a gecko that has been disturbed by our arrival here. They are timid little chaps and they do seem to be happiest when buried in dark corners away from the harsh sunlight.

Some days the heat is so thick, so extreme, that the early-morning dew sops the plants and leaves them drooping. Moistness is everywhere. Nature's way of making sure they do not go thirsty, I suppose. I think that is why I choose to water our recently potted geraniums in the evenings.

It is sunset. My first evening alone. I am in the garden with the hose. Circling above me are two buzzards. I tilt my head (still rather the worse for the port) and watch them wheel and spin, wondering what they are stalking. I hear one of them screech. It is a distant, echoey cry, reverberating on the still air. Then, suddenly, there is another noise: heavy footsteps. Someone is coming up behind me. I freeze. There is the unmistakable sound of heavy breathing. I go cold. How can I, singlehanded in this deserted spot, grapple with a burglar? I consider the hosepipe in my hand. I could spray the intruder, drench and confuse him for a few seconds while I make my getaway. I take a deep breath and turn slowly. There, standing on the terrace a few feet behind me, is a monstrous-sized *sanglier*.

No doubt it is a female, the more lethal of the species. She must be here on the scavenge for food for her young or she would never have approached this close to habitation. I know by reputation how dangerous wild boars can be if angered or distressed. She might charge me if I move or frighten her. The sheer weight of her could kill or maim me. I stand frozen to the spot, almost wishing that it had been a burglar. With an intruder there is the possibility of prevailing on their reason, but not with this great hairy beast. I don't dare to move but equally I have no wish to dally. Slowly, imperceptibly slowly, I twist the nozzle of the hosepipe to close off the water and, half crouching, lower it to the ground. I take my first steps towards the house.

The giant pig holds her ground, watching me. What is she

thinking? Jean-Claude with his shotgun may be a match for her, but I am not. I glance up the hill, scanning the thicket of pine forest to see if I can spot a mate or offspring. I see no others. So there is only this female to contend with. I make it to the house, close the door fast and lean against it, listening to the palpitations of my heart. Even dear old Pamela would have scared her off. I have to admit that I am missing that fat Alsatian. I convince myself that what I need is my own dog. A guardian, and company, too, on lonely evenings.

Michel arrives. We drive directly to the local dog pound and choose a lively, wiry fellow named Henri. He looks rather like an overgrown red setter, except that his coat is jet-black. I wonder why he has been abandoned. His fur is as glossy as a well-polished limousine; he appears in every way to have been cared for. According to his record sheet he is only three years old, and the note on the vet's card confirms that he is in excellent health. When I enquire, the lady who looks after the refuge begrudgingly admits that he is uncontrollable. In what way? I ask. He runs off. Constantly.

Oh.

'Yes, but you have plenty of land, you say,' she reassures us. 'He can work off all that excess energy. He is ideally suited to your needs, and you to him.'

Michel is not convinced. 'Let's think about it, *chérie*. We have no fence yet,' he murmurs.

But Henri's expression breaks my heart, that please-don't-leave-me-here look in his eyes, and he is panting with such keen anticipation that I cannot bear to walk away, to condemn the poor brute to that cage again.

'Could we take him out, just for five minutes . . . to be sure?'

She shakes her head. It is against the rules. It raises the animal's hopes, often in vain.

The woman, a true salesperson, plays on my softheartedness.

'You have a month. If it does not work out, and you return him within the month, we will accept him back. But I am sure that won't be necessary. He'll settle with you.'

Henri pants his eager accord.

We pay our money, sign the authorisation document, buy him a collar and escort him to the car. Or, rather, he drags us there. I can barely hold him. He has the strength of a grizzly bear.

That first evening, Michel insists that we chain Henri, on a generously long lead, to the trunk of the magnolia tree. He can sit with us while we prepare and eat our barbecue dinner, but at the same time he will start to develop the habit of staying quietly at our sides. He must learn a little discipline, explains Michel. That way he will know not to go wandering off. Henri puts his head on his paws and goes into a sulk.

He remains in that position all day Saturday.

'I don't think he's very happy,' I say.

'He's adjusting.'

Henri's black eyes glower at me with pain and accusation: 'You have given me freedom only to take me prisoner,' he seems to be saying. I cannot bear it. I spend hours stroking him and talking to him, but he will not relent. He refuses to eat. Oh, what a contrast with Pamela!

We have guests for dinner. An Italian artist and his Danish wife. *Très chic*. A trend-seeking couple keen to be seen at the right parties and in the company of the rich and famous. He is short and plump, and a frightful womaniser who has, on occasion, after a bottle or two, embarrassed me, but beneath the Casanova routine I have discovered a warm, generous-spirited man.

I was introduced to them in the early eighties when I was performing in a theatre in Copenhagen. Now they have bought a house here in the south of France, in Biot, and we find our-selves relative neighbours. They arrive late, not unusually, armed with taped copies of the samba music to which they like to listen during dinner. Wait till they see our pathetic little cassette-player, I think as I accept the tapes with a broad smile.

He, as always, is dressed from head to foot in moody black. She, the Dane, is tall and slender as a willow. By contrast, her temperament is cool and reserved and she wears a long, flowing, perfectly ice-white linen dress. He, the artist, is not fond of dogs, although they have two of their own.

Henri, still on his lead, is alerted by their arrival and stands up to greet them. He is animated, bucked up, for the first time in over twenty-four hours and begins to wag his tail and yodel.

'Why is he tied up?' our artist friend enquires.

'We only collected him from the refuge yesterday, and in order that he doesn't run off . . .' I am blathering on about the problem of Henri while our friends with their tropical suntans crack open the bottle of champagne they have so generously donated to the evening's proceedings.

Michel, across the dust patch, is fanning the barbecue. Smoke ascends into the night air, giving off the aromas of Provençal herbs and charcoal-cooked meat. I uncork a bottle of red wine, a Saint-Joseph from Saint-Désirat.

'He'll only settle if you leave him free. He has to discover his sense of boundary in a free space.' What Olga says makes sense. In any case, I am dying for an excuse to release him. I run to Michel, who is calling for me and, while replenishing his glass and laying the various cuts of grilled lamb on to a serving plate, I repeat what Olga has said.

'If you think so,' he replies, though I sense he doubts his own words.

In one movement, I charge up the steps and release Henri. He is over the moon with glee. In twenty-four hours he has had four pee breaks and one long walk on a lead, during which he dragged me up and down the hillside. His tail is wagging like a crazed pendulum.

'Come on, boy,' I coax, expecting him to follow me down on

to the terrace beneath, where our chums are sipping champagne and imbibing the view. But he does not budge. The movement of his tail is gaining speed. I fear that this bodes ill but before I can act upon my instincts, Henri takes a gigantic leap and lands on the backs of both our guests. They find themselves splayed out in the dust around our non-existent lawn. Their glasses, thankfully, are not smashed, but the couple are drenched in bubbly and Olga's dress is patched with green stains from the few remaining tufts of grass.

'What an excessively friendly fellow,' says the artist, picking himself up from the ground and dusting himself down. 'It's how I encourage my mistresses to greet me.'

The following Friday I receive a telegram from Mme B. There has been a mistake in the price of the property. I go cold. I knew it! All summer I have been dreading news such as this. And then I read on. Due to the fact that the second half of the land, known to us now as the 'second plot', has measured out at a third of an acre larger than the plot with house – the half we are currently purchasing – we are entitled to a reimbursement of several thousand francs. I whoop and shout in the lane as I watch our fat, bearded postman, who has just handed me the telegram, disappear round the bend. I cannot help remarking that he and his moped are a precarious marriage of large man and modest machine. By the time he reaches us, his daily load is almost delivered. How does he negotiate the early rounds of the journey, setting off from the sorting office loaded down with the entire morning's letters and parcels? And how does that little yellow two-wheeler manage to transport the weight of him and his bundles up and down the steep and winding hills?

But for the moment I have more important matters to think about. I hurtle off to the local phone booth to telephone Michel at his office in Paris.

What it boils down to, he says, is that we can buy a bed.
Yes!

Within the hour I am in Cannes, ordering the largest bed on offer. I leave a deposit; the rest of the money will be paid when the bed arrives in eight weeks' time. I come out of the shop flushed with excitement. We have blown our entire refund on that one piece of furniture.

At the sound of the postman's moped pootling along the lane, Henri bounds down the drive and positions himself on the bend to say good morning. As the postman slows to round the corner, Henri leaps into the air in front of him, paws splayed, barking furiously. Alas, his effusive greeting sends Monsieur *le facteur* flying.

I hear shouting and barking and run from my desk to find out what is up. There, on the bitumen in the lane, the poor plump chap, on all fours, is shaking with terror and grappling with his letters and parcels, which have flown in every direction. Henri is still close at hand, yapping and growling. The postman is a trembling wreck, gibbering at Henri's bared teeth, and the front wheel of his bike is sadly damaged.

Henri is triumphant.

I drag the great hound away to threats from the postman of action by the post office. '*J'avais presqu'une crise cardiaque!*' he yells after me furiously.

I take the coastal road, passing by the old town of Antibes, skirting the Baie des Anges, to visit the antique market in the old town of Nice. I find it situated in the ancient Italian quarter, where the buildings are painted ochre and a deep Siena yellow. There I discover stalls laden with antique linen and lace pillowcases. They are so big and square, and cheap, and the condition is as new. Some are embroidered in white cotton, white on white, with initials. I wonder who they were so caringly embroidered for and what became of the original owners. What in the story of their lives prevented these luxurious pieces from ever being put to use? A jilted sweetheart, a death? In anticipation of the delivery of our generously sized new bed, I want to buy them all. I dream of smothering it in freshly starched, lavender-scented, crisp linen. Crisp and white and inviting. Of sunburnt afternoons lying together. Of winter nights, huddled close listening to the crackling of the fire.

The stall-holder, a tiny woman, hidden behind banks of sheets and tablecloths, is sitting with a man and a child. They are eating lunch. I notice that the spread includes a hot chicken dish in a thick tomato sauce, several bottles of red wine, fruit, two baguettes and an assortment of cheeses. It seems remarkable for a market, but I remind myself that this is France. Food comes first. We make a deal which seems to delight us both and she shoves linen sheets, pillowcases and a tablecloth into several plastic bags, collects her modest sum of money and returns to her meal. While I am here, I begin to scout the various stalls on the look-out for large glass jars, carafes or demijohns which I can use later to store our olive oil. I find none, but there is always next week.

When I return, I pick flowers from the garden. Marguerite daisies, eucalyptus leaves and palm fronds, taken from six tiny potted plants I found at the nursery at 20f a pot. I gather them together and place them, decoratively arranged in *confiture* jars, next to our mattress on the floor, and in the hearth.

Michel is coming home tonight. I cannot remember when I last felt this excited. In preparation, I am stuffing a chicken. Suddenly, I hear Henri barking like a mad fool. I fear another *sanglier*. I peer out of the kitchen window towards the pine forest and, to my amazement, see troupes of people moving in and around the trees, thrashing at the undergrowth. I hike up the hill, thorny brambles ripping at my flesh, and introduce myself. They are mushroom-picking, they explain. I, in return, inform them in a friendly manner that they are on private land. They retaliate by advising me that they have gathered mushrooms on this hill all their lives and they do not intend to stop now.

Chastised, confused, I return to the house and leave them to it. Next year, I will know to get up there first and pick the mushrooms myself, but at this stage I run the risk of poisoning us both because I don't know one variety from another.

Later, in the afternoon, when I go to the village to buy freshly baked bread, I see that the local chemist's shop has large display cards in the windows illustrating in colour the different mushroom varieties. I learn that it is a local service here. Anyone can take their baskets brimming with harvested mushrooms into the chemist and the *pharmacien* will sift the edible from the inedible or downright poisonous. So we will be safe to harvest our own *funghi*. I stare at the coloured cards. Here, among dozens of others, are drawings of ceps and chanterelles and boleti, which, I read later, were originally grown by the Italians. There is another, birch boletus, which grows on the trees and is as large as a child's head. I am not convinced how delicious that sounds.

Over dinner, by the fire, I feel obliged to confess to Michel the tales of Henri's exploits. He is not pleased. But worse is to come, for the postman is true to his word. On Saturday morning, an official notice arrives from the post office warning us that if we do not control our dog we will be taken to court and the animal might well be impounded or, worse, destroyed. I stare at it in dismay while Henri pants gleefully at my side.

'He'll have to go, *chérie*,' says Michel.

'But since Henri, we have had no wild boar prowling the garden, and he keeps me company. Please let's keep him.'

Michel frowns. 'We need to give the matter serious thought,' he replies.

That afternoon, the last straw: Jean-Claude arrives with the news that an officer from the central Cannes police station has telephoned him to say that a large black dog known as Henri (the refuge have identified him by the name on his collar and put them in touch) is terrorising the guests sunbathing on the private beach at the Majestic Hotel. Michel thanks Jean-Claude for taking the trouble to come and tell us. He is then obliged to drive to Cannes, collect the dog and pay a hefty fine – Henri has been charged with disturbance of the peace.

I walk over to Jean-Claude with a bottle of wine and apologise profusely for the intrusion. His booming laugh reassures me that everything is perfectly fine. In fact, he invites us back for another *apéro*. Having barely recovered from the previous one, I fix no date but agree to telephone him, adding that on the next occasion they should come to us. Over dinner, Michel and I discuss the problem of Henri and I miserably concede that it would be best for everyone, including the dog, if he were returned.

On Monday morning, the woman at the refuge seethes visibly as we sign yet another set of documents, this time relinquishing all responsibility for the poor beast.

I weep copiously as we kiss him goodbye and he, bemused, is led away again to his horrid cage, but I have to admit that I have been hasty. Next year, I say to myself, when we are better organised, I promise to return for you, Henri.

Treasure Islands

It is a crystal-clear, sunny autumn morning. Yesterday, it rained for the first time in over two months. Today, the air has a nip to it which foretells the changing seasons and reminds me that these long, dry summers are not truly endless. Only a few days more, and we must close up the house. Michel and I are flying to Australia to shoot the film based on the storyline of my novel, in which I am to play the main role. It is an exciting challenge. Even so, it's going to be a wrench to tear myself away from Appassionata. Australia, the other side of the world; there will be no popping home for weekends.

'If my story had been set here . . .' I mumble, folding away linen which I am storing with lavender bags in a cupboard inside the front hall.

In spite of all that is left to do – I have my work and papers to pack up yet, my luggage to sort out and we are still trying to nail down a most elusive *notaire* for a firm date for the final exchange – Michel announces: 'Leave everything, we're going hunting.'

'What?' I laugh.

'We're taking a ferry to the islands. To look for treasure.'

I agree readily, for the prospect of any boat ride always gives me a childlike joy and the notion of a mystery tour is too irresistible. Besides, I have never visited the Îles de Lérins. 'What kind of treasure are we hunting for?'

'You'll see. We will visit the farthest island first, return to the nearer, where we can lunch, and then cruise home on the late-afternoon boat.'

We purchase our tickets from a booth nestled alongside the harbourmaster's office and the customs quay in the old port of Cannes. As we wait for the boat, we stroll the length of a neighbouring jetty and from that prominent aspect peer back towards the lofty Tour du Suquet, the weathered tower which crowns the very pinnacle of the rock known as the Suquet upon which the old town of Cannes stands. Here was constructed the original fishing village initially christened Canois, meaning 'cane harbour', after the canes that grew profusely so many centuries ago along what was then nothing more than a marshy saline seafront. Cannes as wild nature barely seems conceivable in this day and age. Returning our gaze seawards along the quay, we are back in the twentieth century; a breeze whispers and a curved necklace of pearly-white yachts stirs noiselessly at the water's edge.

'Who owns all these?' I ask, a private musing spoken aloud. I cannot envisage how many millions one has to accrue to be able to cough up for one of these swanky numbers. Several of the cruisers are the length of a train carriage and, surely, would have cost more than the lifetime's earnings of the average working person.

'There is a lot of foreign money here. And a great deal of corruption. One of the erstwhile mayors of Nice, for example, fled to Uruguay.'

'Why?'

'If he had stayed in France he would have been imprisoned for corruption and tax evasion. Apparently, he embezzled considerable sums from the city of Nice and shifted the money to South America in readiness for his retirement.'

'That's right! Jacques Médecin, of course!' I laugh, more out of incredulity than merriment at the breadth and panache of such Riviera skulduggery. 'They got him, though, eventually, didn't they?'

'Yes, they did.'

I remember that Graham Greene, who lived in Antibes and who I met on several occasions, published a book in 1982 entitled *J'Accuse*. It was concerned with corruption in Nice and the close involvement of M. Médecin with the Italian Mafia. There was a casino scandal. Greene believed that a worrying percentage of the police force and justice system were engaged in nefarious dealings with the *milieu*, the criminal underworld. Later, Médecin fled the country.

'Do you suppose,' I ask Michel, 'all Riviera vice and turpitude ended with his flight and subsequent imprisonment?'

'Somehow I doubt it.'

'Might there be zillions of Mafia francs, never smuggled out, buried somewhere on these islands?'

'Who knows?'

'So are we going to dig them up and pay off Mme B.?'

'No.' He smiles at my fooling. 'That's not the treasure we are after.'

'What, then?'

'You'll see.'

I smile, enjoying the game. Looking around us, I notice hosts of bronzed, barefoot young men, clad becomingly in shorts, at work on the string of yachts. Several are shinning up aluminium masts, like monkeys climbing for bananas, while others are scrubbing teak decks, washing, hosing or treating the impressive fibreglass hulls. Varnishing the varnished. All busy as ants, lost in dreams of seafaring adventures.

'We'd better get moving,' says Michel, taking my hand.

The clock tower up in the Suquet strikes ten and the ferry prepares to depart. But a straggle of latecomers are steaming along the jetty; all calling and waving. The captain grins. The boat waits. Everyone shakes his hand amicably and lumbers aboard.

During this short delay, I glance about. I have to admit that there is still great charm in this old port. The Hôtel Splendid ahead, for example, with its colourful array of international flags and simple white façade. But then my attention lights on a sign in large, black lettering, 'Jimmy'z *club*', above the dull beige of the palais block and the plastic blue lettering which reads: 'CASINO'. It is hard to imagine an uglier sight.

The boat is wheeling and we are exiting the port. I lean against the rail, a rush of excitement sweeping through me. A water baby by nature, I am at my happiest on or by the sea. Gulls circle overhead; the misty ambrosial hills of the Estérel and the foamy bubbling spray, as white as the yachts, rise up to cool us as the ferry ploughs through an otherwise calm sea. We pass an anchored five-mast luxury liner with 'Club Med 2' painted on its hull and a glass-bottomed pleasure boat packed with pensioners.

From the sea Cannes still manages to give off an illusion of gentility but, on closer inspection, this luxury resort always puts me in mind of a rather desperate, ageing whore. I recall a long-forgotten group of transvestites with whom I spent some time while working in Brazil. At forty or forty-five, they were all past their prime but, with plenty of slap, a little kind lighting and some distance, they managed to look good. I smile to myself, recalling their coked-up energy, some of the wild places they dragged me and the outrageous stories they recounted. I concede that probably Cannes, too, has many faces.

The Carlton Hotel, situated bang in the centre of the Croisette, dominates the bay. It draws the eye instantly to its crisp, white elegance. None of its meretricious marketplace mentality can be discerned from this gathering distance. Feeling the sun's mounting heat penetrating my flesh, I shade my eyes to pick out the observatory tower high above the town. I scan the *fin de siècle* villas, their windows winking in the light like pirates signalling the all-clear to sailor companions marking time on the open sea. Splashes of autumnal colour – reds, yellows, gold – patch the palmy hills while dozens of umber bodies in richly coloured itsy-bitsy swimwear rest recumbent on the ever-busy golden beaches. This boat ride is delicious. There is barely a handful of passengers aboard the ferry and most appear to be locals who have crossed at dawn to the mainland to shop at the Forville vegetable and fish market, weatherworn biddies clutching woven shopping bags bulging with brilliantly coloured fruits and vegetables. Two old toothless crows, arms wrapped tightly around their trophies, huddle close and gossip contentedly. Their flesh may be creased, tamped olive and leathery by the sun, but their eyes glisten wickedly.

'How many people live on these islands?' I enquire of Michel.

'Île Ste Marguerite is inhabited. I don't know by how many. Twenty households, maybe. The second, St Honorat, is unoccupied. Well, except for a community of Cistercian monks, and one very overpriced restaurant at the water's edge looking out over the canal that separates the two islands.'

'Who goes there?'

'To the restaurant? The yachting fraternity. It is a fashionable weekend haunt. During the season, boats rendezvous here from as far as Monte Carlo or St Tropez. They drop anchor in between the two islands and motor, by dinghy, from one yacht to another, rounding up their parties, and then to the shore, disembarking for a grilled lobster lunch.'

'That doesn't sound too terrible.'

'The canal gets so crowded you can barely move,' laughs Michel.

We are approaching Ste Marguerite.

'*Pour St Honorat, la deuxième île, vous restez abord,*' calls a voice from a loudspeaker. My eye is drawn to a bastion atop a cliff at what appears to be the eastern tip of the island. 'Is that a fortress?'

Michel grins mischievously. 'The Fort Royal. I knew it would fire your imagination. It was built by Richelieu to protect the island from the Spanish, who invaded anyway. But I'll tell you all about it later.'

'There lies our trove? Or there, in that building on the beach? What is that, a deserted hotel?'

'All are for later. After lunch.'

Michel knows that my patience will not easily last out till our return and he relishes the few moments he has to hold on to his surprise. I smile, and, allowing him his secrets, choose not to persist. Not yet, anyway. He tightens his arm around my shoulders and nuzzles his lips against my breeze-kissed cheek.

'*Je t'aime.*'

'*Moi aussi.*'

Every passenger, apart from ourselves and the crew, prepares to disembark on to the planked-wood jetty which rises out of the shallow, crystalline water where shoals of tiny silver fish are darting to and fro. A few tourists, their laden bags at their feet, clot the jetty, impatient to board. But they don't; they must be bound for Cannes. So we have the boat to ourselves. It reverses, heels about and scoots out to sea, negotiating the rocky bed beneath us. Dinghies bask like seals in the sun and a series of small yellow buoys bob like discarded mustard pots. Parasol pine trees and a few look-out bunkers, abandoned since the Second World War, border the island's western beaches. The air is clear and fragrant.

I am fifteen minutes from home, I am thinking. I turn and study Michel, his face in profile, deep in his own thoughts, gazing at the sea. Even during this brief journey, the sun has coloured his skin a light golden brown. He tans easily and evenly. His curly hair is blowing in the salty slipstream. Such a strong, handsome face. Michel's thirst for adventure, his delight at seeking out the mysterious, discovering the unknown, marries with my own. We are fortunate.

In between the two islands, there are a scattering of yachts moored in the narrow strait. Slender, shark-toothed vessels with equally slender women aboard, lying topless and oiled, soaking up the sun. Paunched men stare smugly at our passing ferry, brandishing goblets of whisky and ice. I glance at my watch. It is half-past ten. We pass the 'posh' restaurant, which appears deserted. Perhaps it has already closed for the season, or is immersed in preparations for another lucrative lunchtime.

The passage to this second island has taken no time at all. We negotiate a series of large, rather dangerously jagged rocks and then we arrive, landing safely at the harbour. Michel takes my hand and leads me ashore. The instant I set foot on the bank I am greeted by, no, swathed in, a pine-scented silence, soft as a human pulse. The place radiates harmony and peace. I breathe deeply and turn about. There is nothing in sight, in any direction, except pine forest, coastline and clear Mediterranean, a patchwork of blue and milky turquoise. Salt water laps the sandy beach, licks the bleached skeletons of driftwood and then gently folds away like a sated lover. Save for the departing ferry, we could be marooned on a desert island. It is hard to believe that we are so close to home and that this paradise of eucalyptus and Aleppo pines is visible from our terrace. I spy a statue of the Virgin Mary. High among the treetops, she holds her arms outstretched, looking out over and blessing the canal.

'Come on, we'll visit the monastery, the Abbaye des Lérins, buy lavender oil at the abbey shop, skirt the island and take the boat back to Ste Marguerite for lunch.'

We turn inland, and proceed, flanked by vineyards, towards the abbey, the epicentre of the island – only five minutes away – where we will find a church and a stone arched walkway which leads to the shop and gardens. Stone benches have been placed at strategic points along the route to allow pause for reflection and prayer. I want to dally a moment to commune with the natural beauty here, imbibe the scents of the pines and eucalyptus, but Michel chivvies me along.

As we approach the abbey, he delivers me a swift, potted history. The two islands were once the most powerful religious centres in the south of France. This one was first occupied by the hermit St Honorat (hence its name) in the fifth century, when the Bishop of Fréjus encouraged him to come and create a site for holy retreat. A monastery was built and, under the auspices of St Honorat, it became a training centre for novice priests as well as a school for the study of Christian philosophy. St Honorat, later Bishop of Arles, died in AD 429, but the traditions of the monastery lived on long after him and have been continued to this day, except for a short period during the late eighteenth and early nineteenth century, when the island was snatched by the state, put up for auction and bought by an actress from the Comédie Française.

I chuckle with delight at the notion of ownership by an actress. The exotically named Mlle Alziary de Roquefort, was, according to Michel, a great friend of the painter Fragonard. I long to learn more. Was she as bewitching as her name suggests?

In 1869, Michel does not know for what reason, the island was returned to the Cistercians, who have occupied it, farmed it and laboured for it and for the renovation of its fortified monastery ever since.

'But, see, we've arrived.'

The Cistercians are an order of silence. There are discreet signs requesting us to speak in whispers, dress appropriately and respect the ethos of the island's inhabitants. An incongruous spectacle in this historical setting is a public telephone box situated at a crossroads of dusty pathways lined with pine trees. Seconds later, ahead of us, we are greeted by the sight of a group of portly Americans, shirtless and in shorts, who have congregated outside the abbey gates, snapping cameras and calling loudly to one another to come and take a look at this or that. Can't they read? I ask myself crossly, or do they simply disregard such requests in the belief that they are not intended for them? But then I remind myself, less judgementally, that of course the notices are in French. They may not have understood the message. On the exterior side of the abbey walls, tall palms shade and decorate the approachway. The trees are laden with bunches of dark ruby fruit reminiscent of fulsome berries rather than dates. Agapanthus, past their blooming season, line the pathways, as well as *Ficus Indica* cacti, tall as trees and crowding the flowerbeds. These, too, are fruiting their terracotta-ripe prickly pears.

Entrance to the abbey and its church are by iron gates ablaze with lustrous skeins of flowering bougainvillaea. I read an engraved cornerstone which tells me that St Patrick studied here under the guidance of St Honorat before travelling north to Ireland. As an Irish Catholic, this information tickles me. Patrick landed up in Ireland, and I here.

The shop is managed by two middle-aged ladies, one of whom sells us lavender oil as well as a kilo jar of rosemary honey, which she earnestly recommends. Gregorian chants are playing softly in the background and can be purchased on compact disc. The Americans have arrived. They are buying bottles of the monks' renowned liquor. One of them pulls his directly from its paper bag, unscrews its cap and swigs thirstily from it.

'Jesus!' he guffaws. 'That hits the spot!' The bottle is passed among his companions, and drained.

The women look on in bewilderment. We head back out into the bright noonday, leaving them to it.

On the far reach of the island on the windward shore is the fortified monastery. Weatherbeaten, solitary, awesome. A high austere monument, it has been hewn from hefty chunks of stone. Constructed on the very tip of a minuscule but windy headland, it faces out across the sea towards, I estimate, Calvi, a town on the north-west coast of Corsica.

Everything about its exposed location is windswept, which makes the delicate, peachy tone of the stone somehow even more enrapturing. I notice samphire sprouting from the walls flanking the water's edge, and unknown purple flowers pushing through like tomboyish daisies. On this open coast, the slap of the waves against the rocks has a relentless, overpowering brutality about it. We pay 15f apiece to a lone student, a blonde-haired girl who sits peacefully on a rusting iron chair, reading a book whose pages are blowing to and fro. This gives us entry to the ruin.

As we mount the stone stairs I, compulsively curious, steal a quick glance back towards the abbey living quarters. There is not a monk in sight. What had I expected, to see them peering out like nosy neighbours? I am taken aback by the filth of their windows until I realise that the distance has fooled me. Their cells are protected by the same anti-mosquito meshing we found installed at our farmhouse. The place exudes quietude, almost a forsaken air. I picture solitary monks on their knees at prayer in their cells. I am intrigued by the weight of thought, the depth of spiritual reflection that is being cultivated beyond those walls. These are mysteries for ever closed to me. I will never know what such a life, the life of an oblate, claims, nor the courage and sacrifice, the unstinting dedication, such a vocation must demand. The Cistercian order was founded at the end of the eleventh century in an attempt to return to a stricter, more disciplined obedience to God. The rule of St Benedict, the founder of this particular order, is *Ora et Labora*, pray and work. Spoken aloud, it sounds pleasingly achievable.

I return my attention to the fortified monastery. How different the energy on this island must have been when this edifice was built to protect its inhabitants against marauding Saracens. Within – should I say within when the roof is merely a space open to the blue skies? – there is little to see save for the ancient walls, which date back to the eleventh and twelfth centuries, and the pockets of restoration work. The *salle du chapitre* is a dark, dank room cluttered with broken wooden chairs and a discarded wooden icon of Madonna and child. There are some fine marble and stone pillars and arches, and marble stairs but, all in all, the fort's stately majesty lies in the breathtaking views offered by its position. Unfortunately, these cannot really be appreciated or savoured because everywhere the apertures have been closed, fitted with metal-framed glass like frightful, second-rate double glazing. This addition is hideously out of place and so out of keeping with the restored masonry work that it bemuses me. Why have the openings been sealed off? To prevent brokenhearted tourists from leaping to their deaths on the treacherous rocks below? Or to discourage monks who can no longer stomach the solitude of the life to which they have committed?

I wander from the *salle du chapitre* to the *cloître du travail*. In the centre of this work cloister I discover what I take to be a baptismal font until I peer into it and discover a deep well. At first, I assume the water lying so far beneath us is sea water but, although the building is constructed *pieds dans l'eau*, this seems doubtful. It is too still. From this distance, it looks impenetrable and stagnant. Midges or mosquitos skate its surface, circumventing a dozen or so jettisoned Coke cans. I look about in search of Michel, but he is nowhere to be seen.

I find him perusing a few historical facts, mainly dates, posted up on one of the inner cloister walls. In 1073 work began on this fortified monastery. In 1635 the islands were occupied by the Spanish, and in 1791, the notice informs us, the island was sold at public auction to an actress, Marie-Blanche Sainval, who owned it until 1810. So who was Alziary de Roquefort? Perhaps that exotic creation was her stage name? Whatever the case, I fancy the sound of Alziary better. The deeds of sale might be written in the name of Marie-Blanche Sainval, but I shall continue to think of this actress as Alziary. In my mind's eye she is a tempestuous, flaming redhead; *une femme d'un certain âge*. Lord knows why.

Nearing the top floor, we enter the prayer cloister, *le cloître de la prière*, where, we are told, the walls date from the twelfth and thirteenth centuries. A hundred years it took, then, to erect another storey. Oh, that modern property developers could be so stayed! On the same level we cross to the Chapelle St Croix which, we are informed, was consecrated in 1088. This confuses my sense of logic.

Here there are wooden benches placed at angles, facing a stone altar where hangs a painting of Christ on the cross. Once again the environment, as well as the strategically positioned seats, invites contemplation. So I settle on one of the benches and listen to the waves crashing against the rocks three storeys beneath me. I tilt my head towards the open sky. The blueness is pacifying and airy; a visual balm.

Our footsteps echo back at us as we climb one last flight of ever-narrowing, winding marble stairs to the summit of the keep, where elegant metal railings gird the surround. Against accident or suicide? There, from that top terrace with its stone bell tower, we behold a 360-degree view which is nothing short of divine.

'The Lord often had his prophets climb mountains to converse with him. I often wondered why he did that, and now I know the answer; when we are on high, we can see everything else as small.' The words are those of the writer Paulo Coelho, who spent his early years in a seminary and with whom I once had the privilege of dining in Rio. Everything else as small, yes, including oneself. How could you not be close to God here?

The light breeze at this altitude is very welcome. I walk to the metal railing. Although I am not usually afraid of heights, the clear yet rock-infested water far beneath sends a frisson of icy fear down my spine. Still, I long to plunge the hundreds of feet into the sea and swim and frolic like a carefree porpoise.

A fabulous two-mast cutter ploughs across the distant horizon, making for where? St Tropez, Marseille?

'Great location, what a place to shoot a movie,' I remark, gazing out across the Med and back towards the distant Provençal hills. Constructed in the monks' vegetable gardens are two large banks of solar panelling.

'If you lived here, would you want a film crew invading this serenity? About on a par with those barbaric Saracens, I'd say!' The clock on the terracotta tiled tower chimes noon. 'We should move on.' I smile and nod.

Our promenade around the island is crazily romantic. Water licks our feet and soaks our shoes, which we remove. Fish the size of salmon slip beneath rocks, playing hide-and-seek with our shadows. We clamber from eucalyptus-perfumed bay to lavender-scented shade, kicking our toes in the sand, racing miniature crabs, grabbing hands, touching backs, necks, hair. Warm, damp flesh. Crunching our sodden, sandy feet on the sponge-like cushion of beached and dehydrated seaweed, dragging our wet swimming towels like lazy kites, salt drying on our pinched, damp flesh. We dally, kiss, linger, taste the salt, lick it clean, then keep pace in blissful silence. Or hurry, chattering like euphoric monkeys. Toppling over one another. Falling in love: such a free, expansive fall. There's no knowing where, if ever, we'll land, but today we're in paradise.

All in all, the circumference of the island is approximately three kilometres and takes us, strolling and with a pause to swim, little less than an hour and a half. We had been intending to bathe naked, or at least I had. Whenever it's appropriate, we do. Here, even though there has not been a single sighting of a monk, I cannot rid myself of the feeling that they see us, wherever we are on the island. Their spirituality is omnipresent.

Peace and harmony impregnate this place. The rhythmic lapping of the water, the silent beating of distant sails, the breeze slapping against the waves, and the birdsong. Gulls and swallows wheel overhead, starlings chirp like tiny glass bells, and a brilliant, electric-blue hummingbird zips past us, skirting the shore at the speed of light. My thoughts return to the actress from Paris, reflecting on the seventy years when the place was not in the hands of the monks. Did Mlle de Roquefort invite artists and bohemian friends here to share nature's delights with her? Was she inspired by the votive vibrations created over centuries through prayer and meditation, what today we might speak of as the feng shui balance, or was she given to wild Rabelaisian parties swimming in a surfeit of home-grown wine? As an actress myself, these images amuse me. Or maybe Alziary dreamed of creating on St Honorat what we dream of at Appassionata? To transform our overgrown jungle and restore its original purpose, allowing it its fecundity as an olive farm. Her farm, of course, would have been on a far grander scale. For there are vineyards on this island, sweetly scented lavender fields and bees for the production of honey. Might this island have been her retreat, her escape from the world of drama and illusion? Without the power of television, was Alziary (or Marie-Blanche) known to the people of Cannes? Did they raise their eyes in horror at her arrival here, at her carryings-on? Theatricals! Would she have excited the same interest as, for example, Catherine Deneuve might if she were purchasing these acres now? I very much doubt it, but still I make a mental note to discover more, if possible, about this lady who sailed in and took possession of the monks' terrain. I would be fascinated to learn if she, like me, dreamed of living another kind of life. Was it love that seduced her south? Might that explain the two different names?

'When we return from Australia, I want to come back here and picnic on that grass bank overlooking the turquoise water.'

My thoughts return to our treasure hunt as the chugging ferry delivers us back to Ste Marguerite in time for lunch. We are famished and don't dawdle along the jetty.

'The restaurant is right over there.' Michel is pointing to a white-painted veranda on the waterside several hundred yards along the coast. Behind it a half a dozen or so houses with light turquoise or pale lilac shutters, hidden between trees, peer out towards Cannes from their watery eyries. I notice early clots of autumn-yellow mimosa blossom. Then, once again, my gaze is drawn up towards the hilly incline and the royal fort which, until now, I had completely forgotten.

'Lunch!' grins Michel.

As we near the restaurant, we realise that it is closed and pause in the lane while we consider what to do next. 'There is another,' he says. 'I've forgotten its name. On the beach down behind the fort. We have to climb and then go down the other side of the cliff. It's not far but we should hurry. It's getting late. We'll see it from the clifftop so, if that one is closed as well, we won't bother going down there. It tends to be seasonal.'

We break into a jog and come abreast of the disused building I spotted from the early-morning ferry. A scruffy sign, cobbled out of broken bits of ceramic, reads: 'Hôtel du Masque de Fer'. The Iron Mask Hotel. An intriguing name. I approach the tall, glass-paned doors and peer in, believing the place to be empty. But I see a stooped, bleach-haired woman inside, tottering across a poorly lit, high-ceilinged dining room. 'There's someone in there.'

Michel is intent on getting to the restaurant. He holds out his arm as if to encourage me away. 'We can look later.'

'I think it's open. Maybe they serve lunch.'

He returns to my side and peers in alongside me. 'Do you really want to eat here?'

I have a fanatical attraction to buildings in ruin. 'Let's ask.'

We open the door and an old man materialises from behind what looks like an exceedingly outdated pizza oven. At first, he is reluctant to take us, professing that lunch is over and there is nothing available. We accept his refusal graciously and turn to go, but then he continues: 'Still, if you are not in need of anything too fancy, I can offer you . . .' The surroundings are deeply shabby yet the setting so picturesque. We agree to order his suggested pizzas, along with salad and a local rosé wine which, according to our bald-headed host, has come from the vineyard on the adjacent island of St Honorat. Perfect. We seat ourselves at a grubby table by the window and stare out at a disused landing bay. The water is rippling like corrugated iron across to the busy restaurants on the beaches of Cannes. The view is stupendous. Our wine arrives.

'If we hadn't found Appassionata, this place would set us a challenge. Not a farm, but . . . Why is it called the Iron Mask Hotel?'

'Because the fort on the clifftop has dungeons dug deep into the rock and it was in one of those cells that the man in the iron mask was imprisoned.'

My eyes widen to the size of our approaching pizzas. 'The Alexandre Dumas character?'

'For three hundred years writers have been inspired by his story.'

'He was a real person? I didn't know that.'

Monsieur serves us our plates, and retreats.

'He spent eleven years incarcerated here, and never once was his face revealed.'

'Tell me about him. *Bon appétit.*'

'Legend has it that he was the twin brother of Louis XIV, or his bastard half-brother.'

'So he was imprisoned by Louis XIV? How disappointing! I thought old Louis was one of the good guys. He was the king responsible for sending the botanist Plumier off in search of new species of plant and of cleaning up the Rhône Valley. Without him we may never have had our *Magnolia Grandiflora*.'

'What about the Rhône?'

'The waterways had grown stagnant. They had been deteriorating since classical times and, due to the pestilence, the populations of the cities were dwindling. Many of the river towns had degenerated into little more than fever-infested hovels, so Louis ordered an engineering survey of the region which resulted in his decision to strengthen the embankments. I have always rather admired him for that. So it was his brother imprisoned here, eh?'

'There are many theories. Some have suggested that the masked man was Molière. Others claim that it was a woman disguised as a man. What does seem to be certain is that whoever he was, he was famous.'

'Why?'

'It's logical. Why go to such lengths to keep his face hidden if he was not easily recognised? When he was imprisoned at the Bastille in Paris, not even his doctor was allowed to look upon his naked features.'

'How did he shave?' I ask. Our carafe of water arrives and I fill our glasses, enthralled by the mystery of this personage.

'*Il vous plaît, le déjeuner, Monsieur, Madame?*'

'Delicious, thank you,' we nod enthusiastically, although it is little better than passable. The dough is rather soggy and the salad, lying in a chipped dish, looks as lively as the seaweed we found washed up on the other island. But we don't really care.

We are having a wonderful day, and Michel knows that he has whetted my appetite with this story. Then I remember that I was equally fascinated by this hotel with no guests but us.

'Has the hotel closed?' I enquire of our host.

'It is sold, and is to be turned into a magnificent new Carlton with a small marina for private yachts,' Monsieur tells us, staring longingly across to the mainland at the outline of the real McCoy. My heart sinks as I picture the scene. 'There is only one small problem,' he adds.

'What's that?'

'The inhabitants of the island have signed a petition. They are intending to block the permit I hope to acquire for the construction of a helicopter pad.'

Good for them, I think, but say nothing. At that moment the door opens and a tall, dark-haired gentleman in his early forties, dressed in what must be a Cerruti suit and Italian leather shoes polished to a mirrored shine, enters. He is accompanied by eight or nine others. Henchmen on the payroll, it seems, running after his every need. Our shuffling proprietor abandons us instantly, legs it across the dining room and all but genuflects at the feet of the new arrival. Then Madame comes scrabbling out of some cobwebbed corner or other, bowing and welcoming with the same servility. We are riveted. Tables are dragged together, chairs drawn from here and there. Paper tablecloths are pressed into place and ironed flat by desperate hands. The new arrivals are seated. Bottles of wine begin to arrive. Rosé, red, white, followed, moments later, by heaped saucers of local olives and sliced *saucisson*. Dishes of marinated aubergines swilling in oil and herbs land splashing on the table. Carafes of water and glasses all but jump of their own accord from the dingy kitchen. Nothing is too much trouble for this bunch, who eat and drink with gusto. We have been entirely forgotten. In fact, we do not exist for anyone in the room save one another. Everything centres around the sleek-haired dandy who reminds me of a second-rate matinée idol: everything he does, every gesture he makes is, to my mind, studied and overstated.

'Might he be local Mafia?' I whisper to Michel, hoping that he is and that I can eavesdrop on some hideous tales of local corruption. I watch the man vigilantly, attempting to be discreet but failing hopelessly, spellbound by the mannerisms that I might be able to put to fruitful use at some later stage: the way he constantly slicks back his immaculately groomed hair or adjusts the cuffs of his shirtsleeves, the fact that he never touches his wine, even when a toast is made. He raises his glass, allows the rim to brush his lips and then sets it back on the table. 'Always on the alert,' I conclude and, as I do, he glances in our direction, allowing himself a discreet nod. He is aware that we are watching him and appears to bask in any, in all, attention. Michel is ready to leave, keen to begin exploring the fort and to visit the dungeons, but I cannot drag myself away from the *commedia* that is being played out before us. As it happens, we have no choice in the matter. The *patron* has grown so negligent towards us that the guests at the other table have finished their lunch and are preparing to depart, and still we are obliged to sit there hoping for our bill.

The proprietor and wife, tea towels in hand or, in his case, tossed over one shoulder, are poised patiently like dogs awaiting some titbit or expression of what, gratitude? Acknowledgement? A tip? The customer shakes their hands and thanks them. His smile is of the unctuous American soap series variety, dressed with thousand-dollar capped teeth. The proprietors bow and thank their esteemed guest for the time and trouble he has taken to visit them. Then every member of the group shakes hands with the old man and his wife. This extended '*merci, merci beaucoup. Non, non, merci à vous*' ceremony is followed by the eventual departure of the party. Gratified, our hosts set about clearing away the debris. Michel is now able to attract their attention and requests *l'addition*.

Without a word of apology, Monsieur nods and shuffles away
to calculate it.

'Did you see that?'

'What?'

'Those guys didn't pay for a thing.'

Michel grins at me. 'You're right. Maybe they have an
account here.' This makes us both giggle. When the restaura-
teur returns, I cannot resist enquiring after the identity of the
tall, well-groomed gentleman. Our host's rheumy eyes swim
with pride as he inform us, '*Mais, c'est Michel Mouillot.*'

In unison we reply, '*Qui?*'

'He is to be the new mayor of Cannes, and has promised us
the construction permits we need. We will achieve a far better
price for the hotel with permits.'

In the distance, the smoky blue hills. Replete, intent on the
continuation of our little adventure, we saunter, hand in hand,
up the verdant incline in the afternoon sunshine, our minds
refocusing on the masked mystery.

'Victor Hugo said of him: "This prisoner whose name
nobody knows, whose face no one has ever seen, remains a
living mystery, shadowy, enigmatic and problematic."'

'I wonder how he is described in the prison registers?' My
eyes light on a lovely old boat. The beach, on to which it has
been hauled and winched for the winter for repairs, is a sheer
drop beneath us. Four majestic palms surround it like sentries.
We pause for breath and to take in the magnificence of scenery
and coastline.

'If the unidentified captive had really been a woman, then it
seems certain some of the prison staff as well as the Paris doctor
would have discovered it. I think that hypothesis is a little far-
fetched, but I am interested to know how he shaved and ate. If
the mask could be removed, someone else must have kept the
key. Surely it follows that at least one other knew his identity.

In today's world, they would have sold their story to the papers.'

We reach the walls of the fortress. A rickety wooden sentry box bears the sign: '*Billets*', but it is closed up, the season over, and we walk on. Cobblestones, vast spaces and a garrison enclave greet us. Rows of two-storey salt-weathered stone buildings, all with identical burgundy shutters, line the cobbled lanes and lead to open squares where nothing more lively than a lizard's retreat is taking place. The site appears to be ours alone. Seagulls and terns wheel overhead. There is nothing of today's world about this settlement, and to all intents and purposes it is deserted, yet there seems to be life here. I sense basic habitation.

'What is the place used for now?'

Our footsteps echo around us. The air is clean and scented, the light sharp. The wind murmurs, carrying sounds of the sea, bird cries.

Michel does not know. We come across a painted sign which points us towards an oceanography museum. We make for that. Inside, behind a desk littered with pamphlets, a bespectacled woman sits on a chair, knitting. 'I am sorry, we are closed.'

'A quick peek?' I beg, but she shakes her grey head adamantly.

'Then, please, can you direct us to the dungeons?'

'They are not open either. They are very rarely open to the public. Usually only to guests.'

'Guests?'

Stony-faced, she returns to her knitting needles and balls of wool, revealing nothing else, and we are none the wiser. I recall that character who is always knitting in . . . which story is it? *The Scarlet Pimpernel*? We retreat out into the late-afternoon sun where, suddenly, I become aware of music, the beat of distant rock music, and I am grateful for its normality.

'Hear that?'

We decide to go in search of it. The trail leads us across an immense courtyard where the cobbled cracks at our open-shoed feet are sprinkled with yellow-flowering alpine plants and fragrant arrays of mildly sweet herbs. In this arid environment, they are soft and pleasing. Yet I sense an unsettling presence here, a hazy, indiscernible danger which is closing in around me and which I cannot shake off.

'The music must be coming from a radio or cassette-player.'

The guitar-strumming draws us into an alley, a dusty cul-de-sac. At the end, a crumbling stone wall and grassy banks. We turn about, confused. The notes waft across the bleating afternoon heat, but from where? Retracing our steps and then branching off, still within the fortress environs, we wander down a widish avenue, parallel to the museum, and come upon a wooden door that looks as old as the very foundations of the fort itself. I push against it. It is locked. On it, written in tired, flaking white paint, we read: '*Plongée*'.

'There must be a diving base here.' The music is still audible, but remains tantalisingly, inexplicably remote. We plod from one empty space to the next, lured by the ghostly melody. The place seems deserted yet, in a very different way from the other island, I have a notion that we are being watched, spied upon. The fort is empty but not tranquil; it exudes a troubled nagging power. Suddenly, clouds of small dark birds, starlings, I think, rise up from nowhere and disperse like smoke in the piercing blue sky. The unexpectedness of their movement has alarmed me and I find myself trembling.

I mention my discomfort and Michel squeezes his arm tightly around me and smiles. He is growing used to my dramatic interpretations, or my sixth sense, whichever it is.

Somewhere to the left of us, I see a bronze cannon, a great brute of a weapon. It is trained out over the fortress walls upon the open sea. No doubt in its heyday it would have had the capacity to blow any unwelcome visitors clean out of the water, separating limbs from torso with its solid missiles the size of modern beach balls. I lean my body way out over the bastillion wall and see ferns and shrubs sprouting from the weathered fortification and glinting wavelets glistening in the axis of the sun. Yet where the water breaks against the island, the waves are crashing relentlessly. It is as though we were in a storm. They smash against the mighty rocks rising up out of the sea, upon which this place has been constructed. 'It looks as if there are some very dangerous currents down there.'

There are straggly branched, wind-torn trees and scrub plants growing everywhere on the cliffsides. Still, the elevated terrain is bleak. Wriggling further out on my stomach, feeling both the blood and the rosé rush to my head, I notice an opening cut into the rocky wall beneath me. 'Look, that must be one of the dungeon windows.' Certainly, it is too narrow for any man or even a child to pass through. It offers no escape. I am feeling giddy and shimmy my body back to cobbled terra firma. 'How many years did you say the mystery man was imprisoned here?'

'Eleven.'

I reflect upon that. While an order of monks was freely incarcerated at work and prayer on the neighbouring island less than half a mile away, another was forcibly imprisoned here, stripped even of his identity. Locked in a dank underground cell with only a slit of an opening for fresh sea air and a view of the world beyond this fortress. I am wracked with pity for this unknown human being who for three centuries has been an inspiration to writers and film-makers. His existence must have been intolerable. How did he cope? How did he bear the loneliness, keep madness at bay? Might this prisoner have requested his confession to be heard by a monk from the order across the water? The opportunity to unburden his heart to one trained in compassion? Did he beg the fathers to remember him in their prayers, to aid him carry the burden his life must have become

to him as he paced his cell, manacled at the feet by ball and
chain and masked in iron? And then I remind myself that there
are still, even today, parts of the world where such barbarism
continues to exist. Where liberty is snatched for no good
reason. Internment against faith, colour, political convictions or,
as it seems it was in the case of this pitiable being, birthright.

'It is also possible that the poor fellow was cursed with some
hideous affliction. Locked away because he was judged too
repulsive to behold, you know, like the Elephant Man,' I muse.

'Why don't you write a story set here?'

I laugh at Michel's suggestion. 'I think many far more talented than I have already achieved it.'

'No, a modern story. A children's television series. Set it partially here, research locally and you can work from home. Write
a role for yourself as well, and then you can work from home
twice!'

That is the carrot that hooks me. I consider our olive farm
and the work and time it is about to demand. One of us will
need to remain here on a regular basis once we begin the business of restoration.

'Set the story between Germany, England and France.
Thirteen episodes, please.'

I smile at him, considering. 'So, we have been story hunting?'

'Yes, if you are inspired. But even if you are not, I thought
the islands would entrance you.'

They have. But this island in particular has captivated me.
And troubled me. And, yes, inspired me.

The last ferry departs from the island at 6 p.m. We are on
it. During the short trip across the bay, the faintly descending
light grows opalescent beneath a light Wedgwood blue sky.
The clouds are the white patterns on the teacups. The lovely
Italian tones of the properties along the coast towards the
Cap d'Antibes . . . My train of thought is interrupted by what
I take to be a small girl's scream, followed instantly by an

excited male calling from somewhere behind us, '*Regardez,
là-bas!*'

'*Où?*'

'*Dans la mer!*'

I fear that a child has gone overboard, though I have no
memory of having noticed any children board the vessel. We
swing round to see the crew and the handful of passengers
travelling with us leaning over the leeward side of the boat,
pointing and squealing.

What is it? We cross swiftly, my stomach clenching with
anxiety at the prospect of a helpless drowning child, and
there in the water, not twenty yards from the ferry, is a sleek,
grey creature leaping in the calm, limpid sea. And then
another. '*Dauphins!*' '*Oui, ce sont les dauphins. Regardez
comme ils jouent!*' A pod of dolphins are leaping and flipping, rising, as they do, four, even five feet above the water's
surface. Stubby-nosed athletes with shiny, midnight fins,
somersaulting. They change course and stream on ahead of
our vessel, forward of the prow, as though leading us to
shore. Then one of them breaks away from his party, circles,
tacks and speeds in close alongside us, riding the wave created by our ship cutting through the sea. He spins over
playfully, revealing a whitish, plump belly, and back over
again. I can almost read his mischievous grin. What a sight!
What sheer joy!

As I watch these mythical creatures, I recount to Michel the
story of an extraordinary American, Charlie Smithline, I met
years ago in the Caribbean. He it was who trained me for my
PADI open-water diving certificates. On several occasions we
dived together with bottle-nosed dolphins, which, I believe, is
relatively unusual, because they rarely allow humans close. But
Charlie was a regular visitor among them, and they trusted
him. I remember learning from him that dolphins emit and
perceive sound at frequencies higher than those at which we

humans are able to hear. In fact, the human ear is not equipped to hear in the water at all.

Our dolphin companion speeds off and turns back, bobbing his head above sea-level. He is looking our way and then, almost without any preparation, he soars into the air and arcs back into the water.

'Look at him!'

'You know, they can jump out of the water at a speed of thirty or forty miles an hour,' the captain tells us.

The fading light is playing on Michel's face. He looks animated and relaxed, his head thrown back in laughter. I laugh, too. Around us, others are applauding and snapping cameras. Even the crew and our salty old ferry captain, Gitanes glued to slightly parted lips, are transfixed. It is impossible not to be joyously charged at the sight of these creatures. Every leap thrills you, launched as it is out of pleasure and a pure celebration of life. What a finale! What a curtain call nature has provided to bring to a close the most perfect yet haunting of days; the most perfect of summers.

A Hair-Raising Purchase

Jet-lagged from my flight from Australia, where I have spent the past nine weeks, I land in London. The city is in the grip of shopping fever and the temperature seems to have settled at around freezing. The bookies are taking bets, short odds, on whether or not it will be a white Christmas. After the blinding white heat of Sydney and a crippling film schedule, I am spinning and want nothing more than to get directly out of the city and on the road again, south to the villa. To spend our first Christmas at home. For weeks now, staring out at the Pacific Ocean from my hotel terrace, a script constantly in front of me, pining for Michel, who was back in Paris, watching one bleached surfer after the next 'hang nine', trussed up in corsets and Victorian frocks in an ambient temperature of forty Celsius, I have been dreaming of barbecued turkey on our open fire. The only cloud on that mental idyll has been that we are still not the legal owners of our farm, and we are both growing very apprehensive. The purchase has not been going smoothly and, while we bite our nails and wait, worrying about the money we have already invested, the sterling currency alongside the franc is going through the floor.

As far as we can gather, because no one is exactly keeping us informed, the delays seem to lie within *le bureau des impôts*. Apparently, the French tax authorities are querying M. and Mme B.'s right to dispose of the estate. Investigations are now in progress into both their own and their offsprings' inheritance deeds. The Belgian owners, through the offices of the French *notaire*, have written to declare their foreign-resident status, have furnished letters from the daughter for whom they originally bought the place to support this fact and relinquishing all claims on the estate. As far as we can ascertain, they have filled out and supplied every document the French patrimonial tax system has ever drawn up on the subject. Now, it seems, we are awaiting only this unfathomable body's acceptance of the situation.

Save for the death of poor ailing M. B., which would complicate matters horrendously, Michel and I have been assured that all hiccups have finally been ironed out, all stumbling blocks removed, even the division of land satisfactorily registered, without any heart attacks, on the commune survey plans, *le cadastre*. Nothing else can further hinder or delay the sale. All we need is the official thumbs-up on the Belgians' declared status and then an agreed date when the three parties – the *notaire*, M. and Mme B. and ourselves – can assemble to sign and settle the matter. Given that France and Belgium, unlike Britain, do not close down for two full weeks over Christmas, Michel has telephoned to suggest 28 December. The *notaire*'s assistant has faxed back to say that she will be in touch. It's a cliffhanger.

We take a ferry at some dead-of-night hour which lands us at Calais before dawn. We drive directly to Paris, where Michel needs to spend some hours at his production office, and then we speed like rockets to reach the house before the morning of the next day. This self-imposed itinerary, wacky as it seems, actually suits me because my biological clock is still on Sydney time.

A few days ago, Michel put through a call to an Arab we ran across briefly in the summer who owns a Provençal gardening business – in fact Amar seems to have his finger in a mind-boggling number of pies – asking him to supply us with a Christmas tree. A blue pine is our preference, but not essential. When we arrive, well after midnight, we find the tree slumped against one of the villa's exterior walls on the top terrace. Its height and size make it better suited to Trafalgar Square and we are obliged to lop almost three feet off its crown before dragging it like a corpse through the French windows. Laughing insanely, loony with exhaustion and the pleasure of being together again, dying of hunger because we haven't eaten a thing since a stop in Beaune early in the evening for a delicious but snatched snack, we saw and hack at our tree by moonlight. We have decorations from Bon Marché, the Harrods of Paris, which I purchased while Michel rushed from one meeting to the next. I suggest staying up all night to decorate our monster. Michel recommends sleep.

'We have our new bed,' he reminds me.

I had forgotten. We stagger through to our bedroom to find, staring up at us from the floor, our old lumpy mattress, now laced in cobwebs as well as sprinkled with months of settling dust and gecko droppings. What the hell. We fall into it like shot soldiers.

The following morning, Michel sets off for the market while I walk to the phone box to telephone the furniture store in Cannes. I am informed by a most disdainful *vendeuse* that their driver kept the rendezvous, cutting a path with his load all the way up the corkscrew hills, but was obliged to take the bed all the way back to the depot because there was no one at the farm to receive it. Our neighbours, Jean-Claude and Odile, who had promised to be at the house for the delivery have disappeared, gone away, are not contactable even by phone.

I apologise profusely, attempting to explain the problem, but this saleswoman remains unrelenting and *froide*. It is no longer her responsibility, she says. They have honoured their side of the agreement. Our delivery, which next time around will cost us 400f, will have to wait until well into the new year. The date I eventually manage to drag out of her is weeks beyond our planned closure of the house. So no new bed for Christmas. But we are not too disappointed. It is so rejuvenating just to be back. I wander the rooms, reinhabiting them, breathing in the evocative scents of pine and citrus wafting on the warm air. I peer through the glass at vistas cradled in my memory during distant weeks. A fire piled high with pine, oak and olive wood crackles in the hearth. Freshly made soup is bubbling in the makeshift kitchen: a whole free-range chicken in a bouillon spiced with bouquets of Provençal herbs, leeks, onions, carrots and bay leaves picked from our tree in the garden. Randy Crawford croons from the tape-deck; high, plaintive notes drifting through the near-empty rooms.

Holding hands, trekking from here to there, up stone steps, down rocky tracks, we re-encounter our terrain and remain upbeat in spite of the clumps and thickets of weeds, the brush and thorny climbers. All have shot up as tall as sunflowers in the spaces we had cleared. So much summer threshing for nothing.

I glance back along the terraces towards the villa. Beyond the open French windows, our towering Christmas tree is garlanded with winking silver lights. On a table, a radiant blue glass vase for which I bartered in the old town of Nice after a visit to the Matisse exhibition at Cimiez is crammed with long-stemmed yellow gladioli Michel picked up for a song at the market this morning. It glints in the winter sunshine. Gently hued bulbs blink on and off at a sleepy pace alongside the pool, where I have hooked up a string of them. Hours of simple pleasure I shall take from these colours and twinkling illuminations. This *mise en scène*, with its early art-deco feel, puts me in mind of a shabby yet elegant liner setting sail once more for the high winds, the open seas.

'This place suits me so well,' I say to Michel. 'Its combination of farm and nature on the one hand and, on the other, the faded glamour of a past era, a Hollywood just beyond my reach.'

My reverie is arrested by a strangled cry coming from somewhere near the parking area. We run to investigate and discover a cat tucked away in a dark corner of one of the stables. As I approach her, she spits a malevolent warning at me to keep my distance. Michel presses my hand and inches me back. This wary creature is thin as a wisp, a scraggy-coated, white-and-marmalade feral, protecting a very newborn litter of blind, pink faces. She could turn vicious, so I step back, contemplating her and her young. What should we do? Cats are good ratters, and there are plenty of rats and mice about – or so we presume, though we haven't actually seen any. But we have seen the tell-tale black pellets, rodent droppings, left on terraces and steps. Should we try to tame one or two of the kittens? As if in response to my unspoken question, the cat hisses her disapproval of us. No, let's leave those furry orange balls to their destiny, to the same wild existence as their mother. Besides, after dear, much-missed Henri, how can I accept responsibility for any animal?

And then I remember our kidney-shaped pond and the prehistoric carp inhabiting it, and I feel sure that this feline intruder will have poached them. But when we hasten to look, we count not seven, as we had calculated in the summer, but eleven. We dig out two of the sheets of curled mosquito netting slung in the garage and secure them across our pond. The squatting cats can fend for themselves.

Michel has disappeared to the fish market in Cannes in search of oysters. They are one of the mainstays of the traditional Christmas Eve and New Year's Eve menus here and are deliciously cheap: approximately 30f for two dozen. I am at my desk pegging away, trying to get to grips with my ideas for the story I want to set across on the Îles de Lérins, when I hear the hooting of a vehicle in the garden. I look out of the window. There, beneath in the driveway, is a fire engine. Naturally, this concerns me and I hurry downstairs to be greeted by five stunningly fit, handsome young men clad in tight-fitting, navy-blue uniforms.

'Is there a problem?' I ask, trying to resist the temptation to be flirtatious. '*Bonjour. Nos meilleurs vœux.*' Each shakes my hand before a tender-faced member of the team shoves a swathe of calendars at me and asks me which one I would like. Not caring for calendars, I don't particularly want any of them, but guess that this must be a local tradition – in return for donations to a local charity, perhaps? – so I choose one and all five nut-brown faces light up, and wait expectantly while I run back upstairs to find my purse. There is no set price, I am told, so I offer a sum which seems appropriate because each of them shakes my hand one more time. Again they wish me warm *félicitations* of the season. They depart and I return to my work. But not for long. Now it's the turn of Monsieur *le facteur* who climbs the drive on his Noddy-yellow bike. He hoots, waves and settles. I go down again and am greeted by yet another swag of calendars.

Having lived all my adult life in a big city, I have never been aware of any tradition of calendar-giving. Does it exist in villages and small towns in England? I wonder. I decline Monsieur *le facteur*'s offer, explaining '*Merci*, we have one.' I have assumed that they are all selling on behalf of the same charity, but I quickly understand by the scowl that runkles his bearded face that this answer is simply *pas acceptable*. Images of a triumphant Henri confronting this corpulent fellow on his knees, as well as a sackload of threatening letters from the post office, flash before my eyes. Best not make an enemy of this *fonctionnaire*, or he'll have us all in the doghouse. Smiling stupidly, I dutifully choose another calendar and race back upstairs to retrieve my purse once again. I proffer the last cash I possess, a 100f note, which seems to satisfy our portly pal. He now wishes me the best of the season, steadies his overloaded moped and pitches off, skating down the drive at a precarious angle.

It is the refuse-collectors who arrive next. We go through the same rigmarole. Unfortunately, I am now out of cash, which does not please them at all, so I am obliged to hurry to the *salon* upstairs, where I all but wreck our luggage in a harassed search for my French chequebook. I pick my calendar, write out a cheque and wave them off merrily. I toss the three calendars, all offering identical aspects of our village, on to the makeshift kitchen table, pour myself a large drink and begin to prepare lunch.

Michel returns, hooting and smiling, laden with salads of every shade of red and green, and clementines from Corsica still bearing sprigs of sharply scented leaves. They are so gnarled and misshapen that they remind me of small ugli fruits. I press my nose into the orange-and-green nobbly skin and inhale the tangy perfume. 'Christmas!' I whoop. I unpack several plastic containers of Provençal olives. Dark, fleshy drupes pickled in brine; others marinated in oil and garlic or pimentos; and then, our oysters, still locked within their salty corrugated shells: a dozen *chanteclairs* from Brittany. We place them, with all the care due to newly laid eggs, in the darkest, coolest spot at the back of our little fridge to await our evening meal. Christmas Eve is the slot traditionally set aside for the French family Christmas dinner and, because the girls are spending their holidays with Maman in Paris, we are looking forward to ours, by candlelight, *à deux*. While we are busy unloading the shopping, I recount the story of our host of visitors. Michel, uncorking a fresh young Chablis, laughs heartily and asks, 'So, the police haven't come by yet?'

These winter evenings are enticingly mild. A new moon, slender as a child's pearly hairslide, appears in our cornflower heaven. I am spinning ideas with Michel, my thoughts for the television series, as we huddle on the terrace, keeping at bay the chill which descends with the fading light by wrapping ourselves in one another and thick cable-stitched woollies. I am describing my main character as she takes shape in my imagination while enjoying an al fresco glass before the silvery shimmer on the water disappears into jet-blue night. Nutty, ambrosial whiffs of woodsmoke waft our way on the still late-evening air. A neighbourly owl hoots a waking greeting. Bats swoop low, whizzing by directly in front of us before wheeling and soaring like excited birds. Then we catch the distant call of the *muezzin*. The Arabs are at prayer. I fall silent and listen.

Although our house and its modest olive farm are situated in an area designated as *zone verte*, at the far end of the valley, tucked away beyond gangling and bushy pine trees, is a settlement. It has been constructed on land compulsorily purchased from the proprietors of Appassionata thirty or more years ago. At that time our local council, managing to overlook the small detail of the land status, stamped a permit which assigned to a syndicate of developers operating out of Marseille the right to construct upon the green-belt site.

Although there were no immediate neighbours at that time, the local community were up in arms as only the French can be when they get mad and feel their rights have been abused and, we hear, lobbied furiously, but lost. One can only speculate on how the permits ever negotiated the system in the first place, when to construct a garden shed or even a very humble lean-to in this zone requires a mountain of forms and months of badgering for planning permission. Such a blatant flaunting of the land codes would, of course, have contributed to the racist sentiments rife in southern France against all foreign workers, but aimed particularly against the Arabs. South-east France is the heart of Le Pen country. No matter that the firm of developers, also the managing agents and therefore the beneficiaries of all profits from the rudimentary housing, are French.

But we have no argument against the Arabs, and we love their tinny summons. I find it both plangent and exotic. It feeds my imagination, my attraction to diversity, and unlocks fantasies of caravans led by camels, treks across mystical Arabia on horseback, guided by the new moon. Then, as the prayers grow silent, I settle back into life in the south of France and the prospect of our delicious oyster supper.

We wake to the distant bray of a donkey – again a new sound on our horizon – and flocks of small, chattering birds. These winter mornings are glorious, gentle and pine-scented. The sun has a lusty amber glow to it, ruddy as an autumn leaf, but viewed from the upper terraces, it streaks across the sea in chilly silver strips. It is winter decked out as I have never known it. But encountering our future home in another season also lays bare some ill-considered responsibilities. During our absence, without anyone to clean and care for it, the water in the swimming pool has turned a rich emerald green. Its floor is carpeted with decaying fig leaves. It cannot be neglected like this for months on end. It needs regular attention – skimmers emptied, pipes unclogged, filter system rinsed out, walls and base hoovered – otherwise the work in which we have invested will have been a waste of precious funds. We add Maintenance of Pool to our growing list of chores to be addressed.

I, who will swim in the most arctic of conditions and dankest of waters, decide to take a dip anyway. The water is so icy as I plunge into it that I hoot and holler. The blood courses fast through my veins. Afterwards, I run and leap about in the garden like a madwoman, gathering soil on my naked, throbbing feet. Michel, passing by, shakes his head and disappears to collect wood and cones for the chimney. He makes up monumental fires which thaw my chilled, goosebumpy flesh. They roar in the hearth like winds from Siberia. Their blaze envelops and heats me; their toasting flames roast and redden my flushed, damp cheeks.

Our winter existence centres around this commodious sitting room. For this season, it has become the heart of the house. For hours we sit here with our books and laptops, me at work on my prospective script, plumped on cushions at the hearthside. The light leaping from the flames makes shadow play on our faces and shapes on the peeling walls. Our tranquillity, the peace we have found in one another's company, allows us plenty of energy for work, which we will need if we are to make a go of this place. Bowled over by love, we have rushed into this acquisition on a cloud of romanticism. The purchase of Appassionata does not make sense on any practical level and we, living from one contract to the next, are sailing tight against the wind. Still, we don't regret it, not a jot – not yet, anyway – but the enormity of the challenge is becoming clear to us. And so we beaver away feverishly in our separate creative worlds until late afternoon, when we switch off our machines, close our books and lay our scripts and pencils to one side. There they stay until the morrow, piled next to stacks of sawn and gathered logs.

Sunsets, the close of the day, and evenings we dedicate to one another and to the world we are attempting to build here. It is a sublime happiness; two souls perfectly synchronised.

Without resources for a kitchen, we are cooking our Christmas meals, as Michel had promised, on the open fire. When the piled embers have settled into hillocks of simmering orange and scarlet red, blood-orange like the sunsets, Michel sets the meat on the makeshift grill to sizzle and spit. Our fare is modest for this festive season: slender *faux-filet* steaks with crispy fresh salad from the fantastic food market in Cannes, accompanied by new potatoes, round and smooth as pebbles, boiled in a copper skillet I bought in Nice on Michel's elementary gas ring fueled by bottled gas. Instead of Christmas pudding or dessert we have cheese, crumbly Parmesan and creamy St Marcelin preserved in olive oil with herbs, washed down with glasses of deep red wine. The heat of the fire, the Bordeaux and the food seduce and inebriate us. No meal has ever tasted this luxurious.

The room is perfumed with cloves I have scattered on the embers and the skins of the consumed Corsican clementines, which sizzle and hiss, turn crisply brown and curl like potato chips. They give off a tangy, sweet scent and recall memories of childhood Christmases and stuffed stockings ripped open at the foot of the tree. We crawl into bed early, to treasure the joys of love. Even our lumpy mattress, which we have dragged through from the room we had elected to be our bedroom to the warmth of the jumping flames, cannot spoil these days for me. Cuddling up close, we count five geckos on the chimney breast.

'I wonder if they are aware of us being here?' I ask Michel.

'Surely. They are guardians of the house. They are watching over us.'

Irrationally, it has a ring of truth. Every cupboard unlocked or door opened reveals a gecko scuttling from the glare of the light and discovery to darkness and anonymity but now, within our simple festive sitting room they have taken up residence on the warm chimney breast to share Christmas with us.

'I doubt we could ever be this happy again,' I whisper as we close our eyes and listen to the crackle of olive branches burning on the open fire. It is a passing comment spoken in a moment of blissful contentment but it should never have been voiced, for it has risen up from a dark, unconscious prescience.

The following morning Michel finally manages to get hold of Mme Blancot at the notary's office. Unfortunately, the paperwork has not arrived from the tax office in central France and, in any case, M. and Mme B. have informed her that they are not available to travel during this period. When Michel replaces the phone, he smiles encouragingly and I, for my part, attempt cheeriness. This will be resolved, we reassure one another. But we are growing concerned.

Caught up in the biomass of weeds and herbs, cobwebby trailers and tangled climbers, are the fruiting olive trees. Their abundant offerings are dropping from the unpruned branches and disappearing into buried clods and sods of soil. Hidden among the overgrowth, they rot secretively. These fruits are returning unused to the earth, leaving only their stone hearts as witnesses. How it pains me to see such a potent elixir go to waste.

It is essential, I suggest to Michel, that as soon as the sale has been concluded we hire a professional to cut back the entire acreage of land. Amar would appear to be our man, if we can agree a price. Amar is a Tunisian who has been living in the south of France since he was a teenager. Unlike many foreign workers, who spend certain periods of the year in France and then return to their families in one of the various north African countries for the remaining months, Amar has married here and is raising his family as young French citizens. He is a rogue, but a kindly one who wishes no real harm to anyone. He has a full-moon face rather like a newborn baby's. Add to that the darker

African tones of his skin and I am reminded of a polished chest-nut. Set within that shiny innocence, however, are shrewd, calibrating eyes.

That same afternoon after a call from Michel, Amar pays us a visit . A fact we have yet to learn is that all foreigners buying properties in this part of France are automatically judged *les riches* and therefore easy pickings for the huge labour force – cowboys as well as true artisans – living off the villa trade close to the coast. Amar studies the width and breadth of the terrain, silently calculating the value of the property, and then the road-weary, battered vehicle parked in the drive, which hardly suggests wealth. On the basis of his estimate he weighs how far he dare go and then speaks with due care, testing the water, naming his fee. The figure is astronomical. He reads our shock and instantly retracts. 'But that is the market price, *cher* Monsieur. Obviously, for you, I would consider a special offer.'

Michel frowns, studies the ground, shifting dust with his shoe. He appears to be evaluating the proposition and, after due thought, counters it with a ninety per cent discount. Amar grins like a playful child, appreciating the daring of the coun-terplay. The ritual has begun. The bartering goes back and forth between the two men until a price is warmly agreed: one fifth of the sum originally requested. Everyone shakes hands. Amar accepts a soft drink – as a practising Muslim, he never touches alcohol – and prepares to wend his way home, but just as we reach the parking area, he turns, smiling broadly.

'Ah, Monsieur . . .'

'Yes?'

'We have forgotten the Christmas tree.' And indeed we gen-uinely have. We apologise profusely.

'Yes, of course. How much do we owe you?' Michel is dig-ging about in the pockets of his jeans for cash, for these matters are always dealt with in cash.

Amar, his smile still as broad as a Cheshire cat's, demands

2,000f, which, with the falling pound, is the equivalent of approximately £236.

Now it is the beginning of March. At long last a date is suggested for us to gather in front of the *notaire* at his panoramic office up in the hills behind the perfume town of Grasse to sign the papers for the purchase of the house. Unfortunately, I am in England, rehearsing a new play which is due to open out of town, run for three weeks and then go straight to London's West End for a season of at least three months. The date fixed by Mme B. is a Monday towards the end of March, the only date that she has available this century. It is the week after the play has opened in Bromley, where I am currently rehearsing.

'I can't be there,' I say to Michel on the phone. He is in Paris. 'I will have to assign you power of attorney.'

'Would you prefer it if we waited until the play has opened in London?'

'No. If we do that, it could be another year before we own the house.'

'That's probably true,' he agrees. 'We'll organise the power of attorney. It will involve you going to the French Embassy in Kensington. Will you be able to arrange that with your rehearsal schedule?' Compared with requesting permission to fly to France, an hour in Kensington does not seem such an unrealistic demand and I reassure Michel that a brief trip to London is entirely feasible.

Two hours later, the *notaire*'s assistant, Mme Blancot, telephones Michel to inform him that *le maître* will not agree to this arrangement.

'Why ever not?' I moan when he calls to pass on the news.

'Because we are not married and, here in France, with the Napoleonic laws in force, my daughters have certain inheritance rights. *Le maître* is insistent that the signing takes place when, and only when, you can be here. Madame Blancot assures me that it is your interests he wants to protect.'

'I see.' I am deliberating long-distance. 'Do you think you could charm Madame B. into bringing the date forward? Why not suggest the week before I go into production?'

'I'll try but . . . *Chérie*, there's one other small point the *maître* pointed out, which we have overlooked . . .'

'What's that?'

'Our *promesse de vente* runs out at the beginning of April.'

The impact of this hits me instantly. In Brussels, the contract we signed bound us to purchasing the property before 4 April. If the house purchase does not go through by that date, we will forfeit our hefty cash deposit as well as all monies spent on building works we have either already accomplished or to which we have committed. Worse, we lose all preferential rights to the purchase of the property and it will go back on the market. It does not bear thinking about. 'But these delays have not been of our making. French bureaucracy is enough to send anyone to the madhouse.'

The fact is, Michel reminds me, that Mme B. had offered us *one* date in mid-February – which we were obliged to refuse because both he and I were back in Australia for a month of post-production on the series I shot before Christmas – so any grounds we feel we have for complaint will be judged *inacceptable*. The long and short of it is that we both stand to lose everything. I am sitting silently at the back of a smoky rehearsal room – a church hall to be precise – weighing up my options over a polystyrene cup of coffee so disgusting it might have been brewed with water from our bracken pond at Appassionata. If the notary does not accept Michel acting for the both of us, the bottom line is that I will be forced to find a way to slip off to France. But how?

Where I am, things are not going great. The director is on his fifty-ninth cigarette of the morning. I fear that the leading actor, who is playing a psychopath – the play is a thriller – may be close to crossing the boundaries between acting and life. The other actor (the cast is a mere trio), an affable, easygoing fellow, looks ready to lose his cool with his colleague's uncontrolled outbursts. We are only eight days into rehearsal, and already there are daily confrontations between these two; moreover, the situation shows signs of growing uglier. I am depressed and wish that I hadn't accepted the job; now, in the light of my own predicament, more than ever. Because this is a new play, the chances are that we will be called to rehearsals every day until after the first night in London, when the critics will have reviewed the piece and all damage to our sensibilities and to the box office, if any, will have been achieved. Until then, there will be cuts, rewrites, new plot twists, different stagings, a host of directorial and managerial responses to the reactions of both the out-of-town audience and the newspapers. This is all perfectly normal and to be expected with a new play, but it does not help my present dilemma . . . And there are no scenes without me. The only reason I am not up on the rehearsal stage right now is that the two men are 'debating' the finer details of gun-toting. The tone of the conversation taking place at this very moment goes something like: 'Don't keep sticking that f*** thing in my eye!'

Timing is of the essence, in real life as in theatre. I am going to have to seize my moment to speak to the producer, who is a charming and reasonable individual. I decide to put the problem out of mind for now, wait till matters look a little more sanguine, and concentrate on my work.

During my lunch break, from a call box a discreet distance from the theatre, I telephone Michel in Paris. 'Confirm the date,' I tell him, 'and I'll settle it with the management this week.'

'Are you sure?'

'Yes.' The truth is I am not the least bit sure, but we have no choice.

I still have another fifty minutes of lunch break so, rather than returning to sit hunched up in a dressing room learning my lines, which is what I would normally do, I opt to browse around the suburban high street. Coincidentally, I spent many years of my youth, my salad days, in Bromley, so its dreary, homogenised modernisations hold a certain depressing fascination for me. I range around, trying to remember how it was when I was a girl and which formative experiences took place where until, passing one of the high-street pubs, I catch sight of our supporting actor sitting alone on a stool and leaning on the bar. His head is bent over a glass and he looks desperately glum. Although we barely know one another, having met only eight days earlier at the read-through, I decide to intrude on his mood.

'Hey,' I say, both by way of a greeting and to alert him to my presence. I notice that his drink is a tonic and something. Gin? Vodka? He turns to face me and I realise immediately that he has downed more than this one. His bloodshot eyes glare out from a face that looks bemused, hurt and desperate.

'How are you doing?' I ask. The question is redundant. The barman saunters my way and I order coffee. 'Would you like one?'

My colleague shakes his head mutely. 'I can't work with him. He's a f***ing c***.'

I can see this actor's point but I won't say so. After all, there are only three of us and we have five months of work ahead in a piece that is demanding and intimate.

'I guess he's nervous. Probably pinning a lot on it. Big role . . .' My coffee arrives, for which I am grateful, because I do not believe a word of what I am saying. My fellow thesp takes advantage of the barman's presence to order another double. I look at him quizzically. He says, 'Listen, why don't you do a spot of shopping? I'll catch you back there.'

I nod, leaving the coffee, some coins on the bar and my poor workmate to his angst and alcohol.

When I return to work, our leading player is sitting with the director in the rehearsal hall, where they are sharing anecdotes, one firing off after the other. I find this a common practice among actors in rehearsal, and I have never quite understood why it happens. It is a performance within a performance. I concentrate on my script. The next time I look up, it is fifteen minutes beyond the allotted lunch hour and my friend from the pub has not returned. The leading actor has begun to pace. His face reddens; his blood pressure must be mounting. He is growing manic. The director is chain-smoking. A few moments later, the company manager, a caring young woman in her mid-twenties, enters with a note which she hands to the director. He reads it, frowns furiously, screws it up into a ball and tosses it on to the floor. 'Tony has gone home. He's not feeling too good.'

The leading actor explodes like a canister left too close to the heat. We are all knocked backwards by the sheer vehemence of his response and the foulness of his language. I turn to the company manager, who returns my duplicitous look. The director rises and announces that probably the best plan is to spend the rest of the day with the wardrobe mistress, who will take measurements for our costumes.

When Michel calls in the evening, I say nothing of the problems I am facing and merely assure him that all is well and that I will be in France to sign the documents. I sleep fitfully.

My call for the next morning is slightly later than the others. When I arrive, I discover the same trio I left behind the evening before – all wearing long, murderous faces. Before I have the opportunity to say good morning, I am informed that Tony has left the show. A treacherously unprofessional thought then creeps into my mind: with only two left in the cast, and only one week to go before we begin technical rehearsals, production days etc., there is too little time. The management will be obliged to cancel, or at least postpone the first night, *and I will be free to go to France*! But obviously, I keep such rising delight well in check.

The morning is spent ringing round agents, casting directors and chums to find a replacement for Tony. I offer no suggestions because I cannot in all conscience recommend any of my pals for what I am beginning to see as a sentence rather than a job. Our star is fulminating and cursing. Suddenly, he rounds on me. 'I suppose it'll be you next!' he hisses poisonously, out of earshot of the others.

'To do what?' I reply calmly but shakily.

'You'll be walking out on me, too.'

I refrain from pointing out to him that the play is not about him, but a team effort. 'No I won't,' I answer.

I have never walked out on a job, but at this very moment there is nothing I desire more. However, for many reasons, high on the list being the cost of house renovations and land maintenance equipment, it would be a foolish and irrational act. So I stay put and go on with the business of learning my lines and worrying about how I am now going to persuade the management to give me a Monday off, less than two weeks hence, to fly to France.

'So you're going to stick it out then, are you?'

'Please,' I say. 'Let's just drop it.'

A replacement is found. A jolly chap, resilient and good-humoured. I try hard not to feel disappointed that the production has not been cancelled. I need this job and the actor is someone with whom I have worked before and who I like. He makes me laugh. He is exactly what we need and, astoundingly, learns the piece in two days. As far as everyone else is concerned we are back on track. The other poor victim has been forgotten, written off as unprofessional. Interestingly, our lead has met his match, for every time he starts to become even vaguely malevolent, the newcomer bats back with a quip or joke and the star has no brunt for his sadism. Or has he? As the days creep towards the out-of-town opening and he grows jumpier, he settles his attentions on me. After one of the early runs of the piece, he accuses me – in front of cast, technicians, management and crew – of being entirely without talent and timing. Alone in my dressing room, I shed a few tears. Then, like every actress in desperate straits, I call my agent, who cheers me with, 'Oh darling, he's famous for it. When so-and-so finished working with him she went to bed for a week!' Now he tells me.

The sole good point of my week is the blissful and unexpected news that we will not be rehearsing on the Monday after we open. It has been deemed a much-needed rest day. In the light of this development and all that is going on, I take a precarious and highly unprofessional decision, which is to go to France and not mention it. Such a move could lose me my job, but by this stage, I would almost be grateful. Even so, it goes against the grain for me to behave with such dishonour so I decide, for form's sake and to offload a little of my guilt, to confide my plan in the company manager who, when she hears of it, stares at me in sheet-white horror. 'You have no understudy until we reach London!' she yelps. 'I'd have to cancel the show.'

'I'll be back, don't worry,' I reassure her. 'The signing is at nine-thirty. It will be over by eleven at the latest. There are two British Airways flights leaving Nice after that. Either would land me at Heathrow in plenty of time, and with a taxi to chauffeur me to the theatre, there's no way I'll miss the show.' She relents. What choice have I given the poor woman? Her sole request is that should the worst come to the worst, I am never, *never* to mention that she had an inkling of my plan, or her career will be in ruins, alongside mine. It seems a fair bargain. I agree.

On the Sunday Michel, whose plane from Paris has landed earlier than mine, is waiting to greet me at Nice Airport. It is a glorious spring morning. In spite of a tense week and a dawn departure from London, the prospect of the following day's trip up into the hills exhilarates me. Added to which, after such an interminable wait, we are finally taking legal possession of our home, our farm. When we arrive at the house sitting atop its hill of dusky olive trees, having not visited it for almost three months, it is unrecognisable. Amar has cut back the entire expanse of land. We are gazing upon a new geography. The bosky acres, the brush and brambles, the jungle have been strimmed, laid bare and raked into hummocks ready for burning. However, this fleecing has left Appassionata looking naked and vulnerable; a deserted, crumbling shell. Yet newborn, with much to discover and to come to know. We count sixty-four overgrown olive trees (ten I had not seen before), as well as seeing space on the upper terraces for dozens more;. terraces cut back in their entirety for the first time in many a year. Freed to breathe, to grow anew and to produce.

'I thought you had agreed with Amar to wait until after . . .'

'So did I,' says Michel.

It is both a lovely and troubling greeting for of course we have no gates, no fencing, no boundary partitions of any kind. This will have to be addressed next. Unfortunately, there is so much that will have to be addressed next . . .

But, aside from all future cares, there is a revelation too exquisite for words. The cutting back of the land has exposed a fabulous flight of stone steps. Unbeknown to us, it has lain buried beneath the layers of brambles, forgotten and unused. Now, its secret unfolded, it rises like a bird ascending from the foot of the hillside to the house itself. Michel suggests that it must have been the original entrance to the house before the tarmac drive was put in, before a route for cars was deemed necessary, before the lane which crosses between our entrance and our caretaker's cottage was ever thought of. Judging by a series of small rectangular holes cut into the stones, it looks as though a rose bower covered pretty much all of it, a distance of approximately 300 metres. In full flower, it must have been an impressive sight, and what a perfumed entry!

Our approach along the drive also reveals to us soft pink almond blossom, past its best and fading now, and, all around us, bursting from the branches of the deciduous trees – figs, cherries, plums, pears – fresh, shiny, bamboo-green shoots, as well as hundreds, literally hundreds, of flowering wild irises, white and violet, bordering the terraces at every level. Pale pink, bamboo-green, white, inky violet: a palette I have never associated with the south of France. We inch forward in the car, taking in these sights, these explosions of unexpected colour. What release must nature be experiencing? When did this earth, the soil of these terraces, last feel the beat of sunlight? I consider the millions of creatures and insects who have been rendered homeless, who have lost their bearings and, alongside them, the plants that have been given back the light.

As if to confirm our impending ownership, our new bed is waiting for us in the house. What a treat!

After lunch on the upper terrace, the sky clouds over.

We make the most of our chilly Sunday afternoon by working, keeping warm through activity. It is such a pleasure to be out of doors, to be physically busy; it is invigorating and reassuring. I am weeding the flowerbeds; Michel sweeps the steps, which are knee-high in mulchy leaves, then strips and prepares the garden chairs to be painted in combinations of lilac and ochre. I discover tiny spring-green shoots appearing at the base of the chopped trunks of what we had believed were dead orange trees. Somewhere in the middle distance I hear gunshots, a hunter out after rabbits or small birds. I feel my skin, which is tired and tight from layers of stage make-up, begin to breathe and glow in the sharp, brisk air. As the day draws to its early close it starts to rain. I jump into the brilliant green pool and swim for my life in the freezing water, circling and paddling like an otter in the drizzle while Michel banks up the fire – we have unlimited supplies of firewood now – ready for the evening. A propitious moment in time. Our last evening as official squatters, for tomorrow we will become *les propriétaires*.

Lounging on cushions in front of the fire, we listen to the rain beating hard and fast against the windowpanes and splashing into our well-used bucket in the makeshift kitchen. But we don't care. Tomorrow every leak, every flaking crumb of plaster, will belong to us.

The rain grows tropical in its intensity. All night it beats and slaps against the flat roof and, when we wake in the morning, bright and early ready for our excursion into the hills, our driveway is streaming with water. It runs in rivulets, bringing sticks, a dead rabbit and rotting leaves in its wake. Only in the rainy season in Borneo and in the last throes of a hurricane in Fiji have I witnessed such a torrential downpour. As we belt to the car, it drenches us. The wipers are barely able to beat back and forth, the force of it is so overwhelming, and, in any case, they achieve little. Fortunately, Michel knows the route. We arrive on time, but dripping like river rats. Mme B. awaits us, dry as a bone and impeccably turned out. Robert is not with her. The *notaire* looks on in operatic horror as we squelch across his pristine beige carpet to our appointed leather chairs.

The panoramic views in this area beyond Grasse, about which I have heard so much, are masked by the blanket of sheeting rain. '*C'est dommage*,' shrugs the *notaire*, who sports a pince-nez, a well-cut but rather old-fashioned, double-breasted navy suit and is as manicured and pointy-faced as a poodle. His elbows are poised on the armrests of his chair, and they never leave that position. He joins the tips of his fingers together regularly, as though in prayer, and I discover that he has an infuriatingly meticulous attention to detail. Here is a man who puts brackets between verbal brackets and then parenthesises. Every law, bylaw, clause, full stop is thrown open for consideration and then explained at a rattling pace. The history of the estate of Appassionata is not only written into the contract page by page, franc for franc – husband of, wife to, born of – but is now read aloud, repeated and commented upon by him.

The villa was constructed in 1904. This was the year the great Provençal poet, Frédéric Mistral, was awarded the Nobel Prize for literature. Because the process is ponderous and I have already lost the thread, I search my mind for a quotation of his I learned by heart recently but it slips beyond recall when the *notaire*'s droning drums me back to consciousness. I try again to concentrate but find myself completely, hopelessly, lost. *Le maître* – all *notaires* in France are addressed as *le maître* (literally translated – the master), an acknowledgement of rank and learning equal, I suppose, to us addressing a judge as Your Honour – *le maître* swivels his leather chair, the only one not fixed, and talks at great length to Michel. Michel nods and interpolates every now and again and, once in a while, I am galvanised because I have caught a word or phrase. I am unclear as to why this notary's words are directed exclusively at Michel. As far as I can make out, they are discussing the fact that Michel was born just outside Cologne, but that he has been resident in France since his late teens. Mme B. does not appear to be listening. She is crossing and marking her contract, which is spread out on the desk in front of her as though it were a script in need of drastic and immediate rewrites.

Every so often, when the pinched, parchmenty fellow pauses to draw breath, Mme B. interjects, politely but firmly, '*Maître, s'il vous plaît* . . .' I haven't a clue what finer points they are debating, and I cannot possibly ask Michel. I long for the distraction of the view and I am struggling not to steal a quick peek at my watch. A tiny worm of concern is wriggling about in my English language interior monologue: is all this just a teeny bit longwinded, or does it just seem to be because I am on the outside looking in? And is it going to take all morning? I have to catch that lunchtime flight . . .

The rain is percussionless; no rolls of thunder, no crashes of electric white lightning, nothing but interminable rain.

Suddenly, when I have drifted far away, the *notaire's* chair swivels once more and stops like a ball on a roulette wheel, directly facing me. 'Madame Drinkwater?' All eyes turn to me.

'*Oui?*' I reply weakly.

'*Avez-vous compris?*' Have I understood what? I am asking myself. I shoot a glance at Michel, who is gazing at me warmly. He speaks for me, explaining to the *notaire* that I am not familiar with all of this.

'Aaaah,' sings the man, as though it explained my mute inattention, my lack of delight in dissecting these sacred deeds paragraph by paragraph. And then he launches into a history of my life. Where and when I was born; the name of my parents; which bank I bank with in England, and which in France; my annual income (a figure I must have pulled out of thin air, for I have no guaranteed income); my profession; my mother's maiden name; the sum I have contributed towards the overall price of the estate; the fact that no debts remain unpaid by me. I am stupefied. And then he pauses, throwing his text on the table. 'So, you are from Ireland?' I nod, and he removes his glasses and opens up a personal parenthesis about Ireland and the various holidays he has enjoyed there. Green. I understand that word. Yes, I nod, very green. And wet, *malheureusement*. Yes, Ireland is wet, I agree. Everyone laughs and shrugs and throws their hands about the way the southern French do when they are discussing the living habits of poor unfortunate folk forced to live in climes less blessed than theirs. '*Mais . . .*' and he gestures Shakespearian-fashion towards the window, which opens on to nothing but the blanket of rain. There is a pause while the rain is considered. I and my history have been forgotten, or so I think. Seconds later, he is back in his role, text in hand, and other details of my private existence are shared with the room, which includes Mme Blancot – who is taking notes, though heavens knows how anyone could possibly keep pace with this man – and, silently tucked away in the corner, like an outcast, the estate agent, M. Charpy, who first introduced us to Appassionata.

And so it goes on. And on. I am asked if I have been informed about the existence of Michel's daughters, of his ex-wife. The whole business feels like a preposterous interrogation. Then I am gravely warned about the risks I am taking in signing these documents and in part-purchasing a property with a man who has offspring elsewhere. I fear that were my understanding of legal French any better, I would pick up my bag and make for the door without signing a single page of what turns out to be five copies of a twenty-nine-page document. We are all of us obliged to initial every page and sign our full names at various strategic points after we have handwritten the words: '*Lu et approuvé.*' Read and approved. The contracts are passed round the table in a circular fashion as each one of us – Michel, followed by me, then Mme B. and the *notaire*, as well as his assistant, Mme Blancot – silently and carefully initials and signs.

The whole process is really quite comical, a merryground of papers and pens, with only one person, the estate agent, doing nothing. He, I realise later, is there to receive his dosh, a settlement begrudgingly given by Mme B., which he receives in cash. The thick wad of 500f notes is quite literally passed under the table from richly bejewelled fingers to grasping hands, but only after every last 'i' has been dotted. I am amused by the *notaire* who, while this black-market activity is taking place right beneath his own desk, pulls out an enormous white handkerchief and busily blows his nose. The size of the handkerchief, little short of a sheet, manages most conveniently to cover his eyes and most of his face; he has 'seen' nothing!

It is after midday when we finally get out of there and say our *au revoirs* to Mme B., who we will meet once more when we go through the whole tedious process again for the purchase of the second five acres of land. Outside, the rain, if possible, has grown heavier. The sky is dark and brooding. Mme B. disappears in a chauffeur-driven limousine and we stand, huddled tight, beneath the *notaire*'s porch. We had planned an early lunch at the farm; a toast to our new, elevated position; to our home, the hillside, the new bed. But none of this is now possible. We look at one another and smile.

'The airport?' Michel asks, and I nod. The drive is horrendous; the roads are silted with mud and rivers of water. Everyone is driving with headlights on full beam and the corkscrew hills and bends are treacherous. Descending through Grasse, where the road is perilous at the best of times, is a muddle of impatient, bad-tempered motorists. But we still have time: I try not to be anxious. We are silent because Michel is concentrating, and I am sorry to be leaving, knowing that I shan't be returning until the end of June, which, at this moment, feels a lifetime away. There is so much I want to do.

On our arrival at the airport, I run on ahead to check in for the flight while Michel returns the hire car. When I arrive at the desk, it is ominously deserted. No staff, no passengers. I look at my watch. The flight is not due to leave for another thirty-five minutes. It is tight but surely the check-in hasn't already closed? They will only just be beginning boarding about now. I look around wildly and spot the British Airways enquiry desk, where there is a worryingly long queue and gaggles of troubled and angry passengers. At the desk I learn that, due to the weather conditions, the flight has been cancelled. My stomach feels as though it has just taken a punch from Mohammad Ali. Everyone, including myself, is scrabbling to book themselves on to the next flight. While doing so, I upgrade to Club Class, reasoning that, should there be any further problems, it will give me an advantage. Michel arrives. I explain what has happened. His flight to Paris is not for another hour and it is due to take off from the other terminal, the terminal for internal flights. He hurries over to the Air France desk and changes to a later one.

'Well, then, let's have lunch and celebrate,' he says, and leads me to one of the airport cafés. I do not want to stray too far. I feel I must keep a careful eye on developments here, even though the later plane will still give me plenty of time to reach the theatre comfortably before curtain-up. Nevertheless, I would have felt calmer if I'd already been on my way.

After we have eaten, we bid one another a passionate, heartfelt goodbye, and Michel waves me off through security towards passport control. As I look back, I see him hurrying for the bus to Terminal 1. We will not see each other for three weeks. In spite of the events of the day, the securing of the farm after almost a year of delays, my heart feels heavy. I am torn between two worlds, the past and present and the present and future, and two countries: my heart and home are in France now, but my work is still in England. Preoccupied by these thoughts, I have been only vaguely aware of information coming over the loudspeaker. It is repeated in English, and this time I pay attention. Due to the weather conditions, the British Airways flight has been delayed!

'No!' I cry, and run to the boarding gate, where a pretty young Frenchwoman is switching off the microphone she has just used for the announcement. 'How long is the delay?'

She shrugs. 'We don't know.' We both stare out of the window at a waterlogged runway and a fleet of planes standing idle. Should I telephone the theatre? Could I hire a private plane? But if the regular Boeings cannot take off, what hope has a small jet? I decide to enquire anyway. My fears are confirmed: all air traffic has been grounded. I return to the departure lounge. There is nothing to do but sit it out.

The delay turns out to be a little over an hour. Throughout,

I go over and over constantly shifting calculations in my mind: likely arrival times; how long it might take to get through passport control, to find a taxi. Fortunately I have no luggage. Should I book a taxi to the theatre from here? But I don't know when we will be departing. My brain is beginning to scramble. It is going to take a miracle . . . Should I telephone the company manager? But, if I do, what can she do? I have no understudy . . . I am going to be fired. In a career spanning almost twenty years, I have never yet missed a show, not even due to illness, and certainly not through an act as irresponsible as this one. I am still berating myself when the boarding is announced.

As the stewardess directs me to my seat, I mention to her that I have a show and I ask if there is any possibility of being given priority disembarkation. 'We all have problems,' she snaps. 'You should have taken an earlier plane.'

Admonished, I spend the flight trying to rest. I am exhausted with worry and a surfeit of French bureaucracy. A plump woman, an American from Texas, seated beside me tries on several occasions to engage me in conversation, but I am in no mood and close my eyes firmly. Until I am stirred by a hand resting on mine. 'Honey,' she says, 'I wanna tell you something.'

I open my eyes. 'What is it?' I ask irritably.

'You sure as hell are worried about something, and I want you to know that I *know* about it.'

'Know about it?' I echo weakly. If she has some secret, I am so desperate I am ready to hear it.

'I *see* things,' she continues. 'And you have nothing to worry about. You're gonna make it.'

'I am?' I look at her in amazement and then I realise that I am grasping at straws. It is only my need for everything to be all right that is persuading me to take heart from this utterly vague assertion. 'No,' I say. 'I can't make it. There is no taxi in the world that can transport me across rush-hour London in time for curtain-up.'

'Oh, my God, you're an actress? Have I seen you in anything? Anything on TV that shows in the States?'

I wish I had never been drawn in, but she is well-meaning enough and it is I who am moody and anxious. I give her *All Creatures Great and Small,* which is the usual key that unlocks the door to my curriculum vitae. She is thrilled and 'sooo happy! Let me tell you, honey, you will make that show, I have no doubt about it.'

I smile and thank her for her optimism and then close my eyes. Whatever she says, it is now a physical impossibility, and I have decided that as soon as we land I must call the theatre and warn them, which is what I should have done from Nice, and explain to our very dear company manager that she has two choices: hold the curtain or cancel the show. Either way, I am finished. We fasten our seatbelts and the plane prepares for landing. As we hit the runway, the stewardess makes the usual announcements. Following them with: 'And would Miss Drinkwater please make herself known to the cabin staff . . .' I press the overhead button and she approaches.

'We'll be disembarking you first,' she tells me. 'Please have your bags ready.'

I nod gratefully, though I know this favour cannot help me now.

My Texan friend brushes my hand and wishes me well, reassuring me once more that she *knows* I will make it. She shames me by beaming with the pleasure of having met me and declaring that she will tell everyone I am equally charming in real life.

As I exit the plane, I find a member of British Airways' groundstaff waiting, holding a card with my name on it.

'Miss Drinkwater?' he enquires.

I nod. 'Follow me, please.' He strides on ahead purposefully. I follow obediently, although I am confused. 'We have a short car ride across the tarmac. It won't take more than a couple of minutes. Your pilot is ready and waiting.' He smiles with professional reassurance.

My pilot? Now I am completely bemused.

Accompanied by the BA man, I am driven in a car across an area of Heathrow Airport I have never seen before and deposited alongside a capacious helicopter. The car door is opened, I step out and the man shakes my hand. 'Nice to have met you. Good luck.' And off he goes. The pilot waves and sees me aboard. I settle into the helicopter, which is equipped to seat ten, and prepare for yet another take-off.

'Sorry it's so large,' he says. 'We had nothing smaller available.'

I merely shake my head because I am speechless. 'It's fine,' I manage to mutter. Have they made a mistake? I dare not ask.

'We'll be across London and landing at Biggin Hill Airport in ten minutes. All being well, there should be a taxi waiting to take you to the theatre.'

This *is* a miracle. I simply cannot figure it out. Did that rather charmless, or perhaps just harassed, air stewardess thaw during the flight and notify the pilot, who notified ground-staff? Even if she had, surely they wouldn't have gone to this much trouble? Or has the Texan woman some miraculous powers she only hinted at?

Finally, I ask, 'Did British Airways arrange this?'

'No, your husband booked it.'

'My husband?' I am flustered. I am not married. Have I taken someone else's place? But no, it was my name that was written on the arrivals card, and they have a taxi waiting to take me to the theatre I need to get to.

And there it is, a taxi waiting on the tarmac. A bit of an old banger, but what do I care, and into it I fall gratefully. The traffic is heavy because we are hitting rush hour, but my driver seems to have been briefed that this is an emergency. He shoulders his way in and out of lanes of vehicles with a cut-throat determination usually shown only by the French, and deposits me, fifteen minutes later, outside the stage door. It is twenty-five minutes before curtain-up. My knees are weak, I am soaking with perspiration and I feel like a damp rag, but I am here. I collect my dressing-room key and stagger along the corridor. The company manager finds me. She looks ashen. Officially, contractually, all artists are due at the theatre by what is known as 'the half', a theatrical abbreviation for half an hour ahead of curtain-up, though curiously, the half is actually announced thirty-five minutes beforehand. Don't ask me why. All I know is that, right now, it makes me ten minutes late.

'Sorry,' I mumble.

'Thank God you're here,' she whispers, shoving me into my room and closing the door behind her. 'No one knows a thing but, Christ, have I been having kittens.'

I nod. I cannot speak. I am trembling like a leaf.

'Are you OK?'

'Fine,' I manage.

'Want anything?'

'Rescue remedy.' I know she keeps a bottle of Bach herb-and-flower remedy for shock in her first-aid kit.

'You've got it.' She rushes to the door and opens it. 'By the way,' she throws after her as she leaves, 'he's in the foulest of moods.'

I take this in. 'Make that a double brandy.' I never drink before a show, but tonight, without some kind of boost, I doubt my knocking knees will transport me to the stage.

After the performance, which has gone surprisingly well, I pour myself a large glass of wine and ring Michel in Paris from my dressing room. 'How did you do it?'

He laughs and recounts his afternoon. He had been sitting in the national terminal waiting for the departure of his Air France flight to Paris when, by sheer chance, he glanced up from his laptop out of the window and noticed a British Airways plane sitting on the sopping tarmac. When he enquired he was informed that it was the delayed Heathrow flight. There was no way he could reach me, but what he did know was that every second that ticked by without that plane leaving the ground reduced my chances of reaching the theatre before curtain-up. With the brilliance and agility of mind of a film producer, a breed that lives by the motto that every catastrophe must be turned to advantage if financial disaster is to be avoided, Michel knew that what he had to buy me was time. He cancelled his own flight, bought several phonecards and began ringing helicopter firms operating out of Heathrow. It was the helicopter company who gave him the name of the taxi service which regularly picks up from Biggin Hill.

When the bill arrives, the whole exercise will cost every penny I am to earn from the out-of-town contract – money that might have purchased us a gate or contributed towards the laurel-bush fencing we have decided upon – but I am no longer counting. The show has gone on and my professional reputation has been saved.

As night falls and I curl up and close my deadbeat eyes, the extraordinary catalogue of the day's adventures (and misadventures) plays out again in my mind's eye. In all the gut-wrenching stress, I had almost forgotten that today we bought ourselves an olive farm in the Midi, overlooking the Riviera.

Pride and contentment wash over me for the first time and the reality of our act sinks sweetly home. Then I contemplate the strikingly generous gesture of the tender, loving man, for whose presence I ache but who lies sleeping far beyond my hungry arms in the *chic*-est of all cities across La Manche. To have cancelled his afternoon meetings for my sake! How many human beings would have attempted and carried off such a coup? As my eyes grow heavier and my body slips warmly and safely towards sleep, I am lulled by the certainty that I have finally secured the shambling house for which I have searched during so many years of travel, and, what is even more delicious, along the way I have encountered the one person with whom I desire to share that corner of paradise. All that remains is for us to find the means to transform that crumbling shell into a home and, later, an olive farm. Still, for the foreseeable future, until my West End run is over, I must set such dreams aside. There will be no more snatched escapades in France.

A Melon and
Leather Boots

The instant I step off the plane, I feel that whoosh of heat enveloping me and the sun beating like a great fan against my tired face. What a welcome relief to be back. To be home. Michel, who flew down from Paris a couple of days ago, is here to greet me. He takes my bag and leads me to the car, while I breathe in the scent of eucalyptus wafting from the towering trees which dominate the airport parking. I take in the distant frantic hooting of horns, the gently listing palms, the pure white buildings and clean blue skies, and settle back into my seat to watch the Mediterranean world flash by me. And then, he breaks it to me: the villa has been broken into. It's as though he has just slapped me.

'When?'

Michel has known of the burglary for several weeks but chose not to mention it to me because there was nothing I could do about it. Worrying about it at a distance, he argues, would have been both distressing and frustrating. 'I would have preferred to have known,' I state emphatically. For three months I have been looking forward to this day. I cannot deny that the news has clouded the pleasure of my return.

At the house, Michel unloads the car – my luggage and the fresh salads he bought before collecting me – while I roam from room to room, assessing the extent of the damage to our dusty foreign home. Little has been stolen, but then, there was precious little to steal. I am very relieved to find that our new bed has not been soiled, or even touched. However, our cassettes and tape-deck, modest as they were, have gone. Every tune had a place here, a memory. My fusty workspace is bare. My books, my precious books, have all been taken, every one of them. Dictionaries, guides, a history of the Îles de Lérins, manuals on local horticulture, even the dog-eared, beach-stained paperbacks. As has a brand-new espresso machine, a frivolous purchase I made the day before our New Year departure. I hid and locked it in a cupboard and, due to the brevity of our last visit, we never even used it. Curiously, the bed linen and tablecloths from the market at Nice have been left behind. They are surely more valuable and saleable than my modest library but, angry as I feel, I am grateful that we have not been denied at least a few souvenirs of our first days here.

Michel finds me standing alone in the *salon*. 'How did they get in?' I ask. He points to splintered spaces where our old peeling shutter slats have been hacked out and made good, to new windowpanes replacing those smashed by the thief when he made his entry, as well as to a recently fitted lock on the main door, through which he made his escape. Who repaired them, and when? Amar, Michel answers, studying me. I think he is taken aback by how hurt I am. Though the damage has been put right and the loss is minimal, I want to cry. I take it personally. It is an intrusion, a despoilment and, more crucially, a warning.

Outside the kitchen window, I come across a discarded

Marlboro packet. Should I keep it, present it as evidence? I try to picture the character and face of that smoker, but the discovery of this clue is five weeks too late. I ditch the empty pack in the dustbin. Best to let it go.

The cropping of the land has exposed us. We are vulnerable now. It forces us to address the need for security. The hill might never have been fenced in before but we cannot afford to remain romantic about these matters. In the beginning, there was nothing else, no other property for kilometres in any direction. As far as the naked eye could see, it was owned and inhabited by one family, the Spinotti clan. Life was almost certainly less cut-throat in those days, but, more importantly, in the dependencies, the *mazets* of Appassionata, lived gardeners and permanent staff, a cluster of people who tended the place all year round. We are not as privileged, so another solution will have to be found.

After lunch on the terrace, Michel telephones Amar, who arrives before evening and quotes for the laurel bushes we want to plant to border the grounds. For the time being, we do not have to face the enormous expense of fencing in the entire property because flanking our terrain on either side is the same overgrown jungle we had here. We have no idea who owns these two plots but, unattractive as the weeds and climbers may be, they are a deterrent to burglars.

My behaviour towards Amar is antagonistic. This is partly due to my frame of mind, but mostly because I am conscious that he knows we are beginning to count on him and I can feel him stealing the advantage. His estimation of the number of bushes we need far exceeds mine, and I tell him so. Eventually, over a fruit juice, aided by Michel's appeasing charm, we settle upon a more reasonable quantity, and a price. Yet even after hefty negotiating, it is still expensive. Added to which, the cash we give him to settle for the land clearance, he now informs us, is insufficient.

'A rate has been agreed. Hands were shaken on the deal!' I bark.

'Allow me to explain, *chère* Madame.' And he proceeds in an irritatingly apologetic manner to argue that he has underestimated the total number of man hours required for his two workers to climb up and down the hill and is obliged therefore to add this to the bill.

I am speechless with fury at his audacity and invention. Here, in the Midi, I am discovering, there are always reasons why the valuations change or why the work is not done in the manner or to the standard agreed. In this part of the world, quotations and budgets might as well be used as barbecue kindling. But Michel pays with good grace and we order the laurel shrubs because we cannot afford to delay while we look around for a less sharp gardener. And better the devil you know. Still, before *plein* summer is upon us, with all its distractions and aggravations, its onslaught of tourists, queues, traffic congestions, when even the tiniest chore takes twice the time and every factory, *société* and office closes down for the entire month of August, we would do well to find ourselves some able-bodied help. We have a daunting list of tasks. Most will be left to me to oversee because Michel must return to Paris and will be here only at weekends. I am tired from the run of the play and grateful to have an excuse to stay here and hang out. Besides, I have my writing project, inspired by our day trip to the islands, to complete. And then there is the leaking roof . . . Yet again, after evening calculations over a bottle of wine, we realise that our funds are desperately insufficient. We will have to choose what to attack now and what to leave for some future date. But we are not downhearted. My initial bad mood has improved; I grow cheery again and optimism returns.

Last summer we managed and, better still, enjoyed magical months here, and there is no reason why this year should be any different. Now that the property belongs to us, certain pressures have been lifted. We can work at our own pace. The installation of a kitchen; rewiring throughout; a shower room in between two guest bedrooms; replastering and painting upstairs and down; the transformation of an ancient scullery, or *souillarde*, complete with its magnificent blond stone sink, into a summer kitchen; replacing lengths of piping and cracked tiles; repairing of and painting Matisse-blue all shutters and doors; the planting of palm trees, fruit trees, flowers, more flowers; the creation of vegetable and herb gardens; the purchase of the second five acres; even my precious olive farming . . . it is a never-ending list. But it can all be achieved in the fullness of time. If, in the meantime, this summer, I can study the basics of olive farming and we can find ways to secure the house against the undesired entry of thieves and rain, we will have accomplished a great deal.

I am standing on the roof in the company of M. Di Luzio, our chimney-sweeping plumber. He has agreed to coat this flat, leaking expanse with a layer of bitumen and gravel. Although it is only a temporary solution, and the work does not carry a damp-proof guarantee, he assures me that it should keep the rain out for up to a year, even two; certainly until we can raise the hefty sum needed to do the job in a more professional way (the three quotes we have received have left us reeling). Pacing out the metreage, he spins in a kind of lumbering pirouette, a 360-degree turn, scans the length and breadth of our land, then screws up his face and peers south towards the bay. The view from this *hauteur* is breathtaking, exceptional. In true Midi fashion, M. Di Luzio grimaces his approval. Coming from him, this is a rare compliment for, until this moment, he has recommended repeatedly that the best advice he can offer us is to raze the villa to the ground and construct a new one. But today, the early-summer warmth, mingled with an agreeable breeze coming off the hills, seems to have put him in good humour, for he concludes, '*Pas mal, Madame,*' with, as ever, the authority of God.

I nod, gratified.

He turns to survey our pine forest. 'You have plenty of wood.'

I agree. It is hardly a debatable point, for the felled trunks and branches are lying at angles all over the grounds like pick-a-sticks.

'You know, a word of advice, if I may be so bold . . .'

I brace myself, expecting to be counselled that we should build ourselves a cabin and abandon all hope for this erstwhile neglected farmhouse.

'There is enough wood here to pay my bill for the roof work.'

'Really?'

'*Mais oui*, Madame. Sell it for cash, and then pay me in cash. It will be a *très bonne affaire* for you.' His eyes are ablaze at the thought of a good business proposition, particularly one that is *noir*, and therefore tax-free. We saunter towards the roof's edge, preparing to descend the rear wall of the building by means of a ladder which I have placed there for the purpose.

M. Di Luzio signals me to go ahead. I twist my body and lower myself on to the first rung, stepping cautiously because stepping backwards down ladders always makes me queasy. I leave him to follow. He is a hefty man, and I assume he will wait until I have reached solid ground before climbing aboard. But he doesn't. I am only two rungs beneath him when I feel the ladder begin to shift. 'I have discovered your secret, Madame,' he bellows from above. I wish he wouldn't talk now. I try to hurry, concentrating on reaching terra firma. 'I have told my wife, but no one else. I'll keep it to myself. You don't want the entire village gossiping.'

Whatever this secret is, it is amusing him greatly. I glance up, and stare into the soles of his thick, workman's shoes, trying to avoid the not-very-pretty sight of his blue trousers flapping around extremely hairy legs. He is laughing so loudly that the ladder is now slapping back and forth against the wall. I picture us crashing to the ground, a damaged heap of limbs and metal.

'Tell me in a minute!' I yell, lunging into midair and flinging myself to the ground, which seems a preferable alternative. From there, flushed and giddy, I await his revelation. 'What secret, Monsieur Di Luzio?'

His eyes are twinkling like those of a big kid who has uncovered the whereabouts of stashed sweets. '*Pas un mot.*' He raises one filthy black finger and presses it against his pouting mouth.

'But, surely . . .'

'Ssssh. My lips are sealed.' How he loves to play-act, to revel in his moment of drama.

I shrug and lead the way to the front terraces. I have no idea what he is talking about. Surely, not that *le monsieur* and myself are not married? He winks and shakes my hand ferociously, transmitting soot to me in the process. 'You are busy, Madame, I must leave you to your work. Don't worry, your secret is safe with me.' And off he goes, clattering down the drive in his rickety truck, filled to bursting with old sinks, bits of pipes and blackened chimney brushes.

I am baffled. Still, his suggestion about selling the wood appeals to me. Unfortunately, I am not quite sure how to go about finding myself a buyer until, one morning a few days later, returning by the back lanes from a gym I have recently joined at the wheel of an antiquated Renault 4 I have just purchased for 5,000f, I pass a fenced field stocked metres high with lengths of tree trunks. I park the car to take a look. Beyond the gate, which is locked, is a small wooden hut. A notice is pinned to its door. I clamber on to the lower of the wrought-iron rails and peer over, searching for a telephone number or the hours of service, but the sign is too faint to read. I glance at my watch. Twenty past twelve. No doubt the patron has closed up for a convivial two- to three-hour lunch. It's no problem; this little enterprise tucked away in the woods is barely five minutes' drive along the circular lane which skirts the foot of our hill. I resolve to return later and, in the meantime, dash to the village to buy myself an olive and tomato *fougasse* before the baker closes for his own lunch and another bout of bread-making.

Approaching the village square on foot, I espy M. Dolfo, our bumbling, good-natured electrician. The poor fellow, hot and flustered, is locked in desperate combat with his van, whose engine is screeching. It whines and starts to overheat, as does he, with the effort of reversing into what seems to me to be a perfectly generous parking space. When he claps eyes on me, he abandons all further attempts at parking and simply switches off the engine. I am a little taken aback because the vehicle is skewed at a rather dangerous angle, a fact which concerns him not a jot as he steps out and greets me heartily, shaking my hand as though I have just informed him that he's won *le Loto*. '*Bonjour*,' say I, still contemplating his atrocious parking. I am ravenous and fearful of losing out on lunch. My breakfast consisted of two cups of black coffee, I have worked out for two hours and I have nothing edible in the house. I make a move to leave, but he grips my hand fast and murmurs in a highly confidential manner, 'We had no idea, Madame. *Je suis désolé.*'

'About what?'

'*Et enchanté.*'

This has to be Di Luzio's doing.

On the far side of the *place*, the automated shutters of the *boulangerie* are creeping towards the ground. 'I have to g—'

'Monsieur Di Luzio said *pas un mot*, so *pas un mot*.' He winks, releases my hand and wanders off aimlessly with a wave and a complicitous nod.

Haring across the cobbles to purchase my loaf, I am all but

flattened by a speeding Peugeot 5 which, after missing me, narrowly escapes swiping the entire bonnet off our electrician's ill-parked van. In the smoke-filled *tabac* alongside the baker's, a village resident I have noticed once or twice presses his thick, speckled nose against the window and, beer and smoking cigarette in hand, ogles me lasciviously as I hurry back to my car.

I cannot imagine what story our plumber is spreading abroad.

Before M. Di Luzio begins work or guests arrive I have a few days to organise my summer. I have scripts to write, gardens I want to create, books to buy to restock after the robbery. I browse in air-conditioned *bibliothèques*, hunting for the ABCs of olive farming. In my quest for knowledge of the olive, its history and the farming of it, I buy everything I can lay my hands on. I learn that there are certain esteemed connoisseurs who hold that the olive oil produced around Nice has only one rival, which is the Italian variety from Lucca. Others pronounce that the fruit produced here on the French Riviera is second to none. It yields the finest virgin pressed oil, as well as the most expensive, in the world. Legend has it that Adam's grave was planted with an olive tree. I cannot think how this could be substantiated but, given the Middle Eastern setting of the Old Testament, it is not totally implausible. As tales go, I prefer the one about the battle between Poseidon, god of the seas, and Athene, goddess of wisdom, over the naming of Athens. The gods named the city after her rather than him because she planted the first olive tree there, within the Acropolis, as a symbol of peace and prosperity, and they judged her legacy to mankind more fruitful than any of Poseidon's trident-bashing, art-of-war chicaneries. (Women had the ruling vote on this: there were more goddesses than gods.)

Getting back to the facts: olive trees thrive best in Mediterranean climes. They will grow and produce in stony as

well as well-drained soils and will survive happily at lofty altitudes where other fruit trees would perish. Once established,
they need little attention, minimal water and can withstand all
but the severest of droughts. Even frost, if it is not too extended
and the temperature does not drop beneath eight degrees for
any length of time. These gnarled and characterful plants survive for centuries but commence production at a tortoise-like
pace. They do not produce their first fruits until they are seven
or eight years old and will not deliver the full extent of their
crop until they are anything up to fifteen, even twenty years
old. So, for any farmer who is beginning from scratch the olive
is a long-term investment. This may explain why it is illegal in
southern France to chop down an olive tree. Any road or building must be constructed around existing trees.

I stroll our dusty tracks, flanked by the silvery trees, the sky
above me Gauloise blue, digesting the knowledge I am amass-
ing, seeing the cleared land anew. Now that we are rid of the
stranglehold of weeds I spend delicious time alone examining
trunks and roots, the hang of the branches, the fattening
drupes. The ancients deemed the olive tree a healer, and I feel its
soothing power at work on me, chilling me out, slowing me
down.

On my return to the house, to my work, I observe two magpies warning off a russet fox. The magpies send the sleek
creature scuttling off into the undergrowth, its battle for territory lost. Little fascists!

I have been at my trestle table, scribbling notes, lost in the history of the olive, leaving my return visit to the wood store till
late in the afternoon. But when I arrive I find the place still pad-
locked behind its iron gate. I hang around for a bit, kicking my
heels, wondering if I should leave a note, and if so, where best
to post it. Several retired horses are grazing in a neighbouring
field and I stroll over to stroke them. I have driven by these

creatures on numerous occasions but have never had reason to stop here before.

This is a pretty uninhabited country lane and I decide to while away some time examining the hedgerows in the hope that a woodman might eventually appear. Scraggly clematis vine is climbing everywhere. A flattened milk carton lies in the road. It attracts my attention because its lettering is Arabic. I pass a bay tree tall as a fully grown cypress. There is a peppery perfume in the air which I cannot identify. Is it wild sage? Yellow broom in full blossom brings a sweet, bright colouring to the roadside brush. Shards of green-tinted glass from bottles thrown carelessly on the tarmac threaten my feet, shod only in rope-soled espadrilles. Around the next corner is a tiny vine-yard which I have noticed frequently on my trips to and from the inland village of Mougins. The vines are years old; short and stubby and gnarled. The green fruit hangs like breasts heavy with milk. There are several cherry trees growing in among the neat vine rows. Should I seek out the vine-tender and ask his advice on preparation of soils, planting seasons, fruit flies, harvests, oh, a million questions? A jeep rattles past and I am suddenly aware of how perfectly silent it is here. It is a meditative silence. There is no breeze. The day is still, intense.

I pause by a narrow, shady lane speckled with shoals of pebbles and the crumbling remains of last winter's forgotten leaves. Michel has pointed out this little pathway to me on several occasions. It leads to the rear side of our hill, he says. I notice, because I am on foot and not beetling by in my battered old car, that a few yards down the lane, the route has been barred but is not impassable. There is no red and white '*Défense d'entrer*' sign, which probably means that the land belongs to the local commune, who have installed the gatepost in an attempt to discourage the infuriating habit of jettisoning disused sinks, fridges and rusty electrical junk anywhere and everywhere, be it country lanes, gutters or roadsides. The

Arabs are normally blamed for it but I have no idea how sound these accusations are.

I hear a mewling, or is it a bird? It is so unexpected in the silence that at first I take it to be the whinnying of one of the horses back near the wood store. I hear it again, and trace its source to further along the dirt track. I had been intending to turn back, but decide to take a quick peek. As I slip beneath the wooden barrier, the sound grows more audible. Either side of me the brush is thick with dozens of misshapen Portuguese oaks. They have repeatedly seeded and now struggle for light and space. In among them are many fluffy-fronded mimosas. There is a small clearing ahead, at the farthest point of which lies half the carcass of a burned-out car. The sound is coming from there. As I approach I see a gorgeous, golden-bay animal lying on its side, panting heavily. It is a dog, a large shaggy one, shockingly thin. I bend and kneel, too timorous to reach out in case it snaps at me. One of its rear legs is bleeding badly. It must have ripped its flesh on the jagged, jutting metal. Gingerly, I put out a hand and the creature bares fanged teeth in a ferocious grin. For a moment I wonder if it is not a dog after all. Might it be a wolf? It could very well be. Whatever it is, it is a magnificent animal, and in distress. I rise, considering what to do for the best. Although I am not far from home, I couldn't possibly carry it, even if it allowed me to. And because of the barred entry, I cannot bring in my old car. I decide to hurry home, find the name of a local vet and arrange to meet him here. I start to run and the dog lifts its head and whines miserably. I halt and look back, my heart torn, and then scoot back down the lane as fast as I can.

When I reach my Renault I discover a shooting brake parked by the gate of the wood firm. A short, silver-haired man is unloading two chainsaws from his boot. I call out to him and he spins round. His face is flushed and friendly and kind. I tell him about the animal and ask for his help. He reloads the chainsaws into the silver estate and motions to me to get in. I jump on to the passenger seat and we motor along the lane as far as the barrier. Together we return for the dog, who is yelping helplessly but grows defensive as we draw near. Eventually, after we have made several fruitless attempts to get closer, the wounded animal allows us to approach and carry her – I see now that it is a her – to the boot of the car, where she is settled on her side, hemmed in by the chainsaws, a profusion of wicker baskets and dozens of empty wine bottles.

We drive back to Appassionata, and I run inside in search of a couple of torn sheets and a pillow. The dog is installed on our obsolete mattress in the stable where we found the wild cats at Christmas. My companion introduces himself as René. I explain to him that I had been waiting for him with the intention of asking him if he would like to buy some recently cut wood. Pine, olive, oak. 'Would you be interested?'

'*Pourquoi pas?*' His eyes are blue and creased with laughter lines and I like him instantly.

While I slip off to telephone the vet René has recommended, he examines the wood and offers me 1,000f more than the sum M. Di Luzio is charging for the temporary sealing of the roof. Even better, he pulls from a leather pouch in his shooting brake a very healthy bankroll of notes and pays me, on the spot and in cash, the entire amount.

'Don't you want to wait until . . . ?'

'No, no. I'll be back with my son tomorrow. We'll saw it into logs here, if that's all right with you. It will be easier to transport.' I agree happily, and we arrange a mutually convenient time for his return. He offers to take me back to fetch my car, but I tell him I will wait until the vet has been and then walk back and pick it up. So off he goes, leaving me staring at a satisfyingly thick wad of 500f notes.

The dog has no collar, no name and no tattoo. In France, a tattoo is obligatory. If a dog is found without one, it can be destroyed, explains the vet. Worse, it can be sold and used for experimentation. I am horrified and promptly arrange to spend more than half the cash René has given me on a whole host of treatments and medications for this magnificent hound. Her paw needs a minor operation and stitching. Two teeth have been broken, almost certainly while she was being thrashed. On top of which she has a stomach complaint and bleeding lacerations on a mauled hind leg. The vet is hugely tall and equally rotund. He is a good-natured, bearded German from Bavaria, a really delightful fellow who exudes a love of animals from every pore.

'Leave her with me,' he says, 'I will call you in a couple of days. You can collect her when she is a little healthier. Do you know her name, by any chance?'

We are talking in English because he enjoys the opportunity to test his linguistic skills. I shake my head. 'I have no name,' I say.

He looks surprised, then chortles and writes something on her card, wishes me a *bonne soirée* and assures me that I am not to worry.

I return to my work and thoughts about what to do with the dog when she is well again. I have not forgotten Henri, and the promise I made to bring him back as soon as our circumstances allowed. These concerns prompt me to telephone the animal rescue centre.

When I enquire after Henri I learn that a home was found for him shortly after we returned him. My heart sinks, and yet I cannot begrudge dear, wild Henri a decent bed. '*Il est très, très content*,' the administrator informs me. I thank her, wish her well and replace the receiver, bidding a silent *au revoir* to the big, black hound who sent our lives into a spin for a few short weeks.

René does not return the next day for his pre-purchased wood. Or the day after that. I have no telephone number for him. I didn't even catch his surname. I am puzzled. Am I in possession of stolen or home-made notes which I am about to pass on to the vet and to M. Di Luzio, who is clunking up the drive, ready and eager to begin the repair work on the roof?

I look on as he unloads the most gruesome collection of tools and bitumen-heating equipment, including something not unlike a giant Bunsen burner. All the while he sings and whistles and grins, nodding and bowing every time I am anywhere near him. On one occasion, as I pass by, he slaps his thigh as though he were the principal boy in a pantomime and grins, his shining white teeth exposed like an open zip within his soot-smeared face, '*Pas de bottes, eh!*'

No boots? It is July. I am running about in shorts, tube top and flat espadrilles. I have no idea what he is talking about and I don't want to ask. I am beginning to fear that he might be completely barmy.

Until the end of the twentieth century, when dieticians the world over pronounced the Mediterranean diet the healthiest in the world, the olive and its byproducts were predominantly a southern food, used exclusively in southern cuisines. The hue of the oil is as golden and luxuriant as a summer afternoon spent dozing in a hammock in the Midi. It is as familiar and vital to the kitchens of this region as, say, garlic or *bouillabaisse*. Quintessentially Mediterranean, it evokes the climate, land and character as instantaneously as any wrinkled-faced Niçois playing boules in his dusty village square.

It was the Greeks, some 2,500 years ago, who planted the first olive trees on this southern coast of France, but they spent precious little time cultivating or reaping here, for essentially they were not an agricultural people. They were navigators, explorers, seafaring traders. Moving westwards, they founded such seaports as Nice, Antibes, and, of course, in 600 BC, Marseille – its original Greek name was Massilia – and then they moved on. For the Greeks, the bustling port of Massilia was a watering place and spa where they paused before heading inland, hell bent on securing their tin and amber routes. The citizens of Massilia spoke perfect Greek, dressed and comported themselves like Athenians and kept well away from what they perceived as the contamination of the barbarians living all round them, the tribal Celts.

I give up on my writing and olive studies because M. Di Luzio is above me, marching to and fro on the roof. His every step is acoustically exaggerated and sends shudders through the house as though a giant were striding the heavens. And he whistles and sings. How he whistles and sings!

So I close up my laptop and go outside for a swim. But almost as soon as my body plunges into the pool, he calls down to me, asking for a beer. He is very thirsty. Fair enough. The day is hot, and he is up there with a flame as high as a laurel bush. When I scale the ladder, dripping wet, to take him his beer, I have to stifle my desire to burst out laughing. The heat and activity have caused him to break out in a sweat. The perspiration running down his face has washed the soot away in stripes, and he looks like a zebra. Fortunately, I am rescued by the ringing telephone. I hurry across the semi-surfaced roof. It is as hot as hell up there, with the gas flame roaring and spitting. As I turn to go back down the ladder, he holds up his bottle: '*À la vôtre!*'

'Good health to you too, Monsieur Di Luzio,' I smile. His cheeriness is quite extraordinary. I am about to enter the house, dashing for the phone, when he leans out over the roof again, and calls, '*Et votre mari, il porte un melon aussi?*' And he roars with laughter. I am thinking about it. And your husband, does he carry a melon as well? What on earth is he talking about?

I grab the receiver.

' 'ello?'

It is the vet's young receptionist. 'No Name is ready to be

collected.' I smile at the tag and tell her that I will be by in a short while. I have decided to keep the dog until she is fit and then . . . well, I haven't thought that far ahead yet. Michel is arriving later this evening. I will discuss the dog with him. Although the vet's bill is somewhere in the region of 5,000f, he refuses to accept one centime.

'Why?'

'Because No Name was not your responsibility, and because you have given us many hours of pleasure. In Germany, your vet programme is called *The Doctor and His Dear Friends*. I will accept a signed photograph of you, and that will be my payment.' I am bowled over by his kindness and delighted to see the dog, who is indeed now answering to No Name. She is bandaged from snout to neck, ears exposed and erect, and has another dressing protecting the wounded hind leg, though fortunately it does not inhibit her ability to walk, albeit with a limp. She wags her tail at the sight of me so I cannot have been entirely forgotten. Armed with a dozen boxes of antibiotics, I lead her gingerly to the car and she follows without a whimper.

'It's hard to believe,' says the vet, who accompanies us, 'that anyone would abandon this creature. She's a pure-bred Belgian Alsatian, and a particularly splendid example. If you can't keep her, let me know. I'll have no difficulty finding a home for her.'

When I return, our chirpy plumber has packed up for the weekend, but the wood has still not been removed. I settle No Name in a makeshift basket and set off for the airport.

Michel is tired. Actually, he looks exhausted, and speaks only in monosyllables about his production affairs, but I can read in his expression how pleased he is to be here. On the journey home, I am recounting my week's adventures while he listens, silently stroking my shoulder and hair.

My pride at selling the wood, the vet's kindness . . . 'Oh, yes, there's a dog, and I have understood correctly, haven't I? The word *melon* means melon, doesn't it? As in English?'

Michel considers, pondering Di Luzio's comment. 'That was all he said: "Does your husband carry a melon?"'

I think so.

'Ah, *porter*, to wear!'

'Do you wear a melon?' I am giggling. We are now kneeling beside No Name, who is uncertain about the arrival of this unknown male. But she does not bare her teeth.

I take Michel on a swift tour of the garden to show him various shrubs and flowers I have potted and inform him blithely of my purchase from one of the village stallholders of a hundred roses, paid for in advance, to be collected when the market next passes this way. Without a hint of criticism, he tries to point out that I lack symmetry and that I am not necessarily choosing the plants that will withstand the heat. 'Where will you plant a hundred roses?' he asks. 'If the fellow ever comes back, that is.'

'You are cynical. Of course he'll come back.' I wave my arm vaguely to the right. 'Up there.'

'But *chérie*, the earth is full of stones there, and there's no shelter or water source. It will be blazingly hot, which is not ideal for roses.'

'Sometimes you are so full of logic!'

'*Überblick*,' he replies warmly, which I think is his favourite word – the German for 'overview'. 'Are you sure Di Luzio didn't ask you whether your husband *is* a melon?'

I burst out laughing. 'Why would he ask such a thing?'

'A melon is a fool, a simpleton.'

'Are you?'

'I hope not.'

Michel is preparing the barbecue while I make up a salad. We will be eating on the upper terrace looking out over the moonlit sea. The crescent of lights along the promontory of Fréjus string out and camber, winking in the darkness. Standing in the centre of our makeshift garden table is my oil lamp, a warm ball of pale toffee light. It is already past nightfall and the evening, because we have not yet reached full summer, has turned coolish. Clad in slacks and long-sleeved shirts, we pour ourselves glasses of mulberry-red wine. The sizzling lamb cutlets spiced with herbs from a small vegetable patch I have been creating arrive on a platter as I return from the house carrying the cash paid to me by René. I pour it on to the table for Michel to examine. It has spent the past few days stowed in the bottom drawer of an antique Irish pine chest we found in a junk shop in Paris, buried among our lavender-scented linen. He looks at it, then at me, queryingly.

'Why didn't you bank it?'

I have to think for a moment because I am not exactly clear why I have left the equivalent of £1,000 to sit in the chest. 'In case it's counterfeit, or stolen,' I confess.

Michel roars with laughter. '*Chérie*, you are so dramatic. It is black money, no doubt, but surely *tu as déjà compris* that a considerable percentage of all money that changes hands down here is earned on the black market? It is the modus vivendi. I am sure this René fellow didn't physically make it!'

'Then why hasn't he returned for his wood?'

'He will. This is the Midi. Everything is accomplished in its own time.'

Yet again, I have forgotten to remember that time is interpreted differently here. Tomorrow does not necessarily mean tomorrow. It means at some point in the future beyond now. And the only way to know when that might be is to cheerfully wait and see. For a woman as impatient as I am, this is a steep learning curve. But I accept Michel's wisdom and we spend a blissful weekend without sight or sound of workmen.

As ever here, we rise at the first call of the sun. Now that the land has been cut back, we like to walk. This morning we pick our way up the winding narrow track, ascending through the steep pine forest, hiking to the very pinnacle of the hill. Puffed, we drop to the needly earth, inhale the heaven-sent perfumes, sharp with a twist of early-morning dew, and watch the sun come up. As it lifts, its rays stream through the squiggle of treetops and blank out the crescent moon. Daybreak. I have watched the sunrise, the breaking of the day, in myriad different locations all over the world with companions or past lovers, but nowhere has it felt this blessed. Here it belongs to us and to our intimacy. I close my eyes and breathe deeply. Sometimes, for a moment, it feels scary to love this much.

Wending our way back down the hill to the house, we take an early-morning dip in the still, cool pool, followed by a warm bath. Together, through the window of the cavernous blue-tiled room, we watch families of rabbits steal out from beneath the stacks of wood. They poke cautious snouts and whiskers into the new day and then scamper freely, hopping about, taking stock of their newly undressed playground.

These early mornings are a treasured time of day for us, a part of who we are, and what we share. Most of our waking hours are given over to work, weekends too, because if we don't work we won't have a gnat's chance of restoring, or even holding on to this ruin of a farm. But now, in the bath, a generous old-fashioned porcelain one, our flesh is wet and soapy and we are slippery as seals.

Beyond the window, splashed with droplets of running bathwater, the day is waxing. The light is growing golden as the sun rises higher. Then, in an instant, it explodes through the loftiest branches of the tallest trees, oozing heat. I yield and sink. I am immersed in heat. Heat from the bathwater, heat from Michel's flesh and the heat of the sun baking me through the glass.

'Breakfast!' calls Michel. His curly hair which he has allowed to grow, has turned dark in the water and clings to the nape of his neck. His flesh has been tanned by the sun. Almond oil from our creamy shampoo perfumes him.

The days are growing too hot for us to breakfast on our hidden terrace so we shift our wooden table and chairs to the front of the house, which the sun will not hit until after ten. Over eggs and coffee I begin to fill Michel in on some of the olive material I have been reading. 'It was like a journeying caravan, like good news or a creed spreading, the way the olive tree and the production of its fruit travelled. The Greeks brought it here to southern France, but it was also exported across northern Africa to Tunisia, Algeria, Morocco. There, right across the northern littoral of that continent, the Arabs began to cultivate it. Oil was produced, fruits marinated, recipes and methods passed on, adapted to their cooking. It found its way quite naturally into the local cuisines. Later, the olive tree was transported across the waters north to Portugal and Spain, along with Arab traders, perhaps? The two migrations in that direction from Africa were the Arabs and the Sephardic Jews.'

'Did you know,' Michel chips in, 'that the Koran speaks of it as a blessed tree neither of the East nor the West?'

'No, I didn't. I have been wondering, though, if priests, seers, ancient gurus, the family cook, a tribal grandmother, whoever, understood its mythical powers, its curative properties. Facts were handed down, passed along until somewhere in the melting pot of a more modern world, the second millennium migrations, wars etc., this knowledge was lost, and only now are we beginning to rediscover it. The power of the olive to stave off certain cancers, for example. Longer life expectancy.'

As we natter, we watch a band of bushy-tailed auburn-red squirrels leap from the cypresses to the lower almond tree. They are stealing the nuts we have not harvested. Their expeditions are surprisingly orderly. They jump down on to the tree two at a time where the branches bounce like trampoline nets as they gracefully land; they collect their share of the hoard and then make way for the next pair. The only argument develops when a greedy magpie swoops down and begins to screech and rattle the branches. He is furious that the squirrels have beaten him to the nuts. Several landowners I know shoot magpies; observing the birds on this estate, I am beginning to understand why.

After breakfast, work. Buried in my space, my *atelier*, I hear the distant clip-clipping of Michel's fingers busy at his laptop. I open my book on the history of the olive and read that after the Greeks, it was the Romans who came to the south of France. Unlike the parched topography of Greece, the landscape of Italy was sylvan and lush. It was more verdant and rolling. Because of this the Romans were more at home on land than at sea. During their trek north and their taking of Provence – it was Julius Caesar who christened the region 'Provincia' – they quickly grasped the potential of the dusky groves growing everywhere on these hills, their recently conquered territory, and they wasted no time in cultivating the fruit.

Both the Greek and Roman cultures have left lasting and profound impressions on Provence. Both were Mediterranean peoples, and both stamped their systems, philosophies and architecture on this more northerly region of what we now call Europe. The differences in their natures have had a deep-rooted effect on Provence. The Greeks introduced the olive to the Romans and the Romans, in their own country, husbanded it and created a thriving industry from it, perfecting its storage, and then they began to do the same here.

In the afternoons, we make love, screened from the relentless heat by the spill of shadows from closed, slatted shutters. The century-old house creaks and shifts, waking like Rip Van

Winkle after decades of sleeping. Then it relaxes into peaceful stillness, as do we. Our sole companion is No Name, who heals by the hour. Afterwards, I read or scribble while Michel dozes. Beyond the walls of the cool room, our magnolia has flowered. Its blossoms resemble teacups sculpted from clotted cream.

During an evening stroll on the upper reaches of the land, we find that many of the drystone walls have sunk into rubbled piles and are slowly spilling across the terraces. They will need to be rebuilt. The removal of such a mass of vegetation could be the cause: the root systems may well have been holding the stones in place. Or perhaps, Michel suggests, it is *sangliers* in search of food. Although we have seen no wild boar near the house since that very first encounter, it is unlikely that they have deserted our farmland entirely. We take a little tour and find their footprints everywhere, and untidy holes where they have been snouting for grub.

During our stroll back, Michel asks me how my story is getting on. Slowly, I reply. Might you have it finished by the end of summer?

I smile and nod, knowing he is inching me towards our agreed deadline. The acceptance and production of these scripts would make a monumental difference to our chances of acquiring the second five acres of land and holding on to the farm. It would also mean a great deal to me personally, to the fashioning of this new life, the redefining of myself.

Dusk falls, shadows lengthen and we bathe in the pool, basked in moonshine. Afterwards, we cook supper on the barbecue. I have taken to preparing even the simplest of meals with lashings of garlic. Olive oil, garlic, herbs. Bliss.

Monday arrives and we crawl out of bed before the lark sings. Michel needs to be on the earliest flight to Paris, which means we must leave the villa at 5.30. At the terminal, huddled in my rather temperamental fossil of a Renault, we kiss goodbye. I try not to allow a sense of abandonment or sadness at the prospect of yet another week apart to wash over me. In three more weeks we will be together for the rest of the summer.

When I return to the house, having stopped off for a much-needed croissant and several *cafés au lait* in Antibes, M. Di Luzio turns into the lane and grinds up the drive behind me. Before we have barely exchanged a good morning, he announces, 'You're an actress, aren't you?'

I nod, feeling, at this particular moment, more like a bag lady. He roars triumphantly. I am puzzled as to how he has acquired this titbit of information, but I know that it must please him for he has been regaling me regularly with stories of a highly renowned French pianist and chanteur who, according to M. Di Luzio, lives not too far from us and whose pipes he has replaced. 'Plumber to the stars!' he cries exuberantly, and I picture his vision of this slogan, written in bold paint across the beam of his clonking banger.

One of the characteristics I most love about the French is their appreciation of art and the arts in general. We are all, even the humblest of entertainers, *artistes* in the eyes of the French. The very mention of the word 'actress', or even better, 'writer', fills them with paroxysms of delight and awed respect. M. Di Luzio is no exception.

'I saw you on television, didn't I?'

I shrug. It is possible, but I cannot think what he might have seen. Little if anything I have ever acted in has been bought by the French networks. I understand that *All Creatures Great and Small* has been shown all over the world, with the one exception of France. Even in Poland before the fall of communism, when all American and English programmes were banned, it slipped through the system and continued to be screened.

'You are very famous. I had no idea.'

I head on towards the house, because he has overestimated my fame, because I fear that our plumbing bills are about to escalate, and because I am feeling lonely. Not for long. Presently Amar arrives with an army of *ouvriers* or *jardiniers* who unload what looks like an entire forestry commission project's-worth of shrubs and laurel bushes, and definitely far more than we ordered. Then he departs, leaving his *équipe* to set to work. I steam down the drive. Shovels, rakes, garden utensils of every shape and size are digging, hacking at pine branches, throwing sods of earth every which way, transforming the face of our border land.

'Stop!' I screech.

There is no leader to take heed. I am just the madwoman from the top of the hill. Sunbaked faces stare, eyes glare but they return to the job in hand, the contract they are being paid for, no doubt at a menial rate. I dread to think what Amar will charge for all this. I hurtle back to my papers in search of his telephone number. This has to be called to a halt before I find we have purchased an entire garden centre.

While this performance is taking place, René arrives, followed by a bevy of cars, all of which have open trailers attached to them. Our drive is now completely blocked by vehicles.

René, a little over five feet five tall, fit and stocky, with a wine-tinted red face and a shock of healthy grey hair which grows so thick and lustrous it almost doubles his height, leads his party up the hill. There, he begins organising his gang, all of whom are wielding chainsaws. No Name begins to bark. As M. Di Luzio, above me on the roof, melts and pours bitumen, unloads and rakes kilos of gravel, singing his socks off, five chainsaws start up, zirring at full whack in the pine forest, while, lower down the terraces, shovels are slapping against stones, branches are cracking and hitting the earth, and voices are yelling. I cannot hear myself think or speak. I scream like a lunatic into the telephone, insisting that Amar comes over right now and puts a stop to all this planting.

'But the plumbago will be magnificent. Blue creeping up through all those cedar trees. It will be splendid.'

'We didn't order plumbago and we can't afford it. We don't even have a fence yet.'

He sighs and agrees to get here as soon as he can. The risk of not receiving his money seems to have clarified his sense of reason. I put down the phone and run my fingers through hair that hasn't been combed since I got out of bed, when I barely had time to brush my teeth. I catch a glimpse of myself in the mirror and see how utterly dishevelled I look. Somewhere in the distance, in the village of Le Cannet, where Pierre Bonnard painted some of his finest works and Rita Hayworth lived out many of her lost, later years, the midday siren sounds and, as though a switch has been flicked, all activity stops. Ah, silence. From a dozen quarters, men tramp to the parking area and pull from their various cars, vans, lorries or, in the case of Amar's Arabs, satchels, their lunch. Each seeks out the shade or a step on which to perch. I watch from a window, fascinated. The Arabs have small plastic lunchboxes similar to those given to schoolchildren. Within I see sandwiches and a piece of fruit, an apple or a banana. They also have bottles of still water; the Crystal which is for sale at 1f a litre. They sit on the ground alongside or close by one another, all choosing the deepest shade.

Meanwhile, René and his chainsaw gang – the native French – are unfolding and setting up a portable table. On it are placed unlabelled bottles of rosé and red wine, water, pâté, salad, plates, saucepans of hot food (how? I ask myself), as knives and forks are passed out like leaflets among them. These are followed by glasses which, when filled, are raised by each man to drink the health of the rest. M. Di Luzio, who is alone but French – though his family originally hailed from

Italy – hovers close by his fellow citizens, wishing them *bon appétit*.

As the Arabs munch in businesslike silence, the French still have preparations afoot. M. Di Luzio shambles over to his prehistoric van and pulls out a cooler, from which he extracts chilled water and two bottles of beer. He paces the parking area slugging back the beers, one immediately after the other, in thirsty need. The water is then poured over his head, which suddenly gives him the complexion of an albino. He saunters over to René and his troupe and begins to make conversation. His voice is loud but his accent is so thick I have no idea what he is talking about. Whatever it is, the subject calls for a great deal of gesticulating. The others are entranced. So am I, but for different reasons. I find this social spectacle fascinating. Even the Arabs, whom Di Luzio swings to face once or twice in order to include them in his audience, seem to be hooked. Di Luzio is now acting out, with great pizzazz, what looks like a bank robbery. Two fingers go up in the style of a child's gun play. Then he slinks his portly body in imitation of a woman, slaps his calves, aims a kick into the air as though booting someone off the face of the earth, and, finally, raises his gaze reverentially in the direction of the house.

It is only now that it dawns on me, as all eyes turn towards the villa and I jump guiltily out of range of the window, that the female he was impersonating was me.

Monsieur *le plombier* then makes a gesture that is very common here in the Midi: a shaking of the hand, thumb turned upwards, which denotes wealth or power or serious money. Even his French audience have stopped eating, so spellbound are they by his gossip. Is he telling them that we robbed a bank? But he hasn't even been paid yet, and if the cash stashed in the linen drawer and burning an illicit hole in our sheets is stolen, it is René's money.

Fortunately, the arrival of Amar breaks up the show. He

heads over to his workforce and wishes them *bon appétit*, repeating the same sentiments to the French contingent. I exit the house and make my way over to him, feeling just a mite self-conscious. As Amar and I approach one another, René calls to me: *'C'est vous qui jouez dans chapeau melon et bottes de cuir?'*

Everyone awaits my response. Is it you who is playing in a melon hat and leather boots? Having no idea what this means or what to reply, I take the Midi approach and shrug. This they translate as an exceedingly modest affirmative. René rises and comes across to shake my hand, as does one of his companions, who already looks the worse for wine and keeps repeating: *'Enchanté, Madame. Vous êtes charmante, charmante.'*

Panic drives me to grab Amar by the arm and drag him down the hill. Nothing I say now will convince him that we purchased this olive farm and are attempting to renovate it on an already fraying shoestring. Di Luzio has scuppered everything. Nevertheless, after persistent nagging, Amar reluctantly agrees to dig up those shrubs which were not sanctioned in our deal. But, he says, because he cannot take back the bags of fertiliser and horse dung that have been laid and shovelled everywhere, they must all be paid for. When I query the astronomical figure charged for horse manure, he tells me that it is a particularly potent mix, having been collected from a stud farm. 'The finest stallions,' he smiles wickedly.

I can barely credit the sheer ingenuity of his invention. Yet again, he has managed to augment his contract fee by a substantial sum. I thank him for his co-operation and resolve that this will be his last, his very last, job for us. Thank goodness I ordered the roses elsewhere.

Later, when Michel and I talk on the phone, he agrees that the time has come to look around for someone else. We say goodnight, sending love through the airwaves, and I almost

forget that I haven't told him about M. Di Luzio's latest pantomime. I narrate it briefly and Michel is highly amused. 'A
bowler hat and leather boots,' he explains. 'Yes, I didn't think
of that.'

'A bowler hat and leather boots?' I repeat like the simpleton
described in French as a *melon*.

'*Melon* also means bowler hat. Because of its shape. In this
instance it is the French name for a very famous and successful
television programme.'

'Which is?'

'I can't remember the title in English. I'll think of it and tell
you tomorrow.'

'Have I acted in it?'

'I don't think so. I'll remember it, don't worry.'

Meanwhile, word is spreading with the relentless persistence
of the bush telegraph. As a result, the entire community now
has me identified as the actress who played the role of Emma
Peel in the hit television series *The Avengers*, which is cult view-
ing here in France. Its French title is *The Bowler Hat and
Leather Boots*, a reference to Steed's headgear and Mrs Peel's
footwear. No amount of denials will shift opinion; in fact, they
serve only to confirm the conviction. The locals smile patiently,
reading my effusive rebuttals as modesty and a plea for the
rights of *les artistes* to live their lives in peace. In their eyes, I am
a glamorous actress. But what most amuses me about this
whole affair is my crazy response to it.

I was scruffy and at ease here, but now that I have been
identified and labelled, albeit mistakenly, I switch like a pro-
grammed puppet into actress mode whenever curious eyes are
upon me. Instead of leaping into my battered banger and haring
down the hill to catch the postman or pick up a forgotten
baguette, I now take the trouble to run a brush through my
pool-bleached curls. I put on lipstick and mascara and trade in
my faded cotton espadrilles for varnished toenails and leather

sandals with tiny heels which show off my legs to advantage. Such vanity! The image is all; the public perception which so easily ends up defining the boundaries of character. It is part of what I have been running from.

Not long after the Romans began to press the oil here in France, rather than going the route of the more popular Italian family-run businesses, the co-operative system was established. Small community mills were constructed where the olive fruits were taken by the locals to be pressed or cured. Although there were, and still are, many single estates and farms cultivating their own olive groves, very few if any own a private mill. It has long been the norm in France to take the harvest to one of the nearby co-operatives to press the fruit as a single-estate extra-virgin oil to be sold or used locally. Modest as Appassionata is, Michel and I agree that this is the system we would like to opt for. The finest olive oil is extremely costly because producing it is a very labour-intensive process. The trees do not demand heavy watering but they need to be fumigated, pruned regularly, usually biannually on a rota system, and they need treating once every twenty-one days from around mid-July to early or late October, depending on the weather. Although I am learning all this, it is not until I finally encounter 'our man' and we begin to work with him that I come to understand the challenge we are taking on.

Calm returns. M. Di Luzio's repairs are complete and I hand over the agreed sum in cash. René's cash. Di Luzio counts it carefully, requests one last beer for the road, which he drinks in two gulps before bowling off down the hill, a contented man.

The laurel bushes are planted. Begrudgingly, I settle Amar's account with him: the agreed amount plus many hundreds of francs on top for the manure. I must water the shrubs on a daily basis, he advises. Then, as he takes off, he calls his parting shot: he cannot be held responsible for their life expectancy because, due to the escalating heat, nothing should be planted at this time of year. 'It's too perilous!' I want to throw my gardening tools at him.

Fearful that the precious new bushes will begin to wilt before my eyes, I abandon my writing and rush off to buy several lengths of hosepiping which René very kindly offers to help me fit together. I am grateful for the generosity of his gesture because the whole business is unnecessarily time-consuming and complicated, involving many plastic sockets which in my hands simply will not marry. After much frustrated fiddling, we eventually lay the hose, which winds like a yellow serpent, nudged up against the Italian stone staircase, all the way to the bushes at the foot of the land.

While I was at the hardware store, René sawed the last of the trees. The logs have since been carted away in *remorques* by various members of his family. All activity is at an end. As evening is approaching, by way of thanks for his much-needed assistance, I invite him to stay for *un petit apéritif*, which he accepts. Pastis? No, he would prefer to join me in a glass of red wine. With the bottle, a Côte-du-Rhône Villages, I serve a humble dish of local olives and another of pistachio nuts, because I haven't had time to shop. We sit in contemplative silence listening to the frogs, and inhaling the perfumes of dusk.

'Are these from your trees?' He has an olive pinched between his workman's fingers.

I shake my head.

'You know, since I retired I live my *rêve*,' he tells me. 'The wood business is not my affair. I am helping a friend who cannot afford an assistant.' He asks me to guess his age. This is a dangerous game which I always try to avoid, but in this case I decide not to subtract five years and instead to speak my mind. 'Early sixties,' is my verdict.

He sits upright in his chair and shakes his head, thrilled by my inaccuracy. 'Seventy-four,' he announces with pride. And indeed he has every reason to be proud, for I am genuinely amazed.

His two great pleasures in life, he tells me, now that he has passed seventy and has settled into retirement, *la retraite*, are his boat, which he takes out most fine days to the islands – ah, the islands! – where he spends lazy hours fishing, and the husbanding of olive farms. He oversees and runs four, the largest of which boasts over 200 trees. That particular estate is owned by a longstanding chum of his. They were boys together; both were educated here in the village. His schoolpal, René continues, without the slightest hint of jealousy, is now a multimillionaire and the proprietor of the largest and most famous chain of hardware stores in southern France. When René speaks of his septuagenarian companion it is with fondness, but when he talks of himself it is with pride. 'He works too hard, has too many responsibilities. *Mais moi*, I do what I love in life. I have over 650 olive trees in my care.' And he sweeps up his glass, proposing a toast to doing what one loves in life. I drink to that. Then with a twinkle, and not without a *soupçon* of Provençal wiliness, he adds, 'You have the perfect position here. The fruit from your trees must be excellent. Tragic to let it go to waste. Why not allow me to care for them for you?'

I am silenced by his offer. This is so much more than I had hoped for at this stage. My sole regret is that Michel is not here to share this fortuitous moment.

The bottle on the table in front of us has grown lighter as evening has fallen. I pour what remains into our glasses and he gives me the deal. He will prune and treat the trees, gather the olives and deliver them for pressing at the *moulin*. For this service he proposes to take two thirds of everything farmed and pressed. We will receive the remaining third.

I had thought we might share the harvest on a fifty-fifty basis, but he shakes his head firmly. He is adamant. *Ce boulot* requires a great deal of labour, skill and expertise. I know this to be true from my books and so I accept René's proposition without debate. We raise our glasses to the partnership.

The sun is sinking. Its colours are underbelly tones, gold seeping into tender flesh-pink. I have lived my life through my senses; looked at it, experienced it through prisms of light and emotions; touching, feeling. Now I am attempting, not to be less romantic, but more practical. Particularly about the renovation of this villa and the re-establishing of its farm. Michel describes this as honing new muscles. I hope that when he meets René he will agree that fate has dropped a nugget of good fortune into our laps, for instinct tells me we have chanced upon our man.

Our Desert Prince

My father spent his war in Africa. He was a corporal in the Royal Air Force, but his remit was not to fly planes, bomb cities or fight. Always a big kid at heart, he happily occupied himself during the Second World War dressed in high heels and women's clothes, sporting face powder and streaks of carmine-red lipstick. All in the broiling desert heat. This, along with sliding out of camp, hitting the hot spots and getting roaring drunk with such veteran comedians as Peter Sellers and Tony Hancock. Together this trio spent the night in the cells on several occasions after they were found by their commanding officer falling about the streets of Cairo completely plastered, attempting to hitch a ride back to base, when they should have been tucked up in their bunks. Never dejected by a night in the slammer, my father continued to sing his heart out and play the fool and was applauded enthusiastically for it, for he was a proud and dedicated member of one of the most renowned of the wartime entertainment troupes, the Ralph Reader Gang Shows.

I spent much of my childhood sitting on his knee or on the floor at his feet listening to his stories of those days in far-off Africa. They were outclassed in brilliance only by my grandfather's equally outlandish tales of big-game hunting, though now, looking back on it, I don't believe my grandfather, my father's father, ever set foot in Africa. Whereas my own father's tales of high jinks were certainly true, if a little over-embellished.

Those stories painted in my mind's eye a scintillating and colourful picture of the dark continent, of Arabs and bazaars, of South African beaches and Zulus. It was one of my favourite bedtime victories to persuade my father to sit with me awhile and speak to me in Zulu. All that clicking on the upper palate, short phrases spoken in deep and resonant tones, used to thrill me. I pictured those seven-foot black natives clicking and communicating and banging tall, hand-painted spears, all to do little more than enquire after your general health. If there had been an Oscar awarded for ham acting my father would have been a serious contender.

But nothing matched up to his tales of the Arabs. In retrospect, I see that, in some ways, his attitudes were shockingly racist: 'Never trust an Arab' was a regular piece of wisdom administered to me, and one which I took to be the gospel truth. How many times did I hear the sorry tale of the day he was sitting on a train outside Cairo returning to camp after a few days' leave in England, where he had purchased new reading glasses, only to have the spectacles snatched from off his face as the train was pulling out of the central station, leaving him unable to see, let alone recognise the escaping culprit? His only certainty, of course, was that the blasted thief had been an Arab.

For many years France was the imperialist power in northern Africa, and the horrors of Algeria are known to us all. Today, France's second labour force is African, predominantly Arab.

Jean-Marie Le Pen, the extreme right-winger who preaches France for the French, is their enemy, or rather, they are his. He is more extreme in his rabble-rousing than the late Enoch Powell, and less intelligent in his rhetoric. In spite of the stories bequeathed to me by my father, although I have never felt the slightest empathy with Le Pen, or with any other xenophobic demagogue, I had never reckoned on the possibility that one of the local Arab workforce would become one of my closest friends and our greatest ally in the dark days which lay ahead for us and Appassionata.

I have settled in for the summer. I have no plans to travel any-where, my scripts to complete, the hill to maintain, the arrival of guests to prepare for. I could not be more content, and then the telephone rings. It is Michel.

'We have won an award,' he announces.

My first book, which we filmed as a mini-series in Australia the previous autumn, has been screened at a highly regarded festival in the States and has picked up an accolade. I am speechless. I hadn't even known the series was being presented.

'The Australians want you to publicise it for them.'

'Where?'

'Australia.'

'When?'

'Leaving on Friday.'

The line goes silent while I take this in. Actors are used to living with their passports in their pockets; calls can come at any moment. But this time, I am not prepared. The publicity would coincide with the opening across Australia any minute now of another film I've shot. I know I should go but I am in a quandary.

I am thinking about No Name. I am worrying about my schedule, which is of no one's making but my own. But the trip, it turns out, is only for one week. I won't even suffer jet lag because I'll be there and back before it hits me. 'Fine,' I say eventually.

I begin to set matters in motion. All I really need to do is to close up the house and ask René if he would be kind enough to pop by twice a day to feed No Name. Or, as a last resort, I could telephone Amar, who I know will do it – at a price. Happily, René agrees without a second's hesitation to house my beloved Alsatian, *chez lui*, for a week. No Name will be in loving hands. I have nothing to be concerned about.

It is Thursday. I am leaving at the crack of dawn on Friday, flying to Sydney via Paris. Alone in my gecko-infested workspace, I am settling down to a day's writing when I hear the whirr of machines starting up like an orchestra tuning. They are right beyond the window. Puzzled, I go to take a look and, to my horror, I see three men, their heads and faces masked by plastic helmets, cutting back the strip of land which borders the roadside to the left of us and lies alongside our olive groves. The jungle of vegetation there has been the only deterrent to entry to our property from that quarter. Recalling the unsavoury sensation I experienced when I learned that we had been burgled, I throw my pen back on to my desk and go running to stop them.

They have been sent by the *mairie*, one of them informs me. The land has to be cut back; the neighbours along the lane have complained. It is a fire risk, *très sérieux*. I look back along the winding lane to where the man indicates. I cannot even see the house he is pointing at.

'What neighbours?' I squawk. Their concern exasperates me. 'But we are at more risk than those neighbours should a fire break out,' I protest. To no avail.

'Have you been here during a fire?' he asks.

No, I have to admit that I have not, which seems to be the concluding point. The workman, who is covered from head to foot with bits of vegetation and sheets of aluminium protective clothing and looks rather like the tin man in *The Wizard of Oz*, shrugs, dons his helmet and starts to walk away.

'Couldn't it wait just one week?' I plead. I am thinking that when I return we could buy some fencing to secure this section of land.

He reiterates that he has been sent by the local council and the decision has nothing to do with him, takes up his machine and resumes cutting. Stones, strips of split bramble, roots, all go flying into the air. I move out of range of the travelling herbage and shooting flint. I know there is nothing I can say or do to stop this now. I return to the house and telephone Michel.

'I can't leave,' I tell him.

'Don't be foolish. The publicity tour has been arranged. You can't *not* leave.' He is right, and I know it. 'We will have to take our chances. No Name will be there.' At this stage I don't bother to explain that I have agreed with René that No Name should stay with him. I drop it. We must continue as planned and hope for the best.

Tormented by the steady drone of the brush-cutters baring our home and farm to all and sundry, I give up on my script and set off for the village to buy a week's supply of dog food. As I round the bend I am forced to a halt by two large vans, parked one in front of the other, which are blocking the road. There are also several workmen standing in a huddle, pointing and shouting upwards to one of their crew, who is strapped on to a crane extension and is slicing chunks off the tops of the complaining neighbours' pine trees. At first I assume this to be part of their disquiet over possible fires until I notice that there are cables swinging freely in the road. Some of the telephone wires seem to have broken loose, or a tree has fallen down. Cars are banking up behind me, hooting insanely. So little traffic ever passes this way that I am bemused by this queue and cannot think where it has come from. There must be a road closed somewhere else, other cables down. I sit patiently waiting, listening to the discordance of chainsaw, whirring brush-cutters, French and Arab voices disputing the length of time all this is taking and asking myself whatever happened to the tranquillity of this barely known corner of the coast *arrière*.

Suddenly, I hear two men in front of me begin to shout loudly. '*Non, monsieur! S'il vous plaît, non!*' I crane my neck out of the window and see a car approaching from the opposite direction attempting to pass the parked lorries. This is a perilous madness, for our narrow little lane is bordered by a sheer drop to a busy road a lethal hundred metres beneath the cliffside. Everybody takes up the call, 'Danger!' Arms are waving, men are haring to and fro, yelling, jumping, all engaged in the frenzied business of refusing to allow this driver's impatience to risk lives. I, along with several other motorists, temporarily abandon my car and wander along the lane to take a closer look, for what else is there to do? Beyond the lorries and the furious driver hell-bent on getting through, no matter what the consequences, are several stationary vehicles, their drivers stony-faced, waiting to move on.

Behind this caravan of rising blood pressure and ranting workers, I spy the postman on his moped, weighed down as always with his satchels of letters hanging like floppy leather ears either side of his post office-yellow bike. He draws close, weaves his way in and out of the stationary traffic, circling the screaming, hysterical human beings. Engaged in their fury, no one notices him, and in his turn he pays the show in progress not a blind bit of attention. Instead he presses his foot on his accelerator, intending to whizz by the lorries on the inner side of the lane. Unfortunately, he has either underestimated the portliness of his own figure or misjudged the width of the gap, which is no wider than the narrowest of mountain defiles, because he finds himself sandwiched, along with his bike, between lorry and cliff. I alone am aware of his plight, for his cries are lost amid the general furore.

Wriggling like a trapped insect, he attempts to dismount but cannot move. His lower limbs are crammed too tightly in among his satchels and letters. His plump frame shakes and jitterbugs as he tries to dislodge himself but succeeds only in entrenching himself more deeply. I know that I must help him, even though the temptation to leave him to stew is almost irresistible. Decency prevails. As I hurry to seek out the driver of the offending truck I throw a final glance at Monsieur *le facteur*, whose arms are now stretched wide and waving high above his head, eyes turned skywards, mouth gaping open in frozen horror. His blue postman's cap has fallen to the ground behind him.

It is only then that I grasp what is about to happen. High above us all, the chainsaw worker in the crane has remained diligently at work. A fairly substantial upper trunk of pine tree is about to give and, any minute now, will come barrelling to the ground. Our postman is a sitting duck. '*Attention!*' I yell, '*Attention!*' My actress's voice booms to full capacity. As a man, all turn. I am shouting, pointing and running. There is a general cry of '*Mon Dieu!*' as half a dozen men scuttle like a twelve-legged beast to save the postman. The obvious solution is to shift the truck, but this cannot be done because the driver has disappeared down the lane for a *pipi*, so the crowd is obliged to push and drag both postman and moped. Several other bods are yelling to the *mec* up on the crane, who eventually gets the message and halts work, leaving a very wobbly-looking pine tree. The driver returns, whistling and zipping up his trousers, just as the group to the side of his lorry are yanking the postman by the shoulders and literally hauling the poor fellow backwards off his bike. Everyone, including the postman, is yelling hysterically. To be more accurate, what Monsieur *le facteur* is doing is yelping. He also seems barely able to stand even with the assistance of the rock face behind him. I feel sure, as he leans there gibbering and puffing, frantically rubbing his face with a large, spotted handkerchief, that he is recovering from the shock of yet another of his narrowly avoided heart-attacks. Fortunately, he cannot blame this one on us.

By now, cars are streaming freely to and fro while the workers are shaking hands and congratulating themselves and one another. A crisis of monumental proportions has been averted.

It is then that I happen upon one of the Arabs who has been lending a hand and who is now making his way across the lane towards the house of our neighbour, Jean-Claude. He sees me, nods and resumes his task: trimming the hedges. I watch him for a moment. I have often seen him here and, more importantly, I have frequently remarked on the gardens and well-pruned orange groves. I walk over to him and introduce myself. He smiles shyly, revealing one tobacco-stained front tooth and a golden nugget further to the back on the upper left side in an otherwise gaping mouth. He also sports in the centre of his forehead a small blue tattoo reminiscent of the red spot worn by Hindu women. His eyes are warm, if yellowed by age. He knows who I am, he says; he has seen us coming and going to and from our property. I ask him if he would be interested in doing a spot of work for us. I explain my dilemma and we both stand and watch the men relentlessly cutting back the triangular strip of land. He accepts without hesitation and introduces himself. '*Je suis Harbckuouashua*,' he says. Or at any rate, that is what it sounds like. Sorry? He repeats his name again and I still cannot grasp it, which tickles him.

'Call me Quashia.'

He agrees to begin the following morning. I explain what needs to be done. He lists what he requires and I set off for the builders' merchants in search of metres of meshed-wire fencing, cement and iron pickets in addition to the almost forgotten dog food.

The following morning, Quashia arrives late. I am afraid that he is not coming. Anxious that I will miss my plane, I am about to give up on him when I catch sight of his silhouette sauntering along the lane. Trust me, he reassures. And so I do.

When I return from Australia a week later, zapped by an over-load of radio, newspaper and television interviews, not to mention a body clock that has been turned on its head twice in the space of a week, the fence is in place and completed. What a blissful homecoming to find that Michel and I have acquired the able-bodied man we spoke of at the start of the summer. Quashia's skills include masonry, tiling, strimming, and tree-pruning as well as any other odd job I can come up with.

He is proudly claiming Michel and me as '*ma famille française*' and henceforth, he addresses Michel as *mon cher frère*. This greeting is followed by four kisses, two on each cheek, much hugging, rounded off by back-slapping of a force that leaves Michel limp. At first I have to confess to a certain mistrust of such hearty bonhomie, but I am soon obliged to reconsider my unvoiced reservations.

On the other hand, I am not always regarded as a *chère sœur* but, on occasion, as a potential second wife. When Michel is away or out of sight, even on no more than a quick trip to pick up some fresh salad, I have to watch my step. 'Sleep with me once, just for the hell of it!' pleads Quashia, and I flee indoors. Glancing back, I catch the tobacco-toothed grin light-ing up his sun-cracked face.

High summer is approaching fast, which means the influx of guests. The first this year will be my parents, who are visiting us for the first time. After their concerns about the purchase of this farm, I fear they will be testing, rigorous, difficult to please. So the prospect of their imminent arrival makes me edgy. Added to which, Michel has been called to Paris and will not be back until the day after they arrive. This leaves me alone running around like a headless chicken. I have never claimed to be a good housekeeper – in fact, I am pretty hopeless – but here I am now, dragging such sticks of furniture as we have, garden chairs to use as clothes horses or dressing tables and the like, from room to room, corner to corner, in a pathetic attempt to create ambience and a home which might reasonably be judged as up to scratch.

An hour before I am planning to set off for the airport to collect my parents, believing that all is about as together as it is going to get, I flop over the balustraded terrace, breathe a deep sigh of relief, peruse the shorn grounds all around me and smile proudly down on our swimming pool. Michel has spent hours hoovering and treating it and now it is crystal-clear. That will impress them, I am thinking, rather too overconfidently; they can't call this place a pig in a poke. Then, to my horror, I notice movement. The sanitation cover on the terrace alongside the pool is heaving. An emission of dark brown waste is creeping out from beneath it. Another twenty minutes and the excrement will be slopping like green-jellied aliens into the pool. 'No!' I cry, but the only soul listening to me is No Name, who runs for cover. I scoot inside. My heart is pounding fast. I have to combat this impending disaster before I leave for the airport, otherwise, the image on our return does not bear thinking about.

I rip through the pages of our address book, searching for the number of M. Di Luzio. But it is eleven in the morning: he will have left for work hours ago. Crazed with panic, I ring anyway. I must meet that plane. I have to stop the seepage. There must be an underground leak in the pipes. By this stage I am yammering to myself, my brain spaghetti. What in heaven's name is the French word for 'leak'? I simply cannot recall it.

Mme Di Luzio answers '*Je vous écoute?*'

I am still trying to get my head around how to explain the excrement oozing across the terrace beneath me. *Truite*. Yes, that's the word I'm searching for.

'*Allo?*'

'*Truite!*' I yell into the phone.

'*Allo?*'

'Hello? *Madame Di Luzio, c'est Madame—.*'

'*Bonjour Madame.* Yes, I recognised your accent,' she laughs kindly. 'Are you all right?'

I have no time for such chit-chat this morning. My parents' plane must be sweeping over Lyon by now.

'Madame, I have a serious problem. It's very urgent.' I am speaking in French, of course.

'*Oui, Madame?*'

'Please, contact your husband and ask him to come over here right away, please. It is *gravement* urgent. There is a huge *truite* which has . . . somehow . . . come up through the plumbing and is now moving along the downstairs terrace. It must have escaped through . . . ; through the, er . . .' I cannot think of how to explain the problem. By this stage, I cannot even recall the English words for what I am trying to put across. '*Une truite* . . . in the thing. Yes, and it's making for the swimming pool. *La piscine.*'

Mme Di Luzio is giggling. '*Une truite, Madame?*'

'Yes, it's heading for the swimming pool.' I am a demented being, shouting and waving my free hand in the air, worse than those lunatics who are convinced that if you speak sufficiently forcefully in English anyone, no matter what their mother tongue or how non-existent their grasp of our language, will understand you. 'IT'S MOVING TOWARDS THE SWIMMING POOL AND IS ABOUT TO SLIDE INTO THE WATER ANY SECOND NOW, AND MY PARENTS WILL BE HERE WITHIN THE HOUR!'

'I'll call my husband,' she laughs, and puts down the phone.

I cannot drag myself away from the upper balcony. I am standing stock-still staring at the excrement seeping like poison across the terrace beneath me. No Name approaches it gingerly.

'Get away from there!' I yell from way above her. If she treads in it . . . I scream at her again. 'No Name, get away from there!' Her tail disappears beneath her, she glances up at me curiously, studies what from her point of view must be a red and furious face, and then slinks away, completely baffled. Within ten very drawn-out minutes, M. Di Luzio's cranky old motor croaks up the drive. He climbs out, covered from head to foot in soot, as ever, white teeth grinning like piano keys. 'Where's this monster fish, then?' he chortles.

'What fish?' I cry, believing this to be yet another of his witty cracks alluding to my television career, or rather, the career he continues to insist is mine. Right now I cannot contemplate programmes with fish in their titles; I am in no mood for it. 'Look! Look there!' I lead him to the drainage and he laughs long and loud, his fat stomach heaving with merriment.

'Why are you laughing, Monsieur Di Luzio? This is serious! My parents are on their way. My mother already thinks I have no common sense. Please, do something. Help!'

And help he does. Out of his van, he unwinds kilometres of thick, coiled piping. The underground canal is suctioned and emptied in no time, along with two others situated at various points down the drive, which, according to our sooty plumber, could also cause us distress. Then off he rolls, explaining happily that he and Michel can discuss a cash price over the weekend 'for the removal of the fish'.

I am completely baffled but extraordinarily grateful, and I do not have the time now to try to get to grips with his sense of humour. I need to leave for the airport instantly. I am late.

I arrive frazzled, zipping about like a demented lizard. Naturally, I am not on time. The plane has landed, my parents have collected their luggage and they are awaiting me outside, smiling and unruffled. 'Hello, dear.'

Back at the villa, I install them in their clean but basic room, improved by plentiful bunches of marguerites picked from the garden, and then take them on a tour. They drink it all in in silence. 'Well, what do you think?' I ask at last.

'I'm glad you've got big windows,' says my mother. 'I don't like those small ones the French foreigners always have here.' My father's response is: 'I think you might have bitten off more than you can chew.'

While I have been occupied with my family, word has been spreading fast on the village bush telegraph. I am now known as the actress who can take on the world as Emma Peel but who calls in the plumber to remove a giant trout from her drainage system. In my scatterbrained panic, I muddled *fuite*, which means leak, with *truite*, which is a trout. It's time to learn French, I concede when my linguistic confusion is repeated back to me. Sheepishly, I take myself off to Nice, to the university, where I enrol in an intensive summer course.

During my lunch breaks which, being French, last at least two, if not three hours, I wander the streets and coastal strip of Nice, keen to learn a little about the city at close quarters. It has flavours to it that are different from those of Cannes. For one thing, it is a university city and, even though it is summer and the students have disappeared to the countryside or mountains and the professors are on *congé*, which means the university is catering only for linguistic numbskulls like me, the city still gives off a very different energy. There are myriad bookshops, a healthy majority of young people, a wide choice of cinemas, an abundance of excellent museums and restaurants and a working population which is not dominated by the idle rich. It teems with bustling life, the inhabitants going about their days trying to make a living, and sports a magnificent harbour where colossal white passenger liners lie in dock preparing for departures to Corsica or Italy, even to the Nordic lands or as far afield as Russia.

Set back from the harbour is the old town, where the street

names are written in both French and Niçoise, the patois once spoken here. Perhaps the crowning glory of the *vieille ville* is the flower market, to be found a few steps from the famous opera house, where this evening *Rigoletto* is to be performed.

The language I am hearing everywhere around me is Italian. Every week, the most avid French shoppers cross the border to buy produce and very reasonably priced Italian clothing (and booze) at the frontier market town of Ventimiglia. The Italians, in turn, are drawn here to spend their lire on antiques on Mondays and fresh produce every other day of the week.

Along the Rue St François-Paule, written in patois as Carriera San-Francés-de-Paula, is a *huilerie*, an oil shop, belonging to the Moulin à Huile d'Olive of Nicolas Alziari, a famous name in the business of oil production. His groves are situated in the granite hills behind this city and the fruit is a mix of the *cailletier*, the same small Nice olive as ours, and the *picholine*, which is longer and thinner. *Picholines* are named after a M. Picholine, who developed a method of curing green olives using the ash from the green oaks that grow everywhere in this region – we have plenty on our land. I would have enjoyed a brief browse but the shop is closed for lunch. Across the street, also gone for lunch, is a competitor, the Huilerie de Caracoles, which claims, although I have not come across this *maison* before, that its products are *regionaux, les articles Provençaux*.

Making a short detour along the Rue de la Terrasse, or Carriera de la Terrassa, I am drawn to a sign reading: 'Cave, Pierre Bianchi & Cie.' The shop's painted glass windows are proof of its heritage. Hand-painted, the sign announces proudly, *trois siècles d'existence*. Three centuries of trading. Quite a feat considering the history of this city. It means they were here before the French – Nice was not ceded to France until 1860.

I step up to the glass to read its hours of business, thinking that I might return later after my afternoon course, and am amused to learn that it reopens at two, has no particular hour of closing, and on Sundays is shut only *si grosse fatigue* – 'If enormously tired'.

The colours and architecture of the tall, shuttered buildings crammed alongside one another in streets so narrow a bicycle can barely pass through them (and certainly not our postman) are Italian-influenced: vibrant red ochre, yellow ochre and mustard hues, all decorated with faded green or bleached turquoise shutters. Or pale dusty lilac, a colour so fragrant you can almost inhale it.

Until the integration of Nice with France, this ancient city was governed by the House of Savoy and was adjoined to the kingdom of Sardinia, Piedmont and Liguria. Shortly after 1860, these other provinces became part of a new, unified Italy. But even today there is much about Nice that testifies to its Italian heritage, not least the fabulous Mardi Gras carnival, with its masked balls which date back to the thirteenth century and are known by the Italian name *veglioni*. This famous carnival still parties here non-stop during the three weeks leading up to Lent and proudly claims the use of a ton of papier mâché for every float.

I glimpse behind partially shuttered windows local craftsmen beavering away in *ateliers* barely larger than postage stamps. A bald-headed cobbler repairing the soles of a pair of leather sandals puts them to one side and shuts up shop for lunch. Along a crooked dead-end alley leading off one of the many squares, I encounter a mechanic disgorging the engine of an ancient pram-sized Fiat Cinquecento. He is seated in the driver's seat with the door hanging open, looking out on the world at large. In his lap is a dish of what looks like pork in a rich, winey sauce. On the ground at his feet are a half-empty carafe and a glass of rosé wine, fruit, cheese, a half-eaten baguette and two hungry curs salivating at a safe distance, waiting for scraps.

Washing lines of sheets, shirts, underwear are festooned like bunting everywhere above me, reaching across the narrow lanes from one side to the other. I hear the hum of a carpenter or cabinet-maker planing great sheets of wood. He must be the only craftsman still at work, for the midday siren has sounded and the world of *les ouvriers* has downed tools.

I am growing hungry, too, and make for the Cours Saleya, or Lou Cors, to the marketplace. It is sensational. The central square is an amphitheatre of ancient coloured buildings, the most magnificent of which is now the home of the Préfecture des Alpes-Maritimes and was once the palace of the Dukes of Savoie. The flower market operating alongside the fish and food stalls is a glorious blaze of colours and perfumes, crowned with pot after pot of brilliant green aromatic herbs. It is a feast for all my senses and I cannot resist a dozen long-stemmed birds of paradise. Now I must hurry, and move on to the food. One stall is selling, they tell me – and I take their word for it, as I haven't the time to count them and they are in any case being whisked away and stored in the rear of a van parked in the cobbled square – 150 different varieties of spices. All are neatly laid out on dishes dressed in brightly coloured Provençal cotton fabric. The name of the spice is handwritten in black ink on its dish: *muscade, poivre concassé, poivre Sichuan, exotique* . . . Another trader offers olives. His array is a *fête*. Among a mind-boggling choice are some from Puglia in Italy, singularly the largest I have ever set eyes on, which resemble, in size as well as shape, small green lemons. I help myself to one and slip it into my mouth, sucking on it with the glee of a child savouring a boiled sweet. It is sharp and peppery and delicious.

At various corners and angles in the alleys near the market there are dozens of busy restaurants, where there are knives and forks clattering, glasses chinking, voices chattering, peals of laughter, meals being served al fresco. The acoustics of the ritual of lunch are amplified by the tall buildings. I press my nose against the windows of one or two enticing *traiteurs*, hungry to gorge everything on offer. I must decide, for everyone is packing up for their own lunch. I creep inside one whose flagstone floors are cool and clean, whose pastry smells so warm and soft and yielding you might lie down on it and where every plate on offer is of psychedelic shades. Mayonnaise has never looked so rich, so yellow and creamy.

The dishes of Nice are not necessarily the same as those of Cannes, for here again, in the cuisine, the Italian as well as the Provençal influence is in evidence. I buy myself a working man's portion of *tourte de blea*, which is a local speciality. Still piping hot from the oven, its pastry is as delicate as *papier poudre* and I carry my thick slice in a paper bag like a trophy to eat, washed down with a bottle of mineral water, on a bench along the beachfront overlooking the Med, now bobbing with oily, shrieking bodies.

The beaches along the Promenade des Anglais are filling up by the day. To the right, half a kilometre along the coast, the planes sweep low, disgorging yet more batches of holidaymakers. Summer is upon us, with its whiffs of Ambre Solaire; its sounds of children splashing and screaming with joy, the bells of ice-cream vans ting-a-linging and the ceaseless impatience of drivers leaning on their horns. Two youths, skinheads with radiant pink mohawk spikes of hair, come to a standstill alongside me. The one farther to the left takes an asthmatic drag on a joint, then passes it to his friend, who does the same. They gaze out at the languid sea flopping against the beach in small curls of foam. 'S'foockin' grea' 'ere,' says one, in a thick, lazy Scottish accent. His pal grunts and they move on.

In the hazy, heat-drenched distance, I am able to discern the contours of the Alps which form, whatever the season, the magnificent backdrop to this sweeping seafront. Few of these visitors ever see this coastline at its most breathtaking – for me, at any rate – which is on a sharp, wintry day when the limpid sea is a brilliant turquoise, the coast depopulated, save for a lone inhabitant or two strolling, windblown, close on the heels of racing, excited dogs while behind them the mauve mountains rise up, crisp, clear and snowcapped.

Ambling towards the university, along a return route previously unknown to me, I spot a *poissonnerie* which has reopened and I slip in to buy succulent *clovisses* and *praires* clams, perfect for spaghetti *alle vongole*, which I now decide to make this evening and serve on the terrace by candlelight. As I consider my family, and how they will enjoy this dish, a memory flashes by of my father's mother, who sat by her fireside in the east end of London, cigarette smoking between her nicotine-stained fingers, a glass of stout on the tiled hearth, picking cockles and winkles with a pin from their shells. Here cockles are known as *fausse praire*. How many worlds make up a life!

In a labyrinthine lane somewhere towards the heart of the city, I pass a butcher specialising in game and poultry and pause to take a closer look. Beyond the glass is a still-life menagerie, crowded with heads, curly-tailed haunches attached to hind legs and an array of furry bodies washed by hosepipes and dangling from meat hooks. There are rabbits and hares, unplucked pigeons, quails, chickens and ducks, plump geese alongside tiny birds no bigger than sparrows. And on an oval silver platter in the foreground, like John the Baptist as presented to Salome, the *pièce de résistance*: the heads of two wild boars. Their fanged teeth jut from semi-closed mouths, smiling with misplaced confidence. Still, although their days of hunting are over, they remain tusked and bristly but, decapitated, they have lost much of their menace. Even so, I have no desire to rekindle such a short-range intimacy with any of their cousins living on our land.

Back at Appassionata, the days slide by and the gentle splash of bodies paddling to and fro in the pool is the music of the afternoons. My script moves on apace. No Name grows healthier by the day, springing from one terrace to another like a gazelle in flight. While my mother siestas or reads and my father – with No Name constantly padding or sleeping at his side – snores in the shade or bakes himself a lurid red in the sun and my mother nags him to get out of the heat before he gets sunstroke, Michel and I wander endlessly and aimlessly, taking stock and sharing our visions with one another. Perching on stones buried in the drying grass, plucking daisy heads, we chalk up our lists of projects. Mine are creating orchards, vegetable beds, compost heaps; planting fruit trees; paving terraces and furnishing them with succulents in tall terracotta pots. The produce of the earth surrounded by space and tranquillity, and the freedom to write. Self-expression.

Michel's perspective on the future features a more communal *esprit* and architecture. He has a more structural approach to the place. There it is again, his favourite German word: *überblick*. I am passionately involved at close quarters while he is pursuing the larger canvas. He reads the lines of the terraces, the symmetry of the olive groves which I haven't even noticed, the shapes and curves of walls. He detects cracks, fissures, the balance or imbalance of windows, aberrations that have been added to the property over the years and have destroyed its overall elegance, its simplicity of form. He draws up plans for a future irrigation system and reflects upon a practical choice of plants for this mountainous region. Agave cacti, palms, yuccas, citrus fruits, eucalypts, olives. He would never have handed over cash for a hundred rose bushes to wilt in the hot sun obliging us to pass half our days hiking hosepipes or buckets up and down the hill in a never-ending attempt to keep them watered. But we don't talk about my roses, or about the trader who took my money for them and never returned.

And he talks of artists, film-makers, writers, in wooden huts buried away at work in corners of our pine forest. Here, we disagree. But it is all amiable debate in our shared idyll. Nothing is acrimonious. Harmony, passion, intensity of heat and colour and perfect love are the fractions which make up our union. I, who have never claimed a practical bone in my actress's make-up, begin to discover the roots from which I came: the Irish farmers on my mother's side. They must have been lying dormant waiting to surprise me, for what I find is that the *haute couture* of Cannes interests me not a jot. What I love are the nurseries, the builders' merchants and the *quincailleries,* the hardware stores.

I may, in a moment of stress and dementia, have mistaken a leak for a trout, but during my days at the university in Nice, when it comes to vocabulary I surprise everyone, above all myself. For while other students are struggling with the imperfect or the past perfect, I am constructing sentences which include lists of pieces of equipment, garden tools, building products, swimming-pool parts – nouns I never had need of in English, if indeed I ever knew them. I spout the most curious exchanges and the class stare at me open-mouthed. Inwardly, I, too, am gaping in speechless amazement. Perhaps this shift, this rudder of change, is actually leading me somewhere.

Back at the villa, I catch my mother watching Michel and me. Clearly she is concerned, while my father, a useful aphorism always on the tip of his tongue, is baffled: 'You've got a career back home, love. A bird in the hand . . .' He has risen from his post-lunch slumber and is playing with the dog, or rather, she yields to him like a puppy, on her back, legs in the air, while he strokes her stomach and examines her. I see him fiddling with her teats, a frown crossing his beetroot-flushed face.

'What's wrong? Is No Name ill?'

My mother continues: 'I've seen you do some daft things,

Carol, but . . . If you want a swimming pool, why not work in Hollywood? Think champagne and you'll drink it!'

I giggle. It's true that for the sake of 'art', my untamed nature or the whims of passion I have dived headlong into some 'daft things': hung out in Rome, doing little better than extra work at Cinecittà and learning Italian; lived a week inside a live volcano; dived the seven seas; had a crack at tracking snowy regions of Lapland with a sleigh and six huskies; got blazing drunk on some deeply suspect concoction with head-hunters in a long house in Borneo; travelled unaccompanied up the Amazon . . . oh, the list is endless, and I don't regret most of them (though the long house was a bit precarious – one more glass and my head might have ended up on a keyring), but the purchase of Appassionata does not equate. It is an exploration of another kind because it requires commitment and faith. It is a canvas. My parents' final words on the subject are: 'Well, I hope you know what you are doing.'

I don't. It would be arrogance to claim that I do. I know where I have come from, what I am attempting to leave behind, the habits and experiences I want to shed like a skin, but not where I am going or even exactly what I am seeking. I am taking it as it comes, making it up as I go along. Pushing the boundaries of identity in the hope of enriching, deepening, cultivating the spirit. And alongside me is a man I love. Or – more essential to me, with my history of broken romances – a man who cares about me. Who knows where this mad enterprise will lead us, but better to give it a shot than to stare at the rain through wrinkled, rheumy eyes, sighing, 'What if . . . ?'

'This dog is pregnant,' my father pronounces. This stops all metaphysical philosophising. Within seconds we are all of us on our haunches surrounding No Name, who looks from one person to the next, uncertain and puzzled. She nuzzles close to Daddy.

'No, it's not possible,' I say, staring at the swollen black nipples.

'We should call the vet.'

'No, she's fine. There's no way she could be pregnant.'

If Quashia is to continue his sterling fencing work then we must, by law, call in the *geometre* expert to stake out the boundaries of the land. Once this has been done, Monsieur *le géomètre* will notify our neighbours in writing, including maps to scale as drawn up by the Département de Cadastration, of our decision. If no boundary neighbour (there is only one) contests our rights within a period of twenty-eight days, then the same expert forwards the necessary documents to be signed by the adjoining landowners, which will confirm that they agree they have no claims against us as to the ownership of our land.

All this to fence our property and keep out the burglars! Farmland and buildings, every square metre, every stone fence, every stable, are clearly defined in numbered plots and detailed sketches on the maps and plans filed with both the *notaire* and the local council registers. Still, it has to be done. French bureaucracy is French bureaucracy, and it is tireless.

In order that the *géomètre* can actually find the boundaries of the property to stake, the weeds and jungle need to be cut down so that a traversable pathway can be hollowed out. This means hacking land way beyond the acres cut back by Amar which, in any case, to our dismay, are growing faster than we can earn the cash to keep them at bay. And by law, due to the enormous fire hazards in the area, all landowners are responsible for the safety level of their herbage. I am beginning to get a sense of the never-ending battle that lies ahead if we are to keep the tangle of growth on the farm under control. And the prospect of it exhausts me.

Quashia arrives. He and Michel are going to attack the grounds together. Strimming machines on their shoulders, water bottles in plastic bags, visors to protect their eyes swinging from their wrists, the pair of them hike up the stone track behind the house and disappear into the forest.

As he heads northwards up the hill, Michel at his heels, Quashia points to a mass of small, spindly stalks which are growing everywhere. Wild asparagus, he tells me. Delicious. I pick a huge bunch and steam them with the idea of adding them to a salad, or preparing them with prawns, or as an accompaniment to another spaghetti *alle vongole*. In the end I serve them to my family as a first course for lunch. 'They're rather bitter, dear,' says my mother. I add lemon juice, olive oil and pepper and we find them . . . bitter.

'I can't eat this! What is it, some type of grass?' says my father.

I chuck them out and decide to leave the rest in the garden.

While I am cheerfully chanting verbs in Nice, Michel's parents telephone to say that they have decided to accept his invitation and visit us for a holiday. They will be arriving in two days. My parents are not due to leave for a while yet and before they go, Michel's daughters are flying down. We lack habitable bedrooms. So, while the two men work the land, my mother offers to help me tear out what Michel and I have christened 'the brown room'. It remains as we found it: a hideous, smelly space. Still, after scrubbing, buckets of Eau de Javel and a slap of whitewash, it has the potential to become a cool, airy retreat with a fine view across the valley and a perfect situation right alongside the swimming pool. Its previous function seems to have been a nursery for puppy-breeding. The tenant who did a bunk must have run some kind of kennels here. We have come across one or two rather ghastly examples of her workmanship, but in this room she surpassed herself. It has been divided into eight nests which are entirely covered in a foully stained brown carpet. Not only has she carpeted the entire floor in this dank rugging, but all four walls as well. Add to the lack of air and years of puppy pee seeping into the rotting weave an outside temperature of thirty degrees, and you will understand why we have left this room till last.

My mother loves to clean and scrub, to make bonfires and burn great mounds of rubbish. She seems to find in all such activity fanatical joy. I, on the other hand, loathe it, but she soon has me up and at it. Dragged away from my computer, I am armed with mops, sponges, scissors, bread knives, ladders, hammers and hot water. As we rip and tear at the walls, dead plaster and white dust crash down upon with us with the force of an imploding mine. Within minutes I resemble a baker. My throat is as dry as a bone and I am giddy with trying to hold my breath to stop the acrid air sending me reeling, but worse is to come. Living beneath the carpet is an entire micro-world of insects and small black worms, disgusting little things wriggling free from the shock of having been unearthed. Everywhere around us creatures are on the move. Perspiration stings my eyes, dust is engrained in my hot sticky flesh. Spiders and other bodies are marching over my feet, some ascending my calves. I shout across to my mother that we should give up. 'Why, dear? We are getting on nicely.' I glimpse her across the room, scraping and scrubbing, ripping and tearing: she is having the time of her life.

I can tolerate spiders as long as they are not too large and hairy, but these small black worms look venomous. We begin to lift up the floor covering. Beneath the carpet are twelve-inch grey breezeblocks which have been stacked and grouted into a maze of small walls, presumably to discourage the puppies from crossing from one nest to the next. Settled in among them is a mass of black, stirring life. I think I am going to throw up and suggest most emphatically that we leave it, but my mother shakes her head. 'We're nearly finished, dear,' she says. I have to get this over with fast. I cannot bear one more black being mountain-climbing over me. I run to the tool shed, where I dig out a mallet. Back I come, swinging my arm like a discus thrower, and begin to smash at the breezeblocks. I am sweating and heaving, thrusting and crashing. Shards of cement shoot all over the place. Furry and shiny carapaced creatures are whizzing through the air. My mother is yelling at my incompetence. My legs are bleeding. I have no skill for this but I am determined until finally even my mother runs for cover. 'Stop!' she cries. 'Stop!' She pleads with me to leave the dislodging and dismantling to Michel or Quashia 'before there's an accident'.

I am satisfied. With brooms and black bags, we begin to shovel up the mess we have created, stripping the room bare. It is then we notice the floor. 'Look at this!' Yet another original find. The tiles are obviously Italian. Each has a blond stone base with terracotta triangular inserts and, at the centre, sunflowers in brilliant yellow. They are exquisite and, as far as we can tell, given the mounds of general detritus and rotting carpet and insects that won't stay where they have been swept, barely damaged. How could anybody in their right mind have cemented breezeblocks on top of such craftsmanship? I am bemused but thrilled. I can picture this bedroom in days to come: crisp, white linen, sunflower-yellow walls nestling behind our Matisse-blue slatted shutters. Well-rested guests waking to the music of water trickling into the swimming pool, opening the shutters to a new day, swallows wheeling overhead and there, on the tiled surround, tall terracotta pots ablaze with scarlet geraniums to greet them. It has been worth the work and the worms.

We stagger out into the hot afternoon, promising to reconvene for tea. My mother disappears to shower and put the kettle on while my father reminds me that we should call the vet, which I agree to do after I have dragged myself up the hill in search of Michel and Quashia. I am too excited to await their return, and I need an oxygen tank full of fresh, clean air.

At the summit, it is a veritable rainforest. The broom bushes have been left for so long they are twice any man's height. Even here there are olive trees hidden among the canopy of rampant growth. Branches whip against my arms, unknown leaves prick and jab me as I force my way through. A holly scratches my damp, plastered shoulder. It stings unreasonably. I am calling every few minutes but the whirring of machines and cicadas drowns out everything. I spy Michel. He is bent over, hacking away with a scythe, liberating strangled trees, disentangling brambles, suckers and vines. Quashia is working at ground level, clearing roots with the strimmer. They crack and thud as they break and fall.

As I draw near, I pause for breath and to take in the staggering beauty of the surrounding hillsides. In every direction there are pines and dusky olive trees, drystone terraces falling away like snow slopes and, way off in the distance towards a dense, cobalt horizon, the seductive sight of the sunkissed sea dotted with clear, white sails. Deep, hot stillness.

On the terrace beneath me, I see a twisted, ailing pomegranate engulfed in trumpet vine. Roots and stripped branches lie like dead men on a battlefield. Michel straightens up, lifts his visor-helmeted head and spots me. Quashia is grateful to switch off the machine for a moment's respite from the sweltering graft. I recount the news of the treasure buried beneath the muck. I watch Michel's delight, the smile spreading and breaking across his sticky, muddied complexion. 'We have a surprise too,' he grins, pointing.

Way off to the left, on a parcel of the acreage we don't yet own, is the ruin, uncovered for the first time in at least a decade. We hike over to it and discover the remains of a picturesque little cottage. In what still exists of the living room, there is a fireplace and chimney, terracotta tiles – no roof – crumbling walls; beyond are outhouses where the animals would have bedded down, a fabulous semi-circular staircase which leads us up to a higher terrace shaded by a fig tree and a monumental, very ancient Judas tree. I had often wondered why Lawrence Durrell described this magnificent deep rose flowering tree as 'tragic' until I read that legend has it Judas hung himself from the branches of one. In the distance, back beyond our land, our tiled terraces, the pool where my family are relaxing, swooping down past the olive groves, a wide blue expanse of Mediterranean. Perfect.

Time for tea.

Quashia and Michel collect their tools and we trail in single file back down the stony pathway. Quashia pauses to point out a clump of pale green plants which I don't recognise.

'What is it?' I ask him. An aromatic herb. The name he gives is Arabic.

'Excellent for the stomach. Drink it as an infusion.' The leaves have a pungent scent, sweet yet spicy, but we cannot place it. 'Shall I pick some for tea?'

I tell him next time. After the wild asparagus saga, I prefer to leave well alone.

We are all of us seated in the garden in the shade beneath the *Magnolia Grandiflora*, drinking tea (Indian). I am fascinated to watch my father with No Name perpetually at his side. Though neither he nor Quashia can understand a word the other says, they are fooling together, and an image returns. I picture myself as a child on his knee, entranced by his exotic tales of those Cairo nights, of that wicked Arab who stole his glasses, and I look at the two men in front of me now, a million worlds apart, clowning like schoolboys. My father is attempting to recall a word or two of Arabic but gives up and instead offers his welcome greeting in Zulu, to which Quashia falls about with toothless, good-natured laughter.

Fire!

I wake in the sweltering night, perspiration running from my damp body, to the sound of scratching. It seems to be coming from the hill above our rear patio. I lean up on my elbows and peer out at the shadowy shapes of trees, the dark, silvery contours of the boscage. What is it I can hear shuffling or cutting its busy way through the foliage? My first thought is that it is a snake sidling towards our open doors. I tap Michel's shoulder. He mutters in his ocean-deep sleep, wriggles and returns to his dreams, oblivious of my presence. Now there is a tiny squeaking which accompanies the rustling. I reach for a sarong, not out of modesty, for there is no one to see me, but because, illogical though it is, I am afraid I might be attacked or bitten when I am naked. I get up and patter barefoot out on to the terrace. The moon is full and shines across the treetops, as though we had forgotten to switch off the lights. The sky is brilliantly clear, not a cloud in sight, galaxies of stars twinkling within a sharp navy heaven. The rustling continues but remains concentrated in the same place, which is at the foot of the largest of our green oaks. I cannot make out any shapes or movement because the trunk is enveloped in deep, bushy growth. Fearful of going closer, I sit at the breakfast table, my knees drawn up tight against me, and try to concentrate on the other sounds of the night, whiling away time, savouring the riches of the clammy-sweet air.

Everywhere smells intense, gorgeous. The eucalypts embrace me, heady as a narcotic. Perfume from the twenty-four lavender bushes I have planted – one of the gardeners from our local nursery, who knows me well now, advised me that positioning lavender close to the house keeps the mosquitos at bay – wafts in glorious drafts from the lower terraces. High on the hill there is a bird trilling, even at this hour. I catch an owl's hoot, and then the squeaking again. It must be mice. I wander back to bed and lie listlessly on top of the sheet. I turn and watch Michel's peaceful, handsome face. It never ceases to amaze me how anyone can sleep so deeply. Nothing troubles him.

The squeaking is growing more insistent now, the intervals more regular, as though it were multiplying, and the rustling continues. If it is mice, there are plenty of them and they do not trip lightly on their feet. I rise from the bed for a second time and search for sandals and a wrap. Slowly, I make my way the few metres up the hill to the tree, crouch low on my haunches and discover No Name, surrounded by a writhing mass of life. At close quarters, the cloying smell of blood thickens the humid night. She glances my way but makes no effort to greet me or even acknowledge her recognition of me. I move in close and she growls. It is not a real threat, more an atavistic maternal response. In any case, she seems exhausted. Birthed out.

Gingerly, I touch her head. Her coat is wet and sticky. Viscid fluff heaves against my arm. Overhead branches dapple the moonlight. Dawn has not yet broken, so I cannot make out how many puppies there are. Five, maybe even six. I sit on the ground and keep watch with No Name. Pride surges within me for my elegant, procreating Belgian shepherd, while a longing to rush round the house, beating on doors to rouse every sleeping person, is quelled. I doubt that our parents or Michel would welcome such a rude awakening: it is not yet five o'clock. But I am too overwhelmed to go back to bed, so I decide to stay here, keeping guard over the newborns and awaiting their first sunrise. Although their eyes have not yet opened, I want to share with them that first miraculous moment of light and heat; dawn erupting into day, bursting with the joy of new life. . .

Around 7 a.m., Michel finds me conked out, dead to the world, curled up amid the stones and dusty dry earth at the foot of the tree. Twigs tangle my hair, indentations and dirt have creased and daubed my cheeks. Scantily clad in a bedraggled sarong, I am brushed with blood and bits of gummy afterbirth. '*Chérie?*' he is shaking me gently. 'What are you doing up here? I have been looking for you everywhere.' No Name's half-hearted growl draws his attention to the nest alongside me while I awake slowly, aching and sore, stones piercing my back, trying to work out where in heaven's name I am. And then I remember.

'The puppies, have you seen them?' I cry.

Aside from a zillion worms and ants and spiders and caterpillars and ladybirds and bats and lizards and geckos and carp, and those horrid feral cats which scratched us and took off the day after we found them, and probably snakes, but I prefer not to consider them, and thousands of rabbits and, with luck, dozens of those almond-munching bushy-tailed red squirrels, these blind little mewling beings are the first, the very *first* life born to us on our farm. No Name's puppies.

'How many are there?' I ask sleepily.

Michel puts his hand into the nest, which has been extraordinarily well fitted out. She must have been secretly foraging for this for days when we were not around to notice. 'Seven, I think.' He is moving furry balls aside to see if there is yet another furry ball beneath them. 'It's hard to say, but you know, I don't think she's finished.'

'How can you tell?'

He shakes his head. 'Look.'

I cannot see anything besides a mass of shining wet pelt like a damp, moth-eaten fox wrap unearthed from a long-forgotten attic. A second look reveals ejected placenta and something similar to a plastic bag filled with murky water. And No Name is not moving.

'We should wake my father.' Yes, we should wake my father.

'How many now?'

'Ten.'

'*Ten!*'

'I think so. There won't be any more.' My father pronounces this with such certainty that no one questions him. He has a way with dogs. After all, it was not until our splendid vet confirmed his suspicions that any of us believed the dog was pregnant.

So ten is the final count. 'See how she cleans them with her tongue.' The puppies are now as round and pristine and furry as mink tennis balls. Michel is taking photographs while my father and Michel's mother, Anni, keep watch, communicating with one another through sign language and intricate mimes. My mother is making tea and Michel's father is sitting at the table waiting for his breakfast, scribbling a list of ingredients for the cake he plans to bake later today. As for me, I am taking on board the reality of eleven dogs gunning all over the farm.

By evening there are only nine puppies. The general opinion seems to be that it was not a miscount; that either No Name ate one or it perished and she has buried it somewhere, even though, as far as we know, she hasn't left her post all day long. Any day now Clarisse and Vanessa will arrive. They will be entranced, although I am not altogether sure how Pamela will respond. We will be eight people, two dogs and nine puppies in addition to the prehistoric carp surviving in our murky pond. Our menagerie grows. It's becoming exactly the home I craved as a child: carefree and casual, with animals and people falling over one another, books everywhere and guests dropping by to while away a happy hour or two, jam a few tunes with whoever can play whatever instrument, nobody being quite sure where anyone else has disappeared to because there's loads of space and everyone is quietly getting on with their own thing. Heaven – just so long as I can creep off to my cool, stone room and write in peace.

The farmyard spirit is taking hold of Michel, too. He is eulogising about the possibility of planting a vineyard; acquiring a donkey, goats and bees. 'Think of it, our own honey! And the goats can roam the terraces and eat the vegetation. It will save us the cost of cutting back the land.'

Yes, and of ironing the laundry.

Alas, his suggestions are impractical. The olive does not need babysitting, but the animals do. And we are both still living itinerant professional lives. Somewhere beyond summer, beyond days drenched with heat and families and the scrubbing of walls (and the fumigating of the brown room before the girls get here) and endless puppy care, we have another existence, one all too easily forgotten as the days drift listlessly by and we swelter and burn under the relentlessly seducing sun. Retirement, even as producers of olive oil rather than television, is not yet on the cards. I think of the scarecrow farmer and his weekly visit to the village *crémerie*. I can't quite picture myself in that role yet, although, after a night in the garden, I do look rather like him already.

What does amuse me is a shift I notice taking place. I have never been a practical creature, whereas Michel is very down-to-earth, but the pendulum is swinging. We are changing places, changing roles. He begins to fancy while I plant my feet on the ground.

Later, towards the end of a sun-blessed afternoon, we receive a call from the girls to confirm the hour of their arrival two days ahead of when we had agreed. In other words, tomorrow, and can they, please, please, Papa, bring their cousins Julia and Hajo with them?

'But where will we sleep everyone?' I cry.

The plumbing is creaking, the water has turned a rusty autumnal shade – we cannot work out why – and half the house is crumbling. The cottage has not been touched yet, restoration of the 'brown room' has barely progressed since my mother and I attacked it, destroying half the walls in our attempt, and we are, as ever, almost out of money. Rooms at Monsieur Parking's hotel are no longer available, even if we could have afforded them, for he has sold his *petite affaire* to a restaurant-owner from New York who has closed the place down for extensive renovation works, intending to reopen it in readiness for next year's film festival as an illustrious, exclusive hideaway set back in the hills overlooking the glamorous bay of Cannes.

'They are bringing tents and will sleep in the garden, and before you say another word, they want to. It will be an adventure.'

Tents duly arrive, and with them appear a quartet of teenagers. How is it possible that the two prepubescent girls of last summer have been replaced by two stunning young females teetering on that first delicate step into womanhood? The French have the perfect word to describe that awakening flush: *pulpeuse*. I love it. Pulpy, ripe. Their bodies and senses have awoken to the world. Of course, with such awareness come hazards. Julia, with her nubile figure, bewitching blue eyes and swathes of long, flowing blonde hair, is two years older than the twins, and a sleek and enticing temptress she is, too. Hajo, her younger brother, is a few months their junior and, as so frequently happens with lads, seems to be five years younger. He is a boy scout of a boy. He helps Michel and Anni in the garden, collects wood, treats his grandparents with extraordinary love and respect and, when evening falls, happily accompanies the trio of girls to town but remains completely, innocently oblivious of their real interests: *les mecs*. Guys.

The days spin out. Contented guests laze around, doing nothing in particular, or find themselves chores to help us out while I write like a driven fury. My scripts are ready, or, rather the first draft is completed, Michel is reading them and I have set to work on a novel. And then, a delicious diversion. A klaxon sounds as a lorry coughs up the drive, stripping sprawling fig branches and denuding ripening fruit as it ascends. We have all been waiting for this delivery, I more feverishly than the rest. At last I am to have my ancient wooden table the size of a railway sleeper. We bought it in a sorry condition, months back, from a fabulously eccentric second-hand furniture store on the Left Bank in Paris, near St Sulpice. The shop owner arranged to have it restored for us by an artisan in Mougins. But when the carpenter delivers it, he takes one look at the exterior stairs, the terraces, the length of the arched walkway and pronounces his work done. He and his two associates, with the aid of a pulley system in their truck, unload our precious teak table, deposit it in the parking area and vamoose.

It will take six men to carry it and install it in its place. Quashia goes off in search of a makeshift team, and his Arab colleagues rally to the call, shouting to one another in a language that none of us understand from under their assortment of hats. Polite men with decaying teeth, shabby clothes and shy expressions on dark, tobacco-ravaged faces, always willing to lend a helping hand if there are francs in it for smokes. They troop up the hill shaking hands with one another, shaking hands with us, and set to work, moving as one, like our train of caterpillars, at the yell of a nasal, high-pitched order, until the table has been hoisted up the steps and positioned beneath the towering, majestic *Magnolia Grandiflora*. There it will stay, we hope, for a hundred years. Sweating, and resolutely keeping their gaze averted from the three tender beauties sunbathing in itsy bits of string by the pool, the men refuse refreshment.

Each lines up solemnly for his 50f *billet*, dished out to him by Michel, then nods his thanks and wanders off contentedly down the drive, slapping his fellow countrymen on the back, and Quashia, too, who has found them this rare moment of employment.

Pamela is the first to settle beneath the table. She waddles over and takes up residence like a rotund queen bee, then drops like a log and begins instantly to snore.

By and by, the puppies appear. They creep forward inquisitively, one by one or in twos or threes. Unkempt, fluffy curiosity converging from everywhere. One cocks its little leg against the great wooden beam of table leg. I run, screaming, to chase it away and they all scatter like a swarm of frightened rabbits, tumbling over one another in confusion and uncertainty, only to sneak back again as soon as they sense that the coast is clear. They are still so awkward, so unsteady on their limbs, making nuisances of themselves at every turn: chewing feet, climbing bronzed, creamy legs, uprooting flowers and covering everything in earth. One little culprit steals one of Anni's new sandals, which makes her laugh, but when she turns her attention back to her book he drags it to the murky fishpond. There he ditches and loses it. Only later, when a carp surfaces with a sandal strap trailing from its flesh, are we able to retrieve it. At feeding time the puppies are easy to locate: nine hungry mouths packed greedily beneath No Name with her splayed legs, sucking at her tired, chewed teats. But she is a model, patient mother.

Yet how my father indulges them. Whenever I mention the inevitable – finding homes for them – he offers to take all nine of them back to England until my mother shrieks and quite sensibly reminds him that they would have to go into quarantine to be allowed into the United Kingdom. Vanessa has volunteered to take one, a golden-russet chap whom she has christened Whisky. The other eight, heavenly as they are, will have to be given away.

Meals are a hullaballoo of pleasure. Our long-awaited table is the focus of life, the epicentre of the day. Like a clock striking, a yellow or cobalt-blue ceramic and terracotta plate clatters lightly on to its surface. The salad it contains is a masterpiece of Michel's culinary art: variously variegated leaves – striated, mottled, speckled reds and greens – seasoned with herbs, olive oil, lemon or lime and lashings of garlic. A cork is drawn; liquid shot through with sunlight tumbles into glasses. A rainbow of fruit appears and each one of us, no matter what we are doing, recognises the signal. A meal is waiting to be laid out, to be devoured. Hajo returns from the village, laden with warm bread which divides at the touch. The epitome of the perfect house guest, he roams the inclines searching out kindling to bolster Michel's collection of sacks of pine and magnolia cones to store and dry during the winter for the specific purpose of fuelling our summer barbecue, which is working overtime.

We eat and drink and talk and go silent at the pleasure of the delicacies being passed along the length of our table. As the days progress we eat and drink in greater quantities and the meals grow longer and more cheerfully abandoned. We have three languages here: French, English and German. At night, candles flicker and the warm light glows and dances across our faces, animated by conversation and flushed with wine. The bats swoop low and spin off. I lift my head and watch them flying 'after summer merrily', just as they must have done when Ariel first sang those words to Prospero in *The Tempest*. A trumpet – delicate and exquisitely erotic – reaches across the terrace from a makeshift system Michel has rigged up in the cool storeroom/summer kitchen. Miles Davis playing *Sketches of Spain*.

When Michel's parents first arrived, my mother came looking for me to ask what language they were speaking.

'German,' I replied absentmindedly, busy with my work.

'For God's sake don't tell your father!'

I glanced up, not really paying attention. 'Why not?'

'We fought them in the war.'

Here, at this table, we pass bottles, lift empty glasses to accept yet another refill, and such frontiers don't exist. Michel is the conductor, for he is the only one of us who speaks all three languages fluently. With the turn of his eloquent head, he switches tongues. A glance to the left, and he is with us in English; to the right, and words unknown to me flow from his lips. His French daughters and their German cousins, Julia and Hajo, are able to converse passably in whichever language is currently being spoken, but we Anglo-Saxons and Irish are a sorry lot. A lack of language is a poverty, and I resolve that I must add German classes to my list of chores and also brush up on my Italian and Spanish, both as rusty as the plumbing. The odd German word is growing familiar. *Essen* for example: a meal or to eat. Another, *schnecken*, is being repeated frequently and debated on, I think, a great deal this evening but I have not heard this before. What is Anni saying? I ask Michel.

'She is talking about the snails.'

'Ah, *schnecken* means snails, does it?' I sigh. Yes, the plants are infested with snails. I have spent several hours on dewy mornings picking them off the stalks of various shrubs only to find that, by evening, they are back, and in even greater numbers, crowded on top of one another like hippy bracelets.

'She is telling us that she has a solution for them and that I must take her shopping in the morning.'

I look at Anni and she nods wisely.

'What is it?'

'You'll see.' She laughs loudly and her merriment rings across the valley and is absorbed within the murrey-mauve hills.

The next day is a brittle, dry day. Baking. Eerily still. The still, deep heat which often precedes a mistral. My father and I are returning from the vet, where we have delivered a cardboard box of restless puppies to be inspected. All are in good order and as far as the doctor can say at this stage, these little ones are also pure-breds. No Name must have been days, even minutes, pregnant when I discovered her. He has agreed to put a notice up in his surgery soliciting homes for them. No Name is hovering, concerned by the disappearance of her brood, when Michel comes rattling up the drive with Anni. They have been shopping. As well as the usual provisions and the daily mountains of fresh food being consumed by our party, I notice that they have bought black pepper. Not one container, but twenty. This is Anni's answer to the *schnecken*. They can't abide pepper, she explains to me.

I shake my head in wonder. How can she possibly know such a thing? Is it black pepper to which they are allergic, or all pepper? Are they fine with salt? I take myself off upstairs to my den.

Towards noon, staring idly from the window, nursing my work-in-progress, I observe our various guests at their holiday activities. My father is by the pool, sleeping, dogs crawling over him like flies on a cow's rump, the girls are perched in an elegant trio alongside the pool, varnished toes dangling in the water to keep them cool, sunglasses hiding the mischief in their eyes, whispering hot secrets to one another and laughing skittishly. I discern wind in the trees. It looks as though a weather change is coming in from Africa. Hajo and my mother are both alone in private worlds. He is whittling a branch he has retrieved from somewhere on the land while she, on the pretext of reading, is in fact staring at her feet, frowning, worrying about something. Michel's father, Robert, I cannot see, but I can hear the clatter of tins and pans in the upstairs makeshift kitchen where he is baking yet another round of cakes, which probably won't get eaten by anyone except himself, and where he is creating utter chaos, showering flour and sugar everywhere, transforming our inadequate cooking space into a ski resort.

But where are Michel and Anni? Leaning closer to the glass, I catch sight of Anni, bent low, vigorously shaking pepper over twisting flowers. She moves on to the tender young orange trees, which are shooting up at a remarkable pace and soughing in the wind. Michel trails behind her, shirt flapping, with a tray of pots. Half of them are empty. He accepts another drained container from his mother and hands her a full one, and so they continue. I will be fascinated to learn the outcome. My guess is that the wind will pick up and the pepper will be blown away while the snails continue to cling fast.

I return to the world of the novel I am writing. In my imagination I am on a sugar plantation in Fiji and a young arsonist has set fire to the crops. 'Fire!'

Later, I have no idea how much later, minutes or hours, Michel is at my door. 'Carol! *Chérie!*' I look up but barely register his presence, lost as I am again in my imaginary scenario.

'Mmm?'

'There's a fire. We should prepare ourselves.'

It sounds too incredible to be true. 'A fire?' I repeat, stupidly. Michel has no idea what I am writing, and his news has bemused me. 'What fire?'

'*Chérie*, there's a fire on the other side of the main road. Can't you hear the planes?'

I have heard nothing. I rise from my trestle table, padding after Michel, and then scoot back to save my work on the computer and switch off the machine.

'The others are getting dressed.'

It is Saturday, mid-afternoon. As I leave the house behind Michel I am hit by a blanket of windy heat and by the roar of engines coming directly towards me. I lift my head and look skywards, and there, probably no more than twenty metres above our heads, a red plane swoops low and shaves the flat roof of our house, sending the gravel stones laid by M. Di Luzio into rising whorls before they scatter and clatter like running feet on to the terraces. There is dust everywhere, leaves are being whipped from the trees and swirl about, lost. This feels like an attack.

'I think we should drive to the end of the lane and find out what's going on.'

Our little lane has been cut off by the fire brigade. No one can enter and we cannot pass. A barrier erected within the last hour is being watched over by half a dozen hulking young firemen. Clots of people are huddled in groups. There is great activity, much argument. Most look like Parisians, lean and mean, smoking furiously, dressed in chic shorts, bathing costumes with silk shirts thrown hastily over their shoulders, jogging clothes, gold watches, designer purses clutched tight to their well-honed, neat-bosomed bodies. They are probably the occupants of the summer villas beyond the rear of our hill and along the multitude of narrow tracks which wind inland towards the heart of Mougins. I ask one of the firemen what the chances are that the fire will leap the bridge over the road. He shrugs. 'So long as the wind does not change direction, you are safe.'

'And if it does?'

'If it does, get into the swimming pool and wait for an airlift out.'

We are not to worry, he assures us. They know where we are

and how many we are. 'How many are you?' he asks then, as an afterthought.

'Ten, and two dogs and nine puppies.' One very fat dog, I am thinking, who will not be able to run for her life. If the worst comes to the worst, one of us will be obliged to carry Pamela. And what of all those puppies? I will have to pack them back into the cardboard box and try to keep them calm.

We hurry back down the lane to the house, where the cinders are falling like huge, dove-coloured snowflakes and settling on the surface of the pool. All around us the sky is changing colour. Our loved ones are grouped together, clinging to bags and various bits of belongings. They are staring skywards, where the reflection of the fire has twisted nature out of recognition. It is impossible to concentrate on anything except the fire. The distant cries of people carry on the wind, the force of which sends a towel left by the pool flying into the water, where it sinks like dead meat.

Michel moves to and fro, making mental notes about the wind's direction. He is unwinding every hosepipe we own, calling to anyone who might be listening for assistance, and attaching the hoses to the water supply at strategic points in the garden. Hajo is dismantling the three tents and taking them into the house for safety. I cannot stop myself surveying the scene for details I might extract for my story. The fear, the uncertainty and the threatening sky. Almost every word shouted is drowned out by the skirring of the brilliant red Canadair planes purchased from Canada, where they are used to fight fires to great effect. Their presence is everywhere. If they are not overhead or passing to the rear of the hill, they are visible before us, diving into the sea, swooping like dragonflies. Their presence gives an urgency, a reality to the fire, which is still out of sight. The roar of their engines, no more than a few feet above our heads, brings real terror to the mood.

'I think it wouldn't be a bad idea to begin to soak the vegetation,' suggests Michel, which is what he and I, along with Hajo, are about to do when Quashia appears, damp from exertion, wearing a battered old panama. 'I think you need help.'

'How did you get through?' calls Michel.

'I saw the flames from the village and followed the towpath by the stream in the valley. The bridge has been cut off. There are fire engines everywhere.' I am relieved that our parents cannot understand this, for I fear it would distress them. 'The wind's picking up, too.'

We all look out to sea, where the waves are foamy and white; a sure sign that a gale-force wind is blowing in.

'How much water do we have in the *bassin*?' Michel shouts to Quashia.

'I switched on the pump on my way up here.'

Michel nods, relieved, and hands out hosepipes. 'We can manage this, *chérie*. You ought to stay with the family.'

I retreat as the men begin to run the pipes up and down the hill, watering wherever the nozzles will reach. The susurration of water spraying and falling on a day as relentless as this has a cooling, tranquillising effect of its own, for which I am grateful, because whatever posture of artistic detachment I might be laying on the occasion, the truth is I am scared and trembling.

There is nothing more we can do but wait, eleven of us, plus the terrified animals, staring at an aubergine sky. We sit silently listening to the crackling, even though for the moment the fire is still on the opposite side of the bridge. Or we make inane jokes to keep the fear at bay. Those who smoke are smoking too much; the rest of us are trying to remain calm. Quashia, perhaps because he is too restless to sit, or does not feel comfortable being a part of the family, has gone off to climb the hill. Michel tries to stop him, but he insists that he can better warn us from there.

It is a question of the wind, which is building in force. Trees are bowing and swaying, twisting and turning as though attempting to tear themselves from the earth to fly free and unencumbered. And then it changes direction, an instant about-turn. Within seconds the flames leap the bridge that crosses the road and are now right behind us, burning fast towards the pinnacle of our hill. We are all of us on our feet.

'*Fire! Fire!*' It is Quashia.

We run to the rear of the house, and there, at the very summit, beyond the unfenced limit of our own terrain, where the vegetation has not been so rigorously cut back, is a scorching wall of fire which reaches the tips of the tallest pines. It is perhaps the most terrifying sight I have ever witnessed. The flames leaping towards the bruised and overwrought sky seem to be performing a war dance. I stand gazing up the hill, horrified. And petrified.

Beneath us, the first of the fire engines comes hurtling up the drive. It is shortly followed by a second, and then a third.

Michel tells us to collect our passports and keep them at the ready. Clarisse admits to being scared and wraps an arm tight around my waist. I love her for the confidence. Pamela whines like a frightened baby. Robert, munching on one of his cakes, is still covered in flour. Anni, stalwart and unafraid, empties the last remaining pot of pepper on to a rose bush and lights yet another cigarette.

'The hills are on fire and you are cut off,' announces the hirsute chief of the four *pompiers* who have disembarked from the fire engine. 'Someone set light to the trees in the pine forest over on the other side of the hill. We almost had it under control, but the mistral is picking up fast, changing direction and we can't contain it.'

I am weeping now, the effects of the smoke as well as his words. The heat is beating like a drum and twisting my flesh taut. It is raining ashes. They are drifting through the air and falling on the terraces and floating in the swimming pool. It is like a blanket of grey snow. I have no idea what will happen to us. 'Should we dive into the pool?' I ask weakly.

'No, go on with whatever you were doing. We'll keep you informed.'

Continue with what we were doing?

Men are pouring out of the red vehicles and begin pounding up the hill. Each carries what looks like a knapsack on his back. In all, approximately 120 of them are beating their way towards the summit. I have never seen so many fine-looking, fit fellows. Whatever fear had taken hold of Julia and our two girls has been forgotten. They are giggling and posing as dozen upon dozen of handsome, lithe young firefighters in their navy-blue uniforms go charging past. I confess to being thrilled by them, too, by their maleness and phenomenal physical prowess.

Now, the pool is being sucked dry and the chlorinated water is being transported up the hill by metre after metre of ample piping to be sprayed on to the fire. The dogs won't stop barking. Puppies are peeing and scooting all over the place. We are overwhelmed by noise and activity and chaotic fear. What when the pool is emptied? I ask myself, for certainly there is not sufficient water there to quench this conflagration. Will the fire then beat its way down the hill, killing the men and burning all in its wake? How can they even hold such a fury at bay, never mind put a stop to it?

Suddenly, three or four of the small planes arrive, droning and circling like great, angry insects. They fly low, barely ten metres above the treetops, dumping tons of red, liquidy powder on the wall of flames. Then they circle back round, heading for the bay in front of us. I watch them dive, plunging their noses into the sea, nozzling up gallons of salty Med water. They return, one after another, a ceaseless aggressive procession hell-bent on beating back this twist of nature. Gallon-loads of the Mediterranean Sea mixed with the red powder are dropped like bombs on to the flames. And so it goes on. Four planes, each making ten or fifteen trips an hour. It is a mesmerising spectacle, supremely dramatic.

'Rather puts to shame those memorable Biggin Hill air shows you took me to when I was a kid,' I whisper to my father, who is as always deeply impressed by such displays of organisation.

'You've got to hand it to the French,' he mutters, but he's not really talking to me. He's somewhere else. Lost in his war, perhaps. I cannot say. I lean in and give his hot, peeling flesh a stroke.

I want to walk up the hill to get a closer look, but Michel and Quashia call me back. The weight of the red avalanche, they warn me, is sufficient to kill anyone foolish enough to be standing wherever a plane tips its load. I listen to shrill crack after brutally shrill crack as whining trunks snap and collapse, thud and roll to the needled earth, and I consider the fate of those firefighters, all of whom are at risk should the plane misdirect its lethal cargo. I have always harboured a child's romantic regard for firefighters and lifeboat men. They have always been my heroes, and nothing I see today dents that illusion.

By evening, the flames have been beaten back. Slowly, the engines begin to reverse and depart. We are left with an empty pool, an overwhelming exhaustion and a strange sensation of deflation mingled with immense relief. Something tremendous and sinister has roared through our day and now a disconcerting, cautious tranquillity has taken its place.

'We'll be back tomorrow,' the chief tells us. 'To refill your pool. We'll be keeping a few men on the hill tonight in case the wind picks up. It only needs one burning ember . . .' It is usual here for the mistral to drop at night. No matter how strongly it has blown during the day, by evening it quietens. I have always found it a curious feat of nature how the wind knows when the sun is setting, but it is so. And we are left with a view which is as clear and pure as freshly drawn water.

Michel and I clamber up the steep, stony track to survey the extent of the damage. Four young men are standing together. Their eyes shine blue and bright beneath faces smeared with soot and sweat. Everyone shakes hands. They are welcome to join us for dinner. They thank us, but do not accept. It is not possible for them to leave the site. In any case, as always, they are well prepared. Stores of water and food have been lodged beneath a living tree. Its verdant life is almost jarring amid so much blackness. Charred tree trunks are lying like history everywhere the eye can see, but not on our land. Not one tree, in fact barely a blade of grass, has been touched. Now I understand why the local councils are so strict about keeping the land cut back. There was nothing for the fire to take hold of, nothing to burn.

Still, the sickening aroma of burning is everywhere, mawkish and lethal. My cheeks are scorched just from standing so close. Heat rises like a sauna from the charcoal earth. Everywhere, black tortured skeletons are etched against the fast-fading day. Our water *bassin* has been drenched in red powder.

'You should cover that,' a young fireman remarks.

It is true. Quashia has been nagging us about it all summer. I step up on to a three-rung ladder attached to the side of the *bassin* and peer in. The water within is tinted pink and there are several birds floating lifelessly on the surface. Did the fire carbonise them, were they caught in a slipstream of wind and heat, or have they fallen victim to a normal day's drowning? Pine needles are inches thick on the bed of the basin. The water looks stagnant as well as pink. Its murkiness could well be the reason for our rusty water.

'We'll clean it out for you tomorrow,' one of our night-watch team soothes us.

A curl of smoke can still be seen here and there among the embers in what remains of the dwindling light. And curling roots, snapped and torn from the dry earth. Pines that were dead but not burned have been uprooted, ripped from the earth by the sheer weight of the water disgorged from the Canadairs falling on them. The newly dead surround us in an arboreal cemetery, life laid waste against a ruined sky.

We should leave them to it.

'*Bonsoir*. If there's anything we can do . . .' calls Michel.

They shrug shyly, and then an earnest-faced, dark-haired fellow in his early twenties steps forward. 'Monsieur?'

Michel turns.

'*Nous avons vu les chiots . . . ils sont à vendre?*'

The puppies, are they for sale? they are asking.

We have eight to give away, I tell them.

Two young men now step eagerly towards us, assuring us they would give them good homes. *Sans doute*. It is agreed that they will take one each. Tomorrow morning before they go off duty they will choose their respective puppies.

The following morning, Sunday, is almost as eventful as the previous day. A huge tanker arrives, bearing almost a reservoir of water, and negotiates the winding drive, splintering what is left of the fig branches in its wake, to refill the pool. This is followed by an official from the council administration, who arrives in a sleek silver-grey Renault. He is a short, stocky individual with a dark grey moustache who struts like royalty with his hands clasped behind his back. Most unusual, I think, because a true Provençal uses his hands for half his conversation. When I run downstairs to greet him he asks to speak to the man of the house, which infuriates me. It is typical of a certain machismo that is very prevalent on this Riviera coast.

'He is busy,' I say firmly. 'How can I help?'

He shrugs, wearied by the prospect of dealing with a woman. 'I need to inspect,' he informs me curtly.

'The fire damage?'

He nods impatiently. But, of course! And, squinting, he looks about him with a calibrating eye, ascertaining what we have, or rather what we have not, because the turn of his mouth and pout of his lips tell me that he considers the place a ruin. '*Beaucoup de travail*,' is his informed opinion. It makes me laugh because he is echoing the words of the estate agent, M. Charpy. I am way past bothering to explain that as far as we are concerned renovation is part of the joy of the place. Instead I offer to escort him up the hill. We make our way to the back of the house, where he halts and tilts his head skywards. It is clear that he was not expecting such physical exertion. Glancing at his watch, and heaving a monumental sigh, he begins the climb, his squat body leading, not following me.

The young men who have kept guard all night look very tired and desperately in need of showers and clean clothes, but they are as cheerful as they were last evening. We all go through the handshaking routine and they lead the council official on a guided tour of blackened trees and grizzled brush. I stay where I am, taking in the view. The dense scent of charred wood pervades the early-morning air. He takes his time, this official, crunching across acres of ravaged land before finally returning to me.

'You are to be congratulated,' he announces.

I am quite taken aback.

'*Vous, votre mari, vous êtes des bons citoyens*, and you are most welcome here in our commune.' And he shakes my hand warmly. 'I want to meet your husband.'

As we traipse back down the hill I feel as though I am in the company of a different human being. He is whistling, looking about him, pointing at this and that, nodding his head at the ruin and at our olive terraces. The young men follow on behind us, carrying their rucksacks. They move wearily. Michel offers everyone coffee but the firemen prefer to get off home. They leave promising to return later to choose their puppies. Over a glass of *vin rouge* – it is not yet ten o'clock and our respective parents stare in shock – the council official asks Michel what we do for a living. '*Ah, les artistes, maintenant je comprends!*' Would we object to a photographer from the local gazette, the *Nice Matin*, dropping by? Not to photograph us, of course, he adds hastily, but to take shots of the damage. Our privacy is sacred. Michel gives our consent.

The rest of Sunday sees a series of comings and goings. The fire brigade return to make a reconnoitre, and decide that two more men are to be posted here – 'There is a light wind and you can never be too sure.'

The photographer arrives, an unshaven scruffy chap who appears far more interested in the girls in their bikinis. They lap up every glance of attention. And then the crowning moment of the day, late in the afternoon: the firemen appear, spruced up, shaved, showered and dressed in civvies, handsome as mytho-logical gods, all four of them in one battered, outdated car. They have now decided that they all want puppies. The girls rush to and fro, combing their hair, changing their clothes, searching out lipsticks, pinching mine, and then return to stud-ied composure in deckchairs in the garden, having made quite sure that every puppy has been dragged to their sides.

Much bending and caressing and displaying of helplessly adorable creatures takes place and, I suspect, arrangements are made to meet later in Cannes for cups of coffee. Finally, four yawning puppies are chosen. Of course, they cannot be taken away tonight. They must spend a little while longer with their mother, which means that each of the young men promises to return here at regular intervals to keep an eye on 'his chosen companion'. One young fellow must have lost out, I mutter to Michel, who is blithely unaware of what I am talking about.

After supper, the girls, with dear Hajo as their escort, scuttle off for the bright lights of Cannes while we, the veterans, settle sedately on the upper terrace to watch the new moon and the stars appear. After a mistral the view is always crystalline, as if the whole of nature has been polished. We can see every detail on every hill, though fortunately for the girls, we cannot see what they are up to in Cannes.

Tomorrow, both sets of parents are leaving. It is a sad yet complete moment. We have experienced a whole range of life's offerings here together: birth and death as well as time spent together discovering the world anew. As always, farewells create a profound and melancholy emptiness within me, and I feel the wrench swelling as Michel opens the last bottle to be shared between us all for this summer. The six of us sit in silence, quaffing, listening, appreciating the soft sounds of deep evening. And then, suddenly, there is a noise which none of us recognise. Short, sharp, tiny and repeated.

'What's that?' asks Anni.

We all of us listen carefully. Frowns and bemused expressions take shape in the candlelight.

I watch the families puzzling over the distant hiccup of sound and I simply cannot resist it. 'It's the *schnecken*, Anni. The snails.'

'What about them?'

'They're sneezing!'

Tracking the Olive

Summer is slipping away, like the silent falling of petals.
Everyone has left, and we are on our own. The swallows gather,
autumn sets in, rustic and rather rainy. The land grows green
again, restored, revivified. The grass, dry and brittle as old
bones all those hot months, shoots up overnight and, in among
it, daisies sprout everywhere. They are crisply white, innocent
and childlike, an unpretentious flower. I stroll along the terraces, studying the ripening olives, which are a light violet now,
or piebald green and mauve, picking slender-stalked handfuls of
wild flowers as I go. These I carry back to the house and place
in jars on the tables. They swoop and lift towards the first tendrils of sunlight creeping round the corner of the house, and I
am delighted by their ordinariness.

It is Saturday morning. Herby scents in an immaculately
well-washed day. Michel is somewhere at the foot of the hill
planting a wheelbarrowload of purple and white irises which
we have dug up from the terraces, where they are multiplying in

wild profusion. He is using them to create a border to our new fence and the *arbuste* of laurel.

René arrives bearing two plastic shopping bags full of small, black grapes.

'*Framboises*,' he announces. I am confused.

He laughs at my expression. 'These grapes are known as raspberries.'

'Why?'

'Taste them.'

And, surprisingly, they taste *exactly* like raspberries.

René has come to escort us to one of the farms he tends in the *arrière-pays*, the hinterland (we were expecting him the day before yesterday, but no matter). He and I make ourselves comfortable on the upstairs terrace and settle down to *un verre* while we wait for Michel to complete his gardening chores. I glance at my watch as René pours our chilled beers, and smile silently. It is not yet 10.30. Years of restraint, of broken diets followed by insufferable guilt, sleepless nights and a sense of inadequacy, all to stuff myself into costumes a size too small but befitting the television or silver screen, someone else's notion of sex appeal, and here I am, bright and early on a Saturday morning, dressed like a Mediterranean construction worker in boots and shorts, facing with delight the frothy liquid on the table in front of me. Learning to live peacefully with the hedonist in my soul.

'Thirsty work,' proclaims René, lifting his glass. For a second I think he must be referring to my inner reflections, but then I notice that his attention is directed towards poor Michel, whose silhouette moves in and out of view as he bends and rises in the process of digging and planting.

I listen as René begins to recount tales of his life as a lorry driver before he retired. He has an extraordinary assortment of stories to tell of the years of German occupation here on the coast, when he and his lorry were used by the Resistance to ferry food after curfew so that no French families went without. He paints a tantalising picture of man and his trusty steed – in this case his lorry – of rations redirected, *une petite escroquerie* here and *une petite escroquerie* there, as he followed the trail of Robin Hood.

Escroquerie. I love this word. Although it is not specifically a Provençal noun it does seem to sum up so much of the way of life here: *une escroquerie* is a swindle.

Our olive man is now describing to me in detail, using his hands for emphasis and dramatic effect, how to skin and eat a hedgehog. The cooking is not complicated, he assures me. Boil it first in a *bouillon*, then slit it open down the middle of its soft side, its belly side, 'as though cutting open a cushion', and peel off the skin in the same way you would a diving suit.

'What about its quills?'

'Bah, they fall away as easily as unpicking cotton stitching once the animal has been boiled.'

I cannot picture adding this recipe to my cookbook, but I refrain from saying so. Another staple food here during the Second World War occupation was the guinea pig. According to René, guinea pigs, *cochons d'Inde,* are an excellent source of fat, a commodity that was always in short supply in the wartime diet. It made the meat edible, too. Any animal that has plenty of fat on it makes good eating meat, he explains. I am beginning to think I prefer the rigours of the actress's diet. René reaches for another bottle of the blond beer, tops up his glass and embarks on descriptions of the occupation of the grand hotels and *maisons particulières* along the coast, of shells exploding, of the Maquis preparing for the liberation. Here he interrupts himself: 'Do you know why the Resistance or underground forces were called Maquis?' He does not wait for my response. 'That is the name of the brush or scrubland that grows all along these Mediterranean and Corsican coastlines. And so they were named le Maquis because they took to the bush, went underground. They were very active here in Provence, and without them it is unlikely that the allied invasion of 1944 would have proved such a success.'

I do know this but I feign surprise, and René shrugs that Provençal shrug. He genuinely delights in the telling of his tales and I seem to be his perfect audience. Swiftly on he goes to the nights spent in the shelters – not all misery, he claims – which leads him quite naturally to the wartime romancing of a nightclub singer in Marseille. '*Diable*, she had great legs!' he grins, and begins a saucy observation about his height and the length of her legs, seems to think better of it, glances at me in an impish way, blushes and deflects. Now he has cut to the courting of a local girl. He reminisces about their lovemaking on the beaches while guns were firing all around them. She was three years his senior, and in those days, he says, was deemed a daring and romantic choice. Later, she became his wife. She is housebound now.

Michel is coming up the drive with the wheelbarrow. He waves.

René turns his attention to more pressing matters: plants and *l'entretien* of the *oliviers*. Pruning and maintenance in general and of the olive trees in particular clearly ignites his passion as readily as his longings for the good old days. While I listen and watch him, I perceive in his piercingly blue eyes the joy of a life richly lived.

'Quite a lady's man, eh, René?' I tease.

'Ah, yes, I'm very lucky,' he mutters, gazing out across the view, sipping his beer. 'You don't know the half of it.'

When Michel is ready, we set off. The first trip of what is to be our pre-harvest *petit pèlerinage*, our olive pilgrimage. This morning we are driving inland, winding up and around the leafy corkscrew lanes, gazing back on to spectacular coastal scenery: sweeping bays, a lone helicopter traversing an electric-blue sky, forests of sailboats like miniature flags waving back at us from the glassy expanses of the Med. We are climbing to a cooler altitude, a remoter province, a rural world where little traffic passes save for a few trucks and grunting, soil-beaten tractors. Everywhere, with the exception of the olive and the cypress, the trees are turning striking tones of amber and ruby red. And there is a remarkable stillness in the air. Twenty minutes inland and we might have turned back the clock half a century.

This particular olive farm is approached along a well-hidden track, a bumpy, rutted trail better suited to tractors than René's diesel-powered Renault. The gate is worn, askew and held fast with a rusted padlock and chain. Inside the grounds there is a long, straight climb ahead of us along a steep, stony path flanked by terraced groves. This leads directly to the farmhouse, set, rather like ours, halfway up the hillside. The salmon-pink house with its fading grass-green shutters is an ancient *bastide* all but forgotten in this deep countryside. Situated south of a rocky mass of land known as the Pre-Alpes of Castellane, it looks out in sunlit seclusion across the valley towards a hilltop village named Gourdon. The Parisian proprietor, now well into his eighties, visits the farm for only one month during the year, at the height of summer. For the other eleven months the place is locked up and unused. No one except René comes near it, which saddens me as I recall how neglected Appassionata was when we first found her.

To the left of the farmhouse are the stables, which have been converted into a second bathroom so the old gentleman can shave in peace and not be pestered by his grandchildren first thing in the morning. A vine laden with green, pendulous grapes gives shade to a cracked concrete patio. The look of the place reminds me of one of those early Dubonnet commercials I used to watch on television when I was knee-high to a grasshopper. I had never visited France in those days, but those images struck me as so gloriously foreign, so happy-go-lucky, and so much the French idyll. Perhaps that's why I'm here.

This farm boasts 130 trees, thirty of which are the originals and have grown on these terraces for somewhere in the region of 250 to 300 years. Their trunks are wrinkled and gnarled like old elephant skin. The younger trees, planted by our absent proprietor, are barely twenty-five years old but, for the most part, are fruiting well. They are of a different variety, an olive known as *tanche*. The ancients, with their thick, tormented trunks, are the *cailletier*, the variety we have inherited.

René picks off a drupe and hands it to me to examine. 'The *cailletier* is renowned for the rich, golden oil it produces as well as its superior quality. It is a rustic tree perfectly capable of sustaining long periods of drought and, in times gone by, its oil was sought after by the perfume houses, particularly those in Grasse, because that golden hue was judged a marvellous addition to any scent.' Locally it is known as the Nice olive, and exists predominantly along this coastal strip. It grows taller than any other olive tree yet produces the smallest fruit. Take a trip deeper into the hills of Provence and you will discover shorter, stubbier varieties offering a natural protection against the harsh mistrals which blow fierce and unrelenting at higher altitudes.

We trail from terrace to terrace, watching René check on the progress of his purpling fruit. Suddenly he stops, pulls a mottled leaf from one of the young, zinc-grey trees and turns it over with a frown.

'*Paon,*' he says sombrely.

'*Paon?*' I repeat, surprised, looking around for a peacock.

He nods and then explains. The peacock was a domestic bird on many farms in this southern part of France. The olive tree malady *Cyclocodium Oleaginum* is commonly known as *œil de paon*, peacock's eye, because its fungus scars the silvery green foliage with round, black spots like that in a peacock's feather before jaundicing the leaves, which eventually drop from the branches. René hands us the leaf and we both examine it. 'Watch out for it on your trees.'

Even to amateurs such as ourselves it is obvious that there is something the matter with it. The leaf has turned a dusty yellow and is dappled with dark brown blotches. I am concerned for the welfare of the fruit, but René assures us that this particular ailment will not harm the olives. However, if it is ignored, the leaves will fall, denuding every branch. Within a year, he warns us soberly, the entire tree will be bald. And the blight is highly contagious. 'After the harvest – it is too late now for this season, I would risk poisoning the fruit – I will be obliged to treat every tree on every terrace here on this farm.'

It is naïve of me, of course, but I have not even considered the dangers of olive tree maladies and I am rather horrified to learn that there are nine insect-borne or fungal diseases for which we will need to keep an eye out. Some of them can be carried by the tools used to prune the trees. If one of these should occur, the tools need to be disinfected after the pruning of every single tree. René laughs when he sees my expression and assures me that such cases, though more common in Algeria, are rare here.

During the drive home, I remark on the number of hilltop villages in this part of southern France and learn from Michel that most are built on strategic lookout points originally chosen by marauding Saracens for the building of their fortresses. Once these bloodthirsty invaders had been defeated, villages were constructed on the ruins of the reclaimed territories to protect the people against the return of their enemies or the arrival of future aggressors.

The Saracens, a collective name for Arabs, Moors, Berbers and Turks, painted by history as a thoroughly disreputable lot who did nothing but rape and pillage, in fact made some contributions to local learning and tradition. They taught the

Provençal people much about natural medicines and how to utilise the bark of the cork oaks to make cork – where would the wine industry have been without them? – and to extract resin from the numerous regional pines. Their other significant addition to the culture of the region was to teach the native people how to play the tambourine. Not that I can own to having noticed a single sun-wrinkled Provençal roaming about the village streets or his *places des boules* happily tapping his tambourine.

Dropping back towards the sea, descending into a gentler clime, we drive by squads of people mustering in the numerous country lanes and hidden grasslands. They are sporting baskets and sticks and do not look as though they are embarking on jolly weekend rambles; they seem intent on some far more serious activity. And indeed they are.

'It's the *funghi* season,' Michel reminds me. Ah yes, I remember the troupe I confronted on our own hill last autumn. I suggest to Michel that it might be fun to try our hand at mushroom-picking.

There is a village in Italy in the Apennines named Piteglio where, in the late nineteenth century, the inhabitants used to gather together during the *funghi* season and collect between them 3,000 lbs of mushrooms every day. We are neither so actively committed nor in possession of a hill quite so fecund. Nevertheless, on the Sunday, a gentle, sunny late-October morning, mushroom-picking we go. Clad in wellingtons as protection against the brambles and wet undergrowth, we proceed up to the brow of our hill, where blocks of sunlight cut sharp right angles through the lofty trees. This is a delightful way of working up a thirst and an appetite for lunch, I soon discover. I hear and then catch sight of a woodpecker, and a pair of whoopers. The earth is spongy underfoot and crackly from the sinking layers of pine needles. The scent of humid pine hangs in the air around us as we bend and forage. Fat cones, like sleeping Humpty Dumpties, turn and roll in our wake. The mushrooms are everywhere, barely hidden, soft and slippery, pushing up through the damp earth and the pine needles. I have to watch my step or I squash them, or the big, brown snails hidden on twigs and runkled leaves. Rich, dark soil slides beneath my fingernails as I scratch and scoop at its surface. I want to feel the silky, mushroomy textures, but I am unsure about touching *funghi*. I am no expert and have little idea which of these *champignons* are edible and which are poisonous, and Michel is barely better informed. Still, we tramp the woods merrily, searching and gathering with vigour, stashing our hoard in woven wooden baskets. Back at the house, working at our long table in the garden, we sort them carefully into floppy heaps according to their shape, size and possible variety. We have done rather well, and I fear we may end up wasting them.

'No, if they are all edible,' returns Michel, 'we'll cook some in vinegar to preserve as antipasto.'

We place one example of each kind on a tray, taking care not to damage them, and hurry down to the village. Our regular *pharmacie* is closed on Sunday mornings so we visit another, where a thin, stooped chemist with greased, flat hair peers at our pickings with disdain.

'I wouldn't touch any of them,' is his pronouncement.

We are silenced by disappointment.

'Are you sure? None at all?'

With the tips of two tweezer-like fingers, his pinky curled in the air like that of an old maid supping tea, he begins lifting one after another by their tufted or fleshy stems, still thick with dried earth. He twizzles each one in turn, glares at it and then tut-tuts.

'*Faux, faux,*' he accuses, dismissing each poor vegetable before dropping it back on to the tray as though it were excrement. 'Eat them if you like, but I wouldn't.'

Michel picks up a vaguely mottled ochrey example and offers it up for the pharmacist's consideration. 'I thought perhaps this might be *un lactaire, non*?'

'Perhaps it is, perhaps it isn't.'

Michel turns over the mushroom the better to convince the pharmacist. Beneath its fleshy cap, its corrugated belly, the gills are undeniably reddish. He breaks the stalk in two. The flesh inside is also red.

'*Oui, peut-être ça c'est de la varieté lactaire,*' this dry-spirited chemist concedes without enthusiasm. 'You might try that one, but none of the others. They are *champignons vénéneux*. Even that one might be riddled with maggots.' And with that he disappears, determined not to be moved to any joy.

'*Merci, Monsieur,*' we call after him with a twinkle.

We return home with our tray, heavy with its assorted poisons, to our table in the autumnal garden piled high with stacks of seven different varieties.

'I think he may have been a little damning of our efforts but we'd better not risk it.' Dear Michel patiently gathers up our morning's efforts and dumps the entire harvest into the *poubelle*. We now have one dustbin full of decomposing, deadly mushrooms and are left with just eight edible *lactaire*. Hardly competition for the Italian peasants in the village of Piteglio, but more than sufficient for our own consumption. So, not even vaguely downhearted, we lunch sumptuously on our eight home-grown mushrooms, sliced into slivers and simmered lightly in olive oil seasoned with garlic, salt and pepper and chopped herbs from the garden, served with grated Parmesan and washed down with a bottle of red from Châteauneuf-du-Pape. All on the terrace in the autumn sunshine.

We learn later from our own pharmacist that the mushrooms we have eaten are known as *lactaire délicieux* – in English, saffron milk-caps. 'They grow beneath pine trees and are excellent.'

We vouch for their delicious, nutty flavour and confirm that we gathered them from the summit of our hill in the pine forest.

'The Russians preserve them in salt, you know.' He shows us the chart he keeps on display for ignoramuses such as ourselves and we notice at least one other of the varieties we gathered and threw away. It is the large white variety known here as *faux mousseron*, the fairy-ring mushroom. I am very taken with the notion that we have fairy rings of any sort on our land. On the way home, still in mushroom mood, we stop off at the vegetable market and buy half a kilo of ceps to add to a risotto.

It is a perfect evening at the end of a tranquil, uneventful and too-short day, even though the clocks have gone back an hour. Already the sun is setting and it is growing chilly. Lights on the hills are illuminated. Everywhere the comforting whiff of woodsmoke trails the dusk. Michel is stoking the fire while, a terrace beneath him, I creep naked into the still pool. A fig leaf turned saffron with the season falls from the tree and floats into the water to accompany me. The cold shocks my system and my toes and fingers start to tingle. I splash and throw my body in unflinchingly, swimming fast and determinedly, growing accustomed to the icy temperature. I pound up and down, not daring to slow in case my flesh numbs. Then I leave the pool, heart pounding, flesh zinging, and run around the garden whooping like a squaw on the warpath. The dogs are barking at me and Michel runs out on to the terrace to see what is going on. I am laughing lightheartedly.

'I think there must have been hallucinogens in the mushrooms,' he calls as he goes back inside to more constructive chores.

A deluge of rain descends. Tropical in its intensity, it shocks. Day after day, it sheets across the hills, making it impossible to discern the horizon between sea and sky. The sky glowers blackly. The days are sombrous. Raindrops the size of dinner plates splash into the pool, which looks as though it may burst its banks and roll like Niagara, swamping the terraces.

We are confined to the house, to our books and projects. To wine and food, to one another. I am at work on my scripts again, reshaping them to include Michel's observations, but there are times when the labour goes slowly, I lose confidence and spend restless hours pressed against the long, steamy windows, staring out at the clouds which have hidden the valley from sight. We are very short of money. I need to press on if we are to secure a contract to shoot next summer. The rain drips and sloshes, gushing and gurgling urgently from every pipe. Lightning strikes, the electricity goes dead. We run through the rain to the garage and flip the trip-switch back on. The power flickers on and then off again. We live by candlelight. Thunder rolls and roars. The dogs howl and whine, terrified. We drag them in by the fire to soothe and dry them. Everywhere the rooms are pervaded by the smell of wet dog.

The baked land welcomes the weather, and the plants suck up the water greedily. We are less grateful, for we are discovering cracks and fissures we didn't know existed. Rain is pouring into the house. Under the French windows, it sneaks in and settles in puddles on the tiles. I hasten to the bathroom to fetch towels and spread them out across the floors. I hear dripping and running and splashing everywhere, a cacophony of water music. Back and forth I go, armed with bowls and plastic pails to plug the invasive percussion. Fortunately, M. Di Luzio's roof is holding. I expect the whole thing to come crashing down on top of us at any minute but this is an ancient house built of sterner stuff. It may shift and leak and groan like an old man sleeping, but it will never fall down.

Eventually the rain stops. The sky clears instantly and returns to its crisp, laundered blue. It smiles seductively as though the torrents were a figment of our imagination. The sun bursts brightly forth, the days grow warm again and my mood lifts. The wise men of the olive world say that, as with the grape, it is the September sun that determines the quality of the fruit, but the difference is that rain in October and early November is essential to the olive, because it gives that final, essential, extra burst of growth to the drupes. Unlike most northern hemisphere produce, the olive is not harvested in the autumn. It still has another six weeks' to two months' growth in it, and a nicely plumped olive, with its pulp rich in minerals and vitamins, produces a greater quantity of quality oil.

But this year, nature's waterworks have overreached themselves. We stalk the terraces taking note of the damage and the phenomenal growth that has taken place in the space of a week. Fascinated by the light and the luxuriance of the vegetation, I seek out the scents and sounds of a rainwashed world like a dog trained for truffle-hunting. The orange trees, dead as mummies when we bought the house, we have watched creeping back to life throughout the summer months. They are now sharp, five-foot-tall, brilliant green spears of life. And, what is more miraculous to me, they are laden with round green balls. Minuscule oranges. Such renascence hardly seems possible. I close my eyes. Like a squirrel preparing for harsh days, I store the fact that rebirth is a resource of life. Some creeping shadow warns me that I will need to keep this in mind.

A few feet to the left of the oranges, amid the tufted grass at the root of the prehistoric olive trunks, I detect puddles of purple and green, tiny, hard pellets. I pick one up to examine it and identify it as unripened olive fruit which the force of the rain has driven from the branches. I call to Michel, who is elsewhere, bent on his haunches photographing a harvest of bulbs which have metamorphosed into dwarf-sized narcissi overnight.

'We ought to net the trees before we lose the crop,' he suggests.

I try to reach René, but he is not at home. His wife promises to *faire le commission*, which means that she will tell him we called. He does not ring back, not this day or the next. We make another tour of the sodden, springy earth around the roots of the trees and agree that the ratio of fruit on the ground to fruit on the branches is still shifting. Whether the rain started the downward flow, or whether the olives have been attacked by a fly, or by another of the nine maladies René mentioned and which we know nothing about, or whether the fruit has simply ripened too early we cannot tell, but we decide that the grounds must be netted.

I am confident we can manage this part of the operation on our own without René and suggest to Michel that the Co-operative Agricole might be the very place to guide us. He agrees and waves me off in the Renault, which is becoming a greater health hazard every day, to purchase netting while he reads through my latest pages of work. Naturally, the purchase is not as straightforward as I had hoped.

The chief gardener at the co-operative, a ruddy-cheeked, bespectacled young man, is sent out to deal with me: the foreigner attempting to go native. His patience for such an animal clearly ran out seasons ago.

'*Oui?*'

'I would like to buy netting, please, for our olive trees.'

'Which colour?'

Colour? Price, quality, even dimensions, I was vaguely prepared for, but not colour. The French bourgeois obsession for matching and designing every item of house and gardenware cannot, surely, have stretched to the shade of olive-grove nets, can it?

'Does it matter?' I ask sheepishly, certain that my response is only going to bear out his already formed opinion, which is that I am a city-bred ninny wasting his precious time. He sighs loudly and theatrically and stomps off. I stay hesitantly where

I am until he spins round and orders me to follow him, which, obediently, I do. We arrive in front of a massive roll of bright red netting spooled on to an iron bar operated by a rusting handle which looks as though it has been plucked from one of those nineteenth-century laundry-wringers.

'*Rouge*,' he says.

I cannot disagree.

'Is this the one you want?'

'*Oui, peut-être.*' I am doing my best.

'*Deux francs vingt*,' he tells me as though, for someone as ignorant as myself, cost will be the deciding factor. I am taken aback by the price, which strikes me as extremely reasonable. Approximately 22p in English money.

'A metre?' I feel I should confirm the good news.

'*Par six, le longeur.*'

By six in length. We are getting somewhere. Sounds good, I tell him. He looks disappointed and slightly impatient with me and proceeds to tug at the red netting with his fingers until a small strip of it begins to split.

'*Eh, voilà!*'

I assume he has made this little test to prove to me that the net is not too difficult to cut, but no.

'You see, if you had decided upon the green . . .'

'Ah, the green . . .?'

'Two francs ninety.'

Tucked away at the back of an enormous hangar area, protected by corrugated roofing, is the green. Similarly rolled, marginally longer, but otherwise, to my eye, identical. He strides towards it, unfurls a few feet and begins tugging at it. Nothing happens.

'*Costaud*,' I confirm with the nod of a sage who knows what she is talking about. It is tougher, more resilient. It won't rip when, by mistake, someone – me – treads all over it. I understand and he is pleased with me. At least I think he is, because he grunts and begins to unroll a length of many metres in readiness for the cut.

'How many metres would you like?'

I smile, attempting charm. 'Well, I'm not exactly sure.'

The netting is dropped to the ground. A fellow gardener from somewhere far off calls, 'Frédéric!'

'*J'arrive!*'

I feel my time is running out. I begin to talk fast. 'We have sixty-four trees, so that would be . . . ?'

'What are the size, the reach of the branches? What age are the trees? Are they facing south? Have you measured the circumference of the root areas? What variety?'

To each question I shake my head.

Poor Frédéric is growing exasperated and I am mortified, knowing that I have played my part of the amateur olive farmer only too convincingly.

'I tell you what,' he suggests with a warmth I had not counted on at this stage. 'Buy a roll. *Pourquoi pas*? It is considerably cheaper and that way you can measure the lengths at home and cut the nets accordingly.'

It sounds like an excellent idea, and it lets us both off the hook. I agree wholeheartedly. He points me to the *caisse*, situated inside the shop, and asks me which car is mine. I signal the wreck parked near the gate and hurry off to pay. While in the shop, I pick up the odd extra purchase – oil for the chain on the chainsaw, blocks of olive-oil soap as hefty as building bricks, thirty kilos of dog biscuits – and pull out my chequebook. The girl rings up the items and announces a figure which is a little short of 5,000 francs.

'Five thou . . . ?'

It is then that I learn that I have just purchased 1,000 metres of green netting. I dare not change my mind so I smile wanly and write out a cheque which will just about empty my account.

Outside, I find Frédéric and his colleague closing up the car, which looks as though it has sprouted wings. Not surprisingly, the roll could not be squeezed into the boot, nor would it fit in the car's interior, so it has been wedged between the front passenger seat and the rear seat directly behind my driving place. On each side it is protruding from the open windows a full eighteen inches or more.

'Isn't this a little dangerous?' I mutter. Frédéric is not interested; he is now serving someone else. I start up the engine. Blue smoke billows forth, and off I roar, trying not to take the garden-centre gates with me.

By the time I haul up the drive, I am exhausted and my nervous system is shot to pieces. Half of Provence has hooted or yelled at me and, while I was being rudely overtaken on a roundabout by a very impatient gentleman, my precious netting actually dislodged his offside driving mirror and he seemed about ready to run me into the gutter. Still, I am home more or less in one piece and, more importantly, we have our *filets*. Michel is laughing loudly, No Name and her three remaining puppies are scrambling around my ankles, barking and mewling enthusiastically – they can smell the biscuits – but nothing we do, no matter how we shove or pull or tug, will shift the 1,000-metre roll of netting wedged in the car.

Exhausted, we finally manage to contact René. When he arrives and sees the netting he stops and stares at it in puzzled amazement. 'But why didn't you buy the white?' he demands.

How difficult can it be to lay a length of netting around the foot of a tree? Is it feasible that this work could take three men, and myself, as many days? There is a skill to it which I would never have foreseen. First, the brush-cutting machines need to clear a circle of approximately six metres in every direction around the foot of each tree. This is to make sure that the net does not get tangled in growing herbage and to facilitate the collection of the fallen olives later. After Michel and Quashia have completed this part of the process, the first day is almost over and the evening air has an oniony scent to it. I love it. Freshly mown grass never has quite the same piquancy. I assume it is the mixture of those extra ingredients: felled wild garlic, dandelion for mesclun, wild and unidentified Provençal herbs.

When the auspicious moment arrives for the laying of the first net, René explains that the ground needs to be covered to the farthest reach of every branch, wasting no metreage, cutting the netting as infrequently as possible and marking out the lengths immediately, by numbering both tree and net, so that next year the whole process is not a complete muddle while we *casse* our *têtes* trying to work out which length goes where. And while all this is going on, you are trying to decide how best to keep the overexcited puppies from sitting on the netting or on your feet every time you want to unroll a length or readjust the positioning of it. How much netting can three puppies chew and destroy while your back is turned for five minutes? The men allocate me the task of puppy patrol.

René's white netting is tougher than ours in the sense that it is harder and less flexible but it is not necessarily more durable. And it doesn't blend into the colours of nature so well. I prefer the green, but I keep that opinion very close to my chest, which is just as well, because when the sun shines through the branches hanging low like full skirts and the nets and the silvery underside of the leaves begin to glint, I am forced to revise my opinion. The entire effect resembles a cascading platinum sea. Green or white, nature creates magnificence.

Towards dusk on the third day, when the nets are in place, carefully arranged in a symmetrical formation that will allow not one poor migrant olive to escape, we lay boulders and sticks at strategic points to hinder movement and to create a cradle, so that with any wind or heavy rain the fruit will not roll away. I place a large stone at the border of a net and rise, feeling worn out in a positive, healthy way. The men are at work a terrace beneath me, unrolling the last of the netting, shouting to one another, debating. René, Quashia and Michel bathed in the golden light of evening. The late-autumn sunlight, honeyed and still, that is particular to this climate. The sight of the men on the land amid metres of netting calls to mind preparations for a rural wedding feast, with veils and dresses and local produce. A feast, yes, for at the end of all this, the ritual of the harvesting and pressing, there will be a grand *fête*. A street party held in the villages, a Mediterranean thanksgiving to *l'arbre roi de Provence* or *l'arbre immortel*.

The work we are doing here is keeping faith with the past. It has been acted out for thousands of years. The olive is *un arbre noble*, a noble tree. It survived the greatest deluge in history: that of Noah and his ark. Its branch was brought by the dove as a sign of peace and to show Noah that the rains had finally subsided. Even then it must have been highly respected. It is considered a divine tree, too. René has said to me on several occasions that there is no other artisan who works with tools which are several hundred years old. Indeed, in the eyes of the *oléiculteur*, the older the better. There is dignity and humility in this work. In the yielding to it, to the power and, sometimes, the cruelty of nature as well as to its phenomenal generosity, the fruits of which should not be wasted. I read somewhere this morning, in one of the many French books on *horticulture pratique* that litter the wooden table in my still undecorated *atelier*, yet another version of those bygone beginnings of olive farming, which is that the cultivation of olive groves and the pressing of the fruit began in Iran long before it was thought of in Greece. Old Testament territory. The Iranians took the olive to Greece, but it was the inhabitants of Phoenicia, an ancient territory which consisted of a narrow strip of coastal land bordering Syria, to the north-west of Palestine, who brought the trees to France some 800 years before Christ. That would be approximately 300 years before the Greeks arrived here. Or was it the Greeks those three centuries later, as most contend? The fact is that the history of the olive is so buried in the distant past that no one seems certain of its precise beginnings. Still, what is certain is that we are here today, Arab and European, embarking on a method of farming revered in both the Koran and the Bible – a gathering and pressing, almost as old as life itself.

Pressing the Olive

At long last the moment has arrived. We are about to begin our very first harvest: *la cueillette des olives*. It is a critical period because the fruit has to be gathered at precisely the right time and in the correct manner. The olives will not produce top-quality oil if they are picked while they are still too green. On the other hand, if the fruit is left on the trees too long and it overripens or grows wrinkled, from the moment the drupes are off the trees, they begin to oxidise, which gives the oil an unpleasant, bitter taste. This year, our first as olive farmers, we have a bumper crop and we will lose some of the fruit if it is not gathered and then delivered to the *moulin* within forty-eight hours. René advises us that we will need help, particularly in the light of our lack of experience. We accept his counsel and the following morning – the first occasion since we met him when he turns up on the day he has said he will be coming – he brings with him a motley collection of harvesters. Each of the five gatherers, one woman and four men, is presented to us, and each steps forward and gives us his or her name and profession. They treat us deferentially with, we suppose, the respect normally shown to proprietors, *oléiculteurs,* of a grand *domaine.* This is puzzling and makes us both a little awkward. We have not come across this class barrier here before. We would prefer a less formal relationship and I offer them bottles of water, for the day is warm and I want to lighten the mood.

'*Nous avons. Nous avons tous,*' they assure us politely, and retreat. They set about unloading their cars, which are parked on the flat, grassy bank that skirts the base of the hill and the lowest of the terraces. It is a beautiful late-November morning. The birds are chirruping and there is heat in the day. We leave the harvesters to their work and head off to begin our own picking stint at the top end of the land, promising to return later to see how their part of the *récolte* is progressing. I suspect René has divided us into two groups in this way so that should Michel and I, with our city fingers and clumsy unskilled ways, damage the fruit, which is all too easily done, our basketloads need not be mixed in with those collected by the professionals, where they could destroy the acid balance at the pressing.

What excites me is the thought of that first taste. I have read that there are over fifty different varieties of olive and I have bought and tasted and cooked with an assortment of oils. Some have been virgin, others extra-virgin, while a few have been of a lesser quality or made from mixed varieties of olives. We will soon be trying a single-variety oil, cold-pressed exclusively from our *cailletier* fruit. Perhaps at some point in my life I have used oil pressed from this southern French variety grown on these rocky coastal hills without being aware of it. Still, even if that were the case, they were not from *here,* not from this very hill. A geographical nuance, but it makes a world of difference to us. Part of the thrill lies in the anticipation. Does this farm, our humble terraces, produce fruit which can be ranked as first-class oil? We can only wait and see. Until then there is hard work to be done.

The gathering is backbreaking. And time-consuming. And there is no way round it. René does not hold with wooden rakes. No, every olive is picked from the tree by hand. That means stretching from ladders or climbing up in among the branches and reaching out to collect each olive individually, for they do not grow in bunches.

'But I read that the wooden rakes are good. They are used on many of the well-known estates,' I protest.

He shakes his grey-haired head adamantly. 'No. Whatever anyone says, the rakes can cause damage. Where there are two or three olives growing close to one another, almost in a cluster, the rake is bound to bruise at least one. No, we will climb the trees. You, Carol, can take a ladder.'

So here I am, battling with branches that flick me in the face, stretching, wobbling and gripping on for dear life. On top of which, when I have managed to clutch hold of an olive or two, I must not squeeze it too hard or hold it too long in my sticky palms and overheat it. And I have to take care not to split the nets, whether they be white or green, which encircle the base of the trees. Or, worse, if the foot of the ladder gets caught up in the netting, the ladder and I will go toppling over, spilling two hours' work on to the ground. It is about now that I am beginning to wish we had bought a vineyard. At least cultivation and harvest are at ground level.

Our first visit to the *moulin*. Heading off into the hills with René once more, we are planning to visit two mills within about twenty minutes' drive of one another. René wants us to choose where our fruit is to be pressed, particularly given my preferences for all matters organic. Our first stop is the mill recommended by him, where he takes the harvests from his other farms. Like so many of these traditional agricultural concerns, it is a family-run business. Altogether, on his four farms and including ours, René is husbanding 720 trees so, not surprisingly, he is a familiar and well-loved face at the mill. When we arrive he takes us first to the shop set on a cobbled hill above the mill, which is the tourist arm of the family's trade.

Inside, everybody kisses and embraces and we are introduced as the patrons of the villa farm in the hills overlooking the coast. During a brief tour of the merchandise on sale – Provençal napkins, various jams and soaps and objects such as pepper and salt pots carved out of olive wood – we observe the steady flow of men with children, or lone adolescents, bringing their farms' early-season pickings. Their olives are delivered in large, woven panniers, about the size of a modest laundry basket, resembling those which in bygone days were strapped to the side of donkeys or packhorses. Other loads are delivered in plastic crates, and a few arrive in bulging sacks which look like outmoded coalbags, though these are now discouraged because they do not meet the latest European Union standards of hygiene. The fruit is placed on a whacking great metal scale, where it is weighed, and then it is stacked on the floor in a queue alongside a chute which will shunt the drupes down to the mill itself.

While all this weighing and stacking is taking place, a lady cashier is filling in lilac tickets and handing them out. The tickets provide each farmer or gatherer with a receipt which states the precise quantity of olives delivered. Later, after the *pression*, it will also confirm the quantity of oil produced from those olives.

How the oil is measured is fascinating but somewhat difficult to grasp, convoluted, I'd say, and dates back to the days when farmers arrived with their olives in measures known as *une motte*. Literally translated a *motte* is a mound. One measure – *une mesure* – is equal to twelve and a half kilos of olives, the cashier (one of only two staff at the mill who is employed and not a member of the family) explains to us.

'Why twelve and a half kilos?' I ask ingenuously. It seems a curious and rather complicated figure for calculation. Apparently the containers used in the olden days to carry the olives held precisely twelve and a half kilos, though I refrain from asking why. Across the lip was a measuring stick. When the loaded olives were flush with the measuring stick it contained twelve and a half kilos of fruit. Twenty of these containers equalled *une motte*. Now it grows a bit foggy, at least for a mathematical pea-brain such as myself who is silently trying to calculate twenty multiplied by twelve and a half!

Until today, I have always blithely assumed that kilos of pressed olives liquefy into litres of oil, which seems logical to me. When I mention this, Michel nods his agreement, but René and the staff and family of the *moulin* shake their heads gravely. '*Mais non*,' they tell us. 'The production of oil is valued and measured by weight.' One litre of oil, we learn, weighs 900 grams, or nine-tenths of a kilo. Lord!

If the fruit is ripe and healthy and plump, and therefore rich in oil, it is hoped that a measure (twelve and a half kilos) will achieve 2.7 kilos of oil which, divided by 900, equates to approximately three litres. In other words, after a phenomenally complicated system of calculation, the ideal is to produce fruit which will yield three litres of oil for every twelve and a half kilos of olives, or sixty litres for every 'mound'.

Phew! We are exhausted, my head is spinning, and it is not yet 8.30 in the morning. I am about to ask why the system is computed in such a mindbogglingly difficult way when Michel grabs me by the shirtsleeves and says, 'While we're here, *chérie*, why don't we buy some of their house-produced tapenade?' Anything to stop me further scrambling our brains.

To reach the level where the mill is operating, René ushers us back out of the shop on to the cobblestoned street, through another door to the left and down a narrow and stupendously rickety flight of wooden stairs. I feel as if I am going backwards in time. Added to which, the temperature is falling. At mill floor-level it is almost arctic. Every exhalation of breath is visible.

We *have* gone backwards in time. As we enter the mill, our senses are socked by the thumping and turning of a whole array of machines, and the air is so heavy with the dense aroma of freshly pulped olive paste you feel you want to shove it off you, as if it were an unwanted blanket. At 8.30 in the morning, it makes my head reel. As does the rough red wine handed to us along with thick wedges of locally baked bread topped with ham cured from a pig reared and slaughtered in the village. It is a peasants' breakfast, offered to us by a wan girl of no more than fourteen who is accompanied by a brother of about nine.

Once we have been fed, the children retreat politely to stand guard at the table groaning with their family produce. Silently, arms at their sides like small soldiers, they await the next batch of ravenous *oléiculteurs*. René is battling against the din to explain the mechanics of the machinery, but I am more fascinated by the children. They look like waifs, serious-faced with dark, penetrating eyes that, though gentle, might have witnessed a thousand hard seasons. Alongside them is their loaf, whose circumference is little short of that of a juggernaut tyre. Their clothes are outdated and stitch-worn. They could be extras from a BBC Dickens drama, characters out of a Thomas Hardy novel. It seems incredible to me that we live somewhere equidistant from this scene and the gaudy glitz and *escroquerie* of Cannes.

The noise down here is impossible. I cannot hear or understand a word that is being spoken. René talks on, lips moving. I have no idea what he is trying to tell us. I turn to the miller, who says nothing. He has returned to his work. Both he and his assistant are wrapped in scarves knotted at the neck and substantial jackets even though they are moving continuously, shunting trays of mashed olive paste and enormous bottles filled with the freshly pressed green oil. All around me, machines are turning, milling, thrumming, spewing out liquid or excreting dried paste. A fire is roaring behind a small glass window, no bigger than a portable television screen. It is fuelled by dried olive waste. Each ancient machine feeds the next, it seems. They are interconnected as though they were all part of some enormous Heath Robinson invention which today, according to the miller, talking with his fingers and beckoning us over into a corner away from the racket, is taking four and a half kilos of olives to press one litre of virgin oil. Most of these early-season fruits are not quite ripe enough, he explains. The fruit arriving after Christmas which will have had longer on the trees to plumpen and grow black, should be better, should produce the optimum.

We are led through to a *cave* where labelled bottles glow with oil turning from green to gold as the sediment settles. They await the return of their owners, who will cart them away and store them safely in cool, darkened depositories. This mill, I see, is rigorous about making certain that no grower's olives are mixed with another's if they are a single-estate press, as ours will be.

I am fascinated by how the remains of everything are put to good purpose. Olive-oil soap is made from the residue of the third or even fourth pressings, and the desiccated paste is burned in the fire which heats the water and operates as the central-heating system, such as it is. Ecologically speaking, the olive is an all-rounder. Nothing goes to waste. Every last drop of oil is wrung out of the fruit and only in the making of tapenade is the stone extracted and thrown away.

Before we set off for the second mill, the longer-established of the two, everybody shakes hands enthusiastically. 'Next time, Christophe will be here,' we are assured. He is the patron and has gone hunting today. There is much kissing and back-slapping and promises to meet again soon. They enjoy the idea that foreigners take an interest in this most venerable of trades. '*Beaucoup d'Américains visitent içi*,' we are told. Thumbs and fingers are rubbed together, heads nod gravely to express the sums of money handed over by the Americans in return for trinkets, souvenirs and glossy books detailing the history of the olive and Provençal life in general.

'And the English?' I ask hopefully.

As one, the family shake their heads. I appear to have touched upon a sensitive and sorry subject. '*Mais non*,' returns Madame in a conspiratorial tone. '*Les Anglais* have no interest in anything!'

The second *moulin* is an altogether different affair. Situated in a field at the end of a deserted lane, in the middle of nowhere, it was founded in 1706. It looks as though it must originally have been a peasant farm with an outbarn which at some early stage was transformed into a mill, and has never been decorated since. The crumbling outer walls are of a washed pink that is popular in certain parts here but which I often feel belongs more comfortably in Suffolk. First impression: there is little about this place, aside from the surrounding countryside and mountainous backdrop, that is welcoming. One step through the door and we are directly in the mill, a cavernous space with a room temperature barely above forty degrees Fahrenheit. It is sunless and gloomy. There is no shop here, no tourist attractions of any sort, which rather pleases me. As before, we are instantly knocked backwards by the dense, palpable odour of crushed olives. Here, though, there is no offer of comforting slabs of bread and ham and red wine to douse our senses. Here there are no trimmings whatsoever. The place has one sole function: the cold pressing of extra-virgin oil.

The pressing wheel and floor have been hewn out of massive slabs of craggy stone rendered smooth by centuries of use. Somehow the heavy stone adds to the keen, wintry atmosphere.

I exhale and watch my breath rise like smoke. Ahead of us are two farmers engaged in business with the miller, or perhaps she is the miller's wife, who appears to be discussing their accounts – René, because he has been here only once before, is not quite sure who she is. We are all of us strangers, which suits me, because it allows a sense of discovery.

René guides our attention towards the stone wheel which crushes the fruit. It is imposing, almost monolithic, and I shiver at the thought of someone getting fingers, or any other body parts, trapped beneath it. It is stained with what look like clumps of dark peat but on closer inspection we see that, of course, it is coated with trapped olive paste. Passing along to another completely indescribable contraption we find at its base oil trickling at a snail's pace into a wooden (olive wood) dustpan-like box. The arrival of the oil appears to be a very discreet and low-key affair. There is none of the slosh and flow of the last mill. Nor the horrendous, ear-splitting noise, though to be fair, the machines here are no longer running, having completed their last pressing for the day even though it is only a little after 10.30 in the morning. Looking closely at the system, with René drawing our attention to certain features here and there, we learn that it requires more fruit for less yield. It takes approximately six kilos of fruit to produce a litre of oil, even with the ripest and richest of drupes. René closes his eyes and goes through a swift mental calculation. If we use the other *moulin*, Appassionata can expect, on average, depending on the weather and the harvest, to press approximately 250 litres of oil a year. Here we would net less than 200.

'Yes, but here it is cold-pressed, extra-virgin.'

'The other, too,' he assures us.

'In any case, two hundred litres is more than sufficient for our needs,' I counter.

Michel quietly reminds me that our share would be eighty-three or eighty-four litres from the first *moulin*; if we press our fruit here, somewhere around sixty-five litres. The remainder is René's. I glance at René, who merely shrugs. The miller woman, dressed in boots, full woollen skirt and velveteen shirt, her grey hair slicked back in a tight, uncompromising bun, is paying us no attention, engaged as she is with her clients. They are weighing panniers of violet olives and calculating figures: the cost of the pressing, no doubt. Perhaps for the first time, I am made acutely aware of this as a business, not a dream. Olive farming and oil-pressing is a livelihood, and these people are close to the land and bear its vagaries and hardships. They cannot afford the romance which swims about in my actress's head. I wander off to investigate further, and to be alone.

Beyond the mill, though still under the same roof, I discover a *cave* with storage spaces dug out of rock and cut with stone-shelved corners. It is windowless and dark. Two or three dozen glass jars encased in wicker are kept there. Each must be capable of holding fifteen or twenty litres of liquid.

'They are called *"bonbonnes à goulot large"*. In the olden days, the Romans stored their oil in amphorae, tall clay jars with handles, which were originally turned or baked in Spain and then shipped to Italy. They were not dissimilar to the oval terra-cotta pots you keep in your garden and fill with flowers. These are a more modern version, if you can describe anything in here as modern.' It is René. He and Michel are once again at my side.

Some of these thick-necked demijohns, the *bonbonnes*, are still empty, while others have already been filled with the deep green, freshly pressed oil which, from this distance and in this crepuscular light, resembles seawater or steeped seaweed juice. Judging by its colour and by the viscid juice slipping heavily into the dustpan apparatus, the quality of the oil here is richer, more luscious and aromatic.

'I like this place better,' I whisper to Michel, who laughs and replies, '*Mais oui, chérie.* The question is which mill would better suit our needs, not which would serve as a film set.'

'I still prefer this one,' I insist calmly.

Outside, the morning is warming to a bright, clear day, so clear that we can see for miles the shrubby details on the surrounding hills and valleys and the snowcaps on the high, distant Alps. I close my eyes and inhale the fresh air, rich with the smell of pine resin. The heat of the sun against my eyelids is a comforting relief.

Strolling back to our car, we learn from René that there is an olive tree growing in Roquebrune which we might like to take a look at. There are several villages down here with that name, but the one to which he is referring is the rather glamorous Roquebrune-Cap-Martin, situated on the cloud-capped road between Monte Carlo and Italy. Michel knows the place; in fact, he has visited it on several occasions. Its marvellous restaurant, Le Roquebrune, which has been owned and managed by the family of Mama Marinovich since its inception, has been a favourite of his for years. The village is also known for its mediaeval houses, which have been carved out of the rocks. At Roquebrune, a few kilometres from Menton, the gateway to Italy, grows an olive tree believed to be 1,000 years old. Who planted it? I ask. Does anyone know? It is 1,500 years too young to be a souvenir left by the Greeks and almost a millennium too young to have been planted by the Romans during their marches north from the heart of their empire as they constructed the Via Aurelia, the great highway stretching from Ventimiglia to Aix. The Romans, with Agrippa as their consul, were building roads and tracing out this land of Provincia, creating cadastrel surveys and scientific mappings, before the tree was ever in existence. Even Charlemagne, crowned emperor of the West in AD 800, preceded it, as did the Saracens, who were looting and sacking the littoral even as Charlemagne and his children were dividing up the country for their heirs.

Might it have been a peace offering to the counts of

Provence from Rome? A thousand years after the birth of Christ, somewhere around the date the tree was planted, Provence was being returned to Rome and inaugurated as part of the Holy Roman Empire. The Saracens, having created havoc and terror for a hundred years, had been conquered and driven out and Provence, though back under the ruling thumb of Rome, was enjoying a certain independence, a bit of peace and quiet after so many centuries of strife. Alas, it was not to last. For within a century or two the counts of Provence ceded the province to the counts of Toulouse, and they in turn to the counts of Barcelona, and so the chain goes on, right up to the liberation of Provence by the allies from the Germans in August 1944, an event to which our friend René, standing beside us now, bears witness. Still, this noble tree is believed to be one of the oldest in the world. By what stroke of fortune has this single specimen survived?

Michel suggests we make a detour, a slightly elongated one, a round trip of approximately 110 kilometres, to pay homage to this most holy of trees. I agree wholeheartedly. René, who does not want to come with us, bids us *bon appétit* and leaves us to it.

Less than an hour later, we are swooping and turning like a bird in flight along the alpine road. It is a giddy, spectacular altitude. The endless hairpin bends above the sea on this infamous descent and then ascent from La Turbie, with its magnificent Roman ruins, make you catch your breath and pray your brakes won't fail, and there's precious little chance to enjoy the view if you are driving. Michel is at the wheel. He drives fast, but with great skill, and I am leaning out of the window, unafraid, hair flying in the wind, whipping my face, eyes watering, thrilled by the panorama all around me, following the sweep of the hundreds of metres of rocky face that lead dramatically to the Med.

Somewhere near here, Princess Grace of Monaco, formerly

the actress Grace Kelly, lost her life. Her sports car went over the cliffside and she was killed instantly. From where I am now, you can see why. The memory of that accident sobers me for an instant and I crawl back into my seat and gaze at the rock towering to the left of us. It's then that I spot the village high above us. Rising out of the stone towards a linen-blue sky, it resembles a drawing from a book of fairy tales illustrated by Arthur Rackham. Even more so when I realise that perched atop its pinnacle is a castle with a tower.

We park the car at the foot of the village, in what was the ancient castle's barbican, and hike the winding lane to the *vieux village*. Much to our dismay, because we are starving, every single restaurant is closed. It is *la fermeture annuelle*, 15 November to 15 December, a time when many businesses shut up shop in preparation for the upcoming festivities – Christmas and New Year are a busy season on the Côte d'Azur.

We stride and puff and arrive at a perfectly empty square, and what strikes me instantly is that although there is not a soul abroad, there is no sense that this is a ghost town. In the centre of this pleasingly airy *place* is an olive tree fenced and surrounded by benches. It is unquestionably an aged specimen, and well preserved, but I am disappointed. I had expected something more spectacular. The girth of its trunk is probably three metres, which is barely more than our own trees. I stroll to the cliff's edge and look out across the rippling water, lambent in the sunlight, towards Cap Martin and, in the other direction, to the principality of Monaco with its curiously out-of-place skyscrapers. Michel comes up behind me and wraps his arms around me. 'I've had a good look. I don't think that's the tree we're after,' he says. 'Let's investigate.'

We make our way through the *vieux village*, up a hill, down a winding stairwell, everywhere tiled and cobbled and polished with the gleaming shine of a proud housewife's doorstep, passing through Place Ernest Vincent, with its obsolete prison before us, until we spot a sign for the *olivier millénaire*. 'Look!' I cry.

Triumphantly, with the air of adventurers reassured that their navigations are on track, we begin to descend. A profusion of hillside trees, fluffy with green leaves similar to the willow – a variety of tamarisk, if I am not mistaken – overhang the pathway. We are plunging down a steep path. In former days, a donkey trail, no doubt, used to transport victuals from the fields at sea level up to the homes fashioned out of the rocks. We are walking in the footsteps of a billion and more travellers – soldiers, other lovers, farmers and farmhands – to pay homage to a tree. And lo and behold, 200 metres or so further along, there it is, growing out of a wall on the terraced cliffside. This elephantine miracle is not fenced in. It is not on display. It is simply there. Being. Branches reach out like the tentacles of an octopus. Its roots, like those of a banyan tree, are sprawling everywhere, spilling over, bursting forth with their sheer determination to live, to survive. The force is taking earth and stone with it.

Michel and I stand side by side, silenced, gazing in awe at this monumental symbol of creation. Then we spin round, seawards, to take in the view unfolding before us, flocks of starlings swooping and tacking against a vigorous blue sky. Even at this precipitous height we can hear the gentle lap of the water washing the coastal rocks and beaches so far beneath us. We incline our heads and gaze down upon the coastline, eyes eastwards to the cap of St Martin, where W.B. Yeats once spent a holiday, Queen Victoria was a regular visitor and the architect Le Corbusier drowned.

Everywhere is warm and still and calm. *Calme* in the French sense, meaning untroubled and at peace. Without a word our bodies reach for one another and I feel the warmth of the sun on Michel's skin.

'*Je t'aime.*'

Rarely have I felt so in harmony with life, so humbled by its magnificence. I pace out the distance between the farthest visible reaches of the trunk extensions of the tree and measure fifteen metres. Here we are, some 900 feet above sea level, in the presence of a growing organism which has stood sentry over this landscape for ten centuries. At this moment I can comprehend the millennia of reverence given to the olive tree, to its wisdom and unmatched nobility. For a heartbeat, all seems clear. The world is pure and the miracle of life washes through me.

We return to the village, deciding to continue up to the castle, moving closer to the sun, passing open windows which look out on to one of the most breathtaking coastal views I have ever laid eyes on. I pause and catch snippets of language, barely audible radios transmitting in both French and Italian. We are on the border of both cultures, yet so much about this village was born of times when France and Italy were not divided as they are today.

The climb is winding and the lanes are cobbled and tiled and pristinely clean. From the keep, the views are, yet again, stupendous. Several hang-gliders are drifting on slipstreams high above the water. What a spot for it: to take off from here like a bird and wallow in the boundlessness.

We walk on. I read aloud from a booklet given to us by the friendly lady at the ticket booth. We are about to discover the oldest castle in France, the sole example of the Carolingian style. It was built by a count from Ventimiglia, Conrad I, to keep those dratted Saracens at bay. Later, it was remodelled by the Grimaldi family who, of course, still reign over Monte Carlo.

What a coup for one small village to be in possession of both the oldest castle in France and a tree claimed to be the oldest living olive in the world. The leaflet also informs us that the inhabitants of Roquebrune believe that the creation of the world is a 'thought from God' and that while He was creating this particular village His mind was particularly well disposed to man. For that reason, they value their good fortune and make it their business to honour their environment. Too right! With such a philosophy, they deserve their daily sightings of this seascape and their miraculous olive tree.

René telephones to inform us that the *moulin* of my choice is to be closed down. Almost 300 years in existence, and the very winter we decide to take our custom there it ceases to trade.

'But how can that be?' I cry.

'It doesn't meet the European Union health standards.'

His advice is that we had better take our olives to his mill. Half a dozen crates of olives are sitting in the dark at the back of our garage waiting to be pressed and if we delay, they will be oxidised. Though stung by an initial bout of mistrust and suspicion, I have no reason to be disappointed with the mill we saw first. The proprietor – the chap we did not meet on our initial visit – is a splendid fellow with cheeks as red as his checked shirts and a paunch which flops over his sinking jeans and causes his string vest to protrude in a comical, bib-like fashion. He welcomes us extravagantly, takes care of us admirably. And I warm to him all over again when that long-awaited first trickle of oil from our own pressed olives drizzles from the stainless steel tap.

'*Venez vite, mes amis!*' he bellows. 'Come quickly!'

By now, it is spluttering and gushing green-gold gallons in fits and starts. Nervously, excitedly, we pick our way across the mill floor, skidding and skating because the surface is an ice rink from the dregs of a season's oil and paste, to taste, please God, our ambrosial liquid. It is a tense moment.

Michel, Monsieur *le propriétaire*, known to us now as Christophe, and myself lean in close over one single dessert spoonful and inhale its aroma. Will we like it? Will we be satisfied? We sip in turns. I go first. Six eyes meet apprehensively, but there is not a shadow of a doubt. The texture is velvet-smooth with a flavour of lightly peppered lemons.

'Oh God, it's delicious!' I croon.

We are mightily proud. Christophe, after filling a wooden spoon with another precious few drops, dunks a chunk of the local rough bread into the cloudy liquid and chews pensively. Save for the thundersome turning and clunking of machines, there is a gripping silence. His *fils*, the young miller we met the first time we came, looks on while a motley clutch of farmers who are awaiting the results of their own *pression* flock round us eagerly. How they love these *petits* dramas. And then, in thick Provençal accent, Christophe declares our produce *beurre du soleil*. Butter of the sun, he cries loudly, followed by the all-important quality distinction, '*Extra!*'

Everybody cheers. There is much shaking of hands, slapping of backs, kissing and hugging and, of course, pouring of wine while Michel and I, grinning from ear to ear with the pride and happiness of a birth, are also doing our damnedest not to fall about laughing.

Outside, at our table in the garden, lashings of burnished oil, our very own oil, are being decanted by Vanessa and Michel from the five-litre plastic containers supplied by Christophe at the mill into numerous elegant or uniquely shaped wine bottles. All year we have been merrily quaffing their contents, cleaning them, collecting them and storing them away for this most auspicious day. Christmas is upon us once more, and this one is to be celebrated. Clarisse is designing some delicate, exquisite labels and while the others pour, we are spending our hours in front of a roaring fire ticketing the full bottles and dating them before Vanessa's friend Jerôme carts them off and stows them away in the crepuscular cool of the summer kitchen downstairs. There, over the coming weeks, the olive fruit sediment will settle and the clear oil will become a glorious primrose-gold.

Mellifluous carols, broadcast live from Notre-Dame Cathedral in Paris, are playing on the radio. A blue fir tree perfumes our home with a spicy happiness. Michel purchased it from a bankrupt antique-dealer in the square opposite the old port in Cannes where, aside from this festive season, retired gentlemen with dubious histories pass their afternoons playing boules. To honour this, our very first harvest, he has decorated it entirely in swathes of golden trimmings and glass.

The girls are spending their holidays with us this year and along with them has arrived Jerôme, who is eighteen and disturbingly gorgeous. Twice I have invited him to come and help me in the kitchen and on both occasions Vanessa has lovingly whispered in my ear: 'Please, *chère* Carol, resist flirting with my friend.' In a day or two, Anni and Robert, Michel's parents, will arrive, followed by my mother, for St Sylvestre, New Year's Eve. My father and sister, both being in the entertainment business, are working in England. Still, Appassionata is stocked for a full house and the holidays are set to be a joyous affair. Our turkey – for now we are in possession of an oven, which stands alone in our empty, still-to-be constructed kitchen – is being lubricated with oil from our own reserve. It is a moving and significant moment which we honour appropriately with long-stemmed flutes of champagne. To accompany our *apéritif*, as a pre-lunch appetiser, I prepare bruschetta, toasting thick slices of six-cereal bread which I top with sliced tomatoes straight from the vines in my thriving vegetable patch and season with dried herbs and salt and then grill. While the toast is still warm, I decorate it with strips of fresh basil leaves picked from our herb garden and then generously oil them – Appassionata oil, naturally – adding only black pepper.

We gather at the table in the garden and eat in the end-of-year sunshine, chattering noisily in French – French language, French manners: we are knitting together as a French family – knowing that later, when the winter sun has begun to sink behind the cypress tops, slipping out of sight beyond the mountains, we can curl up indoors with books and music and doze in front of the fire. While the others clear the table and stack the washing up, I disappear to my den for a few hours to print out my scripts ready for Michel to take back to Paris after Christmas. He has clients waiting to read them. Afterwards, I intend to close the door on my work and forget about it for a few days. I need to rest, relax and partake of the holiday season with our loved ones.

As evening falls, the wintry sunset patterns the sky a pale, streaky rose. My work done, I run my fingers across the stacks of freshly printed pages standing on my table in thirteen neat piles and turn to gaze out of the window. The Mediterranean coast is growing dark and still. I cannot see the fortress and dungeons where the Man in the Iron Mask was imprisoned, cannot even detect the silhouettes of the islands, but the images live on in my memory and have fed me my story. Thirteen episodes, partially set on the isle of Ste Marguerite.

Beyond this private space of mine I hear the ripple of laughter. I smell that woody smokiness of crackling logs burning briskly. The others await me. Michel and his teenage girls, so staggeringly grown-up, so suddenly filled with a confidence I am sure I have never known, and Jerôme, the first of what will no doubt be a long procession of handsome young suitors over the summers and winters to come. Summers to come . . .

I don't go to join them, not immediately. I linger by the glass, aware of my reflection. Of me looking back at myself. I am in pensive mood, assessing what has been achieved, often my way after a long work stint. After many years of wandering, I have found my base. We have our shabby home. We have produce too – oil – and good men to help us. We have a story to sell; with luck it will be our way forward. With luck, it will settle our affairs with Mme B. Maintaining the house is a struggle, but we are just about managing. It has been a productive year, and I am grateful for it. Nonetheless, something is nagging at me, tugging at my floating balloon. Can life really turn out this good? Can I really be this happy? What if it should all fall apart? I have opened myself up now. Yielded to love. Trusted someone. The loss would be twice as devastating.

Steeped in these dark evening musings, I am not at first aware of the diesel van coming up the drive. I stare at it almost without seeing it and then move through to the *salon*, where the others are gathered.

Michel jumps to his feet. '*Jerôme, s'il te plaît.*'

'Who's that?' I ask no one in particular. 'Are we expecting somebody?' The men hurry from the house while the girls, basking on cushions, pay me no attention. I stare at their concentration. Clarisse is sketching; Vanessa, ears plugged to her Walkman, is learning Russian from a tape. Whisky, the last of the puppies and no longer a puppy, is snuggled in Vanessa's lap. I hear several male voices shouting.

'Do we know what's happening?' I ask again. Neither girl responds. Curious, and bewildered by their lack of interest, I stride back to my *atelier*, to the window which overlooks the parking lot, to find out what is going on. Quashia has arrived. He is accompanied by a faithful quartet of Arab colleagues who are all hovering by the rear doors of the van. I frown, puzzled. Michel is climbing into the van and he and Quashia are conversing or debating. Two of the Arabs are then instructed to cross the parking area and collect a wooden pallet which they place at the foot of the rear doors on the bitumened ground. Something is being delivered, that is clear, but what?

'Do either of you girls know what this is all about?' I shout through to the *salon*.

Still they don't seem to have heard me. I am about to get cross when, from out of the van, comes a curious-looking plant, sitting in a saucer-shaped terracotta pot the size of an early television satellite dish. The plant must be exceptionally heavy because it is being lowered painstakingly on to the work pallet. Then slowly, awkwardly, Jerôme and the Arabs hump it along the walkway beside the pool and mount the outside staircase to our open front door, which is where I am now eagerly awaiting them.

'What in heaven's name—'

'Where shall we put it?' begs Michel. I turn, swamped by indecision. Half the room is already taken up by the Christmas tree. There are cushions everywhere. Presents, shoes, sweaters, general holiday detritus have all spread across the room. Michel does not wait for me to respond. The men are sweating and staggering.

'There,' he commands, and the plant is delivered into the house, lifted ever so carefully from the pallet and placed on to the tiled floor. Quashia and the men bid us *bonsoir*, shake hands and retreat. Michel sees them out and returns to survey his gift. Or rather mine, for clearly I am the recipient; the only person who has not been cognisant of the arrival of this wonder.

'Happy Christmas, *chérie*,' whispers Michel, and kisses me on the mouth. 'It's not as ancient as the *olivier millénaire*, but it's as close as I could find.'

I am speechless, gazing at this extraordinary gift which stands six feet tall, has a trunk like a sculpted rhino's leg and, according to its label, is named *Beaucarnea*, hails from South America and is 150 years old. What most puzzles me is that this spectacular exotic is growing in a saucer-deep pot. Doesn't it have roots? All eyes are upon me, waiting, the girls grinning, as I turn to Michel and kiss him. '*Merci*,' I whisper, for I can barely speak, so overwhelmed am I by the sheer craziness of this man's love. All niggling fears evaporate. What am I worrying about? It has been a magnificent year.

Dark Days

After the holidays, some time around late January (the month Matisse described as a 'rich and silvered light essential to the spirit of the artist'), when every last straggly olive has been culled from the trees, pruning will begin. Alas, Michel and I cannot stay for it. Quashia, who took the train to Marseille a few days ago, bound for the boat which, by now, will have transported him home to the town of Constantin in northern Algeria, where he is spending the remainder of the season of Ramadan with his wife, seven sons, one daughter and sixteen grandchildren, will return to look after No Name and caretake for us. Vanessa and Jerôme have agreed to stay on for a day or two to await his return. She is taking Whisky with her when she leaves. Michel and I have work to do. For this year, our first as olive farmers, our contribution is at an end. Sadly, we will also be absent from the celebrations of the *fête des oliviers*, held on the last Saturday in January in the streets of many of the inland Provençal villages, during which strangers and natives alike are invited to tastings from the various mills and single-estate oils or simply to party. The one local to us is to be held in the streets of the village of Vallauris and, we understand from René, our own mill is represented. As is their tradition, Christophe and his three sons will deck themselves out in local Provençal costumes and offer *dégustations* of the various oils they produce. They even display a small working model of the mill which actually presses olives.

Meanwhile, Michel and I are returning to our separate, bachelor-style existences in London and Paris, meeting when and where we can, grabbing a day here or a weekend there, burying ourselves and our desire for one another in professional energies. Going back to our 'real' lives. But can the cut and thrust of the metropolis still be thought of as our real life? It is confusing. I have frequently heard friends who originally hailed from various far-flung corners of the globe and ended up in London complain that they don't know where they belong. I am beginning to understand that displacement, although I myself have been a traveller all my adult life. But now my heart is in France. Here, I wake in the mornings thinking: I am where I want to be. Here, I swim, garden, spend hours at the outdoor markets shopping for vegetables and fresh fish, natter with the local stallholders about the quality of this or that home-grown produce, marvel over the range and choice on display and then bury myself away in my studio, writing stories.

Still my work and history remain in England. Back there, I stare out of rehearsal-room windows, dreaming of what? Of shrubs and herbs, of the possibility of rearing goats and vines, and of the man I love so passionately. At the end of the day, I race to the local shop, negotiating a trolley around row upon row of shelves and neon lighting, grab some prewashed salads in bags and then gratefully close the door of my little flat, which these days feels as impermanent as a hotel, shutting out the fractious bustle of city life. There I prepare a solitary meal, unless I have managed to catch up with a frantically busy friend or two not seen for months on end, and when I set off again for work, some kind lady plasters my face in make-up while I fret about my figure and ever-increasing wrinkles and the problems of an actress who is fast saying *au revoir* to forty.

Life's rich pattern. I am more than fortunate to have both the gregarious life of an actress and the solitary days of a writer, but, from time to time, it is confusing and on occasion unsettling. And there is no doubt that, because I am in England less and less often, the spaces I had staked out as mine in the circles and worlds I have long inhabited are disappearing, filled by others. Friends call less regularly, unless they happen to be passing through the south of France and decide to drop by for a few days. My agent calls less frequently: actresses who are on the spot are offered the roles I might have played had I been around. Sometimes I feel people think I have emigrated to the moon.

But when I mention this dilemma to Michel, he looks bemused. 'I don't know why you feel you have to choose,' he says. 'Why can't you encompass the whole? A woman who has a multilayered existence.' And perhaps it really is that simple. It's me who complicates it.

It is St Valentine's Day. Michel is attending a television festival in Monte Carlo, which means he can spend a week at the farm. I am on location in Wales and cannot get away. I send him a dozen red roses and receive a dozen from him. And then the telephone rings in my hotel room. I catch the background bustle of festival activity, the chink of *apéritif* glasses, issuing from the hotel bar, and I hear excitement in Michel's voice. I miss him so badly it hurts.

'The English are in!' he says. For a moment I am nonplussed. And then it dawns on me. My thirteen-part series will need several partners but, given that it is the story of a thirteen-year-old

English girl, it would be almost impossible to film without an English network. Monte Carlo was to be Michel's first attempt to finance the production. I am staggered.

'Any chance that you could fly down here for a couple of days and meet up with the head of drama?"

Well, I am not filming at the weekend. I could drive to London and take the plane . . . Yes!

Saturday at Appassionata is the date. The English television executive, delighted to have an excuse to linger in the south of France for an extra day or two and to wriggle out of the mind-grinding business of buying and flogging programmes, is more than happy to have lunch with us at our home.

February is traditionally a wet month on the Côte d'Azur. So, just in case, I prepare lunch at the table inside. From the dining room, through the tall French windows that command a view over the front terraces across to the sea and distant horizon, I gaze down upon the splendidly pruned olive trees. They are a magnificent spectacle. With their height lopped and their remaining branches hanging low and wide, tumbling almost to ground level, they remind me of whirling dervishes.

One of the great joys of Appassionata is its ability to surprise; the ever-evolving, complex shift and balance of the surrounding nature. According to time of day, season and the vagaries of the weather, the hills, mountains, forests and the sweep of the watery bay transform themselves. We live in a world of kaleidoscopic colours, softening or deepening shades, and an array of perfumes; tantalisingly sweet, fragrant, musky or dusky. Now, in this month, when the sun is busy elsewhere and the dove-grey skies lour and clouds bank up thickly above us, the deciduous trees are naked skeletons tightly withholding any promise of spring. Save for the almond which, though leafless, has already begun to burst with the palest of pastel-pink blossoms. Beyond our farm, the distant mountains appear as dense, stubby shadows while the sea, an ominous battle-grey, is lifted to poetry by slender rays of nacreous silver.

This is an altogether unencountered tapestry. These nuances of shadow and light are steelier than in the brighter, warmer seasons. Still, February justly claims its own stark beauty, and it is always wonderful to be home again. My sole concern is No Name, who is angry with me and will not draw close. She glowers at me from various corners of the room or peers in through windows from the terraces, refusing to approach. Whether her anger is born of grief for the loss of her puppies or my absence I cannot tell, but nothing I do consoles or appeases her. And what is worse, while her reproachfulness towards me is unrelenting, with Michel she is playful and tender.

I hear the smoky cough of Michel's old powder-blue Mercedes. He is returning from the station in Cannes, where he has collected Harold. I have met Harold before. In fact, I have worked with him, as an actress. He is a well-meaning Brit who has spent his entire career in the poorly paid service of children's and adolescent drama (why it is that networks feel obliged to cut the cloth so tightly when it comes to creating programmes for the young I have never quite understood). I hurry out on to the terrace to greet them. Harold calls out, 'Yooey!' I smile at the sight of him for, even in this wintry season, he has arrived in a crumpled off-white linen suit and panama, with his *Times* clutched tightly in the crook of his arm. I find his appearance touching, so wonderfully British. He looks as though he has ambled absentmindedly out of the pages of a Somerset Maugham short story.

He has read my scripts and likes them very much. He speaks with a mild stutter, which I had completely forgotten. We talk of the filming as though we might be commencing the following day. I am thrilled by his enthusiasm, and he is delighted with lunch and with the wines on offer. As far as he is concerned we can begin picking the key members of the production team and start the joyful process of location-hunting. The development budget he offers is generous, and sufficient to take us into preproduction. This leaves Michel with ample time to slot the remaining financial partners into place. Business matters are concluded satisfactorily and, as a natural accompaniment to the cheese, glazed apple tart and dessert wine, Harold's conversation, growing more frivolous, turns to gossip within the British television industry. He revels in his topic, attacking it, along with the *brie de Meaux*, with a salacious appetite.

As afternoon pitches towards deepening dusk, Harold is transported back down the drive. Disappearing out of view, head poking out of the car window, he gazes back up at me on the upper terrace, waving his panama in the air like a man setting sail for the ends of the earth.

Later, alone together by the fireside, Michel and I discuss two essential matters. The first is my distress about No Name. Was it thoughtless to have given all the puppies away? Should we have kept one? Whisky was her companion for many months and now she is lonely and bereaved and I feel wretched about it. The second is the new series. As soon as my work in Wales has been completed, Michel will employ a line producer – he has the ideal man in mind – and with luck, by summer, we will be in production on my first entire series as screenwriter.

Miraculously – anyone operating in the world of film finance will know that these affairs are usually tortuous – the money falls into place with ease. By April, everyone has committed the sums Michel has sought. We have a major French network, our Englishman abroad, Polish national television and a prestigious German company. I am both excited and overwhelmed. My summer is to be spent travelling with the producer and designer to the various countries, meeting the network executives, listening to their requirements and making any requested script adjustments. Then, later, towards autumn, once principal photography is underway, I will be employed to play the role of the mother in the series. I have structured the scripts so that most of her scenes take place on Ste Marguerite and I will therefore be able to work from home. The future looks rosy.

Michel bases the production office in Paris. Early in May, we find a very pretty girl to play the main role. During those same weeks, many of the other major players are also contracted. Three weeks from now, carpenters will start building sets in London; from there the crew moves on to Paris. I am finding this early process of film-making very thrilling. There is much to be said for being on the other side of the camera.

I, with the producer and designer, am bound for Warsaw, Kracow and Gdansk and then on to Bialystok, close to the Russian border. We are in need of a Polish property master and master carpenter. There are props to be made, most importantly a huge wooden windmill to be constructed in a remote field in the countryside outside Bialystok, which, during the course of the film, will be set alight and burned. In Paris and London, a team of design assistants, property-makers, set-dressers and costumiers have already been brought on to the payroll and are out shopping, sewing, building, measuring and painting.

The evening before my flight from Paris I am in my element and happy as a lark but, during our last supper together for a few weeks to come, Michel mentions to me that there is 'one small concern clouding the horizon'. The English money hasn't arrived. Well, the early development funds have, but nothing since. According to the contracts, which as far as I can comprehend are stacked like a pack of cards, the English money was scheduled to be the first in place, followed by the contribution from the French, who are due to come in at a slightly later stage, then the Poles, and so on and so forth, right through to the completion of postproduction.

In my naïveté and perhaps blind excitement, I don't pick up on the gravity of the situation. Harold and Michel have shot numerous television film series together, one or two of which have picked up awards, and the station he represents in England is solid and wealthy. Whatever the delay, it can be nothing more than a minor bank hiccup, surely? Then I learn that the contract has not been returned. This has never been a concern before. On at least two of the programmes they have shot together, the contracts did not arrive until after the films were delivered. But in each of those cases, though the contracts were delayed, the money was not.

I replace my fork on my plate. I fear I am beginning to get the gist of this. 'Are you worried?' I ask, attempting desperately to keep the jitters out of my voice.

'Well . . . no, not really.'

I recognise that bluff, the smoothing-over, mellifluous tone Michel has fine-tuned over the years. One sentiment a producer can simply *never* convey is panic. Rather like the captain of a torpedoed ship, he cannot fall to pieces and bellow with fear. I am staring across the table in shocked silence. 'Give me the worst-case scenario,' I say, barely audibly.

This rattles him, which was certainly not my intention. 'Why do you have to look for the worst in everything?' he snaps.

'Don't.' My hand has leaped the distance between us and is attempting to meet his, but he withdraws, rises from the table and goes in search of a corkscrew. I stay where I am, listening to the opening and closing of drawers, silently calculating how many members of the team in how many countries across Europe have been contracted. And what of those already on the payroll? If the English funds are not covering all their fees, who is?

'That early development budget must have run out . . .' My palate is dry. My words stick in my throat. I cannot complete the sentence because Michel has returned to the table and, while opening our wine, is looking at me in a way he never has before.

'The French network advanced several hundred thousand francs,' he replies, filling the glasses.

'So, there's no real problem, then?' I hear the plea in my question, the need to know that everything is right with the world. It is quite pathetic.

'No, probably not. I shouldn't have mentioned it,' he mutters, and the subject is closed.

I lie awake while Michel sleeps. I am a perennial insomniac and our evening together has given me plenty to toss and turn over.

The following day we say our goodbyes. I promise to call from Warsaw. He promises to keep me abreast of what is happening. It is a muddled, unsatisfactory parting and I hate to go like this.

'Everything will be fine,' he assures. I nod and set off for Charles de Gaulle Airport, leaving him on the telephone.

Warsaw is extraordinary. Poland is a heady mix of reformation, modernisation and long-lost chivalry. Every colour shrieks like a drunken song in streets which have known only the greyness and deprivations of communism for so many years. I am fascinated and attracted and, occasionally, repelled by the weight of recent history here. Blocks of ugly buildings lean in over me, oppressing me, as though they will squeeze my presence right off the streets, and I want to run for my life. And then I stroll to the old town, entirely rebuilt after its wartime bombings, during which it was razed to the ground, sit in a quaint café and listen to the accordion-players and to the bell-like chatter of waitresses, plump and girlish and innocent whatever their ages, and pleasing and polite, and I am seduced. I love the fact that we are here to film and create and fuse with these people who see the world through eyes that are so different from mine;

artists who have known mental and creative imprisonment. And I know I can add this vision to my story. Poland is a country emerging from communism. My tale is of a girl emerging from the pain caused by the break-up of her parents' marriage.

The work is going well. Our team and the Polish production company are enjoying one another's contribution. The only drawback is that everything takes twice as long as I would have expected because everything needs to be translated. Our interpreter, not always accurate, I fear, sits between us or trots along at our sides as we hurry from meeting to meeting, location to location, and repeats in Polish all that we have said and vice versa. Dear Gruzna, whose shiny, plump face is buried beneath layers of bright blue eyeshadow and thick block mascara, has been assigned to us by the local production company. She is a rather lazy girl who has no truck with our Western ways and longs to return to the security of the old regime where she knew that at half-past four she could go home, her work for the day done. All day long she jabbers empty-headedly of romance and tells us how she and her husband are starving and surviving on love alone, but her heavily painted, black and blue eyes light up like a magpie's when she sees currency or jewellery and she sidles close, hoping for a gift. She, like everything here, is a curious paradox.

One evening, after eleven hours in a van without suspension travelling country roads that seem never to have been completed, so rutted are they with deep potholes, I stagger exhaustedly to the reception desk at my hotel to collect my room key. The porter hands me a message, left early that morning, asking me to call Michel. Frustratingly, but not unusually, it takes me a while to get an international line. When I do, I know instantly from the tone of his voice that all is not well, so the words 'the English have withdrawn', only partially stun me. Still, I am silenced. I have no idea what to say.

'Why?' is all I can think of.

'Restructuring within the network. It looks as though Harold might be given early retirement.'

'Poor Harold,' I bleat, unable to contemplate where this leaves us.

Michel is used to the rollercoaster of film-production crises. Unless an actor has invested his own money in a film, he is rarely, if ever, burdened with such problems. Actors are cushioned, cosseted, so this is a completely new and rather scary scenario for me but, I remind myself, I am sitting on the other side of the fence now. I have to take the blows with the rest of the team. 'What now?' I ask eventually.

My question is returned by a silence broken only by the crackling on a very inadequate and antiquated telephone line. Eventually Michel says, 'I've spoken to the French and German networks today. Both are willing to up their investment and make first payments earlier than originally scheduled. It doesn't cover the shortfall, but it will pay the production salaries and keep us going for the time being. I'm flying in to Warsaw tomorrow and I'll see Agnes mid-afternoon.'

Agnes is the head of drama here. One of the other discoveries that has surprised and impressed me about Poland is the power given to women. I am delighted that Michel is coming, but I am very troubled by the reason for his trip. We say goodnight and he sounds as tired as a 1,000-year-old man. I cannot sleep.

Over a drink in the dimly lit bar, I hear from Michel and our producer that the meeting with the Polish network has gone smoothly. They are still very keen and are offering to double their commitment to the project. I, in my naïveté, am thrilled, believing this to mean that we have jumped this tricky hurdle and are out of trouble. Michel gently explains that because the Poles are not rich and are operating in a currency which has no buying power on the international market, they are offering their extra commitment to us in 'below-the-line' costs.

I stare blankly.

'It means the Poles will make available to us extra facilities here in Poland. Hotels, crew, provisions . . .'

The three men sitting with me around the table read the bemused look on my face. I have never been confronted by this problem before but I am not so blind that I cannot discern from the mood of less than abundant joy at the table that the matter is not fully resolved. I attempt a lighter approach. 'Such things never concern actresses. We learn our lines, climb into our frocks and are driven to the set.' I look from one to the other. 'Help me,' I add.

'We will shoot a greater chunk of the story here, more than we had originally envisaged. This means that we, or rather you,' says the producer, 'will have to relocate certain episodes.'

'Relocate?' I repeat stupidly.

'The story will not begin in London. It will begin in Paris, and then, instead of two episodes in Poland, we will have four set here.'

I take this in. 'But it's not possible—'

'It has to be.'

'Fine,' I mumble. I have absolutely no idea how I will fulfil this unexpected order.

Later, alone with Michel in my hotel room, I learn that there is still a shortfall of over half a million pounds. He is returning to Paris at first light to begin the process of finding another source of finance to cover it.

'Wouldn't it be better to cancel the series?' I ask. No. We are already committed to such an extent and to so many contracts which would still have to be paid that in fact it is cheaper and less risky to keep going.

'I see,' I mutter, but I don't.

Michel leaves and I am driven to the studios to meet Agnes and a script editor before being put to work. Apparently, there is a considerable amount of Polish history that I must learn and include in the storyline. I dare not ask what Polish history has to do with our rites-of-passage tale. I am at the point where I think the best course of action is just to do as I am told. We are ten days away from principal photography and I am now five scripts short of my thirteen – the thirteen it took me the best part of a year to write, shape and perfect. If I cannot produce four acceptable Polish scripts, we will have no film, and then what? I do not allow myself to dwell on it.

Everything I need is installed in my hotel room. Food is brought in at intervals, as well as limitless supplies of dark, stewed coffee. Then arrive reams of paper to feed a monstrous-sized printer which barely succeeds the original printing press. In Paris it would sell in a fashionable Marais boutique as a techno-antique converted into some natty home device, but here it is dumped on the floor because there is no shelf or table-top in the room capacious enough to contain it. Cables festoon the room. Every time I stand up to stretch, I trip over them or the printer itself.

For forty-eight hours I work without sleep, feeling guilty if I pause to brush my teeth, and emerge at dawn on the third day having produced two rewritten scripts. I am gibbering with exhaustion and, to remind myself of what is wonderful in life, I pick up the phone and call Quashia. Extraordinarily, I get through without a problem. The chuckle in his voice, his light-hearted good humour, warm and relax me.

'How are you?' he hollers. Quashia seems to believe that talking long-distance on the phone still involves a great deal of shouting. But it's him, part of who he is, and I am deeply glad to be in touch. It all seems a lifetime away.

'Terrific,' I lie. 'How is No Name?'

I am buoyed by the news that all is well back at the farm. No Name is in good form and has adopted Ella, the small golden retriever puppy we bought for her, who is now four months old. I close my eyes and picture them prancing across the terraces in the bright sunlight. I try to draw energy from the image of tranquillity. Whooper birds flitting to and fro in the garden; the two white doves who have appeared since Christmas and fly in and out daily, cooing and nuzzling on the phone line by our bedroom terrace; buzzards wheeling high in the deep blue sky. All is right with the world back there and I am profoundly grateful for it.

During my retreat it has been decided by the drama department that what the story lacks is a plane sequence and a chase set in one of the famous Polish opal mines.

'What?' I stammer, barely able to comprehend what is being suggested to me. 'But this is the story of a thirteen-year-old girl in search of her father.' No matter, I am assured; the proposed sequence will dovetail into the story nicely. I am given a sheaf of material which tells me (in halting English) all I need to know about the local mining industry and sent away to write the scenes. Back I go to my room, encased once again within four walls and my imagination.

I am cheered by news from Michel. He has found an independent company in Paris who have guaranteed the missing finance. Everything is back on track. I return to the opal sequence with optimism in my heart. Perhaps my heroine can find a stone or two. Why not?

By Friday, I am certain that if I do not get out of the hotel I will not be held responsible for my state of mind. I have had four hours' sleep in as many days. I stagger down to reception, where the sight of so many people milling to and fro in a brightly lit, bustling area almost sends me into trauma. I leave a note for the producer telling him that I have four scripts. They are ready to be read and I don't care what he says, I want to go out to dinner this evening and will he and the designer please accompany me because I am starved of human contact and laughter.

Later that evening, along with the English director, who has flown in from London the day before, we stroll to the old town and order vodka and fresh fish and settle down for the evening. The producer and designer update me on all that has happened during my missing days, but I am so tired, so punch-drunk and, after one straight vodka, so slewed that I can barely take in the sequence of events. The mayor of Bialystok has telephoned to discuss the newly constructed windmill, which he has spotted in one of the surrounding village fields. He is refusing to allow us to burn it. The designer laughs as he recounts the conversation. Why? Is there a local fire risk? No, not all. He is so taken with it, with its unusual design – essential to the story – that he wants to buy it and keep it there as a tourist attraction. We laugh wildly and order more vodka, a blissful palliative to me this evening. The restaurant fills up, candles are lit, accordion-players in national costume serenade us at our benched table with searingly sweet romantic tunes. We are talking and giggling hysterically because we are all tired and stressed. And so I chill out and heal. The money is back in place. The English director, a gentle, intelligent soul, is an excellent addition to our small team and in one week, so long as my new scripts are accepted, I will return to the haven of Appassionata and deal with the remaining rewrites from there. My work in Poland will have been accomplished, and the film will have reached the starting gate. Life is not so bad after all.

My thoughts drift to our garden, to the olive trees and dogs, and how good I shall feel writing in my own precious space, my sanctum, surrounded by shelf after shelf of books and warm shafts of moted sunbeams. Of course, if the scripts are not accepted, the start of principal photography will be delayed, the budget will be at risk, jobs on the line . . . I choose not to reflect on such negatives tonight, nor on the incredible weight of responsibility I feel. Tomorrow – no, today, it is now Saturday – there is to be a mammoth afternoon script conference at the studios, where my work will be discussed and, probably, dissected. What a baptism of fire for any young scriptwriter.

It is two in the morning when we enter the lobby of the hotel and I find an urgent message waiting for me to call Michel.

Back in my room, dubious about ringing at such a late hour, I pick up the phone. His voice is grave and I know before he utters a word that what I am about to hear will not be good. 'It's your father,' he says.

The effect of the vodka, which had left me sleepy, slurry and mellow, is whipped from me just as surely as someone slapping me with a cold, metal object.

'You'd better ring England.'

I crash the receiver down clumsily almost before Michel has finished speaking and telephone my mother. It is a frustrating age before I can get another line out and another age before she answers.

'We've just got back from the hospital.' I hear her breathlessness, caused by rushing to the phone, no doubt.

'The hospital?' I seem incapable of uttering anything other than parrot-like responses.

'There's nothing you can do.'

My father has had a stroke. He is unconscious and paralysed. He could live a day, he could go on for an indeterminate period.

'If you came, he wouldn't know you were here and we know you have difficulties there. There's no sense in risking everything you have been working for.'

'No.'

We say goodnight and I promise to call again in the morning. I walk to the window, tripping over the accursed printer on my way, dragging a carver chair with me which I place facing the leafy, deserted square beyond the hotel.

I sit there for the entire night. Exhausted, spent as I am, I cannot go to bed, couldn't sleep. I think of my father and try to comprehend the reality of what has happened to him way across the waters in a land of Englishness so alien to this place, with its remnants of grey communism, its fast-growing Mafia, its distant, grim echoes of concentration camps and its desperate hungry hand reaching out to a new world where pop music is not banned, kids smoke dope and, supposedly, salvation lies. In my story, the young girl searches for her musician father and in the Polish episodes she finds him and loses him again. The streets beyond the window are deadly quiet. My own father, lying dying in a hospital bed in a place my mind refuses to conjure, is a musician and has been the inspiration for the central theme of my story. It was to have been a spiritual present to him; a gift of my work. I had been looking forward to talking to him about it, to taking him to the islands, to the fortress where the resolution of the story is set. I close my aching eyes and picture him at Appassionata, sleeping the afternoons away with No Name at his side, his sunburned body covered in puppies.

At first light, I make my way to the dining room. There is not a soul in sight. When the waiter comes I order coffee and stare at the phenomenal buffet on offer, which includes mountains of caviar and every marinated herring you could dream of. All so at odds with the miserable poverty and deprivation I have witnessed everywhere. I stare at it blindly and then, in my mind's ear, I hear a voice. It is indisputably my father's. 'Carol, Carol, darling, it's Daddy.' And I know that whatever the weight of responsibility here, however many actors' and technicians' jobs are at risk, no matter if the Poles hate every word I have written and call this huge production machine to a halt, I must go. If only for a day. Today is Saturday. I could take the weekend off and be back to face the music on Monday morning.

At reception, I learn that travelling in and out of Poland is not as simple as I had thoughtlessly assumed. There is one flight to London later this afternoon and another back tomorrow evening. They are fully booked. In fact, there is not a flight with a single seat available in any class for the next five days. What if I went through Paris? Or Amsterdam? Or Frankfurt? In my vulnerable, barely coherent condition I blurt out my dilemma, unbosoming myself to the desk clerk. He is kindly, sympathetic and promises to look into the matter and get back to me. I return to the dining room and drink several more cups of black coffee before calling the producer's room.

'Of course you must go,' he tells me when I disturb him at 8.30. 'I will drive you to the airport.'

By whatever miracles make these matters possible, flights are found and I am booked to London via Berlin. There is no time to waste. The producer has read the scripts overnight and seems relatively happy with them. He envisages few, if any problems. We grab a hurried bite, or rather he does, while we talk through various scenes. He plans to attend the prearranged Saturday and Sunday script meetings on my behalf, take notes and, on my return, he and I will collaborate on whatever has been requested by the television network and I will have the corrected scripts on the network desks by Monday morning. I merely nod my agreement to this insane schedule. I cannot think beyond what awaits me in England. I have moved into a different pace, another zone.

Standing in the centre of my hotel room on Sunday evening, I survey my temporary habitat. Nothing has changed except that the bed has been made during my thirty-six-hour absence and my papers, which were strewn everywhere, have been tidied into bundles. I stare at nothing in particular except its orderliness. I have a meeting in the bar in fifteen minutes with director, designer and producer, who have spent practically the entire weekend at the studio. I have begged the time to wash and to phone my mother.

I slept, or rather didn't, at the hospital, at my father's side. I have just replaced the telephone receiver having learned from her that my father died two hours ago. I would have been on the plane somewhere between Berlin and Warsaw. I gather up my scripts and head for the lift. In the bar, my three colleagues await me with a tall glass of champagne, which costs the earth here.

'Ready to go back to work?'

I nod and decide to hold back my news until we have gone through the scripts. It is four in the morning when our pow-wow breaks up and we head towards the lifts. I am clutching my papers tight against my chest. Empty, bleak emotions are churning up my guts. Unanswerable questions hang in my mind like smoke trails. One phone call, and life has taken on an entirely different perspective. The men are talking among themselves, small talk, the banter born of exhaustion. As we leave the lift, the producer and I say goodnight to the others, whose rooms are elsewhere. He accompanies me, knowing.

'It's curious. When you rang my room on Saturday morning I was lying awake thinking about my own father. He's not well. I was wondering what I'd do if I got that call. You were luckier. Mine's in Australia.'

I drop my eyes and stare at the carpet. Luckier?

'Have you told Michel?'

I shake my head. 'Not yet,' I murmur. 'The funeral's next Monday. I'm going,' I snap, too sharply.

'Of course. In any case, you should be out of here by then. You've done well. Against all the bloody odds. Thanks for it,' and he leans over and gives me an awkward hug.

The days bank up, each one like the last. We attend meeting after meeting. While the others talk and debate, the producer fighting my corner with a ferocious loyalty to the story we had set out to tell, which now seems to be disappearing behind action sequences which bear no relationship to it as far as I can see, I close down. I stare at the blank, faded white walls or the conference table around which we sit. None of this seems relevant, and yet I know that it is. So many livelihoods at stake. And a story dedicated to the father I have just lost.

As we approach the end of the week I discover that there are no flights out of Warsaw. Not at any price. I will walk then, if I have to, I tell no one in particular, and set about trying to rent a car. I shall drive to London, or drive across the frontier and pick up a plane in Germany. I am going, I repeat angrily. These dark days have crept up without warning, no pointers to alert me that they were approaching. I was not prepared for this. I am hurting with life and ready to lash out.

Miraculously, yet again, flights are found. But this time the route is more circuitous. Warsaw to Frankfurt, Frankfurt to Nice and then Nice to London. This extraordinary tour includes an overnight in Nice which means, incredibly, that I can briefly go home. I am profoundly grateful for the opportunity to touch base.

I phone Quashia to alert him of my imminent arrival and am told that No Name has gone missing. In between script sessions, budget and design meetings, I begin to ring all the refuge centres in the south of France. No one has found her. I am beside myself with worry. I call the police and the fire brigade, who also respond with negatives. I telephone the vet. What shall I do? He has a record there of the numbered reference he tattooed in her ear when I first found her. He will call the central office and alert them. He reminds me that when I gave him the signed photo he had requested, I also gave him a photograph Michel had taken of No Name running in the garden. He offers to have photocopies made and distribute them in our local shops and to put one up in his surgery. My heart is troubled as well as numb but I am thankful for his support. 'I'll see you when I get there,' I mumble, and replace the receiver.

*

A blanket of heat greets my weary arrival. Here, at home, it is a blazing, glorious summer. It had been warm in Warsaw as well but because I had been incarcerated in meetings and cold with grieving, I had not noticed. The tropicality of the Côte d'Azur takes me by surprise. For the first time ever, I feel a stranger to the plumes of palm fronds and the gloss and bustle of Riviera life rather turns my stomach after the paucity of Poland. But as I climb up into the winding, twilit hills, breathe in the fragrance of scarlet and pink oleander and sky-blue plumbago, my heart begins to settle. And by the time I have reached the land of olive groves and our own in particular, a great weight seems to lift from me and a peace descends; albeit a lamenting peace.

At Appassionata I find a fax from the producer saying that all four scripts have been accepted. The network is delighted with them. So once I have mourned with my family and shared a farewell to my father, I can return home and begin to write the new first script, now to be set in Paris, from the serenity of my own stone-walled space. Any last-minute changes required by the Poles can be faxed. Principal photography has been given the green light and my task has been accomplished.

Devastation

Soon, the weather will begin to break. Already the crush of holidaymakers with children have packed up and left, and with them has gone that distinctly pungent tang of Ambre Solaire which has dominated the Riviera coastline for the past two months. Michel and I are lunching on the beach. Early autumnal winds have blown in, driving off the heavy summer lethargy and previewing the shift of season, bringing with them fragrant whiffs of late-summer flowers. Light gusts lift and settle the paper napkins on the table in front of us. Dragging a stray wisp of hair off my face, I glance about me. On the shore, at the water's edge, two wiry setters are barking incessantly at a retired couple in matching swimming caps who are splashing lazily on their backs in the warm sea. Cries of distant voices drift towards us on the welcome breeze. Closer by, well-fed bronzed bodies, Nordic, Dutch, German, British, chatter and prattle, ordering drinks, lighting cigarettes, oiling one another, while tame waves spume and curl just a few yards from our feet. Michel and I have barely seen each other for weeks. Our eyes shaded by Ray-Bans, we gaze across the table but do not smile. Michel looks shot to pieces, needs a haircut and a break, while I am shell-shocked by the news he has just imparted. Behind me, the steady thwack, thwack of ball hitting bat acts like a salty metronome. Time to make a decision.

'What are we going to do?' I ask eventually.

An entire film crew is on its way. Shooting will finish in Hamburg in a week, which means that the full caravan – actors, make-up and costume, cameras, lights, electrics – is about to converge on this resort by road and air. In the meantime, the advance team of designers, carpenters, buyers and so on has already been installed in a small hotel three streets back from the main coastal drag. The rushes have been well received by all the various international networks involved, and the young girl playing the leading role has been described as 'magic' on screen. We should be delighted. And so we were, I thought, in a worn-out sort of way, until this morning.

The French company who stepped in to cover the deficit incurred by the loss of the British network has gone bankrupt. They are not alone. In Paris, during these past few months, somewhere in the region of twenty independent production companies have gone to the wall, and we are likely to join them if we cannot find a solution to this crisis. Michel learned this news three days ago. He said nothing to me but went immediately to his bankers in Paris who have, after much wrangling, telephoned this morning to say that they agree to advance the monies and keep the production running – which right now means getting a host of salaries paid before the middle of next week – on one condition.

'And that is?' I ask as a plate of freshly grilled sizzling sardines seasoned with curls of parsley is set in front of me and the waitress, a pretty, darkly tanned, middle-aged blonde in shorts, refills my glass of rosé.

'That we put up the farm as a guarantee.'

'Appassionata as a guarantee? No!'

Sleek heads at nearby tables turn at the sound of my raised voice. I sigh. We are both exhausted.

Since collecting Michel from the airport and driving along the busy stretch of coast road, negotiating corkscrew curves in the old fortressed port of Antibes, swinging by the palm-fringed, art-deco villas along the cap, I have chattered without pause for breath about various horticultural difficulties I have been experiencing, as well as about my preparations for the arrival of the girls, who are flying in later today. This was to have been our first home-based family weekend in months. I was excited. Having completed the rewrites on my scripts weeks ago, I have spent my late-August days immersed in affairs of the garden and wanted to share my news.

'*Cicadelles*. They are small white flies, smaller than moths. They're everywhere and lethal. According to René, there's a local epidemic. They've laid their eggs on our orange trees. The underside of the foliage has been invaded, and the leaves have been robbed of their colour; all viridescence sucked out. I treated them twice. Quashia has, too. But it's made no difference. They just fly off and settle somewhere else. They move like a soft, pale-grey blanket fluttering across the terraces. Now they are on the roses and the bougainvillaea. When you touch the plants, they are all sticky. I was scared they'd attack the olive trees, but they haven't gone near them. And just when I was beginning to feel safe about that, I discovered *paon* – you remember, the blight René showed us when we went to visit that farm near Castellane? Remember, he told us to watch out for it – leaves turning yellow, round brown spots? Well, I have found the fungus on nine of our olive trees.

'You're very quiet, Michel. I'm talking too much. I'm so pleased to see you. Are you all right?'

And that was when he broached the subject. By then we had

parked my little car and were crossing the street, heading beachwards for this café.

'We can't give them Appassionata,' I repeat. My voice is quieter now, strangled, almost, but emphatic. Behind my dark glasses, tears prick my eyes.

Michel picks up his wine and takes a sip. He smiles at the waitress as she places parma ham and a mesclun salad in front of him. '*Merci.*'

We begin to eat, but the delicious fish tastes like cardboard in my mouth.

Michel says 'If you don't mind going back to the airport later and picking up the girls, I'll make some calls. See what else I can come up with.'

'Such as?'

'I have plenty of contacts in Germany. I'll try to pick up a cable sale. I'll talk to the Swiss. A children's channel in Italy. I don't know yet, I'll think of something.'

The girls are clearing the table after dinner when the row begins. I don't know where it explodes from. I'm feeling fraught and deeply upset because we have decided to go ahead and sign Appassionata over to the bank as a guarantee. Frankly, we have no choice. Salaries have to be paid, hotel bills met. Whatever solutions Michel can cobble together, they will not solve our immediate problem. We agreed the matter at the beginning of the evening and then promised ourselves to leave it until Sunday, when we will put aside part of our afternoon to arrange the paperwork.

Now, suddenly, here we are, standing around the table shouting at one another. I rise easily, being quick-tempered by nature, volatile; Michel is more steady in his emotions. Vanessa lunges forwards and screams at me, unkind words which send me reeling. 'No,' I stammer. 'No, you don't understand.' Have I spoken too sharply to the man I love? Do I act as though I blame him for what has happened, even though I know that the difficulties are not of his making? The girls must think me culpable. They side with their father, naturally. And yet, in many ways, I had thought us a family. I wanted to believe it. I am more sensitive to cutting words, accusations, precisely because I am not their mother. Were we flesh-and-blood kin I could dismiss unkindnesses more easily. As it is, dishcloth in hand, greasy plates clutched before me, I turn and flee to the kitchen.

Glancing back, my eyes hazy with tears, I see a sight which curdles my heart. Michel standing at the head of the table staring at the floor, lips puckered, frozen in speech, one daughter either side of him clutching him fast, their heads pressed against his chest. I settle the dishes in the sink and, without washing them, creep off to bury myself beneath a cave of sheets and pillows.

Everyone is sleeping. The dew on the early-morning grass glints in the sun like crystal stones. The soles of my feet are damp from walking in it. A cock crows in the far distance. The blue of the sky is as smooth as velvet. It caresses my fractured senses.

'They will hold all deeds of the farm until the film has been completed and sufficient profits have been made to pay them back, plus their interest, of course.' Michel's words of yesterday echo in my mind. This must be hurting him as much as it is me.

Seated on one of our many drystone walls, I scan the misty morning hillsides, drinking in our ravishing land and seascape, and my heart swims sickeningly. Our lives had seemed golden until this summer. Even if we don't have a cent to renovate it, even crumbling alongside its romantic ruin, this place is magnificent, magical. To lose it all – myriad moments of crazy happiness – does not bear contemplation.

Ella, our little puppy, is nudging her cold nose against my naked arms, begging for attention. I stroke her soft, russet-auburn head absentmindedly. We never found No Name. We advertised everywhere. She just walked away, vanished from our lives. We cannot fathom even how she got loose. She must have made a hole in a fence somewhere. I looked for it, spent hours scouting the terraces in search of a point of exit, a clue, but without success. I still blame myself. Even though, in the wake of her disappearance, the most extraordinary incident occurred. I might almost claim it a *petit* miracle.

It was my father's birthday, two weeks ago now, a hot, sultry lunchtime. I was aching with the loss of him. I sauntered down the drive, taking heart from the birdsong, to collect the post from our letterbox. I unlocked the great iron gates, which Michel has painted the Matisse-blue of our house shutters, and there, curled up like a snake in a shaded corner among the irises and beneath the swathes of bird's-egg-blue plumbago which festoon the cedar trees, was another Alsatian. For one euphoric second I thought it was No Name, blackened with mud or tar, until I saw that the shivering, skeletal creature was darker and smaller, a German not a Belgian Alsatian. Her fur is not as long. I put my hand out but she growled ferociously at me and I was reminded of that first encounter with No Name, a damaged fawny mess who feared to trust. What was this dog doing here, settled right outside our gate, miles from anywhere? I could not contain the thought that she had been brought to us by the spirit of my father, on his birthday, to keep our little Ella company.

I bent low and she bared her teeth, so I decided to leave her be and turned to retrieve our mail. As I locked the gates, she staggered to her feet. She was unsteady and limping, in pain, but she trod the length of the hilly driveway; a shadow stalking me, keeping her distance. What a scrawny sight. I hurried to the stables and dug out No Name's bowl, which I loaded with chunks of meat, biscuits and water. This I offered her but she backed off mistrustfully. I placed the food on the ground and returned to the house, upstairs to my writing room where, through the window, I could watch her discreetly. She did not touch the meal but slumped on the ground about three yards away from it and glowered at it, as though waiting for the aluminium dish to approach or challenge her. It made me smile. I noticed then for the first time that her left side and haunch were completely bald. I wonder if she belongs to anyone, I was thinking. She wasn't wearing a collar. I telephoned the vet.

She bore no tattoo. Lucky is her name. Or so I have christened her. She is still with the vet. She was suffering from internal bleeding, a perforation, stomach problems from where she had been kicked repeatedly. She has two broken ribs, worms, and a highly strung, nervy disposition which the doctor suggests is the result of continual maltreatment. This is why she is still with him. He wants to be sure before we take her in and foster her alongside a small puppy that she will not turn nasty.

I was intending to collect Lucky later today. I had been looking forward to introducing her to the girls.

Wordsworth said that the past, present and future are strung together, as it were, on the thread of the wish that runs through them. Running through my mind this morning is everything we have achieved, the contentment I feel here and the happiness Michel has brought me, but the future now seems beset by hurdles and fears. And this morning, justifiably or not, I blame myself.

At my side Ella begins to wag her tail as arms reach round me and hug me tight, drawing me back to the present, to this 'spot in time', from my memories and misery and from an uncertain future. It is Vanessa. She says nothing; neither do I. We only hold each other tight. The sun, flooding through the treetops beyond the flat roof of the house, begins to heat our backs, invigorating us, healing us with the promise of a whole new day.

The weather is breaking. Pale rain falls across the hills and turns the sea bluish, misty and opalescent. Michel has gone travelling, to sell our now completed series. He is working all the hours God sends. Travelling as though he is trying to squeeze in an extra day, catching the sunrise on both sides of the world. He never rests, never takes a day off. He behaves as though he could keep it up for ever, as though he were invincible. I want to tell him that he'll wear himself out, make himself ill, but I know that such negatives will only disable him. I want to believe that he is as powerful and capable as he is forcing himself to be. I want to believe in his strength, because I dare not consider the alternatives. But most of all, I think we should relinquish the farm, sell it, hand it over to the bank; throw it at them, release ourselves. But Michel won't agree. He won't hear of it, will not discuss it. 'We'll get there,' he keeps saying to me, as though it were a secret mantra which, the more he repeats it, the truer he begs it to become. It is a heavy burden to carry. I am anxious and depressed for him. And I see our dreams turning to dust.

Quashia leaves for Algeria. He is preparing for his retirement early next year. His departure all but finishes me. I have no idea how I will manage without him but I lie to him, tell him I've found someone else to help because he has his own life and family in Africa and it is not for me to hold him back.

'If you need me,' he says, when he comes to say goodbye, 'call the village café, *comme d'habitude*. I'll come back.' I nod and wish him well, knowing that I will not ring.

'Remember, we are family, you and I. I will never let you down.' I nod again and kiss him on both cheeks, twice, fighting back great, blubbing tears.

This is beginning to feel like the year of loss.

Loss. The fear that has haunted me. It is why every farewell, every parting, no matter how trivial or short-lived, seems to tear at me. It's why I never found the courage to love until I met Michel.

'Say hello to your wife and children,' I manage. I have never met them, but Quashia talks of them so often that I feel as though we are old friends.

'You tell Michel from me to stop working so hard. He's needed here.'

I smile bravely, wondering if he has any idea of the deep trouble we are in. I suspect so. He has a wise man's instinct. I watch him walking away down the drive, fur hat on his balding head, waving as he goes and smiling that warm, toothless grin of his.

I stay on alone at the farm, thinking out devices for the salvation of Appassionata, living from hand to mouth. The bank is growing impatient with us. They are threatening us. They hound us regularly with registered letters, vowing to snatch the farm and put it up for auction. Worry haunts me. I pace the tiled, sun-slanted rooms and windy terraces like a lost spirit who has a code to decipher but cannot find the root clue. Round and round in my mind the fears and responsibilities churn like souring milk. Some nights, before the first cock crows, sleepless with concern, I press my face against the glass, staring out at the moon while, down in the farthest valley, the Arabs are at their prayer, their *muezzin*. Their cry to God.

Count me in, I whisper.

I write from dawn till dead of night. Alone in the ancient, creaking house, candles burning, logs crackling, I stare into Bible-black darkness. Stories, children's books, script synopses, I beaver away, wearing myself out in an attempt to change the tide of our fortunes.

And I seek out small day-to-day joys to cheer me. I jump into the freezing pool to save the life of a drowning bee, twitching his legs every which way, backside down on the surface of the water. I talk at length to a surprisingly large cicada who has pitched up out of season in the bathroom, lonely in a corner like a displaced twig. I chance upon a pair of hornets copulating against one of the flowerbed walls. He, embracing her, is moving rhythmically while she strokes her small, black, insect face with her front feet until, suddenly, she begins to emit high-pitched noises. A love song sung with passion on a warm Sunday afternoon. Lucky is a miracle, too. Nervy and snappy, but less so. She requires much tending with creams and potions but her fur is beginning to grow back and she is proving herself a loyal and loving guard dog. I tell her how thankful I am for her company, her gratitude and need of me, and I stroke fluffy little Ella and reassure her that I feel the same way about her, too.

René drops by to take a look at the *paon*, which he won't treat now because the spray he is suggesting – one I absolutely oppose because I have been running our farm by organic methods – might damage the fruit. He hands me a set of papers given to him by Christophe, the mill-owner.

'What are these?' I ask, puzzled and barely interested.

'Forms to fill out and send to Brussels. Christophe mentioned your names specifically.'

I stare at them in a lonely, unmotivated way. They appear to be as complicated and longwinded as all French paperwork, so I stuff them into the pocket of my jeans.

'Don't ignore them, Carol. To support the olive industry here in France, Brussels is offering every *oléiculteur* financial assistance. For each litre of oil pressed, we will all receive a designated sum.'

My eyes light up, my attention seized back. I am considering our crisis. Could this be the answer to our problems? 'How much?' I ask.

'Well, it is not retrospective, but if this farm produces the same volume of oil this coming season as last, then it would be approximately six hundred francs.' Six hundred francs! That's barely £60. He must read the disappointment in my face.

'It's not a great deal but . . .' and he shrugs his wonderful

Provençal shrug and that canny look of his tells me that anything is better than nothing, which is true, of course.

'I'll fill it in,' I smile. 'I won't forget.'

Before climbing into his Renault estate, which is laden with
the largest, frizziest lettuces I have ever set eyes on, the size of
lavender bushes, he reminds me that before too long we will
need to begin netting again; the harvesting season will be upon
us once more. A swift tour of the terraces shows us that the
trees are laden with bullet-hard green olives. We are in for
another bumper crop. 'With that load, you might even make
seven hundred francs from Brussels,' he jokes as we return to
his car. 'Do you want a salad?' He is pointing at the produce
cluttering up his boot. I shake my head, explaining that I
bought mesclun and lettuce earlier at the market. Still, I cannot
help but remark on the size of them. His eyes glint with pride
and that knowledge of a *bonne affaire* as he explains that he
grows his salad on someone else's *terrain* where the water is
free because the owner has a private *source*.

'And don't forget,' he calls as he leaves. 'We can't do this
alone.'

It is a fact. Without Quashia, and with Michel away for
weeks at a time, René and I will need extra help. We were so
blessed in the early days in the way both he and Quashia
seemed to turn up out of thin air that I have no idea how to go
about finding anybody. Finally, I decide to scribble a card, a
four-line *annonce* to pin up at the local *épicerie*. I have always
been rather fond of this particular store because it reminds me
of countless village shops to which my grandparents took me
when I was a country child back home in Ireland. There they
sold their great, clanking churns of milk and it seemed to me
that every item in the world was on sale for us to choose from,
particularly sweets. Jar after tall, glass jar of rainbow-coloured
sweets.

The burly wife of the owner of the *épicerie*, pregnant again, greets me loudly and, having glanced at my advertisement, tells me that there's no need to post it. I can take their chappie.

'But what about you?'

'Winter's coming. There's nothing for him to do here 'cept rake leaves and burn. Manuel's his name.'

'And you recommend him?'

'*Mais bien sûr*, he has worked for us for six years.' She quotes the hourly rate they pay him, which seems affordable – the olive crop will pay for it – and I can think of no objection to offering him the job.

'*Bon*, we'll tell him to be ready for you tomorrow morning. You can drive him back with you.'

Relieved, I agree, and proceed to do a spot of shopping. This includes a dozen small bottles of lager. Madame shakes her head. '*Désolé*,' she tells me. 'We have run out.'

I am puzzled, for I requested the same only a few days ago, and she informed me that she was expecting a delivery the following afternoon. We have long passed the full throes of summer, so tourists with tongues hanging out are no longer raiding the fridges of every corner shop and leaving them bare.

'Your delivery never came then?' I remark innocently. She glances at me sheepishly and heads off to collect the coffee I need.

'Don't forget Manuel,' she calls after me as I close the door.

When I return for Manuel the following day, as arranged, I find no one and head into the store to enquire after him. Monsieur, usually a fairly convivial bloke, who is proprietor, *boulanger* and *pâtissier* and is right now covered in flour, glowers at his full-bellied wife in an accusatory fashion and disappears in to his back-room bakery without a word.

'Try the woodshed,' Madame mutters, pointing towards a section of the grounds I have never visited before.

I am a little taken aback to discover not a Spaniard or a Portuguese, as I had expected, but a scruffy, weatherbeaten

Arab no bigger than a sparrow, currently fast asleep on a pile of logs. At his feet is a small, frayed satchel. I hover a short distance in front of him. 'Manuel?'

Startled, he cusses incomprehensibly and drags himself up on to unsteady feet. Staring at me with the air of a guilty child, he grabs the satchel and raises one arm in the air as though leading a posse to the charge.

It is only when he is seated beside me in the car, lighting a cigarette without checking whether I mind, that I notice his bloodshot eyes and inhale the fumes of alcohol on his breath, which are so overwhelming I fear the flame from his lighter might blow us and my little buggy sky-high.

I need this man, I need this to work, I am thinking desperately. We have been shopping in that little corner store ever since we moved here. Madame wouldn't palm us off with a drunk, would she?

It appears that she would.

When we arrive back at the villa, and once Lucky has been chained up because Manuel refuses to get out of the car while the Alsatian is at liberty, he asks immediately to be shown to his room.

'Room?' I retort, for it has never been my intention to provide him with board and lodging.

He lifts his battered satchel into the air and swings it as though he intends to set up residence wherever it lands, or smash a window or two.

'I need a shower and then I'll go to work,' he groans.

I am perplexed and uncertain as to what to do for the best. Should I just shove him in the car again and deliver him back to the shop? Should I release Lucky and hope that he runs off in terror, thus relieving me of the problem altogether? Or am I being hasty? I decide to humour him until I can speak to Madame on the phone. Why not work now and shower later? I suggest. He harrumphs, throws the satchel on the ground, kicks it, lights a fag and shrugs. 'What do you want doing, then?'

I look around in desperation. Nothing that could involve breakages or damage, I am thinking; certainly not the preparation of the olive nets. 'A spot of weeding' is my reply, as I point to the largest of the various flowerbeds. I unchain the dog when Manuel is not looking and leave them to it, making for my work room where I can discuss the matter with his former employer in privacy.

Searching for the number, I realise that although we have shopped at that little *épicerie* since our arrival, participated in their Christmas raffles, bought numerous tickets for gallon-sized chocolate Easter bunnies and generally been neighbourly with this couple, I have never actually observed the name of the shop. It is the only one on a manicured private estate set in the hills to the rear of our home, but that does not help me. I have no way of finding it out short of going back there and leaving Manuel here alone. I have been careless in this arrangement and I am grumpy with myself. And I have so much work of my own to be getting on with, I wail silently. Finally, I hurry downstairs intending to explain to him that I will be back in a few minutes, but he is not in the garden and I cannot find him anywhere.

'Manuel!' I call.

Lucky comes loping towards me, barking.

'Manuel!' There is no response. Eventually I find him hovering like a spectre in the darkness of our windowless garage which, with two cars as ancient as ours, never houses vehicles but is packed to the gunwales with gardening equipment and a beaten-up but useful fridge.

'What are you doing?' I demand crossly.

'Looking for a hoe,' he explains. I point out the switch for the electric light and hurtle off down the drive in the car, hurrying along the lanes to be there before the shop shuts at midday. This *épicerie* is one of those small family businesses which closes at noon and does not reopen until four in the afternoon. When I arrive it is already closed. I bang on the door and call out. No one answers. I wander round the back to the area with the woodshed and rap my fist against a glass door. Still no reply. It is only a few minutes after twelve but the place is as silent as a deserted ship. Infuriated, I pile into the car and rush back to the farm. Manuel is nowhere to be found. His satchel, which he had ditched on one of the terraces, has also gone. The only sign that he was ever here at all is the hoe, which I find in the flowerbed, slung carelessly across a cluster of now-wilting tiger lilies. No weeding to speak of has been achieved. I call his name several times, peer into the garage but do not find him. He must have disappeared, driven away by fear of the dog, perhaps. Lucky is supine on one of the terraces, panting contentedly. Little Ella, dozing, has her head resting against her companion's stomach. I return to my writing, mightily relieved. The incident has been settled with far less consequence than I had dreaded.

Michel is in Paris and I have been trying unsuccessfully to reach him by phone. Given the extreme nature of our crisis and my natural propensity for worry, I am concerned that something could be wrong. I telephone his office and ask his assistant where he is. She has no idea.

'When did you last see him?' I beg, eager to keep the alarm out of my voice and not to panic his team.

'Yesterday morning.'

'What? He hasn't been at the office since . . . Is everything all right?'

Isobel, a stable and well-balanced woman, cannot see what I am so concerned about. He's probably working from his studio, she suggests. But I have been ringing there and there is no reply. Michel has never installed an answering machine at the little studio where he sleeps when he is in Paris because he guards it as a private space. Endless hours of his days are spent on the phone and he has always claimed to need this sanctuary. We speak so frequently during the course of the day that this has never been a problem before. But now I am unsettled. I ask Isobel to get him to call me when he comes in. By evening I have heard nothing and try his studio once more. Still no reply, and the office has not seen him all day. He has probably been in meetings elsewhere is Isobel's latest explanation.

'You don't think you should go to the studio and break the door down?' I urge.

Clearly she considers me preposterous. 'I work for him,' she replies tartly. 'I am not in the habit of beating down my boss's door.'

'No, no, of course not. Sorry to have troubled you.' I replace the receiver but I know that if all was well I would have heard from Michel. Something must have happened. If he had been obliged to go away at short notice he would have telephoned. So what is the problem, and how am I going to reach him?

I am sitting on the terrace, tormented by worry, trying to take heart from the wintry sunset, when René appears unexpectedly. I am overwhelmingly grateful to see him. As is frequently the case, he has come with a little offering. A jar of fig jam, brown and slippery as a seal, made from our own freshly picked figs. From the eight trees on the property, Quashia and I gathered more than 200 kilos of fruit during late September and early October before he left. I thank my silver-haired friend and offer him a glass of beer, trying to disguise my anguish. I am in a fix. Quashia has gone, I have no one to look after the dogs and I am thinking that, broke or not, I must go to Paris.

'Wine or beer, whichever is easiest,' he says, and settles himself contentedly at the garden table on the upper terrace to enjoy his drink. He likes to do this, René. He has a key to the gate and will occasionally drop by to while away an hour, discourse a little, recount a tale or two and take pleasure from the burned-orange sunset.

I head down to the fridge in the garage to collect a beer and a bottle of rosé. To my amazement, the fridge is bare but for a bottle or two of wine; certainly it is empty of all beer. Puzzled, I pull out the sole remaining bottle of rosé. I know I am stressed, but I definitely remember buying a crate of beer at a local supermarket the previous evening when the *épicerie* had been out of stock. Given my state of mind, it is possible I have forgotten to put them in the fridge. I try to recollect where I might have left them. In the boot of the car, perhaps? And then I remember Manuel who, with all my concerns about Michel's unexplained disappearance, had completely slipped my mind. The blighter must have made off with all the Stella Artois! I return apologetically to René, with wine and a dish of our own olives.

'You look tired,' he remarks. 'Did you remember to send that form in?'

'Which form?'

'For the olives.'

Ah, yes, that form. Yes, I reassure him I filled it in, signed it and posted it on to Michel for signing and forwarding to Brussels. It is dealt with.

We raise our glasses, offer the usual French *à la tienne* and sip our drinks.

I am about to ask for his help with feeding the dogs and holding the fort for a few days while I fly to Paris when a strident trumpeting interrupts me. Amazed, we both turn towards the second plot, from where the sound has emanated. 'It's a wild boar,' I croak.

René shakes his head. 'I don't think so.'

'What could it be then?'

'We'd better take a look.'

Leaving our drinks on the table, we set off into a wilderness of grass, brambles and weeds. Due to lack of resources and earlier torrential rains during this autumn season the second plot has been transformed back into a gentler version of the wilderness it was when we first discovered Appassionata. It is a sad spectacle. Lucky and Ella trot at our heels. Lucky is barking wildly, but the peculiar bleating or calling has stopped and we cannot trace it. René suggests that it may be a trapped animal.

'Trapped in what?' I ask, a mite defensively. I am totally opposed to hunting and when this portion of land was first cut back, I personally saw to it that every trap still buried beneath metres of herbage was ripped out and burned or, if fabricated out of some lethal metal, slung in the dustbin and removed.

It is not too long before we come upon the source of the bellowing. Manuel, though not a single drop of Latin blood runs through his knavish veins, is spreadeagled on the ground, dead to the world, beneath our spreading bay tree. Head pillowed on his satchel, he is snoring contentedly. All around him, like a spray of stars, are our emptied beer bottles.

'*Diable*,' grins René. 'Who is he?'

'He was meant to be your assistant for the olive harvest.' I laugh and swiftly recount the story of Manuel.

We lift him between us and haul him, dragging him by his heels through the grassy earth, the entire length of the garden to René's Renault shooting brake, where we dump him in the open boot. His breath is like dragon's fire.

'Let's finish that bottle,' suggests René, giggling. 'We've earned it. And then we'll return him to his woodshed.' Which is exactly what we do. Manuel never once so much as stirs during the whole operation.

During our little excursion to the *épicerie*, René agrees to hold the fort for me as of the morrow, assuring me that I am not to worry. He delivers me back to the gate. I thank him and begin my climb up the hill. As I do, he calls after me, 'Do you want me to look for someone to help with the olives?'

'I'll let you know tomorrow,' I answer, too whacked to think about it now.

Up at the house, the telephone is ringing. It is Isobel to say that Michel has been taken ill. I knew it.

The dogs have been fed for this evening, so I phone René, who is just walking through his door, to let him know that I am leaving for the airport and intend to catch the last plane to Paris tonight. I promise to be back as soon as I can.

Paris is damp and wintry. Streetlights refract and rainbow in the rain. By the time I arrive at the studio it is after eleven and Michel is in bed, doubled up in pain.

I am shocked by the sight of him but fight back my desire to quiz him about what is wrong. I learn that he was taken ill yesterday morning during a meeting with his lawyer. His lawyer called in a doctor friend and a specialist, who has performed some tests, sent Michel home to rest and promised to call as soon as he has news.

'Why didn't you phone me?' I manage.

'I didn't want to worry you.'

I refrain from mentioning that his silence over the past forty hours has nearly driven me round the bend. Instead, I slip into bed beside him, wrap my arms around him and we try to sleep.

The specialist phones at what seems like first light. In fact, the louring grey skies make it feel as though day has not broken. He wants Michel at his clinic before the end of the morning. I feel everything within me tighten.

'Did he say why?'

Michel shakes his head. I insist on going with him. At first he will not hear of it but I am adamant. Michel is not a man to ease up on his workload. On the few occasions I have seen him ailing, with a common cold or minor health problem, he has ignored it. He will not accept or even acknowledge any form of physical incapacity. This is not going to be easy for him. Or for me. I am little better, and I hate hospitals. I am the world's greatest coward when it comes to blood and I can barely stomach the sulphurous and alkaline aromas of unguents, tinctures and disinfectants. Those long, narrow corridors give me the shakes. Supine bodies on trolleys bring nausea and fear to my senses. But I want to be there. I am not prepared to sit around at the studio all day chewing my nails.

Even though Michel is set on taking the Métro – taxis, he says, are beyond our means – we hail a cab because I insist more vociferously and he is, frankly, too weak to argue.

The doctor is a youngish, handsome man with a warm, reassuring manner. He leads us through to his office and informs Michel that he wants to begin a series of tests right away. Michel is in so much pain – stomach cramps – that he can barely speak. There are many French words, medical terms, that pass me by. I have a dozen questions but I say almost nothing. Michel is led away and I am left alone in the office.

It is not even six months since I sat at my father's bedside. The memories return and I try to drive them away, for they are too terrifying. I stand up and begin to pace the room. I open the door and peer out along a corridor where figures in white flit in and out of other opening and closing doors. Many are wearing face masks, carrying clipboards. I have no idea where Michel has been taken. Suddenly, the foreignness of everything hits me and I begin to tremble.

I love this man with every fibre of my being. I could not bear to lose him. Suddenly, I am tormented by images of my father, of his deathbed and the funeral service. My fear is getting a grip. I must hold this together, I am thinking. And then the doctor returns. To give me an update, put me in the picture.

'I am zo zorree zat I kennot zpeek Engleesh,' he smiles. I nod without looking at him, because I am ashamed of my desire to weep, because I am terribly afraid and because I feel I am about the most useless woman ever. If this were a film, if I were playing a role, I would be bearing up. A mountain of controlled energy, stalwart, docile; the rock upon which a marriage is built. Or, at the other extreme, the alcoholic who can't hold anything together, the kind of role I am frequently offered these days. In reality I am neither, just ordinary and insignificant, lost in the labyrinthine world of another language and a situation over which I have no control and in which I can see no signposts to guide me forward.

The doctor begins to explain to me what they are testing Michel for but the words are long and incomprehensible and I cannot follow until I recognise one and lock on to it, as though I have been slugged: cancer.

Have I understood correctly? These days, most of the time, I move between French and English almost as easily as changing my clothes, but there are occasions, like now, when I panic and the language becomes scrambled. It is as though I am on the outside looking in, a moth fluttering beyond glass intent on reaching the light. Instead of being in communication, I feel lost and cannot grasp what is going on. Desperate to be sure, I repeat the word. Once, and then again.

'This is difficult for you, *n'est-ce pas*?'

I nod.

'What I am trying to tell you is that we do not think there is a cancer, but we must test, *non*? Come with me.'

And he leads me down one corridor after another to a vending machine, where coffee, tea and various other beverages are on offer. Pulling out a 5f coin, he asks me how I take my coffee. I cannot remember. He orders me an *express*. At that very same moment an aluminium trolley rolling on big black wheels appears from behind a swing door, followed by a young, bleached-blonde girl, thin as a wisp, who offers me the choice of croissants, *pain au chocolat* or ham or cheese baguettes. The

doctor sits with me and we eat breakfast together. Then he
leads me to a quiet corner, rests a kind hand on my shoulder
and hurries off to work.

The day passes, long and slow. When I am too drained to
pray any more, I cheer myself with lists of heavenly moments to
keep me company:

*Late warm evenings: returning home in evening dress, after
film and dinner at the Cannes Festival, to the song of
nightingales, lyrical beneath a blanket of stars. Dancing to
their music on the terraces, arms wrapped tightly round one
another, my head on Michel's white silk jacket.*

*Summer Sundays on our own, floating together naked in the
pool, in the world's largest azure-blue rubber ring – a birthday
present from me to Michel – water trickling through our
fingers and toes. Heat baking our backs, circling on a cushion
of bliss. The taste of chlorine on our lips. White flesh where
watches and rings have hidden centimetres from the sun.*

*Cool white linen sheets bearing the weight of sunburned
flesh.*

*The notes we have secreted in one another's luggage each
time we were separating, if only for a few days.*

*Lines from songs we have sung to one another: 'You taste
so sweet, I could drink a case of you,' and 'When you need
someone to love, don't go to strangers, lover, come to me.'*

*Airport goodbyes and then crushing kisses at the week's
end which say how much we missed one another.*

*How Michel paints every mundane article in striking
colours, even the hosepipe rollers – all of them inspired
contrasts. Picasso, when he lived close by our farm, was
unhappy about an electricity pylon which blighted the view.
The EDF refused to remove it, so he painted it a rainbow of
colours. We have one too, which Michel intends to
camouflage in similar fashion.*

A door opens. By now it is early evening. The doctor is returning. I leap to my feet, piercing his expression in the hope of
gleaning news. He does not speak directly and I fear the worst.
My stomach is churning.

'How is he? Where is he?'

'He's five minutes behind me, getting dressed.'

All has been discovered. Michel is suffering from a mild
form, early stages of, diverticulitis, probably caused, and certainly aggravated, by stress. The doctor is confident that it can
be treated with plenty of rest, no work, an extremely strict
diet, no wine and nothing that will irritate Michel's nervous
system. If, after all that has been tried, the condition has not
been resolved, then an operation may be required. The best
news is that Michel does not have to be kept in. He can come
home. Now.

During our return journey to the studio he does not even
question the choice of a taxi. He is very silent. Exhausted by
tubes and machines.

Over dinner – a chicken *bouillon* and Evian – we discuss our
predicament. With his usual brand of tenacity, which in this
particular situation I would describe as stubbornness, Michel
suggests that he will rest over the weekend and go back to work
on Monday. I will not hear of it and we begin to bicker until a
stomach cramp reminds us both that he must be kept calm.

The positive news, he tells me, is that the series is out on
offer all over the world. With a few healthy sales we can release
the farm. I smile encouragingly, but the battle to keep hold of
Appassionata has paled for me now. After all, magical as the
place is, we could always find another farm, another property
and begin again. It's the journey together that counts, not the
points of departure or disembarkation.

Once upon a time, oh, it seems a long while ago now, I
dreamed of a natural haven, of paradise winking down upon a
tranquil blue sea. I had pictured friends and family at ease in

my Garden of Eden, sharing and at peace, where artists worked and lovers loved. But it had been a vague sketch, a dream without connections between the dots, until I met Michel. Then it began to gain wattage. To take on a shape, develop light and shade, rhythm, sinew. Together, with the potency of our passion and creativity, we breathed eloquence, colour, fragrance, joy into those blurred images. Together, we have discovered how to live a new life. What has blossomed out of those dreams surpasses any bricks or mortar, or even the loveliest of pearly terraced olive groves. Our paradise lies in the depth of our love for one another. Its complexities and generosities. Our passion and exchange, our trust and commitment and sharing. To what geographical points our travelling takes us is no longer important.

Whatever Michel, with his dogged determination, believes, I suspect that our chances of hanging on to Appassionata are slim. But, painful as it is, I am ready for the loss now. Prepared to watch our quirkily dilapidated farm be seized by bankers who cannot begin, for all their grim-lipped numeracy, to calculate the wealth in every silvery leaf, each golden orange, the glittering of early-morning dew drooping in clusters from foliage and richly coloured petals. We began this enterprise on a shoestring. Love and tenacity have held it together. We can do it again if we have to. And in the discovery of all this, I have shed skins: driving ambition, materialism, a need to control my life. I am learning to let go and I feel empowered. My heart has found heart.

Poetry, or Love Song

Michel's health is improving. He works from his little studio in the mornings, then we meander for an hour or so up and down the crooked cobbled lanes of the Latin Quarter, pausing for stillness in the small garden facing Notre-Dame before poking about in the musty corners of the Shakespeare and Company bookshop until it is time for him to return and put his feet up for the remainder of the day. The pains have subsided. Our last visit to the doctor at the clinic was very reassuring. If Michel's health continues to improve at this rate, there will be no need for the operation and, before too long, he will be able to return to a more civilised diet. I feel a little quieter about leaving him. In an ideal world I would stay, but there is work to be done and in a few more days, he will join me at the farm for a simple and restful Christmas.

However, I cannot get home. The airport at Nice is closed. Each day I telephone Charles de Gaulle and am told that the situation has not changed. René is holding the fort but the olive season is commencing and he has over 700 trees to tend. I must return. What is going on in Nice? When I finally get through to the airport on the telephone, I am informed by a member of the Air France ground staff that the problem is the weather. Yes, but for five days now I have been trying to get a flight. What weather could possibly close an airport in a climate as temperate as ours for such a long period of time? She doesn't know. I check the weather pages in *Le Monde* and *Libération*. In both newspapers, alongside Nice is a miniature drawing of the sun, beaming at me beatifically. I am baffled. Eventually, I hire a little car and set off by road, taking with me everything we will need for the holidays. Just before my departure Michel receives a fax to say that the first sale of the series has been made, to Greece. We are over the moon. And how fitting it seems to us both that Greece, the spiritual home of the olive tree, will allow us to make our first reimbursement to the bank. It buoys me, for the thought of separation never gets easier. These days together have been harmonious and dulcet. Parting, particularly under these conditions, hurts.

I love to drive long distances. The solitude and the passing landscape clear my thoughts. Whenever I am blocked with my writing or have a problem to unravel I will get in the car and go for a spin. This trip offers me the perfect opportunity to mentally catch up on the time I have lost on my work. I stop for a quick lunch and, to stretch my legs, stroll around the mediaeval town of Beaune, gazing in the windows of antique shops, before continuing on my journey. It is a pleasing drive. The weather throughout the day is crisp and topaz-bright. The passing countryside is naked but for row upon row of twisted, wintry vines, smoking hillsides, frozen runnels of dark earth and occasional sightings of farmers or country folk clad in gloves and scarves and overcoats.

It is somewhere around Montelimar that night falls. Early,

because we are fast approaching the shortest days of the year. The sky is clear, a deep wistaria blue and the stars resplendent. At first, I mistake the glaringly bright light behind me for a car approaching on full beam and am irritated by the selfishness of some drivers. Then I glance in my wing mirror again and look more closely. There is no traffic. The great globe of light reflected there is the moon. I slow down, move over into the crawler lane and, because the road is deserted, pull up on the hard shoulder.

Everything on earth seems to be illuminated by its lunar glow. I have never seen the moon this bright. Waves of flaxen light on the silent, distant hillsides. I step out of the car and tilt my head to gaze heavenwards. The moon seems so close I could caress it or draw it down, cradle it in my arms. A platinum balloon, a great, round scoop of Montelimar nougat. Its proximity is eerie, awesome, but it lights my path all the way home.

Journey's end. I cross the bridge and turn into the lane. The familiarity of the approach is gratifying. Here are sweet-scented orange groves and agave cacti to welcome me. Here, silhouettes of lofty, coned cypresses. Here there is peace. I draw up outside the gates to search for my keys. The cottage, meant for a caretaker and sadly empty since the departure of Quashia, is lit up. For a fleeting moment I think that someone is in there and then I see that it is this same extraordinary moon casting beacons of light across the desolate garden, knee-high in weeds. Illuminating it as though with electricity.

The dogs plunge down the drive to meet me. Three of them. Ella, Lucky and who? No Name? No, the third animal is too small to be No Name. They yap and bark, panting and frolicking with excitement, following the unknown car the full reach of the ascent. Flanking us are the olive groves and, at the foot of each tree, our circular sprays of netting. Ah, it is a joy to be back. I wind down the window and breathe in the perfumed air. An owl screeches from somewhere in the forest high

above. I step from the car and am instantly bowled over by
three pairs of paws landing on my hips. There is much licking
and tail-wagging happiness. The third dog is a fellow, a black
and white hound with long, droopy ears and an even longer
piebald body. He is compact and muscular with legs like a
footballer. 'Who are you, where did you come from?' I ask
him, but he backs off shyly and begins to yowl like a country
and western singer, which makes me laugh. Before going inside,
I walk the terraces for a few minutes. Stretch my legs. Twisted
galaxies of stars dazzle like tinsel in the moonshine. The world
is as clear as broken daylight. Dare I take this as a sign that our
days of darkness are coming to an end? That soon life will be
reconciled and polychrome once more?

I am dead to the world the following morning, coming to consciousness only when I hear the diesel spit of René's sturdy
Renault climbing the drive. His arrival is greeted by a chorus of
barking dogs. I turn over and glance at the clock. Seven-thirty.
Downstairs, I hear the clatter of aluminium dog bowls scraping
the ground as they slurp and guzzle greedily. I grab a robe and
head out on to the terrace barefoot, calling as I go. The tiles are
cold. The air is brisk. The day is clear and ominously still.
René looks up and waves '*Bonjour! Tu vas bien?*' I nod, yawn,
stretching my sleepy, bed-warm body as I glance out across the
sweeping valley to the sea, where white horses are discernible
on choppy waves. A sign of wind. Bad weather coming in. '*Tu
veux un café?*'

He tells me yes and heads to the boot of his car, drawing out
a chainsaw. One of ours. Needed sharpening, he explains.

'By the way,' I call as I head back into the house. 'Whose dog
is that?'

'The hound? He turned up about a week ago, following your
Alsatian. Never leaves her side. I tried to shoo him off but he
won't budge. He's only a puppy.'

Coffee mugs in hand, on the terrace by the pool, we study the olive groves. Birds trill and echo in winter song. Overhead, a buzzard tracks and circles.

'Have you looked at the trees?' he asks.

'Briefly, last night. What is it? The *paon*?'

'No, no. I said it would be a bumper crop, but even I under-estimated. We'll need help. When's Michel back?'

I explain the news and he nods thoughtful concern then asks me to take a walk with him. We leave our cups on one of the garden tables and set off to tour the terraces. The trio of dogs canter at our heels until our new arrival emits a curious and rather comical baying, then takes off like a streak of lightning. The other two follow.

'He's a proper little hunter, that chap.'

'I wonder where he's come from? I'll have to call the vet and the refuge, find out if he's been reported missing.'

'Runt of a pack, I'd say. You might be stuck with him.'

I laugh, wondering what it is that makes our home such a popular hostel for stray dogs. Is it possible that they can sniff the old kennels here, in spite of our renovations? Do scents linger like memories?

During my absence the olives have grown plumper, slightly softer, but remain purply-green. The weight of such a crop is dragging the branches low. A few are brushing the nets. René drops on to his haunches and scans my famous green netting. There is barely an olive in sight. 'They are clinging fast to the trees. Not ripening. It's the same everywhere. I don't want the branches to start snapping.'

'What's the forecast?' I ask. 'It doesn't look too good out at sea.'

'I didn't hear. We should harvest some of this fruit. Of course, it won't yield the same quantity of oil, being so green, but I have – I don't know, a feeling in my bones.'

'What about?'

'Not sure. Never in all my years of *oléiculture* have I known the fruit refuse to ripen like this.'

'Could it be the *paon*?'

'It's not only your farm, it's all over.'

The hound returns, tail wagging, a dead rabbit hanging limply from between his jaws. His front legs are bloodied. I am appalled and want to chide him but what's the use? The little fellow is a hunter. He pants, pleased as punch with himself. Even so, I confiscate the still-warm corpse and carry it to the dustbin. Three disappointed mutts stare at me miserably as they watch their post-breakfast treat disappear before their eyes. I pretend to be cross with the little dog but I cannot help grinning at what a splendid threesome they make; retriever, Alsatian and hound, tails awagging.

René and I agree that he will make a start within a day or two. If I can find someone to lend him a hand it would save him some time; otherwise he can try to rope in some of his own cronies, but the problem is they are harvesting elsewhere. I promise to do my best but thoughts of Manuel stunt my expectations. As René settles in his car, he says, 'You'd better collect your oranges. My wife makes excellent marmalade and I'll make you the finest *vin d'orange* you've ever tasted. By the way, did you see on the television that this region is going to be granted an AOC next year? Of course, it won't be for the likes of you and me, but it should improve the local oil prices on the national market and that can't be a bad thing, can it?'

I smile. I have never tasted *vin d'orange*.

'*Diable!* I'll make you bottles of the stuff. You won't forget it!'

An Appellation d'Origine Contrôlée for the finest of the olive oils from this region. One or two areas of northern Provence have already been granted this coveted mark of respectability, and certain connoisseurs believe the olives from our coastal strip, particularly the modest *cailletier*, which is the variety we farm, to be the ones that produce the most delicious of all oils. I think it would be a splendid tag.

After combing the employment pages of the *Nice Matin*, our local rag, phoning one or two possible candidates – I even interview one rather pompous, ex-military chappie who arrives with a list of rules of what he will and won't do and then, due to his overaggressive demeanour, gets bitten by Lucky and I spend the rest of our farcical meeting bandaging his hand and generally pampering him for fear he might report both us and dog – I give up and put through a call to Quashia in Africa. It takes me several attempts. Each time I struggle to make myself understood in either French or English while at the other end a male voice – *le patron* of *le café*? – replies in Arabic and replaces the receiver. 'How are you?' I ask, several hours later when I eventually touch base with Quashia.

'What's happened?'

'Any chance you could get back? René is inundated with work and—'

'And the olives need harvesting. Yes, I've been thinking about it. I gave you my word. If you need me, I'll come.'

'What about your family?'

'I'll be there. Don't you worry about them. Is it urgent?'

'Pretty much. When could you be here?'

'I'll find out about flights tomorrow, or I'll organise a boat ticket. It shouldn't be too hard. All the traffic is going the other way, men returning to their families for Ramadan. Call me Saturday.'

We linger a while longer, exchanging trivialities about his life at home in Constantin, news of his ever-expanding family. I can hear the background hubbub and chatter of the Arab café. That world, so alien to mine, surrounding him. I picture him – where? – leaning up against a counter occupying the proprietor's one crackly phone line. In the background, well-worn plastic tables and chairs are crowded with creased-faced elders, sticks at the ready, drinking minuscule shots of pitch-black coffee, putting the world to rights. Who else, aside from us, I am asking myself, telephones a bar in northern Algeria to book the gardener? I smile; the image amuses me.

'Saturday then,' we agree, and say our goodbyes.

'If there are any problems, I'll ring you tomorrow,' he shouts, as an afterthought.

The next day, around one, I am working and hear the phone. As a rule, I would let it ring or leave the answering machine to take a message but I have a hunch it might be Quashia, which it is.

'*Bonjour.*' My ears are keen to the fact that he is not calling from his local café. The background is silent, apart from a truck or two roaring by. Is he in a callbox in some dusty Arab side street? I fear the worst but try hard not to reveal how desperately I need him to return. 'What's the news?'

'I am in Marseille. My train gets me to Cannes at fifteen-seventeen.'

'When? Today?' I am speechless. 'But how did you . . . ?'

'I took the boat, travelled overnight. I'll see you later.'

We say nothing about me meeting him off the train in Cannes. I have no idea if that is what he has in mind, but by 2.45 I am down at the station, sitting in front of an *express* at a café across the street. From a well-placed seat, I can keep an eye on all the comings and goings of passengers, in case his train should arrive early. His TGV is on time, and then I see him. Black Persian wool hat on his head, carrying not even so much as an overnight bag. One split carrier bag with Arabic lettering printed on its side is his sole piece of luggage. He looks exhausted and unshaven. I wave and shout and run to greet him. His warm eyes dance merrily and he grins his tobacco-toothed grin and we embrace like long-lost family. People look on, some with disapprobation. This is, after all, Le Pen country and here am I embracing an Arab workman.

'Here, I brought this for you.' He hands me the carrier bag. Inside are swags of fresh, sticky, treacly-coloured dates clinging fast to skeletal fronds. There must be a thousand of them. I thank him and picture the little pencil-box of dried dates my mother used to buy us as a treat at Christmastime. On its lid were coloured illustrations of camels trekking a desert. How exotic they seemed to me then.

'My grandson picked them from the garden before we left for the port. He said next time you and Michel are to come and pick them yourselves.'

'We will,' I promise.

'My family want to meet you. We'll go to the desert, take off on a trek.'

Arm in arm, we thread our way through the tangle of vehicles, impatient scooters and pedestrians to Michel's ancient Mercedes, which is barely more roadworthy than my car was and is twice as unmanageable as it lacks power steering.

'Where's the Quatre L?' he asks. Quatre L, pronounced 'Katrelle', is the nickname the French use to fondly describe that most typical of all workman's cars, my sadly missed Renault 4.

'It drowned,' I sigh.

'Drowned?'

'A storm in Nice swelled the banks of the river alongside the airport. The place was closed for days. I couldn't get back and when I went to collect the car, I found the parking lot had been flooded and all the cars had drowned. How forlorn it looked, the little Quatre L. Swimming in silty mud, rusted, tyres sinking . . .' I recount, smiling. 'The attendant said to me, "No charge for the parking!"'

Quashia roars with infectious laughter. Climbing the hills, smutty black smoke billowing from the exhaust, I listen to his

tales, at ease in his company. First, his journey. At such short
notice, there were no bunks to be had. He travelled across the
sea sitting on the upper deck, perched against a lifeboat, watching the stars.

'You must be dead.'

He grins and a solitary gold tooth glints his happiness. 'Yes,
but it's how I like to travel. Not a soul around. Constellations
of stars and a full moon to guide us, and the roll of the sea
beneath me, wending my way back.' I glance towards him. His
wrinkled, baked-brown features are animated with the recol-
lection of his voyage and any guilt I may have felt about having
dragged him out of his early retirement disappears instantly. I
understand him well enough to know that he is positively
delighted to be back. Quashia is not a man made for retirement.
And this corner of France is for him, as it is for us, a spiritual
home.

The following bright winter's morning, when we are alone
together gathering our first crop of oranges from the regrown
trees, Quashia begins to talk of his past. He was twelve years
old when his father died, leaving behind him a wife, three sons
and two daughters, but not a penny. Their sole possessions
were two barns. It was during the Algerian war with France.
French soldiers came, the family fled and the soldiers burned
the two barns. Quashia went up into the mountains and began
to collect and cut wood, which he sold to buy food for his
mother and younger brothers and sisters. His eldest brother left
for France, where he found work, sending back money each
month to help feed and clothe his kin. With the modest income
Quashia acquired from his wood sales, he constructed a small
homestead for his family which even today, he assures me – he
will show it to Michel and me when we visit – is still standing,
although it has now been abandoned. He had never placed one
stone on top of another before, but he managed to build the

little house by watching others at their work. Reassured that his family were safely ensconced in a home, a roof over their heads at last, he left by boat for Marseille to join his eldest brother here on the Provençal coast and to learn the masonry trade in earnest. He had been in France only a week when his brother was run over and killed instantly by an American army jeep. Marines on shore leave driving along the seafront in Cannes. There was no inquest. Nothing. Quashia returned to *la mairie*, the town hall, day after day, begging for justice, but his French was minimal, he was just a lad of fifteen, and no one listened. The Americans were the liberators here, the Arabs had been the enemy, and those living in France were – still are – no more than a secondary labour force. The matter was never investigated. Eventually, a couple of years later, his mother received a cheque for the equivalent of 5,000f, a settlement for the death of her eldest son. Strangely, Quashia bears no grudges. He tells the tale of fifty years ago as though he were recounting the history of another man's life. It is the way of Allah, he shrugs. And the healing of time, I am thinking.

The weather is strange, unpredictable. Yes, clear and warm, typical for this pre-Christmas season, except unnaturally still. And then, every now and again, the vegetation shivers a warning. Out at sea, there are still white caps on the waves but there is no wind coming in. René arrives and we begin to gather olives. 'If they don't fall at the touch, don't force them,' he commands. Quashia cuts himself a long, sturdy stick to beat the upper branches but René forbids him to use it.

I leave them to their debate and drive to the airport to collect Michel. First, though, I make a stop at the fruit and vegetable market to buy the fresh food essential to his diet. There I fall upon kiwi fruit on offer: twenty for 10f. Delicious for breakfast along with mandarins, bananas, grapes and two succulently ripe mangos flown in overnight from the Dom Tom –

Départements et Territoires d'outre-mer – islands belonging to the Republic of France, in this instance, Martinique. Michel prepares the best fruit salads known to man. They are a feast not only for the tastebuds but also for the eyes. He serves them sliced and arranged in a rainbow of colours and shapes which would rival any decorative plate designed by Picasso in the nearby village of Vallauris.

I arrive at the airport to greet him, merrily swinging my carrier bag of exotic fruit and crunchy, verdant salads which have cost me in total the princely sum of 57f, 90c. Michel is looking far more relaxed but has lost a great deal of weight. At first this scares me, and then I remind myself that anyone who has spent a month or more living on chicken broth, mineral water and herbal teas would have lost weight. Our Christmas diet will be regulated but not untenable. We hurry to the car park holding hands. It seems an age since he was home, and I want nothing more than to cherish and feed him.

Back at the house we find a message from René. He delivered our olives to the mill this afternoon where they were pressed immediately. Six and a half kilos of fruit required for every litre of oil. He sounds very depressed. If the fruit does not ripen and the yield is no greater – it is taking a third more fruit to produce each litre of oil – the season will be a catastrophe for the local farmers.

I understand his deep concern in a way that I might not have done a year or more ago. We are not dependent on our farm for our livelihood but we have known the icy winds of scarcity ourselves this autumn, and we are still battling against very unfavourable odds. A shortfall in a film budget or a poor harvest, what's the difference? All the hard work and determination in the world cannot change the tides of fate, it seems. The point is, somehow or other, to ride it out. *Gardez le cap.*

*

'Funny valentine,' croons Chet Baker from the CD-player. We stoke up the fire, ditch the dishes from our *pâté à langoustines* in the kitchen and prepare for an early night. From the terrace, while closing the shutters, I notice the waves rippling fast across the sea. They glint in the soft shadows of night like chain mail, while high up on the hill behind us an owl screeches raucously and I hear creaking and moaning in the treetops. The weather is spooky tonight, and unsettling. It is as though nature were on the move, shifting, readjusting, reclaiming its territory. I think of Macbeth. I don't know why. That forest, or wood, rather, creeping closer. 'Stones have been known to move, and trees to speak . . .'

We curl up in bed together, tight in one another's arms, and I feel grateful not to be alone in this old house tonight.

It is the crashing of pottery on the flat roof right above my head that wakes me, jolting me back to consciousness. Outside, beyond the solid stone walls which encircle us and keep us safe, a storm has whipped up. I lie still, listening. There have been storms here before, many of them, but this is furious. At my side, Michel sleeps on. I creep from the bed and tiptoe across the cold tiles to peer from the windows. Beyond, everything is pitch-black, which means that the electricity has gone. Not only ours – whenever there's a storm our trip switch in the garage cuts off the current as a safety precaution – but all the way across the hills and valleys. I can make out nothing but black shapes that look like hunched goblins. Out at sea the horizon is murky with cloud or spumy spray. In the foreground, the tall, pointed cypress trees are twisting and turning, bending and swaying, wraith-like beings lost in a frenzied voodoo dance.

I pad back to bed and close my eyes. I want to sleep but the storm grows. Its force escalates from one minute to the next. It blows relentlessly, screaming, not whistling. Howling like a banshee, the Irish fetcher of the dead. This image terrifies me and I rise again. My heart is beating too fast. I want to wake Michel but decide not to. He needs to rest. The shutters everywhere in the house are slapping against their locks. I fear this wind will rip them from their hinges. I light a candle, which gutters furiously and then dies. I return to the window. I consider the dogs curled up in their stable. They must be petrified. I am. I would go out and fetch them, but if I opened the door it would be whipped from its hinges and carried off into space. Garden chairs are flying everywhere. A table sinks to the depths of the pool. Things – Lord knows what – are crashing and shattering. Nothing stands in the way of this untamed wind. Its raging has risen to tempest, even hurricane force. I press my trembling body against the glass, recalling lines from Eliot's *The Waste Land*.

> There is not even silence in the mountains
> But dry sterile thunder without rain.

Every tree is bowed over, mastered by the gale. And then a groaning, a destruction, which is akin to a werewolf's howl; a tearing of life to shreds. Freaked, I retreat to bed and curl up like a squirrel. Michel, from somewhere within his slumbering subconscious, must be aware of my restlessness because he stirs. 'Be still, *chérie*,' he whispers, and wraps his arms about me, drawing me to him, and I fall in with his breathing, breath for breath, heartbeat with heartbeat, and drift off to sleep, dug into the crook of him, from midnight to dawn.

Morning comes. Eventually. The wind has not abated. We are woken around six by a furious thumping. The wind beating at our door. We leap from the bed and rush to shove furniture against it. A wooden chest, two chairs and a bookcase, which totters in the panic, slapping my precious, well-thumbed, orange Penguins to the floor. It takes all this to hold the door in place. Peering from the one unshuttered window in my work-space, we see that the landscape has been flattened. The views are wider where trees have been ripped from the ground, crashing like tin soldiers everywhere. But still it is not over.

'How will we get to the dogs?' I ask.

'I'll go out by the front door. As soon as I'm out, push the furniture back in place.' We haul our wooden pieces into the hallway and the door begins thumping again. Michel turns the key and opens it less than an inch. A blast of wind and the pungent scent of pine engulfs us. Felled, like a monster, an underwater sea beast with tendrils, is our beautiful blue pine tree. It has swamped the entire length of the upper terrace. There is no exit.

'My God, that must've been what I heard crashing. It must've taken part of our renovated wall and some of the balustrades with it.'

We cannot make coffee as we have no electricity. There is nothing to be done but wait it out. I return to the window, staring out at this raging, chaotic world. This perturbation of nature. We could go stir-crazy on this windswept hilltop, and what of those three poor dogs? Have they fled in fear? And then I light on a sight which warms my heart.

'Michel, look!' Michel comes to join me and together we watch Quashia, hand pressed against his sheepswool hat, mounting the drive, tacking in wide zigzags, blown from one step to the next. A slow, heavy slog as he battles against the weather. When he reaches the summit alongside the pool, in front of the garage, he pauses and stares about, horrified. We cannot see what he sees, but the devastation must be shocking. I beat on the window, but he cannot hear me. And then, as a reflex, he looks up, sees us and beckons. Michel signals our dilemma.

Once dogs have been reassured and the blue pine has been dragged away from the door, we are free to go out. I consider

Noah and what it must have been like to step from that ark. Our wind has not abated. It is calming, but it is far from done.

We check out the wreckage. As far as we can tell we have lost about fourteen trees, mostly pines, our glorious blue among them, and possibly one oak further up the hill. At the foot of our recently discovered Italian staircase, a very tall pine has been ripped from the ground. Its roots have dismembered the lower part of the ancient wall while the massive trunk has smashed and sundered into thick chunks a romantically sequestered stone table and banquette. A cypress, one of a dozen which encircles the parking area, has been uprooted and taken with it a drystone wall and an *Opuntia Ficus Indica*, a giant prickly-pear cactus. We should be grateful that it has fallen towards the vegetable gardens – though missing them, mercifully – and not the parking area, or our sole means of transport, the thirty-year-old Mercedes, would have been flattened. I am heartbroken to discover that four of my antique Barbary pots, a birthday present from Michel, have been smashed to smithereens.

We set to work, clearing up the devastation of this first night, dragging away entire branches of wood pregnant with clusters of pine balls. Small yolk-yellow flowers gild the dusty blue boughs of our favourite pine – the only one of its kind on the estate – while the potent perfume from its seeping, sticky gum pervades the clear, sharp morning. It is as though the dying tree is bleeding, or weeping.

The wind is bitter. It has an arctic bite to it and stings our sweating flesh. As we work, Quashia talks again of his youth, of the long, cold winter after the death of his father. He recounts stories of endless journeys, marching alone for several days into the mountains in search of wood for his mother and her brood. There, among the snowy mountains, he gathered and stacked until he had all that he could carry. Then he began the slow march back, like a donkey, his body weighted down with strips of wood, to the humble dwelling where he and his grieving family were hibernating. In my mind's eye I picture that small, dark-skinned Arab youth, his loss and his determination, and I feel honoured that through the sharing of his memories he has taken us back half a century to an Arab world that we might never have entered without him. He has lifted moments from his adolescence in a land unknown to me and pulled them forward to the present, where they can co-exist with our own experiences. It reminds me that the Australian aborigines have no words in their language for yesterday or tomorrow.

In return, Michel talks of his childhood in northern Germany, not far from the Belgian border; of a countryside ravaged by war, of a father who, before Michel was born, spent several of those years in a prison camp, though he was an army cook and not a soldier. I am moved when I hear that Anni, Michel's mother, walked from their village all the way to the camp, a trek which took her several days, carrying her first-born son with her to introduce him to his father. And then it is my turn. I spin tales of my English and Irish past. I paint the rolling, verdant landscape, the incessant soft rain, salmon fishing down at the coursing, bouldered river with my uncle, the lingering smell of potatoes boiling on the wood stove, losing my sister in a cornfield, a maze of gold taller than both of us, the warm, cackling voices of my grandparents' neighbours, as well as illicit friendships with 'those Protestant kids' huddled in packs behind the village post office. And I recall the scenes of violence I witnessed. The bloodshed. Hesitantly, I touch upon those.

And so we pass our day. At sunset, we settle around our big table and drink hot mint tea sweetened with lavender honey, and Michel reminds me that we should be thinking about acquiring our own hives and planting vines. I invite Quashia to stay and eat with us – we have electricity again – but he waves his hand and smiles. He has a pot prepared, he says, and bids us goodnight, wending his way down the drive to the cottage where, because it is situated in a sheltered nook, there has been no damage whatsoever. I wonder at his solitary existence, but it seems to suit him. Months in Algeria and then other months here with us. His two families.

And now the wind is rising again, but according to the news on the radio it will be less forceful tonight. We are worn out from the physical work of the day but also deeply grateful, because in one of the neighbouring villages the toll this morning was eight dead. At its peak, the wind on this Alpes-Maritimes coast reached 150 kilometres an hour. The roads are closed, even our little lane. We cannot get out by car to buy food. If we need supplies we must walk the towpath by the stream to the village. We learn that 3 million families in France are without electricity and half as many again have no telephone. Thousands have been left homeless and the death toll is rising.

The following morning, this holocaust of nature is at an end. We step from shuttered darkness out into blindingly bright sunlight and a sky as clear as cut glass. Still, the air has a frisson of danger; every now and then a branch stirs, and shivers a reminder. Bushes and trees have been twisted and split out of all recognition. They will for ever bear the imprint of this tempest's passage.

There is so much work to be done.

The hillsides are thrumming with the whirr of chainsaws. I find it a reassuring sound, like the summer song of the cicadas. On neighbouring peaks, folk are beginning the work of cutting and stacking the trees torn from the earth and riven. Sawdust floats like snow in the bright, clean air. Nature's quiescence of today feels almost as alarming as the roaring winds of the past two nights, its quiddity disturbingly manifold.

Michel and I repot the yucca plants lifted from the smashed

Barbary pots. When we are less up against it, I will buy more. We shovel debris, wheeling the barrow backwards and forwards to the compost and to dozens of small hillocks piled high with stripped branches, ready for burning. I lift the plastic cover off one of the pool skimmer baskets and put in my hand to dig out the fallen leaves, and there to my horror, coiled like a spring, is a snake. My shrieks bring gales of laughter and the perfect opportunity to pause for refreshment. Amid the devastation, early cyclamen are flowering rich reds and luscious pinks. I come across an uprooted palm, one of a dozen baby ones we planted which had grown tall, furnished with long, prickly fronds. It will not survive.

All day we labour in a garden bathed in seductively warm Christmas sunshine. High above us, in a perfectly hyacinthine sky, the birds are returning. Gulls turn and pipe lazily, on the look-out for food. In the treetops, tiny, busy birds are chirruping insanely. Their chatter seems so urgent and engaged. What fun to be able to understand, to eavesdrop or even participate. And three, no four, even five, cooing turtle doves settle in the *Magnolia Grandiflora. Les tourterelles,* welcome, timely visitors.

René arrives. He is very depressed. Damage to his olive farms everywhere. Trees destroyed. Magnificent centuries-old *oliviers* split, amputated, fallen. The moon, they say, is the cause. Its proximity to the earth. Once in a century, it draws so perilously close. What of his crops? Tons of fruits lying on the ground, scattered everywhere. Now the olives will never ripen. We take a tour together of our own groves and discover that a pair of our trees, growing alongside one another, have been severed in two by the storms. It is as though a colossus has come by with an axe and sliced right through the heart of the trunks. Sheer, like a knife through butter. In each case, one half of the tree remains upright, bearing its semi-ripened fruit, while its twin lies on the ground like a smashed bird, wings limp and broken. Its fruit is still intact but drying up fast, wrinkling towards death. It is a tragedy. We must begin collecting the fallen fruit without delay. Our windblown nets are all over the garden, curled like sleeping caterpillars. Inside is the fruit which fell to the ground before the storms.

Elsewhere, the olives have been blown hither and thither and need to be collected individually by hand. The four of us, baskets at our sides, spend the sunny afternoon on our hands and knees. Gathering the windblown fruit is a slow and painstaking task. All my nails crack and break as my fingers root between the grass shoots and dig into the winter earth to lift out the buried olives. Many of them have already begun to wrinkle, or, worse, to rot.

Later, we relax with several glasses of rich, ruby-red *vino* from Chianti – except for Quashia, who accepts only *eau cit-ronné*, with sliced lemon which has fallen from our own tree – as the sun sets behind distant hills. The view as dusk falls is as clear as shined windows. All at once, the sky grows gentian with bold, untidy streaks of brilliant orange. Somewhere along the coast it must have been raining, for a rainbow appears and straddles the calm sea. This earth made out of chaos is settling back into peace.

The following afternoon, Manuel turns up. He happened to be passing, he says, though there is no reason on God's earth for anyone to pass this way en route to anywhere else. He staggers the length of the hilly drive, spluttering and perspiring, shakes our hands enthusiastically and asks after a spot of work. 'A bit of tidying after the wind?' Our answer is a most emphatic no. He shrugs amicably and, as he turns to go, remarks on how very much he enjoyed his time working for us.

The New Year comes and passes tranquilly. The olives are ripen-ing at last; each day we watch the shift in colours as they turn from green towards violet, then a luscious grape-purple and onwards towards deep, succulent black. They are plump, fleshed out with oil and there is a packet of them, or as the French would say, *un vrai pacquet*. Christophe greets us at the mill with a dramatically sullen expression. This year is a tragedy, he repeats over and over again, shaking his shaggy, hangdog head. He peers into one of our brimming baskets, picks up a fruit or two and pulls that Provençal face which could mean one of many things. In this case, *pas mal, pas mal*. Michel needs to make some phone calls, so he and I take off for a coffee and leave René to oversee the pressing. When we return the pair of them are as gleeful as children. René grabs Michel by the arm and asks anxiously, 'You did post that form, didn't you?'

Michel is confused. 'Which form?'

Christophe pushes forward, impatiently. 'I gave René a form for you to register yourselves as *oléiculteurs*. Did you or did you not fill it in and send it to Brussels?' He is bawling like a madman while Michel responds with a composed, '*Mais oui. Pourquoi?*'

Christophe heaves a theatrical sigh of relief. We are puzzled by the intensity of his concern. 'Your farm is the first this year,' he goes on to explain in a more reasonable manner, 'to produce oil at less than four kilos a litre. And what is more the quality is exceptional.' And with that he yells for wine. His young son, the miller, obliges. René is pouring glasses. Their ebullient mood is contagious. The wife is called down to the mill floor, as well as the brawny chap who shovels the olives into the chute, and who I have never seen without a cigarette glued to his lips; also the youngest son, who is responsible for the quality of the tapenade, and even a customer or two are roped in to celebrate what they are all but claiming is the future of the local olive industry.

Everyone congregates in a grand circle while in the background noisy machines belch and deliver. More glasses are poured, biscuits flavoured with essence of orange are offered. This is a real *fête*, and all in our honour, it seems.

'Any week now,' Christophe bellows, 'the inspectors from the AOC body will be arriving. How could I admit that not a single farm in the vicinity is producing oil at anything less than six kilos a litre? And even that is of average quality. I would be disgraced. All my new equipment, transported from Italy to comply with Brussels – bah, it would count for nothing. *Rien! Rien de tout!* We, this region, would be a laughing stock. Dismissed! *Nul!* Zero!' By now he is roaring at the top of his very forceful voice. It must be because he spends his life battling against this thundersome machinery, I am thinking. His red cheeks are shiny with exertion and proclamation while his long-faced audience hangs on his every word. This could be a rally. *'Mais, vous, mes chers amis,'* here, wine glass in hand, he points at us while René, flushed and proud, smiles on benignly as though we were his children, 'have proved that this area is worthy of the honour. *A la vôtre!*' And all glasses are raised to us.

Back at the house a fax awaits us from Michel's production office in Paris. It tells us that the Greek money has arrived. With this information have come pages of news of a dozen or more other sales. Dollars are finally en route to the bank. We should whoop and dance, open bottles of champagne, pour them over ourselves, yell and jump for joy. That is how I have imagined this moment, over and over in my mind, and prayed for it. But we don't. We stand quietly, reams of floppy fax paper in Michel's hands, and smile at one another.

'Looks as though we're going to make it,' he whispers.

'Looks like it.' I smile.

And so we can be confident that, in the fullness of time, the debt will be cleared entirely. We will not lose our farm. Not this time. Our crazy little ramshackle farm, which boasts herb and vegetable gardens but still no kitchen, and where the walls continue to flake and chunks of plaster still occasionally fall on our heads, and which now, thanks to Christophe and to René and to the work of dear, loyal Quashia, looks set to be awarded an AOC status for the quality of its olive oil. How did this all happen? We never intended to be farmers!

The girls, *les belles filles*, are arriving later this evening. Tomorrow we can, we will, party. We are taking them to Menton, where a street festival in celebration of the lemon is to take place, *la fête des citronniers*. Menton, the Franco-Italian border town where every garden is gilded with sweetly scented citrus fruit. And where every hot-blooded Latin lover will be ogling our two teenage beauties and not giving a damn for the tons of lemons and oranges adorning the floats (and which, by the way, have been imported from Spain).

Spring is returning. Baby geckos scuttle out from behind the shutters. A red fox sits in the sun on one of the upper terraces in among the wild irises which deck the drystone walls. A beetle-like insect trundles over a rose-pink wild garlic flower. Today, his carapace is a deep, iridescent bottle-green. In a month or two, he will be bracken-brown. The almonds are in palest bloom once more. The lizards who spent the winter holed up in a million fissures in the walls are zipping to and fro, shy as ever. Shiny lime-green leaves are breaking out everywhere. Orange blossom embalms the air. I pause and gaze upon our ruin, bathed in flaxen stalks of dappled sunlight. Budding Judas trees, peaches and figs encircle it, and I know I woke up in a poem. Soon, there will be heavenly purple and white lilacs, pear and cherry blossom, and apple blossom on the trees in the little orchard I am creating in memory of my dear, much-missed father.

Yet another year is unfolding, flush with romance and exploration. And while I am musing on where to place a sundial, Michel comes running towards me, smiling and healthy.

News of another sale has just come in. An important market, rich in dollars. A small percentage of which can go to the bank.

'Yes!' I whoop. 'Yes! I was considering a sundial,' I say. 'I have always fancied a garden with an antique stone sundial.'

'You are such a romantic, *chérie*.'

We chatter on about the projects we might begin when we return from our travels, of the baby olive trees we want to plant. Michel sees beehives and vines on the hillsides; I picture myself atop a tractor trundling up and down the terraces, mounds of *fumier de mouton* behind me to feed our sapling trees.

Arm-in-arm we hike the terraces, three loyal dogs at our heels, including our comical hound who answers to the name of Bassett. We are searching out the first spiky tulip shoots when unexpectedly, from the radio, on our balustraded balcony, I hear, 'I'll Be With You in Apple Blossom Time', and I am reminded that love is timeless, and regenerative. Like the wind, love leaves its imprints everywhere.

THE
Olive
Season

A cknowledgements

My very special thanks go, as always, to my loyal agent, Sophie Hicks, and to the team at Ed Victor, whom I regard as champagne-quaffing buddies and without whom my professional life would grind to a halt: Maggie Phillips, Hitesh Shah and Grainne Fox.

While out promoting the first volume of this story, *The Olive Farm*, I met some of the people whose job it is to sell books. I understood then what a vital role booksellers play in the publishing process, so my thanks to them, too, for supporting me, welcoming me into their stores and promoting my work.

Almost without fail, when working on a film or television drama, I get a really uplifting kick from the team spirit it engenders. Now, for the first time since I have been pottering about in the publishing world, I know it elsewhere: at my publishing house, Time Warner Books. The group of people who have worked on *The Olive Farm* and *The Olive Season* are too numerous to name. They include the sales guys I have travelled about with, signing books and grabbing sandwiches; the marketing people; the design team who have given me such stunning jackets; fabulous publicists and, of course, the editorial team. I mention one out of such a splendid force because he has become an inspiration to me, my editor and friend Alan Samson.

Contents

For Michel,
I was born in love with you.

And for my mother. Our friendship has been a
long time in the budding. But now that I have
understood what she was fighting for, I want
her to know how much I love her.

The Ancients sang their way all over the world. They sang the rivers and ranges, salt-pans and sand dunes. They hunted, ate, made love, danced, killed: wherever their tracks led they left a trail of music. They wrapped the whole world in a web of song; and, at last, when the Earth was sung, they felt tired.

Bruce Chatwin, *The Songlines*

This is a true story. A fragment of my own and, because it is my own, I have taken certain liberties: bent time, changed names, rejigged the script here and there. 'To protect the innocent,' as they say in the movies. As well as a few of the guilty lurking within these pages.

CD

Getting Spliced, Polynesian-Style

The car draws to a halt in the leafy lane that not so many years ago was barely a mule track. In front of us is a set of tall, Matisse-blue gates. Ours.

'*C'est bon*, we'll walk the rest of the way,' Michel informs our driver.

Our man at the wheel is puzzled, and so am I.

Michel smiles, and insists. '*Vraiment*, there's no need to take us further.'

In the boot of this Mercedes taxi is an extremely heavy suitcase, an aluminium briefcase containing Michel's video-camera equipment, two laptops and one hand-painted didgeridoo measuring close to four foot in length, as well as sundry pieces of rather battered hand luggage. It is evident to anyone that carrying all this will be no easy exercise. It is also obvious that beyond the locked gates there is a drive which snakes up a steep hillside, and we are both exhausted and jet-lagged. We have been travelling for more than twenty-four hours. Yes, the prospect of carting our luggage by hand and tramping the hill on foot feels like more than I am able to face, but now I see what Michel has seen.

Our three dogs, led by Lucky, the Alsatian, are bounding down the drive. Lucky, who had been abandoned, and who I found curled up like a moth-eaten mat at the foot of our property, bone-thin and nervy. We decided to adopt her, and here she is now, airborne at the gates, barking and growling at the innocent driver.

He stares fearfully at her. '*Ah, vous avez raison, monsieur.*'

Our bags are swiftly unloaded, the fare is settled and, once the car has safely rounded the corner, Michel unlocks the iron gates. They creak like a mummy's tomb as I pull them open and three sets of canine paws land firmly on my stomach, tails wagging.

We are home.

I scan the terraces, planted with row upon row of ancient olive trees. It is April, late spring. Here in the hills behind the Côte d'Azur, the olive groves are delicately blossomed with their tiny, white-forked flowers. Beyond them, perched halfway up the slope of the hill, our *belle époque* villa comes into view. Abounding in balustrade terraces, nestling among cedars and palms, facing out at a south-westerly angle, overlooking the bay of Cannes towards the sun-kissed Mediterranean, there it is, Appassionata, awaiting us.

'Mmm, it's good to be back,' I murmur.

'Would you like me to carry you?' asks Michel.

'Carry me? I know I'm tired, but I'm not that exhausted!'

'Over the threshold, *chérie*,' he adds with a grin and a wink.

Ah, yes. I had momentarily forgotten. We are returning to our olive farm as man and wife. We tied the knot a week ago at the whackiest of wedding ceremonies. Our nuptials took place on the tiny tropical atoll of Aitutaki, one of the Cook Islands in the South Pacific.

'You know, I never thought I'd go through with it,' I giggle.

'What's that?'

'Getting married.'

'Well, there you go.'

I smile, reminding myself of how it all came about.

The first time Michel proposed to me was in Australia on our very first date. We were sitting side by side at a table in an open-air restaurant in Elizabeth Bay; shy strangers awaiting two plates of Sydney Bay prawns.

'I think we have a problem,' Michel said to me.

I looked across at him in surprise.

'I've fallen in love with you,' he muttered softly. 'Will you marry me?'

I confess that I was completely blown away and reacted as any amazed woman might, which was to gulp down a huge mouthful of my Brown Brothers Chardonnay and shrug off the proposal with a confused laugh. The fact is, I didn't take this handsome, blue-eyed man seriously. In any case, I was a career girl, a thirty-something actress, independent, ambitious, in demand and not the type to settle down. Or so I was perpetually reminding myself in those days. Terrified of commitment, scared of losing or being hurt was probably closer to the truth. And although within months of that first dinner in Australia we had scrambled together the rather substantial cash deposit to secure this gloriously dilapidated property, I hedged my bets as far as marriage was concerned. Until one morning, the following autumn, Michel flew in to London from Paris, arrived at my flat, went down on one knee, small, square jewellery box in

one hand and the other holding mine, and said: 'We have
known each other a year now. A year to the day, exactly. We
have our olive farm. Soon all the papers will be signed and
it will officially belong to us. I think we are very happy.
Both my daughters adore you, Carol, *chérie*, and I, *je t'aime
avec tout mon coeur*. So will you, please, accept to be my
wife now?'

My heart was beating like a clapperboard. I love Michel
passionately, but was I capable of taking that final step?

Out popped my answer. 'Only if the King of Tonga marries us.'

What did I know of the King of Tonga? No more than
anyone else: that he was famous for his massive girth, was
the ruling monarch of a small archipelago of Pacific islands
and that he was Polynesian. It was a flippant response
intended only to buy me more time and keep that final itsy
bit of commitment at bay. But even then, after so many
months of living with Michel, I was underestimating the
measure of his love for me and the tenacity of a film producer's spirit – or this one's, certainly – for they can usually
be counted upon to provide whatever mise en scène has been
requested.

A few weeks later I was back in Sydney and at work. I was
filming a series based on a book written by me and produced by Michel. A fax arrived at the hotel from the
kingdom of Tonga, addressed to me. Buried in the make-
believe world of the role I had created for myself, I had
completely forgotten my careless riposte of weeks earlier
and so the fax bemused me at first. It was handwritten by the
King's personal secretary. Standing in the hotel lobby, I read
on. The communication sought photocopies of my and my
parents' birth certificates and my current passport, details of
criminal record, if any, religious adherences, etc. I flipped to
the next page, heart palpitating, beginning to anticipate what

was coming. Continuing, His Highness's secretary explained that the King insisted all betrothed visiting his island be scrupulously investigated before any 'joining in holy matrimony blessed by His Royal Highness could be approved'.

I dashed upstairs to my seaview suite, telephoned Paris, woke Michel and immediately began to interrogate him. 'Is this a practical joke?' I cried. 'Is it? I mean, what's it all about?'

I could almost hear the smile in his voice as he confirmed that, as I had entreated, we were to be married in the royal kingdom by none other than King Taufa'ahau Tupou IV, the King of Tonga. To say that I was stunned when I replaced the receiver would be an understatement. Still, after a minor panic attack, my enthusiasm for the idea began to grow. A South Sea-island wedding, warm, spumy waves lapping our naked toes as they sank into golden sands, a portly Polynesian potentate waving a scarlet hibiscus or two over our heads, muttering blessings in an incomprehensible tongue . . . Mmm, I thought, if I've got to go, then this is the way to go.

Having furnished the necessary mountain of paperwork, I then learned that the wedding ceremony would be a very different function to the one I had been dreaming of. The King was a devout Methodist. There would be no beach celebrations, no champagne. Prayers, countless hymns and a protracted service would be the order of the day, and no alcohol. I have nothing against such weddings for those who select them but it was not what I had envisaged for us, and so I rang Michel again. This time to explain, rather sheepishly, that I didn't fancy the wedding he was organising.

'Couldn't we just forget it?' I muttered, all too aware of the trouble he must have gone to to bring the arrangements thus far.

He accepted my reservations without complaint. All plans

were halted, and not much more was said on the subject of marriage until three years later, which is to say a little more than a month ago.

We were back in Sydney, the city where we met four years earlier, having dinner with a fellow television producer and longstanding friend of Michel's, Roger. During the course of the meal he asked, in the rather blunt manner Australians sometimes favour: 'I thought you folks were getting spliced. What happened? Decided yer don't like one another? I warned yer she'd be too much for yer, mate!'

I blushed as Michel recounted my objections to the almost forgotten Tongan escapade. Roger guffawed and laughed. 'Bloody lucky escape, I'd say, mate. That old bugger's a religious nut. And they're all still cannibals at heart. You must have heard the story about his mother, the old Queen, when she travelled on the *QE2*?' And before we could reply, Roger proceeded to recount the well-known anecdote about Queen Salote who, when handed the dinner menu at the captain's table, perused it briefly before passing it back to the waiter, saying, 'There's nothing there I fancy. Please bring the passenger list.'

'Listen, why don't you go to Rarotonga? The — Hotel will put on a good do for yer, and no questions asked. Won't even check if y'er already married! Get yerselves spliced, Polynesian style.'

Rarotonga, I learned then, is the capital of the fifteen Cook Islands, which remain, loosely speaking, a protectorate of New Zealand. As it turned out, Michel and Roger had filmed the pilot for a television series on one of the southern islands, Aitutaki, which they claimed was 'absolutely gorgeous'.

'I'll send a fax to the manager. He knows me. They'll do it for yer almost on the spot and it'll only cost yer thirty dollars. Lot cheaper than the divorce'll be.' He grinned at me with a wink. 'Two days on the island is all you'll need. Buy the certificate on yer way in; they'll stamp and date it for two days later and Bob's yer uncle. Sit on the beach and tank up on a few tinnies while they get all the festivities rolling. I'd come along, be worst man for yer, but I can't leave, mate, I'm in pre-production.'

And so we arrive in Rarotonga, where blustering rain greets us, armed with a copy of the telex sent to the hotel by best mate Roger as well as his rather splendid, if a touch cumbersome wedding gift to us: a hand-painted, hand-carved didgeridoo which stands chest-height off the ground and which neither of us can raise a sound out of.

The rain rattles like gunshots against the corrugated roof as we enter the customs shed.

'Film producer?' enquires the customs officer.

Michel nods.

'Are you carrying any unsuitable film material or pornographic magazines with you?' Michel assures him that we are not while I, waiting alongside them, silently marvel at the proportions of this man. I am reminded that when I visited Fiji for the first time I never ceased to be amazed by the size of everyone's feet. Great paddles, they were, in sturdy brown leather sandals, creaking and slapping against the dry, dusty earth. The locals here are Maoris, Polynesians, not Melanesians, as the Fijians are. Still, this officer's feet, his whole physique, are simply stupendous. Michel is over six feet tall but in order to look this man in the eye he is obliged to crane his neck. My husband-to-be explains that the purpose of our visit is to get married. The man smiles jovially and we are, as Roger promised, furnished with a piece of paper – our wedding certificate – dated (but not yet signed by a church minister) for two days hence.

A taxi takes us through the sloshing, muddied capital of

Avarua and delivers us to our beachside hotel, where the native staff greet us in a friendly, if ponderous way. We introduce ourselves to a pretty desk clerk at reception and she plods off in search of Jim, the manager. He is a complete contrast: a harassed New Zealander who bursts from his office as though on the run and greets us anxiously. 'Welcome,' he mutters distractedly, not looking us in the eye, while pumping our hands. 'Yes,' he says, he has been expecting us and, yes, he received the telex and he has come up with an idea. He will arrange for one of his staff to row us and the minister out to a speck of an islet about forty yards offshore, where the service will take place, and then row us back for a champagne breakfast in the dining room.

'Sounds good,' we smile uncertainly.

We are standing at the entrance to the lobby, hemmed in by streaming rain. I glance towards this balding manager – what hair remains is powdered with dandruff; his eyes are bloodshot, bleary-looking with heavy, puffy bags semi-circling them; his nicotine-stained fingers are trembling and it occurs to me that he might have a drink problem – and then I peer out to sea, squinting at where he is pointing, but I see nothing. The sheet of rain coming in off the steel-grey ocean has obscured the islet in question.

'Don't worry, it will be clear and dry by Saturday. There might even be a nice breeze, if the weather forecast is to be believed.' But his nasal whine suggests that nothing in life can be counted on. 'The monsoon season finished a month ago. This shouldn't be happening,' he adds, desperately attempting to conceal concern.

I smile again and stare back towards the dining room. It is remarkably dark. In fact, everywhere in the hotel is dark. The place has a neglected, lost-in-the-middle-of-oblivion feel to it. In all the hotels on all the Pacific islands I have ever visited I have always been thrilled by the beauty of the brilliantly coloured, erotically shaped flowers displayed in vases at reception, the robust succulents growing in the surrounding gardens. Here there are none. None at all. I don't like it here, I am thinking. We have been flying for five hours, so it is probably my mood and the depressing weather. Tomorrow, after a good night's sleep and a bit of tropical sunshine, I will be bursting with excitement at the approach of our wedding day. I must buck up. Still, standing in this godforsaken lobby, I find it hard to believe not only Rarotonga's claims to have one of the densest tourist trades in the South Pacific but that it is a much sought-after and applauded holiday destination.

Our room is up two flights of darkly varnished wooden stairs. It is a simple space, not dissimilar to a room in a downmarket motel. Simple and damp. It smells musty, of mothballs and well-trodden carpet. The furnishings are worn. There is one chair covered in a threadbare fabric, limp burned-orange curtains, our double bed, with its sickly-white counterpane and sunken centre, a built-in wardrobe and one wooden shelf at knee-height which now holds our suitcase, Michel's camera equipment and our didgeridoo. Adjacent to this is our en-suite, cupboard-sized bathroom with its slanting tiled floor and a shower nozzle in the ceiling a couple of feet to the left of the electric lightbulb, which is screened by a white plastic, tulip-shaped shade with a crack up one side of it.

The view from our only window looks out over the car park towards the interior of the island where, in this filthy weather, the volcanic mountains tower, black and threatening.

Perhaps my desire for these days, this occasion, to be perfect is unrealistic. But however naïve and sentimental I may be, by any standards this is not promising. I feel choked with emotion but unable to communicate any of it. I am thirty-eight years old and have never been married before. Fear of commitment, a violent childhood and an over-acute sense of romanticism have kept me single. I wanted this to be *special*. I have travelled a fair amount in my adult life and ended up alone in some dead-end dives, yet I have almost always managed to retain a modicum of humour or at least my sense of adventure by assuring myself that at some point in an unforeseen future the situation will make good copy. But this is different. Or so some inner voice keeps repeating.

Is this Roger's idea of a bloody good practical joke, cobber?

I decide to put on a brave face and unlock our suitcase ready to begin the unpacking. Michel is on the telephone alongside the bed – an ancient cream appliance with no dial which looks as though it has been thrown out and found its way to a bric-à-brac stall. He is trying to contact reception. Finally, he gives up and decides to walk back downstairs.

'I'm going to see if they have another room,' he mutters impatiently as he closes the door. I cross to the window and gaze out at the rain. It is falling like a barrage of knitting needles. I cross to the bed and lie down, sinking into the pillow, which smells awful and is humid against my clammy cheeks. A tear falls, and I feel miserable.

The storm persists throughout Friday. Its density prevents us from going out in the rowing boat to visit the islet where the wedding is to take place. Jim, desperate to keep his cool, now suggests a contingency plan which is that, should the rain not let up, we will be married at the point of a roofed pontoon that juts a few metres out to sea from the hotel beach. We see little alternative but to accept, and so the plans are rearranged.

Miraculously, fortunately, somewhere around eleven on Saturday morning, the weather clears, blown away by a tradewind approaching from the south-east, from the direction of the Tropic of Capricorn and Easter Island. The sodden, palm-covered pontoon is now swaying back and forth in the surging swash like the tail of a gigantic prehistoric reptile.

Still damp from my shower, I stare at it from our room on the first floor – we moved yesterday – while water from my shampooed hair drips on to my shoulders and runs in rivulets down my naked body. I have no idea where Michel is; I have hardly seen him these last two days except during our meals together in the cheerless dining room. It has been too wet to consider wandering in to town. I dress myself in a bathing costume and sarong and decide to dry my hair in the wind on the beach. Anything to get out of this bloody room.

A glimmer of sun breaks through the banks of fast-moving clouds. My hair is whipping against my face, streaking my eyes, as I perch on a boulder and look out across the South Pacific to a horizon barely delineable. I am thinking about life back at our olive farm, and our future plans for it, wishing I was there, when, suddenly, carried on the wind, I hear my name and turn to see Michel running towards me, waving wildly. I leap to my feet.

'What's up?' I cry.

'Get dressed, we're leaving!' he shouts as he approaches.

'Leaving? But I thought we were getting married!'

'We are, but not here. Come on, let's go. I've packed the case.'

Blown by the wind, I stagger after him, completely bemused.

'Where are we going?' I call, but Michel cannot hear me, or he is not listening. He has a scheme afoot, and it involves settling the bill, organising someone to collect our case and ringing for a taxi to take us to a strip of the airport reserved for private inter-island aircraft. Amid the scramble I have to bullet back to the room after the taxi has pulled up because we realise that the bellboy has not collected the didgeridoo, and then scurry to the lobby loo to change from bathing suit and sarong into shorts and a top dragged from the case.

So it is only once we are seated, squashed together at the back of a plane loaded with sacks of unripe bananas, do I receive an answer to my question.

'Aitutaki. I telexed yesterday and have just received a reply. A representative from the hotel there will collect us at the airport and we will be married in their garden later this afternoon.' He puts his arm around me and draws me towards him. 'I have told them we would like something special. So, we'll have our Polynesian wedding after all, and because the storm has not touched that island, we'll have sunshine, too. After the service we'll drink New Zealand champagne and swim in the crystal-clear lagoon. It's the most magnificent I have ever seen.'

Aitutaki.

Stuck in our Rarotonga hotel, I have been reading a bunch of South Pacific guidebooks I picked up in Sydney. I know that Aitutaki is one of the most northerly of this southern group of Cook Islands. Other facts I have learned: the Pacific Ocean is larger than all five continents put together; its depth is deeper than all other oceans; reef sharks and plentiful other more dangerous family members inhabit these waters; sharks have not evolved in many hundreds of thousand of years, which is proof of their perfectly proportioned form; coral is the fastest-produced structure of anything created by any living beings. Some of these fascinating if not terribly useful bits and pieces I have gleaned while trying to keep myself sane during the interminable rain, dreading a dismal beginning to married life, which I, with my acutely superstitious Irish nature, might have read as a bad omen.

The pilot arrives, apologising profusely. He is in his early thirties, has lustrous, bleached hair and a thick Aussie accent. There will be a short delay because the wind is too strong to take off, but once we are airborne, he assures us, it will be a smooth and pleasant ride.

I cannot deny a silent moment of scepticism.

The engine of our plane drones like a snoring bee, the air in the cabin is stifling, the bananas, green when we left Rarotonga, smell so fruity that I think they must have ripened during the two-hour flight. My head aches from the lack of fresh air and because I haven't eaten a thing all day. But I am thrilled by what awaits us below.

Michel is filming our approach to Aitutaki through the window on the left-hand side of the plane. Occasionally I lean against his sticky flesh and gaze down upon what he sees. It is little different from what I am looking at: tiny, sand-banked atolls, *motus*, in turquoise water so clear you can almost see the fish swimming. Here and there a lone, dark-skinned fisherman leans out from his canoe to draw in his net. The triangular-shaped lagoon is fringed with small, white waves breaking against the coral reefs which, in turn, are ringed by deeper, greener waters, winking and sparkling in the sun like precious stones. There are lagoons within lagoons. Turquoise, white, green, aquamarine smudged with golden shafts of sunlight: a sultan's jewellery casket.

I hear the shift in the engine's whine and the plane inclines to the right. Bags of bananas slide heavily against my feet as we swoop and then dip gently seawards. The pilot calls to us from the cockpit to get ready. 'Landing in ten,' he shouts. And then I catch sight of 'our' island. It slides into view as though from the other side of the curvature of the world.

Aitutaki, a slug-shaped mass of pale honey sand peppered with sparse patches of one- or two-storey shacks and buildings buried among forests of palms whose fronds are waving and flapping in the wind like happy dancing girls.

'Yes!' I turn and press my head into Michel's chest and kiss him hard. 'Thank you.'

A short, fat, local woman holding a page torn from a notebook which reads, 'Carol and Michelle' awaits us in the shade out of the broiling afternoon sun. I step into and immediately out beyond airport customs, which is little more than a corrugated shack, home to no more activity than a dozen flies buzzing in circles. Sealing-wax red flowers are in blossom everywhere in large, square-shaped tin cans. A Cook Islander, wearing a straw Stetson and chewing, sits patiently in an open Jeep, the only vehicle in sight. I wave and hurry towards our female guide while Michel remains busy with the pilot. Our case is unloaded; dollars exchange hands; the pilot gestures his thanks and climbs aboard his aircraft. Aitutaki is not his destination – he has made the stopover only to accommodate us. I introduce myself to the woman, whose name is Gladys, and point to Michel, who is approaching. Gladys frowns, looking confused.

'Who's he?' she asks, in an unexpectedly accusatory tone.

'Michel,' I repeat.

'Michel? But we thought Michel was a woman! We thought Carol and Michel were two women!' She rocks with hammer blows of laughter, pulls two garlands of sweetly scented white frangipani flowers out of a raffia shopping basket and hangs them like necklaces round our necks, then waddles to the Jeep, gesturing us to follow. 'Well, that's a relief! The minister was shocked. Come on, climb on in.'

Gladys and Harris, her tall, robust son, the driver of the

Jeep, Michel and I are now floating towards our hotel aboard a raft ferry. Gladys uses the ten-minute journey to inform us that because the plane was delayed by the winds and it is now half past five, the wedding will have to take place tomorrow.

'The minister is keen to talk to you,' she says. 'He hopes to meet with you after his service in the morning which you will, of course, attend, and then, if he finds everything in order, he will perform the holy rites a little later in the day. But you're not to worry, he'll see you at the church hall this evening for the singing.' I am admiring the lush vegetation and listening to the creek water slapping against the raft, aware that Michel at my side has also cottoned on to the fact that the minister she is referring to, as well as herself, her family and probably ninety per cent of the inhabitants of this corner of the island, is clearly either a member of the Cook Islands Christian Church or a Mormon. As far as we are concerned, both faiths, as practised here, lean towards zealous. I have been reading during our rainy sojourn in Avarua that since the missionaries left these islands the American evangelists have moved in and have found great success here.

Everyone disembarks. Harris, carrying all our cases, plods forth, leading the way to reception, which is hardly difficult to find because the hotel and complex, even with its dependencies, are compact. Well, tiny. The resort consists of the main reception building with its dining room and eight guest huts, the *bures*. We sign the register and are escorted to our *bure* by Pururangi, a pretty, if rather beefy, black-haired Polynesian woman in her early twenties who informs us gaily that she has been chosen to be our bridesmaid and witness.

'I love weddings,' she trills. 'What a special weekend. We have the Pearly Stars for two days, too.'

I look heavenwards and see no stars – it is still light – and then out across the lagoon in both directions. This vista is mind-blowing. Black herons are stalking about in the sand or wading at the shore's edge like cautious holidaymakers mindful of what they might step on. Our hut is the very last between land and Pacific Ocean. There is nothing else except a comma-shaped sandbank and one rather round-shouldered palm between us, the shimmering lagoon and the distant blue horizon. A few yards from the shoreline, I spot shoals of tiny, slender fish leaping up out of the water. They leap as one, an arc of silver, a platinum rainbow, and return to the unseen leaving shimmery ripples in the limpid ocean. Michel suggests that our wedding take place under that very palm. Married on a shelf of sand surrounded by lapping lagoon water, with palm fronds as bower? Too romantic – everything I have dreamed of – but will the minister agree?

Later, when we stroll back to reception, we are greeted by the New Zealander, Tony, who runs the place and his local wife, Bundy. They invite us for a beer, which we readily accept.

'Never had a foreign wedding here before,' remarks Tony. 'If it goes well I might start advertising the idea. Get the tourists in. One of our guests caught sight of you earlier,' he says to me. 'Claims you're a TV star. Is that right?' Before I can answer he goes on to tell us that they have another celebrity staying. 'Mabel Burt.' He stares at us wide-eyed, awaiting our reaction.

We shrug.

'Mabel Burt, mate, the Maori singer from New Zealand. You haven't heard of her?' We shake our heads apologetically. 'She's here with her husband and her trio, the Pearly Stars. Funny thing, tomorrow's her wedding anniversary, so it's all go here this weekend. I could advertise in the *Cook Island News* and the *New Zealand Times*: "Aitutaki: the wedding of your dreams – live like the stars".' I am smiling to myself, wondering if Tony is referring to the Pearly Stars or to myself and Mabel Burt who, I calculate, is probably about as internationally celebrated as I am. The idea that anyone would cross the world to play out the same wedding fantasy as Carol Drinkwater or Mabel Burt strikes me as highly amusing and I burst out laughing. Tony is nonplussed by my reaction and, as if to compensate for my irreverence, his wife announces that the minister will interview us later at the village hall after the community singing, and then finalise the arrangements for the wedding after his service in the morning. It is then that Michel deals the blow that almost changes our fortunes on the island. 'We are neither of us regular churchgoers. We were hoping for something a little less conventional. A tropical wedding, Polynesian-style,' he states warmly and with great grace. 'Obviously, we are looking forward to meeting the minister and arranging the ceremony with him, but I doubt that we shall be attending the service in the morning.'

The silence that follows this announcement is as heavy as lead.

'Well, I'll pass on your remarks to the minister, but I don't know what he will have to say about it,' states Bundy curtly, and with that she rises as though the very idea of dallying at a table with beer-guzzling heathens is an affront to her faith.

What the minister has to say about the matter is perfectly straightforward. He refuses to marry us. In fact, he refuses to meet us at all. As far as the hotel and the church are concerned, we are no longer suitable candidates for the holy sacrament of marriage.

'Funny, it seemed OK to them when they thought we were both women. Oh, well, now what?' I ask Michel later, after the community singing in the village hall which we have dutifully attended, and where we have been introduced to the renowned songstress Mabel Burt, who is an affable, broad-faced New Zealand Maori and about as glamorous as her name suggests.

'We'll find another solution,' replies Michel.

I am spreadeagled across the iron bed in our *bure*, an open book on my stomach, listening to the cadences of the hot, dark night. The air is thick and still. There is no air-conditioning. Instead we have a metal ceiling fan which creaks and spins erratically but does little to shift the lethargy. Beyond the open window the blackness is irradiated by brilliant constellations of Southern Hemisphere stars and by the moon, which is an apple peel off being full. I am mesmerised by it, glowing like a topaz in the ultramarine sky.

It's daytime in Europe, back at the farm. I wonder how our dogs are getting on. 'There are no dogs here,' I murmur. 'None of that incessant yowling and barking one hears so frequently on remote islands.'

I shift over on to my hip, feeling deliciously at peace, south of the equator, in the tropics, where the towering vegetation barely stirs in the sweltering darkness and where I close my eyes for a second and drink in the rhythmic lapping of the waves. I am toying with the idea of a midnight swim, so invigorating to immerse myself naked in the water's phosphorescence, when Michel interrupts my reverie.

'Look at these guys.'

'What?'

He reaches for his camera, directing it at the flaking white wall where two large shiny-brown cockroaches, the colour of the leather sandals worn in Fiji, are butting up against one another like stags in combat.

'Jesus, Michel, I hope they don't bite!'

The following morning at breakfast in the deserted dining room – everyone else is at church – Pururangi serves us eggs. Back and forth she plods with plates, pots of coffee and

Carnation tinned milk, looking very downhearted. Eventually, she owns up to her disappointment. She had been so looking forward to attending a *papa'a* wedding and, even better, to have been chosen as bridesmaid, that instead of accompanying her family to the singing at the village hall she had spent her Saturday evening weaving garlands for her hair.

'Papaya?' I repeat.

She giggles and explains shyly that *papa'a* is the Maori word for foreigners.

'We would still love to have you as our bridesmaid.' Michel asks her if she knows anyone else on the island who might agree to marry us.

The question perplexes her. She furrows her brow. 'I think,' she pronounces, and trundles off to the kitchen.

We take a small boat out on the lagoon. I want to do some snorkelling and there is precious little else to do to pass the time if we are not now getting married. Michel rows while I watch the gorgeous, technicoloured angel fish darting playfully to and fro before disappearing beneath the hull of our skiff. 'Coming?' I ask.

'You go ahead. I'll swim in a minute and then I'll wait here for you.'

I dive overboard, slip on my flippers and scud off towards deeper waters out by the coral reef, hoping to see sharks.

It is a while before I am aware of the sun's rays burning into my wet, salty back, at which point I turn like a porpoise to cool my flesh and to gauge how far out I have travelled. I catch sight of Michel instantly. He is upright in our bobbing boat, waving and gesturing to me to come back. I flip over on to my stomach and crawl fast back towards the shore. 'They've found someone!' he shouts when I am within earshot. 'Let's go!'

Sand crabs run for cover, vanishing with the agility of

liquid into tiny holes as we haul the boat out of the sea and secure it to a tree. An egret circles overhead. The sun is high in the sky. It must be about noon. According to Michel, Pururangi's husband has gone off on his scooter to one of the neighbouring villages to search out a man he knows who would be more than willing to help us out.

'Is he another minister?'

Michel has no idea. All he understood from Pururangi's cries from the shore was that we are to be ready for two o'clock.

We shower and dress. My brightly coloured wedding dress is shoulderless and sleeveless but has a whale-boned bodice and a full, short skirt plumped up with yards of netted petticoat. Within seconds of climbing into it I am perspiring and the netting is scratching my tanned-raw skin. Michel attempts to adjust the speed of the fan at the wall switch but it whines a complaint and beats on at the same monotonous pace. It is half-past one. He suggests we go to reception and find out what the plans are but I cannot face the blistering sun in this frock and wait on the bed. Sitting proves too uncomfortable because the whalebones are pressing into my sunburned buttocks, so I lie back and count the cockroaches. There are seven. At home, geckos, not cockroaches, hang from our whitewashed ceilings and walls. When we return we intend to keep bees.

A short while later, I am woken by excited male voices beyond the window. They are chattering incomprehensibly in what I take to be their local language. Cook Islands Maori is rather similar to the Polynesian languages spoken in Tahiti and Hawaii, or perhaps they are discoursing in a local Aitutaki dialect. I haul myself back on to my feet to take a look. Four burly men are transporting two trestle tables, which they place in the sand alongside 'our' palm tree. An island woman, not Pururangi, carrying a pink plastic laundry basket stacked with champagne flutes, brings up the rear.

Who are they expecting? We have no guests.

I see Michel hurrying along the beach. One of the natives who has deposited the table and is returning to the hotel greets him with an enthusiastic handshake. They exchange a word or two and then Michel hurries up the steps to our hut.

'So, it's finally happening, is it?'

'Well, there's no sign of Pururangi's husband. According to Tony, it's nothing to worry about. However, it's unlikely the ceremony will take place promptly at two. Mr Pururangi rang reception from a callbox a few miles away to say that the man he had in mind has left the island, so he's going to find another fellow who has been recommended to him.'

'Right.' I pad back to the bed. 'Maybe I'll take this frock off for a while. It's killing me. And have a shower.'

'There's no water. The generator's off for a couple of hours. Tony said to apologise. It'll be back on around four.'

I lie down again, convinced this wedding will never take place.

I am wrong.

At almost five o'clock, Pururangi's husband pulls up with a male passenger on the back of his scooter. The other man is a Maori chief dressed in shorts and muddied boots; he was working in his garden when Pururangi's husband called on him and explained the *papa'as'* predicament.

'Why are you telling me?' the Maori asked.

'They would like you to marry them. I've been everywhere, can't find a soul.'

'Good Lord! Well, why not?'

Our chief is a jolly sort, if a touch confused about the wording of the vows. We settle to discuss it but are interrupted by Tony and Bundy, who have come to warn us that we had better get on with it or the light will fail and it won't

be possible to have the ceremony outside. Darkness falls
swiftly in the tropics.

'Quick, then. Do you want "obey" left in in the sentence
to love, honour and obey?'

I decide against obey and, with that, the proceedings
begin.

I am rather amazed to find, as Michel takes my arm and
solemnly walks me to the tree, that a modest crowd has
gathered. Mabel Burt and her trio, the Pearly Stars, each
with his ukelele, who have offered to provide the wedding
music and entertainment; Mabel's husband who, it turns
out, is a cameraman employed by a New Zealand television
station and has agreed to film the occasion with Michel's
camera; a lean, handsome Danish couple and their two
naked children who are more taken up with their seashell-
hunting than paying attention to our nuptials. The guest
who apparently 'spotted' me is present with her husband
and another middle-aged couple also holidaying at the hotel.
All four are originally from England but emigrated to
Australia in the late fifties, when the £10 single passage to a
new life Down Under was on offer. The first couple are now
living in Wellington. They moved to New Zealand, I learn
later, because they found that they were less homesick there;
its landscape felt more familiar to them. The second are
based in Melbourne. They are a curious-looking quartet.
Each is sporting a safari hat woven out of freshly cut coconut
fronds made especially for them by Pururangi, who stands in
splayed bare feet looking solid and resplendent in a brilliant
pink shift dress. Her thick, black hair has been plaited with
garlands of purple and yellow flowers.

I have slipped a virgin-white hibiscus into my own curly
locks.

Mabel and her group strike up the music. A little ditty
entitled: 'She Wears My Ring'.

'Ring! Oh, Lord!'

It is only then, as we – I in slingback heels – are sinking into soft sand, stepping towards our Maori chief, still in his shorts but now wearing reading glasses and a very serious expression, that it dawns on Michel and I that we haven't thought to organise a ring. I swiftly slip off the little emerald-encrusted engagement ring he bought me three years ago and shove it into his trouser pocket.

'We'll have to use this,' I whisper. My hands are trembling and I fear I will drop it. 'Turn it the other way up so you can't see the stones and don't, for God's sake, lose it in the sand.' My voice is quavering, nagging almost, because I am horribly nervous.

There is little reason to be. The ceremony goes off without a hitch, and even though we cannot claim this to have been an authentic Polynesian wedding – for since the Christians and evangelists have got hold of these islands, what is a Polynesian wedding? – the register is signed and witnessed by plump, dark-skinned, hugely warmhearted people with unpronounceable Polynesian names. All this once our Maori chief, in his khaki boy-scout shorts, has pronounced us man and wife. (No one, not even us, notices that the date on the marriage certificate is incorrect – it still bears yesterday's date.)

In the waning light of this gloriously bizarre and unfor-gettable day, as the sun is sinking and pinking a benign gathering of clouds, Michel makes a speech which so guts me that when it comes to my turn to say a few words I cannot utter a sound. Tears are streaming down my face. I hastily toast absent family and friends and hand over to Mabel and her trio, who hum and strum and croon while many bottles of the hotel's NZ bubbly are quaffed and this motley gath-ering of complete strangers begin to acquaint themselves with one another.

Our Maori chief, champagne flute in hand, is smiling merrily now. He raises his glass, wishes us years of enduring happiness with many healthy children running about our olive farm, and then thanks us both for inviting him, before admitting shyly that he has had 'such great fun, far better than spending the afternoon gardening' and continues: 'I never thought when I got out of bed this morning I'd be here, performing a *papa'a* wedding. But if the chance comes along again, I'll do it like a shot.'

It is only then that he owns up to the fact that he has never performed any form of marriage service before.

'Are we legally married?' I am on the point of whispering to Michel, but then I look about me, marvel at the colours streaking across the ocean from the setting sun, feel the squeeze of a hand wrapped around mine and decide the question is irrelevant.

Back in our *bure*, we discuss the possibility of lingering a while longer, having a honeymoon. But we have so much to crack on with back home. We are still awaiting the final decision about whether we are to be awarded the coveted AOC award for our virgin olive oil. We settle for an overnight stop in Tahiti, where we hire a red Jeep and drive out of town to the Gauguin Centre. The following morning, after a starlit night in a wooden-stilted house built out in the ocean waves, we catch a dawn flight to Los Angeles, change planes at breakneck speed and land in Nice, exhausted but thrilled to be home.

Fruits of Spring

I am alone in my book-lined den, enclosed within the century-old, metre-deep stone walls of our villa standing at the heart of our hillside olive farm. Above my head, a newly installed fan is gently spinning. Its breeze flutters the papers strewn across my desk while I continue to make notes: research for a new book.

Unfortunately, my work, though well-intentioned, is faint-hearted. My concentration is erratic, my brain befuddled, my thoughts swimming all over the place. I rise and sit and rise again, toking on swigs of Badoit mineral water direct from the green plastic bottle, attempting to allay both nausea and the torpor that has taken hold of me. Why can my mind not settle? Why must it whizz off in incoherent directions? I smile at my foolish questions, knowing the answers; chuffed to bits.

Beyond my sheltered refuge, the sun is beating down out

of a cloudless, forget-me-not-blue sky. It is May, the final weekend of the Cannes Film Festival, and the temperature is unseasonably hot. I rise once more, then, tossing Biro, notes, mineral water and intentions aside, I walk to the window, fling it wide open and loll listlessly against the casement, inhaling the scents of the season. Heavenly drafts from the flowering lavender bushes – such an intrinsically Provençal perfume – reach into me, clearing the heaviness in my head, alleviating the sickness in my stomach. We have planted dozens of these canescent shrubs up against drystone walls and along the borders of the tiled terraces where we spend so many hours of our days. Aside from the pleasure of its perfume, according to Frédéric at the garden centre, lavender is a wasp deterrent, but nothing, as far as I can see, not even meshed netting, seems to disenchant the carnivorous little blighters who gatecrash our meals and drill into our hams and cheeses, brazenly gorging themselves. Many of the lavenders are coated in a carpet of bees. These furry gatherers are dipping and rising as they pollinate, winging from one purple cluster to the next.

Our lavenders are of the *Lavandula dentata* variety, more commonly known as French lavender. It is drought-tolerant, has a longer blooming season and is the species most frequently found here along this Mediterranean coast.

I should be jotting this down, but I stay put.

I stick my head out into the afternoon and my ears are assaulted by the zirring and zinging of male cicadas busy with their friction-driven mating call. Stretching and straining beyond the casement, I lean to survey the land. The herbage has grown knee-high and is shot through with lofty, lipstick-red poppies. Come evening, I love to roam these grasses, these endless stretches of soft, breezy greens and audacious scarlets; to canter a passage through and feel their caress and tickle, their lick against my calves. The scene puts me in mind of a Gustav Klimt painting, *Poppies Amongst the Poplars*. Though of course, we have olives, not poplars.

Returning from our wedding six weeks ago, we roved the garden by starlight, wine glasses in hand, rediscovering our terrain, making love in the spring grass, recumbent on the earth; flushed embraces beneath sprays of apple blossom. Might that have been when . . . ? I smile at the possibility.

Turning my head to the left, I sight our two cherry trees, groaning with shiny burgundy fruits, so ripe their skins are splitting. We should have harvested them a week ago but now it is almost too late; the fruits are falling or have been pecked at by my enemies: the magpies.

Nature at its diverse work of propagation. Yes, indeedy.

I reach for the bottle on my desk once more and knock back another mouthful of the mildly fizzy water, but the reeling sickness remains.

In between the late wistaria and the bougainvillaea seasons, perhaps beneath the apple trees, I have fallen pregnant. Six weeks is all I am gone, but the being inside me, not yet the size of a snail, has me in its grip. My body's rhythms are being shunted about by its minuscule presence. Mostly, I feel drained and, like today, spaced out. I hide away in this writing room attempting to immerse myself in study but the days pass, I remain unfocused and my condition leaves me with zero tolerance for this unseasonably early heat.

But I am over the moon.

To date I have borne no children of my own. This little being will be my first. I have two stepdaughters, twin girls from Michel's first marriage, Clarisse and Vanessa. They visit us regularly but they do not live with us. In any case, they are growing up fast and taking charge of their own lives. I am late to be starting a family and this pregnancy was not planned, but it has long been hoped for. I have miscarried more times than I care to remember.

The pregnancy test, which is three days old, remains in the bathroom. I have left it there, in its plastic casing, next to the soap dish on the side of the old porcelain bath that was in this long-abandoned house when we found it. When Michel comes home he will not be able to see the result of the test because its reading has faded, but I have kept it anyway. The soft pink which turns to blue in positive cases, such as mine, looks like nothing more than a used square of blotting paper. He will probably ask me why I still have it and I won't be able to explain, except to say that I wanted to relive the wash of delight I felt when the discovery was actual.

I haven't breathed a word to him yet, about having his baby, and I won't until he arrives. I won't blurt out such special news on the telephone. I won't write it in an e-mail. I want to be there standing in front of him – the best seat in the house – to watch the smile break across his face. I want to share the joy of that first moment of knowledge, of all that this baby will mean to our lives. I feel jealously possessive about this moment to come. He arrives this evening and, impatient as I am, I am hanging on, savouring the scene, playing it out in my head, over and over again.

In the meantime, when I am not horizontal on the bed, victim to physiological changes, my days are taken up with research for my new book as well as with our projects here on the farm. We are still grappling with the unfathomable bureaucracies involved in gaining the coveted AOC – the Appellation d'Origine Contrôlée, the highest accolade given for fine quality produce – in our case, our excellent olive oil; the green-gold olive oil that we press from the drupes of our venerable *cailletier* olive trees. Olives of Nice, the fruit is known as locally, harvested from the variety that prospers along this stretch of Mediterranean coast. We had hoped for a letter on our return, but still nothing. Michel is chasing.

Quashia, our loyal Arab gardener, is building us a fine

new woodshed constructed from honey-toned stones and locally fired terracotta tiles. I hear him shovelling and hammering as I write. We could not run this place without him. Due to our frequent absences, he has taken charge of the vegetable garden and planted it up for us. The only snag is that he has failed to create variation and our beds are now swamped with big-leafed, yellow-flowering courgettes that have grown into monstrous-sized marrows, great green appendages that won't fit into the fridge, and tomatoes, the vines of which are bending and breaking under the weight of the pappy red fruits – more than we could ever eat or cook with.

And I, when I am not scribbling, am locked away indoors studying the nuts and bolts of beekeeping. We have decided to find ourselves an apiarist who might be interested in placing half a dozen of his hives on our hills and sharing the honey harvests with us. Michel wants us to strike up an arrangement with a local bee farmer along similar lines to the relationship we have built up with René, our olive-tree guru. René assists us with the pruning of the trees and the gathering and pressing of our fruit and in return he keeps two thirds of our olive produce. We were lucky to find him. Our little farm, this most unexpected enterprise of ours, has got off to a fortunate start. Quite by chance we have fallen upon a plot of land that yields first-class olive oil. But we have much to learn, a long way to go, if we are to honour the AOC we have our hearts set on and gain a deeper understanding of the Provençal way of life.

I know nothing whatsoever about beekeeping, or *apiculture*, and in order that I do not present myself as completely ignorant in this complex business, I have bought myself a textbook, a hefty tome in French, that claims to tell me everything I will need to know about hive construction, the rearing of the queen, extraction of honey and royal jelly, the nutritional value of pollen for humans, manners, the social activities of worker bees and the husbanding of the whole. These stripy little insects are arthropods, as are butterflies: species with bilaterally symmetrical bodies divided into segments. Fascinating reading, but it grows exhausting during my bouts of morning sickness, which last well into the afternoons. They will pass, I know, and are a small price to pay for the joy of the child to come. Still, I am unaccustomed to lethargy and thankful it won't endure for months.

When I arrive at the airport to collect Michel I see that his Paris flight has been delayed and is not scheduled to land for another hour. Instead of hanging about the crowded, Friday-evening concourse, where the noise, cigarette smoke and film-festival hullaballoo will put me in a grumpy humour, I decide to drive to Nice where I can while away the time at a beachside café, watching the sea and quietly studying my *Beginner's Guide to Beekeeping*.

Sitting alone outside the café-bar in the soft evening light, engrossed in my manual, I am only vaguely aware of the arrival of a moustached man who settles himself and his newspaper at the small round table right alongside mine until he shouts loudly to the waiter – 'Henri!' – and lights up a Gauloise. The waiter brings the man a pastis and they chat animatedly together. His exhalations of smoke drift my way and draw my attention. I feel a sweep of nausea wash over me and decide to move, but before I can scoop up notepad, pen, book and bag, my neighbour – a middle-aged, leather-skinned, fubsy Mediterranean with the florid complexion of one who lives out of doors, victim to winds and sun – makes a totally bizarre comment which stops me in my tracks. 'Have you seen them dancing?' is what he asks.

I assume that he must still be talking to the waiter, and glance behind me to see if Henri is standing close by. This provokes my neighbour, who grows noticeably hot under the collar and begins waving his hand at me. Before I know what's happening, he is leaning over my table and rapping his finger (one of the two holding the burning cigarette) hard against my manual.

'The bees, madame,' he says. 'The dance of the bees.' He repeats his words in an emphatic way, as though he considers me deaf or simple. 'Danced till they were stunned. So, you're wasting your time.'

'*Excusez-moi?*'

With a bulging-eyed nod, he raises both hands, fingers heavenwards, 'You won't find such matters in books. Books won't give you the truth!' And with that he downs the remaining swig of his pastis, tosses a few coins on his table, calls *bonne soirée* to Henri, picks up his *Nice Matin* and struts off.

I am left feeling both irritated by this bumptious individual and curious, and as soon as he is out of sight I riffle through the pages and then flick back to the index in search of a chapter or heading on Dancing Bees. There is no mention of any such activity. Stupid of me to have bothered to look. I dismiss his comment, laughing at myself for having paid him any attention at all.

Once we are back at the house, Michel busies himself in the kitchen chopping the parsley, chives and basil I have collected from our maturing herb beds. During these last days I have been planting baby lollo rosso salads and rocket, which have shot up so fast that I am able to harvest some of the tender young leaves for supper. We are having *loup*, sea bass, which I have marinated in five tablespoons of Bourgogne Aligoté white wine, generous dribbles of olive oil, pepper, ground sea salt, sprays of fennel, a sprig or two of celery and slubs of freshly picked lemon, ready to bake in tinfoil on a bed of sliced onions and tomatoes – our own, of course.

I prepared everything earlier so that we would have little to do this evening. The plane's delay has meant that we are eating late, but the temperature is heavenly and we can dine by candlelight beneath the stars.

I have said nothing yet to Michel about my news. Still savouring the moment. While the oven is heating I walk round to the big old fridge we bought second hand and have installed in the garage by the stables, where we store our wine and keep our washing machine, and draw out a bottle of champagne. Once I have uncorked it and placed it in a cooler, I take it, with two long-stemmed flutes, to our wooden table to await Michel, and set it down next to a plate of small, round toasts generously spread with a creamy and very garlicky *crème d'anchoïade*, anchovy paste, which is made locally and which I buy at the *épicerie* in the village.

The cicadas have given up for the day, but the dogs have awoken, no longer beaten by the heat. They smell dinner and have begun pacing the terraces, marking time until we sit down to eat, at which point they will settle under the table in the hope of being thrown the odd morsel, even though they know I refuse to indulge them in this. Presently they are barking, demarcating their territory, warning off intruders, most especially the wild boars, those great hulking beasts who scour our hill in search of roots and acorns.

One evening, during our very first summer here, while I was alone – Michel had returned to Paris – occupied in the garden, watering the first of the plants we had purchased, geraniums, a passiflora, some herbs, I was frightened by strange gruntings and heavy breathing. I turned my head fearing a burglar, but found myself staring at a huge, hirsute wild boar. She was a female, the more dangerous of the species, foraging for food. An awesome sight, she stood her ground, eyes fixed on me, until I crept stealthily but determinedly away.

Although we are aware that they have not abandoned these ten acres of ours, since that evening there have been no more close encounters with these strapping pigs. We assumed the dogs were successfully keeping them at bay until we began to notice damage to our renovated drystone walls. This is usually a clue that *les sangliers* are about. They leap and stamp from one terrace to the next, displacing the stones which, as they loosen, sink into piles of rubble. Months of Quashia's work destroyed with the careless kick of a hefty hoof.

They enter our holding from the rear of the hill, approaching us from its summit – up there, we are not fenced in – and, as they gain courage or grow hungrier, they shuffle ever closer to the house. A few nights back, Quashia spotted a family of four stalking the land, tearing up the grass.

'Are we celebrating?'

'Mmm?'

'I see champagne.'

Lost in my boar concerns, I had briefly forgotten. Michel is at my side now. He sits at the table, looking at me quizzically, then leans forward, lifts the bottle from the cooler and begins to pour. He hands me my glass and raises his. '*Santé*,' he says.

I lift my flute and gently trace it against his. '*Santé*. Here's to us and – our baby.'

My eyes prick with moist emotion and I rub at them, attempting not to be a softy.

Michel is on his feet and draws me to mine. '*Chérie! Félicitations!*' Arms around my waist, he seeks my lips. '*Je t'aime*,' he whispers, holding me tight. 'That's wonderful news. The best.'

Later, when the bottle is empty and we are laughing senselessly with joy and a surfeit of champagne, the scent of burning from the upstairs kitchen arrests us and reminds us that our delicious sea bass is still in the oven. I rise to hurry up the newly tiled steps that skirt the side of the house to retrieve our supper but Michel presses me back. 'No, you don't. No overexertion.' And off he goes, returning a few minutes later with the barely recognisable remains of our fish, charcoaled and bubbling inside the scalded tinfoil.

It is half-past ten on Saturday morning. The sun is already high and the temperature is mounting. I am crouched on the ground observing a minnow mayfly resting on the stone surround of the pond. René was meant to be coming by at half-past eight. We had arranged with him that he would accompany us to the farm of an *apiculteur*, 'the best bee-keeper in all Provence', who happens to be a dear friend of his. 'I've known him since we were lads.' But not for the first time there is no sign of our silver-haired olive master and no news, either. I go inside and ring his mobile, but it is on answer machine so I don't bother to leave a message. Instead I take the opportunity presented by his tardiness to prepare myself grilled tomatoes on toast as a second breakfast, which I tuck into out on the terrace.

'What are we doing about this beekeeper, then?' Michel refills our coffee cups. 'I've never seen you eat that before,' he adds.

'I know, weird, but I really fancied it. There are a couple of other names on my list. The first is M. Manneron. He has a stall at the Forville market in Cannes. I met his daughter there when I was buying our poor sea bass. The other I contacted after reading his details on the label of a honey jar. They both live further afield than René's pal, but we could go anyway, make a day of it.'

Both beekeepers are expecting us, but both live in the distant hills, one inland towards the mountains and the other in the Var. Michel thinks that we may have left our outing a little too late in the day. It will be a long and sticky journey in his ancient, non-air-conditioned Mercedes, we have tickets to see a film at the festival later and he is concerned that I should not wear myself out. We argue the point in an amiable way, because I am determined not to allow a little nausea to spoil our plans for the day or stand between us and our modest farming ambitions. In any case, I have been looking forward to the outing while poring over my bee tome.

'Think of it, Michel, beehives standing in rows the length of the terraces.'

'Steady on, we're only talking five or six hives.' He laughs, picking up the phone, still expressing misgivings about the taxing nature of such an upland reconnaissance in my condition.

The first apiarist informs him that he cannot wait in. '*Je suis très occupé*,' M. Le Beekeeper advises us, and goes on to voice the view that we live too far; the journey would be unprofitable unless he were to install a minimum of seventy hives. Undeterred, Michel replaces the receiver and rings M. Manneron, who is less dismissive and assures us that he will be waiting for us.

'If you're not feeling up to it, we can postpone this,' Michel reasserts, but I shake my head.

Within the hour, we are heading off in the direction of Digne-les-Bains, leaving the Alpes Maritimes behind us, taking the Route Napoléon, where the roadsides are buttoned with summery white and yellow wild flowers, heading towards the Alpes de Haute-Provence.

Once we are through the chaos of modern day Grasse, with its commercialised perfumeries and overconstructed high-rises housing most of the region's bureaucracy, the traffic begins to thin out. At 600 metres we pass glowing, bald-pated men dressed in shorts, walking purposefully. Here, in the environs of Grasse, there are dozens of *maisons de retraites*. Even today it remains a fashionable place for the French to retire to, and many of the ornate *belle époque* buildings have been converted into luxurious nursing homes or apartments, standing high on the hillsides looking out towards the distant sea.

Succulents grow everywhere out of the rocks, their sharply needled fronds reaching heavenwards like wailing women or the tentacles of giant octopuses. It was the British who brought succulents to this side of the world, transporting them from their distant colony of Australia. Also from Australia came eucalyptus trees. Their heavenly perfume always reminds me of home, because it is the first to greet you when you exit the arrivals hall at Nice airport and walk towards the *parking*.

Alice de Rothschild had a vast and very fabulous garden here in Grasse at her austere Villa Victoria (now converted into flats) to which Queen Victoria paid a visit in 1891. As was the custom with all Mme Rothschild's celebrated visitors, Her Royal British Majesty came bearing a gift of a tree which she was invited to plant in the grounds herself. Unfortunately, in the execution of her task, our Queen, who never tripped lightly on her feet, trampled all over one of the flowerbeds, destroying several rare plants in the process. Madame de Rothschild sent her instantly packing.

'I like the idea of inviting guests to plant a tree,' I say.

Continuing our climb inland in this solid yet ancient car, we reach the mountains, the most southerly of the Alps. Here the views plummet into lush, emerald-green valleys and sometimes, through a break in the ranges, we catch the sparkling blue of our own doorstep Mediterranean. The vegetation is not yet alpine; there are still the occasional reminders of hot lands. No palms at this altitude, but tall, willowy eucalypts perfume the air. Cork oak, *chêne liège*, is growing profusely everywhere – an indigenous tree to this region – but there are no more olive trees to be seen. We are saying a temporary *au revoir* to the land of baking sun and beloved *oliviers*, leaving them behind as we ascend towards a cooler clime. Herbs spice the wind. We turn a corner, a delicious scent hits our nostrils. Juniper. It grows wild up here in the scrub. As does the aromatic broom, with its tightly clustered butter-yellow blossoms, now in full flower. The altitude begins to slacken the heat. I breathe deeply, more easily. This old car burns oil, exhaling clouds of navy fumes which make me dizzy, so I am grateful for this milder climate. It clears my head, offers comfort to the journey.

Eight hundred metres. The landscape is changing. The dense, chocolate-red earth, so evident at sea-level along the Esterelle coast, is in sharp contrast to the stark white stone at this elevation. Clefted white rocks loom all about us, runnelled with tracks which resemble fingernail scratches across naked flesh. Small furry blue flowers at the road's edge. Forests of pines, not the generous-branched *pin parasol* which so elegantly shades the coastal diners, but the pointy-tipped Christmas ones that put me in mind of rows of paintbrushes. Even the buildings up here have an alpine look to them. Wooden homes with slanted roofs that resemble Swiss wall clocks. I half expect little hand-carved people to pop out, twirl and disappear again. Their shutters are solid, workaday wood. None are painted the electric colours ours are; here they are varnished to protect against the fierce climatic changes. The artists' hues for which the Côte d'Azur is so renowned have been bleached out at this altitude, all but erased. We are travelling through a world of dun brown, white stone, deep conifer evergreens, softwood forestry tones, with dashes of russet. It is a less audacious, less vibrant palette. Bare nature, no livestock. Little activity.

Swinging the *lacets*, the hairpin bends, we begin to encounter another breed of tourist: the cyclist with his trim, busy buttocks in brilliant blue Spandex body and hard hat, pedalling for all he is worth.

And turning my attention to the left side of the road, I spot a sign with an engraving of an eagle and the letter 'N' beneath it. 'La Route Napoléon.' 'We are following the tracks of Napoléon Bonaparte, Emperor Napoléon I.' As I speak the land takes up the eulogy. Everywhere we see Café Napoléon, Camping Napoléon, Parking Napoléon.

On 1 March 1815, having fled incarceration on the island of Elba, Napoléon landed at Golfe Juan – his escape had been financed by his doting sister, Pauline, who, the year before, had sold her jewellery in Nice and, as he was escorted through St Raphaël, a heavily guarded prisoner en route for Elba, she had slipped him the cash needed 'to make flight possible'. Today Golfe Juan is a buzzing resort, sandwiched with beachside cafés, boutiques and clubs thumping with the beat of popular music; a playground for the young and trendy. But when Napoléon set foot on that shore with his 1,200-strong army, it was a humble fishing village. From there he marched on Cannes, conquered it, and the very next day began his trek northwards.

Keen to avoid the Rhône Valley, where he knew he would be greeted with hostility, he chose this mountain way, the route to Sisteron, which today is more famous for its deliciously tender lamb. By the time he arrived in Grenoble, throngs of people had amassed and were waiting for him. He marched into their city to the resounding cries of: '*Vive l'Empereur!*' Like the soaring eagle on his insignia, he must have felt invincible. His triumphal return to Paris, the seat of his omnipotency, must have seemed reassuringly secure.

Roadside shacks are in evidence now, selling kilo pots of honey, predominantly lavender. And lavender bouquets advertised at two for 10 francs. Signs tell us that we are at 'La Source Parfumée'. Rather splendid, I remark, to know that one is living at the source of a perfumed world. It cries out to be the setting for a fairytale.

We pass though a hamlet with a garage offering all manner of repair work yet chock-a-block with rusting husks of vehicles, a spattering of houses and a trim whitewashed *auberge* decorated with a faded hand-painted advertisement. It reminds me of those Dubonnet commercials I used to see on television when I was a small girl and the perfect universe they depicted: tranquil summer lanes in the heart of the French countryside. In my own childhood I rarely knew that warmth, that peace and sunshine of mind and I have some-times asked myself whether, somewhere deep within, I wasn't seduced by those commercials. In my search for happiness have I sought a world where jolly French workmen in jaunty automobiles motor about with not a care in the world? The *auberge* we are approaching displays a less genial image, however. It is a larger-than-life silhouette of tricorned head and shoulders. A haunting, black shadowy figure stencilled against a white wall. We draw close and I see that the adver-tisement is for cognac: Cognac Napoléon, of course. A small man enlarged to many times his own dimensions.

I think of product placement and the fortunes certain stars are paid for lending their names to merchandise. 'I wonder what our Corsican hero would have been paid today for all this,' I laugh. 'He's a bankable icon, that's for sure. And there's no copyright to stop anyone from reproducing his image.'

As we pass through Castellane, heaving with tourists and the only traffic jams we encounter throughout our journey, we see signs everywhere for the Grand Canyon du Verdon –

the largest gorge in Europe – which I have never visited. But no time for that today.

I return to the purpose of our outing – honey – and share with Michel what I have been studying. '*Apis*, a genre of bee that collects pollen for honey-making – not all do – has been around for somewhere between ten to twenty million years. Incredible, eh? It seems that bees and honey have been on this planet longer than man as we know him. *Homo erectus* dates from the Newer Pliocene period. The earliest bee fossils found date back to the Miocene period. There is a fossil in the Smithsonian Museum in Washington which is nine million years old. Man was already consuming honey somewhere between three to eight thousand years before Christ. An ancient industry, on a par with olive farming.'

I fall silent, stunned by the beauty of the nature around us.

Winding through one of the mountain passes, *les cols*, a coach approaches, driving fast, blasting its horn like a demented beast. The sound alone might sweep you away, send you spinning into the ravine that plummets more than a thousand feet beneath us. The rush and drama of the coach whistling through the mountain pass has sent a flock of rather large swifts scattering, screaming, regrouping and sweeping in and out of the clefts and crevices of the carved limestone alongside us. Are they swifts? Yes, alpine swifts, with white underbellies. In winter these *cols* must surely be impassable.

Our journey takes us through a lush valley where we drive in and out of a pretty and inviting town, Barêmme. A fertile oasis where Napoléon spent the night of 3 March 1815. We pass fields of apricot trees, cherry, bamboo.

Bamboo. I had thought that the origins of bamboo were in China, but I have read that its early history includes India, America, even Africa. In the Mediterranean, the Romans cultivated it as a decoration. Indian bamboo, which grows to great heights, encircled many of their temples. There are over 200 different species. Its cane was believed to carry the magic of the Orient within it.

The fruit trees prompt thoughts of lunch; I am hungry again. Michel suggests that we eat after our rendezvous with Manneron. 'I'm sure we can find a mountaintop restaurant in Mézel serving delicious local produce. What do you fancy?'

I consider his question as a steam train comes puffing along a track that flanks the road. Written the length of its three carriages is '*Nice à Digne*'.

'Something with tomatoes,' I answer.

There are maybe a dozen passengers aboard, all peering from the windows. It resembles a blue and white Dinky toy, a lithe Thomas the Tank Engine from a world of children's literature which precedes Harry Potter. We watch it rock and sway and then the signal goes down on the track in front of us and the train steams across the street.

The signalman's house to the right is green and shiny, with a carapace of ivy. Cut into it are red oblong window-boxes crammed with scarlet geraniums and, in the garden, two crooked tables dressed in red checked cloths.

Matisse wrote: 'Red becomes a sound like a note escaping from a musical instrument.' When I look upon the ruddy richness of these flowers, I see what he was getting at. And our poppies in the garden; so hot is that colour, I hear the heroin-cracked voice of a jazz singer, scarlet lips flush against a silver mike, crooning the blues.

The signal goes up and on we go. Now the train is to our right until it disappears into a small tunnel, chuff-chuffing cheerfully out of sight.

We have reached 1,200 metres above sea-level and the out-skirts of Mézel, where the air is heady, knife-sharp and spicy.

It is fragranced with the scent of wild lavender, which cannot grow so easily closer to the coast: it needs an altitude of over 900 metres to survive.

The sky, the light, the land are a delicate chromatic tapestry; the chalky earth is as pale as faded butter or goat's cheese, the sloping fields are a deep, inviting amethyst and the cloudless blue sky seems almost within reach. My head out of the window, hair blowing freely, I inhale the piquantly aromatic herbs, brush plants and trees known collectively as *garrigue*.

La garrigue Méditerranéenne includes a vast selection of wild and sweetly scented bushes and plants. What a paradise for bees . . .

As we close up the car to ask about Manneron and stretch our legs, I hear the echo of our footsteps on the dry, empty pavements. There is a hint of wind for which, after the length of the journey, we are very grateful. I crane my neck to release the stiffness and sight an eagle drifting effortlessly on the windslip.

'*L'aigle volera de clocher en clocher jusqu'aux tours de Notre-Dame*,' said Napoléon, the returning hero. The eagle will fly from belfry to belfry until it reaches the bell towers of Notre-Dame. Flushed with early success, his dreams must have soared with those overhead birds as he and his retinue marched northwards, cutting a celestial route through these Haute-Provence Alps. Above him, the lords of the domain, swooping, hunting, killing. He would have been watching those raptors, living in proximity with them, planning his campaigns, inhaling rushes of their potent power, hell-bent on his own resurrection.

Looking out across these mountains, where the natural peaks rise sharply skywards, not dissimilar to bell towers, I can picture where his image might have come from. Today, over a thousand birds of prey are executed every year by the power lines the EDF, the electricity board, have installed in these ranges. If their wingtips brush against two lines at once, they are electrocuted instantly. Others are wiped out by forest fires, pesticide and fertiliser poisonings or illegal hunting.

Napoléon would have had the opportunity to observe nests built in treetops on the cliff faces and to hear the broad, flapping wings of a variety of diurnal and nocturnal raptors hunting between one range, one peak, and the next. Instead of the sombrous tolling of church bells, he would have been listening to the eerie, resonant skirls of those mighty predators echoing through the stillness, cutting across brittle streams of light.

Nearly two centuries later, numerous birds of prey have become a rare sight. Bonelli's eagle is now an endangered species. Probably no more than fifty pairs survive in France.

'I think it's a young Golden,' murmurs Michel. I tilt my head and fasten my attention on the mighty bird. From this distance it does not look golden at all. Its underbelly is a dark, chocolatey brown.

'Why do you say that?'

'It has a golden head and nape. See how it glides, the "V" of its wings? See, it has white markings on its wings and tail.'

A tractor purrs by in the main street of Mézel and draws me back to earth, to this friendly little mountain town, where I notice chamomile growing in stone pots at the road's edge. This is a very different Provence from our coastal strip. It is far removed from the glorious *belle époque* splendour and glitz of the Côte d'Azur. The tourists here are in handfuls; they pass in dribs and drabs or sit in the roadside cafés studying maps. Not the roasted packs shuffling about by the coast, stuck in traffic, gorging despondently on ice creams and cola, or the film festival crowds. Here they are fresh-faced and purposeful, walkers in sensible sandals and batik shorts, no-nonsense haircuts or hippy-long curls, swinging woven swagbags from their shoulders.

Beyond the town, crossing a rather unattractive bridge, we go in search of the Manneron holding. An umbrous-featured local points out the route. 'But you can't walk it,' he warns. 'It's too far. It's way up there,' is the sole indication we are given.

Back in the car, we begin to scale a track, a *sentier muletier*, probably once trodden only by mules and *les bouquetins*, the splendidly horned goats that used to roam freely in these southern Alps but are never seen these days outside the national park. Slender-trunked trees rise up all around us. The higher we climb – and I thought we had reached the summit – the narrower and more perilous the path grows. The ground has turned to a shade of bleached nutmeg. There are numerous butterflies: minuscule citrony ones and larger, darker fellows and then another, a rich, creamy butterscotch. I am sorry to say that I cannot identify any of them, though the small ones could be Clouded Yellows which are habitués at this altitude. I dare not look down; the verticality makes me giddy. So I zero in on what is aloft and catch sight of what looks like a *village perché* hidden high above the trees, squeezed between bouldered rock formations.

'Look!'

I cannot believe the car will make it. It whines and wheezes as we snake our way round the mountain until eventually we reach the tiny hamlet, which bears no sign to tell us its name. We pass a man and boy leaning together against the wall of a house. They stare at us as though we have come from outer space, intruders to these dizzying heights. We park in a square, the only square, at the end of the road. Literally. The only way out of here is retreat. We

must have climbed a hundred metres since leaving Mézel.
The view is stupendous. One lone man is tinkering with his
car, which has a Paris registration plate. I ask directions to a
café or bar. He laughs. 'There's no bar here. There's nothing.
Eight houses. Not even a baker. If you want bread you must
return to the town.'

Does he know where we can find the beekeeper, M.
Manneron?

He shakes his head. 'I'm *en vacances*, sorry,' and off he
goes, up a narrow cobbled lane, the only lane, to one of the
other five properties – we have already passed three that
look out over the view. I glance at my watch. It is minutes
after midday and I hear the echoing clatter of plates and the
chime of voices behind semi-closed shutters. It is baking hot
and there is the familiar zirring of cicadas which I haven't
been aware of since leaving the coast.

A dog barks, and then another. Within seconds a
cacophony of howls and barkings has broken out. We sight
one rather dusty-looking hound chained in the square
behind several rusting, wheelless trucks and then a second
further over in a pit of earth. Both are dun-brown. Why
would anyone need a guard dog here? What's to steal?
Who is there to steal it? Beyond the yowling mutts is a
small walled cemetery. We take a look. Neat graves
adorned with plastic flowers. The family of—. Sadly
missed mother of—. Shiny enamelled photos, oval-shaped
like cameo brooches; pre-war portraits of severe-looking
men and women in starched collars and swept-back hair. I
am suddenly fascinated by the history of this place. Who
left? Who stayed? Who married whom? Every villager
turning out for a birth, a marriage, a burial. Who went to
war, who came back? To live so intimately with one's
neighbours. No secrets. Or might the entire hamlet harbour a dark secret? The Parisian tourist is calling to us. He

has enquired after our apiarist and the news is that he doesn't live here. He lives in Mézel.

'But we have just come from there.'

'No, his place is outside the town. There's a hillside, an escarpment, where he has a holding with many hives.' Yes, that sounds like him. We thank the young Parisian for his trouble and begin to stroll the few yards back to the car, making one more stop to take in the magnificence of the location and its utter isolation. It is then that I see the sign.

> La Réserve Géologique de Haute-Provence est une Réserve Naturelle Nationale, spécialisée dans les Sciences de la Terre. Sa mission est de protéger le patrimoine géologique. De la fin de l'Ere primaire au Quarternaire, ce sont, trois cents millions d'années que roches et fossiles nous racontent.
>
> Dans ce territoire de 145,000 hectares, immense musée en plein air, les géologues de la Réserve Géologique de Haute-Provence font revivre ces époques disparues.
>
> . . . découvrir et d'aimer le monde des roches.

The notice is informing us that we are gazing upon 145,000 hectares of a natural, open-air museum. This is a geological reserve. We are standing smack in the centre of one of the oldest inhabited regions of the world, where the rocks are impregnated with fossils and prehistoric signs of life. For 300 million years these rocks, these mountains, have been telling their stories, or so claims the Haute-Provence Geological Reserve. History written in stones; in their wrinkles, folds and eruptions. Every curve, every hollow is a language in granite. Michel tells me that among the fossil deposits found in this vast region are hundreds of examples of ammonites as well as footprints of prehistoric birds. Footprints of prehistoric birds who circled these mountains, landed, fed, procreated here.

Hills, valleys, forests of green folding one into the next, far-off mountains, distant crickets, all beneath the crystal midday sky. It is as though time has stopped and we are gazing into the memory of an ancestral brain which is both stupendous and terrifying. The world revealed, omniscient, staring back at us across the ages. I feel my heartbeat quicken.

'But Paris is a very old city and we were very young . . .'

Why, suddenly, do I recall and find myself mouthing these words of Ernest Hemingway's from *A Moveable Feast*? I cannot say. Perhaps because this place *is* so very old and we, by comparison, are still young. Our future is undrawn. Our love is young; this baby within me certainly is. And in the earth's stillness and age, its continuity, its witnessing of time, its wisdom, I sense a warning – the distant echo of an ancient haunting.

Hemingway was referring to the temptations outside his own marriage, an adulterous affair which damaged for ever love's trust. In that sense our love remains shining and untested. But it is not invincible; what if it all goes wrong? What if I should lose this child, too? I slip my hand into Michel's and he squeezes gently on it. A bird high above screeches. I turn my face up towards the light, scrunching my eyes to close out the noonday glare. The buzzard's shadow crosses over me, darkening the day. My head begins to swim and nausea returns; the height grows vertiginous and I turn and walk silently to the car feeling as though I have travelled a great deal further than two hours' distance from the coast, from our farm and from the happiness I seek to create.

As we return towards Mézel, Michel warns me that M. Manneron will probably consider our site too far for him.

But still, he may have good advice for us. 'You are not to be disappointed, *chérie*, if he refuses us. It is a great deal further and a more arduous drive than the map suggests.'

Manneron's stock farm is situated in an isolated backwater in the Alpes de Haute-Provence, and although he and his family live *en ville* in Mézel, the beehives are some distance out of the town, and off the beaten track. When we eventually find the narrow, grass-rutted goat run that leads us to his holding, the beekeeper is leaning against the gate clutching his mobile phone – which is how we have finally tracked him down – waiting for us.

He greets us with a shy shaking of the hand. His pebbled glasses are so thick I am surprised he can support the weight of them. A taciturn individual who has been awarded the Red Medal, the highest honour in France, for the quality of his honey, he speaks impossibly softly in response to our questions and otherwise not at all. Accompanied by M. Manneron, who strides with the ease of a country-dweller, one who spends his days negotiating rugged terrain, we climb a steep incline and then follow him, in single file, along a trail crossing an escarpment. 'Any special tips you might share with us on the husbandry of bees?' asks Michel.

Manneron does not reply. I am uncertain whether he has heard. He pauses to catch his breath or to give us the opportunity to do so – Michel is discreetly watchful that the effort is not too much for me – and then we continue our ascent in silence. Now the path has widened and we are walking side by side. The view in every direction is simply magnificent. I glance furtively at this myopic man striding with his head bowed, deep in thought, and I am curious to know what is going through his mind. From here we descend the scar, moving into an alpine valley, a shallow plateau scooped out between two peaks, and keep moving through windblown grass until, eventually, we reach the hives, *les ruches*, which

are laid out in two long rows. Large, white, square boxes
standing on short wooden legs amid the tufty mountain
grass. A quick calculation tells me there are approximately
one hundred.

'Where exactly are you based?' he asks Michel, who pin-
points our location. Manneron nods, contemplating it.

'I understood you had many more hives?'

'Ah, yes, but they are not all here. These have been gathering lavender honey. I have others at work on the *sapins*.
These little girls collected from the *romarin* before I brought
them up here. And a good season they've had, too.'

'So you move the hives to the flower sources?'

'Transhumance. Most *apiculteurs* practise it.'

'Have you heard of bees dancing?' I ask awkwardly.
'What I mean is . . . might there be a dance of the bees?' I am
not convinced that the activity exists but, if it does,
Manneron strikes me as a man who might know of it, and I
am keen to find out. Besides, the memory of that fellow at
the beach café has stayed with me. Our beekeeper leans
towards me, peering so close I feel as though I am wearing
his glasses. 'They have two routines, but it's only the workers who dance,' he confides.

'Two?'

'Yes, there's the waggle and there's the round. Each dance
is a different configuration and communicates a different
message. Sometimes, early in the mornings, I open up the
hives and there they are, dancing away.'

I am amazed. 'What's it all about?'

'A means of communication. A way of informing the foraging bees where they can find a good source of pollen, of
notifying the others of a change of address, you might say –
the repositioning of the hives. The language varies slightly
between one geographic race of honeybees and another, and
thus resembles birdsong and human languages in having

local dialects. Looked at that way, you could say that my little girls dance in Provençal.' He grins, pauses and frowns, as though trying to recollect something, and then smiles before continuing in a thickly accented English: 'A swarm of bees in May is worth a load of hay; a swarm of bees in June is worth a silver spoon; a swarm of bees in July is not worth a fly!'

'Did you write that?' I venture.

'What? *Mon Dieu*, no. I think it's a load of nonsense! Folklore. My wife found it on the internet this morning. Listen, I won't be able to help you myself. Your farm is too far. *Desolé*, but I'll lend a hand in finding you someone. You can count on that.'

Silver Side of
the Coast

Parking in the town of Cannes during these fifteen days of the film festival is a nightmare. The Croisette, the internationally famous lido that borders the seafront, is cordoned off. All general traffic must make circuitous detours and sit snarled up for hours on end in narrow lanes and back streets. Only official film-festival cars have access to the Palais, where they disgorge stars and filmmakers of every nationality who pose for the paparazzi while climbing the red-carpeted stairs, watched by thousands of attendant stargazers, eyes agog, alongside the old port. During these days in May, Cannes metamorphoses into a beargarden, and, frankly, the only way to negotiate it is on foot.

But how to get from our farm in the hills to the coast without finding ourselves lumbered with a vehicle that we cannot arrive in or park? Michel has come up with a rather natty solution. We don our evening clothes and fly down the

hills on a scooter he has bought for me, but which I don't
dare use without him, because the first time I took it out I
drove it slap-bang into our neighbour's wall, buckling the
front mudguard and smacking my nose so hard I was left
with a bruise the colour of winter pansies. I have been
behind the wheel of cars since I was sixteen – it is illegal to
drive in England at sixteen, but that's another story – yet
when it comes to two-wheelers I seem to lack the aptitude. I
have no sense of balance and I fear the exposure; I have
grown used to the security of the metal carapace of a car and
believe myself to be protected, but on a bike I panic and
wobble all over the place, like someone's granny after several
whiskys. Still, for the festival, the scooter is the ticket. We
park and lock it up in one of the back lanes of the old town
and from there we stroll to the Palais, our coveted film invitations at the ready. At this time of the evening the back
streets of the *vieille ville* are relatively quiet; the action is
taking place around the Palais, known to the local Cannois
population and those who work in the film and television
industries as 'the bunker' due its consummate ugliness and
desultory ergonomic values.

Arriving on foot rather than in a chauffeured limo provided by the festival for official guests of the festival – this
honour is reserved for those who have a film in competition – means that we must push and shove our way through
the crush of crowds as plentiful as spectators at a Premier
League football match. What an assault to our senses after
the tranquillity of Appassionata and our day out in the
mountains with the shy beekeeper, M. Manneron. As we
approach the glaring lights, music – as usual a well-known
film score – blasts from the humungous loudspeakers while
the glitterati shove and kick like fishwives to get to the front
of the queue, for once inside the huge cinema, the seats are
not numbered; it is a first-come, first-served affair.

Everywhere people are begging for spare invitations, hopefuls in makeshift evening dress whose dream it is to walk those red-carpeted steps and maybe, just maybe, have their photograph taken by one of the paparazzi who flank that stairway to fame. Between street level and entrance to the Palais, there are twenty-four steps and then, if you are up in the grand circle and not at auditorium level, which we are, another eleven to climb. I know because I count them regularly – it gives me something to concentrate on, helps me feel less shy. The attention of the world is spotlighted here: every television station, every international newspaper and magazine have sent representatives. Each May, approximately 25,000 people converge upon this coastal resort, amphitheatred by its deluxe hotels, to partake of the mayhem and madness that is this festival.

Cannes is about this moment. Ever since 1946, when the first film festival was inaugurated here to celebrate the town's liberation after the Second World War, it has become its raison d'être. Every other festival, every other season, is a pale reflection of this glitz. The buzz, the hype and, it has to be said, the tackiness. Spot the celebrity. The photographers are everywhere, pointing lenses, flashing cameras at well-known faces, sequinned, fishtail frocks, backless gowns and plunging cleavages, any trick in the book or fashion accessory to grab the attention of the thousands of snappers congregating the length of these hallowed steps. Stunning women hanging from the shoulders of drop-dead gorgeous men pose and pout before the strobe of flashbulbs and the blinking, adoring crowds.

As we negotiate our way through the scrum of overexcited people, Michel wraps a protective arm about me. 'How are you doing?'

'Fine,' I smile.

'Ready?'

I nod.

He takes my hand and we begin the ascent.

It is important to look cool, composed and, above all, to smile. It is no good concentrating on one's feet in an attempt not to trip or hitching up one's frock or frowning like a sourpuss. Smiling and swanning are all part of the show, the parade, the masquerade. The music is 'Thus Spake Zarathustra'. Up we climb, arm in arm. No selfconscious rictus grin this evening; I have the best reason to be gleeful and I am sailing up the stairs, savouring every minute of it. I turn my head and glimpse my husband, the father-to-be of my child, at my side. Flashes explode around us. I barely notice them; I am fathoms deep in my own happiness, our happiness. Michel squeezes my wrist, a tiny recognition of the swell of joy within me. The paparazzi always snap him, not because they recognise him – they don't – but because he looks magnificent in his black waistcoat and white *smoking*, which enhance his imposing, Prussian good looks and that long curly hair of his, and I am chuffed to be the woman on his arm.

Once up the stairs, we are jostled inside, huddled and shuffling like a colony of emperor penguins, and directed to vacant rows of seats by one of a dozen uniformed girls. Tonight, just as we are about to take our places, someone yells out Michel's name, bawling it across the rows of chair-backs. Coiffured heads turn. We spin around to see who it might be and catch sight of an eager, middle-aged man elbowing his way through the shimmering crowds to reach us, all the while shouting and waving. He seems to know us well and is almost jumping for joy to find us here. His stomach is straining in his outdated dinner jacket, he is flushed and perspiring, but he seems thrilled to see us, if the huge smile animating his shiny-complexioned face is anything to go by. I know we know him, but I cannot place him.

'Who is he? Have we worked with him?'

Is he a business associate of Michel's from Paris? But his accent is Provençal. He presents his chunky wife, who is clearly overcome to meet us both, particularly me. 'Now I can put a name to that English accent, madame,' she teases. 'And we love that television series of yours.'

And then it dawns on me. We are in the company of M. Di Luzio, our sooty plumber-cum-chimney sweep, and his wife. Tonight, as spruced and scrubbed as a newborn baby, he is quite unrecognisable. What is clear, though, is that he and his wife still insist on believing that I am Emma Peel from *The Avengers* – a series in which I have never played so much as a guest role. Even here, amid the madness of industry posturing, M. Di Luzio slaps his thigh like a principal boy in a pantomime, wiggles his hips and winks at me triumphantly. Then he turns his head and, through the assembling crowds, roars to another couple, friends of theirs, apparently, seated high up at the back of the upper auditorium. 'It's her!' he bellows in his thick, Provençal twang. 'Her off the telly!'

Later, after the screening and before going for supper, Michel and I stroll the Croisette arm in arm. It's fun to gaze, to miss as little as possible and to bear in mind that as far back as the late nineteenth century this famous lido has played host to the rich, the royal and the famous. Along its waterside arena an astonishing aggregate of destinies has become interwoven.

Prince Leopold, Duke of Albany, the youngest son of Queen Victoria, died here in 1894 after an accident at the Villa Nevada. Her Royal Majesty, his mother, paid a visit to Cannes three years later, with an entourage of over a hundred, to mourn her son and to visit the church of St George which had been built in his memory. However, much as she loved the French Riviera – the name was bestowed on the place by the visiting British – and was a regular visitor to these shores, she quit Cannes after only four days, declaring that she strongly disapproved of the immoral carryings-on here.

'I would be fascinated to hear her opinion today,' I say to Michel as we weave our way through blasting horns and autograph-hunters.

In 1949, the glorious, flame-haired film star Rita Hayworth married Prince Aly Khan here and lived out most of the rest of her sad and lost life in a villa in Le Cannet, which overlooks this renowned bay. In 1953, a seventeen-year-old nubile French girl, the daughter of bourgeois parents, posed on these golden sands (the sand is imported) for the paparazzi and caused such a sensation that from that day onwards her rise to fame as world sex kitten was assured. Brigitte Bardot. In some ways, she did as much for the perception of women in the fifties as her feisty suffragette predecessors, because of the new attitude she displayed to sex. BB was portrayed as a woman with carnal values who cared more for her own pleasures than for the men who partnered her. These days she is pretty much dismissed by the French. Though reaching sixty is not a setback – in France, women *d'un certain âge* are revered – she has not aged with the grace or poise of Catherine Deneuve. Pictures show her looking plump, wrinkled and rather vulgar, and I suspect that her marriage to a senior assistant of Le Pen, the leader of this nation's extreme right, has been the final nail in the coffin of her image.

In 1955, just a couple of years after BB's explosion on to the world scene, a very different breed of woman, the American model-cum-actress Grace Kelly, met Prince Rainier of Monaco here and, in marrying him a year later, renounced film-star status for that of Beautiful Princess endowed with Kingdom and Untold Riches – the ultimate escapist fantasy.

And that, it seems to me, is what Cannes is about. This

fringe of Provençal littoral remains the land of make-believe, but what fascinates me is, at what cost?

Occasionally, a fellow producer from Paris or London, some industry person, waves to us, or a harassed American executive, here for the market rather than the festival, stops to say hi to Michel and to enquire, 'How's business?'

While they exchange news, I take the opportunity to drink in the scene.

Although it is almost eleven at night – the second competition screening starts somewhere between 10 and 11pm – this famous beachfront drag is jam-packed with people. All along it, folk are sitting in cafés or restaurants or at tables on the pavements doing business, a few rather too ostentatiously. Others are acting chic, being famous, spending money, while others still are talking serious film. Many are sporting black tie. These tend to be the professionals who, like us, have just attended a screening or are about to sit through the later performance, for *smoking*, evening dress, is de rigueur here during the festival. You cannot climb those renowned red steps after 6.30pm unless you are attired in evening dress. Michel and I both rather enjoy this custom. These days it's about the only occasion I drag out the glad rags, and it adds a certain elegance to proceedings which, after all, purport to be about the celebration of filmmaking.

Beyond this nucleus, looking keenly and hungrily about them, are surges of star-spotters, wannabes, tourists, and make-believers and, to keep these motley swarms controlled, there are police at every corner, lining the streets, whistling at and redirecting the noisy streams of traffic.

This evening the weather is perfect. Balmy with a lilac sky as clear as a bell. Constellations of stars light up the night. Yes, it's the season for stars, but the terrestrial ones won't be spotted here. No, they are to be found hanging out in heavily guarded villas, attending exclusive parties in châteaux hired by distribution companies desperate to promote their latest multimillion-dollar extravaganza, or they are staying at the Hôtel du Cap, where the management refuse to accept payment by cheque or credit card, where attendance at one breakfast meeting at least is essential if you are to be hailed as a member of that most exclusive of all clubs, the A list, and where you can lose yourself in the sumptuous grounds, *le parc*, play langorous tennis in diamond-studded *baskets* (plimsolls, to those of my generation) and where, it has to be said, the view from that strand of the Cap d'Antibes out over the Mediterranean is truly breathtaking. But we are not members of that A list, and nor do we particularly wish to be. Well, if I am honest, I have hankered after that fame – I began composing that dreamed-of Oscar speech when I was ten years old – but not Michel: he is far more grounded, far less Hollywood-oriented. Or, as the French might say, '*pas très 'ollywoodien*'.

So here we are, strolling contentedly along the Croisette, hand in hand, enjoying the brush of palm trees soughing lazily in the hint of breeze – palms, by the way, were yet another British legacy to this coast. They imported them here in the nineteenth century along with the fluffy, sweet-smelling golden mimosas that are today celebrated at dozens of Provençal mimosa festivals in late January – when, suddenly, from out of the huggermugger of people, looms an unshaven, scruffily dressed journalist. He calls my name and I try to recall his. Jacob. Yes, that's it. I became acquainted with him in Madras, India, when I was a guest at the annual film festival there. I introduce him to Michel, and without further ado he gets straight to the point. He is here with his girlfriend, he explains, covering the festival for a German magazine, but the girlfriend, Barbara, of whom he spoke frequently in India, is at a loose end and not feeling well. He asks for our phone number and enquires whether she could come up to the house, use the garden and pool, hang out with us?

'Where we are staying is pretty grotty,' he moans, 'as well as being horrendously expensive, but it's in a good position for me. Still, Barbara can't sit in all day and she hasn't managed to find tickets to any films because she doesn't have any accreditation. Any chance that you guys could dig up a festival badge and a few tickets? Or if you have a spare room, maybe we could move up to your place?'

Before I can open my mouth, Michel tells him, '*Desolé*, it's not possible.'

We say our goodnights and he hurries away. I turn and glance after him. I am remembering an occasion several festivals back when I went into my bank and witnessed a scene that quite distressed me. A youngish but balding Englishman with an air of down-at-heel desperation was at the front of a rather long queue attempting to cash a cheque for the princely sum of £30. The teller refused him. He became loud and upset and an assistant manager was called to the scene. He begged her for the money, regaling her with his hopes for his first film, while the rest of us waited patiently. Eventually, the assistant agreed to telephone his branch in London, but while she was away making the call, he turned on his heels and fled like a hunted rabbit.

I recount this tale to Michel and then reflect on the fact that, whoever you are and no matter what your reason for being in Cannes during these fifteen glittering days in May, there is one thing you can bet your life on: it's costing the individual or the corporates an arm and a leg.

'The town of Cannes must be so rich,' I say.

'I am not at all sure about that,' replies Michel. 'In fact, there are whispers of financial problems.'

'Really?'

Smiling, he leads me off the Croisette into a side street. We are making for a friendly, family-run Italian restaurant he favours.

'I'm starving,' he says. 'Let's eat. What do you fancy?'

'Stuffed tomatoes. I'm dying to know what you've heard.'

'Didn't you have tomatoes for lunch?'

'Yes, and breakfast.'

Our Sunny Surroundings

After early-morning coffee, while the sun is rising into honeydew clouds that drift out of sight to reveal a clear blue sky, Michel begins a full day's work, even though it is Sunday, while I swim, shower and beetle off to Cannes.

The first performance of this, the last day of the festival, is due to screen at the Palais at 8.30am. The dress code is casual, seats are marginally less fought-over and I will find space for the ancient Merc in a *parking* we use above the historic fruit and vegetable market. From there, it is a pleasant stroll to the Palais.

Here lie aspects of Cannes I relish. It was at this hour, in this season, that I discovered this seaside town. Michel and I, sleepy off the first flight in from Paris, drove by hire car into the washed winding lanes of the *vieille ville*. Everywhere was amber-lit with the warm glow of early sun and the euphoria of newly tasted love. Little did I guess on that heady spring morning that this southern coast of France was soon to become my home.

Today, the promise of the sun's eternal heat caresses my flesh anew. There are handfuls of festival people abroad. The street cleaners have been at work, and few signs of last night's revels remain. From a dozen smoky cafés, bustling with Cannois locals, freshly brewed coffee tempts my taste-buds. At the water's edge, rows of yachts, rented at fall-over-backwards prices for this festival, sway gently in the harbour wash, sheltering sleeping guests, heavy-eyed from a surfeit of champagne and partying. Alone, I climb the hoovered red steps, not a photographer in sight, claim a seat and yield myself up to my first and original love: the magic and illusion of cinema.

After a rather disappointing film, I decide to stretch my legs. Strolling in the sand along the seafront, kicking my toes into the curls of waves, I pause to observe the comings and goings as the town swings into action, rolling its cameras on a whole new hard-bitten day. Everywhere along the Croisette are signs of the film festival winding down. Fleets of taxis are parked outside the hotels, preparing to depart for the airport carrying sales executives. All films in competition have been screened. Tonight is *la clôture*, the closing ceremony at which the winners are announced and the coveted Palme d'Or, the golden palm, is awarded by a jury of professionals to the film of their choice, the equivalent of the Oscar for Best Picture. I spy two police officers moving along a pair of beach dossers with sleeping bags and a tawny-haired mongrel. Cannes cannot afford to expose the fissures in the image, cannot reveal itself in a less than ideal light. There is too much at stake. Contrary to what I had believed, the town is not accruing wealth. Michel was right. It is in a great deal of debt. This has been a revelation to me. In my naïveté, it had never occurred to me that towns, municipalities, are obliged to balance their books just like the rest of us, and it certainly never occurred to me that a glitzy and expensive resort such as Cannes would not be rolling in spondulicks, lolly, palm oil. But Cannes is indeed up against it.

Michel Mouillot, the mayor, a man we once lunched alongside, before he was elected, at the Hôtel du Masque de Fer on the island of Ste Marguerite, is being leaned on from every direction. Shops along the beach strip and the streets and lanes to the rear are closing down at an alarming rate, while those who are managing to hang on are struggling for dear life to pay their rents and taxes. This is all very unfortunate for the local *commerçants*, and it puts the town in a difficult position vis à vis its traders.

So it tickles me to scout this illustrious beach parade and peek at the methods the town is adopting to keep up its illusion of wealth. The Côte d'Azur sells itself on its image of open-top sports cars speeding, carefree, along the Corniche, the cliffy coastal road between Nice and Monte Carlo; movie stars and princesses in darkly shaded sunglasses; palm trees swaying in the barely discernible but welcome breeze; champagne on the terraces of hotels and villas with linen-white façades and, at the pinnacle of it all, the advertisers' ultimate dream, fairytale romances, such as Diana in love with Dodi, holidaying on his playboy yacht. *La jeunesse d'orée* living out their brief days of bliss. Cannes cannot risk even a sniff of bankruptcy when what it is about is selling lifestyle, especially when it is the lifestyle of movie stars and international playboys. I see the windows of several empty shops are togged out with development projects. The displays include photographs, cuts of green and blue plastic representing golf courses and miniature swimming pools, all flanked by plastic models of homogenously designed apartment blocks bearing such names as Bougainvillaea Park or Sunset Haven.

A rather garish ice-cream parlour has opened up where a designer dress shop has gone under. Billboards harnessed across the façades of several buildings bear gigantic posters promoting films that will never see a movie house, possibly not even the video stores. A new Hilton has recently been constructed. And there are plans for extra gambling facilities: tongues are wagging at the prospect of another casino in Cannes and its boost to the economy. A rather splendid *belle époque* hotel has been torn down and replaced by a sugary-pink block of flats. This has caused a *petit* scandal, but Michel Mouillot stands his ground. His interests are the interests of Cannes, he declares brazenly.

The strip remains dominated by high-priced restaurants, cafés and estate agents, even while the price of real estate, *immobilier,* is plummeting. The rich and famous, or the rich and unscrupulous, bought in here at top-dollar prices, invested further fortunes in renovating their villas, equipping them with every modern amenity, installing Jacuzzis and state-of-the-art whatnots, and then, when they came to sell again, found that their properties were worth less than fifty per cent of their disbursements. Not surprisingly, the local community, shopkeepers, hoteliers, agents, are growing jittery.

It's a crisis. We await the outcome.

It was Somerset Maugham, who lived for many years on the luxurious and lushly verdant peninsula of St Jean-Cap Ferrat, who described Monte Carlo, the small tax-free kingdom between France and Italy, as 'a sunny place for shady people'. In his day, I am sure it was an accurate and witty observation of those who took up residency on that tiny horn, but today, Maugham's phrase could be applied to a broader area: it rings true everywhere along this palmy littoral. The French Riviera is a magnet for hopefuls and no-hopers in equal proportion, in the same way Hollywood draws the would-bes and wannabes to the world of celluloid. The south of France, predominantly Cannes, promotes itself as the California of Europe, the multilingual film centre of the world, at least for the fortnight when this, the most famous film festival in the world, unveils its latest package of stars and stars-in-the-ascendant. In the hills above Cannes, a kilometre or two away from our crumbling farm, there is a residential quarter named La Californie, twinned with Hollywood, which boasts some of the most expensive real estate in France, much of which is hidden behind tall, thickly fronded palm trees and equally tall, electrified iron gates. To rent a villa on that strip during the film festival can set one back something in the region of £5,000 a day.

Aside from this film festival, there are two television festivals held in Cannes, one in the spring, the other in autumn. There is a music festival in January, as well as festivals for the worlds of multiactive media, young aspiring actors, short films, advertising, television commercials, antiquary, clairvoyancy, yachting, parlour games, real estate and, for the town of Cannes, the most lucrative festival of all, the Duty-Free Festival, which is held in the late autumn. Yes, festivals are big business here. International companies fly in chairmen, presidents, vice-presidents, any and all executives by the planeload, and they are all on generous expense accounts.

'A duty-free festival?' I asked incredulously when I first heard mention of this one. Particularly since Europe is now a united body whose duty-free borders have been dismantled and across which travel no longer offers this perk. But that has made little if any difference, it seems, to the thriving duty-free market elsewhere. This festival is heavyweight money for the town. Prices escalate during that autumn week. For anyone who is not a card-carrying duty-free merchant, a hotel room is an impossibility at any price. These traders are the guys who call the shots. So much so that Cannes has been warned that if it does not build two new five-star hotels, providing every amenity required and desired by these visiting sales people, the organisers will move the whole shebang to Barcelona.

A few years ago, when I was in Fiji researching a novel, I pulled out a six-page supplement which had been slipped beneath my hotel room door, delivered with my daily copy of the *Fiji Times*. The entire leaflet was devoted to a Fijian Indian lauded in the headline as 'the Duty-Free King of the World'. Perfect. I was looking for such a figure for the novel I was there to research. I telephoned his office to request an interview. Thrilled and totally puffed up by the notion that his ideas and opinions should be of interest to any foreigner, he invited me to dinner at his home. During the course of the meal, learning that as well as earning my living as a writer I am also an actress, he bragged: 'I won the golden palm at Cannes.'

Naturally, this claim puzzled me. I must have shown my disbelief because my host hurried away from the table and I heard him rooting away in one of the many other rooms of his palatial bungalow. He returned clutching a statuette which indeed announced him to be the International Duty-Free Palme d'Or winner of the previous year. I was highly amused but duly congratulatory, and have taken a far more active interest in the flow of traffic in and out of the town ever since.

In the olden days, indeed from 1923, when Coco Chanel made her first summer appearance on the Côte d'Azur, when the first open-air swimming pools were constructed here and the summer season as opposed to the winter season was hailed as a fashionable affair, wealthy families – including, no doubt, Signor Spinotti, the Milanese businessman who built our villa – or families of *haut standing* from Paris or the United States would descend by train or motor car, take suites in the deluxe hotels and occupy them for the duration of July and August. These days, those who can afford such luxuries have villas of their own, or have found other equally fashionable, less tramped-over destinations. Even so, Cannes, up to the present, preserves those two summer months as trade festival-free. Hotels do not have to tout for such business while the heat of the sun is at its zenith and the Mediterranean is milky warm.

Much has changed since Mme Chanel first put her elegant toes in the clear, blue Mediterranean and trilled, '*Ah, les délices de la mer!*' These days, during the summer months, the coast becomes infested with a very mixed bag of visitors. First there are the jazz and art aficionados who, like us, frequent the Jazz à Juan festival and the Jazz at Cimiez fortnight held among the starlit olive groves in the Parc des Arènes, where a magnificently renovated, red-ochre, seventeenth-century Genoese villa houses a permanent collection of Henri Matisse's work. Cimiez, in the hills above Nice, where Matisse lived, worked and died, and where both he and Raoul Dufy are buried, in the cemetery of the Monastère Notre Dame de Cimiez, remains a fashionable residential area. As well as the jazz-lovers there are the family holiday-makers. Usually they come cruising through in their laden BMWs and Volvos, making for nowhere in particular just so long as it is southerly and sunny. The bourgeoisie from Paris flock here to their *résidences secondaires* to dine on fresh fish and *crustaces*, jog through the oleander-blossomed parks and bake themselves on the beaches, sipping Evian and wearing designer next-to-nothing. To these add a whole host of transients, including troops of coal-black Africans from the Gabon and Senegal in gloriously coloured batik print *jubbahs*, who traipse the beaches and the exteriors of the fashionable *restos* and cafés, attempting to sell their imitation Louis Vuitton bags and purses, trays of watches, lucky charms and sunglasses galore.

I enquired of one such African how he came to be living here and he told me that he had been brought over from his native village by a *patron* who was housing him and many others like him in two dingy rooms in Nice. It seems that these *patrons* set up these immigrants with their merchandise and if, after a certain period of time, they have not sold sufficient trinkets and earned handsome cash returns, they are kicked out of their living quarters and, if they are fortunate, booted on to the next boat out. If they are not, they are left penniless, without work permits or prospect of employment, to fend for themselves.

Aside from these Africans, whose skills appear to me to be far removed from those required for a heavy sell – most seem far happier whiling away the hours showing me scruffy photos of their kids or chattering about their homeland villages or their uninspiring experiences in southern France – there is a whole host of other, less salubrious, illegal immigrants, in addition to the professional criminals. Crime pays here, particularly during these summer months. Kids on scooters will target a chicly attired tourist. They ride up, ask the time and then, while the unsuspecting stranger, usually a woman (it has happened to me), has her arm raised to check her watch, they snatch her handbag and make off with it.

And thieves in vans descend from other *départements* of France. It is a busy season for them. They cruise the hills and case the villas. A practised eye tells them when holidaymakers are in situ and when they are out, and holidaymakers are renowned for failing to lock away that extra bit of cash and jewellery in a safe.

During our first penniless summer on the farm, before we had gates and fences and dogs, a procession of tired-looking men on motorbikes or in Citroën vans ascended our hill at regular intervals. Armed with catalogues and brochures, they attempted to sell us one of a selection of the alarm systems they had on offer. Many of these blokes looked completely unscrupulous and we both agreed that we would not trust them with our shopping lists, never mind our modest and pitifully empty farmhouse.

A Dutch producer friend of Michel's bought a villa in the neighbourhood of La Californie and paid exorbitant sums to have an alarm system installed. A few months later, the company telephoned to inform him that the equipment was antiquated and needed to be updated at a further cost of something in the region of 20,000 francs. The Dutchman refused. A salesman from the company telephoned again when his wife was there alone. He talked her into allowing him to send one of his representatives over to either confirm their opinion or find some way to modernise the present system. The woman agreed. She let the man in and, busy with her own chores, left him to his work. After he had spent a tedious amount of time fiddling with and readjusting various clocks, he informed her that there was nothing to be done and that she and her husband would be obliged to invest in the company's newly modernised equipment.

When Michel's friend returned from his business trip in the Netherlands, his wife recounted to him the latest development in the affair. He hit the roof and telephoned the company to make clear that in no circumstances would he pay them another sou to install a new system. The very next day, the couple were burgled in broad daylight. When they returned from their lunch on the beach and walked in to find their house in disarray, he checked the alarm system and discovered that it had been disconnected. Naturally, the police were called. Their enquiries revealed that the monthly *abonnement* our friends had been shelling out to the security

firm to link up their alarm to a twenty-four-hour surveillance
service was actually connected to a fax machine. When the
couple in question drove to the firm's last given address in
search of the culprits, they learned that the *société* had been
out of business for eighteen months. The police shrugged
and said there was nothing more they could do. Stories of
such swindles and rackets have passed into local legend. At
this level, they are unfortunate for those who are stung, but
we are on the Côte d'Azur, 'a sunny place for shady people',
and when the heat is on, there are degrees of shade.

Returning to the house, I potter about at my desk for an
hour and then, while Michel goes through a thick envelope
of papers that arrived when we were in the mountains yesterday, I whip us up a salad of mozzarella and tomatoes
dressed with basil, ground black pepper, our own oil and
slivers of fresh mint. And, to follow, plates of fresh vegetables braised in oil, herbs and garlic.

'There is no debating the fact that the French have a
mania for bureaucracy,' I remark while tucking into generous
helpings of lunch. My observation is borne out yet again by
the veritable suitcase-load of forms piled on the garden table
in front of us. They come from ONIOL, the organisation we
have been waiting to hear from for the best part of a year. It
is they who are considering our AOC rating as producers of
quality olive oil. Over a glass of Chablis, we set about trying
to fathom out the forms, fill in the various questionnaires,
which comprise several columned boxes requesting information about the number of fruit trees we have, what sectors
they are planted on (our smallholding is divided up into seventeen sectors, *parcels,* of land) and the distance between
them and the olives.

'I think we ought to meet up with these people. According
to all this, we may not qualify for an AOC at all,' says Michel.

'But Christophe, the mill owner, said our oil is of the finest.'

'That doesn't appear to be the concern. Well, not at this stage, anyway. Formalities first, and these forms seem to suggest that the details I supplied do not conform with their requirements. If I understand correctly, a farmer needs a minimum number of olive trees to qualify as an *oléiculteur*, and unless we are registered as bona-fide olive farmers, we are not eligible for any grants or awards, hence we cannot be promoted to AOC status.'

I ponder this over a mouthful of cheese. 'What is the requirement?'

Michel stares at various pages, frowns and then replies, 'It doesn't specify. I can never get through to these people so I'll have a word with the Chambre d'Agriculture tomorrow morning. We must find out what this is all about.'

The following morning, he telephones the Chambre d'Agriculture in Nice and is informed that he must discuss it with ONIOL, which is precisely what he has been attempting to do for the past year. When Michel explains this, the *fonctionnaire* at the other end of the phone suggests a particular woman at the organisation. 'Ring her, say you have spoken to me and you'll get an appointment.' This Michel does and, miraculously, we are offered an appointment for the very next morning. Michel postpones his return to Paris and we drive to Marseille for our long-awaited interview with the ONIOL representative. I am a tad nervous, for if this body, which regulates olive plantations and oil pressing, does not back us, our request for the dreamed-of AOC will be rejected out of hand before our oil has even been sampled.

I had naïvely assumed that the sole criterion was the quality of the produce.

'*Mais, non!* There are rules,' we are informed as we sit down.

'Ah yes, *bien sûr.*' I should have guessed. How foolish of me to have assumed that here in France it might simply be about the quality of the oil and not also about the maze of paperwork involved at every level of government funding, not to mention union considerations. In this case the farmers' union and the union of *oléiculteurs*, olive-growers. Will we be obliged to join a union of beekeepers, I ask myself silently, when – if – we eventually find someone who is willing to share a few hives with us?

'And they are?' enquires Michel, smiling disarmingly at the young lady in black who, behind the mountains of untidy files sliding all over her desk, sits opposite us smoking furiously. I feel prenatal nausea creeping up on me again.

She sets sail, listing at full rattle a host of must-dos and have-to-bes. I am lost. It takes me back to our early days in Provence. Legal French then and legal/agricultural jargon now: both have me beat.

What I do understand is that Michel's summing-up of the situation was spot-on: we need a minimum number of *oliviers* on our farm, our *verger*, to qualify.

'How many?'

'Two hundred and fifty.'

'Two hundred and fifty! But all we have are sixty-four mature trees and a dozen small fellows I planted last year,' I stammer.

'*Hélas*, monsieur, madame, that is the regulation.' She begins to rise. The interview that has taken us months to achieve is at an end.

'What if we planted another two hundred?' suggests Michel.

I stare at him open-mouthed. Who will pay for them? Who will oversee them? Water, prune and harvest them? Our irrigation system is rudimentary, humping hosepipes and watering cans by hand, and we are soon to have a baby!

'Well, that's a different matter.' She sits again, then rises, lighting up yet another dark-tobacco cigarette in this windowless, airless space. 'But that is not my department. I oversee the *versements*, the funding, for the quantities of oil produced. You must talk to my colleague. She looks after the grants for plantation development. But first, I need photocopies of your passports and your bank RIB.' Michel furnishes our Relevé d'Identité Bancaire, our bank-account identification slip – experience has taught us always to attend official meetings such as this one with these photocopied documents at the ready, because you can bet your life they will be asked for – and she leads us through to an adjoining office where we are introduced to another young woman, also clad in black, with layers of raven hair pinned carelessly into a nest. She appears equally frazzled, rather more vague, and smokes just as furiously.

Half a dozen forms are dug out of drawers to be completed here and now, more photocopies of our passports are requested – this causes a minor hiccup as we came with only one of each, but it is satisfactorily resolved when Michel suggests that the first young woman make copies of the copies we have left in the adjacent room – and then another batch of forms is handed over to us, to be taken away, studied, signed and returned *assez vite*: 'Time is running out. You have left it very late to qualify.'

Her remark is exasperating. Still, I resist the temptation to point out that it is almost a year since we sent in our letter requesting an application form and only a couple of days since we received the rather unhelpful reply.

'You understand that if you decide to plant the requisite number of trees they must be purchased from an ONIOL-approved *pépinière?*'

Officialdom. Small print, large print. I sigh loudly.

'How do we go about finding the nurseries?' asks Michel, unruffled.

'I will send you the list. But first there are regulations to study,' and off she goes again to organise the photocopying of another five pages of bureaucratic stipulations.

As we leave she adds: 'Here is the representative you need to contact at the Chambre d'Agriculture. Without his approval, and it must be his, the file is invalid. Mention my name and he'll see you without delay.'

Michel jots down the details of the gentleman in question, thanks the young woman for her *gentilesse* and *accueil chaleureux* and assures her that we will be in touch again in the near future.

France is a country renowned for the quality of its agricultural produce and, along with its mania for bureaucracy, it requires stringent adherence to the rules. The Chambre d'Agriculture oversees every aspect of French farming, be it beef, rapeseed, cheese, olive oil, horse meat: whatever it is, nothing gets past the eagle eye of this government department. Its designated olive oil *bureaux* are in Nice and Marseille (there are none in the north of France, because it is a southern industry, an exclusively Mediterranean product). When we return home, Michel telephones Nice to make an appointment and is informed that the chief of the department himself will come along to visit us. Fortunately, he is the very man suggested to us by our contact at ONIOL. Might we finally be getting somewhere?

While I am still struggling to make headway with what I am beginning to discover is a most elusive breed, the apiarists, the bee-masters, a delicious piece of scandal is rocking the town of Cannes and sending the waters roiling beneath those gleaming, sleepy yachts.

The snappily dressed, savvy mayor, Michel Mouillot, is arrested. For corruption. A small matter which the local rag, the *Nice Matin*, and restaurant gossip assure us will be ironed out in a jiffy. I take to buying the local paper. It is not a journal which up until now I have bothered with, but it does have its own brand of soap-opera-style 'reportage' which, given the case in question and the subject of my research – the changing face of Côte d'Azur–Provence – I find delightfully appropriate. Watching Mouillot across the salon of the crumbling hotel out on the offshore island of Ste Marguerite several years ago, I had playfully cast him as a leading figure in an American soap, and now, here he is, star of his own scurrilous show, whose ratings are rising as *le petit scandal* gets out of hand. For the scoop is being picked up by the national and, indeed, international press. It seems that these frauds concern dealings in London, in the heart of the City. Rather large sums of money have been changing hands. There is a suggestion that someone is seeking a permit. Briefcases, carried as hand luggage, are stuffed to bursting with cash. *Le marché noir, la caisse noire.*

As the beaches begin to reflect with glistening supine bodies, the scandal escalates. Local folk talk of little else. Meanwhile I, in my den, am yet again on the telephone to M. Manneron. Yes, I tell him, we have understood that he does not wish to commit to the *emplacement des ruches* on our land, but he has promised to pass the word around. Indeed, he confirms, but so far, not one beekeeper has expressed interest. Oh dear.

The morning of the departmental visit from the Chambre d'Agriculture is upon us and I am quite taken aback to find myself greeting a handsome, dark-haired, vigorous young man of twenty-five or -six who arrives in jeans, T-shirt, walking shoes and briefcase. This is the chief inspector. I had been expecting someone a little more sedate, mature and office-bound. While Michel goes off to fetch a bottle of wine and three glasses – de rigueur when negotiating such matters – the young gentleman and I seat ourselves at our wooden table in the garden. Behind him, I see branches of tender fruits: pears, apricots and peaches, and the orange trees decorated with their tiny green balls. I am fascinated to know how, at his age, he has acquired his position but feel that at this stage to comment on his youth might not serve us. However, as usual, my insatiable desire to glean facts gets the better of me. I broach the subject delicately: 'Have you been employed in this line of work for long?' He stretches his long legs, strokes our golden retriever, Ella, who is nuzzling his arm, and smiles.

'The chief before me was retired from the office. I came to it pretty much directly from university.'

'Really, why? Was he . . . ?'

'Couldn't handle the stress. He had a nervous breakdown and nearly went mad.'

I may know little of the demands of working for the Chambre d'Agriculture, but I would have put the stress level of such an occupation reasonably low on the trauma scale, compared with, let's say, air-traffic control, mining or television production.

'Is the appointment so taxing?' I venture.

Michel returns with the tray and begins to uncork the rosé. Our friend leans back in his chair, rocks on two legs, splaying limbs, physically expanding at the prospect of a chilled glass of wine in the noonday sunshine. He looks about him, calibrating the holding. 'Nice spot you have here. Well situated, close to all amenities yet private.'

I am desperate to know why his former colleague nearly went mad. I see little sign of any such infliction damaging this wholesome young man.

'*Santé*,' smiles Michel when the drinks have been poured and served. We all three sip our wine and sit silently relishing the moment.

'I was just hearing from monsieur . . . that the previous chief of the olive department was retired early due to unstable health. And I was interested to know what caused it.'

Michel shoots me a glance, fearful that I may be opening a can of worms we won't want to get into, but our companion seems perfectly happy to discuss the affair.

'It's no secret,' he begins, taking another sip of his rosé, 'that the Provençals, and most particularly the farmers, have developed their own ways and methods and don't take kindly to interference, as they call it, particularly from official bodies such as ourselves. My predecessor was given the unfortunate task of visiting every registered olive farm and informing the farmers that Europe was now one entity, which meant that new standards for agriculture – health, sanitation, farming equipment etc. – were to be enforced. Well, to a man they took it badly and refused to be ordered about. And to make sure that the poor chap understood their sentiments, they fired at him with rifles and shotguns. The second his Renault passed through the gates of an *oliveraie,* he was blasted with bullets. His front windscreen was shattered, his tyres were punctured, dogs bit him, sticks were hurled at him, to say nothing of the verbal abuse. I only encountered him once or twice, when I was still a student and was working in the offices as a *stagiaire.* On both occasions the poor chap arrived back at his desk, clothes torn, shaking and gibbering, reeking of alcohol. It was shortly after that he requested early retirement and I was offered the post.'

'Aren't you afraid?' I ask him.

He laughs. 'No, the farming community is getting used to the changes, slowly accepting the new order, and where they remain obstinate – well, I find ways of gently persuading them.'

Lucky, our Alsatian, comes loping towards us and I fear this may be the day he finds himself savaged by an olive farmer's dog. We should have chained her up. I rise hastily, preparing myself for the attack but, no, she approaches at speed, sniffs at his fingers and settles herself like a docile puppy at his feet.

Before I can ask him what his gentle persuasions might be, Michel suggests a tour of the land and off they go to pace out the distances between the trees which takes them the best part of the lunch hour. When they return, *le jeune monsieur* seems satisfied. We have breached no rules as yet, and as long as we agree to plant the extra quota of trees and maintain the required distances between olive tree and olive tree and olive tree and fruit tree, he sees no reason at all why we shouldn't be given an agricultural registration and, from there, be awarded our AOC.

We are getting somewhere.

A few days later, we receive a letter from one of the unions informing us that an officer will be coming to inspect our land. This is followed by a visit from a serious-faced inspector who needs to interview us and register us as olive farmers. Passports photocopied yet again, we find him waiting, an hour early, at our gate when we return from a shopping expedition. He is in time for lunch which, naturally, we offer him and, equally naturally, he accepts. Then, as coffee is served – '*Un petit noir pour moi, madame, s'il vous plaît*' – out come the papers from the briefcase. 'Which of you is registering?' he asks.

Michel and I look at one another and shake our heads. Does it matter?

'It's up to you. It's a security, insurance for your health.'

'We are covered,' I retort. 'And please can I make it clear that we both also practise other professions? We don't wish to deceive anyone.'

He frowns. 'That's not the point, madame. You have to

register and pay the fee, which is negligible.'

And so Michel signs his name on our behalf, and with this insignificant spill of ink he has been transformed, in the eyes of the French law, French tax offices, social security bodies, and the farming union, as well as the Chambre d'Agriculture, into an olive farmer. Or so I thought.

'Ah, *non*, madame, not the farmers' union. *Non*, that is another matter.'

'But we thought that you—'

'*Non, non*, we are *la mutualité*. I will give you the name of the man you must telephone at the union . . . It is important that you don't tarry in this matter . . .'

And so it goes on, and on and on. Who can blame our poor, scowling postman for his miserable frame of mind? Every morning I am obliged to keep an ear open for his moped, and the second I hear it come putt-putting round the foot of the hill I have to leg it downstairs to the garden, play catch with Lucky, who loves every minute of this frenzied game, up to the point when I chain her to a tree, where she remains sulking and uncomprehending until the traumatised fellow has delivered his load and motored off well out of biting range, and I am left with the large brown envelopes containing magazines and pamphlets all offering assistance with *la culture et entretien des oliviers*. As well as letters informing us that several other *fonctionnaires* from official oil *syndicats* will be arriving; delegations of them, it seems, and they all bear names that sound in translation like mouth-watering delicacies: Mr Lemon (M. Citon), Mr Duck (M. Granard) or Mr Jam (M. Confit). All stride the land, counting aloud the metreage between trees, counting the trees, noting the numbers of fruit trees which have been planted on the same terraces, while I prefer to gaze at the blue heavens, a splendid background to the fruit burgeoning all around us, or to drift off to other more pressing agricultural concerns of my own.

For example, it occurs to me now that I had been intending to research the origins of the cherry tree, and that in all this wooded land of ours I have never once seen a bird's nest. Certainly, none in the olive trees, and I am curious to know why that might be. I am about to ask one of these learned gentlemen when I realise that a very perplexed member of this particular party is addressing me.

His troubled expression has been caused by the sight of my humble pomegranate tree. It has stopped him in his tracks. He is staring at this unassuming sapling as though looking down upon something quite disgusting.

'*Mais ça, c'est un grenadier, madame! Pourquoi? Pourquoi?*' he demands with extreme gravitas, as though I have committed a mortal sin, which in his eyes, of course, I have. Why, he wants to know, have I stuck a pomegranate in the middle of the olive terraces?

I stare at him, shamed and open-mouthed. I have no satisfactory explanation. Other than the fact that I dreamed of looking down from the poolside upon its vermilion-red flowers, its hard, crusty fruits with skins like a country maid's complexion, there was no deep or meaningful reason except, damn it, why not? I fancied putting it there.

He shakes his head in sorry bewilderment – he is dealing with a foreigner, tantamount to an idiot – and continues with his inventory while I, somewhat humiliated, take heart from listening to the songbirds who are in lusty throat on this glorious day.

I make a mental note to look up the history of the pomegranate, and on we go.

On we go, moving to the age of each of the *oliviers* and their varieties. All our trees are *cailletiers* except for four young ones, which yield larger drupes than our venerables but less fine oil; these are known as *tanches*. On each inspection these saplings also stop the visiting *fonctionnaire* in his tracks. *Mais pourquoi?* they ask dryly, and I am obliged to launch into yet another explanation as to why we have a mere four trees, obviously recently planted, of this other variety. The reason is quite simple. In the early days, when I purchased and planted these babies, I was unaware of such delicate nuances as single-variety farming. Indeed, it never entered my unProvençal head that we might one day be standing here going through this rigmarole at all – all in the hope of gaining one very modest AOC.

Once I have explained about the *tanches* they shrug, note down my faux pas and warn us solemnly that we cannot farm these drupes and press them along with the others.

'Of course not!' we cry in operatic horror, which seems to appease them.

'Marinate them in brine is my advice to you. Use them for serving as *les hors d'œuvres,*' is their suggestion, and we nod colludingly.

'You are probably not aware, madame, that the *tanche* olives were originally from Nyons in northern Provence, though I expect you have noticed that they are very black in colour. They are excellent for making *anchoïade*. Best to pick them when they are slightly overripe. Wait until they are showing signs of paper-thin wrinkles, caused by the first frosts, and for heaven's sake, do make sure to use lashings of garlic. Or you can make a most excellent *tapénade* with them. Now, I have a particularly fine recipe, less well known than most. I make it up myself and it's a personal triumph *chez nous*, even if I do say so. It includes a little cognac. My secret, of course, but . . .'

All that is left to do, it seems, once these men have tracked every inch of our land and given us their opinions, hints and inside information on every last detail, is to order the trees. This will have to be done from a *pépinière* in the Var; there is no ONIOL-approved grower any closer to us.

'You will be sent a list,' we are informed. 'When it arrives, make an appointment, go and have a look at the trees. Make yourselves known to the growers, that's my advice.' Michel assures everyone that if necessary we will hand-pick each and every one of the 200 trees ourselves, which seems to thoroughly delight them. That's the spirit, I hear them mentally declare.

And then we are told by one or other of this endless stream of suited visitors that we will not be eligible for agricultural water rates until we have furnished proof that we hired a *sourcier*, a water diviner, who has come to the farm, tramped the land and confirmed that there are no natural *sources* anywhere to be found. Any, that is, that could be used to supply us with natural water so that we do not have to apply for a subsidy from the Lyonnaise des Eaux.

'A water diviner? You are kidding me!'

But Michel shakes his head. The condition is for real. 'And we'll have to do it, *chérie*. Do you remember when we bought the farm, Madame B. mentioned something to us about a *source* here, the well that we have never tracked down?'

'How do we go about finding a water diviner in this day and age? Do you think they advertise in *Les Pages Jaunes*?' I giggle.

And you know what? After a truly fascinating half-hour trawling through the Provençal Yellow Pages, I come across an advertisement in the 'Water Suppliers' section under the heading: '*Rain Bird, Hunter*'. Could this be what we are looking for? Just for fun I telephone their number, but receive a frosty response. Of course they are not an agency for water diviners; they are suppliers of garden watering systems. Do we need a quote? The answer is we badly need an automated water system, an entire irrigation system, in fact – summer watering is the bane of our lives because it takes so

long – but such an installation is way beyond our means
right now, and when I admit this the woman hangs up. The
whole business is mind-bogglingly exhausting and, with a
baby on the way, I confess to being a touch reticent at the
prospect of extending our olive plantation to such a degree.
With so much extra work, how will we cope?

Still, the more I chew it over, the more I come round to the
idea. Our little farm will truly earn its title of olive farm.

And what to do about this water diviner?

Water divining is surely an ancient trade, part of the old
order. Its practitioners have been dismissed in a world of
modern technology, cast aside as perpetrators of jiggery-
pokery. To insist we find ourselves one might well be a novel
attempt – and not without a *soupçon* of Provençal cunning –
at protecting, reincarnating the local heritage. Well, I'll go
along with that. In such a frame of mind, I determine to
find us one.

Quashia, who is busy strimming the terraces – felled are the
seeding poppies and spring wild flowers – shakes his head
solemnly when he hears what I am about. 'There's no water
source on this farm,' he pronounces.

'Well, according to the *vendeuse* we bought the house
from . . .'

He shakes his head again. 'You're wasting your time and
your money. You tell the Lyonnaise des Eaux, as well as all
those clowns who've been marching about here sticking
stakes in the ground, that if there was water here, I'd be the
first to know it. I spend my life scaling and strimming these
terraces. No one knows them better.'

A fact that cannot be argued. And I tell him so, while
inhaling the scent, borne on the breeze, of newly cut herbage.

Then, to cap it all, Quashia announces his need to leave.
'What!'

'Don't you worry, I'll be back. I won't abandon you. But I must go and marry off my last son. I promised my wife we'd have him wed before the year's out, and it's more than my life is worth to break that promise. Besides, he's given me an ultimatum. He says he'll be married next week without me if I don't get there. That's impossible, of course; he doesn't have the wherewithal. Even so, I'd best get on my way.'

'Why, no question about it, you must go, Monsieur Quashia,' I tell him.

And so he must. I smile and pat him on the shoulder. I cannot allow myself to dwell on the labours that lie ahead knowing that, for the foreseeable future, without Quashia, we will have no one to lend us a hand.

Treating the Trees

The evening before his dawn departure, our loyal farm manager strolls up to say his *au revoir*s. This involves walking the garden with Michel – a male ritual they always play out before one or other leaves for any length of time – and then sitting at the table beneath the spreading magnolia tree to partake of a pot of mint tea with us, sweetened with spoonfuls of coppery Provençal honey. As we watch it plop into the cups, we promise ourselves that this time next year it will be from our own hives. On this occasion, Quashia has also come to collect a salary advance because 'weddings are such expensive affairs'. I am rather taken aback by the sum he has calculated the whole business is going to cost him. Until he explains that, in Algeria, the preparations are the responsibility of the groom's father, as is 'footing the bill for every darn thing', and that involves more than just the protracted wedding festivities.

'What else could there possibly be, Monsieur Quashia?' It amuses me that, considering the length of time Quashia has been working for us, I still address him as 'monsieur' and use the formal *vous*, rather than *tu*, when speaking to him. I never call him by his given name. I have no idea why this is. We are family, in our way. Certainly he has become more precious to us than any run-of-the-mill member of staff, and infinitely more than a hired hand. Still, unlike René, Quashia maintains a professional distance. 'Are you expected to build them a home as well?' He has mentioned in the past that he single-handedly constructed each of the dwellings his other sons and daughters and their offspring inhabit. I had presumed he had chosen to do this out of his profound sense of duty and generosity, but now we learn from him that, yes, he will build his son a house but first, over the coming days, his entire village will be invited to his home and fed at several feastings that take place over a period of days. But, above all else, the bride has to be purchased. 'And this young lady is not cheap!'

'You must buy her, I see.' Again, I had taken it for granted that, if there was a dowry to be paid, it would be the bride's parents who would be shelling out, but in this part of Algeria, north of the Sahara, apparently not. I had also assumed that such customs as the buying and selling of marriage partners had died out altogether. Evidently not, in dear Quashia's case.

'I am still in the middle of complicated negotiations with her family,' he tells us. According to him, they hail from a distant part of the country where the customs are marginally different. It has been agreed that the ten days of feasting for both partners' families, friends and fellow villagers and the building of the marital home are all to be paid for by Quashia. 'On top of which, they're demanding three dozen sheep and a certain amount of cash.'

'Seems a bit tough on you,' I venture.

'My lad wants her, and they know it.'

His son, the very last of his children, is twenty-two. Both Quashia and his second wife (not the boy's mother) have been deeply troubled by the fact that he remains single.

'But he's still young, Monsieur Quashia, give him time,' I have advised on several occasions in the past.

'I was married at sixteen, and it's better that way. He has to get on with building us a family.' Quashia, who is the proud grandfather of close to thirty, is adamant. Whatever the cost, he will purchase this bride. 'If only,' he tells us plaintively, 'to keep my wife quiet. She's such a worrier.'

I am up with the rabbits the next morning to drive him to Cannes to catch the dawn TGV to Marseille. Even before I have downed my coffee, I see him trudging our hill loaded down with presents trussed up in cardboard boxes and squeezed tight into tartan nylon bags.

'*Pour les gosses*,' he grins, as he swings his load of gifts for his grandchildren into the boot.

We say our farewells at the station and off he goes in his checked orange shirt and moth-eaten Panama on his leave of absence which, he has assured us, will last no longer than six weeks.

'If you need anything, I have left the number of a good friend of mine, a Monsieur Halaz, in the pocket of my work clothes in the garage. Give him a ring. He's a decent sort.'

Brandishing fistfuls of cash, he bids me a fond *au revoir*. I wave him off, picturing the stages of his journey with all those bags – the train to Marseille, from there a boat to Algiers on the northern coast of Africa, and then on by country bus to the small village south of Constantin where his wife and extended family reside and await him excitedly – and, as always, I feel sadness at his departure.

*

Back at the farm, summer is approaching at a galloping pace. Every living plant is showing early signs of wilting in the heat and for the next two months most will need to be watered on a daily basis. And I am alone here, well, without Quashia and now Michel, who has returned to Paris to resume work on his animation film, but with three newly installed house guests. An actress pal of mine from way back, who I haven't seen since we were in our twenties because she has been working in Hollywood on one of those glamorous, highly remunerative soaps, tracked me down and arrived with two teenage daughters, proclaiming a need for 'peace and retreat, darling' and declaring that our 'sweet home' is the 'dreamed-of haven'. She is in the process of a bordering-on-bankruptcy, highly publicised divorce. The 'ex', many years her junior, is apparently 'poor as a church mouse but mean as a skunk'. So here I am, pregnant, with a house full of hysteria, and no one to lend a hand.

I telephone M. Di Luzio to see what arrangements might be made for a watering system of sorts and to ask if he knows of a water diviner, but his answer machine is on, and he is away on holiday. I leave a message and then call René, because the disease *Cyclocodium Oleaginum*, known as *paon* and caused by the fungus *Spilocea oleginea*, is spreading at a virulent pace and is visibly jaundicing the leaves of the olive trees.

'This malady must be treated with a fungicide as soon as possible,' he tells me when he drops by to take a look.

'Is there no way round it?' I beg, because spraying the olive groves does not fit in with my desire to run this place organically.

He shakes his head solemnly. 'You should have done it at the beginning of the year when you were pruning the trees. I warned you, Carol.'

'Yes, I know you did, but . . . are you absolutely certain that there is no natural antidote we can come up with?'

Again he shakes his head, and I sense a hint of impatience at what he perceives as my romantic approach to farming.

I now learn that our tender young olive drupes must also be protected against, *la mouche de l'olive Bactrocera olae*. This is a fly they are prey to during this approaching season of extreme heat.

'It's rife everywhere this year.'

I stare at them in dismay. Now, more than ever, it is essential the trees remain healthy; we could be visited at any moment by heaven knows what organisation, and infected trees could prejudice for ever our status as olive farmers. But I have dreamed of, and maintained, up until now, whenever possible, an insecticide-free policy, and I am loath to change course at this critical juncture.

'I read of another system being tried out, to combat these flies. Traps attached to the branches that attract them . . .'

'It is not efficient, and far too expensive. Any farmer will back me up on this. Ninety per cent of the olives are attacked anyway, fall too soon and rot. Still, it's up to you. They're your trees. But you'll have to count me out if that's to be your approach,' declares René with an edge I have rarely heard before. 'Trust my expertise. I'll mix the products together, *un seul traitement*. It will lower your costs – the hire of the machine, for example – to spray them together, but I can't manage it without assistance,' he tells me squarely.

Fair enough. He is seventy-six. The fittest seventy-six-year-old I have ever encountered, but still there are almost seventy trees to treat over many terraces and Quashia would have done the lion's share of the work.

'Can it wait until Michel is back?'

But when we calculate the days between now and Michel's next scheduled return we both realise that to tarry would put both this year's harvest and the viability of the trees in jeopardy. René suggests bringing someone with him, one of his chums who would accept a reasonable daily rate – in cash, *bien sûr* – but no one is available: they have all committed themselves elsewhere. I am deeply relieved because, as is so frequently the situation for us here, money is scarce and we are struggling.

We have a baby on the way, a watering system to plan for, a water diviner to unearth and bees to track down. My head is beginning to spin.

'Carol, are you listening?' René is reiterating the fact that he cannot accomplish this job alone, and so I suggest myself for the role of assistant.

His immediate response is to guffaw and then, to cover this rather impolite reaction, he sighs, coughs and mutters incomprehensible misgivings which I fear amount to nothing more than the fact that I am a woman.

'I'd like to,' I encourage.

He is mulling it over, harrumphing and breathing at my side. '*C'est vrai,* Carol, that you are always willing to learn, and the truth of the matter is that I have no alternative. All right, I'll hire the machine and see you at half past seven on Saturday morning. Or is that too early for you?' He asks this with just a hint of sarcasm, the insinuation being that show-business folk, *les artistes,* such as myself don't get out of bed till noon.

'René, you know me better—'

'Yes, yes,' he mutters. '*A Samedi.*'

Artiste or no *artiste,* nothing alters biology and I *am* a woman and, to René's way of thinking, this is no job for a female. I shall have my work cut out to prove to him otherwise. What I have avoided disclosing to him is my condition. If he were wise to the fact that I am pregnant, he would never agree. But I have telephoned my local GP and confirmed that there are no risks involved. In any case, my share of the workload will not be taxing, and I will take care.

Saturday rises warm and bright; it threatens to be baking. I am awake and out of bed before six. Dogs fed, coffee made, e-mails answered, I head off down the drive to wait for him. I fear that the noise of René's diesel-powered Renault, plus the petrol-generated machine for the tree-treating, might wake my house guests, who demand their beauty sleep, so I ring my silver-haired olive guru to warn him and we decide to begin at the bottom of the hill and work our way up.

As soon as he arrives I see that he is in a business frame of mind. I am no longer Carol, but the lowly assistant. The first task, he orders, almost the moment he arrives, is to mix the products in with the water. It is unusual for him not to greet me with the customary double French kiss on both my cheeks and I am aware that he has not got his head round doing this job with a female.

'Fill this with water, please.'

The plastic container he is referring to, which fuels the machine, holds 150 litres of water. Machine and water container, along with hundreds of metres of piping, are in a trailer – *la remorque* – hooked up to the back of his Renault. The length of hosepipe in the cottage garden will not extend to his car but we have plenty more rolls up at the house. I offer to run up and fetch one.

'No, no,' he dismisses, and I sense the early signs of his ill humour. 'I have a plastic bucket in the car. You can use that.' And so here I am, in the lane at the foot of our land and alongside our caretaker's cottage, empty because Quashia is away, sloshing and carting buckets back and forth, filling them from an outside tap.

The cottage garden has one olive tree, an ancient one and fairly laden with ripening fruit. René decides that we'll begin with that. He barely needs my help because he can reach it easily from where his car is parked. I stand back and watch, paying careful attention. There appears to be little to this tree-treating business and I cannot think that, as assistants go, I will prove to be a disaster. What could possibly go wrong?

Once inside our grounds at the foot of the hill, his car and its trailer strategically parked off the driveway on the grass, he begins to instruct me in earnest. 'Your job is to keep the hosepipe supplied. It needs to remain flexible at all times, do you understand?' I nod. 'Don't let it get snarled up on any of the drystone walls, and don't let it curl back on itself or the flow will be restricted.'

Yes, I nod again. It sounds simple enough. He trots off along the lowest terrace to the farthest trees, holding the spraygun from which trails the hosepipe, or part of the hosepipe, which in turn is attached to the giant water container. The rest of the piping remains unfurled in the trailer. Five hundred metres of it. To me it looks like any other garden hose, but René has told me that he drives kilometres into the hills to borrow this specific one for us.

'Couldn't we just buy our own? Then it would be here whenever we needed it,' I have asked on several occasions.

'No, it is special.'

'Really? In what way?'

'It is lined and protected, so that it won't easily wear. It needs to resist the force of the product flowing through it, and it costs a pretty price. The amount you need for here would make it prohibitively expensive because you can't get near the trees with a tractor. There are too many terraces and no accessible routes up and down the hill, nothing but mule tracks on this property. No, you must walk it and haul the piping by hand, which is time-consuming. On top of which, you need hundreds of metres of piping.'

All this sounds a touch fantastical to me but I acquiesce, silently plotting that the next time I am at the Co-operative Agricole I'll acquire a few hundred yards of the stuff, and we'll hear no more about it.

'Switch on the machine,' he shouts to me bossily, 'and hold the hosepipe the way I've shown you. And make sure it doesn't rub against the trailer, or the piping will get damaged and spring a leak and then we'll be in serious trouble.'

I signal my assent and loop a few metres of the pipe loosely over my shoulder, creating some slack. I am watching René at the far end of this lower section of our land; he is staring up into the branches of a gnarled old olive tree. Beneath it, he stands no taller than a matchstick and resembles a small sentinel insect. I switch on the machine, which starts to make a rather disgusting slurping sound, like an old man drinking soup, and then the solution starts to feed through. This sends the hosepipe into dancing gyrations.

René is circling the distant tree, spraying up into it, and I am trying to keep an eye on him as well as concentrating on the line of pipe which is skittering through the dry summer grass. It weighs heavily against my shoulder, twisting and turning against me like a snake in pain, or in love. Still, I have it under control and I own up to actually rather enjoying myself. It is a beautiful morning. The sun is shining through the trees and the water mixed with the blue fungicide powder – which I am assured is the next best thing to organic but which looks worryingly lethal to me – is rising and falling through the branches and creating streaming rainbows. It is quite lovely. Our silvery trees are streaked with cold, sharp colours.

There is a very light wind, indiscernible really, but it is sending the spray whorling downwards. René signals to me to switch off the machine, which I do as he strides bowleggedly back in my direction. 'I need my mask.' And into the boot of his Renault he disappears.

'It's like a factory in there, René,' I tease.

'What is?'

'Your car. No matter what is needed, you have it to hand.'

'It's not a factory. I am an artisan; it is my *atelier*.'

'Yes, well, that's what I meant.'

He reappears now from the trunk of the car with what looks indisputably like a Second World War gas mask and a floppy desert hat. He pulls the mask over his flushed face and plonks the hat on his head.

I stare at him, amazed. 'I'd love to take a photo later,' I grin.

He says something in reply, but I don't understand a word through the mask. The sight of him on this hot morning, a little man standing with a spraygun in his hand and this outmoded military equipment covering his whole head, is quite ridiculous and I burst out laughing.

He pulls off the hat and then the mask. 'Start up the machine. I told you once, why aren't you listening?' And off he trots. 'And I will need more pipe.'

'Yes, René.'

We have a good rhythm going. René does occasionally wave a frantic arm at me, signalling me to clear out of the way, but before I can run for cover, my hair, face and sunglasses are rained upon and I am speckled in blue liquid. To protect against fumes, I have tied one of Michel's handkerchiefs over my nose and mouth. My shorts and T-shirt are filthy. Dog turds decomposing in the grass, dust and bits of straw-like weed have fouled the pipe and are now stuck to me, too, but otherwise I am performing my role without too many hitches and we are making good progress. It is hot and tiresome work. The further we go, the more piping I am obliged to lift, negotiate and release. I must look like Houdini, or a snake-charmer, with coils of the whirligigging stuff wrapped around my waist and hanging from both shoulders. I am sticky with perspiration from the effort, and covered in bits of twig, but I don't really care. It's farm work, and I enjoy mucking in and learning and I feel sure that

René must be just a little impressed with his female sidekick. Until, all of a sudden, when my silver-haired friend is at the farthest point in the garden, I am caught off guard by a cry coming from above me at the swimming-pool terrace level. 'Darling! Darling!'

Ali, my actress friend, is out of bed. She descends a step or two, clumping in stiletto-style mules. I turn my head to acknowledge her. 'Sleep well?' I shout through the handkerchief, aware that I must not be distracted.

'The girls fancy hamburgers for supper,' she cries. 'Shall we have that, or would you prefer to do a barbecue, darling?'

The pipe in my now gloved hand – the speedy movement of the rubber had been burning my palms – is being tugged, unbalancing me, and I need to release some slack. 'Whichever.'

'Do decide, darling. The girls and I want to go shopping. We can pick something up on our way back.'

I don't want to deal with meals and menus now. 'You can't get out,' I shout up to her.

'Why not?'

Can't she look? I am thinking. Can't she see that there is a car and trailer blocking the driveway? I gesture with my head and turn my attention back to my task. I am now being dragged across the new stone path Quashia has laid on our Italian staircase, beneath the rose bower which shades a part of it, my arms being scratched by thorns, heading generally, and inelegantly, in René's direction. He must be getting impatient, wondering what I am doing.

'How long?' I hear from on high.

'An hour, maybe two.'

'Oh, that's all right, darling. We'll have a swim and make a pot of café-o-lay. Oh, that looks like fun! You're like the baddie in a Western. How are you getting on?' But she wanders away without waiting for my response.

René is approaching, trotting towards me, bowlegged but still agile, tearing off his ridiculous mask to reveal a flushed, rather cross, stiff-lipped face. 'What are you doing? I can't reach the farthest trees.'

'Sorry.'

'I want to have this finished before the sun gets too hot. Please give your attention to the job in hand!'

I nod, and he stomps away.

'Actually, Carol? Darling!' It is Ali again.

I untie the hankie and sigh. 'What?'

'I think we'd like to go out now. The girls fancy a cappuccino in the village.'

'You can't!'

'Surely someone can move that little van?'

'Carol!' Now it's René calling.

Wouldn't I rather be somewhere else? Wouldn't I rather be back sitting in a make-up caravan on location somewhere divine, being pampered, running through lines in my head, concentrating on the scenes to come while chatting amicably with the likes of drop-dead gorgeous Hugh Grant, or in London drinking champagne with pals at the celebrated Ivy restaurant?

'Carol, please ask the little man to move his car.'

I pull the handkerchief away from my face. 'I think that might be difficult.'

'Well, the girls are getting restless.'

'Carol! Carol!' René is marching towards me again. Now what? 'I have no pressure. What's happened to the pressure?'

'I don't know. I haven't got a clue,' I squeak. As far as I can tell there still seems to be liquid running through the Michelin suit I have wrapped around me. I can still feel it agitating against me, as though I am dancing a rumba with an invisible partner.

'There must be a leak somewhere. We'll have to turn off the machine and then look for it.'

René is shaking his unmasked head from side to side. Chastened, I follow him back to the car and we discover that where the pipe is resting on the back of his trailer, due to the fact that it has not been properly protected – my fault, undoubtedly – and to the hours of vibration it has endured, it has worn through and sprung a leak. The water container is empty. Our carefully mixed (and rather expensive) blue, foamy liquid is gushing like a special-effects river down the hill. René sighs loudly and begins rummaging in various toolboxes in the boot of his car. 'We'll have to cut it and rejoin it.' He glances up towards the sun, which has risen high above the tallest of the towering pines. My head is swimming with heat and exhaustion and, although I haven't suffered from morning sickness for more than a week, I am beginning to feel woozy.

'Ah, good, is he moving?' Ali has arrived, dressed to the nines. She introduces herself to René with a beaming and slightly pert '*bonjour*'. He is instantly entranced. All the irritability written across his face disappears in an instant.

'*Quels beaux yeux,*' he croons. '*Beaux yeux bleus.* Tell her, please.'

'René, this is Ali. Ali, René has asked me to tell you that you have lovely blue eyes.'

Ali simpers and then asks if I could persuade 'the nice man' to move his car. This I do and René agrees in a flash. Seconds later, the trailer is temporarily disconnected and all vehicles are being shunted and moved as the girls file by.

'*Diable*, what a family! Please compliment the mother on the breathtaking beauty of her daughters.'

I do as requested and the trio of bronzed females swans off down the drive, waving and giggling at our olive guru. I have rarely felt less feminine as we trudge back to work.

An hour later we are sitting on the terrace enjoying a well-earned beer when my house guests return with cartons of ice cream and suntan lotions and glossy magazines and disappear into their rooms. Within seconds they reappear, three lean, creamed bodies in skimpy bikinis, and begin splashing and frolicking in the pool. René swigs at his beer, watching them.

'Wait a minute! That's not . . . ?' He gazes at me pop-eyed, as though he has just been visited by the Virgin Mary. 'From the series . . . ?'

I nod and smile. He slugs his beer.

'*Mon Dieu*,' he mutters. 'Fancied her ever since I first saw her on the box. She's smaller in real life. Even so . . . Man, I love women. You know, I haven't changed. I'm still . . .' he pauses, looking wistful. 'It's the years that have changed.'

I smile. He may be seventy-six, but those sharp blue eyes of his are burning with desire.

'What's she doing here?'

I shrug. 'A friend of mine.'

'*Diable*,' he mumbles, still transfixed by the dripping-wet vision of Ali. 'By the way,' he continues, finally turning his attention to me, 'you worked well this morning.'

'*Merci*.'

'You know, you work like a man.'

I roar with laughter, a long throaty outburst. 'Is that a compliment, René?' I ask.

'*Mais, diable,* of course it is.'

Our tomato vines are producing fruit that is ripening so quickly and in such abundance that this particular section of our vegetable garden looks vaguely like an advertisement for Red Nose Day.

'Why on earth did Quashia plant so many vines?' I ask Michel when he returns for the weekend and we are occupied with watering, traipsing buckets, feeding hoses back and forth.

'I think that, aside from the dozen plants you picked up at the garden centre, he must have taken seeds from the garage and thrown them into the soil. Don't forget he can't read French. He may have confused the labels on the packets and mistaken them for another vegetable. We will have to find ways of using them or they'll go to waste. Have you ever made chutney?'

I shake my head and suggest instead that, as we already have plenty of courgettes – marrow-sized – I should invest in an aubergine plant. 'Then I can try out a recipe for home-cooked ratatouille, prepared with fresh, garden herbs and our very own olive oil.'

'Great idea,' says Michel.

I take a quick peek in the garage to check where all the seed packets are stored. It is difficult to find anything in there amid the chaotic clutter: chainsaws still spattered with wood shavings, strimmers covered in tufts of dried grass, petrol canisters, flagons of oil, brushes and hoovers and tablets for the swimming pool, a zillion tools and contrivances of every conceivable shape and size, chunks of old rusty iron that Quashia is saving for a rainy day, boxes of Lord knows what that came with us from London or Paris and have never been opened or used. I sigh. It is a miracle Quashia planted tomatoes and that nothing more lethal has ended up in the ground. This space should be put to better use, I am thinking, as I move next door to the stables to feed the dogs. Only then does it occur to me. We will be needing quarters for our baby. Not in the early days, but once he or she has been weaned. This is the perfect place.

'The garage and the two stables could be converted into a two-bedroom extension. I know we don't have the money to do it now, but what do you think?'

Michel laughs, drawing a cork for our evening glass in the garden. 'It's exactly what I had planned to suggest to you. I will make up some rough sketches and we can get some estimates.'

A day or so later, I make a trip to our hand-made tiles man in Mouans Sartoux to begin the approximate costings.

''My word, you look well!' he exclaims.

I smile shyly and then regale him with our olive and bee tales.

'I know a bloke, bit of a toff, but he's a farmer and his sister keeps bees. I'll give him your number. They might help you out.'

I nod gratefully, choose the tiles I fancy for our proposed extension, give him the measurements I have drawn up, and he promises to post us a *devis*.

On my way home, I spot a sign I haven't noticed before. It is advertising a nursery, right off the roundabout, a short drive towards the old Grasse road. I pull over, turn off the main intersection and there, to my utter delight, I discover a splendidly equipped garden centre. I make directly for the vegetable plants, which are outside in a spacious yard that vaguely resembles a miniature rainforest. Fully grown tropical trees shade me where the air is damp and cool. Water is falling in crystal sprays from strategically placed pipes and there is that vibe here which I adore, of silent, lusty growth. I stare skywards through the cupola of fronds, trawling the alleyways, smelling and touching, intoxicated by the scents of the damp roots, earth and leaves, until I come across the aubergine plants. I choose two, both of which look robust and have several small, pendulous fruits hanging from them. As soon as I get back to the house, I plant them.

Although my pregnancy brings serenity, it also rules my every waking and sleeping hour. Few physiological changes

have taken place yet and the morning sickness has finally
abated, but cravings and dietary predilections are taking an
uncontrollable hold over me. I am developing an aversion to
meat, I cannot sit within a mile of anyone who is smoking a
cigarette and I have developed an obsessive craving for
tomatoes, preferably raw and straight from the plant,
though I fear this is because I do not have the patience to
wait until they are cooked. Given that our garden is chock-
a-block with the red beauties, if a craving must take hold,
this is a rather convenient one. Still, I find myself at whatever hour of the day or night clambering through vegetable
beds protected by green netting – Quashia has pulled out
some of the roll stored for the olive-gathering, attached it to
bamboo canes and hung it in sweeping swathes to protect
against scavengers, though not against me – searching out
the ripe tomatoes; the riper the better. This is unusual. In
normal circumstances my preference would be for fruit a
tad underripe, green even. Not now. The redder and the
mushier the better. As soon as I have picked them, I stuff
them into my mouth, gorging on them. Juice and seeds run
down my chin and along my arms. I feel sure that I am a
disgusting sight, but I simply don't care; I know no shame.
The need is beyond my control. I devour until the craving
has been sated.

One night I wake, in the grip of a craving. I sigh, knowing
that I will not sleep unless it is satisfied, so I steal from our
bed. Michel does not stir. I slip on some sandals, grab a
sarong and trek off to the vegetable garden. It is a lovely
clear night with sufficient light from the moon to guide me.
I roll away the stones used to pin the green netting against
the earth, lift up the cloth, clip it to the bamboo structure,
climb in among the caned plants, sit on the stone surround
and begin to feed. Ah, such exquisite joy!

Although I appreciate good food, I would never have

described myself as a glutton, not until this evening. Now I am well cast for the role. It is brought home to me when I hear a shuffling in among the cedar trees and I turn to see two of our dogs, Lucky and Bassett, staring at me in the star-lit darkness. I try to picture what they must be seeing. Their mistress, a sarong tied about her waist, slip-on sandals, seated in the centre of the vegetable patch, hands full of tomatoes, munching greedily, sticky with dripping and spilling seeds and fruits. Even the presence of these two bemused and silent mutts is enough to mortify me, and I decide that as soon as the aubergines are ripe, I will find a more elegant way to calm my feeding frenzy. Over the fol-lowing few days, the aubergine plants fruit half a dozen shiny mauve-black gifts, lovely as dark African breasts. With these I make our first dishes of home-cooked ratatouille. Everything required for this recipe has been grown in our own garden, the herbs and garlic as well as the crateloads of tomatoes and the oil. It is the first season we have grown garlic and I am thrilled with the results. I love the piquant sap it leaves on my fingers when it has been freshly picked.

This homespun dish is a huge success, hot or cold. The plates are emptied and cleaned up with soft, freshly baked, hand-torn chunks of baguette *à l'ancienne*. Even Ali and her two teenage daughters who, aside from consuming generous helpings of ice cream, spend their poolside hours counting calories and preening their skinny-as-maypole figures, lift their plates for seconds. I am delighted and picture lengthy summer days ahead with groaning dishes of ratatouille, as well as an end to our tomato surplus. But not with our trio of English beauties. Ali's divorce calls for attention. The fol-lowing evening I wave them goodbye at Nice airport and return to a sky shot through with coral.

Beekeeping. Archaeologists have discovered in certain

regions of the western Mediterranean representations of hives that date back to 2500BC. Might some have been found here in France?

An Egyptian mural from around 1450BC shows a man carrying a tray full of honeycombs.

During archaeological excavations at Phaistos and Knossos, on the island of Crete, hives made of earth dating from 3400BC were discovered. At that time, the husbandry of bees was already practised there. The mythology of Crete contains many references to bees, honey and wax.

In Greek mythology, Aristée, son of Apollo and Cyrene, was kidnapped by Nymos, who taught him the fundamentals of beekeeping. Legend has it that Aristée later introduced the art to the inhabitants of certain regions of Greece as well as to the islands of Sardinia and Sicily.

After an hour or two of reading through notes in my den, I make my way to the vegetable garden to pick two aubergines for supper and find, to my amazement, that the twin plants are now sprouting *tomatoes*. But how can this be? I track the length of the plot, convinced I am going mad. Has someone dug them up and relocated them without saying a word? No, these are definitely the aubergine plants. I glare at them. They are green and healthy and growing precisely where I planted them, except they are bearing tomatoes. And not just any tomatoes, but the Tom Thumb variety, with a soft hue of pale ochre-orange. I am stumped, stupefied. I return to the house to recount this bizarre episode to Michel and discover him at his desk in his office, his head in his hands, holding a sheet of flimsy paper. 'Michel? Are you all right?' He appears not to have heard me, which sends a cold chill through me. Some tragedy has struck. Or rather, one of life's truly extraordinary twists of fate, which will take several years to unfold in its entirety, begins today with devastating

news. Michel was due to return to Paris tomorrow to continue work with Serge, a colleague of many years and
director of the animation film Michel has been developing
since last year. Not only is it a project dear to both their
hearts, it has created a bond of deep friendship between
them.

Without a word Michel hands me the crumpled fax
clutched between his fingers. Sent from Paris, it is handwritten by Serge, whose wife was due to give birth to a child any
day now.

It reads: 'Please don't contact me. Give me a few days.
Lost Melissa and the baby. Don't call; I cannot work.'

I am silenced. 'What can we do?' I manage eventually.

'I'll leave him be for a few days and then I'll invite him
here. I think he might appreciate that. What do you think?'

I met his wife only once, a few months ago – she was
already pregnant – and I, as a pregnant woman, am speechless.

'What happened?' is all I can ask.

'I have no idea.'

The notion of losing both mother and child in this day
and age in a city such as Paris, with medical facilities second
to none, is too incredible to entertain. I am numb with shock
for them all.

'Shall I fetch you a drink?' I ask.

Michel shakes his head. With a brush of his shoulder, I
leave him alone and continue on to the upper part of the
house to lie down.

Later, while I am dozing, Michel comes to tell me that, due
to this devastating turn of events, he has changed his plans
and will stay home for a while longer. I am grateful for his
company because I cannot deny that I am shaken by what
has happened.

*

We are invited to a party at a villa on the outskirts of an inland village, pitted with homes owned by English expats. Neither of us is really in the mood, but we accept. Perhaps it is simply to seek diversion, to get out and be among people, albeit strangers – our next round of house guests are not due for a bit.

Although it is early summer, it rains. A short, swift down-pour that lets up as we arrive. We park in the grounds and approach through a wooded garden where cyclamen-pink strobe lighting sweeps in arcs that make me giddy and paints the faces of the guests fuchsia. Heavy-metal music pounds out an unrelenting bass. Young women in skimpy frocks with exceptionally tanned flesh are gyrating awkwardly. Brits in denim shirts, clutching cans of lager, are hollering at one another. The music thumps on. Lumps of cheddar cheese attacked by everything but a trowel are resting on paper doilies, soggy from the downpour. Rows of empty wine bot-tles litter the sodden grass.

Michel and I falter. I suggest we leave, or perhaps he does. We turn on our heels and shove our way back through the swell of smokers and revellers as the strobe illuminates and darkens our path by turns.

Somewhere in a nearby clump of trees, I hear a deep and menacing growl.

'What was that?'

Then we notice the dogs: green eyes set in thick heads. Three Rottweilers, tightly leashed, panting and growling. Behind them are two security men dressed from head to toe in black uniforms with knee-high, black leather boots. Their presence is disquieting. We continue on round a corner and come face to face with four more dogs accompanied by a quartet of uniformed men. I am wondering if we haven't stumbled upon something kinky when a woman I was once introduced to in an adjacent upland village comes running breathlessly towards us. She is followed by a very young woman whose mascara is staining her face and who is exceedingly drunk. She is staggering all over the grass.

'I know you. You're on telly,' slurs the drunken girl loudly.

'Where are you going?' enquires the other. She seems unnecessarily overwrought at the prospect of our impending departure.

When Michel explains charmingly that we are going home, she wails, 'You can't leave!' And, assisted by the inebriated girl, she begins, quite literally, to drag us back. The young girl is now shouting and squawking.

My desire to get away has both heightened and lessened. I am curious to know why there are so many dogs here and what the villa might contain that requires such heavy-duty protection. I discover, as we are pulled back towards the heaving mass of desperate celebration, that the drunken girl is the hostess and is hell-bent on acquainting us with her partner, the host. She then proceeds to confide that he beats her. She lifts what little skirt she is wearing and displays a shocking bruise on her sunburned thigh.

'He did this,' she mewls.

My curiosity has waned and, like Michel, whose impatience I feel beating at my side, I simply want to go. Unfortunately, at that moment, the host, who bears the look of a fifty-year-old trying to pass for thirty-something – bouffant hair, gold chain nestling against hirsute chest, pink shirt slit to the waist, tight trousers – comes searching for his sweetheart. She folds herself against him as though he were Prince Charming, and then points at me. He claims in a thick Cockney accent to have recognised me and attempts to lure us back. We shake our heads. He offers to escort us to our car. 'You can never be too careful,' he reasons. The girl hangs from him like a bell, humming to herself; he completely ignores her.

I have taken such a dislike to this man that I can feel my flesh horripilate. Evil is the adjective which springs to mind. We pass kennels of dogs, Alsatians this time, and two more men: uniformed, shaved heads, built like bouncers, dandling rifles. John, that is the host's name, pronounced 'Djo', as he speaks it, informs us that he is 'in security'. He whisks a card from his shirt pocket and passes it to me.

'We 'eard you'd moved to the neighbour'ood' – in fact Michel and I live a fair distance from John's neighbour-hood – 'an' knowing your line o' work, you'll be needin' someone like me. Givvus a ring.' And with that he winks at me, shakes our hands and heads back to the party, shrugging the poor dozing doxy from his arm as he retreats.

Sporting a large, floppy hat, white streaks of suncream on my shoulders and nose, I am well armoured against the rays of the sun, but what of the plant life struggling beneath this unrelenting sky? The earth is showing signs of cracking. Every shrub, every blade of grass, is wilting, gasping for water. What impression will this give to any official bods, should they arrive here unannounced and find nothing cared for?

I haven't the time, or the stamina, and Michel won't hear of me carting buckets and hoses across acres of ascendant terraces, so he takes on the task for a day or two, but we must find help from somewhere. Michel is also attempting to locate a particular woman working in the *urbanisme* depart-ment at the local town hall. He is having little success. We have received notification from an officer at the Chambre d'Agriculture to say that we are obliged to file our intention to plant new olive trees with the local council and gain their seal of approval.

'Why? We still haven't even received the list of approved nurseries.'

'Because we are living in a green belt. Didn't Quashia leave the name of one of his comrades in case we needed help? Why don't we ask him to come and water the grounds for us?'

'Yes, you're right. The number must be in the garage. But surely by planting trees we are enhancing the green belt? I don't understand their logic.'

'I wouldn't try,' says Michel, and I trundle off in search of the phone number for Quashia's friend M. Halaz.

I have just learned that 'John', the Brit whose party we looked in on, is an ex-convict who served a six-year sentence at Pentonville for armed robbery. When he was released from prison he changed his name and relocated to the Côte d'Azur. Now he is making a lucrative living keeping a watchful eye on clients' villas while they are away visiting family in dear old Blighty. I have no idea how well circulated this information is, but the fact that he beats his elfin girlfriend appears to be common knowledge, which I suppose, given her frankness on the subject, is hardly surprising. I have also been told that a certain number of the Englishwomen who move in that particular expat circle find him 'masculine and sexy', and several claim to have had an extramarital affair with him while their husbands were away on business.

A swindler or a conman in French is an *escroc*, and *escroquerie* is the act of swindling. The petty crook is a very familiar figure here on the coast. Bloodshot eyes, Gauloise pressed between nicotine-stained fingers trembling from a nervous system shot to hell, voicebox husky from a surfeit of *vin de table*, he is quick to size up any situation and create his chance. He can smell good cash pickings and is expert at securing those cash-in-hand deals. Once paid, he is not seen for dust, seeming to disappear off the face of the earth, until you hear his name, that Côte cowboy or Midi maverick, mentioned in connection with yet another ruse perpetrated on yet another trusting individual. Foreigners are the *crème de la crème* in this regard. Those who dream of a home on the Côte d'Azur, but who don't speak the language and, rather than taking the trouble to learn it and to mix with the 'natives', prefer to spend their time drinking gin and tonics alongside the pools of neighbouring residents with whom, back home, they would not pass the time of day. *Escroquerie* is woven into the fabric of living here. How could it be otherwise when money is the god? It is the yardstick by which worth is judged and valued.

I return to the garden centre, chugging along the pretty country lane that hugs the rear side of our hill. Families of *sangliers* are breeding in the thick mass of woods here. This is the herd which, when there is a shortage of food, emerges from out of the thicket, ascends the back of the hill and steals on to our land. Perhaps they consider it their territory. Occasionally, I see hunters here, armed with rifles and packed lunches. Quashia wants me to call a hunter in to shoot the boars who destroy his walls, but I can't bring myself to do it.

Before reaching the main road which will take me inland, I pass through an area of open parkland backdropped by the Alps. Here, I see a discreet sign which reads 'Chapelle de Notre Dame de Vie'. Picasso spent the final years of his life in a 200-year-old farmhouse right by here. The house, Notre Dame de Vie, named after the chapel, evidently, where the painter died of a heart attack in 1973, has been vacant since the suicide of his second and last wife, Jacqueline.

Once upon a time it nestled among fields and hills; these days there are elegant properties in enclosed estates – *domaines* – constructed all across the plain and the hillsides. Still, the house remains apart; unsold, abandoned, almost forgotten. A decaying *mas* and a neglected treasure trove on the borders of the *commune* of Mougins.

I have secret ambitions of passing a moonlit evening there, communing with the ghost of genius. To fulfil that dream, or at least get a gander at the place, I have been trying to find it, but no one I ask seems to know its precise location. Several have never even heard of Pablo Picasso.

Arriving at the nursery, I make my way through *salles* of fishtanks, perfumed candles and garden furniture, stepping to the rear, where it reeks of damp soil, lavender and murmuring growth. I seek out a salesperson.

Leaning against a pillar in Potted Vegetables, arms crossed, I come upon a frowning, pale-faced adolescent who answers my enquiry with: 'Don't speak French.' She is here from Scotland on a temporary basis, she tells me, revealing too that she is exceedingly lonely, not having a very agreeable time and knows nothing at all about plants.

'How is your French coming along?' I ask, attempting to encourage.

She hangs her head, mumbling tearfully. 'I just wantae go home.'

My instinct is to invite her over for a swim, but I dither. I have a beekeeper to find, a water diviner to hire, ten acres to irrigate, weeding to catch up on; I have almost given up on achieving any writing this summer, and I have a baby to prepare for. Lord.

The girl begins to sniffle. I hesitate, caught in the dilemma. 'Would you like to lend a hand at our place, water our plants? You'd be out in the sunshine. You could stay on and swim.' This sounds relatively inviting to me, but she shakes her head, scuffs her shoe against the earth and repeats that she wants nothing except to go home. I leave her with a pat on the shoulder and go off in search of someone who might furnish me with an answer to my puzzle. I find a young man shunting dustbin-sized black pots of ferns from one spot to another. He rises, sweating. I explain my predicament.

'Bring them back and we'll change them' is his solution.

'But why would aubergine plants fruit tomatoes?'

'Bring them back,' he repeats crossly.

'I can't. They're in the ground and have shot up to five or six feet tall.'

'Well, what do you expect me to do?' he asks impatiently.

'I just thought that you might explain why, what we can—?'

'I haven't got a clue.' And he bends back to the pot at his feet and drags it away. I toy with buying more aubergines, decide against it – God forbid, they might also turn into tomatoes – and return to the car park, where I accidentally drive Michel's dusty-blue Mercedes into a wooden gatepost. No real harm done – the car is built like a tank – but it adds to my growing frustration with it and how it smokes and fumes and splutters like an ageing, ill-tempered dragon.

Back at the house I find a message from a farmer with a Welsh accent: Lord Harry, the brother of the woman who keeps bees. Their estate is situated between our address and the Esterel. He would be happy to meet with me and help in any way he can. I jot down the details, intending to call after a short rest. Michel brings me tea and I learn that Serge, deep in grief, does not feel ready to accept our offer of a sojourn here in the south. Later in the season, perhaps. This means that Michel must return to Paris. If Serge is not able to work, Michel will use the time to hunt out investors for their film. I smile encouragingly. I know that he must go – our work always involves these arrivals, departures and separations – but it never gets easier. I have been enjoying his daily presence around the place. Particularly with our baby on the way.

He strokes my cheek. 'I'll be back at the weekend, *chérie.*

And, shortly after, we will be together for leisurely weeks of summer here.'

The next morning I drive him to the airport, or rather he drives, because the old car has no power steering and is such a bloody bus to manoeuvre. We promise ourselves that, with the next contract either of us secures, we will invest in a tuppence-ha'penny runaround, rather like my much-mourned Renault 4, the Quatrelle, which sank in mud when the river that abuts the airport burst its banks, flooded the car park and drowned every stationary car in silt and water.

Towards late afternoon, René drops by, as he is wont to do, for no reason other than to while away an hour or two and drink in the view across the sea. He delights in watching the sun go down, chilled glass of beer in hand, with me at his side, an enraptured audience for his tales. This evening he comes bearing a wine made from walnuts. I have never tasted walnut wine, which tickles him. He is in a jolly frame of mind and I suspect that the bottle is a peace offering but, of course, he makes no mention of his tree-treating humour. I walk him over to my aubergine plants. He nods as though he knows the mysteries of the universe. 'They have been grafted with tomato plants,' is his diagnosis.

'Really? Well, what would cause them to return to their grafted source?'

He merely shrugs.

'Might it be an act of survival? Rather as a reptile changes colour or sloughs its skin?'

Whether the explanation is too complicated for the likes of me or he doesn't know I cannot say. What he does tell me is that it is not uncommon to graft one plant with another of a different species. He practises it himself, and has been intending to suggest such a graft to one of our *agrumes*.

'You produce so many oranges that I thought you might fancy a yield of *pamplemousses*.'

'Grapefruits on an orange tree?'

'Or tangerines, if you prefer.'

I am amazed and ponder the proposition. One tree, two fruits.

'*C'est pas la peine à se presser le citron*, Carol,' he grins.

'One mustn't press the lemons?' I repeat, bemused.

'No, no,' he roars with laughter. '*Se presser le citron* means to rack your brains. But if you don't fancy grapefruits, leave the tree to its oranges and I will continue to harvest them. I have made a dozen litres of *vin d'orange* which I will bring you once it's bottled – the wine needs to ferment – and I have two dozen jars of splendid marmalade. All from your oranges.'

More than sixty kilos he gathered in the spring while Michel and I were far across the seas getting married.

'Is it your wife who makes the marmalade, René?'

'Lord, no, it's me. A secret recipe, all stirred up in an ancient copper pot. You'll never taste better.'

'How about harvesting our tomatoes and making us some chutney?'

'I certainly will. I'll gather them at the weekend. But dry some in the sun. Dried tomatoes – delicious!'

I marvel at the capacity this septuagenarian has for life and its earthly pleasures, which puts me in mind of Picasso. I mention to René that I have been looking for the great man's house. 'Have you any idea where it is?'

René is surprised that I have had difficulty locating the artist's home.

'Some people I've asked have never heard of him.'

He shakes his head. 'The property's not hard to find. I was there. I paid him a visit. Years ago, of course.'

'You are kidding me, René! You were at Picasso's house?'

'Yes.'

'Was he there?'

'*Mais oui*. Of course, there wasn't the fanfare about him then that there is now. As I say, it was years ago. I was still young. My sister wanted to meet him, so I agreed to go along. She was interested in his pottery.'

'You amaze me, René.'

'Why? He was just a bloke selling paintings from his house. Making a living like the rest of us.'

'Hardly! He was already world famous by the time he reached that address, exhibited worldwide, hailed as—'

'That may be, but he still had groups visit him *chez lui* to see the *tableaux*, and that was why my sister wanted to go.'

'Did you actually set eyes on him?'

'Yes, we shook hands. He welcomed us.'

'René, you are making this up!'

He stares at me as though I am the one who spins tales.

'What's to make up? He lived here and we visited him.'

'I read that after his death the house went to rack and ruin. His wife committed suicide, tired out by the loss of him and the *heritage* wranglings. It is still empty, I believe, which is why I'd like to find it.'

'Just like Maurice Chevalier.'

'What is?'

'His house, up behind La Bocca. He left it to the state for the use of impoverished artists. They didn't look after it, and now it's overrun with gypsies.'

I prefer not to engage in conversations about gypsies and Arabs with anyone from Provence because it usually leads to a diatribe about how the country is being overrun with foreigners, so I return to Picasso. 'What was he wearing? You know, in all the photos, he's in shorts.'

'Lord, no! He was dressed correctly. He had guests – us. Short bloke. Handsome, though.'

I giggle. René is five feet two. Upstairs, the telephone begins to ring.

'I'll let you answer that.' He kisses me on the cheeks and as he climbs into his shooting-brake he points to several cedar branches extending towards the electricity wires. 'You should get those cut back. They're dangerous. You don't want them brushing those cables. If the EDF see them, they'll have something to say.'

'Don't worry, Michel has already spoken to Quashia. When he returns he'll prune them.'

'I'll take the wood off you; give you a fair price.'

I nod, waving him off without tarrying.

'By the way,' he calls as his diesel-powered Renault sputters in the drive. 'I almost forgot why I dropped by. I've found you a water diviner.'

'No!'

'Yes. But don't tell anyone.'

I shake my head in amazement. Why shouldn't we tell anyone?

The call is from Michel, in Paris. He sounds tired, but he has met up with Serge.

'How is he?'

'Silent. I think work is his best antidote. We'll plot the storylines, then I'll leave him to make draft sketches while I go to Australia. I've found a co-producer there.'

'Australia!'

I have no time to register my dismay; the instant I put down the phone it rings again. The female voice enquiring after me is British, pukka and unfamiliar. I assume it is the apiarist sister of the Welsh farmer, but no. The woman announces herself as Lady Edwina —.

I have never heard of her, but she is inviting me to dinner. The invitation is for the following evening, a midweek night.

'We do so hope you can come,' chirps Lady Edwina.

'We're frightfully short of gels. Rather too many single men drifting about these days. We're a wee distance inland from the village of —, but not difficult to find. Take the Vence road and follow the signs to —.' And she proceeds to give me rather complicated directions. I accept the invitation, partly out of curiosity, but principally because I am assured that Lord Harry, the Welsh farmer, will be attending.

The address turns out to be more than a 'wee distance inland' in a locality quite unknown to me, and not shown on any map we own. But as dusk begins to fall, close to an hour after setting out, driving along a meandering lane cut through Provençal brush, I eventually find the sign directing me left by an impossibly remote petrol station Lady Edwina told me to keep an eye out for. Once I have turned left, I assume that I have arrived, but no. I discover as I crawl through dusty scrubland that I still have another five or six kilometres to go. I begin, ever so slightly, to panic. This can't be right. Michel's old Mercedes grinds on, carrying me with it.

Should I turn back?

It is then that I sight a distant twinkling of lights up ahead and, as I approach, an alarmed gate. I dig about in the glove compartment for the code Lady E. has given me. The gate swings open on to another deserted dust track. I look back and see the gate swing shut. I begin to grow anxious, as though I had rolled smack into a David Lynch film or, worse, one of Cronenberg's. Who would choose to live out here? I ask myself. And why?

On I go until I reach a pocket of recently constructed salmon-pink villas and, beyond, another secured gate. This requires another code, which has also been furnished by my hostess. I roll down the car window but the codebox is not within arm's reach and I am obliged to get out to punch in the figures. Nothing happens. I try again. Still nothing happens, aside from the arrival of a small dog who growls and yaps beyond the wrought-iron gates, warning me away. Its insistence would alert anyone to the presence of strangers, but there is no one to alert, no sign of habitation. The dog scampers up some steps and then down again. There is a hut up there, presumably for *le gardien*.

I call. No response. I boom with my actress's vocal cords. Still no response. I go back to the codebox and hammer in the numbers again, to no avail. By now, I am frustrated, furious and hungry. I have started to turn back when a light finally goes on in the caretaker's office. The spill reveals a narrow gate alongside the main one, which is ajar. I push my way through, skip round the snappy dog, climb the steps and beat on the door. A sleepy-eyed man opens up. I explain my situation, who I have come to see, repeat the numbers of the code and, before I can finish, he presses a button and the gates glide open.

'The house you want is the last. You can't miss it. About three miles up the track.'

'Three miles!'

When I eventually pull into the pebbled drive of what, from this aspect, looks like a very modest modern house, I park up behind an electric-blue Bentley convertible with its roof open, two Porsche Carreras, an old banger – probably a staff car – and a sports Jaguar. All, except the banger, display Swiss plates.

I pull on the bell. The door is opened by Victor, husband to Lady Edwina, a Russian who speaks English with an impeccable accent. He pours me a glass of champagne and leads me directly to an exterior terrace.

Behind us icing-pink, mock Palladian colonnades. We are gazing down upon a capacious pool and beyond, across bosky hills and valleys cascading towards a fingernail glimmer of opalescent sea. I must be facing south-ish; I am staring at the Med, but where, in actuality, I am, I haven't a clue. In some obscure, human fabrication of Wonderland.

Victor has made 'his pile in realty'. He buys up thousands of hectares of scrubland, *le maquis parfumé*, for next to nothing – these sylvan acres are designated *nonconstructible* and therefore deemed worthless. He then proceeds to 'sort out' the permits at the local Mairie and, once these are acquired, he builds residential parks, *domaines*, on the land. These consist of several dozen uniform villas, fenced in with oleander bushes and other local shrubs surrounded by electrified fencing and well-fortified gates. Foreigners are his market. They holiday at these second homes, buried away in the pine-covered hinterlands of the Riviera. Here, the enormously wealthy and overly paranoid can vacation with peace of mind, secure in the knowledge that armed guards and coded gates keep the rest of the south of France out of sight and at bay.

More to change the subject than anything else, I ask him about Lord Harry. 'Both the sister and the brother are a little eccentric, but salt of the earth. Still, if you go to visit them, good luck. He'll be here later so you can see for yourself.'

Lord Harry is the last of the guests to arrive at what turns out to be a birthday bash for Lady Edwina, a point overlooked on the telephone, which means that I have arrived empty-handed and inappropriately attired. Everyone else is in black velvet evening dress. Thankfully, I thought to pick up a plant at one of the villages I drove through. Edwina accepts it graciously, though my less than soignée appearance does cause a look of horror to cross her face. But it is only a nanosecond before her well-bred smile saves the day and almost camouflages her shock. 'My dear, you look absolutely charming. Victor, pour Carol some champers,' is her response to my apology.

My glass is refilled while I am introduced to Colin, who I recognise instantly. Colin is an attractive, thirty-something thriller-writer who began life in the east end of London and now resides in Geneva. His is the convertible Bentley out front.

We are nine, including our hosts. Lady Edwina places me between Victor and Lord Harry, a convivial, lobster-faced aristocrat who is puffing and perspiring from the word go. As we sit for dinner, he already looks the worse for booze. His rotund stomach is threatening to explode through his shirt as he unbuttons his velvet smoking jacket and pours himself a glass of wine. I watch as he dabs his streaming face with a handkerchief and I cannot help feeling that I am in the company of a steaming kettle.

'Cotty top-up?' he bellows at me. I panic, assuming this to be a British expression I don't understand.

'Excuse me?'

'Cotty de Ronnie, dear.' And he serves me a brimming tumbler of a Côte du Rhone red and pours another for himself. I notice that he has several glasses on the go. A Chardonnay in one hand and a 'Cotty' in the other, and he has already polished off the rest of the magnum of bubbly.

By now we have dealt with the foie gras, which, for a reason I have missed, seems to have caused a minor fracas between host and hostess, and we are getting stuck into steak and kidney pie served with peas. I feel as though I have walked on to the set of a Noël Coward play. Three seats away, across the round table, Lady Edwina is lolling tipsily against the breast of the writer, strategically seated to her right. They are engrossed in what appears to be a very intimate conversation about matters of the heart. I catch little

more than the general drift because Harry is bellowing and
huffing alongside me. I turn my head to my left where hubby
Victor, blithely disinterested in his wife's table manners, is
attempting to prise details of my marital status out of me. I
confirm that I have a husband who is in Paris on business,
but I divulge nothing of my pregnancy.

Copious amounts of 'Cotty' are being sloshed into tumblers and poured down throats at a rate that simply amazes
me. I am surrounded by the cream of Britain's élite class.
These men, save for the Swiss-resident writer who hails from
the back streets of London, claim education at the finest of
English public schools. Lord Harry's accent has now become
thick, lilting Welsh. He leans close, swaying, and whispers
with the breath of a dragon some furtive secret which I don't
quite catch about his daughter, a svelte English blonde
dressed in gold seated opposite, the youngest by far at this
Mad Hatter's dinner party.

I frown, confused. 'I thought Lydia was Edwina's daughter?'

'Yes, with me! I married her first! Lydia's mine!' he rages
wildly, his eyes bloodshot, but with neither rancour nor
venom. His yelling seems to be more of a flailing in the dark.

Next to Lydia is seated a flamboyantly turned-out gentleman in black velvet *smoking* with yellow silk cuffs, red
embroidered slippers and full, if discreet, make-up. He puts
me in mind of Somerset Maugham. The poor man looks
profoundly bored. Moments later, he leaves the table never
to be seen again, but it is of no consequence because his disappearance goes unnoticed.

The fact is, our hosts are plastered, and I fear we might be
shifting gear here, moving from Coward to something less
frothy: the second act of an Edward Albee, perhaps? It is
time to leave, but before doing so I am keen to arrive at an
arrangement with my neighbour, Lord Harry, about his
sister's bees.

'It might be Mummy's birthday today but I have just had *my* birthday and Daddy must buy me a Cartier watch!' wails Lydia.

'Ah, but which daddy?' quizzes her stepfather, the Russian, nudging me in the ribs and winking at me as though he's nobody's fool.

I smile gamely.

Victor decides that it is time to change the mood with a little music. He staggers to his feet and chooses a smoochy tune by crooner Julio Iglesias. The others seem to find this 'just the ticket' while our host, a well-preserved, regularly exercised, bronze-skinned, lizardy fellow of sixty-odd, begins circling the table and gyrating his hips. He is grinning rakishly at me as he embarks on the tale of a past conquest. In lurid detail he describes how he had his way with a nubile 'thing' called Julia. Only at the tail end of the monologue do I learn that Julia was Harry's girl. Before or after Edwina is not clear to me.

'Are you just remembering this now, old boy?' asks Harry with a sigh. I turn to him and see not the blustering drunk who has been bellowing in my ear all evening, but a sad and defeated individual. Perhaps he is actually the most interesting soul at the table. Still, it is definitely time to be on my way, but first the question of his sister.

'About your farm,' I begin. 'May I pay you a visit, Harry? I would like your sister to place a few hives on our land.'

'Of course,' he sniffs. 'Any time you like.'

I offer my thanks and wend my way.

Trekking back in the dark is no simple exercise but the time passes and, surprisingly, I find my route with relative ease. All the while I am contemplating the evening – a madcap affair, to say the least. What a crowd I have fallen upon. The new Côte d'Azur. Shoving aside centuries of history, digging up the earth, sectioning it off into profitable plots with no thought for the old business of farming the lands. Except perhaps Harry, whose sister, with luck, will become our long sought-after beekeeper.

The name Côte d'Azur comes from a book published in 1887 by a Burgundian lawyer-poet, Stéphane Liégeard. He settled happily in Cannes and decided to write a guide which covered the coast from Menton on the Italian border to Hyères, near St Tropez. He named it la Côte d'Azur as a celebration of the inky blueness of the Mediterranean waters. The book was an instant smash hit, and the name stuck.

I yawn, changing gear, as my thoughts are requisitioned by what lies ahead. Irrigation systems. How will we ever channel water up to the summit of the hill where there is plenty of good earth for planting new trees? It will require new piping – sections of what is laid and in use are metal, have rusted and sprung leaks – and possibly a second electric pump. Costly.

We will need to clear terraces everywhere ready for the planting and this will involve more than just the strimming away of the brush which Quashia and Michel have achieved so admirably. A myriad mountainside stones will have to be removed, the decomposing remains of ancient roots from fallen trees still clinging in the earth will need to be pickaxed out, holes dug, compost and fresh earth supplies brought in. I must find out what fertilisation, if any, we should use for all those olive saplings. The soil will need analysis. And the treating of the trees? If the traps, *les pièges*, I suggested to René, used to attract and kill the flies, are not viable, then surely there must be another organic alternative?

I arrive home to noisy greetings from the dogs, who are busy about their starlight guard duty, catch the distant hoot of an owl as I climb the outside steps and fall into bed exhausted, determined to wake early and, albeit singlehandedly, set to work.

Hives of Inactivity

Over the weekend we find a note left in our mailbox, hand-written in a spidery calligraphy. 'Pedro et Maria', it announces, '*touts mains*'. They are offering themselves for tree-cutting, housework, pool-cleaning, *gardiennage*, dog-sitting, painting, decorating, rewiring and car maintenance, among other things. There is a telephone number at the foot of the list of their advertised accomplishments. Michel is impressed, not only by the diversity of the tasks to which they seem willing to put their energies, but because he always admires anyone who goes out to find work, who shows signs of ambition. 'We should call them,' he says.

I agree that they might be capable of executing these chores – though secretly I am always rather on my guard with those who claim the ability to turn their hand to whatever you will – but, I point out, we are not planning on any painting, decorating or wiring, not at any time in the near future; not until we decide whether to convert the stables into bedrooms. 'And we don't need a pool-cleaner, we have Thierry. We have Quashia to look after the land, and the car is way beyond the help of any form of maintenance.'

'Perhaps I'll ask him to prune back those overhanging cedars in the driveway. They really are dangerously close to those electricity cables.'

I am less than enthusiastic about this suggestion. 'Let's wait till Quashia returns, or ask René. It's a risky business, Michel, and we don't know the extent of this man's skills. One slipshod cut and we could end up with lop-eared branches that bring the cables down.'

Michel reminds me that we have a pair of towering pines leaning precariously over two of the lower front terraces and stealing much-needed sunlight from four of our olive trees; they really should be pruned back.

I cannot argue this point.

'If he's reliable, we'll keep him on to water and tend the garden till Quashia returns.'

And so, at Michel's behest, Pedro drops by: a gaunt, wiry middle-aged Portuguese with a face as lined as a latticed gate and a voice as hoarse as a damaged squeezebox. He smokes like a chimney and infuriatingly chucks the butts in the flowerbeds, which does not endear him to me, but Michel seems set on giving the man a chance. I sigh. It is true that he is friendly and certainly eager for the few days' employment; he is equally eager for his wife, Maria, to be engaged as our *femme de menage* on a more permanent basis, which Michel agrees to. After Pedro has left I protest, but to no avail. Michel insists. He rarely puts his foot down but, on this occasion, he is adamant. 'I have been watching you scooting here and there and it is time for you to take it easy. We are having a baby, *chérie*. I don't want to see you lifting or carrying anything, not even shopping, and certainly not cleaning this big old house. I won't discuss it.' And with that he returns to Paris, and Pedro and Maria are taken on as our temporary workforce.

On the morning Pedro is due to begin the pruning of the trees, four Portuguese cronies come barrelling up the drive. They park up and descend from the oldest, most shambolic Peugeot I have ever set eyes on, armed with chainsaws, manual saws, wicker baskets, hammers and an arsenal of useless, ageing tools in their kit, plus a stack of rather heavy lunchboxes which they ask me to store somewhere cool. I am reminded of the mechanicals in Shakespeare's *A Midsummer Night's Dream*.

'*Bom dia*,' I say. 'Where's Pedro?'

'Pedro arrives last,' they inform me, as though it were an acknowledged rule.

'Show us the trees, *as arvores*, to be cut down, madame, and we will get to work,' one says in a French injected with Portuguese where Js are pronounced as heaving Hs.

'Not cut down, monsieur, pruned.'

'*Sim, sim*, madame, *bom*,' he nods vigorously.

'Down there, towards the foot of the land.'

The men stare at the trees and then at one another with stupefied expressions. This is followed by an explosion of the foulest of Portuguese swearwords, silenced by the arrival of Pedro. He parks his equally rusty banger – thank the Lord we didn't decide to take him on for car maintenance – on the lower terrace by the trees in question and climbs out, cigarette between his fingers, hacking and spitting. The men rush as one, hats waving, tools like sabres, down the drive and lunge at him. I am puzzled as to what is going on but when Pedro yells, literally yells at them, before dissolving into a fit of coughing, they hang their heads shamefacedly, gather up their assorted tools and say no more, and I go inside.

Oh dear, I am thinking, this is not Bottom and his merry

men, it's the Marx Brothers. But no doubt they will settle their differences and attack the job. I am at my desk, lost in a world of my own. A wasp is catapulting itself at the glass of the closed French windows, trying to find a way out. I rise and unlock the door and the insect flies free. It sets me thinking about our beekeeping ambitions. I must telephone Lord Harry.

Outside, the day is hot and still. The cicadas crack on, but little else stirs. It is that, the silence from the grounds, that nudges my attention. I haven't heard the whirr of a chainsaw since the Portuguese arrived. On the pretext of going to collect the mail, I make my way into the garden and descend the track towards the gate. There I discover the quintet at the foot of the sprawling pine trees, shirts on heads like turbans, rowing furiously about *os troncos de arvores,* pushing and punching and shoving one another, throwing tools to the ground, stamping feet, fists at the ready, without so much as a single pine cone trimmed.

'Is everything all right?' I call out.

They turn, waving and smiling as though at a picnic.

I decide, while I am outside, to scale the hill and reconnoître the disused water basin. It is in a desperately sorry state. The main weight of it appears to be resting on an anterior drystone wall, which has sunk into a pile of rubbled stones. I fear that, due to the force of rain or hungry boars stamping about, the earth could shift and that section of the hill could slide, taking the foundation of the basin with it and cracking it wide open. It needs urgent structural repairs.

I try to look inside to gauge the condition of the interior but the walls are too high. I shall have to leave this to Michel, or Quashia, when he returns.

I descend as far as the house, needing to rest in the shade for a bit. There is still little sign of activity around the pine trees. I am feeling less than sure that this pruning will ever be

achieved and conclude that these Portuguese are a disorgan-
ised, hotheaded bunch. Thank the Lord we are paying them
by the contract and not by the hour.

Throughout the day, they continue to fight and seem to
agree only when they down tools for lunch and uncork several bottles of wine, though these merely serve to exacerbate
their tempers.

I stroll in and out of my den at regular intervals, more to
keep an eye on them than anything else, and to caress poor,
tormented Lucky, who is barking and howling incessantly.
She has been chained up since this morning and must remain
so. I dare not let her loose. I fear that an animal as nervous
as she, the victim of early violence, a skin-and-bones vagrant
when we found her, will be unsettled by the constant yammering and shouting and swearing.

The gist of the men's argument, it appears, is not about
how best to attack these gigantic trees but who should be the
one to shimmy up *os troncos*, the trunks, and how come they
are being paid such a pittance for a *trabalho* of such monumental danger. They are hardly a hive of industry, but I leave
them to it. The heat of the sun makes me dizzy and, each
time they catch sight of me, one or other of them attempts to
drag me into the dispute.

Finally, in the late afternoon, I hear the dulcet zirring of
the chainsaws.

It is amber evening, shadows lengthening, the cicadas
silenced, when Pedro comes banging at the door, fag in
mouth, sawdust stuck to his sweating face, to announce
that they are quitting work for the day but will be back
bright and early in the morning. As is my habit, I offer the
team a beer, which they accept without a second's hesitation – one of the few decisions they have agreed on since
their arrival. I direct them to the garden table and make my
way along the covered terrace to dig five chilled bottles

out of the fridge in the garage. Unbeknown to me, Pedro follows and, deep in the crepuscular space, pungent with the aroma of dried herbs left uncleaned on the strimming machines, saucers filled with lethal pink flakes of poison intended for the rats, and trickles of *mazout*, oil, leaking from the ancient central heating system, he creeps up behind me and presses himself against me, breathing tobacco and alcohol fumes into my ear.

Shocked, I spin round. 'Take your hands off me!'

Instantly he backs off, making a gesture which I have come across before. Arms in the air like a surrendering soldier, it reads: hey, cool it, lady.

I return to the group, followed by Pedro, and graciously pour out the offered beers. But I am shaking with anger and aware of flashes of pain at the base of my stomach. Silently, I berate myself for having allowed this man to rile me so. As the gang prepares to leave, I beckon Pedro aside, sounding out the sum we owe him.

'But the work is not finished,' he splutters. 'You haven't seen how well we're doing.'

'Yes, Pedro, it is.'

He smiles, and nudges closer. 'The way you say my name, your accent. Pedro. Pedro. It makes me hot.'

I walk away, seething at his impudence.

'You can't fire me now,' he calls after me. 'There's the second tree to prune.' Given the stress and delicacy of Michel's situation with Serge, I make the decision not to bother him with this matter on the phone; we can deal with it when he returns from Paris. As I walk down the hill later, flanked by the dogs, to lock the gate, I see butterflies everywhere – rich, golden wings tinged with buttery yellow, others pure lime like a watered summer juice. Such pleasure. And then I notice the olive tree.

One of the branches Pedro and his crew have lopped has

plummeted to the terrace below and torn away several of the
fruiting boughs on the left side of one of our olive trees. I
walk over to take a closer look. Ripped from the main trunk,
fresh creamy-white wood exposed, the limbs are hanging in
the evening light like severed silver wings.

I hurry back inside and telephone René. He is not there. I
leave a message, asking him to do what he can to lessen the
damage. This careless destruction of our tree and of even a
small percentage of our olive yield has upset me. The shooting pains abate as unexpectedly as they arrived, but I
recognise the warning sign. I must rest. I decide on an early
night, lie in bed perusing my *Guide to Mediterranean
Butterflies* and find that the specimens I saw this evening
were Clouded Yellows and the lime ones Green Hairstreak.
Such a splendidly punk name.

Until this evening, the tiny being inside me has been only
that; an energy force, albeit desperately desired, that has
been unbalancing my system, changing my eating patterns,
tiring me out. Tonight, though, there is a change. I picture a
child walking the hills with me, its hand in mine. Scuffed
espadrilles, a floppy sunhat, curls, a voice, many questions,
a burrowing curiosity. Podgy arms pointing, requesting
names of flowers and butterflies . . . My mood is appeased.
I am carried into sleep dreaming dreams of a small, emerging
person.

A couple of days later, I am attempting to reroute an army of
large, black ants that I refuse to treat with pesticides. I don't
want to kill them. I want them to get on with their busy lives
cleaning up in the garden but to keep out of the kitchen.
Barbaric to massacre an entire colony simply because I fear
them near our food. My difficulty is that my ploy of leaving
bread and jam at strategic distances from the house has not
worked: the dogs have eaten the crusts and the ants are back,

marching, more resolutely than ever, like a black conveyor belt down a wall from the roof, along a balustraded edge of terrace, and heading in the general direction of the main door of the house. While I am leaning over them, staring at them in dismay, wondering what, apart from insecticide, I can do to make sure they stay out of the house, Pedro's wife, Maria, comes battling up the drive in another rattletrap of a car. I had not been expecting her but I cannot hold her responsible for her husband's out-of-order behaviour, so I put her to work and go about my own.

L'olivier. In my earliest studies, I had assumed that the olive tree, because it is regularly cited in the Old Testament, was possibly the earliest tree known to man. This is erroneous. Think of Adam and Eve and the garden of Eden: figs, apples. I have recently learned of another tree, the bristlecone pine, that does not grow in the Mediterranean basin and so does not concern me here, but what does interest me about it is that there are examples of this species surviving today that are far older than any existing ancient olive trees.

One particular example of this pine, nicknamed 'Methuselah', is believed to be 4,768 years old. It outdates, by a thousand years, the earthen beehives found by archaeologists at the Cretan sites of Phaistos and Knossos.

I hear weeping. I lay down my pen. It is coming from the bathroom; it must be Maria. I deliberate and then choose to ignore her tears, deciding that I should not intrude.

Mimosas and olive trees are not visited by bees. Pollen is not reaped from them; they are not used in the production of honey.

The weeping is unremitting. Maria has shut herself in the

lavatory and is now wailing. I close my notepad, feeling I should offer help or consolation, but it's awkward. I rise from my desk and knock gently on the door. 'Maria?'

'*Sim*,' she hiccups.

'Are you all right?'

The door opens and I find her sitting on the loo seat, stripes of mascara running down a face wretched with misery.

'What is it, Maria? Can I help?'

'It's my Pedro,' she sobs. 'He has another woman.' And off she goes again, wailing like a siren.

The news does not surprise me but evidently it has knocked her for six. In fact, she is so devastated I don't know how to comfort her and eventually murmur something inane like, 'Perhaps you are mistaken.' Trite and inadequate, I know, but I cannot think of anything better.

She shakes her dark head and begins to howl again. 'No, I'm not. He talks of her in his sleep. "*Esto apaixonado por te*," he says. "I love you, your curvacious breasts, your curly blonde hair, your accent when you speak my name. *Esto apaixonado por te*." And look at me, madame!' She is gesticulating angrily now, pulling at her hair. 'Dark, dark, dark!' and, beating at her breast, 'Nothing, *nada* here!'

I step back from the lavatory door, feeling decidedly ill at ease, offering to make tea so that I can slip swiftly away. Infuriatingly, to add to my mood, the ants have made it to the kitchen. As soon as I have a few minutes' peace and quiet, I telephone Michel in Paris, insisting that we put an end to our relationship with Pedro and Maria immediately. I promise to explain when he gets home. Bemused, he agrees.

On Friday, when Pedro drops by to collect his money – I make sure that I am not present – he enquires of Michel: 'What's up, chief? The work we've done is good, *non*?' Michel tells him that the work is not good. He was asked to prune the trees, not hack them. 'And look at the olive tree on the terrace beneath.'

'We haven't hacked the pine, monsieur. We've pruned it real hard so it'll grow faster. That olive's nothing to do with us. It must have been damaged already,' he counters with a shrug, and a drag on his fag.

Michel does not bother to engage in the nonsense of these arguments. 'There are other reasons we cannot continue to employ you,' he says and hands the man his envelope.

Still Pedro does not understand, or chooses not to.

'But what reasons?' he insists.

Finally, Michel, who hates to be forced into any form of confrontation, is obliged to spell out the incident in the garage, at which Pedro stares at him in blank amazement. 'But you can't be upset about *that*, monsieur! I was paying your wife a compliment!'

We are left for months with one over-pruned pine tree and its neighbour listing dangerously. We still have no one to water and, as to the olive, it breaks my heart to see its leaves and tender green fruits withdrawing from life, shrivelling and dying. I cannot reach René.

Later in the afternoon, as I step out of the car, having just returned from the garden centre, where Frédéric has advised me that there is nothing for it but mass destruction of the ants, 'before they wreak havoc in the house and take to biting everyone', Michel comes hurrying out on to the terrace. 'It's your agent,' he calls.

'I bought the dog food,' I yell. 'But I have nothing for the ants. Frédéric suggested some lethal blue powder, but—'

'Telephone,' he shouts again. 'Leave all that. I'll unpack the car.'

I make my way indoors.

'Hello?'

It seems that I have been offered a rather good role in a TV drama for the BBC. In the circumstances my first reaction is to refuse, and then I reconsider. Why not accept? The shooting will only take three weeks, we could most certainly do with the money and, as I need to see my gynaecologist in London, the timing is rather convenient. What is more, the dates coincide almost exactly with Michel's trip to Australia. The only snag is that we have guests, a family of four, arriving any day now and no one to look after the place, no one that is until I finally manage to track down Halaz, Quashia's fellow countryman, who agrees to come up and take on a few daily chores for us until Quashia's long-awaited return. Basically, all that we need is someone to water the plants and sweep the numerous tiled terraces and, during the period when we are both away, to feed and care for our dogs. Normally I would manage these chores myself but the heat and my pregnancy leave me flagging and manual work has become too taxing.

I suggest to Halaz that he comes up before dusk, feeding time for the hounds, and then Michel or I can give him a brief tour of the place and show him what to do.

The man who arrives is a short, bald-pated fellow, partially deaf and totally toothless, wearing a brightly coloured Hawaiian beach shirt, a broad grin and speaking a version of French which surely qualifies as an unidentified language. He shakes my hand enthusiastically and then, clapping his hands as he goes, scampers over to introduce himself to the dogs before I have given the signal. Lucky, interrupted in her evening biscuit and meat slurpings, snarls and lurches at him which sends our prospective help skittering off behind the trunk of the elephantine fig tree, trembling in terror of his life.

'There's nothing to be afraid of,' I shout, running to coax the cowering Arab out of hiding while calling for support from Michel, who is engaged in detaching a small wasps' nest he has found beneath the rear mudguard of the car. 'She's as friendly and faithful as a newborn puppy when she gets to know you.'

'I'm afraid of dogs,' he croaks.

'Then why . . . ?' But I don't bother to finish. Lucky comes loping towards me expecting a congratulatory pat for frightening off the nasty intruder. 'Well, it was kind of you to come. I'll walk you to the gate so that you're not troubled again. Thank you for . . .'

But the man has edged nervously out from behind the tree. 'No, no, it's fine. I'll get used to them. I like animals. It's only that the Alsatian, well, he's rather big. But I promised Quashia that if you called I'd lend a hand, and I will.'

Fruitless to point out that Lucky is a female.

'Truly, it's fine,' he insists, shooting wary glances in the general direction of the stables, where our canine trio are watching on, panting gleefully. Fortunately, Michel arrives about then, wasps' nest dealt with. He calms and charms Halaz, and the two men go off on a tour of the land, which allows Michel to explain the basic workings of our convoluted water system.

Providing our villa and acreage with water involves switching on an electric pump which has been installed in a tiny stone hut in the valley in front of and abutting our land; land that in times gone by was owned by this estate. From there, the water is pumped across the narrow access lane into our grounds and, by means of hundreds of metres of visible black piping, interspersed with the unreplaced lengths of old, rusty, metal piping up to the very summit of our hill and into a gigantic stone basin, from which it freefalls down the hill to the main house, the swimming pool and on to the foot of the land, crossing the narrow strip of lane again, where our entrance gate is situated, to feed our caretaker's cottage. It is a labyrinthine and archaic system but the four neighbouring houses in our forgotten corner of this rather unknown quarter all have exactly the same type of water supply and Lyonnaise des Eaux have no intention of changing it any time in the near future, so we have learned to live with it.

When Michel and Halaz return from their sally round the land, the poor man, who must be at least sixty, is sweating and puffing and looking vaguely puzzled.

'How about we all sit in the shade and cool off with a lemonade?' I offer. I know he won't touch alcohol.

He shakes his bald head, too breathless to speak, chewing pensively, on his gums I think.

'It's a lot to take in, but once you get the hang of it and know what's what, the work will only require a couple of hours a day.' I am trying my damnedest to be encouraging because without him, Quashia's return seems a distant promise and I will be obliged not only to refuse the television offer but, more importantly, to postpone my gynaecological appointment or find another specialist, one I don't know and who does not know me, here in France. Given my unlucky history, I would dearly prefer to be examined by my own doctor. In any case, even if I cancel the trip, I cannot handle this work alone.

'No problem,' he grins, bucking up in the most unexpected manner.

'And the dogs?'

'No problem.'

I shoot Michel a glance and say to him in English: 'What do you think?'

Michel replies in French with a pat on Halaz's back. 'Monsieur Halaz will have it taped in no time, won't you, monsieur? We have the utmost confidence in you.'

'No problem,' the man repeats. 'How much will you pay me?'

'What do you think is fair?' parries Michel.

Halaz stares at his sandals with a frown which seems to carry the weight of the world and then lifts his head and requests a sum which is rather insignificant, tantamount to slave labour, and I think he must have miscalculated. I repeat the figure and he nods nervously.

'I think that's too little,' I answer. 'We will offer you double that, on condition that the tasks are carried out on time and as we have asked.'

He stares at me in amazement and then grins from ear to ear and shakes our hands as though we were long-lost friends. 'No problem,' he says again and again. 'I'll start in the morning, and then you can see how I am doing. I'll be here at quarter to six.'

'Oh, it's not necessary to come quite so early.'

'Yes, yes, it's fine. Quarter to six. No problem.'

At that moment, as matters seem to be reaching a happy conclusion, Lucky comes haring down the hill with Bassett at her heels. They have been off on their early-evening hunt, a recce for rabbits or snakes or stale baguettes raided from some disgruntled neighbour's dustbin, from which they usually return bristling with an excess of triumphant energy. I call her sharply to heel but she heads straight at Halaz, who begins dancing backwards in his sandals while emitting groans of terror. The Alsatian rises on her hind legs, waltzing towards him, and I think the poor man is about to have a heart attack. But she rests her paws against his chest and pants contentedly. His terror turns to an outburst of joy. He attempts to caress her but his contact with her is rather abrupt, the pats almost slaps, and, fearing she will misunderstand, I rush forward. But she seems appeased and remains where she is, front legs now wrapped around his torso.

'See, no problem!' he cries like an ecstatic child. He shakes our hands again and shuffles off down the hill.

'I'm glad that's settled. Did you manage to take a look at that second water basin while you were up there?' I ask Michel as I slip into the summer kitchen and draw out a bottle of Sancerre.

'Yes, it will need shoring up and then some serious plumbing work.' Michel sits down at the table, where I join him, both of us about ready, as the evening draws gently in, leaving the soporific heat of the day elsewhere, to chill out with a glass of wine.

The early-morning sun is rising beyond the rear of the house, beyond the summit of our hill, climbing up behind the tall, narrow pines, framing and transforming their treetops into burnished halos and sending rods of golden light into our bedroom and on to our sleeping faces. I open my eyes to the caress of heat and to the unexpected sound of sloshing water. At first I am confused, and then, glancing at the clock, which reads a little after six, I remember M. Halaz. Michel is still sleeping, which is unlike him. He is usually up with the lark and preparing coffee and fresh fruit for breakfast about now, or already at his computer. Since the conception of our baby I have grown lazier in the mornings and am beginning to revel in idleness. Still, I roll over on to my left flank and clamber out of bed.

Once I have our coffee brewing, I step outside, slip my feet into espadrilles, stretch to scratch the sky and stroll to the terrace's edge to take in the view. The light hitting the distant Esterel is delicate, soft-hued; a purled mist that, later, the sun will burn off. Beneath me, a dusting of dew has alighted on the plants and the grass, which is beginning to turn brown from lack of water, and I am delighted to observe that there are no ants anywhere in the vicinity of the house. I seem somehow to have disenchanted them without needing to resort to killing them. I lean over the balustraded railing and am mystified to see a slender stream of water running down the driveway. To the left of the house, in the *parking*, is Halaz, in a cherry-red shirt, hosepipe in hand, wrestling with its orange plastic nozzle. Suddenly, the nozzle flies off the pipe and a powerful jet of water explodes in his face. He drops the hose fast and the pipe spirals away, seesawing water everywhere. He looks desperate and I see from his lips that he is muttering under his breath. I decide to go and lend a hand. Passing the garage, I notice that the tap alongside the stables has been left running, which would explain why we have a miniature rivulet in the drive. I close off the tap and go to help our man. Drenched, he has taken up the hose again and is attempting to dry himself off with a bright green handkerchief.

'*Bonjour*, monsieur, would you like a towel?' I ask.

He peers round awkwardly, surprised to find me there. 'No, it's fine,' he answers brusquely.

'May I show you how the nozzle works?' I hold out my hand to take the pipe from him but he pulls away, shrugging me off like a child with a prized toy.

'*Jeleconnay, jeleconnay*,' he answers petulantly, in his toothlessly incomprehensible French. '*Cet cazzi*.'

We establish, gently, patiently, that the nozzle is not broken and that it is essential, when one corner of the garden has been completed, before moving on to the next tap, that the other should be shut off tightly so as not to overconsume water, which is mightily expensive. He nods, drags and heaves at the hose and scurries off as though in a race, returning to what he was attempting to do before my appearance on the scene.

Over a delicious breakfast, prepared and served by Michel on the upper terrace – poached free-range eggs and a succulent portion of grilled tomatoes from our endlessly abundant vegetable garden, accompanied by a fresh baguette which he has driven to the village to collect – I express my concerns about Halaz. Michel's opinion is that we need to give the man time to get to grips with the work. As he says this, we spot the very fellow two terraces beneath us, puffing and panting, his red shirt so sodden it clings to his torso as though it had been painted on him, haring from one lilac bush to the next, spraying water everywhere as he trips in his sandals and then heaves and tugs at snake-like whorls of yellow piping.

The next time he appears, hosepipe at the ready and held aloft like an ancient flag of war, he is charging back in the opposite direction, springing from one terrace to the next, as though hell-bent on extinguishing a fire.

'Why is he rushing like that? He'll give himself a heart attack.'

'I have no idea.'

'Lord, I hope it's not because I told him the job should only take two hours!'

The fact is, Halaz explains to me the following day, that he prefers to work quickly so that he has no time to forget what he is doing.

While Michel is at the supermarket stocking up with a mountain of food for my Irish family, who eat like horses and are due any day now, though we have no idea of the precise date because they have not yet let us know, the telephone rings. My cousin's Irish accent greets me warmly. He is phoning to say that they have not managed to get flights and would it be all right with us both if they came later in the year? In fact, the change of plan suits us, but I am surprised by the news about the airline tickets. 'Why not?' I ask.

'Ah, Jeez, I haven't had the time to look,' is the response. I have to smile.

Through one of the tall French windows, as I put down

the phone, I spy Halaz engaged in what looks like a one-man Aboriginal corroboree or a Dutch clog dance. The hose in his left hand is swinging to and fro and irrigating most of the antique terracotta tiles as well as our teak dining table, not to mention feeding the fountain of water rushing down the stone staircase in front of him. Meanwhile, his right hand is flopping backwards and forwards and turning in bizarre circles; all this as he hops excitedly from leg to leg. The sight of these insane gymnastics makes me burst out laughing. What is he up to? I ask myself, and I creep out to take a closer look, but I can find no rational explanation for his performance. What I do observe, though, is that the garden is swimming in ponds of gurgling, bubbling water. We'll be waterlogged before the week is out and I shall be forced into a desperate search for René's elusive water diviner. Where *is* René? I am thinking. Why hasn't he returned my calls? At this rate, Lyonnaise des Eaux will have a shortage if not a crisis on their hands.

Michel returns, laden with shopping, and I greet him with the news that the Irish have postponed their visit. We stock most of the perishable foods in the deep freeze and stack the bottles of wine in the shuttered cool of the summer kitchen. The whites and rosés are left to chill in the garage fridge, and then we begin to address our own departures.

The fly in the ointment could prove to be leaving Halaz here in charge and this does not make my confidence sail. 'I caught him flapping about in the garden like a demented bird.'

Michel tells me not to worry so much. 'He's getting the hang of it, *chérie*.'

But at what cost? I dread to think of the water bill. We will definitely be needing a diviner.

'Do you think we should get a quote from Di Luzio for plumbing that second basin?' I ask.

'Did he call back?'

'No,' I sigh. Summers in Provence.

'Let's wait until Quashia returns. It may be beyond repair.'

I drive Michel to the airport. He is taking a plane to Paris, and from there will be departing in a few days' time for Sydney. We say our heartfelt goodbyes and I weep like a child.

'Please don't be sad, *chérie*. It's only for three weeks, and then we'll be back at the farm and together again. August will be upon us and I shall stop travelling for at least a month. We'll invite the girls down to spend a week with us, and Serge, too, if I can persuade him to accept. I am concerned for him. Think how lucky we are. *Nous avons la chance;* we have a baby on the way and everything to look forward to. *Je t'aime.*' He kisses me tenderly, hugs me tight and then speeds off to his departure gate. I wave him goodbye with a smile but I cannot deny a presentiment that my sadness is not entirely misplaced.

Driving back to the farm I determine to shrug off my downbeat mood. When I arrive Halaz has gone off for the day and I come across two taps at different points in the garden pouring forth. Sun-reflected puddles have collected everywhere and, to keep their coats cool in the increasing heat, the dogs are dozing in them and then transporting the mud and wet all over the place. I rush inside, ruby with rage, intent on calling the man back here right this minute. I intend to give him a damn good trouncing and have the matter settled once and for all but, at that very moment, at the peak of my rage, the telephone bursts into sound.

'*Allo?*' I shout. 'Who? Who?'

It is Jacob, the journalist Michel and I bumped into a couple of months back at the Cannes Film Festival.

'What is it?' I bark at the receiver.

Jacob is calling from the coast. He and his girlfriend, Barbara, have just arrived there, on their way back from another film festival somewhere in Lausanne, I think he is telling me, and are travelling south by car, returning to their apartment in Rome.

'I would love you to meet Barbara.'

'I'm afraid I can't this time . . .'

'She's dying to meet you. She's a great fan. She's read your books, she's seen your films. Would you like to come down and have an *apéro* with us later?'

'Well, I'm awfully tied up today, Jacob . . .'

'Then let us invite you to dinner. Get your work done and then drive down here. "As late as you like," Barbara is shouting to me. But do come.'

My temper has begun to subside and I recall how frequently and warmly he spoke about his girlfriend when he and I were in Madras together.

'Hello, Carol, this is Barbara. Please say yes.'

I have shelfloads to get done before my own departure, which is looming, and I am feeling consumed by misgivings about Halaz but, rather than refuse and be unnecessarily impolite, I suggest to Jacob, who is back on the line, that they come up to the farm instead. I give detailed directions and we agree the hour.

'We look forward to it, Carol. *A plus tard.*'

But my mind is not on this unanticipated rendezvous at all. I am stewing with Halaz's incompetence and determine that when he returns in the early evening to feed the dogs I will speak very sternly to him and threaten to sack him if he doesn't pull his socks up. This I cannot do, of course. At least, not without jeopardising my own trip and my appointment with the specialist, but he does not know that.

Jacob and Barbara arrive earlier than we had agreed, which does not please me, but as it turns out this new acquaintance is utterly enchanting. A late thirty-something, husky-voiced woman with a mane of wild, blonde hair. From her accent it is clear that she hails from one of those upper-middle-class English families who hold themselves in high esteem. The refreshing difference is that Barbara has an air of the gypsy about her. She has healthy, tanned skin and a face as brown as a nut from out of which shine the most mesmerising, soulful green eyes.

I open a bottle of chilled Bourgogne Aligoté, serve two dishes, one of local olives, the other a mix of almonds with pistachio nuts, settle them in the garden, share a few gulped sips with them and then apologise for the fact that I must dash back upstairs and finish the correspondence I was called away from.

'Have a swim,' I suggest. 'There are towels in the spare room. I'll join you later.'

Later arrives all too soon, while I am still buried beneath a mountain of unfinished paperwork, or rather as I am giving up for the moment and leaving it all to go in search of Halaz. Halaz, who, unbeknown to me, has plodded up the drive and paused for breath beneath the spreading fig tree where, in this leafy, shaded corner at the shallow end of the swimming pool, he claps eyes on Barbara, blithely ascending the chlorine-bleached steps, wet, oily as an otter and stark naked. This sighting sends Halaz, whose notion of women is that they should be covered from head to foot, into a state of cardiovascular shock.

Having exited through one of the back doors of the house, I am entirely ignorant of this collision and have no idea, when I find Halaz, what has come over him. All I see is that here he is in the stables, arms outstretched, collapsed against the crumbling ancient wall, fighting for breath with the desperation of an asthmatic, the three dogs' dishes, fortunately metal, having fallen from his grip to the ground and rolled off out of sight. A twenty-kilo sack of biscuits has split open and the contents are pouring all over the floor. In addition to this, three lidless tins of meat chunks swimming in thick gravy have been discovered by the dogs and dragged out on to the forecourt where, heedless of Halaz's state, they are gobbling and slurping with a gluttony which exceeds even their habitual zest. I find them, usually such a harmonious trio, growling deep-throated threats at one another, warning their comrades away from their portion of the stolen provisions.

'What is going on?' I demand of Halaz.

'Where's Michel, where's your husband?' he stammers and pants.

'He left this morning. Why?'

Try as he might, he simply cannot spit out the words. Only the direction of his eyes tells me what has driven him to this state of apoplexy. I turn and observe Barbara, smoking a cigarette, wine glass in hand, spreading her bronzed and naked body out on a towel, luxuriating in the warm early-evening sunshine.

I have to admit that the sight of her does come as a bit of a surprise. I say surprise and not shock, because we have no problem with nudity here at our olive farm, but even so, it is unusual for a guest visiting us for the first time to disrobe themselves so entirely quite so soon after arrival. My first impression of Barbara was that she is a hippy, a free-spirited creature, with a gentle but powerful sensuality. This has been borne out. I only wish that Halaz, an Arab male and a Muslim, had not been the one to discover her, because it leaves me rather on the defensive when I had intended to be stern with him.

'Mr Halaz, you left the taps running again . . .'

He walks away, shaking his head in disgust, deaf to my words.

'Mr Halaz!' I call after him, but he has disappeared. My remonstrations must wait till the morning.

Back in the house, I leave yet another message – a rather bad-tempered one, due to my frame of mind – for Lord Harry's sister, who has not returned my last call. In fact, I have not yet managed to have a conversation with her. I am discovering that these apiarists are an irritatingly cranky and elusive breed, and singularly particular about where their blasted hives will or won't be placed, *l'emplacement des ruchers*. But I shan't be detracted and I say so in my message.

Jacob and Barbara stay for supper. We decide to have a barbecue, but my mood is agitated. Jacob is getting on my nerves, fussing over what he will or will not eat, continuously requesting the use of the telephone, and I am worried about my impending departure. I bury myself in the kitchen, slicing potatoes, chopping parsley and garlic, preparing a recipe of my own composition which I bake with strips of freshly cut sprigs of rosemary in a locally fired faience dish. I am not feeling sociable; I would have preferred to have been alone this evening.

Barbara finds me there.

'I opened another bottle of wine,' she says. 'I hope that's OK.'

'Of course,' I reply, continuing with my culinary distractions.

'And I brought you up a glass. You seem tense. I hope we are not intruding?' Before I can respond, she continues. 'You mustn't let Jacob's neuroses get to you. He can be a pain in the arse, but if you ignore him, he'll stop.' She giggles.

This makes me smile, and I pause to acknowledge her.

'I never take any notice of him and then he shuts up.'

'How long have you been together?'

She sighs. 'Since I was eighteen. I'm forty tomorrow.'

'Children?' I ask.

She shakes her head. 'You?'

'Two stepdaughters from Michel's first marriage and' – I glance down at my delicately protruding, tumescent belly, 'we're expecting one of our own at Christmas.'

She takes a long drag on her cigarette. I have observed that she has been smoking incessantly since she arrived. 'I'd really love a kid.'

'Then why . . . ?'

'Jacob hates children, just as he hates all noise, most music, too much sun, the majority of human beings, red meat, alcohol, smoking – particularly when it's me doing the smoking or drinking . . .' her voice drifts into silence.

I want to ask her why she stays with him, but for once in my life I keep my interrogations to myself. Instead I place my potato dish in the oven, pick up the glass of white wine Barbara has brought me and lead the way back out on to the upper terrace. One level below us, over at the remotest corner, flanked by a quartet of stately cypress trees (*cyprès Florentin*), Jacob is fanning the flames and the narrow column of smoke rising out of our barbecue, and coughing. The air is scented with evening pine and charred herbs. Barbara perches on the balustrade to admire the view out over the sea. To the right of us the sun is moving towards the mountains. Soon it will begin to set, sinking deep beneath the mauve hills, leaving a vermilion sky to decorate the late evening.

'This place is fabulous. You're very lucky.'

'Yes, we are. It needs a load of work and we never have a bean, but in the fullness of time we'll get to it all, no doubt.'

Over supper, aromatically spiced *daurade* lightly marinated in white wine, fresh herbs and slices of lemon from the garden – not forgetting the olive oil, of course – and baked in tinfoil on the open coals, Jacob and Barbara prise out of me the concern I am harbouring about leaving. Almost before I have finished, Jacob suggests that they stay and take care of the place during my absence. The haste with which he has offered, and a fleeting memory of our meeting with him on the Croisette during the film festival, make me dubious. I thank him but assure him that it won't be necessary. Barbara lights up another cigarette, saying nothing. After another bottle of wine, most of which she consumes, they prepare to wend their way back to their hotel on the coast. Before leaving she embraces me like a sister. 'Thank you. I really enjoyed meeting you.'

I notice my watch. It's gone midnight. 'Happy birthday,' I trill, returning her hug. I wait in the drive beneath the clear, starlit sky to wave them off.

My heart is a complex knot of emotions. For Michel and I and our awaited child I carry profound joy and a recognition of our good fortune; for Jacob and his inability to let life in I feel pity, while those green, soul-stirring eyes of Barbara's haunt me, so full are they with fragility and yearning.

The following morning Halaz greets me with the restrained, mistrusting gaze of one who believes he is in the presence of iniquity. My anger towards him, on the other hand, has dissipated. I take him aside and patiently go through all the tasks to be achieved, walking to each and every tap, turning it on, turning it off and then squeezing it tightly shut. I reassure him that he can take his time, that he doesn't have to achieve the work in two hours, that too much water can be as damaging to some plants as none at all, and confide in him that we are counting on him.

He nods gravely. 'In that case, please can I have a new brush?' he asks. 'So that I can sweep to the best of my ability. I'm good at sweeping,' he adds.

'There's an unused one in the garage.'

'No, I don't like those. I prefer the softer ones. The ones you use inside the house.'

Incongruous as I find this, I take the time to go to the hardware store and buy him not one but two new brooms, both of slightly different lengths so that he can have his pick.

When I return our Arab has finished for the morning and left everything in perfect order; not an itinerant splash to be found anywhere. Satisfied, I go inside the house to find two messages, one from Lord Harry, inviting me over later and the second from Barbara, thanking me for the previous evening and leaving a number where I can contact her.

When I return her call, her voice sounds rusty, just-woken-up and unused, and cheerless.

'Have you got something fun planned for today?'

Two Italian friends of theirs have turned up in Cannes and they will get together for a birthday celebration, I learn. 'Sorry about Jacob,' she says, interrupting herself.

'What about him?'

'I don't know, everything.' The line goes silent. I hear a heavy exhalation.

'Why don't you come up here, bring your friends and we'll have a little party in the garden – just something simple?' I suggest. It's a spontaneous offer which I have not thought through. Her sadness troubles me, and for a reason that I cannot quite explain I feel impelled to lift her out of her dejection. In any case, the larder and fridges are bursting with provisions, some of which will not keep beyond my departure, so better to share it all. The idea thrills her.

Just as I am about to shoot off for Lord Harry's, René turns up to rescue the ailing olive tree. 'It's not fatal, but it's a good thing you called.'

'Will the damage affect the tree's performance?' I ask. 'I mean, are we going to lose all this season's fruit from it?'

'Hopefully not, but it will have to be dramatically pruned at the end of the year, and that will affect its yield for several harvests to come.'

I sigh.

He cheers me with the news that he has spoken with the 'finest dowser in the region', who has agreed to visit us. Nick someone.

'It's a drug to him. He has to do it, search for water. He can't stop looking.'

This strikes me as a rather comical claim, but I assure René that we look forward to meeting this gentleman and ask if, given that the man is so hooked, we could please get on with it as soon as possible so that we can settle matters with the Lyonnaise des Eaux who are, in response to Michel's numerous letters, still adamantly refusing to accept our newly endorsed status as local olive-growers.

'We may have to wait until his partner can be here with him.'

'Partner? Oh, I see, I hadn't realised that he might need a partner.'

'Oh, yes. But when you meet him, the partner, that is, you are not to say a word.'

'About what?'

'His identity.'

I suppress a grin. 'Am I going to recognise him?'

'Oh, no doubt about it. Well, *you* may not, of course, but he is very famous in the community. A highly regarded and very wealthy Provençal figure.'

'My goodness.' There are times when I suspect that René is pulling my leg. 'And he does this for pleasure, or . . . ?' I am indisputably his best audience and I cannot help feeling that my keen interest for local learning nudges him towards embellishments that any great storyteller would be proud to have come up with. This might just be one of those occasions.

I scan his robin-red face, those piercing blue eyes, for a clue, but his earnest expression reveals no joshing.

'After he retired he discovered he had the talent for finding water. The pair are old friends; they work well together. One uses a *baguette* – a rod, which is actually shaped like an extended catapult – while the other works with a pendulum. Monsieur— (I'd better not mention his name just yet) is frequently the one to pinpoint the precise spot while young Nick can read to the metre how deep the source is and the quantity of litres flowing there. It's a *vrai* talent. But you will see for yourself. I have no flair for it, *hélas*.'

We have strolled inside now and I see René hovering, hoping for a glass of something refreshing.

'Have you given it a try then, René?'

'Oh, yes, *mais bien sûr*. I hoped it might have become another string to my bow, but it was hopeless. Nothing happened until the gentleman you are soon to meet touched my arm. I kid you not. He literally touched my arm as we were standing over a water source and the baguette I was clutching shot upwards, quivering.'

I listen on with respectful interest and mixed feelings. I am in two minds about what René is recounting. I want to believe that such a talent exists. I am drawn to the mystical element of it; it fits with my vision of the olde-worlde Provençal temperament. But I must admit to a sneaking scepticism. 'Well, I really look forward to it. Can we set a date now, René, please?'

It is essential, with our lovable olive guru, to nail him down, pin him to days and hours. Even so, he frequently doesn't show, but at least then he knows he has let us down. If we leave an arrangement as vague or loose as 'tomorrow', or 'the beginning of next week', it can be weeks before we hear another word from him.

'How about Friday?' he suggests.

'The day after tomorrow? Perfect.'

He takes a sliver of carrot from the dish of crudités in front of him and washes it down with the last mouthful from the glass of Pomerol I have produced, then rises to go. 'Good Bordeaux that, thank you. Expensive?'

I shrug.

'Do you know where the Provençal tradition of serving little dishes of vegetables as appetisers came from?'

I frown, working it out, considering the history of the Greek custom of *meze* dishes, but he is impatient to impart his local knowledge.

'The Spanish Moors. They would originally have been Arab dishes.'

'Yes, *meze*. Turkish and Eastern.'

I have been skipping back through Lawrence Durrell's *Bitter Lemons* and I recall the lovely phrase: 'We sat beside the road in the thin spring sunshine and shared a stirrup cup and a *meze*,' which I do not trouble to repeat to René. In any case, I wouldn't know how to translate 'stirrup cup'. A welcoming glass, perhaps?

'No, Carol, the habit arrived with the Spanish Moors. Definitely. *Ah, oui*,' he insists, nodding triumphantly. I say no more on the subject. I cannot dawdle; I am late for Lord Harry. We have reached the door. 'You do realise, Carol, that you'll have to declare any water we find, don't you?' I shake my head. But I don't foresee any difficulty with registering our find. We have no reason to hide the discovery, should there be one. 'And acquire planning permission to install a drill and pump before you begin excavating. But there shouldn't be any unnecessary delays. Water is the only subterranean product here in France that the state don't lay claim to, did you know that?'

I shake my head again.

'Now, if it were oil, they'd come and take it and you

wouldn't get a centime out of it, apart from compensation
for the damage to your land while they tear it up to siphon
out the juice. But there's still no law against you keeping for
your exclusive use any water found, as long as it is declared
and written into the cadastre plans. A *source* must be registered.'

'Please God we don't find oil then,' I laugh. 'Or gold!' I
see him to the door and as we peck cheeks I ask, 'What time
on Friday, René?'

'Afternoon.'

'Two o'clock, then?'

'No, later. Three or half-past. I'll call you tomorrow and
confirm it.'

I realise that I will get no firmer commitment out of him
today, so I wave him goodbye and return indoors to collect
my car keys. The main thing is that he has contacted the
dowsers, and even if they find not a single drop here it won't
be serious because, with luck, the water board will be
obliged to readjust our price plan. As requested, we will
have made the search.

I am running very late when I arrive at Lord Harry's, but I
don't want to postpone my visit and miss out on the opportunity to meet his sister and finalise bees with her. I drive
through a wide gate, up a winding dust track and into the
sweet, tangy scent of freshly picked apricots. There are crateloads of them everywhere, mostly in an open barn. These, the
most recently harvested, are to be dried for use in preserves
and *sirops*. Elsewhere, all around, there are fresh, succulent
fruits, the main bulk of his crop, which are being harvested
now and which will be sold to a supermarket chain. Lord
Harry greets me with a robust handshake and then takes me
on a tour of the estate, which has been inherited from
Baron —, his father, who made his fortune when he came up

with the apparently inspired idea to breed prime Angus beef in the Camargue district and sell the meat to the French.

'He made a fortune,' Harry tells me. 'And then retired here to farm fruit, a passionate hobby of his.'

The main house is impressive but needs a fortune spending on it and has a bedraggled air about it. The interior is dark, the curtains left undrawn, and old-fashioned. Empty glasses, used cups forgotten on side tables and dressers. Out of doors, in the dusty yards, it is more animated. There are labourers all over the place, moving to and fro on tractors or on foot, shouting out to one another, up ladders, stacking crates in the barns. Certainly the farm is operating at full tilt, but I cannot help thinking that it has seen happier days.

He drives me to a valley, peaceful and green, with leafy rows of well-pruned trees gravid with ripe fruit, and I am trying to recall what I have found out about the history of the apricot tree.

For many years it was believed to have originated in Armenia, but is now known to have existed long before in ancient China. It reached Armenia via the Silk Route, and from there was transported to Greece and then to Rome. The Romans cultivated it throughout their empire. Today, it is considered a quintessentially Mediterranean tree. It would have been the Romans who brought the apricot to this French coast.

'Where is your sister?' I ask, taking in the expanse of his acreage.

'She's in Geneva.'

'When will she back?'

He shakes his head. 'Your guess is as good as mine.'

I stop in my tracks. 'But you still have her hives?'

'Dozens of them. We can take the car and go and have a look, if you like.' Which is what we do. Standing in a modest orchard of espaliered apple trees, the hives are a sorry-looking sight. Desolate and in need of a lick of paint, they put me in mind of rows of beach huts at an out-of-season resort.

'Where are the bees?'

'There are no bees any more.'

'No bees?'

'Well, there are a few,' he explains. 'Those that have not died or abandoned the hives.'

The few still pollinate Harry's apricots, but the swarms are feral now.

'What happened?'

'Bit of a scandal, as I understand it. I really don't know the ins and outs of the affair, except that my sister lost heart with the whole bloody business and took off.' He offers to let us have a few of the abandoned hives. 'If you want to take them, you can have them for nothing. Help yourself to as many as you like,' he says. 'They are of no further use to me, but you will need to purchase a queen and a swarm of drones of your own.' I would like to quiz him further, but one of his farmhands, a fresh-faced English lad, comes in search of him and Lord Harry needs to attend to other matters. I thank him for his kind offer, explaining that we are not apiarists; we do not have the skills or the time to tend the bees ourselves; we are looking for a beekeeper who might be interested in using our land. He nods sadly. 'Sorry I couldn't be of help. Come and visit me again in any case,' he says. 'My wife's left me, gone back to England, and my sister – well, she's disappeared to the Swiss mountains. Haven't seen her in months. I think she's become a Buddhist. It's bloody lonely here. Just me and the apricots.'

I am now running very late. Thierry, the young bullet-headed fellow who cleans our pool, is at work in the garden when I arrive home with a cake for Barbara from an excellent *boulangerie*-cum-*pâtisserie* on the outskirts of Mougins. He is bursting with some gossip which he cannot wait to share and I am obliged to deposit my bags on the ground while he imparts his news. Because of the spread of residences Thierry works at, he tends to have access to delicious titbits. This one concerns a property belonging to a thirty-something German whose pool he has been looking after for several years. Electric gates, armed and vested bodyguards patrolling the grounds, half a dozen trained dogs, the whole caboodle. Some time ago, while Thierry was at work there, the police arrived in two cars and the German was arrested for drug-smuggling. He has been shoved in jail and the house is now on the market for 36 million francs, about £3.2 million.

'Goodness,' I say, politely feigning surprise, gathering up my shopping.

'No, no, that's not it!' he returns excitedly.

Last Saturday, while Thierry was hoovering and treating the pool – his contract has been renegotiated by the firm of estate agents until the place is sold – a young Russian and his wife came to look at the house. According to Thierry, they liked it, said they'd have it and pulled out a suitcase from the boot of their car containing considerably more than the required 36 million francs in dollars. If French law allowed it, they would have bought the villa right there and then.

'The Mafia are moving in here like the plague,' he comments.

I find my attention drawn back to the scandal down on the coast which has been hogging the limelight since the spring.

'What's the latest news on the demise of the mayor?'

Thierry seems to revel in the uncloaking of these *petit* local corruptions, as do I, particularly when they are not so *petit*.

The latest is that a senior official in the Cannes town hall has followed our Riviera mayor into custody on suspicion of trying to extort money from a gambling firm in London. He has been placed under investigation for alleged corruption.

'Some chappie working for him was caught redhanded by a British special investigations squad. At the Ritz Hotel. He was receiving a payment of three million francs in cash.'

'In London?'

'Yes, the sum was being handed over by a British firm in return for permission to install one-armed bandits at a casino in one of the beachfront hotels. It was the British company who tipped off the police.

The mayor's son, Gilles Mouillot, has also been placed under investigation, but has been released under supervision. Father, Michel, is in prison and on hunger strike, which is delaying matters. A lawyer acting for the mayor has denounced the arrests and investigations, calling them politically motivated. He claims that they are connected with wrangling and factiousness between members of the centre-right coalition.

Everywhere here there are echoes of Graham Greene's excellent book, *J'accuse*, which exposed the nefarious dealings of Jacques Médecin, the infamous mayor of Nice, who swindled his city out of millions and then did a bunk to Uruguay, where the said millions had been stashed away for what he hoped was going to be a very sunny retirement. Our chap, Mouillot, hasn't been so nifty.

Thierry promises to keep me up to speed when I return from my trip.

Barbara's birthday is an ebullient yet easygoing affair. She blows out the four candles I have placed on her cake. Much wine is drunk, we sing and talk and play sixties rock music and old Van Morrison records rather too loudly and dance till late on the terrace by the pool. Her only disappointment is that her camera jams and neither she nor Jacob is able to unlock it. They cannot photograph the occasion. It suddenly occurs to me that Michel may not have taken his camera with him for his trip to Sydney. I run up to our bedroom and find it beneath my shoebags on the floor of the wardrobe, which is where he usually hides it.

I have no idea how to operate such a complicated apparatus but I return to the garden with it and suggest a few snaps. I set the zoom and the lens and the flash and everyone gathers round the table, arms linked, glasses raised, and shouts '*Fromage!*'

From the summer kitchen comes the unmistakable voice of Buddy Holly: 'Maybe Baby'. The quartet burst into laughter and raucous song, jigging as they hold their poses.

'Hang on! Wait!' I cry. 'I don't seem to be able to—'

'*Fromage! FROMAGE! FORMAGGIO!*' they shout and call like merry parrots, hammering out a recurrent squawk, clapping their hands. I fiddle clumsily, all fingers and thumbs, until, almost without my guidance, the camera clicks, slides, flashes and snaps, and I feel rather pleased with myself. Glasses are topped up, spilling over, and I promise to send copies on to Rome when the negatives are developed. And then I say my goodnights, exchanging *bisous* with everyone, and leave them all to plunge into the underwater-lit pool, uncork more bottles of bubbly and vino, smoke, chatter loudly and generally behave like Romans at a party, while I disappear off to bed to cries of '*Ciao, bella!*' '*Grazie mille, mille grazie!*' They promise to let themselves out and to lock the gate behind them. Lord knows if, by whatever hour that might be, they will remember, but aside from hanging out all night with them, what can I do?

My last image of the party, as I close the front door, is of Jacob: a lone figure sitting at some distance, a terrace above his loved one and their companions, fingers jammed in his ears to block out the noise, looking decidedly fed up.

I wake about five, climb out of bed and wander out on to the terrace, thinking that I should walk down the drive and check the gate. The pre-dawn is sharply lit by an almost full moon which is reflecting circular pools of luminous, citric light right across the Mediterranean; it is a breathtaking sight. I sit for a while in pensive mood, gazing upon it, considering the lot of Barbara and Jacob.

I am not one for matchmaking and never have been, but I find myself wondering whether I shouldn't introduce her to Lord Harry. Surely they would have more in common. Same background, both lonely . . .

Lost in these fruitless, not to say busybody, musings, it is some time before I realise that I am not alone. The clinking of a glass is what draws my attention to the terrace beneath me. There I see Barbara, perched barefoot on one of the cream-painted walls by the dining table, wearing nothing but a sarong. Her hair is wet and hangs like lengths of damp seaweed down her back; she must have been swimming. She has a lighted cigarette between her fingers and a three-quarters-empty bottle of wine at her side. The dogs, all three of them, are dozing in a semi-circle around her.

I go down to join her. As I approach she holds out her hand. It turns out that the others left several hours ago but she has lingered, preferring to walk back when she is ready to go. We barely talk; there seems little need. She thanks me for the evening and tells me that I won't ever know how special it has been and how appreciated she has felt. To me, these words only emphasise the appalling loneliness I feel this woman is trapped in.

As the sun comes up, she helps me clear the debris from the table and stack the myriad empty bottles ready for the local bottle bank, stays for breakfast and then I drive her to Cannes.

She is off to sunbathe on the beach. 'I'm only really happy when I'm by the sea,' she says. 'It calms me, brings me peace.'

'Me too,' I laugh.

'You are lucky to be having a baby,' she mutters, almost inaudibly, before leaving the car.

We kiss goodbye and agree to stay in touch.

'And don't forget to send the photos,' she calls as our old car chugs away. After dropping Barbara off, I decide to take a stroll along the Croisette. The beaches are humming with activity and the *restos* and cafés *au bord de la mer* are buzzing with a new breed of holidaying visitor, many of whom have bleached, backcombed hairdos. They are ordering drinks, fixing extravagantly painted faces and reading Russian newspapers and magazines.

Once I begin to take notice, I see that every beachside bookstall has Russian journals for sale. The newsagent has *Vogue* on display in Russian for the mafia molls who might enjoy a little light beach reading. Russian restaurants are springing up everywhere, both in and out of town, and the fashions in the women's stores are being slanted towards the new market. This is not the usual seasonal changes or a pitch at the wealthy Arab consumers, who still exist, though since that 'blasted Gulf War' the Arab trade has not been what it was. No, the outfits on sale now have a retro look, but not as in the fashion corridors of Paris. This is fetchingly out of date, late fifties, early sixties, meretricious colour combinations; the dressed-to-kill rocker look that every young Russian might have aspired to during those sealed-off years of communism. Thierry is spot-on: a new Mafia is moving in, but no doubt the town of Cannes is grateful for them.

Three days later, I fly to London. René and his water diviner never made contact, never appeared. On my way through the departure lounge at Nice airport, I notice two posters advertising Russian television stations. My flight is announced, and as I approach the boarding gate I pass a young man dressed in a loud suit. He is shouting into four mobile telephones all at once. The language he's talking is Russian, with a few English swearwords thrown in for spice.

A new page in Côte d'Azur history.

Before leaving for Birmingham, which is where the shooting of my television film is scheduled to take place, I visit my gynaecologist. I admit to my tirednesses and the occasional shooting pains. He recommends that I undergo an amniocentesis. I am wary but agree. The risks are minimal, he assures me, though marginally higher for a woman such as myself with a history of miscarriage.

On the day, it all goes off without a hitch. I learn that our baby is perfectly normal, followed by the even more joyous news that the child I am carrying is no longer an 'it': the life taking form is a she. I leave the Harley Street clinic feeling both nervous and totally exhilarated and make directly for a phone box to telephone Michel in Paris.

'What will we christen her?'

We decide to both choose a name and, just for fun, to keep them to ourselves; a secret from one another until the next time we are together which will be after my filming. Suppose we choose the same name?

'*Peut-être, qui sait?*' Michel laughs happily.

Think how remarkable that would be.

The reality of the approaching birth of our baby, our tiny little girl, is taking hold. Her arrival is months away yet, but now she has a name, no, two names. Spiritually christened, she exists in my day-to-day life. She has moved in, is already a participating member of the family. I pass my days visiting my hairdresser, lunching with my agent, meeting for drinks with my editor; I am city-busy and oscillating between states of excitement and nervousness, which leave me both effervescent and drained. I feel as though my whole being is smiling, glowing from inside.

'You look great,' people repeatedly tell me.

Yes. I am past all the enervating bouts of morning sickness and no longer a prisoner to my tomato obsession; I am a woman in her stride.

Some days my mood is vital, powerfully alive and sharp. I and my baby are omnipotent; a single invincible force. I talk to her, ask her advice, offer her mine. She shares my secrets, knows my shortcomings, forgives me because she is too tiny to know otherwise and, for the present, I am all there is. She is my invisible ally, as I am hers. She is my passport to another earth, another stratosphere of happiness, of bondedness. Together our love, this union of mother and daughter, this sorority, girls together, will make my world go round.

And then, at other moments, friends remark that I look tired, or rather pale. It's true. I feel inadequate. I have sleepless nights worrying that I have left this birth too late, that I am too selfish, too set in my ways, that I won't be able to meet the challenge, that something will go wrong, that our little girl will not be whole. Fortunately, the negative responses are less frequent and are strongly overridden by my more upbeat moods. The designer calls. 'Costume fittings, darling,' she purrs. 'We must meet and discuss your cozzies.'

I have been postponing this important rendezvous knowing that there will be a drawn-out session involving measurements, sizes and styles of clothes and that I may be obliged to give away my secret. I suggest that she and her assistant come over to my flat, where we can discuss the script over a bottle of wine.

When she arrives that evening, accompanied by the assistant, she compliments me on how well I am looking, 'radiant', she says, tactfully observing that I am perhaps a tad on the plump side. I shrug this off with a comment about my French lifestyle: 'The wine and good living, you know.' We settle down to discuss the costumes required for the various scenes when a ring at the doorbell interrupts us. I am not expecting anyone. Excusing myself, I go out into the hall to press the intercom.

'Yes?'

'Flowers for Miss Drinkwater,' a voice announces.

This flat is not in the most salubrious district of north London and though we are well concealed on two floors at the very top of the building I am usually cautious before pressing the lock-release.

'I am not expecting flowers. Who are they are from?' I interrogate, but the crackly male voice does not say. Yet because I am not alone I feel less wary, so I press the button that opens the street door, calling out an apology to the two women in the living room, suggesting they help themselves to more wine and explaining that I will be with them shortly. I open my front door to await the delivery boy who is climbing the winding stairs. I see the bouquet of eighteen red roses before I see him.

It is Michel!

I cry out and both designer and assistant look up anxiously from the living room. The designer hurries to the door. 'Is everything all right?'

I nod. 'It's my husband,' and I run down a few steps to greet him and to throw my arms around him. 'What are you doing here? I thought you were on your way to Sydney.'

'Changing planes in London. I wanted to surprise you. I can't stay, I'll miss my flight. I have a taxi outside,' and he hands me the flowers, kisses me softly on the mouth, whispers

'*Je t'aime*,' and disappears out of sight with a final blown kiss. 'Take care of her,' he calls up softly.

I return to the two women, who look at me curiously. 'My husband,' I repeat. 'He's just flown in from Paris.'

'Isn't he coming in?' asks the designer 'I hope that we . . .'

'No, no, he's on his way to Australia and wanted to . . .' I consider divulging our news and then decide not to. 'He just came to give me these.'

'Shit, that's too romantic!' says one of them.

'He must be French,' declares the other.

Buried within the bouquet – I find it later – is a gold chain as slender as a strand of hair with one tiny emerald worked into it. It matches my engagement-cum-wedding ring.

It is the Irish in me, my superstitious nature, that has decided against broadcasting news of the baby, as well as the fact that I shall be filming for only three weeks. Had I been contracted for a longer period, out of courtesy to the designer, who would have needed to be prepared for the inevitable costume alterations, I would have discreetly included her. As it is, the entire shoot will be over in no time, so there will be few, if any, physical changes and, as much as I hate to, I have promised myself I will diet rigorously. So I guard our cherished secret, and the following afternoon I set off by train for Birmingham.

A Darker Climate

Surfacing from an uncharacteristically deep sleep, I open my eyes into a twilight zone, into the shadowland between drowsing and waking. Though my lids and limbs feel sluggish and my responses dull, I am instantly assaulted by two very different sensations, both of which send shockwaves through my system. Encompassing me is a heaviness, as though life itself has been becalmed, and the other, a raw ache rapping at the pit of my stomach.

I lie motionless, stiff as a board, on my back, staring at the ceiling, attempting to deny this pain which has the nagging quality of a pre-menstrual cramp. I want to close it out, to be attentive only to the bursts of middle-of-the-night London traffic. I lift my hand and brush it gingerly against my stomach. Although heartened by my belly's crescent fullness, I am unable to rid myself of the fear that all is not well. Should I rise, make hot tea, take an aspirin? Or should I relax, breathe deeply and try to sleep again? I close my eyes, hankering for Michel, pining for him to be here alongside me, relieved that I am not filming in the morning and that I can sleep late if I choose to. I roll over on my hip to ease the discomfort but this does not alleviate it. On the contrary, the sensations are worsened; or perhaps they are exaggerated by my focus on them. I grow scared, worrying for the wellbeing of the minuscule female foetus growing with faith inside me.

Supine again, I keep my eyes firmly shut and move my hand from side to side across the rounded flesh, massaging it, intent on creating a pain-free zone down there, to transmit waves of serenity, of security to the tiny girl agitating within me. It seems to work; the pain eases and I drift off, swimming in and out of wakefulness, until, some time later, something alerts me to the fact that my thighs are damp; damp with a sticky warmth that freaks me, sending distress signals up and down the length of my body. I turn fast and put on the bedside light, pressing my other hand tight against the source of this wetness.

Drawing my arm out from beneath the bedding, I stare in horror at my palm, my fingers and my wrist. Sickened, I throw off the cover as though it were on fire and gaze down upon my lower regions, all of which are blotched in haemorrhaging blood. The sight of it, claret-dark and viscous, scares and nauseates me just as violence scares and revolts me. I kick the duvet away and lift myself, breathlessly, to a sitting position, noticing the clock, which shows something after 3am. I don't know what to do. I feel panicked and uncertain and alone and unwilling to face up to what this must mean.

I have to call someone, do something, take action, but who, what? Michel is in Australia. Even if I telephoned him – it is mid-afternoon in Sydney – what could he do? Why alarm him? I lift myself unsteadily to my feet and stagger down the stairs to the lavatory. I feel the blood escaping, slipping down my inner thighs. I am heaving in dry gulps as though I were choking although I know that I am not. It is fear, shock, confusion, as well as a passionate, a desperate need for this not to be happening. Clots as well as steady trickles of blood are slipping out of me. The ease with which they fall belies the gravity of my situation. I am losing my baby. Am I? Am I really losing our precious little girl?

The pains are shooting up my back and pressing vice-like against my stomach. I am dizzy and weak, seated on the loo, chest slumped against my knees, head hanging towards my feet like a vomiting drunk; I have no ability to move, no strength; the pain has me in its grip. But I know that I must take some action.

Eventually I crawl to the telephone and dial the number of Chris, a fellow actor and a loyal friend.

'What time is it?' he slurs sleepily.

'Come over,' I whisper. 'Please. Come now.' He lives nearby; he has keys. Thank God he has keys.

'What? Are you all right?' He doesn't wait for a coherent reply but accepts my stuttering negatives and assures me that he is on his way.

I drag a towelling robe from a hook on the back of the bathroom door, wrap it like a sarong around my lower torso and slump to the carpet in the living room, curled up like the foetus which is tearing itself out of me, because I have no strength to climb the stairs again. I am trembling and cold and frightened and the blood is still raining out of me. The pain clenches in fits and starts. Perhaps it's not too late. Perhaps this is not as serious as . . . but I know that it is. I have miscarried before; nothing quite as dramatic as this, but I recognise the signs. Above all, that dull ache throbbing round the base of my spine, digging into the lower half of me.

Chris finds me there on the floor. He fights back his distress at the sight of me. 'I'm taking you to hospital,' he says manfully.

I manage to convey my wish to be seen by my own gynaecologist. Chris goes in search of my address book, finds the number and telephones the specialist's home. Richard listens, instructs him on where to take me, details of how to get there and what to do in the meantime. Then Chris rings for a cab because he wants to be with me, to be able to hold me instead of having to drive; to care for me, and I am so grateful.

Dawn is rising bruised mauve and tangerine-sharp beyond the city's granite-grey high-rises. This part of London seems unfamiliar to me. I cannot recall ever having been here before. Curled, blanketed figures are dead to the world on the pavement, overturned bottles at their sides, as the cab swings in through the open iron gates of the hospital, and stops.

'We're here,' my friend whispers, leaning across me to open the door.

The damp, chilly weather bites into my senses. I hear the echo of my shuffling feet. I am weak, close to fainting and still bleeding. The morning light lours. It is close to 5am as Chris guides me through into Emergency. I see only two ambulance-drivers, deep in conversation, smoking, drinking coffee out of brown plastic cups and then, waiting by the reception desk, I spy Richard, still in his overcoat. The expression on my specialist's face prepares me for what is to come. With the help of my friend, who then discreetly disappears, he leads me through to a scrubbed, sulphurous-smelling cubicle, slips off his coat and switches on a monitor while I am disrobing myself of whatever ill-assorted clothes I have managed to cover myself in. Once I am horizontal on the trolley-bed, he begins to trace the

ultrasonic scanner across my stomach. I shiver as it contacts my skin, recalling that curiously smooth, ice-cream
cold sensation. The last time one of these instruments
touched my flesh and X-rayed the inner contours of my
body, reading me as nothing else has ever read me, it
reported life within. That was barely two weeks ago. The
gynaecologist at my side now is the same man who performed that earlier sketching of the inner me. On that
occasion he was pointing out the silhouette of the tiny girl
growing inside me. 'See here?' Richard had said then.
'Those white lines are the arms, and there is the head. And
here, see, it's a girl.'

This morning, it is a different scenario. He does not turn
his clean-cut face towards me but frowns, concentrating hard
on the screen, which I cannot see. 'There's nothing there,' he
says eventually.

Stupidly, and because I choose to, I take his words to
mean that the machine is not functioning, or that there is no
problem, until he turns his grave blue eyes upon me. 'There's
no heartbeat, Carol, no life left. Nothing to save.'

I screw up my face and close my lids so tight I see lemony
shapes dancing in the blackness of my mind. I feel dampness
burning the contours of my eyes and my throat is constrict-
ing as though swelling from within. I want to beg him to
look again. 'Nothing at all?' I plead.

'I'm sorry. You have miscarried.'

I cannot utter another sound. Seventeen weeks of joy, of
anticipation, ejected. *Why?*

'Stress, overwork or nature's natural selection process.'
He does not seem to know. 'A great many more women than
you would think suffer similar losses. I doubt there was anything you could have done to save it,' he tells me. Kind
though his words are, they do nothing to alleviate the pain of
the loss.

'I'm going to ask a nurse to get you ready. I'm taking you up to the operating theatre to clean you out. I want to make sure there's no residue to become infected. And then, Carol, you will need to rest.'

'I'm filming tomorrow,' I mutter defiantly, angrily.

'No, you won't be strong enough for that. They will need to change the schedule.'

He rises, places a hand against my shoulder. 'Try not to worry or upset yourself now. I'll call the anaesthetist. Would you like to see your companion before we sedate you?'

I nod.

I wake into a world in which my head is throbbing in a thick and muzzy way, where the base of my spine is as rigid as an iron rod and my innards feel raw, as though my interior flesh and organs have been scraped with a paint-scraper. I moan involuntarily, blinking out the glaring light of consciousness, toss my head from side to side to rid myself of the pain and then close my eyes again, sinking back into the secure cave of darkness, drawn back down into a deep, drugged sleep.

I open heavy eyes. Figures are leaning over me; white masked faces leaning over me. Slender, chirpy young women and men in midsummer leaf-green uniforms. I think I hear white leather clogs echoing along corridors. I must be on a trolley being wheeled. No, I am static and in a bed. Sheets and covers and pillows are being tucked in around me. People are fussing over me. My head is spinning; my mind is turning corners. And I have a desperate thirst.

'Thirsty.'

'Here, drink this.' A glass of water is pressed against my parched lips. A cold hand slips behind the base of my skull, raising me up. I suck and draw and dribble clumsily, lacking control, and then, head resting once more against the newly plumped pillows, I disappear, plunging yet again down the rabbit warren corridors of my damaged self.

When I eventually regain consciousness, Richard is standing over me. 'Hello, there.' He takes my wrist, feeling for my pulse. 'It all went smoothly,' he says. His smile is kind, and professional.

'Was there . . . ?'

'It's all gone. We've cleaned you up. Nothing to worry about.'

A wave of grief presses hard against me, rolling titanically through my guts. In that split second, I have no desire to live.

'There were no signs of infection. How are you feeling?'

I cannot begin to explain, which is what I reply.

Someone, a woman in white, enters the room and takes my temperature. Richard watches on, lingering at my bedside.

'I want you to rest. You are going to need plenty of rest.'

'What time is it?' I drawl, as if it matters.

He glances at his watch. Half past three.

'In the afternoon or the morning?'

'The afternoon.'

I try to recall how I arrived here and where exactly I am, grappling with images of recent events. 'I'm filming tomorrow. I have to be in Birmingham tonight.'

'That's out of the question. You have lost a fair amount of blood and your system is in shock. I will only agree to discharge you if there is someone at home to take care of you. Otherwise, I really would prefer you to stay here tonight.'

I telephone. Chris returns. He drives me back to the flat. He makes hot tea while I lie on the sofa refusing to climb the stairs to the bedroom. I don't want to be alone up there, don't want to return to that threatening space. Not yet.

'Have you said anything to Michel?' he asks, when he appears with a cup of Earl Grey sweetened with two spoonfuls of the Provençal honey I brought with me from France. I think of the beekeepers back home, life back home, our precious, funny little olive farm, and I smile. A tear threatens. I feel emotional and unsteady but determine not to give in to it.

'Are there any messages?'

He plays the machine. A young man, Peter, from the Birmingham location has left me my call. According to his garbled news, they have lost a day due to bad weather. My new call is on set at 6am the day after tomorrow. This requires me to be in Birmingham late tomorrow afternoon. Their loss has gained me one day for myself.

'You'll have to tell them,' Chris says. His tone is unintentionally nagging, almost bullying. It is his manner, I have found, when he is faced with unfamiliar problems and he is concerned. Here he is, my pal and a gay man, attempting to cope with a situation which is well outside the realm of his own experience. 'When did you last talk to him?'

'Who?' I close my eyes, brushing a hand across my forehead, trying to recall. Time and the whole sequence of events are in a warp.

Yesterday – or was it the day before? – I was in Birmingham, standing alongside a fellow actor, my co-lead, posing for a photographer who was on set to shoot location stills for the BBC publicity department.

'Big smile, Carol. That's it. And, Den, eyes this way, please. That's it, and again. Great! Thanks, guys.' And I was beaming, laughing in a carefree way, savouring the knowledge that there were three of us in the photographs, not two, and no one knew it but me. Considering the health risks, I was tempted to ask Den to put out his cigarette, but I decided to remain silent. He would have been amenable but I preferred not to give the game away. Den is one of a breed

of working-class theatre actors who has found success in
television; he is short, stocky, intense and talented but ego-
driven and a heavy drinker. One of the lads, and not an
obvious confidant for me. Still, he is a father and a warmhearted guy, and I may need to confide in him now. Was it
really only yesterday evening that I arrived back in London?

'Carol, are you listening to me?' Chris insists. 'Have you
spoken to Michel?'

Did Michel and I talk before I went to sleep yesterday?
Was it yesterday? Yes, I think we did.

'I shan't call him now,' I answer. Chris brings over the telephone and, instead, I dial Birmingham, asking to speak to
Laurence, the first assistant. He is responsible for drawing up
the schedules; he keeps the show on course and is the right
hand of the director during the weeks of principal photography. Denise, the production assistant, informs me that he
is not at the base right now but is travelling somewhere
between the location and the studios. She promises to have
him ring me back. I thank her and emphasise the fact that it
is rather urgent. Laurence returns my call almost before I
have replaced the phone.

'Carol? Laurence here. Is there a problem?' I can hear the
tension in his voice. The logistics, the smooth running of
the shoot, rest on his shoulders. In the background his radio
mike is crackling, transmitting the cries and orders from the
shooting base.

'Cut!' 'Check the gate!'

'I've been taken ill.'

'*What?*'

'I mean I can film, if I have to, but I was wondering if
there is any chance that . . .'

Chris heads back into the room from the kitchen, teatowel
over his shoulder, waving wildly at me, signalling that I must
not offer to go.

'Carol, there's no way I can change the schedule. Not unless it's a case of life and death. We're already over a day behind and the forecast for the rest of the week is rain, rain and more bloody rain.'

'*Hair in the gate!*'

'Oh, shit, I don't believe it! Hang on, Carol.' I hear him fiddling with the radio. 'Tim, Tim, can you hear me? What's going on over there with the stock? That's the third fucking hair in the gate this afternoon! Tim, Tim, can you . . . Carol, I'm going to have to call you back. Stay where you are, OK?'

'Laurence, I'd like to speak to Paddy. Please could you ask him to call me when he has a break?'

'He's . . . Yeah, OK, I'll give him your message. I have to go. Tim, *Tim?*' And the line goes dead.

Chris is hovering at my side. I don't look up. 'I've asked the director, Paddy, to call me, but it does sound rather tense up there, and I feel sure that I'll have to go,' I explain. 'I won't need to leave till lunchtime tomorrow, so . . . I'll be fine by then.'

'No!' he all but yells at me.

'Please, don't shout.'

'Well, tell them the truth! It's only a telly film, Carol. They can change the shooting schedule if they have to.' But he doesn't believe his own words. An actor himself, he knows that when the cameras roll, for those involved during those few intense weeks the film takes on a paramountcy, an aggrandised significance, that outstrips life or, in this case, death.

When Paddy returns my call, which, surprisingly, he does rapidly, he sounds frazzled and as though the very last thing he needs is a problem with the leading actress. 'What is it, darling?' he demands wearily.

'I've . . . lost . . . a baby, Paddy.' I am met with silence, and so I hurry on. 'I had a miscarriage in the early hours of this morning and . . . and I was wondering if . . .'

I hear him drag on his cigarette, the deep tiredness in the exhalation of his breath and the unspoken accusation: why didn't you tell me when I cast you that you were pregnant?

'All right, I'll speak to Laurence. But the weather forecast is lousy. We'll have to shoot interiors for the rest of the week, and that means you, I'm afraid, darling. In any case John, who's arriving tomorrow, is only contracted to us for the second half of this week. He has another shoot to go on to and I've got to release him on time. It was always going to be tight fitting in his dates, and now, with this bloody weather and the damaged film stock . . . I'll ask Laurence. I am sure that he will say the same, but we'll see what we can do. He'll call you later.' And again the line goes dead. By now I am regretting that I ever mentioned anything.

Chris persuades me to sleep, and it is while I am sleeping that the message comes through: I must return to work. The alternative seems to be that the shoot stops and it – me – becomes an insurance claim. I persuade both Chris and myself that I am fine, that by tomorrow I will have rested and will be raring to go. Now my friend tries to talk me into telephoning Richard, which I adamantly refuse to do.

'And you still haven't spoken to Michel. He has to know, Carol.'

This does it, this breaks me. It takes me out of the realm of the functional, dealing with my professional life, into the fragile, more vulnerable world of what has been taken away, what is no longer the future, our future, and the fact that Michel does not know yet. He is going about his Australian day – possibly getting out of bed as I think these thoughts, which makes it the ideal moment to speak to him – cherishing the knowledge that he is soon going to be father to his third daughter, and our first child. Outside, in the grimy city,

evening is beginning to fall. I hear the horns of frayed drivers attempting to motor home, to make it beyond the grill
and fumes, the roars and disappointments of the city. And I
am suddenly exhausted. How I long to return to
Appassionata, to hide myself away, to lick my wounds, lose
myself in that landscape, shelter beneath olive trees. I assure
my friend that he has done everything and more and that
now I shall sleep.

'I can kip down here on the sofa if you like,' he offers.

I shake my head and stand up to see him out. The room
spins but I manage to keep steady as I wrap my arms around
him. 'You're a real pal,' I whisper. 'Thank you.'

'Call Michel,' he states. I nod into his woollen-sweatered
shoulder. 'And if you need me, you know where I am. I wish
you wouldn't go . . .'

'Sssh,' I say. 'Thank you for being here.' And he leaves me
with a tender kiss on my forehead.

Before falling into bed I telephone Michel. His frame of
mind is upbeat and energetic; things are going very well. He
has negotiated a couple of very good sales, and one of the
networks has watched the promo reel he sent on ahead of
the animation film he has been working on with Serge and
they have expressed a commitment as co-production partners. 'They love it,' he says. 'I've been running to and fro
from their studios over on the north shore to their bank in
the city and back to Elizabeth Bay. The weather is wonderful. A real balmy Sydney morning. Hard to believe it's
early winter here. The only thing missing is you.' I listen to
his positive mood and decide against mentioning anything
of what has happened. There is nothing he can do. The
knowledge will only cause him pain; he will begin to worry
about me instead of paying attention to his work and,
though I hate to deceive him, I cannot bear to trouble or
frustrate him. We say 'Goodnight,' and 'Have a great day,'

and I set the alarm so that I will be up in time to pack my travelling bag.

When I arrive in Birmingham it is evening; a howling wet evening. The chill wind burns blisteringly sharp against my skin as I hurry from taxi to hotel, where a teenage receptionist hands me my key.

'Is there a call sheet waiting?' I ask her.

She checks the message-box and shakes her head.

'Do you know if they've wrapped?'

'Wrapped?' she repeats, having not comprehended the question.

'Are the others back from the set yet?'

'I haven't seen anyone.'

'Has Mr Dunmore checked in yet?'

She fingers through a guest list and confirms that there is a reservation for a Mr Dunmore but that, as far as she knows, he has not checked in and that, in any case, he is not due in today.

Puzzled, I nod my thanks and take the lift to my room, where I set down my luggage, draw the curtains to darkness and curl up on the spacious bed. When I wake it is after nine. I rise and go to the door feeling certain that the third assistant will have slipped my call sheet under it. There is nothing. Concerned, I call reception. No call sheet has been left for me. Laurence is not staying at this hotel so I ring his mobile. He is in the production office somewhere across town. They wrapped late and he is still working.

'I haven't received my call yet for the morning,' I tell him.

'Oh, hi, Carol. There's no call sheet for you because you're not working tomorrow. We've had a hell of day and lost another four hours. We've been landed with faulty stock. I don't know how many duff gates we've had since yesterday. Paddy is blowing his top.'

'Am I on standby, or . . .'

'No, you're free. We definitely won't get to you.'

'May I go back to London?'

'No, I'd rather you stayed. The schedule's all up in the air. You just never know.'

But John's not here, I am thinking, and the greater proportion of my remaining scenes are with him. Still, I decide not to argue the point.

And so the following day I rest in my room. And the next day, and the day after that. It is now the end of the week and I haven't seen a soul in days. If I had returned to London, even to Appassionata, no one would have noticed. Time drags and there is nothing to do but go back over my script time and time again, take the lift to reception, poke my head into the bar and scan the dimly lit interior for other bored actors, or walk the drizzling streets of Birmingham. I promise myself matinée visits to the local cinema to cheer myself up but find myself sleeping the afternoons away, waking after harrowing dreams. I grow depressed. Very depressed. My mood is bleak and empty and my life feels directionless, pointless even. I call Richard, who says that mood swings are to be expected; they are nothing to be concerned about. Even so, he insists that I make an appointment to see him before I fly back to France and I agree to call him when I return to London. I still haven't broken the news to Michel and now I feel unable to do so. I decide that it must wait until we are together again. But the withholding is weighing heavily on me, exacerbating my negative frame of mind.

Finally, I am called to the set, where I learn that during my absence there appears to have been a 'minor' change of the artistic interpretation of the nature of my role.

The character I am playing is an adulteress. She is a glamorous and enigmatic figure as well as being a capricious wife who is betraying her husband (played by Den) with one of their neighbours. This morning we are scheduled to shoot the love scene between the neighbour (played by John) and myself in the 'kitchen set, John's house'. I doubt that any woman who has recently miscarried a much-longed for baby feels good about herself or her body – there are many insecurities, both physical and psychological – and I have not even begun to address these issues rising within me. To act out the motions of lovemaking in front of a camera not five feet away at a moment when you are as vulnerable as this calls for technique, skills, tricks. Actors are schooled at revealing their secret hearts, albeit wrapped in the flimsy mask of character, but there are times when you ask yourself whether you are capable of getting out there and performing.

This morning I need to create the illusion of wellbeing, or as the French so succinctly describe it, *être bien dans la peau*, and an actor's trick I frequently use when a situation requires it is to pick a song and sing or hum it to myself over and over, to try to call up a particular frame of mind, a mood, to replicate an emotional state. So here I am, alone in my dressing room, staring blindly at my well-thumbed script, bottling up a swell of negative emotions, humming 'These Foolish Things', attempting to recreate from memory Oscar Peterson's mellow rendition of this melody. It is a tune that never fails to make me feel feminine, sentimental and in the mood for love or, at least, a little cheek-to-cheek affection. Alas, not this morning. This morning my libido has gone underground.

A knock on the door is followed instantly by the bustling entrance of Tina, my dresser, with an armful of costumes: freshly washed tights and a black nylon negligée and matching housecoat, complete with bows and frills, pressed and ready on coathangers. 'The black nightwear is not mine,' I say casually to this young girl, whose job it is to look after me and see to my costumes and requirements.

'Yes it is,' Tina states emphatically. Confused, I request a brief word with the costume designer.

It appears a new twist has been thought up during my days away. So explains the designer to me when she appears in my dressing room.

'Which is?'

'Are neighbour and wife really at it? Or does the affair exist only in the distorted mind of the husband?' Much of the plot hangs around this question, it now seems, and, in order to underline the torment of the character of the leading actor (Den), the director has decided that he wants to overplay the love scene between myself and the neighbour to 'draw out the eroticism, not to say bestiality', to play up the torturous pictures in the head of the husband. 'Paddy came up with the idea a couple of days ago, didn't he mention it?'

Speechless, I shake my head.

'This black number's a bit in-your-face, I know, darling. Not quite the character we've been drawing with the other outfits, but you mustn't be concerned. It *is* sexy, in its way. You'll look fabulous in it. I've been watching the rushes; you're glowing. You're pregnant, aren't you?'

My heart feels as though it has just been knifed.

'Is that why your husband turned up with those roses? I've been telling everyone. How romantic can you get? No one's ever done such a thing for me.'

I am choking back the tears which threaten to send rivulets of black mascara streaming down my face.

'Don't be upset about the cozzie. You look a bit tired, darling, are you OK? It's all that hanging about in that bloody awful hotel. What a dump that place is. Have you eaten there? Don't, and don't worry. Sue in make-up'll soon put you right. Do you want me to fetch Paddy?'

I consider this, and then before I can give a decision, or

even gather words from out of my choked emotions, there is another knock on my dressing-room door.

'Who is it?' It's the designer asking. She can clearly see that I am utterly devastated, and though amazed that a costume should reduce anyone to such misery, she decides to speak up for me.

'It's John.'

The actor playing my supposed lover, the neighbour in the piece, is a pal, though we haven't seen one another for donkey's years. We were at drama school together, along with Chris, and then, eighteen months or so later, we were both offered a year's contract at the same provincial repertory theatre. Far from London, in a distant unknown northern city, we shared a flat together. It was a rambling, Victorian space which neither of us could afford, but we had great fun together. So, although we have not actually set eyes on one another for the best part of fifteen years, there is a bond between us that goes back to those special days of studentship and actor internship when we were soft at the edges, when one is so open to new friendships, when life promises dreams for the taking, and we were intent on stardom.

'Come in,' I manage.

The door opens and in walks a successful, well-fleshed-out forty-something man, equally handsome, equally prepossessing, with those honey-warm eyes, but long ago gone is that shy, soft-voiced juvenile with his floppy scarves, shoulder-length hair and well-worn sneakers. We fall into one another's arms, hugging tightly, shouting exuberantly. As actors do.

The designer exits discreetly, saying she'll catch up with me before we shoot.

'Has he told you what he wants?' John asks when we finally disengage. I shrug, dreading what's to come. 'He wants, and I quote, "raw lust, bestiality, darling".' John begins to giggle.

I try not to expose the insecurities welling within me. I know that I am not called upon to actually desire John, which I don't, nor have I ever, though I adore him and find him gorgeous, but it would spice up and authenticate the scene we are about to be expected to perform in front of the camera if I felt good about myself and capable of exuding a little passion.

John laughs at my downturned face.

I try to disguise the troubles flipping through my mind. 'He's chosen a costume. I wasn't even here . . .'

'Hey,' says John, wrapping a firm arm about my shoulder. 'I've never known something as trivial as a cozzie get you down. If it's "raw lust" he wants, honey, you and I can provide it. You're not to fret.' And with that he brushes a light kiss against my hair and disappears from my dressing room, leaving me alone in a very empty and unexpectedly alien environment.

When the third assistant's knock on the door comes, panic rises. I fear that I cannot step outside the hidden harbour of that space, let alone reveal this outfit before approximately forty predominantly male crew members. Beneath a floor-length dressing gown of my own is the horrendous and deeply unflattering negligée. But the job demands it. I take a deep, deep breath, and out I go.

Once on the set, there is a tense wait while some technical problem is addressed. Sue, my make-up artist, is tinkering with my hair and chattering away while I stew silently, desperate to fall upon a solution which will not cause a fuss. I catch sight of Paddy pacing up and down, glowering at his watch and casting malevolent glances in the general direction of the electrics lads, who appear to be responsible for whatever has caused this latest delay. Alone on a chair, in an unlit corner, behind our fulminating director, sits John, browsing through a newspaper.

In an instant I decide to take the bull by the horns. I leave my seat and hurry across to him. Blurting out to him the bare bones, a potted version of my history over these last few days, I plead for his support and then, to emphasise my case, I untie my dressing gown and reveal the deeply vulgar outfit. John lifts both hands to his face to mask a grimace of the-atrical horror.

'Leave it to me,' he whispers conspiratorially.

The upshot is that I am led away to shed the scantily clad look and change into a frock and high heels. The scene is then rehearsed in a closed set. With the lights and cameras ready to shoot, the enactment of our illicit passion for one another is played out on the kitchen table. I hate every second of it. Limbs entangled, we huff and puff like creatures in the zoo as we are obliged to exaggerate our carnal cries and heavy breathing. Still, only a moderate amount of flesh is exposed, far less than had been threatened, and John gallantly shields my vulnerability. After the scene has been completed from all of its various angles we are both wrapped, given the all-clear, and we leave the location together to be driven back to the hotel, where we order a bottle of good wine and settle down to catch up on long-lost friends and gossip. I can relax now, knowing that I have few scenes left to shoot and the worst is over.

Back in London, two things are uppermost in my mind: my appointment with Richard and then, once I have been assured that all is well, my safe and speedy return to Appassionata to await the homecoming of Michel and the breaking of news I have postponed too long. Richard agrees to see me at his clinic in Harley Street on the day I telephone. The examination is brief and straightforward.

Afterwards, he leads me through to his capacious consulting room.

'Well, the good news is that no infection has set in and you are healing nicely.' He smiles, pausing to rest his hands on his desk; he glances at my file in front of him though I can see that he is not reading it but merely fiddling with it and shifting it a centimetre or two. His manner alarms me.

'What caused the miscarriage?' I ask 'Was it the amniocentesis?'

He shakes his head. 'No, I am quite certain that the amniocentesis was not responsible, or you would have aborted sooner. A foetal cardiac arrest is my belief. There are signs of intraventricular haemorrhage.' He pauses again. A frown creases his forehead and I can see that he is weighing his words with care.

'Is there something else?'

'As I said, you are healing, but . . .'

This hangs in the air between us as he slowly shifts his gaze from the table to fix it on me.

'But?' I inhale, mouth dry, heart beating fast.

'I suspect another pregnancy might be out of the question.'

'We will wait,' I butt in. 'I know that Michel . . .'

His eyes, those blue-grey eyes set in a handsome, youthful, public-school face, remain concentrated on me. 'It's not a question of waiting. Yes, I would have advised a physical rest of, say, three to six months, but the case is slightly different here. You have a history of miscarrying. Still, until now, I have always held firmly to the belief that with rest and no pressure you would be able to carry a child through its term. I fear that may no longer be the situation. My belief is that it is not possible for you to carry a child the full term. You can conceive, that is not the difficulty, but any conceived foetus will sooner or later abort itself.'

I am stunned. The blow all but paralyses me, arresting my breath as though my life were hanging in the balance. In one clean swoop, dreams have been demolished. My head flops backwards and I exhale slowly, as though expelling from my mind, body, respiratory system the seed of such a prognosis. Eyes staring ceilingwards, determined against tears, against the rising hot anger, I resolutely examine the white cornicework, the central rose, and then I try to speak. I want to ask him if there is anything to be done, but my voice breaks mid-sentence; I bite back the swelling emotion, unable to continue. I am staring at a pair of clasped hands, mine, resting in my lap. A tear falls and wets my finger.

'Before you leave – when are you going? – before you do, I'd like you to see two of my colleagues . . . Or you might want to consider adoption?' He waits, and then, 'I could put you in touch with a therapist who . . .'

I shake my head.

'Well, I'll organise the two appointments, and let's wait to hear their diagnoses. Who knows, my colleagues may disagree. There is always the possibility that I am wrong.'

The Silence of the Sea

Throughout my life, whenever I have been in pain or have felt lost or confused, I have set myself on course for the sea. The sea heals me; its rhythms calm me; its boundless horizons revitalise and free me, easing out those cages I feel closing in around me. Today is no exception. The sea is the healing source I crave now. And tireless physical work. I want to bury myself and my misery in furious activity. No resting, no grieving, no taking stock.

For this I need to be back at the farm. I need the uncomplicated happiness of playing with the dogs, of preparing the house for the invasion of summer guests and the return of my husband, whose intense kindness I can no longer do without. And when I am worn out from work, I want to idle away time on the terraces and stare out at the distant skyline. At the end of each complete and fading day, I want to slip in a CD and drown myself in the blues, drink gallons of wine, take refuge in that Provençal light, those rays of bruised and coppery colours falling across the limpid stillness of the Mediterranean, until it is time to creep indoors and light the candles. And when the night draws in, I want to fall into bed exhausted and curl up like a damaged squirrel, ready to wake early with a list as long as my arm of tasks to be achieved.

Equally, I long to walk the beaches listening to the waves, to sit on the sand, breathe deeply and inhale the intense perfumes of pines and eucalyptus gums, to feed greedily off nature's munificence and, in isolation, unfold the disappointment and the sense of failure raging in my heart.

But I cannot face the airports, the queues, the nightmares of security and luggage, the gaggles of travellers and tourists I am bound to encounter during these early days of the height of the summer season. Even the journey from city to airport threatens to overwhelm me and my jumbled self, which gibbers and trembles as though shot.

My delayed response to my specialist's news is a defensive one, and not entirely logical. It leads me to embark on a series of decisions which threaten my safety because my reason is blinded by pain and is running haywire.

There are six more days until Michel is scheduled to arrive home from Sydney, which means that I have the time to choose *not* to fly, and so I decide to buy a car. The possibility of taking a train simply does not cross my mind. I will buy a car in London and drive it home, travelling south through France, moving at my own speed towards the land of olive groves and Judas trees, keeping pace with my thoughts and my solitude.

We have talked of buying another car since the Quatrelle drowned, I argue to myself. This is a fact, but the replacement vehicle of my choice is not the solution. I shell out every penny I have just earned, and a chunk more, on a second-hand Mercedes sports car. Into the boot I pile my chaotically packed bags and off I head for the ferry. I have not telephoned for a reservation; I barely know the registration number of my new acquisition; I have informed no one of my whereabouts or what I am embarking upon except my mother who, the moment she claps eyes on me when I make a stop at her home, en route for Dover, understands that I have lost the baby. She begs me not to act irrationally, to stay a while and rest or take the plane, but I won't hear of it. I must be on the move, must leave now, hell-bent on a course of my own fashioning: to begin again, pick myself up, dust myself down, be where I believe I am needed and where I have created a world; a world in which life and growth thrive. No self-pity. I must get on with the business of living.

She waves me off with that concerned expression of hers, which I know so well but barely register today.

I cross the Channel without difficulty, striding the ship's blustery deck relentlessly, back and forth like a soul lost in the swell, heaving in great gulps of salted wind, relishing the strength of its whip against my flushed face.

A certain calm descends when we draw in sight of the coast of France, but it does not last, does not stay my manic resolve. The ship drops anchor into a drizzling late morning, and I am on my way, choosing not to pause for lunch or refreshment of any sort. A full tank of *essence* and I hit the road again at rally-driving speed.

By the middle of the afternoon, having shot through the Champagne region with barely a glimpse at my surroundings, I become aware of an intermittent fluctuation in the car's performance. The rev-counter begins to flutter like a nervous butterfly. Peugeots, Renaults, Range Rovers, Porsches and other fast-moving machines gaining ground behind me begin to flash their lights, warning me to get over and out of their flight path. I have no knowledge of mechanics, and what this loss of speed or power means is unclear to me, but I swing to the right and out of the fast lane. I hear a clattering as though some vital part of the whole is trailing me. I mentally close my eyes, determined to believe that nothing is amiss and that this car is bloody well going to get me home in one piece. More or less as soon as I have completed this thought – slap-bang in the middle of the merciless jungle of a French motorway – my new acquisition grinds to a standstill. The engine is still turning, but the accelerator does not respond to the pressure of my foot and the erstwhile fluttering instru-ment has settled at zero. Now what?

Blind to the risks involved, I fling open the car door and step out, waving for help. Juggernauts are thundering by and horns begin to blast all around me, like rapid rounds of gunshots. The drivers, through open windows, are shouting at me in various European languages, threatening me with clenched fists as though I were doing this on purpose, or cursing me with degrees of blasphemy which amount to 'get off the fucking road', while I, stunned, am swept to and fro, weaving my way in and out of cars, until I eventually stagger back towards my stationary vehicle. I continue flailing my arms in the vain hope that one of these truckers will under-stand, stop and take pity. I have no mobile phone so I have no means, without assistance, of contacting anyone. After several dozen monsters have roared angrily by, one slows, his wheels or brakes emitting high-pitched squeals, and draws to a halt a hundred metres or so ahead.

The driver, a barrel of a man with blond, crewcut hair, clambers from the cab of his pantechnicon, waves and advances towards me. His gait is stiff, paddling, creating the impression that his joints are held together with screws. He is wearing a billowing scarlet T-shirt, khaki shorts, has hairy, muscular legs, solid boots and elongated cotton-wool pods sticking out of each ear. It is a means of protecting his hearing, no doubt, from the vehicle's constant rattling and the boom and roar of the motorways, but this, added to his overall appearance, inspires me to believe that I am about to be saved by a cuddly toy from outer space.

He is Belgian. He does not speak French, he explains – he must be one of the only remaining Belgians on God's earth who exclusively speaks Flemish and it's just my luck to fall upon him – but he manages to make himself understood with a spattering of English and jolly-sounding German.

After several exchanges achieved predominantly through hand signals, minutes spent staring beneath the bonnet of my wretched car, head-shakings, tuts and grave sighs, he offers to drive me to the next SOS telephone, which is a half a kilometre or so further along, or that is the gist of what I understand from the statement, 'Hare nix gut. Must you SOS calling frome ze point. Nix longe. Dry hoondred metres.'

While I, in the middle of this scorchingly hot, noisy and traffic-clogged afternoon, want to scream – not at him; he's a sweetheart – or just walk away, yes, that's it, walk off the road into the adjacent brushland, the wilderness, curl up beneath a leaf and disappear. Lose myself in the landscape, leaving everything behind me, particularly this useless sports car.

But this vat of a Belgian is a kindhearted soul who ruffles my hair and tells me not to cry, 'Not zo krying, pliss.' Then hands me his mobile phone 'Vife, you, telefon, want you?' he asks.

I shake my head, uncertain what he is offering. He shoves the phone at me again, more forcefully this time. 'Vife, Herr, Madame und Monsieur, wanting you, telefon?'

Eventually, I understand that he is lending me his mobile to call my husband.

'Thank you, but no.'

'*Pourquoi?*'

'Sydney.' He doesn't understand. 'He's in Sydney. Australia,' I reply with emphasis.

He nods uncertainly but quickly withdraws the phone.

I haul myself aboard his impossibly difficult-to-get-into cab while he rips off a length of ham baguette sandwich and offers it to me. I refuse, he shrugs and we rattle up the road to the SOS point, where he deposits me. He must be 'runnig', on his way, he explains, while writing on a sheet an excuse for his stop. 'Ist verboten de liffts,' or to help anyone out at all, it seems. Still, I am mightily grateful to him for his monumental kindness. He ruffles my hair once more, and I muster a smile for him as he waves like an old friend, calling, 'Bye bye Frau Sydney!', and zooms away in his articulated machine.

At the yellow distress box, I am informed, when I get through, that the wait will be an hour and I am firmly instructed to remain by the car. I decide that I have time to visit the next service station, which I see just a short walk ahead of me.

There, I buy a much-needed coffee, hand over 100 francs for the highest-unit phonecard on offer and put through a call to Michel in Australia. He is sleeping but instantly picks up the anguish in my voice.

'Carol? *Chérie*, what is it? What's happened?'

'We may be cut off. I'm on the motorway going back to the farm; my car has broken down.'

'Car? Which car?'

The sound of Michel's voice over such an immense distance and his concern flood my emotions and I am unable to contain my feelings. The tears pour helplessly out of me. Crouched on the floor in the cabin of the callbox, I am hiccuping and blubbering misery.

'Carol, Carol what is it? What's happened?'

'I lost her. I lost our little girl.'

There is a pause, a parenthesis, a heartstopping silence. Twelve thousand kilometres away, in another hemisphere, another time zone, my husband is taking this in.

'I'm sorry, Michel.'

'*Chérie*, where are you? Are you all right? Well, no, obviously you're not. What are you doing on a motorway? Where . . . ?'

And so I pour out my tale, or incomplete, disjointed parts of it, of the loss of our child. 'We're going to be cut off.'

'Leave the car, get to Paris. I'm coming back. Wait for me in Paris.'

'I didn't go through Paris. I'm somewhere near Beaune, I'm not sure where exactly.'

'Leave the car, then, wherever you can. Does the insurance include a relay? No, don't think about it; I'll deal with it when I get there. Go home. Promise me, you'll go home.'

I promise with a silent nod, but the line has gone dead.

Our home is our shelter from the world. Not only because it sits alone on its hill, set back from the lane and is protected by dozens of venerable, arcane olive trees and modest acres of terraced land. It is a place where Michel and I can be together, where the interface that exists between us can continue to evolve and take on its own shapes, where we can continue to create *us* and ourselves as individuals and where we can heal ourselves, lick our wounds and each other's, from the blows, the calamities and the uncertainties of life. A house is so much more than a house. It is a great deal more than its physical representation. Or it is to me, at least. For this home, this farm, is a place of healing for me in another sense, too. Perhaps in a way that it is does not need to be for Michel.

Certain eminent psychoanalysts claim that we spend our

adult lives attempting to heal the traumas of our childhood. I had never taken that idea fully on board until we moved here. For more than a decade I trawled the coasts of the world, alone, looking for 'my house by the sea', but it was not until I met Michel, until we found our abandoned olive farm, Appassionata, and set about the arduous and satisfying task of singing the place back into existence, of giving it back its elegance and its vibrancy after years of neglect, that I began to understand what I had been searching for and what I am now doing.

I am trying to heal the scars of domestic violence. To release the weight of that entrapment. To redraw the canvas, to paint over with rich, sensuous colours a childhood that was tormented by fear and burdened by guilt. To create beauty where before there was sorrow. The colours that dominate my memories are the red of my mother's painted fingernails and lips, and red again for spilled blood, the result of brutalities, the black nights in my bedroom as I lay awake listening to the hammer-and-tong exchanges in the living room beneath me, and black again for the cavern of despair that engulfed me. My father was a hot-tempered passionate man; a musician of average talent but a superb bandleader, a toastmaster (in red frock coat), a master of ceremonies with a magnetic sense of humour; charming, handsome and an incorrigible Lothario.

Once my mother, who had the lips, curves and cleavage of a Gina Lollobrigida, had given birth to my sister, she and my father grew estranged in the bedroom. Twenty-six years old at the time, she shut down that expression of herself. She believed that she had good reason for her distance – perhaps she had – but whatever it was that happened between them gave him every excuse for his endless stream of infidelities and he began to stay away from home more and more frequently.

My mother is a staunch Irish Catholic, a principled woman with an indomitable and courageous spirit, innocent in the ways of the world yet well able to gauge the worth of the material universe as well as its appraisals of her. Whatever the circumstances, she believed that it was her moral duty and her right to cling to her marriage, to hold it together and, on occasion, I believe, she has mistaken prudishness and punishment for discipline and values.

Both of these people are heedful spirits and they certainly did not set out to traumatise anyone. In fact, at my father's deathbed, as he lay unconscious, slipping away from us, it was heartbreakingly clear how deeply and loyally my mother loved him, but they had spent their lives grappling with a post-war marriage governed by Catholic values which my father did not adhere to and my mother insisted upon, and they never found the common ground where those differences could be resolved. In spite of the emotional bond, the physical differences between them left no space for their individual personalities to come together and their frustrations grew dark and angry and eventually found their outlet in violence.

I was conceived in the early days, the heyday of their relationship, the courtship days soon after the wedding. I sometimes fancy that those months were my mother at her truest, a time in her life when she let herself go and gave flight to her passionate and beautiful self. She was in love, after all.

Although I was not the trigger for their marriage, I became the habitual object of their frustrations, the reason for their imprisonment. In short, I was blamed. Children in unfulfilled marriages frequently find themselves shoved into the role of hostage. My situation was perhaps more distressing: I was cast in the role of jailer. 'If it wasn't for you, we wouldn't be in this mess, this marriage.' These words were hurled out thoughtlessly at all too regular intervals; they turned my blood cold and stripped my ribboned heart to shreds.

The world looked at and lived through my disturbed eyes was an angry, violent place where folk who lived together expressed themselves through physical and emotional brutality; where furniture was slung from room's end to room's end; where tables bearing hot food crashed to the ground like shot beasts spewing clots of baked beans, soggy toast, smashed plates; where I pressed my ear against closed doors and eavesdropped on the tinkly sound of my mother's solitary weeping, hovering, not knocking, impotent to offer succour. In fact, not only was I unable to help, as I understood it I was the cause of the tears. Where friendships made at school disintegrated in an instant when the new attachment was, eventually, like all the rest, forbidden to come to my home because I and my background were judged a 'bad influence'. In among all this there were moments of tenderness for, as I say, my parents were not cruel people, merely trapped in a marriage from which they felt unable to free themselves, or perhaps, deep down, did not want to walk away from.

My newly acquired possession is towed away to the nearest Mercedes garage, who agree to organise its relay to Cannes where, they assure me, the vehicle's British guarantee will be sorted out. I learn from my insurers that I am entitled to a hire car, but I decline it. At this moment in time, I am safer off the roads. They offer me a first-class rail ticket instead. I spend the night in a very indifferent hotel and then, with my ill-assorted bags, cases and confusions, take a late-morning express to Cannes. The TGV I am travelling on is not equipped with bar or restaurant. This is most surprising for a nation of meal-lovers, but my fellow passengers seem to be au fait with the oversight and have come prepared. As *midi* approaches – the hour for lunch – everyone in the carriage, bar me, begins unloading their lunchboxes, well-provisioned with sandwiches, *charcuterie*, a little *fromage*, coffee, mineral water, dried fruits, fresh grapes, oranges and Mentos mints. They lay out their generous portions of refreshment on their laps or on portable picnic tables, accompanying it with plastic glasses brimming with red wine.

Opposite me sits a huge woman with a Felliniesque bosom, kitted out in matching red cardigan and skirt and chunks of gold and ruby jewellery. Her feet planted firmly on the ground, skirt riding up to her thighs, legs wide apart, she has been nibbling since I boarded while at the same time amusing herself with a crossword magazine. Mouthing possible solutions to her puzzle, she is now chewing bovinely on a baguette sandwich of lettuce, tomato, ham and cheese.

Everyone is content with this lovely sunny day, a little light nourishment to keep inordinate hunger at bay and the impressive countryside flying past the window, when two new travellers arrive and a rumpus begins.

It appears to be a question of seat numbers.

It seems that we have all been allocated seats 21 and 23 in carriage 13. It was of no matter as far back as Chalon-sur-Saône. We all took a seat, any seat, and settled down. But now a heavily made-up Arab woman has climbed aboard at some inconsequential station with seven massive suitcases and a child and insists that two seats in our compartment, only one of which remains unoccupied, are hers. Much heated shouting breaks out and the matter threatens to grow disagreeable.

'I've been sitting here since Nancy and I'm not budging!' booms the woman who resembles an extra from *Amacord*, in between mouthfuls of food.

Eventually a guard appears on the scene and the entire carriage, to a man, save me, pounces on him, shouting hysterically, demanding facts, explanations and, above all else, apologies for potential damage to their digestive tracts. 'We were *eating*!' they yell.

'Sit where you can,' he announces. 'Carriage 14 has been forgotten; left in Metz.'

'*Eh, voilà!*'

'*Mais oui, on comprend maintenant.*'

The misunderstanding has been explained to the satisfaction of everyone. Unfortunately, the difficulty remains. The bevy of lunching women, and one rather timid husband who is nervously twisting his copy of *Le Monde*, are not willing to vacate their places, while the Arab woman mulishly refuses to seek out another carriage.

Eventually, when everyone is worn out, it is decided to turf the Arab child into the corridor and install her on suitcases, leaving her mother free to claim the remaining seat. Calm is restored and lunch is resumed. I watch the little Arab girl perching sulkily on one of her mother's numerous *valises*. She is hungrily eyeing the delicious offerings of the various passengers who are munching contentedly while gazing blithely out at the passing vineyards.

Nothing disturbs the ensuing peace now except our large companion in the red woolly outfit, who is travelling with a print-out of her itinerary. At each station she reaches for it and announces to us all the length of time the train is scheduled to stand in the station.

'Mâcon! *Deux minutes!*' At one minute forty seconds her stubby fingers with their burgundy-varnished nails and 'rubies as big as hen's eggs' (in Scott Fitzgerald's words), begin tapping the face of her gold watch. She peers at it and tuts crossly. This is followed by loud huffings and the rolling up of her crossword magazine so that it now resembles a short, thick cane. And then the train pulls out and she relaxes back into her lunch.

I believe I am the only one to notice a rather interesting

exchange taking place about now. The Arab child in the corridor signals to her mother from beyond the glass that she wants food and the mother responds, also in discreet mime, that she has none.

We roll along in silence for a short while until suddenly the Arab woman wails loudly and dramatically: '*J'ai mal au cœur!*' 'My heart! I'm sick! A pain in my heart!'

I am perfectly fascinated.

'*Ah, ma pauvre!* I have pills,' cries the fat woman, and instantly begins rummaging in her handbag for her heart pills and her mineral water – not still water but the *gazeuse*, which, she assures us all, is better for the digestion. 'You must have eaten something which disagreed with you,' she continues.

'No, no, my heart feels tight. No, I haven't eaten. Nothing at all. We haven't eaten since—'

'You haven't eaten? *Mon Dieu!*' The words are chorused across the carriage. Folk jump to it. A *demi-baguette* is found, a lump of Brie. The fizzy water is delivered. As are the heart pills.

'Have you a glass?' the heart-of-gold fat lady enquires as she passes over her bottle.

The Arab woman shakes her head faintheartedly. 'Nothing. No time to pack it.'

'Use mine. Yes, you must. I insist. I am eighty years old. If I had any diseases I would know them by now.'

Eighty years old! This, too, is repeated like a Chinese whisper by one passenger to the next. It is true that the woman does not look such an age. The Arab mother keeps up her play-acting admirably, determined not to let the age of the other detract from the business in hand. She is now drinking the water while fanning herself and moaning softly. She resists the pill, but it is forced upon her and so, reluctantly, she swallows it. We have reached Lyon. The timid husband and his axe-faced wife are now leaving the train. But not before the husband has been ordered by his wife to place all seven pieces of the Arab woman's luggage up on the rack and offer his seat to the ragamuffin girl, who takes it without a second's hesitation. As they depart, they leave the remains of their buffet for mother and child, who eat like greedy street urchins.

I return to my private contemplations both amused and surprised that this little scam has worked so successfully.

The last I hear, as they all descend the train together at Marseille, the very best of friends, is our octogenarian remarking: 'I ask you, what is more beautiful for any *maman* than the gift of a little girl?'

A reminder, a stab of a pain, and I switch my gaze to beyond the window, to the silver sadness of the sea.

From the station, a taxi delivers me up into the sun-scorched hills, to Appassionata. When I arrive – cautious of the dogs, the driver deposits me at the gate – I climb the olive-ter-raced drive, pausing every few yards to touch and examine the drupes, which are green and hard but fattening up nicely. The trees glinting in the sunshine are, in the words of Auguste Renoir, who lived his last years on the coast here at Cagnes-sur-Mer, 'shining like diamonds'.

I pause to pick a purpling fig from our elephantine tree and split it open with my thumbnails. A satin-white milk bleeds out of the still unripe fruit and sticks to my fingers. I lick them clean and then lift the fig to my lips and suck out the pale rose, mildly crunchy seeds.

Le figuier. The fig tree. Its botanical origins are uncertain but, most likely, it has been a native Mediterranean plant from prehistoric times, growing wild with fruits which were at first believed to be inedible. It is possible that this may be the thinking behind its role in the Garden of Eden. Unlike the apple, it could not be consumed. It was a useless thing, good for nothing until its leaf was used as the earliest, most primitive form of underwear. Adam and Eve took it to cover their shame, their sex, their knowledge and nakedness. Or, if Titian's painting of Adam and Eve in the Prado in Madrid is to be believed, it was Adam, the man, who understood shame and covered himself. Woman was the sinner.

Puberty arrived early for me. I was ten. Around this time, men who came to the house, usually friends or associates of my father's, began to whisper obscene desires in my ear or touched me in places on my body which left me feeling ashamed of the fullnesses forming there. I grew to perceive myself as a she-devil who induced inexplicable behaviour in heavy-breathing, sour-breathed men. My parents knew nothing of what was happening and I did not have the courage, or faith, to say anything. I believed that, like their marriage, I was to blame for these male manners. I grew withdrawn and secretive. I spent hour after hour locked in the bathroom, washing myself, not clean but out of existence.

I chew on my fig and feast my eyes, inhaling the mid-year quietude. All around is stillness. The farm is at peace in the summer heat, except for the *cigales*, who are buzzing frenetically, living their final weeks to the hilt, making the most of it, searching for a partner while the going is good, for after their frenzied bouts of mating these little critters pass away. There are no signs of activity and then, in a trice, the dogs come bounding from a dozen different directions all at once, charging at me to greet me with welcoming barks and leapings and wildly overenthusiastic felicity. How pleased I am to have their affection. I bend and stroke and kiss them hard.

   M. Halaz, our watering hero, is nowhere to be seen. He

must have finished his chores and trundled off for a siesta. His presence is everywhere, though, in the fabulous firework displays of growth.

Shrubs, flowers, climbers are explosions of breathtaking colour. Geraniums are tumbling eagerly from their terracotta pots in bouquets of scarlet and pink and striped reds and whites, hanging like swathes of uncombed hair over the tiled edge of the pool, where one or two stray blossoms have fallen and are spinning gently in the movement of the water. The bougainvillaea bushes straddling the four lower verandah pillars have shot up in a lusty tangle of leaves and flowers, reached the upper terrace and are snaking themselves around the balustrades. Our spring wistaria, which rarely flowers twice, is dripping with blossoming racemes, smaller, more fragile, but blooming, while the roses, which never fare well in our devilish midsummer heat, are bursting forth everywhere. Further to the left of the *terrain* are the vegetable patches. I see the aubergine plants are still fruiting tiny golden tomatoes. I cannot bear to look, and instantly swing my gaze a terrace lower, where the branches of our *quatre saisons* lemon tree are bowing beneath the weight of their offerings.

No one is entirely sure where the lemon tree originated. There are no references to it in any Latin sources. The first mention of *le citronnier* in literature appears to have been in south-east Asia, further east than the earliest-known olive-tree topography, but both the lemon and the orange tree have been growing on this south-eastern French coastline since the Middle Ages. Interestingly, that is much later than the Greek or Roman occupations here, so it is possible that it was neither of these cultures who contributed this member of the citrus family to the Provençal way of life.

*

In every direction, the garden is an intoxicating celebration of life, which is precisely what I have been craving, and the tiled terraces are as pristine as freshly scrubbed floors. I have every reason to delight in being back home, and how I do delight in it. This homecoming contributes heartily to my determination to move forward and not give in to the weight of sorrow that is gnawing at my gut. I have already wasted money and time on an ill-considered purchase and now I must re-establish my equilibrium and get back to work as soon as possible.

As I pass the stables, still struggling with my luggage, I see that Halaz has dug out every broom the farm owns as well as others I was not even aware we possessed and lined them all up. The count is nine, all of varying shapes and sizes; an assortment of textures and materials for a variety of purposes, standing sentinel like solemn soldiers against one of the outer walls, heads upwards, airing and drying in the sun.

The villa, which has been closed up during these away-from-home weeks, is heavy with trapped, summer inactivity. It reeks of dried herbs, forgotten flowers and, in the bathroom, lingering whiffs of my Chanel No. 5 perfume. I throw open the shutters to let the light flood in and find dust and cobwebs everywhere. Three bright-green stink bugs fall to the floor and lie on their backs, writhing. They are pests to our vegetable beds. Even so, I turn them over and leave them be. Geckos scuttle into shadows, climbing walls at a speed which amazes. On the dining table there lies a stack of curling mail, mostly bills, which can be dealt with later and, hanging like a tongue from the telephone in my den, is a faxed message from Michel. It welcomes me home, begs me to reassure him that I have arrived safely and acquaints me with great tidings: he has managed to change his flight and will be landing in London at dawn the day after tomorrow. Assuming there is no intercontinental delay, his 9.05 plane from Heathrow to Nice will transport him home well in time for lunch. Thirty-six hours to go till love returns on 'the wings of the morning'.

I decide that, after I have ripped off my clothes and dived into the pool – better to do it now before M. Halaz wanders back up and has another seizure – I will consecrate the remainder of the day to mundane, organisational matters so that tomorrow, tomorrow I can indulge my yearning by making an early-morning pilgrimage to the sea, though to which beach I am still undecided. I am considering Antibes.

Antipolis, the classical Greek name meaning 'the city opposite', was bestowed upon the port they founded west of Nice, directly across the Baie des Anges, in the late sixth century BC. Today it is better known as Antibes or, in the Provençal language, Antibou. There is debate even now among scholars as to whether the Greeks were intending its name to describe the harbour's relationship to Nice – Nikaia to the Greeks and Niço to the Provençal people – or to the island of Corsica or even to their most hostile of enemies, the Ligurians of Liguria, now part of northern Italy.

When the Romans conquered this province, threw out the Greeks and took possession of this northern Mediterranean coast of France, Antibes became as strategically important to them as Fréjus. They used it as a stopover for their coastal fleets travelling between Italy and Arles. So valued was the town that they honoured it as a *civita romana* instead of deeming it a mere colony.

Today, this seaside port and holiday resort is still famous for its harbour and many, if not most, of its inhabitants are foreigners or members of the itinerant yachting community. Soon after we found our farm, while we were embarking upon the lengthy process of moving down here, setting up home and actually acquiring the deeds, I used to make regular Monday-morning coffee stops one lane back from that port after kissing Michel goodbye at the airport, where he was set to board the dawn flight to Paris. I would sit at a table alone in the rising heat of the morning sunshine, drink several large cups of *café au lait* and watch, with a child's admiring gaze, an elderly man frequently seated at the table next to me, who was awaiting the arrival of the London *Times*. He was, and remains, one of my heroes, Graham Greene. Later, I was fortunate enough to make his acquaintance and exchange precious words with him, but in those early days, during that first warm summer of discovery, I was too shy, too tongue-tied and too in awe of him to strike up a conversation.

It was the owner of the café who told me that M. Greene was a year-round regular at his establishment, and that the acclaimed author lived nearby, not in Antibes itself but on its verdant cape a short drive along the coast.

'If you haven't made a tour of the cape,' the patron told me, 'you must. There are fine beaches all along its coastline. And a wealth of artists and writers have passed through the doors of its luxurious villas. The place is legendary.'

Of course, in the years since we first arrived here, we have visited on many occasions the legendary *cap* that M. Greene inhabited and I never tire of its rugged beauty.

Two childhood passions became my lifebelt and gave me the wherewithal to battle on and to dream beyond those early stages of life to a time when I would be grown up, when I could escape and play roles other than that of the bane of someone's life.

Both these pastimes were lived out in isolation, in the make-believe worlds of a damaged child's creation.

The first was Tireless Scribblings. I bled Biros dry expressing heartfelt thoughts in a quest for meaning, for the key to the puzzle, filling notepads with quotations squirreled from books, self-pitying poetry and, later, lovesick sonnets. I wrote plays such as *The Story of Robin Hood*, which I staged at school and at charity institutions. The Cheshire Home for the Retired was one such establishment. Looking back, I am convinced that none of those bemused pensioners had a clue what I and my classmates were about, nor what my almost certainly ill-constructed story was saying. I was twelve at the time. I walked home in the autumnal darkness feeling despondent and perplexed by their lukewarm responses. Twelve, and already staring Critical Acclaim in the back. Curiously, though, the experience cemented my desire to write.

My second survival mechanism was Dressing Up. At some stage my father had acquired an entire costume department from a local amateur theatre that had lost its funding and was closing down. Most of these he stored in a long glass conservatory in the garden, while the rest went into the spare bedroom, which consequently reeked of stale sweat, mothballs and the faint traces of the panstick stage make-up which still stained collars and cuffs. This was where I was exiled as a punishment, and punishment it could be. Late at night the costumes, particularly the dark frock coats, terrified me because I was convinced they were moving, inhabited by invisible spirits.

However, in the hours of daylight I loved this room, because it had a square wooden rostrum in one corner – something to do with the design of the stairs – which became my theatre. Here I painstakingly pieced together a monster circular jigsaw which I kept laid out for reference. It showed a bust of Shakespeare surrounded by a still life from each of his thirty-seven plays. I studied those drawn characters, trying to imagine how they sounded, moved and behaved. Decked out in impossibly large and fraying costumes from those metal racks, tripping over dragging hems, I attempted to breathe life into my interpretations, reciting with intense ardour and dramatic emphasis the master's lines, struggling to find meaning in words weird and unfamiliar to me, such as 'coxcomb', 'palfrey' and 'humours'.

In the course of any one, usually rainy, afternoon I could be transformed into Mistress Quickly, 'Proud' Titania, Hermione, Rosalind, Viola, Shakespeare himself, with his goatee beard, which I drew on my face with a crayon, as well as his wife Anne (my middle name) Whateley of Temple Grafton, whom I had vaguely read about. But the character I loved the best, the queen of them all, the glamorous mistress and goddess of love, was Will's Egyptian monarch, Cleopatra who, in my mind's eye, possessed the luxuriant black hair, the curves, cleavage, low-cut frocks, stiletto heels and red lips of my mother. She exuded passion, had inspired war and epic emotions. She would have no truck with the grubby, furtive fumblings of decrepit old men, which was how the visitors to my parents' house appeared to this pubescent girl.

To recite her lines, enact that embodiment of femininity, would inspire applause, bouquets of flowers and international acclaim. Thus it was here, in those nights of isolated agony as well as in the hours I spent in empty auditoriums watching my charismatic father rehearse with his musicians, that my actress's 'immortal longings' and deep-rooted ambition were born. My dreams grew grandiose. I pictured myself as a movie star – Katharine Hepburn in *Stage Door* – or as a grande dame of the theatre, and I longed for the days when I might stand on a stage, gaze beyond the footlights and be uproariously applauded and adored.

For many years acting and my devotion to its craft gave me a vocation. I channelled all my confused emotions into work and my creative universe, but I discovered early on that there were two areas of this life that were unsatisfactory. The first was that the parts on offer to women, particularly on television or for the cinema, were not as varied or as challenging as those I had allocated to myself in the spare bedroom. Usually the choices were delineated by men's ideas of the woman's role, the woman's look, and, in my twenties, I frequently did not have the right look, did not fit the picture. I was too plump, too voluptuous. Secondly, there always came the moment when it was time to go home: the end of the day or, worse, the end of the shoot.

Home was a rented top-floor flat in Kentish Town where I lived alone. Sometimes, in the early, struggling days, I would let out a room to one fellow actor or another to help pay the bills, and sometimes there were mates staying who were passing through town or who had been thrown out of their own base by an erstwhile partner. In other words, I had company. Frequently, we whiled away the midnight hours listening to rock and jazz music, drinking bottles of rather poor wine, Hirondelle or Bulgarian Bull's Blood. Sometimes, I went to bed with one male friend or another and, occasionally, I had an affair which, for a brief period of time, actually made me quite happy and reasonably excited about life. There was one longish-term on-off romance with a young actor I cared deeply for, but it did not last. He married someone else. So nothing, no one, assuaged the emptiness I carried around within me. It was profound, but it was also relatively unconscious.

I believe now that I shadow-boxed with love, cloaked everything in a romantic haze. Much of the loving part of my nature, the nurturing side, I had cordoned off somewhere during my tormented teens. Outwardly, I was feminine, flirtatious and romantic, but within I was defensive, brutalised and terrified to reveal more of myself than I could regulate. I feared that the *real* me, the angry, abused young person, would explode like a volcano and overwhelm anyone who came too close. I was incapable of entrusting another with my heart; it was way too scrambled an organ. The deepest of my female urges, the atavistic desires for partnership and childbearing, I poured into my ambition. I never disclosed my past. I rarely talked about my private life at all, even to very close companions. I spent my out-of-work days, or my off-set hours, if I was filming away from London, on my own, travelling, searching for what I described as 'my house by the sea', which I don't believe, back then, I thought would ever materialise.

The following morning I am out of bed and clear of the house by sunrise or, in Colette's words, *à la naissance du jour*, making not for the sixteenth-century fortressed town of Antibes, because the town's beach is small and not very interesting, but to that legendary peninsula the Cap d'Antibes. In this season there is no possibility of enjoying the coast or of hoping for a moment to oneself unless you arrive bright and early and are gone before the tourists have woken, for once they are up and about the beaches and the cafés are seething with activity.

Taking Michel's deafening old car because we have no other transport, I hit the coast on the Cannes side of Golfe Juan and from there drive alongside the gently lapping sea, hugging the pearly, calm waterfront. The sun is rising beyond the Alps into a cloudless, iris-blue sky. Chugging past Tetou and Nounou, the two well-known fish restaurants, both deeply fashionable and renowned for their delicious bouillabaisse and, in the case of Tetou, astounding prices, I am reminded of the time Michel and I dined at Nonou, where we were seated at a table next to Vera Lynn and her late husband, Harry. Afterwards, Michel asked me about the elegant woman we had been talking to and I told him that, during the Second World War, Vera had been dubbed the Forces'

Sweetheart. Her name meant nothing to him, which served to emphasise the years and the different lives we had inhabited before our worlds so sweetly collided. Our fathers, neither of whom were actually in combat, were nonetheless on opposite sides of the war in which Vera sang for the British troops.

I drive on, passing through the beach town of Juanles-Pins which, thanks to the influx of rich, partygoing Americans, became the hot spot on this stretch of coast in the 1920s, the Jazz Age. I am making for the western side of the *cap*. Yards from the shore, perched in the sunshine on glistening wet rocks, I spy several black cormorants, and there are Mediterranean, black-headed and herring gulls flocking and swooping everywhere. This is hardly surprising, given that the early-bird fishermen with their baguette breakfasts, coffee flasks and woven fishing baskets inhabit this rocky coastline. I count eleven already.

I am right alongside the Musée Naval et Napoléonien. Stylish tracksuited joggers, sweatbands keeping expensively cut hair out of eyes, remind me that this museum neighbours the exclusive Hôtel du Cap Eden Roc, situated on the south-western tip of the cape. I peer in through its imposing black iron gates at the fabulous palm-lined alleys. This fashionable address was immortalised as the Hôtel des Etrangers in Scott Fitzgerald's novel *Tender is the Night*.

The Eden Roc was the first hotel on the Côte d'Azur to construct an open-air swimming pool. It was also the first to throw open its doors to summer guests. That was in 1923, the year Coco Chanel, in the company of the Duke of Westminster, broke with tradition and escaped Paris to enjoy this coast as a summer visitor. Until then the Riviera had always been a fashionable winter resort and dead to the chic world for the remaining months of the year.

I am travelling along John F. Kennedy Boulevard. Not far

from here, buried in a wooded *parc*, is the Jardin Thuret, created in 1856, where the British planted the very first eucalyptus trees, which they had imported from Australia. President Kennedy was also a visitor to this neck of the woods. Half a mile or so back, I passed the magnificent beachside art-deco villa where in times gone by he was a guest, as was Marilyn Monroe, along with numerous other luminaries.

In the early days, before I knew who had graced its terraces, every time we drove past that well-proportioned cube of white house, sitting *pieds dans l'eau*, from where you can climb straight out of bed, gaze beyond the rocky, shorelined garden across the sweeping, semi-circular bay known as Port de l'Olivette to Cannes and, still clad in your silk pyjamas if that's your fancy, dive directly into the Med, I used to say to Michel: 'I wouldn't mind owning that villa.'

I began to feel like Charles Dickens who, walking up a hill in the Medway town of Chatham in Kent and passing his favourite house, used to make a similar statement to his father every morning: 'One day I am going to own that house.' Later in his life, when he was a bestselling author, he bought the house of his dreams. When this villa went on the market recently and I heard about it, for no more justifiable reasons than avarice and curiosity, I telephoned the agents. Yes, they said, it is for sale. 'How much?' I asked. A snip, at £7 million.

Years ago when I first began looking for 'my house by the sea', I had no clear idea of where that Elysium would be, what it would look like or if it could ever exist, but what I knew for certain was that it would be an enchanted place, vibrant and ringing with joy and passion. My childhood had upped the stakes, as it were, for what was required of that house by the sea. Generations of families, visitors, artists and friends would pass through its doors and leave traces of themselves, their imprints, behind them. There would be animals, there would be music and laughter and a free-spiritedness fed by the nature and the climate and home-grown food and the chaotic, unlikely combinations of the people present. And, at the centre of it, the axis that made it all spin, would be love. A love which would offer me peace of mind and the freedom to creep away and write; a love that would encourage me, enable me to discover who I am. And a love that bore children, innocent infants running about naked, unselfconscious and safe.

I signal and turn right into a seemingly insignificant tree-shaded *chemin*, actually adorned with gracious villas, which leads me to the renowned Plage de la Garoupe.

Here I park and sit a moment to contemplate the awesome beauty of the natural arena laid out before me. In the distance beyond the Baie des Anges, the amphitheatre of Alps. In the olden days, before roads were cut through, they served as a natural protection for Nice against inclement weather and unwanted invaders. In winter, they are a deep purple and capped at the summits by snow. This morning, they are a blueish-mulberry in the early light.

I shan't swim in this bay today. It is full-blown summer and the sea is heaving with svelte ivory yachts. Many of the yachties ditch their detritus overboard, sullying the shallow waters. Before I was wise to their habits, I once swam into a used Tampax and, believe me, I, who will frolic in a turbid puddle, was out of those waves like greased lightning.

I change into sneakers, take my costume and towel and set off along the path, the *sentier pédestre*, which winds its way around the cape and which, at this hour, is almost deserted. As I approach the small easterly point known as Cap Gros I see two wetsuited divers wading into the water, hauling their oxygen masks and lungs. I wonder what they are going after. I have never dived these waters but I know that neither the visibility nor the marine life here is exceptional. Distant sailboats at full mast flag the horizon. Startling white against milky blue.

Behind me, set back from the beach, hidden somewhere within the thickets of the lean-trunked *pins parasols*, is the renowned Château de la Garoupe, rented by Cole Porter in 1922, where Scott and Zelda Fitzgerald got regularly soused on whisky sours.

There are a handful of dog-owners at the water's edge, trailed by their fluffy boutique canines yapping and snapping and jumping up and down on their hind legs. How I would love to bring my rabble-rousers to splash in and out of the wash here but it would be impossible. They'd wreak havoc everywhere and terrorise all these chaps.

The sudden roar of an engine startles me and a young man on his white fibreglass water scooter comes skirring by, churning up the calm sea.

I spy another dawn bather. An elderly bowlegged gentleman in a pale blue swimming cap – the French call them *bonnets*, so delightfully Edwardian – is clambering over the sharp, slippery rocks in his plastic reef shoes. I wriggle into my costume and follow suit. There are saltwater pools everywhere, still as dark night, in among the dun-and-white rocks bleached by the dry heat. They sometimes give harbour to *les oursins,* sea urchins, whose five rose-coloured ovaries, dug out of the belly of the creature, make for one of the great seafood delicacies down here, particularly when used in omelettes or scrambled eggs. Today they are just another reason for the plastic shoes, because you don't want to accidentally step on a sea urchin and end up with one of its black spines through the sole of your foot.

Once at the water's edge, I wedge my buttocks securely

between two boulders, pause to inhale that haunting, sing-song wash of waves licking against a rough barnacled strand, dip my toes into the water, shiver at its delicious tingliness and then plunge myself, stomach first, into the sea.

My father was discharged from the Air Force into postwar Britain. When he met my mother, at a dance hall in south London, she was a trainee hospital ward sister. It was a whirlwind romance. Money was scarce. One Saturday morning, the young couple installed themselves in the top two rooms of my grandparents' rented four-storey house in Brixton, south London, and went off in Grandad's horse-drawn taxi cab to get married. No honeymoon was planned. But one Saturday not long afterwards my father checked his football pools coupon and discovered that he had won £180. 'It was a bloody fortune.' He was due to share this princely sum with his father, who had chipped in fifty per cent for the coupon, but his dad would take only £80, saying that Peter should keep the hundred as he was newly wed.

So my parents treated themselves. They purchased two train tickets and set off at the beginning of October in the observation car of the *Devon Belle* for a week's holiday at the Grand Hotel in Torquay. I was there, in a manner of speaking, accompanying them on that heady honeymoon. A silent, subaquatic witness seesawing about in the womb, my ear to the neck, listening to everything.

Later, they occasionally spoke of those days – how they strolled the beaches hand in hand, visited antique shops and country pubs and made a stopover in a farmhouse in Combe Martin – eulogising the holiday and my father's timely wind-fall. It was out of season, but 'the weather was gorgeous'. It was a benchmark for their lost happiness, I suppose. And I have often wondered if those seven harmonious days didn't sow the seeds of my addiction to the sea, my sense of it as a 'palmy state', a providential environment.

The water is deliciously cool and tangy. Once I have immersed my entire body, I flip over on to my back then kick out a distance so that I can float in peace and quiet without being washed back by the current towards the shore. Bobbing with the beat of the waves, arms and legs outstretched like a Da Vinci diagram, I surrender my traumatised body to the water's saline buoyancy, to its thalassic remedial powers, and ponder the ether. It seems that I will never know the pain of birth, the breaking of waters, the joy, relief and exhaustion of delivery. Ours was to have been a Christmas baby. I had been dreaming of long evenings by the log-filled fireplace, and now . . . the anguish of childlessness.

A gentle offshore breeze lifts dampened wisps of my long hair, which settle across my face. The sun, rising hot and fast to the left of me, penetrates my bare, scrubbed skin while illuminating the ghost of a muslin-white, gibbous moon. Overhead, in that same dense expanse of blueness, soaring over mountains and sea, a plane, no, two, en route for Nice airport, leave vapour trails. Two white zips, dividing up, peeling open, the inexorable azureness of this Côte d'Azur sky.

Why has this happened to me? That is the question to which I am seeking an answer. No, I am not seeking, I am demanding. I want to know *why*. Why *me*?

Perfect silence, save for waves and screeching herring gulls and distant cries from the shore.

Within the breaches of the division above me, no booming voice of God speaks back; no Old Testament explanation is forthcoming. Nothing is answered, nothing clarified. As far as the Man Above is concerned, I must sort it out for myself.

Or does the answer lie somewhere within the realisation that this is not simply another sticky situation? Throughout my life I have managed to engineer my way out of those. I pride myself on quick thinking, finding ways through, but I cannot negotiate or act my way out of this one. This is a given. One of those junctures from which there is no going back. Not dissimilar to the death of a parent or loss of a loved one, it has to be taken on board. I cannot cast this loss, this set of circumstances, aside. I cannot rejig or rewrite this script.

So now it is down to me. I must find a way through, *and I will*. I have everything to be grateful for. Not least the golden splendour of this morning.

And so, that's it, is it? The response to my cry? It is not for me to reason why. My role is to accept – or not – to get on with it, for there lies wisdom, or sanity, at least.

Tomorrow, Michel will be home and I am already grateful, eternally grateful, for his approaching presence, for the spell of his warm embraces and those fabulous blue eyes filled with care and compassion.

And the love that illumines my house by the sea.

Love Rediscovered

I see him approach, wheeling a trolley full of luggage, eyes cast to left and right, searching for me as the doors swing automatically apart.

'Michel!' I wave vigorously and, in among the early-morning coasties in shorts and well-polished suntans, he spies me and smiles broadly. I never grow blasé about this moment, this first sighting of him after a long absence. My stomach flips like a girl's as I hurry through the press of people. He looks zonked. That first embrace. He hugs me tight, so tightly I think I might faint. His lips brush my hair. I hear him exhale as though landing – here, where we belong – then, locked together, we make our way, bumping against one another, out of the arrivals hall.

Having someone there to care makes all the difference. It feeds the spirit. We tend one another. He has been travelling for twenty-eight hours non-stop, those long legs crammed into spaces they were not born for. He needs a shower, or a swim, but first a decent cup of French coffee, and then, afterwards, we breakfast on the terrace: yoghurt and strawberries and slices of honeydew melon and *six cereales* bread, spread with marmalade made from our own oranges.

'You are wearing the necklace.'

'I haven't taken it off, except to film. It's beautiful. Thank you.'

'No more travelling,' he says. 'We are neither of us going anywhere for at least a month.'

His hand on my hip, slipped around my waist, I feel reassured. There is time and there is reason to heal.

Days of intimacy. Talking, listening. I talk, Michel listens.

'I'm afraid,' I tell him. 'And I feel a failure.'

He hammers hooks into the trunks of a great oak and an ancient olive and hitches up the hammock in the leafy shade. We bury ourselves in it, wrap it about us, a vibrantly coloured cocoon, rocking together, cradled out of the heat.

'What name did you choose?' I whisper eventually.

'*Chérie*, please, try not to hurt yourself like this.'

'No, that's not what I'm doing. I'd like to humanise her. It will help me, if you don't mind. If it doesn't hurt you.'

He reflects upon this and then wraps himself tighter about me. I feel his breath against my cheek, the familiarity of his intimacy. One word, he whispers in my ear, and then, in the space of a single exhalation, it has disappeared, spirited away by the breeze in the overhead branches.

'Yes, I like that.' I smile, fastening on it. 'Can you guess what I chose? Well, I didn't choose, exactly. She did, I think. She *became* the name. Shall I tell you?' I insist.

'If you want to.'

'Carrot.'

He frowns, puzzled, I am sure, by the unlikely tag.
'Don't laugh.'
'I'm not.'
'Nothing else seemed to fit. I doubt that she would have been born with red hair or any of the characteristics we might associate with such a nickname. She would probably have been blessed with our olive skin and long unkempt curls. But the name persisted. I tried to shoo it away until, finally, I acknowledged it, welcomed her thus and we began to communicate with one another using it. Carrot.'

I turn towards him, his face in the dappled shadows. He seems to understand, or accepts my madness, at least.

Mornings, rediscovering one another. For ever touching. Growing reaccustomed to the silky or rough feel of one another. To the partnership of love. His medicine: 'strokings'. Hours, he spends, stroking me. Every part of me: cracks, crevices, curves, soothing away my pain. Evenings to ourselves. Sitting in rickety wooden chairs, silently, side by side, watching the sun go down. Waiting for night to fall. Nights in white linen. Pushing out the night boat, drowning in love. *Les nuits blanches.*

There are the occasions, though, when I wake towards dawn in a sweat, crazed, hair in a tangle, haunted by nightmares, and find him, like a Chinese puzzle, entwined about me. Limbs slipped into limbs. His breath on my shoulder. '*Calme-toi, chérie.* Come here, cuddle up close.' Tight against one another like spoons in a canteen of cutlery. Spooning, breathing in unison, I quieten.

And, later, after repose, eyes opening to discover another, baking new day. Glad to be alive. The morning sky the blue of tit's wings, *bleuté*. Yes, the days are as lovely as a story.

Into one of these baking days, these days of 'stroking', comes a letter from ONIOL. I stare at the envelope. ONIOL. Planting olive trees. It reminds me of spring, of our plans for the farm. Of our trip to Marseille. When I was pregnant. The letter lists the approved nurseries for the purchase of olive trees. Nearest to us is one deep in the heart of the Var, behind Hyères, in the *arrière-pays*, La Londe les Maures.

'Before the girls arrive,' Michel suggests, 'we should go and take a look.'

'I'd rather not,' I answer.

This baffles him. 'Why not? We can make a day of it, stop somewhere for lunch, find a *domaine* vineyard and stock up on rosé.'

'I don't want to plant the extra trees.'

He says nothing. Silenced by surprise, wary of where this is leading. And then, eventually, 'We need the extension, *chérie*, if we are to be offered our AOC. They won't accept us as serious *oléiculteurs* without the required minimum of trees.'

'We don't need an olive-oil award. We're happy this way.' I feel the catch in my throat. 'What I mean is, I don't want to get lost in . . . Let's just accept everything the way that it is.'

'Why?'

'I don't think I can . . . I can't cope.'

I gather up our breakfast plates, rise to move inside. He takes my arm. His blue eyes bore into me. Crinkled features burned by sun.

'Of course you can. There's no question about it. But I don't want to force this decision on you. Still, I see no reason why we shouldn't make the trip A leisurely olive-tree recce, and afterwards, we can find a hotel on the beach. We could stay overnight. The girls will be arriving soon, and I have spoken to Serge again about paying us a visit and I think the idea is beginning to appeal to him. So let's visit the nursery, see what we think and make our decisions later.'

'Do you think that old car will stand the journey?'

'It's doing better than yours.'
I smile. So does he.
'That's settled, then.'

We set off the next day at the crack of dawn, because that is what Michel likes to do. We take the inland road, avoiding the autoroute and the south-seeking tourists. Oleander blossoms, vivid colours everywhere and sweeping hillsides furnished in green by the herby brush of the familiar *maquis*. Passing through leafy lanes of chestnuts, with olive fields beyond, moving westwards until we reach the Var wine districts. To left and right climb the cambered hills, green with vines, their dark grapes ripening like pendulous udders awaiting milking.

As morning hails us, so too do the mountains of Maures, almost as if from nowhere; there, rising up in front of us. Lilac and rust in the early light. The wooded summits of the Massif des Maures.

'Oh, my God!' I exclaim, taken aback by the beauty, the stillness, the sheer mountainness rising up out of a burnished landscape. 'It reminds me of Ayers Rock. I don't know why.'

'High, empty sky. Hot, flat land, that's why.'

'The name Maures comes from the Provençal word *maouro*, meaning dark.'

We snake left, following the trace of the road, hugging the curve of the mountain base – no access blasted through its centre – and head for the coast.

'I think breakfast at the beach. What do you say?'

We hit the water west of the city of Hyères and negotiate our way to a very pretty fishing port. The world has woken up. Cars are zipping to and fro, hooting and screeching. Urban sounds. I smell coffee and bakery flavours. My stomach rumbles, and I grin.

'Hyères. A designated stopover for pilgrims on their way to Jerusalem. A favourite spa for the British upper classes in the eighteenth century. Tolstoy lived here, and then, later, towards the end of the nineteenth century, Robert Louis Stevenson. He said it was the only peace he ever knew. He wrote the opening chapters of *Kidnapped* here.'

At the quayside, we settle at a café-restaurant, order peasant-sized cups of frothy coffee and guzzle on them greedily while giving ourselves over to the cinema of the early-morning seaport, which is already in full swing, busy about its business.

From where we are seated, we are well placed to study the world of the fishermen. Several fishing vessels are in dock. Others are arriving, men disembarking. A handful are kneeling or bending over nets on a narrow jetty jutting from the quayside, occupied with the unloading of their overnight catch. I am curious to know what they are spilling out of those bulging nets.

'I could sit here all day,' I murmur, but no sooner have the words been uttered than a white van draws to a halt directly in front of us, blocking out both the early-morning warmth of the sun and our view.

From the driver's side, out steps a small, plump man, whistling, in dusty white overalls and wellingtons. He thumps the side of the vehicle, walks to the rear, opens up both doors and a gangling, spotted youth clutching armfuls of baguettes descends. This callow assistant has an old-fashioned baker's hat set askew on his head, lying flat like a raw mushroom. The baker waves to the bald-headed *patron* of our café, who is leaning against a sliding glass door enjoying a cigarette in the sunshine.

'Don't worry, they'll be gone in a second,' says Michel.

But no. Between them they deliver what must be at least a *hundred* baguettes. One load after another of warm loaves direct from the oven slung in sacks over their shoulders. How can one establishment possibly require so much bread? Finally they rev up and set off to make other deliveries elsewhere along the summer coastline.

The briny sea hits my senses, as does the unmistakable and overwhelming smell of freshly caught fish.

'What's their catch?' I ask.

'Mackerel, I should think,' suggests Michel. 'Or maybe it's sea bass.'

Ah, the delicious Mediterranean white-fleshed fish *loup de mer*. 'If it is, we're taking some back with us,' I smile. It is one of my favourite meals. A fleeting memory of our burned one catches me out; I choose not to mention it. 'In these waters they could have been lucky and found crab, *non?*' Soupe de Pélous, the Niçois name for a truly delicious broth made from locally caught crabs.

'I don't think so.'

Michel is right. I can make out the flapping tails of fish gasping for oxygen, expiring on the quay.

Now, the fishermen have emptied their nets and are attempting to sell their wares. They call loudly in deep-throated, resonant voices, a singsong language I cannot figure out. I hear French, but another, too. Sentences roll out that are incomprehensible to me.

'What are they speaking?'

The language they are talking is Provençal: a foreign tongue to us but, bizarrely, its rhythms are familiar, flirting with revelation until then the sense slips infuriatingly away.

While some of the fishermen start trading, others settle at the narrow wharfside and begin the business of gathering up the nets to dry them or stitch and mend them in the sunshine. Their deftness of hand, their dexterity thrills me. These are burly men with hairy, muscular arms and thick workaday fingers, kneeling on the quay in high rubber boots, wrists turning like dancers. They laugh broadly, with hearty gusto. Vigorously handsome, black-haired men. Lovers, husbands, fathers, hunters of the sea.

People approach to buy the fresh spoils. A few arrivals are tourists, Belgians or Dutch perhaps: broad-beamed, unhurried bodies, solid shoes, light complexions burned pink. They talk with the animated fishermen, choosing carefully, lifting one wriggling sea creature after another, dropping it back on to the slithery heap, digging for another. The hirsute seamen, who have not slept all night, watch on, advising patiently, laughing and joking with their clientele. It is all part of an ancient ritual here on the Côte d'Azur: choosing one's own produce; picking or rejecting each item with due consideration; discussing its quality at length. The serious business of food, of eating, of nurturing the body.

Replete from our several generous cups of *café au lait* and our fresh *tartines*, spread thickly with fig and peach *confitures* and a dark coppery-coloured marmalade that is so delicious it could only be equalled by ours, home-made by René, we want to linger a while longer watching the ruddy-faced fishermen, but we must be on our way. And so, eventually, we leave coins on the table and set off along the waterfront, which reeks of the recently landed fish and of diesel, past the wooden fishing boats bobbing in the deep-green water slicked with a rainbow coating of oil, and return to the road that takes us back inland.

Behind Hyères, bulldozed landscape. Industrial zones. Advertising hoardings. Signposts everywhere, all pointing to the airport. We get lost, snarled up in clutches of fuming traffic. Rush hour. Stressed faces, smokers, mobile-phone users driving like sharp card-dealers.

'Let's get out of here.' Michel swings the old Merc over to the left and, as soon as he can, does a U-turn. On we go for miles, trying to find our way, moving out of the city's breeze-blocked suburbia into the countryside. Hot dusty roads, straight Roman roads flanked by keenly pruned plane trees. Empty but for one rusting white Citroën rising up out of the distant heat shimmer, transporting a band of farm hands to the vineyards.

'*Le platane*. Plane tree. Its first mention in Greek literature was in the *Iliad* and then, a little later, in the *Odyssey*,' I murmur.

'What is happening with your book?'

I shrug, and turn my face to the window.

'Why don't you take another look at it?'

'Not now.'

Michel does not persist. We reach a roundabout. I lean from the window and catch sight of, nestling behind overgrown foliage, a handwritten sign directing us to the nursery. Two or three kilometres further along, we see it up ahead: a disappointing *hypermarché* of a place. Turning left off the road, we park on the gravelled courtyard and Michel hurries to enquire at one of the cash desks.

'The olive trees are not here. Follow the lane. You'll need to take your car.'

Rolling slowly along a pebbled path, past row upon row of fruiting trees – I have never seen so many trees – we come upon a wooden shed with a handful of cars outside. This is the office.

A young man steps forward to greet us; he has been expecting us. He smiles warmly, shaking our hands, the epitome of wholesomeness.

'I'll take you to the *oliviers*,' he says.

He reverses his four-wheel-drive out of the shade and we climb aboard and hit the road again. Down lanes, past entrances to vineyard *domaines* with signs offering *dégustations*, where, hidden beyond winding, vegetal tracks, can be glimpsed gracious *bastides*. Michel asks the young man if he can recommend one or two modest labels. He suggests two local wineries and then moves right back to the business in hand: olive trees.

'Of course, you are fortunate. Where you are situated, you have the *cailletier*, the famous Nice olive. It makes excellent oil. Here, in this region, no particular variety is cultivated. Here is a bit of a hodgepodge, which is why the area is not eligible for AOC status. The conditions, the soil, where you are, are ideal.'

Moments later, we swing off the lane into what, once upon a time, must have been agricultural land but is today the property of the nursery. A vast acreage dedicated exclusively to the propagation of olive trees. In every direction, as far as the eye can see, olive trees.

I step from the car into a silver ocean of foliage. Beyond are mountains and lavender sky.

'We have thirty-six varieties on offer here. Three sizes: three-year-olds, six or nine.'

Michel and I look about us in wonder.

'How many trees?' asks Michel.

'We aim to produce one hundred and eighty thousand a year.'

It is a mighty concept.

'One of our goals is to create the future heritage of Provence. This tree, *l'olivier*, one might say, is the signature tune of Provence.'

I turn to him in surprise. Signature tune? Yes, I like that: to sing the ancient ways of Provence into the future.

'Well, our order would be a modest one. Two hundred of the *cailletiers*. I think the six-year-olds would suit us. But my wife and I will obviously discuss it and confirm it with you in writing. Will you be needing a deposit, or—?'

'Lord, no, there's no hurry. You can settle the bill next year when we deliver them. If you decide to go ahead, that is, which I sincerely hope you will. There's an old Provençal saying,' he continues proudly. '"A hundred-year-old olive tree is still a baby." Yes, its finest fruit seasons are still to come.'

'It's your day,' Michel says to me when we are back in our car, having purchased two dozen bottles of rosé at one of the *châteaux* recommended by our nursery gardener, whose name we didn't learn. 'What would you like to do now?'

'Swim. If we can find a quiet bay.'

'We'll find a spot.'

Wading deep into the yawning blue sea, our thighs are caressed by brown twiny leaves of seaweed which, I discover later, is not seaweed at all. It is an aquatic plant known as *Posidonia oceanica.* In Corsica it is a protected species because it is a vital source of oxygen and nutrition for Mediterranean marine fauna. Waves slap gently against our naked navels. Michel's body is as brown as tobacco, as smooth as velvet. He throws himself carelessly into the warm water and swims fast. I follow, shouting and splashing after him. The exercise relaxes our tired limbs, aching from hours in the car. We float on our backs, staring up at the cloudless sky. It feels like a stolen day. The warmth of the sun beating down on us. Golden-hued. Almost sinful.

The wavy sand is packed with heat. Our bodies are packed with heat. We flake out on a dark, triangular rock which looks out across the semi-deserted beach to the flat blue water and beyond, to the Iles d'Or. Lapping waves and bird cries are our companions while the sun pours down upon flesh glistening with driplets of the sea and runnels of salty perspiration. I am lying on my stomach, deep in thought. Michel rolls towards me.

'Quite a sight, those olive trees, eh?'

'Yes. As is their philosophy. Remarkable. Still, we have all we need.'

He asks no questions, but leans into me and licks my shoulder, tasting the salt. Socks of damp sand cling to our sea-wet feet. A mauvy speckled lizard scurries by, pauses, stock-still, on the rock as though sensing our presence, flicks out its tongue and then disappears.

My fingertips have wrinkled in the water and turned a marbled, death-like white. It reminds me of my loss and I feel a wave of gloom wash through me. 'Please, don't let's order more trees.'

Later, inland, travelling home beneath a dramatic evening sky, we spot hand-painted signs pinned to pine trees announcing a *Guignol* performance this very evening. I beg to go. Michel agrees, although he does not share my passion for Punch and Judy shows.

In a dusty plaza in a lonely rural village, it is a pitiable occasion. Half a dozen kids, a gang of local lads, are running to and fro, a couple of them in bare feet, shouting, mocking the show. The French word for brats is *les mouflets*, which aptly describes these kids. They are slinging pebbles at the puppets, jeering at the sad puppeteer.

I recount to Michel how, when I was a child of eight or nine, I worked as the puppeteer's assistant for my father while he performed his weekend Punch and Judy shows. I can still see the battered navy case that housed the clothed wooden figures, and in which they were transported from gig to gig. I could recite every word of the dialogue in those days, from beginning to end. Even today I can recall chunks of it. How I used to love to peer out from the rear of the tent and watch the sea of entranced grown-ups and children, all sitting cross-legged on the grass, shouting words of warning to the characters:

'Judy! Judy! Look behind you!'

'Where?'

'There!'

'Here?'

'No, there!'

'Crocodile!'

'Policeman!'

'Ghost!'

I grow silent when reminded of my father, of the confused child I was, and of my own girl so recently lost. Michel guides me back to the present by asking me why I don't begin to write again.

I have no enthusiasm for work; no confidence in it.

He lets the matter drop.

The story being enacted here is marginally different to the tale I remember from my childhood. It seems to have a more political bias to it, but it is hard to grasp precisely because *les mouflets* are still screaming and throwing sticks.

I turn my head this way and that, searching for someone to call them off. But all I see is a trio of old men with hand-carved canes, olivewood, perhaps, seated side by side at the square's perimeter beneath a dusty olive tree. They stare into the middle distance, motionless, as though made of stone.

'Well, I wouldn't want to be the proud mother of any of this bunch,' I whisper crossly.

Summer Eclipsed

Les filles arrive, Michel's twin daughters. Eighteen, and beautiful as unfolding flowers. Although still adoring of their Papa, they are growing up, setting out on their own lives. Their talk is of their individual futures. Vanessa, with her long, auburn hair, her cinnamon-tanned skin and full, pouting lips, is intending to read modern languages at the Sorbonne in Paris while Clarisse, slender, soft-curled and poised, who appears to view the world from a more passive stance, is preparing to settle herself in my flat in London in readiness for a foundation course at one of the major art schools.

They swim, they read, they sunbathe, they natter together, they help with the table. Vanessa makes salads picked from the garden and her own style of potatoes, which are coated in our oil, baked with strong, hard cheeses and served up creamy and delicious. They take the scooter to buy the *brioches*, almond *croissants* and the *sablés* for breakfast or disappear down country lanes on outings of exploration, returning, with wild flowers, for meals or for dips in the pool. In so many ways they are independent; they are no longer children. Their lives are ahead of them. They do not notice my sadness and I say not a word. They enquire after my work and sometimes we discuss my projects but their energies are centred on their own lives. They are two regular teenagers; it is as it should be.

'Are you at work on a novel?' asks Vanessa.

The fact is I have no work. The material I was researching all those months back – for my book about this region of France, its changing history, its flora – has been relegated to a drawer, forgotten, abandoned. 'Just an idea I had,' I tell myself now. I still make the ritualistic trek to my den, padding along there every morning, sitting at my table, staring at my computer, or out at the awakening day, but it is habit more than a fervent need to write. I find myself sifting through papers, relocating one pile from here to there or simply gazing out of the window. Lost.

'I am lost,' I tell Michel. 'Directionless.'

'What about the new trees, our AOC, have you thought any further?'

I shake my head and shrug. I cannot throw myself into farm activities. In any case, there is little I can do to further our plans because it is August and the world of the south of France has closed down. Only the amenities for tourists are sparking. For the rest, it is holiday time. I flick through my bee tome, turning the pages, staring at diagrams, but I have lost heart in this project as well. The images remind me of spring and I cannot bear to think back to spring. But I know that I must attack something.

To offset apathy, and because the plants in the flowerbeds are all but strangled by weeds that shot up during the watering reign of M. Halaz I spend the days weeding. Reminded of water, I call René. We have heard nothing from him since before my departure. I leave a message with his wife, but he does not return the call. He is probably out fishing on his boat, and who can blame him? The weather is stunning. The sun shines hotly. The sky is cloudless. It is hyacinth blue and clear as a bell. Lazy summer. Yet, this time, it disappoints me that he lets us down.

I am engrossed in a tribe of wasps, trying to shoo them away – they have congregated round a freshly halved water-melon I left out in the summer kitchen because it won't fit in the fridge – when we hear our unoiled gates creak open and the dogs begin to jump and bark. 'Ah, this could be René,' I call out, and hurry to greet him.

But no, it is Quashia. The return of Quashia!

His nonchalant stroll up the drive, a supermarket carrier bag in one hand, bearing a gift of sorts, I am sure, as though he were arriving back from lunch, is greeted by whoops of joy and much embracing.

'Welcome! Welcome!'

The wedding ceremonies were a huge success. Over a glass of mineral water in the shade of the *Magnolia grandiflora*, he acquaints us with the details of the celebrations, which have cost him every franc he had saved. He has brought us video cassettes of the occasion. Eight hours' screen time.

'Eight hours!'

'Well, it lasted for weeks,' he laughs. The feasting of this family, that clan, the neighbours; the relocating of the bride; the preparation of the food. 'Here.' He hands over the plas-tic bag that contains the tapes. 'See for yourselves.'

Michel assures him that we look forward to it, and I smile to myself, knowing that it will be me who sits through those home-recorded festivities.

'I hope you negotiated a good price for the bride,' I tease.

'I made a fair deal, but now I'm stony, stony broke.' The glint in his eye tells me how pleased our Arab friend is to be back.

'Any news from René?'

I shake my head and Quashia grins. 'The invisible man!' He looks about, appraising the garden. 'I hear it hasn't rained here in months, but Halaz has done his bit, I see.'

'Yes. I dread the water bill but . . .'

'Got yourself a water diviner?' he joshes.

'René found someone, but . . .'

'. . . you haven't heard from René. What's happening about a new watering system then?' he asks.

'Nothing.' I don't share my doubts about planting the new trees.

'Well, let's get to it. We need to get that second basin up and running.'

He rises, rolling up his sleeves. He never wastes a second.

And perhaps, now that he is here, we will get to work.

Michel and Quashia wait while I change into shoes that can negotiate the hill and then, together, we climb up to the basin.

'The front wall must be repaired first. No point in touching the container yet.'

Michel nods. 'Correct. But it's a drystone wall and carrying too much weight. Yes, it must be rebuilt, but also reinforced. It has to be securely shored up or the stones will come loose again and it will disintegrate as soon as any stress or weight is laid on it. Once the wall has been secured, the base of the basin needs to have new foundations.'

Quashia frowns. 'I can join every hose we own and create a water supply from one of the higher taps. We probably have just about enough metreage to reach this spot, but how can we transport sand and cement up here? There's no proper track. If the builders' merchants dump everything in the *parking*, as they usually do, I'll have to transport it by wheelbarrow and I'll be at it till Christmas!'

He has a point. We are practically at the furthest extreme of our land. There is no road up the rear of the hill and nothing except terraces in front. The tracks that cut through the terrace walls would have been carved out for the ease of beasts of burden, mules, nothing else.

We look around, reflecting on the problem.

'How about a chain?' suggests Michel eventually. I don't think either of us understand immediately. 'Let's sit down and work out the quantities of sand and cement we'll require, and then decide how many men could deliver it up here in, say, three days.'

Quashia gets the idea.

'Do you think you could muster some of your cronies to work in this relentless weather?'

'Two of my wife's brothers are staying nearby. And there's another fellow I know. He's a good worker. It's time those buggers sent a few francs back to their families. When shall we start?'

While Michel and Quashia clear the land surrounding the disused basin, I am dispatched to the builders' merchants to place our order. It is deserted. I find both manager and drivers lounging about in the air-conditioned Portakabin, smoking, drinking coffee, bitching about life. As I enter they fall silent, eyeing me as though I have just trucked in from another planet. I smile, offering a breezy *bonjour*, and they return my greeting with grunts, wondering, with barely veiled amusement, what this foreign woman who busies herself with sacks of cement and always debates the price wants this time.

'You can't charge me five hundred francs for a delivery of sand! It's out of the question,' I argue.

Lucien, the site manager, who I occasionally run into at the gym, shrugs. 'It's two tons,' he says. But eventually he proposes 250 francs.

I am convinced they add on a few hundred from the start, knowing that I will insist upon the same advantageous terms given to the professionals. We settle on 250 and he agrees to find a driver who will be able to deliver before the end of the week. I nod gratefully, perfectly aware that there is a quartet of drivers standing right behind me who are engaged in little aside from staring at my rear view in shorts.

I have given up on hanging out in my den, accomplishing nothing. Instead, for want of something productive to throw my energies into, I make an inventory of the garden, scribbling notes on my findings, listing plants, flowers, wildlife. Today, I am following the voracious antics of a praying mantis. I came across her yesterday when I was checking the progress of the grapes. There she was, holed up on the underside of one of the vine leaves. Extraordinarily, she has been there ever since, but her camouflage colouring is very effective and I had to hunt hard to find her again. Has she been taking it easy, caring for her digestion, after dining on her partner? I read that few male mantids are actually devoured by their women. The males seem to know the score and, once coitus has been achieved, they zip off out of the way, sharpish. This morning, I watched her trap and devour a tiny, jewel-skinned lizard. Quite shocking.

Before lunch and his siesta, after he has seen to the watering, Quashia goes in search of his three assistants. Two are as ancient and wrinkled as he, but the third is tall, handsome, young. His heavy boots and sloppy clothes aside, his looks and bearing would cast him as an Arabian prince. They sit with Michel at the round table up behind one of Quashia's newly renovated walls and the negotiations begin. Men's business.

The girls show signs of growing restless. I think they are uncomfortable lying by the pool with such visitors about. They propose an outing, but we are all agreed that it would be too crowded, too stultifying to visit the coast. In any case, Serge is due to arrive any day now. At long last he has accepted Michel's invitation.

Later, when the business in hand has been settled – the materials are arriving tomorrow and the men will set to work the day after – Michel suggests an adventurous alternative. Tomorrow we will take a little trip inland, towards the mountainous region of the Haut-Pays Niçoise, to visit the Gorge du Loup, where we can swim and picnic in relative tranquillity. Serge is travelling alone by car from Paris and, to make his journey marginally shorter, Michel organises a sundown rendezvous in the town of Tourrette-sur-Loup, the gateway to the gorge.

Tourrette-sur-Loup, constructed out of the mountain face, is known locally as 'the town of violets' because those purple-blossomed flowers grow wild there and felt-carpet the olive groves in springtime.

The next morning we leave Quashia to organise the truckloads of materials and set off after breakfast, juddering along in the smoking Merc, which reminds me that I should phone the garage and enquire after mine. But then again, it is August, and I don't much care to think about that car.

En route we make a swift alpine detour to a farm nestling in several thousand hectares of herb-scented pastureland. Its nearest neighbour is a pretty mountain hamlet. The farm is owned and managed by a handsome young goat farmer and cheesemaker we met a little over a year ago, at a Provençal honey festival in Mouans Sartoux. Although that village is not a million miles from our home, on that particular late-spring Sunday we felt like aliens because the locals were conversing in Provençal. The fishermen we observed near Hyères jumped between the two languages, but at the honey fair, French was shunned altogether. There are many faces to Provence, and its history is rich, diverse and embedded in our daily lives, but until that Sunday I had not been aware that Provençal was a spoken language.

Marcel, the goat farmer, is an esteemed figure in these parts because he is a published poet who writes in Prouvençau, but we are not making this stopover to partake of his poetry. It is his goat's cheese, probably the most delicious we have ever tasted, that we are after. Among his specialities is Banon, a fresh, light *chèvre* sprinkled with nuts and then wrapped in a chestnut leaf. Banon is a region in the Haute-Alpes, and by rights the name belongs to cheeses that hail from those pastures, but even if his goats are not reared in Banon, his cheese is an epicurean delight and well worth making the journey for.

Marcel is the proud owner of eighty-five nannies and three dark-coated billies. The nannies produce the newborn kids in early spring, at the end of February or early March, and are milked daily from two weeks after giving birth right through to September, which explains why you cannot find fresher cheese than right here at this farm. From late September until early October, the goats are put to mate.

On one of my previous trips to this hilly hinterland creamery, Marcel explained to me, and I ask him to repeat it now for the girls, that Provençal was one of the languages of Occitan, the traditional language of southern France. It is a dialect of the *langue d'oc*, or Langedocien, which literally means the 'tongue of the Occitan'. Its roots are closer to Spanish, or Catalan, which is prized as a sister language by Provençal speakers, than to French, which has a Latin root.

Once upon a time, Prouvençau was widely accepted as the literary language of all France and northern Spain.

Mediaeval troubadours and poets wrote poems and songs in Prouvençau and sang or recited them to their fair ladies, the mistresses of the courts. 'Their sentiments were of an altruistic nature, which is to say that they sang or recited the idylls of pure love, homages to the women of their dreams, rather than clamoured to consummate the physical passions, the carnal aspects of their desires. They were not looking to conjoin with their loves; it was more to celebrate them in words and music and offer the works as gifts to the heavenly creature of their choosing,' expounds Marcel.

'Might it be from this tradition that we find the root of the verb "to court", to try to win the hand of, the favours of?' I ask him.

He shrugs in the way so common down here. '*Hélas*, in 1539,' he continues, 'a statute known as the Villers-Cotterêts approved French, rather than Provençal, as the official administrative language in Provence. After that, over the centuries, Provençal fell into disuse. It threatened to become a dead language, but we are campaigning . . . *Eh, bien*.' He falls silent, his expression hangdog, as though the loss were a personal affront to him and his heritage. And I can well believe that it is.

I cast a curious eye towards the girls, who are gazing at him, listening intently, with shining expressions. Perhaps they are smitten not only by young Marcel's romanticism and his swarthy good looks but by his dark velvet voice. If so, I can't say I blame them.

'I wonder if you would like to add your names to our collective?' He is addressing the girls, handing each of them a form which contains a bulletin for new adherents to fill in. I have already sent one off on behalf of Michel and myself.

'*Un mouvamen souciau en marcho!*' it announces in this ancient tongue. 'The rest,' he points out, 'is written in both languages. As you can see, the form states clearly that we are neither a political party nor a sect. We are an independent body fighting hard for the recognition of our mother tongue. We want it taught in schools and spoken in our day-to-day lives. It is a quintessential part of our culture.'

The girls read the forms while I decide upon several small circular cheeses encrusted with herbs or peppers and Marcel wraps them for us. Through the window I glimpse Michel waiting by the car. He wanders over towards a small herd of goats. I smile, divining his thoughts.

'Were you able to find a use for all your tomatoes?' Marcel asks me.

I turn back, confused.

'Was the recipe I gave you helpful?'

And then I remember that I have forgotten to thank him. He advised me to halve our harvested tomatoes, lay them out on our flat roof to dry in the sun, and then add them to his very delicious *chèvre à l'huile*. The last time I visited him must have been three months back, during our tomato surfeit, after René suggested the idea to me. I nod brusquely, shying away from the memory.

Elegantly parcelled cheeses in hand, we wave our *au revoirs* – Marcel invites us to return later, if we fancy, to lend a hand with *la traite*, the evening milking – and set off, but not before Michel has reminded us that to accompany our mouthwatering *fromages* we will need yards of fresh, soft bread. 'Eyes peeled for a good baker, please. You know, *chérie*, I still think we should buy a goat of our own,' he says. 'Look at them.'

'What if they eat our olives?' I counter, but I suspect that, in the fullness of time, my objection will be overcome.

A kilometre or so along the way, as we approach the outskirts of the mediaeval city of Tourrette-sur-Loup, we make another stop for the required baguettes. This *boulangerie*, like so many here, is also a local *pâtisserie*, and the fresh fruit tartlets on display look too tempting to ignore. We choose two: a lemon and almond and a pear and apricot, and I ask the woman to wrap a couple of their onion tarts while she's about it.

'Mmm, what's that smell?' I have been seduced by something flavourful that I can't quite identify, sweet yet nuttyish, wafting from the rear of the building. The homely baker's wife grins, picks up a tray and flourishes the house speciality. '*Pâte de guimauve, fait à la maison!*' she cackles.

Home-made marshmallows. I have never seen them on sale before. At least, not direct from the oven like these. We buy a greedy man's portion, white and pink and soft as downy pillows. Our good lady weighs them up and off we go, leaving the shop laden with goodies – I feel the seeping warmth from the bread and the bagfuls of sweetmeats clutched against my chest – and I am suddenly reminded of my late father visiting us here, and what delight he found in the artistry of Provençal bakers and cakemakers.

Before too long, we are parking the car in the village of Pont-du-Loup. We unpack our shopping, our home-made picnic and our swimming gear, and embark on our hike. Passing a small *maison de confiserie* bearing the name of a well-established French confectionery house, we resist the temptation to step inside. Here, in the foothills of the lower Alp region, a few modest farmhouses cling to the twin hillsides that converge at the foot of this canyon. We move into single file and prepare to penetrate the uninhabited interior.

This cleft, riven into two gigantic faces of salmon-beige rock, which, even in this dry season, has a substantial river running right through it, is a majestic sight. Gone is the lush, subtropical beauty of the coast. This is an altogether more awesome landscape.

'Any idea why the river is named Loup?' I yell to Michel, who has taken the lead. He shakes his head.

Loup means wolf. No doubt in former days wolves travelling in hungry packs hunted these mountains; it could be the origin of the name.

The dust track at the river's edge, *la rive*, is narrow and winding. Mountain streams puddle the path. If there is underground water to be prospected from our rocky small-holding, it would be fed by one of a million of these mountain runlets. Which reminds me that I must, somehow, track down René. It only now occurs to me that I have no idea where he lives; all we have are telephone numbers.

In winter this track would be mulched in rust-coloured oak leaves, sodden with water and black sinking mud, but this is the rainless season. Today, the only hindrances to our procession are the broken branches we encounter, snapped off somewhere way on high, or monumental felled trunks which block the route like feudal drawbridges, but we scramble over or circumvent them without difficulty, passing our bags from one to the other.

I feel sure there are raptors nesting or hunting here, but, craning my neck, even squinting, I see only drifting smudges. Any bird soaring above is too remote for me to identify. The sky, a visible curvy mass between the two rims of the canyon, looks to me like an inflated blue mouth. Warholesque. Butterflies on either side of the steep banks flit from one perched plant to the next and I attempt to identify both flora and fauna, mostly unsuccessfully. But this territory is untampered with; whatever grows here is native. Species that have survived for millennia.

La garrigue Méditerranéenne. Numerous plants compose the garrigue. Dog rose, tamarisk, blackberry bramble, rock rose, holly, myrtle, rosemary, ivy . . . others I cannot recall now.

Our marching is hot going. It is a thirst-inducing, dusty activity. Even with the river pounding tantalisingly close and an abundance of verdant vegetation brushing against our sweating flesh, the enclosed space feels dense and airless. We climb up, we climb down, we swing left, we swing right, and each progression seems to take us further from the riverbed. Midges swarm like bolts of mesh netting and irritate.

'Look down there!' calls Clarisse.

Thirty metres beneath us is a sparkling rock pool. A perfect invitation to picnic and swim.

'But how can we reach it? The descent looks dicey.'

'Shall we try?'

The girls turn to Papa – *always to Papa* – who decides that it is more prudent to continue. 'There'll be a well-trodden access soon and from there we'll approach with safety. If not, we'll find another pool. There are several further along. Don't worry.'

No one doubts the wisdom of his words, and so on we step. The day is reaching its zenith and I am beginning to feel faint, woozy with heat and lack of oxygen, but I am keen not to create a fuss, particularly in the light of recent events, and so I fall back, discreetly taking up the rear position.

We travel on for half a kilometre, more or less, before reaching an iron bridge, painted green – almost the same brilliant hue as the praying mantis I have been observing. It transports us over to the far bank and to the left, which means that we have swung back on ourselves and, before long, we find a narrow conduit that delivers us to the very same splendid rock pool Clarisse spotted a while back. From this angle, the descent is perfectly accessible and without danger. Our footsteps crackle and crunch on dozens of tiny twigs.

'Wow!'

'How lovely!'

And it is: a lush and stony oasis. A lonely, hidden place.

Luckily for us, the pool is bordered by substantial balloon-shaped boulders where we throw our bags in the shade of half a dozen leaning holm-oaks – these native evergreens grow everywhere in this region – seeded tight up against one another.

We tear off our clothes and fall into the water. It gurgles and bubbles and takes our breath away as we scream loudly and immerse our sticky bodies, splashing to and fro. The water is fabulous. Vanessa skids her hands across the crystal surface of the pool and a white spume rises, soaking Michel's face.

'Hey!' he cries. And then both girls take up the game. I hear the call of *'Papa! Papa!'* echo round the gorge until Papa dives out of range like a seal hunting fish.

Afterwards, we rub ourselves and one another furiously and fast and then lay out the towels to dry on the boulders. The girls go off to explore the rocky clefts and two rather litter-ridden caves we passed back by a waterfall beyond the green bridge, leaving us alone with river and sun.

'Watch your step,' Papa calls after them, but they don't turn back. They are not listening. Arms linked, then hand in hand, long-legged beauties, hurrying away to share secrets, to lose themselves in rocks and thickets and be grown-up girls together. I watch them until they are out of sight, and then, a moment or two later, I unfold a rush mat in readiness for our picnic. Still thinking of the girls I lie back, supine and glistening wet, against the darkly freckled, porous rock. A tear threatens.

I feel the brush of Michel's damp hand against my haunch, not a sexual caress so much as a supportive one, reassuring and reminding me that here at my side is companionship and love.

And how would I manage without it?

The roaring river cools us with its spray while the vegetation growing out of the rock face is our organic, filigreed parasol. We bask and dry in the dappled heat like lizards on the voluptuous curves of the boulders until a couple of mosquitos appear from out of the undergrowth, approaching from dark, fetid everywheres to bother us. The location is deceptive. You don't expect to find them here but they zirr and dive-bomb, hoping to feed off our blood. I sit up and reach for a bottle of mineral water, flicking my wrist crossly at one of the intruders.

Michel breaks off an oak branch and fans it over me like a switch. 'Are you having a nice day?' he enquires, having surely picked up on my evolving mood.

I stare at the river, the thundersome rush of the river, roaring furiously by. We have to shout to be heard above the din of the fast-flowing crystalline water, but before I can answer, while I am formulating thoughts, we are disturbed by the unexpected ring of his mobile phone breaking into this intimacy.

'Why did you bring that thing with you?' I demand irritably.

'In case it's Serge.'

It is. He has had an accident. He is unharmed, but his car is a write-off. Michel shoots questions, establishes location details, then digs for our car keys and bends to give me a quick kiss. Before he sets off on this rescue mission, we arrange that I will wait for him here with the girls or, if it gets too late, at the café we spotted in Pont-du-Loup close by the mouth of the canyon.

When he has gone, to relax and keep troubling doubts at bay, I plunge myself back into the water. Returning to my rock, I begin to lay out our picnic. Plastic tumblers, even for wine – glasses here may cause accidents – and then the cheeses from Marcel's farm, our fresh bread, the marshmallows and various hams. I cover the whole with napkins to protect against creepy-crawlies and await the girls' ravenous return. Once this has been accomplished I settle with a book, only to be interrupted by something wet pelting the back of my neck. I think it must be a bird and lift my head. The next raindrop splats on my cheek. It is pursued in quick succession by several more, all as large as saucers. Drops are plopping heavily against the overhead trees – I love the sound – while the river in front of me begins to furrow and spin and groove with the force of the rain now sheeting down.

Glancing skywards again, I see chutes of rain descending out of louring black clouds. This is no quick summer shower. Hurriedly, I begin to pack away all that I have painstakingly spread out.

'Vanessa! Clarisse!' My cries echo back to me, but there is no other response. The mountain water cascades forth, thundering by like a high-speed train. Oblivious, on its sonorous journey to the coast, of the potential separation of a trio of women. The roaring, yowling wolf. We don't want to get trapped here. I pull on my shorts, gather up the bags, too numerous for me to carry alone, and look about for shelter. Could I make it to the caves? I doubt it. Not with this load. I am already soaked, sopping, streaming. I haul the bags back against the cliff face and shelter beneath the trees. It is surprisingly dry. The ground at my feet remains dusty, untouched by a single raindrop. Water gutters all around me but I am safe; huddled, shivering, but refuged.

Peering out into the rain, my thoughts turn to the book I had intended to write this year. Listening to René and his tales of days gone by had set me thinking of the wonders of the old order of Provence alongside the new Côte d'Azur. Crouched here on my hams, I could be a cavewoman. Time has slipped away. Nothing where I am has changed in a million years. I should get back to my book; find something. Or the sense of failure will bring me down.

A clap of thunder is followed by a rustling sound and then cries and, from out of a curtain of heavy, wet leaves and sheeting rain, the girls come bounding towards me. Young gazelles, unicorns to the rescue. T-shirts over their heads; helmets of sodden cotton. They are laughing, wide smiles, healthy teeth, exuberant with life and the thrill of this mini-adventure.

'We got lost!'

'*Où est Papa?*'

'Serge telephoned.' And I recount the events.

'We should get out of here!'

'Let's go!' yells Vanessa. They swoop up belongings and hare on ahead. I look back, squinting, checking our spot.

'The marshmallows! I forgot the marshmallows.'

There they are, stuck like rotting mushrooms on the streaming mottled boulder, waterlogged and drowning in the summer downpour.

'*Tant pis!*'

'*Trop tard!*'

By the time we belt into the smoky café – a squelching, giggling hysterical entry – we are drowned rats. '*Chocolat chaud! Chocolat chaud!*' we are screaming.

Large cups of hot chocolate and pizzas with *saucissons* and local free-range eggs are ordered and while we await these, we rub each other's hair with the dryish towels providently stuffed and zipped away inside one of the backpacks. Men, propped against the bar drinking and smoking, stare at us, eyeing the girls.

Surely they take me for their mother.

For hours we sit there, reading, watching the rain, which

eventually gives way to a street potted with shining puddles and a cloudy blue sky. Coachloads of tourists come and go, tramping the village's sole thoroughfare, chomping on sweets purchased at the *confiserie*. I observe it all – this unscheduled mountain day – through the window, including the girls' reflections, all the while asking myself, what if there were no Michel? What would remain between myself and these two vibrant creatures, reading and nattering at my side, guzzling Coke and ordering yet more hot chocolate?

I recall occasions during my troubled teenage years when I was dragged off to partake of disagreeable lunches with one or other of my father's mistresses. I measured them, those unctuous women, none of whom possessed the beauty of my own mother. I mistrusted those who went to great lengths to curry favour with me. And I disliked with an even greater fervour those who ignored me, purring and pouting at Daddy as though I didn't exist.

Who is the intruder in this threesome? I used to ponder.

Still, I am the wife of these girls' father, not his mistress. There is a difference, isn't there? Even so . . .

And finally, late in the afternoon, after we have positively gorged ourselves on cakes and pizzas and hot chocolate, Michel and Serge turn up and we make for home.

When we arrive, we find hillocks of soaked sand in the driveway. Fortunately, Quashia has had the foresight to store the dozens of bags of cement in one of the stables.

Life turns between repose and activity. All around us the Arabs are transporting building materials, shifting wheelbarrows, laying planks up and across the hill while the rest of us are centred round the pool. Michel and I flit between one and the other. I to supply gallons of drinking water, Michel to survey the work process, though Quashia has the chain under control.

Serge is staying on with us. Such a gentle, introspective man who sits alone for hours in a deckchair in the garden. He sketches, mostly.

Occasionally, I see Clarisse crouch at his side on the warm terracotta tiles engaging him in easy conversation about his work. Otherwise he says little, even at mealtimes. I find myself watching him, slyly monitoring him, with awe and curiosity. Like a dog on the scent I keep tabs on him. He seems so unsuited to the practical demands of everyday life that I fear for his future. How will he cope alone? What has he learned about grief, about how to accommodate it, that I can steal from him? I empathise with his desolation. It mirrors my own. He shelters his pain with such dignity, losing himself within the fabulous worlds of his animation storyboards.

He works.

Is the grief of a male different from that of a female? I would like to ask him, but I don't.

I observe him beneath our cream-white parasol, sketching a translucent-blue dragonfly hovering by the pool. And the next day he has created a character: an iridescent, queen-like nymph with a humanised face and the svelteness of the dragonfly. Out of this world.

I should be working too. When summer is over, I tell myself, when everyone has left, then I'll begin again. Dig out my notes. But the very idea of summer being over, of the emptiness it will bring, fills me with terror.

A letter arrives from London, from Richard, my specialist. It reaffirms our conversation in his office. The various tests and scans I have undergone confirm that, though there appears to be no precise physical damage, to carry a child the full term is not possible. I stare at the page, clutching on to it. There is good news, though. In every other sense, I am healthy. All the scans are clear. He rounds off the missive by suggesting that whenever I am ready I should telephone, make another appointment to see him, 'for a chat'. I fold up the letter and secrete it beneath my computer in my den. A lifeline deep within me, centuries old, millennia old, has been severed. Atavistic rights I took to be my God-given entitlement have been withdrawn, snatched away from me, leaving me, in a world bred to propagate, as what?

Standing out in the heat on the upper terrace, I watch the girls and Serge lazing round the pool, see their obvious contentment as they sketch, swim, dangle their toes into the cool water, do nothing more strenuous than basking in their day, and I creep back inside, close up the shutters to block out the tireless light, the singsong cries of the Arabs at work and the trance-inducing heat. I burrow deep beneath the duvet, burying myself in a cave of darkness, beating back despair. Lying in the bed alone, hot tears roll silently down my cheeks. And when Michel comes looking for me, I pretend to be asleep.

He is returning from a trip to the garden centre, where he has bought me *nénuphars*, waterlilies, for the pond. He 'wakes' me, takes me by the hand and together we settle them in the deep green water. Six white blossoms floating like miniature sails. The foot-long carp dart in and around them. They are exquisite. Several blue dragonflies arrive. Darners, I think these are – the females are less brightly coloured than the males. They congregate there, hovering, or anchored to the petals where their tails lift and fall like teeny silver pumps. An expression of their contentment?

In the evening he leads me back to the pond. 'Come and look.' There, clipped to the creamy rim of one of the *nénuphars,* we discover two slender, graceful insects.

'Narrow-winged damselflies,' smiles Michel, who has looked them up in one of my nature books.

I smile too, aware to what lengths he has gone, but his

attentions serve only to exacerbate my sense of inadequacy. I had not bargained on this inner turmoil, had not expected to be so poleaxed by mourning, to be thrown into such isolation by it.

In the not too distant future, we will be the proud owners of a second water basin, but from where will we fill it? We could reroute our exterior pipes, or create an extension branch from the piping fed by the Lyonnaise des Eaux's central reserve, which travels up from our pumphouse, but that will prove to be extremely expensive. I telephone M. Di Luzio, our plumber, from whom we haven't heard a word since the film festival. We need a quote for laying the extra lengths of pipe. But his message tells me yet again that he is away. Yes, it's holiday time. I attempt to find René once more to find out what news there is, if any, of his celebrated colleague, the water diviner.

'Well, I can't ask him to visit you now.'

'Why, because it's August?'

'No. He's driving north for the eclipse.'

Ah yes, I was forgetting that any day now the earth is to be totally eclipsed by the sun.

'I'll call you at the weekend,' he promises, 'when it's all over.' And we leave it like that.

Everyone, everywhere is being whipped into eclipse fever. Even our trio of Arabs and Quashia declare it a holiday. Each night on the news, each day in the newspapers, we hear of the route of the eclipse, which will sweep a diagonal swatch across our eastern hemisphere, namely – as far as the French are concerned – across northern France.

Provence does not figure in what is known as the 'totality zone'; we are too far south for 'maximum coverage'. But it is predicted that we should have between ninety-six and ninety-seven degrees coverage. This offers shops and local radio and television stations an opportunity to take full commercial advantage.

Michel sends me to the village to deposit a roll of film for developing and to fetch eye-protection masks, special eclipse glasses, so that we can stare at the sun without danger. I trudge from shop to shop but all the *commerçants* have sold out. '*Plus*,' they tell me, but assure me that another delivery is expected in the morning.

The following morning I duly return, a few hours before the predicted eclipse. I collect Michel's developed photographs, but have no luck with the dratted glasses. The shopkeepers shrug when I ask what alternatives they can suggest. 'Don't look,' is the best they propose.

Back at the farm everyone is disappointed. We have one pair between us – Vanessa bought a pair in Cannes – which we will share. We will station ourselves outside anyway and take it in turns to wear the special lenses. I suspect that the temptation to look heavenwards will be irresistible.

'Can the glare really blind us?' asks Clarisse.

'Better not risk it,' cautions her father.

Jessye Norman is due to give an eclipse concert at the magnificent gothic cathedral of Reims. Reims, the capital of the Champagne district in northern-eastern France is, today, the centre of the 'totality zone'. In 1429, the newly victorious French Dauphin entered that cathedral to be crowned Charles VII of France, thus becoming the first of a long line of French kings to celebrate their coronations there. At Charles's side was his companion in battle, the eighteen-year-old Joan of Arc. The Maid of Orléans was the same age then as Michel's daughters are today.

Michel switches on both televisions to full volume, opens the French windows in our bedroom on the east side of the house and dusts down our ancient transistor radio. We troop outside: Serge, the girls, Vanessa already sporting her glasses, tripping and giggling on the steps, Michel with cumbersome radio in hand and me at the rear, flanked by the dogs. The morning news has warned that all domestic animals should be kept inside but we have decided, because we are not in the totality zone, that there is no serious threat. Our furry faithfuls will be less perturbed in our company than locked up in the house.

We settle ourselves over near the washing line. Not having bothered to bring chairs, we perch on the drystone wall or squat on the sun-baked grass. Michel is kneeling, trying to stand the radio upright. He is fiddling with the tuning knobs, twisting and turning, searching for the station, while the ancient ghettoblaster hisses and whistles like a drowning kettle.

And then, miraculously, there is music: a blast of ebony notes. Jessye's opulent voice belts forth 'He's Got the Whole World in His Hands', but this is not the tinny reproduction we had expected from our radio. It is a sublime, surround-sound performance assailing us from every direction. Other homes across the hillsides must have come up with the same idea, for the soprano's supersonic voices are airborne; a fleet of aluminium ribbons soaring beyond the hilltops. We are, all of us, silenced and amazed.

'*J'ai commencé d'utiliser le noir pur comme une couleur de lumière et non comme une couleur d'obscurité*,' wrote Henri Matisse.

I have begun to use pure black as a colour of light and not as a colour of darkness.

Bathed in sound from the concert, I attempt to penetrate Matisse's vision. Am I not witnessing the living expression of it? I turn to share this but the others are now engaged in an astronomical debate. All except Serge, who is staring at his feet. He would be fascinated by Matisse's observations, I feel sure, but watching him, I defer, choosing to leave him with the privacy of thought. What memories are haunting him? I wonder. Is he floundering like me, rooting about, trying to reconstruct meaning?

'No, it was Copernicus, not Galileo! Galileo came later.' I hear Vanessa, charged by her young-blooded certainty. Such certainty. 'Copernicus was the first to understand that the earth orbited the sun and not the other way around.'

'That's right, of course,' confirms Papa.

I read that after England's last total eclipse, on 29 June 1927, Virginia Woolf wrote: 'We had fallen. It was extinct. There was no colour. The earth was dead.'

No colour. I try to picture that. The earth dead. Extinction. As I close my eyes to spear her image, I realise that the temperature is dropping. I feel chilly. And there is no birdsong. No songs of nature at all. The exquisite music, yes, and the conversation alongside me. I open my eyes. My skin has goosepimpled. The dogs at my feet are silent and uncharacteristically still. Lucky's ears are standing to attention; she is alert in the way she is when she sniffs intruders or trouble. The other two, Ella and Bassett, are prostrate at my feet, snouts buried beneath paws.

The universe is rotating, turning the clock to another setting. I see shadows lengthening across the earth, distorted elongations of the cherry and olive trees reaching across the groves, creeping towards us like spirits stealing forth. I behold shadows where there have never been shadows before. It is eerie, quite spooky. Souls of the departed tiptoeing out to play. I shiver, casting off this image quickly.

Although the day is growing dimmer it remains bizarrely clear, sharp. Neither dusk nor dawn, day nor night. Rather, a flash of lightning frozen in time. On the terrace beneath us the cacti resemble giant-eared cartoon figures. I hear voices rising from afar, the rattle of shouted conversations, nervous-edged cries in the valley as the world slides into darker mode;

a limboland of quasi-crepuscular noon. The heavens are retreating, as though the gods were switching off our universe, drawing the celestial curtains once and for all. For a moment I feel nauseous. I experience a profound sense of panic. I glance about me, taking in the family gathered here, the people I love. Each momentarily silent, lost in his or her own contemplations; awestruck, perhaps, or pondering similarly gloomy demises to this unnatural day.

Michel picks up his explanation of the death of megastars, describing white dwarfs and what causes them. How long does a star live? I ask myself. And then, bizarrely, I hear Vanessa raise the same question and Michel's response: 'The bigger the star, the quicker it dies.'

'Compared to the sun, how much bigger are these stars?' It is Vanessa once again.

'Varying sizes, but scientists are not able to measure precisely. Twenty times bigger, I don't know. But when they implode they form the most mysterious phenomenon in the whole cosmos. I'm sure you know it, Vanessa?'

She shakes her head.

'The black hole.'

The black hole. Yes, I know it. I've been there. I lift my eyes to stare at the sun, to challenge that black enemy. Throwing my head recklessly back, gazing impudently upwards, knowing I shouldn't, but what the hell; inexorably drawn to the phenomenon occurring billions of light years above. The glare is blinding; it shocks. A sheet flaps lightly on the washing line. It catches my attention and its snowy-white ordinariness drags me to my senses.

'What are you doing? *Chérie!*'

I close my eyes tight before the light brands my retina. I see silver and black rings, crescents, circles, cuticles, wafers of luminosity; my sight has been dazzled, momentarily zapped.

Michel reaches towards me, his hand grabs my wrist. '*Chérie*, please take care.'

Jessye is now singing Gershwin's 'Summertime' from *Porgy and Bess* as the darkening grows darker; a wink, centuries old, received as though in slow motion.

We are each marginally apart, in our space, transfixed, bewitched by music and the coupling of star and planet, this mysterious astral love song. Each of us, that is, except Clarisse, who suddenly rises and shifts places, settling herself at Serge's side. I study her as she draws her knees tightly up against her daisy-stalk frame, wrapping arms round calves to keep warm and then, so imperceptibly, tilts herself in his direction.

I am stunned. I hadn't read the special attachment between these two but now, in this ghost of a light, their future is chalked, pellucid-clear as though it had always been written.

Without ado, I spring up and hurry inside.

On the television, the news report from Reims is taking a dramatic tone: if the clouds don't clear the eclipse will be obscured. An anchorman is counting down the minutes, the seconds. I think I hear that it is raining up there, but I am not listening, not paying attention. I cross through the living room and enter the haven of my den, where I switch on my computer and begin to bang at the keys.

Do I have the right to be jealous of C's attentiveness to S? His loss is unquestionably worse than mine. I don't OWN grief. Am I jealous of their youth without being aware of it? Do I begrudge them their beauty, their shiny futures; the possibilities they hold in their hands, their almost certain fecundity?

'What are you doing?'
'Scribbling.'

'Yes, I see that. Won't you come back outside and join us?'

I don't answer. I can't speak. This day, this darkness, this family gathering is almost too much to bear.

'Please, talk to me,' begs Michel. 'What is the matter with you?'

'It's fine for you, you have children!' I snap, not meaning to, not even knowing what carelessly thought-through thoughts I was about to utter.

'It's easy for you to say you don't mind that we don't have children, that if I can't produce any . . .' I falter. 'That we are still a couple, no matter what. You have your family. Those girls are yours, *yours*, not ours. I am the one who . . .' my voice breaks. I cannot continue. Overwhelmed by the affliction which aches like a deep, black chasm, I drop my head forward over my desk. My forehead brushes against the keyboard which instantaneously produces an alphabet of confusion on the screen. 'I feel so many things. All of them negative. I feel inadequate, a failure,' I mutter.

Michel remains a moment by the doorway, where no door exists now because he took it away to open up the space and create a more luminous living area. He looks on helplessly in my direction.

'Shall we discuss this now, or . . . ?'

I don't respond because I don't know what to say. I had never intended to embark on this, but now that I have I pinch at the corner of the envelope hidden beneath my Apple Mac and slip it out. Richard's letter. Without a word, I hand it to Michel.

He takes it and reads it gravely. And then lifts his eyes to mine. 'Come here.'

I remain where I am.

'*Papa! Papa! Viens! Vite!*' It's Vanessa calling. He hesitates.

'Please go, they're waiting for you. They want to share this day with you.'

'*Viens, chérie*, please.' He holds out his arm. '*Chérie, s'il te plaît.*'

I flip a glance over to where he is waiting patiently for me and rise awkwardly, accepting his outstretched hand. He takes me in his arms and hugs me tight. 'I know it might feel like the end of the world, particularly today, but it isn't. We'll get through this together,' he whispers into my hair. 'I am here for you. *Je t'aime enormement.*'

We step out into a world that has been transformed.

Everything is lit as though by floodlight, everywhere cloaked in silence: an enchanted stage. The gloaming hour before the appearance of the Fairy Queen. Heads are tilted heavenwards – it is safe to look now – entranced faces pearly-skinned, lustrous in a world that is perfectly still.

Two images come to my mind: the parable in the Bible of Lot and his wife looking backwards and being frozen into pillars of salt, and, in the teachings of Zen, the notion of being so at one with oneself, so in union with the universe, that you can hear a blade of grass growing.

The universe shifts yet another notch, such a great lumbersome clock, and the sun's corona, that halo of oyster light made up of the superheated gases surrounding it, is glowing like a translucent wedding band. All five of us are transfixed by the aubergine heavens. We are in communion with the stars which, at the zenith of this supernatural, surreal day, are winking like expiring fireflies.

And all at once the spell is broken. It's over. Daylight returns. It comes like an explosion of shattering glass as a flock of herring gulls appear from out of nowhere and screech angrily, raucously at the silence. Tearing into the sable darkness, they fly low, beating their wings, swooping and turning. They are disoriented, not knowing if it's day or night.

'Surely it must be night, for we have been in darkness,' a

cacophony of creatures cry out in unison. The world is raging with confusion. Crickets, birds burst into song; I hear the crowing of a distant cock which, bemused, probably thinks it's daybreak, the braying of a far-off donkey, the cicadas zirring like there's no tomorrow – and, perhaps, cowering between stalks and leaves, they had feared there would not be one ever again. Noah has unbattened the hatches, lowered the gangplank; time to fly free. We are standing in the midst of a new dawning, a newly lit afternoon. I exhale deeply, sensing ineffable relief. I had never before measured how profoundly the flora and fauna depend on this time-honoured structure of day and night, the customary rhythms of the universe, at least as much as we do. And within these routine yet mysterious daily rounds, this ebbing and flowing, this waning and waxing, there exists both loss and gain, suffering and joy, death and birth. And rebirth?

At our feet, from the radio, Jessye's ivory-black voice belts forth, engendering faith. 'Somewhere', and then 'Praise God and Dance'.

René's Bêtise

The Arabs have said their farewells. Utensils and materials have been transported up the hill, their work achieved. Now it is down to Quashia to begin the construction repairs. M. Di Luzio finally returns my call. He is pleased to hear from me, enquires after my escalating success in films – have I been offered a role in Hollywood yet? – and then announces that he has retired.

Ah. I ask him if he can recommend another plumber.

'Well, I don't usually make a habit of suggesting anyone else, but it can't hurt me any longer so try Sordello. You'll find them in the Yellow Pages and they're in the village beneath you.'

'Thank you,' I tell him. '*Et bonne retraite.*'

'Retirement? Bah! I'd rather be working. My wife stalks me, watching every mouthful that passes my lips. No more beer. Oh, well, that's life. I might drop by to borrow some of your garden tools, if you have no objections; I've got myself an allotment. Well, it passes the time. Greetings to Michel.'

'Indeed,' I smile, replacing the phone.

Michel is not at home. He has driven the girls and Serge to Cannes. During their absence René drops by. As is his habit, he arrives with a gift. Today he comes bearing a bottle of eau de vie distilled from our plums. With a twinkle in his eye, he confides that it is illegal to brew home-made alcohol. Only one location in each village – 'and this is not the case in every village, mind you' – has the right to distil alcohol. Naturally, he has figured out a way to circumvent the system.

I thank him for the precious bottle and ask after news of the water dowser. 'We are cleaning up the *bassin*,' I explain, 'and we'll be needing to feed it some time soon, so if there's underground water here . . .'

'*Malheureusement*, he's not here. After the eclipse he decided to spend a few days in the Champagne district to buy some wines. He only drinks champagne, you see.'

I am beginning to doubt the existence of this fellow and am on the brink of saying so when a rattling screech breaks out above us in the parking area. We both lift our heads to see four magpies pecking brutally at one another, staking their territorial rights over a few figs shrivelling on the tree.

'Bloody magpies,' I curse.

'Did I ever tell you about the pet magpie we had when I was a kid? Margot was her name.'

'No.'

'Good Lord, Carol, those branches have grown!' cries our olive master, now pointing up at the cedars overhead. 'They're damned dangerous. You must cut them back. Otherwise you'll have the electricity board on your backs. It's illegal, you know, for your trees to brush the cables, and it could cause a fire. And I don't have to tell you about bush fires.'

'Yes, we've been intending to cut them back all summer, but what with one thing and another . . .'

'No excuse. I'll cut them back for you right now and, as I told you last time, I'll keep the wood. Where's Quashia?'

'He's working up at the second basin. Do you want me to fetch him?'

'No, I'll manage, but I'll need to use his chainsaw. I haven't got mine with me. I lent it to my son. Has Quashia taken the ladders with him? No, there they are. Good.'

And before I can say another word, René is setting about in a purposeful way. It is unusual for him to be in such a hurry. Usually, he prefers a glass of something and a natter first.

'I tell you what,' he calls out to me as I make my way back into the house. 'Why don't you pour us both *un petit verre* while I get the chainsaw warmed up? And then I'll go to work.'

I smile, and then call back to him. 'You don't think we should have the glass of wine later, after you've finished with the ladder?'

'Not at all. It's almost lunchtime.'

Seated on the terrace, a bottle of Beaujolais to hand, I ask him to recount the tale of Margot, the magpie he spoke of.

'*Ah, notre agace,*' he grins.

Agace actually means an irritation – *agacer* is to jar, grate, set one's teeth on edge, and it is used in Provence as a name for magpies because their wretched screeching can drive you to distraction. As does their habit of filching.

'Margot lived with us for eight years and she drove our neighbours and guests crazy. Us as well, sometimes. She was jealous, you see. She couldn't bear it if the cat got more attention than she did. You know, Carol, we were rather poor and my mother used to feed the cat with leftovers from

our meals. Usually we ate pasta, *pâtes*, and the cat seemed
perfectly content with her scraps of that, but Margot would
go mad. She wanted the same, you see. So, when the cat was
dozing or not paying attention, Margot would sneak to the
cat's bowl, steal the squares of pasta and . . . you know that
magpies hide things they have stolen, don't you?'

I nod.

'Do you know where she hid the pasta?'

I shake my head.

'We were poor, as I told you. We ran around in our bare
feet and, while we were at dinner, the bird would sneak
under the table and slip the pasta squares in between our
toes.'

I stare at him incredulously and then burst out laughing.
René is encouraged by my response. He nods, pours himself
a second glass of wine and then continues.

'Our neighbour smoked a pipe. Margot stole the pipe and
threw it in his pond. Eventually, a week or so later, he found
it, dried it out, cleaned it up and put it back on the mantel-
piece, and then, *diable*! it was gone again. Of course, at that
stage, the neighbour hadn't realised that it was our blasted
bird who was responsible, but we kids guessed. The neighbour searched in the pond, but it wasn't there because the
bird was smart. She never hid anything in the same place
twice. He couldn't find that pipe anywhere and gave it up for
lost.'

René reaches for the bottle and proffers it. I shake my
head. He serves himself a top-up.

'But I knew it must be Margot, so I went round to the
neighbour, knocked on his door and said to him: "Monsieur
Braccio, is there a reward for finding your pipe?" He
laughed, ruffled my hair and promised me two francs if I
found it. It was a fortune to me then. I told not a soul but I
kept a watchful eye on our bird. And one morning, weeks

later, bingo! I found it. The magpie was sitting in the neighbour's mimosa tree with the pipe in her beak. She liked to copy, you see. She had understood that the neighbour held the pipe in his mouth and sucked on it, so Margot mimicked him. There she was, happy as Larry, sitting in a fully blossoming golden mimosa smoking a pipe. *Diable.* I got my two francs.' He laughs triumphantly, downing his wine and refilling his glass. I am beginning to wonder if I should remind him about the tree-cutting, but before I can he has launched into another anecdote about the bird.

'She learned to whistle like my father, repeated our names like a parrot and called and whistled for the dog.' Here René imitates the magpie by whistling and calling in a high-pitched voice: '*Flora! Flora!* That was the dog's name,' he explains. The sound has alerted two of our own dogs, who come running in our direction.

'My father used to keep his work boots in the garage alongside a box of nails. Margot stole the nails and hid them in my father's boots, and he cut his feet when he put his boots on and stood on the nails. How we children giggled! Ah, yes, we loved her. She had fallen from a nest. My father found her and we raised her. Eight years she lived with us. She was so crafty. She taught me a few tricks.' He chuckles mischievously and downs the remainder of his Beaujolais – the bottle is almost empty – then sets to work on pruning back the cedar trees while I return to my den, both amused and amazed by our little Provençal olive guru. Just like Margot, he never misses a trick.

I am answering e-mail when I hear the cries, and because my computer is a laptop and works on both battery and electricity I do not immediately notice that our electricity has been cut off.

'*Mon Dieu! Diable! Putain! Qu'est-ce que . . .?*'

I run to the window and throw it open.

There I behold René, at the foot of the ladder, chainsaw hanging from his hand, pouring with sweat, red as a beet-root, covered in bits of cedar foliage, and sticks and twigs and branches everywhere on the ground. But what is most shocking is the firework display of flying sparks.

'Oh my God!' I cry. 'What's happened?'

But it is quite clear what has happened. The tree has been felled in the wrong direction (or 'it turned on its own in the wind', as René tries to convince me later) and has landed on the four electricity cables running via the pylon close by the swimming pool to the house. While stretching from the ladder to the tip of a branch, René has lost his footing and with it his control of the chainsaw, which has struck the central trunk of the tree, still zirring. The upper portion of the tree, partially sawn through, has cracked and barrelled earthwards, slapping against the overhead electricity cables as it spun. The weight has pushed the highest cable against the one beneath it, and so on, in a domino effect, soldering all four cables as one. Naturally, this has caused a short cir-cuit in the system and our power has gone.

I stare down at the cables. They resemble giant lengths of liquorice, looping towards the ground sending massive streaks of sparks sissing skywards.

I am open-eyed, thunderstruck, by the pyrotechnics taking place before me. 'I'm calling the fire brigade!' I yell. 'Those sparks will set fire to the trees!'

They are indeed ominously close. And what of the summer-dry herbage everywhere on our land?

I hear a female neighbour's cry and then, from down the lane, the roar of another neighbour, Jean-Claude. René, in the *parking* below me stares up at me like a guilty child. 'I think the electricity may have been cut off at the entrance to your property,' he announces sheepishly.

If this predicament weren't so perilous I might be tempted to laugh, because I have never before seen René cowed by anything. The man who made a financial killing out of the Second World War and everything else that has come his way has now landed himself in a very sticky situation.

'I'm on my way down,' I tell him, closing up the window. I tear down the exterior steps to the ground-floor level, bellowing 'Monsieur Quashia!' as I charge alongside the pool, where the skimmers have gone dead. There is little hope that Quashia will have heard me, and, as he will be facing uphill as he works, I doubt that he will have seen the sparks flying, either.

I join René in the *parking*. He looks as though he is about to have a heart attack.

The fireworks are over and the cables have sunk to the tarmac in the *parking* like deflated balloons. I am hit full on by an appalling smell of burning rubber.

'Now what?' I am terrified, but the fact is I have not grasped the magnitude of the accident whereas René has. As I approach, he bursts into action.

'It's because they are *en alu* that they, the cables, are *fondu*. First thing,' he is shouting as he scurries into the garage with the chainsaw, burying it beneath some of Quashia's work clothes, while I follow trying to work out what he is up to, 'I wasn't working here, OK?'

'OK,' I mouth, because at this stage I don't know what else to do or say. 'But what should we do? Call the fire brigade or the EDF?'

'No! No!' He is turning in circles like a small trapped rodent, desperately trying to think his way out of this one. 'I've got it. We must play shocked.'

'I am shocked!' I retort.

There is a high-pitched voice calling my name. I peer out

of the garage. A woman is running up the drive. Who left the gate unlocked? How did she get in?

'Carol! Carol!' she is screaming hysterically.

It's one of our neighbours. 'Oh, God, not her,' I moan.

'*Diable*, I left your gate unlocked,' René confides to me under his breath. 'Quick, run down to meet her. Don't let her up here, whatever you do.'

I do as I am told. He puffs along behind me. 'On second thoughts, keep quiet. I'll handle it.'

'Handle *what?*'

'Er, *bonjour*, Suzanne,' I say to the woman, who I am not in the least fond of and try to avoid even on the best of days. 'What is it?'

'There's been a disaster!'

'Really?' I play-act.

'An accident somewhere. We have no electricity, nothing at all. Do you know anything about this?' Her voice rises and the tone grows shriller and meaner as she grills me.

I shake my head, waiting for René to chip in and 'handle it', but he says nothing.

She continues: 'The whole lane's cut off, as is the motorway – all the way to Antibes.'

'WHAT!!' I scream. 'All the way to . . .' Antibes is close to fifteen kilometres from us.

René steps briskly forward. 'Yes, I was in the garden sorting out a few plant problems, *quelques petits soucis*, for Carol and I thought I was going to be killed when the sparks started flying. Did you see them? I hope you weren't too afraid?'

'I was,' Suzanne admits to him in an altogether softer tone.

'You and Carol must sue the electricity board, as well as the local council, for negligence if the fault is found to be due to an oversight on one of their parts.' His placatory tone, his charming concern, his brazen *lies*, have Suzanne eating out of his hand, and I am left gawping at his audacity.

'Fret not, madame, I will telephone the EDF and get them over here right away.'

'I think Jean-Claude has already done that.'

'Oh, has he?' I hear the edge return to René's voice. 'Well, there's nothing for it but to wait, then. Would you like me to accompany you back to your villa? Although I am sure there will be no further risk.'

'*Mais merci beaucoup. Vous êtes très gentil, monsieur.* What about Carol?'

'Oh, she's fine.'

And René escorts Suzanne back down the drive, leaving me alone, listening to his sweet concern. 'Is there anything you need, *chère* madame?'

Moments later, he climbs back up the path to me and the broiled, perished chaos that is our parking area. He is using the oily rag in his hand to wipe the sweat off his brow, thus blackening his florid face.

'Well, that's dealt with her. Now, we'll have to play this one out,' he says sternly to me. 'According to her, your other neighbour—'

'Jean-Claude.'

'Yes, Jean-Claude, well, he has called the bloody electricity board and they are on their way as I speak. Let me do the talking.'

I nod. I would not dream of interfering. If there is a day to be won, it's René's.

I take a seat over by the pool, wondering whether I should fetch Quashia. I decide that the fewer the people involved at this stage, probably the safer we are. If Michel comes back now . . . At this very moment, a blue EDF van beetles up the drive and two burly technicians get out. They look like they mean business. I rise and move uncertainly in their direction.

Should I leave this to René, or should I come forward, mistress of the house, and say something or other? Offer help, plead ignorance?

René is pointing out the overhead trees, charcoaled by the sparks. They stare heavenwards with sullen expressions.

'*Bonjour, messieurs,*' I call as I approach.

'There's over forty thousand francs' worth of damage,' one of them states in a matter-of-fact manner which I read as a threat.

'All the signalling on the autoroute is out. We have one dead system, burned out back at base. It will take three days' work to repair this lot!' adds the other. 'I think forty grand is an understatement. Someone's going to have to pay.'

I feel my knees buckle. I am not sure if I want to be sick or lie down. What I am sure of is that I don't want Quashia to wander down the hill now and let the cat out of the bag by commenting on René's work. I glance across at our olive hero, who looks, at this moment, no bigger than a pea. 'Any idea what happened?' he asks manfully, but I hear the croak in his voice.

'Well, you are the last house to be affected, so my guess is the problem started here.'

René flashes a look my way. I think he is telling me to get lost.

'Would you gentlemen like a cold drink?' I offer.

'No thanks, ma'am.'

'No, thanks.'

'Well, when I first saw the sparks . . .' begins René, and I am obliged to walk away because I cannot listen to what I know will be a pack of lies. Forty thousand francs is £4,000. I, we, don't possess such a sum.

The next time I look up, from the other side of the pool, where I am seated, worrying, the three men are talking on a telephone. Then they are shaking hands and slapping one another on the back. René is smiling. He comes hurrying towards me while the electricians wait near the cars.

'Quick!' he cries.

'What?'

'Give me some freshly bottled olive oil. The last pressing you have. I'll repay you later.'

I hurry into the summer kitchen, where it is cool and dark and where we store the freshly pressed oil, and pull out two wine bottles filled with our rich, green produce. René grabs them from me, winks and scuttles back to the *parking*. He hands each man a bottle, each shakes his hand vigorously and then they drive off.

'What was all that about?'

'They'll be back later to begin the repairs but we – well, you, that is – are off the hook.'

'Us?' I squeak.

'You would have been responsible for the entire cost of the works,' he tells me proudly. 'But I saved the day.'

'How?'

'It turns out that I know their boss. He used to drive lorries with my son. Well, I know a thing or two about him, a bit of business that goes on here and there, and I told them to give him a call. We had a word. Well, you know how these things are . . .'

I don't, but I don't interrupt him.

'. . . and we agreed all round to register the fault at the motorway. The fact is, Carol, it shouldn't have had such an impact back at their base, so it wasn't really our fault anyway.'

'So that's the end of it?'

'Once they've been back to carry out the maintenance work, yes.'

'Right,' I mutter, not quite sure whether to congratulate him or berate him.

'I need a drink. Shall we finish off that bottle we began at lunch? It seems a long while ago.'

I nod and go off to fetch wine. Frankly, I need a drink too, but there's not much left in that bottle. I dig out another.

Sitting with René on the terrace, I am understandably pensive, anxious even, while he is in high spirits. His mood is triumphant.

'Once we get the dowser here and sort out your well,' he says, chewing on an olive, 'then we'll make that trip to my friend the beekeeper.'

I listen on silently as he promises yet again to introduce me to the 'best beekeeper in Provence', a friend of his since they were lads in the village. Now this gentleman is eighty-three years old but still a professional apiarist.

'When we were youngsters we were competitors for the girls.'

'Who won?' I tease, brightening a little to his mood.

'Oh,' he grins, 'we both did all right. Never touched the local girls, though. Only the foreign ones. Never get into trouble at home, is what I say.'

Well, you can't claim to have followed that dictum today, eh, René? I am thinking, but choose not to say this out loud.

Later, when Michel and the youngsters return, he asks me what on earth has happened. I suggest that we all settle down with a glass of wine in the candlelight.

'It will have to be red wine because the white is no longer chilled. We have no electricity.'

'What's happened?' he repeats.

'Fill your glass with warm wine, Michel, it's a long story.'

Alternatives

During these hot, languid days, while the sun punishes and where nothing but a jet trail disturbs the blueness of the sky, I have been observing Clarisse and how she tends Serge. Her attentions are discreet, unlike mine. Now I find myself studying them both. Pressed against windows, leaning from terraces, always observant of her, my step-daughter, of how she asks to see his work, talks to him at length about the characters he is sketching, the world he is creating. She is prising him out of himself; she listens attentively, chooses subjects that fire his imagination. She is the image of her father. She knows intuitively when to draw near, when to gently intrude and when to hold herself at a distance. Her approaches are graceful. *She* is graceful, never hasty. Tiny, geisha-like steps she takes, and never falters. Yet she has no experience in this – how could she have? – she is playing it by instinct. Still, what I see is her regard for this man so many – how many? Fourteen? – years her senior, and for who he is. I am amazed that one so young, a slip of a girl who has passed her previous summers here collecting wild flowers, a girl I judged as passive, can operate from such depths of compassion and human understanding.

Both Clarisse and Serge are fired by a passion for art and their ability to express themselves through colours and forms. They have that in common. It is their language, as it is a mother tongue to Michel, who lives his own life so richly through colours and forms. He, too, I watch, as he works with Serge at the long wooden table in the garden, pages and pages of artwork for their storyboards spread out before them, fluttering in a ghost of a breeze, pinned down with stones and pens and used cups. I cannot see their eyes, shielded by dark glasses, or hear their words from this distance, but I can read their enthusiasm for their film, their creation. And all the while Clarisse is there, fetching and carrying glasses of wine, bottles of water, or sitting a little apart, chin resting in her hands, elbows on the table, listening attentively, idly studying the sketches, drinking in the process of work.

She has been seduced by the business of filmmaking, that is evident. But there's more. She loves this bereaved man. No doubt about it. Her eyes, flowing over with the vernal joys and palpitations of first love, linger on him and tell their story. And what of him? What he does feel? A shy, physically gauche man at the best of times, he probably has no idea what he feels about any damn thing. I know I don't. Still, he responds to her. Fragile emotions. Unspoken words, tender glances, drawings exchanged – messages only they can read – long walks side by side or, more frequently, one trailing the other until they reach a resting place within the harbour of the fruiting trees. Sometimes they are gone for hours on end, lost among the butterflies and wasps and vintage heat. Love in the olive groves. It certainly is a love affair of sorts. With Clarisse at his side, his unthreatening companion, Serge is healing. I clock the changes taking place within him. He is picking up the pieces. And what do I feel? Bittersweet emotions engulf me. Those youngsters have time. Together, or individually, they have their futures. But what of me?

Vanessa, too, is absent most days. She takes the scooter and goes to the beach, returning late, flushed with sea wind (and kisses, I am sure of it), brown as chocolate licked shiny in the melting heat. She, too, has met someone, and she has flowered overnight. She has become radiant. I mention it to Michel. He frowns. 'I don't think so,' he says. 'Why would you think that?'

Because I am a woman.

Even if these girls are not my daughters, I am alert to them. To the treasures of their enchantments. And if they were my daughters I would enfold them in my arms and hug them with such force and josh with them, begging them to share their secrets with me. 'Recount your happinesses, your discoveries, whisper them to me.' But they aren't, and there's the rub.

The water bill arrives, and sends us reeling. Nine thousand francs for three months' supply. Even when we discovered a leak in the swimming pool a while ago, it was nowhere near as much as this. We have been charged for approximately 1,500 cubic metres of water. It cannot be possible! And then we remember M. Halaz and his remarkable results in the garden. Delighted as we were, they have come at a price. They have left us with a sum to pay three times higher than we have ever shelled out before.

'Think how much more expensive it would be if we were to plant the new trees,' I say to Michel.

'We haven't decided not to,' he returns.

I do not respond. I gather up our coffee cups from the terrace and carry them inside.

He follows with jams and yoghurts. 'What do you say?'

'I don't want to plant trees. I can't take on anything else.'

I may have given up on the olives but I am still struggling with the elusive beemasters, who have all retreated inland and refuse in this escalating heat to visit us here. One woman I have been talking to on the telephone scoffs at the idea of bringing her hives so close to the coast. 'Too many tourists, too much traffic and the area is overconstructed.'

'Not where we are.'

'*Desolée. Non.* It's far too polluted where you are,' she says. I sigh, because from her point of view, this is probably not unreasonable, and we may never find our hivemaster.

Quashia has completed the repair work to the *bassin*. Today, he and Michel will go to work on the interior, which resembles a jungle. We all traipse up the hill to take a look. When I stand on piled stones and peer inside the old stone chamber, I see it is a breeding ground for plants. There are tiger lilies shooting up and wild, willowy canes growing within and Lord knows what else has seeded. The cane of Provence, I tell them, is one of the earliest plants to have been found on this Mediterranean coast. Cannes takes its name from the canes that used to grow along its saline littoral. They are known to survive best in hot, humid environments.

'Here, look at this!' calls Michel. 'The wall bears a mason's name, inscribed into the stone. No date though, which is a pity.'

The terraces up here are bare, save for a few self-seeded baby pines, thin as pencils, swaying gently in the altitude heat. It is ideal land for planting olives, or for the hives. *L'emplacement des ruches.* Yes, I can picture a row of beehives up here, out of reach of the dogs. No one could claim this patch is polluted. I breathe in deeply and the resiny air sings through my lungs.

'What's that noise?' I ask the two men, who are deciding how best to approach the basin cleaning.

'Sounds like chainsaws,' replies Michel.

I look about, wondering where the distraction could be coming from, but the forest is too dense to gauge the direction.

'They are cutting trees over on the other side of the valley,' says Quashia without concern.

'But we're in a green belt. *Une zone verte*. Nobody has the right to cut down trees!' I cry. 'It's illegal!'

'No, it's fine, don't worry. They are only pruning them, tidying up the land.'

When I return to the house to make coffee I hear screams and shouts from the *bassin* and rush out to see what is happening. Quashia hares down the hill with the step of a teenager. A family of deep russet-red squirrels are inhabiting the basin and sticks are needed to encourage them out. 'We don't want to hurt them,' he shouts as he passes. 'Come back up and see.'

But halfway up the hill, I am interrupted by the arrival of the new plumber, M. Sordello. He seems a very excitable fellow, hooting incessantly and bawling from his van, door open, cigarette in hand.

'Anyone home? Hello, hello! Anyone home?'

'I'm coming,' I scream from the hill, puffing and panting back down the track.

'Jesus! How many dogs have you got? Call them off!'

'Three. I have already chained up the Alsatian. The other two are reasonably harmless.'

I outline our requirements and he takes one look up the hill and shouts – I learn later that he always shouts – 'I'm not climbing up there! Not in this bloody heat! It'll have to wait until autumn.'

'Couldn't we take a gentle stroll up so that you can give us an approximate costing?'

He huffs and sighs dramatically, scratching his balding head, twitching his beaked nose. 'Any chance of a cup of coffee first? I'm bloody exhausted. I hate this weather. Roll on winter.'

I go inside to pour the freshly made coffee. He follows me in, still smoking. 'How do you take it, Monsieur Sordello?'

'Black, five sugars.'

Five sugars? No wonder he is jumping like a jack-in-the-box. We go out on to the terrace, and I am pointing up the hill, explaining what we need, when I see Clarisse and Serge up ahead. Michel is waving to me. There is much excitement, but I cannot make out what is going on. Sordello seizes his chance to be on his way, promising to return another day, in the evening, when the sun is less fierce.

'I'll give you a bell later,' he shouts, zipping back out of our lives.

The squirrels have successfully escaped. They have levered themselves on to the olive stick Quashia has lowered into the basin, scurried up it and then leaped to freedom. All except one, a baby that lost its footing on the cane. When Quashia attempted to assist, the little creature freaked and drew blood from our gardener's wrist.

I spend the remainder of the morning treating his wound, which is worryingly deep. I want to drive him to the hospital or to our doctor for a tetanus jab, but he won't hear of it. The little squirrel is frightened but not harmed. We decide to let her go. How she leaps! She flies through the air, landing in a cedar tree, and from there scoots from tree to tree until she is lost in the verdant wild.

Serge left for Paris this morning, loaded down with work for his project with Michel. We said our farewells, with hugs and embraces, and then Michel drove him to the airport. All day long Clarisse has looked downhearted, tramping the hill in search of her father.

I have never felt jealous of Michel's family, never felt any desire to intrude upon or despoil that past life of his, the years he spent with the girls' mother and all that they built together. On the contrary, I have always heartily welcomed that past; it is a vital and significant fraction of the man I love, the man Michel is today, even though I know precious little about that time. Michel is inscrutable and he is discreet. That first marriage and those early years belong to him and those who shared it. Not to me. I have no rights there. The girls rarely speak to me about Maman, even though she and I have met on several occasions. I like her. She makes me laugh; she is neat, witty and pretty. Still, it is their world, their universe, and it does not include me. Only on rare occasions do I skirt its periphery. Michel and I, *we*, came later, when so much was already in place, but I have never perceived myself as an outsider. My relationship with him, his generous love for me, has given me a secure foundation, one I never knew before. It gathers me up, cocoons and protects me. But my misery is eating into it, breeding fears and doubt. Worries nag me. How will I heal? How can I move beyond this failure? What if Michel should leave me? What witness to our love would remain? He and his first wife have the girls; they are the witnesses to that young love. Without children of our own, there will be nothing. Our love will have been a fleeting instant in time; a memory.

The following morning, after a tormented night, I drag myself to my den, not even bothering to dress. I heave down files and riffle furiously through work notes, casting about for a structure that will gel the pages into some semblance of order, grappling for the logical progression I must have been building, because I *have to* get beyond this negativity. I must find purpose and the only way I know how is through work. From my window, I rest my tired eyes on the sprawling fig tree. I return to my table and I write:

The perfume of the summer fig is a heavy fragrance. It is musky, milky and dominates the scents of everything growing around it. Gravid . . . mothers' milk . . .

I throw down my pen and, rising from my chair, return to the window. I look again. What do I see? I see lopped-off cedar branches and scarred trunks. Most of the figs have ripened, fallen to the ground and been squashed by the passage of cars. Their crunchy pulp and seeds, carried by tyres, have spread all over the tarmac drive and left a sticky jam. The magpies zap at it with their beaks, devouring it wolfishly. They ignore the fruit's dark purply skins. Those lie shrivelling like bits of dried leather leached by the heat to the colour of diluted ink.

I return to my table and take a deep breath. Somewhere beyond the room, the telephone is ringing. I barely notice. I am leafing through notes. I find the page.

The fig tree, *le figuier*. The fig tree appears in many paintings and there are, of course, frequent references to it in the Bible. According to Lawrence Durrell, the fig tree was 'owned' by the god Demeter, while Bacchus, the god of wine and good living, carved his sacred phallus from its wood.

Its logs give off an acrid aroma when burned in the grate. It is ill-advised to plant these trees up against stone walls. They require plenty of circulating air or else, in the heat, they smell like cat's pee.

'The garage in Cannes has just telephoned. Your car is ready.

Would you like me to ask them to deliver it, or shall we drive down together and fetch it?' I have not heard Michel's approach, lost as I was in my studies.

'Oh, hi there.' I sigh, placing pen on tabletop. 'No, I'll walk down myself and collect it later.'

'Don't you want me to come with you? To make sure they've done a good job?'

I shake my head. 'No, I'll be fine.'

He pauses. 'It's good that you're working,' he smiles encouragingly.

I bow my head. 'Not really . . .'

'Please don't be so closed off, *chérie*.'

'Am I? Sorry, I . . .'

'I feel as though you resent me.'

I shake my head again. 'No, I don't. There is resentment, but it is not against you.'

'Who, then?'

I cannot answer. Until we came here, until I found Michel and we took on the challenge of Appassionata, I never put my feet on the ground and felt the earth stay firm beneath me. There is not a corner of this place, this olive farm, that I do not love. Every cobweb shot through with light, glinting silvery as old badgers' hairs; every arboreal bird singing its song; the geckos, lizards, every creature (well, maybe not the snakes and rats); every storm, even those that crack and fizz, shut off the electricity, send the dogs into a yowling spin and terrify me; every sunbeam that warms Michel's smooth skin and mellows the shadows I have carried in my heart. I hear and see all of these wonders and more, but I will never hear our child's cry, see her laughter on a summer's day, suffer her fears as she enters the pool before learning to swim. I will never know if, when I took her hand in mine, she would have felt safe in the fundamental way I never did.

'Carol? Are you listening?'

'Mmm?'

'Let me come with you to the garage. We can take the car and go off for lunch . . .'

I shake my head.

Michel nods his acquiescence and turns to leave me. 'By the way, what happened to that roll of film I gave you?'

'What film? Oh, I took it to be developed.'

'And?'

'I collected the photos.' He waits expectantly. 'They must be in my bag or in the car somewhere. I'll find them. Sorry, I forgot.'

The photographs have been hidden beneath the passenger seat of the car in what is now a raggedy wallet. They must have slipped under there as I took a bend in the road and have lain undiscovered for more than a week. Michel finds them while I am at the garage. When I return they are on the table on the upper terrace, where he has prepared our lunch.

'Isn't this the journalist you introduced me to in Cannes?' he asks.

He holds up four photographs, each one taken by me. Of Jacob and the two Italian guests at Barbara's birthday bash. In each of the four pictures, where Barbara should have been, there is nothing, nothing but an illuminated smudge, a grey ghost of an outline. I pick them up and scrutinise them. I am no photographer, but even so.

'I don't understand,' I murmur. 'There were four people . . . Is this something to do with the flash?'

'It shouldn't be.'

'Must have been the glare from the candlelight, then, that bleached her out.' I take the pictures and, later, their negatives too, and slip them into a drawer in my den, disquieted by them.

Some mornings, like this morning, I wake and stretch and

feel if I could reach up and tap at the sky, tap, tap, tap with my fingernails, it would reverberate in gentle chimes. And I know that today will be a good day. Then, carrying our coffee out on to the terrace, we find trails of wet weeds everywhere and muddy pawprints. I am bewildered until I trace them and discover that one of the dogs has devoured the water lilies. Every one of them. Nothing is left but a trail of root systems to prove they ever existed. And the carp, too. All are gone. I am peering at the surface of the pond hoping to catch signs of life, just one living fish, when Thierry, the young man who cleans our pool, arrives on his weekly visit. His mood is buoyant. He has gossip to impart and waves exuberantly. Michel Mouillot, the ex-mayor, has been found guilty of corruption.

'But he is not actually serving his sentence in prison. He has been put under house arrest, *en résidence surveillée*, in a rather elegant villa in the Var. At our expense!' cries cropped-haired Thierry, dragging hard on his cigarette. 'We, who do an honest's day's work for a pittance. We, who pay our taxes and without complaint!'

I smile. I love it when the French get *très chaud* under their collars or, in this trance-inducing climate, their T-shirts, especially when it concerns matters of injustice or workers' rights and white-collar corruption. They rant and rave but our experience has shown us that, at any given opportunity, most would prefer to do business *en noir*, in cash, so that the money can remain undeclared. Thierry is not of that breed. His work is by contract and above board. He is intense and honest. He never accepts a beer because he has other pools and other clients to attend to, but he always stops for a natter, to pass on the latest news of local rackets, and then goes contentedly on his way, with a bottle of mineral water to which he has helped himself from the garage fridge. It does not surprise me to learn that he is originally from another, more northerly region of France.

The scandal of the mayor does seem to have run its course and matters are quietening down along our wave-lapped coast. A new mayor has been elected. Cannes is returning to the erstwhile lucrative business of promoting its perfect sun-kissed lifestyle, and most local enterprises appear to be regaining ground. Even the price of real estate is on the increase again. Although I did read recently that the villa of that old trickster – crook, actually – Jacques Médecin was bought by the state for what many considered was a vastly inflated price soon after he legged it to Uruguay, and has just been sold to a local firm of estate agents for less than a tenth of the sum paid for it. Mmm.

Clarisse flew off late this afternoon. She was headed for Paris, but only for a day or two. Soon she will be setting off for her new life in London. Summer is drawing to a close. Michel will be going away in a few days, too, to begin pre-production on his animation film. It will be almost as though I am alone. Vanessa wants to stay on a while longer, she says, though we rarely see her. She rises late, spends hours in the shower, dresses with meticulous care, endlessly brushing her lustrous mane, and then speeds off, a whirlwind of smiles and flying excitement. These days, she converses with me in English, relishing it as though it were the language of love. And for her it is. The object of her attentions is a young American, she confides. 'He iz verry tall and verry 'and-some.'

'Will we meet him?' I ask her.

'*Ça depend*,' she grins secretively.

'Depends on what?'

' 'e iz verry shay. And 'e is verry frightened to meet Papa.'

'Why?' I laugh.

'Because Papa is my 'ero. But I shall invite him to Paris. I want him to meet Maman.' And she kisses me on both cheeks and hurries away to town, waving as she goes.

She hasn't meant to hurt me.

When Michel returns from the market, he finds me curled up on the bed, red-faced, sobbing into one of our square linen pillows, blotched now with mascara. He kneels on the bed, caresses my tearstained cheeks, kisses my head and then presents me with a cluster of red chili peppers, still attached to their stalks and held together with a pale blue elastic band.

'For you,' he whispers, and lays them out alongside my face.

'What are these for?' I mumble, nonplussed, for we rarely cook with chilis.

'A bouquet for you.'

I sniff and attempt a laugh. 'Are you teasing me?' But no, he takes my hand and leads me through the *salon*, where a bouquet of equally red long-stemmed roses are displayed in a vase, and on to the kitchen, where he places the chilis in the woven basket piled high with raw vegetables.

'I don't understand.'

'I thought it was an interesting alternative to flowers,' he smiles, inching me towards him, hugging me tightly, while tenderly stroking my back.

'This sadness won't last for ever, *chérie*.'

And I see that it is yet more evidence of Michel's kindliness, his generosity and inventiveness. He will transform anything into a form, a shape, a display of colour, but what I don't yet see is how he is encouraging me to seek alternatives.

The Divinity of Nature

Everyone has left. I spend my days alone, endeavouring to write. The weather has grown hot, windy and turbulent. Scribbles of cloud fleet fast across the sky. Our swimming pool is turning green. This will resolve itself at some point, I have no doubt, but what is much more troubling is that the olive trees are growing jaundiced again. Many of the leaves are dull yellow and smudged with black, circular stains. As I finger a leaf, it falls effortlessly into my hand. This is the wretched *Cyclocodium oleaginum* or *œil de paon*, the malady that damages the leaves but not the fruit. It is a fungus, René reminds me again as we scout the terraces, that is difficult to treat. It was apparent last year, but not to such an extent. I thought we had handled the problem at the beginning of summer.

'We'll have to spray all the trees again once the drupes have been gathered. We can't do it now, of course – it would harm the olives.'

'What troubles me, René, is that I don't want to spray the trees again.'

'You have no alternative.'

'There is one organic product . . .'

'Please don't tell me there is another solution, because there isn't. All anyone will advise is to plant the trees a decent distance apart and prune them regularly. Well, we all know that.'

'It's copper-based . . .'

'It'd be preventive, not curative, Carol, and it's too late for that. There isn't a farmer in the area who'd give a sou for your alternatives. Spray the trees or lose the foliage.'

I sigh. This is a sticky issue between us. 'It's irresponsible. The more we spray, the more we unsettle the ecological balance,' I venture as we walk from one tree to the next, patrolling the extent of the deterioration. 'Have you noticed that there are fewer swallows? I read they are being killed off by insecticides.'

'Well, you may be right. I heard that too.'

I turn to scrutinise him. This remark is coming from a man who has always extolled the virtues of treating the trees by raining gallons of water-mixed chemicals on to them. His methods have always been in direct opposition to what he perceives as my whimsical desires to run this place as an organic farm.

'And the fact is, René, we *have* treated them, against my better judgement, and the fungus has returned. There has to be another way to beat it.'

'There isn't. We have failed because we left it too late. You dithered. If we had sprayed in February or March, before flowering, this would not have happened. And these blasted winds don't help anything. They're probably spreading it.'

We are in the throes of the third *mistral* in as many weeks. Out at sea, white horses are chomping the waves.

What has caused these turbulences? The greenhouse effect? The depletion of rainforests? The roads blasted through the Alps, which allow northerly weather patterns to penetrate southern regions when before there was no access? Or might it be the astronomical quantities of pesticides squirted all over the countryside? I have heard, read, been given so many diverse explanations and I have no idea which, if any, to believe. But I do know that the return of the fungus has made me determined to find an alternative solution. Not only is the product we have used possibly harmful, it is inefficient.

'I went to visit an apiarist in the Var yesterday, a gentleman who has been tending bees since he was fifteen,' I tell René. 'He has agreed to visit us in the spring with a view to placing fifty hives up in the pine forest.'

'Ah, well done.'

'He talked to me about an insecticide spray developed to protect sunflowers that has killed off millions of bees. Sunflowers are a rich source of pollen for bees. While the bees feed off the blossoms, this product attacks their central nervous system, stunning them, and the bees' innate sense of distance and location is befuddled, destroyed by the chemical. They die of exhaustion, searching for the flightpath back to their hives.'

René shrugs. He hates these conversations.

'After I left the bee farm, driving back through the countryside, I remembered an old codger who sat at a table next to me months ago in Nice. A man whose remarks I dismissed as eccentric. The dance of the bees; their language for communicating pollen sources and the whereabouts of their habitats. He said they danced till they were stunned.'

'You can't take on the world, Carol.'

We kiss goodbye and he promises to be back later in the afternoon with the long-awaited water diviner. This will not be M. Nick, but the other gentleman. M. Nick seems to have disappeared off the face of the earth since the beginning of the summer break, but we can do it without him, René is confident.

'If this monsieur finds water, then we'll call in M. Nick to confirm it. If he doesn't, then you can inform the necessary parties that a dowser has made a thorough search and has confirmed that there is no accessible water source.' He glances skywards. 'Let's hope this wind doesn't bring rain, or he won't be able to work.'

I smile. It is not something I would have given thought to, but it's logical, of course; a water diviner cannot search for water in wet weather.

The wind does not let up, but nor does it bring rain. I am in my den when the American four-wheel-drive purrs up our leafy approach. It is twenty minutes early and for a moment I am not sure who has arrived. The dogs are barking and I run to look out of the window. They quieten when they see René descending from the rear of the Ford. I bang on the window and signal that I am on my way down.

'Hang on to the dogs,' I call, hurrying to greet my guests.

Monsieur the water dowser is an impressive but unexpected sight. He is very elegantly dressed, in golfing cap, suede bomber jacket and exquisite leather shoes. In all my imaginings among the *dramatis personae* of life, this is not the character I would have created to play the role of Provençal local searching for water. The dogs jump all over him, sullying his clothes, and I am obliged to haul them away.

'Don't worry,' he laughs. 'I love animals.' He exudes warmth and good breeding. 'So does my wife, here.' He glances towards the front passenger seat, and out steps a tiny woman, thin as a twig and no taller than a robin. She has dyed blonde hair, a silk scarf which is blowing into her face, and running shoes. I fear the dogs in their overexcitement to greet the new arrivals might send this Piaf figure flying, but she repeats that she loves them and declares that I am not to tie them up. Her accent is thick and I cannot place it.

René introduces us. As soon as the monsieur's name is spoken I recognise it, and he registers that I do. He is indeed a fabled figure, a person of repute throughout Provence and, as it happens, also a native of our nearby village.

'Right, where shall we begin?' Monsieur looks about him, appraising the width and breadth of the land. 'Is there a track?'

'Yes, several,' say I.

'Are they suitable for trucks?' He is digging about in the rear of his luxury vehicle for the tools of his trade.

I shake my head.

'No point in looking, then. I'm wasting my time.'

'Why not?'

'Well, if there is water, how will the drilling truck reach the source and dig the well?'

I had never considered that problem. The truth is, I don't think either Michel or I have ever seriously believed that water might be found here. This house is constructed on solid rock, the hill behind us is rock and, if appearances are anything to go by, dry as a bone.

Monsieur has retrieved from his Ford a large square of black material which puts me in mind of one of my late father's Magic Circle conjuring props: the black scarf that hid the magic wands. I smile at the memory. Carefully, the cloth is unwrapped and I see two tendrils of metal, each about eighteen inches in length and barely more substantial than cuts of wire. This is the diviner. Wrapped up with it is a chunk of coppery metal secured to a chain.

'The pendulum,' he declares and hands the cut of cloth,

along with the pendulum, to his wife, who is being all but blown away by the wind. He then asks René to fetch his notebook, calculation list and pen from the dashboard. Madame spins off to talk to the dogs while Monsieur exits the *parking* and crosses the lower terrace alongside the pool. He is staring at the tiles, as though his eyes were boring through them. His expression is one of serious concentration. 'There's water here, no doubt about it,' he is muttering.

'We are above the drainage system and alongside the pool,' I offer by way of explanation. He appears not to have heard me, or has chosen to ignore my flippancy. René hurries to keep up with us and whispers in my ear, 'If he says there is water here, there is. He has never been known to be wrong.'

Am I being made a fool of? I am wondering. Might this be yet another example of local *escroquerie*?

Once we clear the house and have arrived at the tiled terrace where our wooden table and outdoor chairs live, he places the elongated, V-shaped divining rod between his two little fingers and his thumbs. He levels the apparatus directly in front of him, like a pair of dividers, somewhere around waist-height, making sure that its narrow end, the joined tip, is pointing outwards. Now he begins pacing. Long, sure strides towards the hill and then left towards the farthest reach of our land in the direction of what we refer to as the 'second plot', because we purchased it later. I trail along with him, holding back a polite pace or so, but surveying him like a hawk. First, I train my attention on his face, and then on his hands. I am the daughter of an entertainer, a musician, a magician; I grew up on sleight of hand. If there's a trick in this, then I am determined to spot it.

Suddenly, and most unexpectedly, as we approach the

four cedar trees that stand sentry on the passage between the two plots, the rod shoots upwards and begins to quiver like an overexcited bird.

'*Eh, voilà!*' he says, and stops. The rod continues to quiver. It looks as though it has a life of its own.

René, bringing up the rear, repeats the maestro's words. '*Eh, voilà.*'

The wife is elsewhere, lost in her elsewhere world, shouting to the wind.

'Are you telling me that we have water right here underneath this terrace?' I ask. We are standing on a patio that we have laid using something in the region of two hundred square metres of antique hand-made *dalles*. If we drilled here, even if we did repair the damage later, we might never find such tiles again.

'Yes. And what is more, it intersects right here. There are two streams: one is coming from the hill and the other is flowing in this direction. If I can find the precise junction and you drill at that strategic point you can benefit from two rivulets, both drawing from the same well.'

'Well, we're not digging up the terrace!' I bark. 'I'd rather pay the water bills. Can't you find another stream further up the hill?'

Monsieur steps away from what he has claimed is the source and the rod wilts instantly. 'But you have no means of accessing it up there.' He wanders off, frowning, as though trying to solve a conundrum. I turn to René, who is occupied with Madame; she is bent double and looks as though she is going to be sick.

'Is she all right?' I ask.

Her husband strides past her and tells her to go and sit in the car.

'What's up?'

'She's freezing, not feeling well.'

'Would you like me to take her inside?' I enquire of her husband.

'Later. First we must find water.'

'Look, it's really not that important.'

'Wait, if it runs this way – the *parking*! Why didn't I—?' And with that he is off, marching purposefully back towards his stationary truck. 'Move those cars!' he commands.

Madame sinks on to one of the swimming-pool steps, head in hands, while I am instructed again to move the cars, which I obediently do, driving them virtually into the trees until Monsieur calls to me that I have shifted them a sufficient distance. His own monster machine he reverses halfway down the drive. And then we begin the divining proceedings again. A few paces here, turn to the left. Rather like square-bashing. I don't know whether to concentrate on him or worry about his wife, who is at my side now leaning against me, muttering. René is taking notes. The rod is up and quivering again.

'Look! Look!'

I am looking. In amazement. You would think it was battery-operated, the speed at which it is moving.

'*Où est la pendule?* The pendulum!'

Everyone is shouting, 'Fetch the pendulum!' No one, of course, can find it. Who had it? Madame. This creates a *petit* drama because she cannot remember where she has put it.

I am bemused by the panic and the rush. After all, the water, if there is any, is not going to dry up in the next five minutes.

While the trio search for the cloth-wrapped pendulum, I ask: 'Please may I have a go?' Monsieur, almost without thinking, hands me his rod. I weave it carefully through my fingers, resting it against my upturned palms, precisely as I have observed him doing, and begin to pace. No one is paying me any attention. I stride here and there and nothing happens, except that my fingers begin to ache, and then, while the others are engaged in trying to find the key to their Jeep because they insisted on locking it and Madame swears that she placed the pendulum carefully on her seat in the car, I retrace his steps. I can just about recall where he found the water and I approach gingerly, pause and wait. Nothing happens. I twiddle my fingers in an effort to manipulate the rod, to give it impetus, to thrust it upwards, to spring the stupid thing into life. Nothing happens. Back and forth I step over the spot. Still nothing happens. If there's a trick to this, a way to manoeuvre this appliance, I am hell-bent on finding it.

'You don't believe me, do you?'

I swing round guiltily. 'Yes of course. I just thought . . .'

'It's neither dupery nor illusion.' He smiles. 'Allow me to guide you, please.' Monsieur plants himself right behind me, lays the heel of each of his hands beneath the backs of mine and negotiates me gently towards the spot. As we step towards it, the *baguette* swings fast with inverted gravity, pointing skywards and twitching powerfully. I feel its strength and this man is barely touching me; certainly, he is not in a position to force my hands.

'I tell you what, let's finish the job. I'll use this pendulum' – he takes it from René – 'to measure the depth of the source and the force of the flow, the cubic metreage per hour, and then, if you are willing, we can go into the house, get my poor wife out of the wind, and discuss all this.'

The pendulum swings and whirls and the source is reckoned to be about forty metres deep which is extremely shallow, I am informed, and therefore should not be expensive to excavate. The flow is sufficient to fill our 200-cubic-metre swimming pool in two days. The only information we cannot glean at this stage is whether the water is *eau potable* or not. For that we will have to drill and then test but, even if it's not drinkable, it will certainly irrigate the garden. It would also irrigate the 200 young olive trees that Michel, in spite of my protestations, is still eager for us to plant.

If what has been demonstrated here today really does indicate the presence of underground running water, then we have fallen upon tremendous good fortune.

Once inside and out of the gale force wind, where they will not accept refreshment – Monsieur drinks only champagne, and we have none in (I should have remembered his preference, René did tell me) and Madame is not supposed to consume anything hot or anything too strong, but she will accept a small nip of port if we have it, though when I serve it she worries that it may contain a tad too much alcohol – we settle to a long discussion. Monsieur asks me if I recognise the name Michel Rocard.

'The former prime minister of France?' I ask. 'Of course.'

'The very same.'

He tells me that Rocard's father was an esteemed research scientist who did some studies in water divining.

'One of his discoveries was that certain people have magnetism sensitivity at designated pressure points in their joints, and this enables them to detect unmapped water sources. Perhaps there is truth in it, I don't know. Certainly it sounds logical, but we in Provence believe that it is not explained away quite so reasonably.'

'What is your explanation, then?'

'It is less tangible. One needs to have a feel for water. How can I put it? To be in tune with it. There are other similar gifts. A cousin of mine, for example – she's dead now – had another talent that is passed on only through women, mother to daughter, mother to daughter, and no matter how hard a man tries, he can never achieve this power.'

'And that is?'

'The relieving of sunstroke. Someone working in the vineyards, for example, who has been weakened, made ill by too much sun, would be sent to such a woman. How does she extract the sun from the victim? She takes a glass of water, any ordinary tumbler of water, places it on the head of the patient and rests her first finger lightly against his or her forehead. The glass remains in position as though glued to the crown. Within seconds, the water in the glass begins to boil. And it boils, believe me, I have witnessed this, like a kettle on a stove. When the glass has been removed, the sunstroke has gone. You won't read of any such talents in your guide books to Provence. These are secrets we keep close to our chest, and women who possess such gifts are regarded with a certain deference. It is not a *métier*, not a profession, you understand. These women have a touch, a feel. I cannot explain it any more clearly than that.'

We are all of us silent. Monsieur rises and removes his jacket, folding it neatly behind him on the chair.

'Water divining is not a *métier*, either,' he continues. 'Though insurance companies regularly approach my colleague, Nick. If there is a lawsuit which is related to underground damp, leaking foundations and the like, they call him in to locate the flow. This is a mysterious land, a puzzling culture to outsiders, and in our language we have rich expressions that cannot be translated but they aptly describe the way we see the world. We—'

'Your language?' I butt in.

'Provençal.'

'You speak it?'

'Of course, I was raised speaking it. As my wife here was raised speaking Corsican. Both languages were outlawed by the French government, who created statutes to enforce the use of French as the official language—'

'Ah, I know about this,' I rather rudely interrupt again. 'The Villers-Cotterêts statute of 1539!'

'How right you are. And it has taken centuries for both Provençal and Corsican – languages rooted in the psyches of their native peoples – to fight their way back. Interestingly, they are not such distant neighbours. I can understand a smattering of Corsican, just as my wife here can partially understand my mother tongue. Carol, you seem to have a passion for this area of France and for the olive tree in particular, isn't that so?'

I nod my assent.

'I will send you a copy of a Provençal poem, in French, of course, that recounts how we believe that the spirit of the ancient Greeks lives on in the olive tree. To a true Provençal all trees are sacred, but above all reigns the olive tree. One reads of many ancient cultures who enforced the death penalty against anyone who cut down an olive tree . . .'

His wife nods her agreement, as does René. I look from one to the other. There is a certain madness in Monsieur's wife but, by contrast, he has a businesslike manner. And yet . . .

'Spirits in trees,' he laughs. 'No doubt you are thinking that we are a little crazy, that all this is far-fetched?'

I shrug.

'I understand the reverence given to the olive tree. All my life I worked in the world of business. Well, I believe you know what my work has been.'

'Yes.'

'These days, I ask myself what all those years were about. Making money, of course. Building a reputation, yes, indeed, but it wasn't until I retired and decided to dedicate myself to my farm that I found fulfilment. I feel in tune with life now, with my olive trees. I have over three hundred and fifty and, like you, we have splendid oil and hope for an AOC.'

*

And so we talk on while, beyond the windows, I hear the wind whistling through the pines. As night falls and the moon begins to rise, I find myself still sitting cross-legged on a cushion on the floor, listening to these two men, friends for over seventy years. They speak of this land – 'this land', to them, is Provence, not France – and recount anecdotes of their childhood and adolescent days here.

Monsieur narrates us the story of a boy he knew as a child in his village, an unprosperous fellow, who took two of the spines from the skeleton of a discarded umbrella, soldered them together and found that he had the skill and all the tools needed to source water. I learn that there is a shop in Paris where you can buy pendulums and divining rods.

Monsieur asks me if I know anything about the Aboriginals of Australia, and I tell him I spent several years intermittently working in and travelling around that prodigious continent, that I have a passionate respect for what I understand of their ancient ways, and that I frequently cite examples of their thinking.

'Australian Aboriginals,' he says, 'can pinpoint an underground stream with no more than an outstretched finger. They also believe, by the way, that the earth, its trees, mountains, every natural thing, is inhabited by its spirit life.'

'Going walkabout! Singing land back into existence!' I cry. 'I have always fancied that we might be doing something similar here with this little farm, which was abandoned and dilapidated when we found it. Singing the place back into existence. Recreating its colours.'

He smiles. 'Something like that. Well, we must be on our way.'

I glance at my watch and see that they have been here for five hours. 'I am so sorry to have kept you. I ask so many questions.'

'Not at all.'

Outside, the passage of the wind has turned the inky darkness into a glittering diorama. Its force has let up now, as it frequently does at sundown. Monsieur and I pause alongside one another, lingering an instant to drink in the beauty of the evening, the frisson of movement that stirs the perfumed air like fluttering chiffon.

From a branch in the *Magnolia grandiflora* – a tree which was originally discovered in the southern states of North America by the French botanist Plumier, who shipped examples of it back to France to enhance a botanical garden created for the pleasure of Louis XIV – we hear the gentle clunking of the bamboo wind chimes I bought in the market at Nice and hung there. Quashia always remarks that they remind him of his boyhood days as a goatherd in the Algerian mountains.

'I can trace water with an accuracy of within inches, but I can't trap the wind,' Monsieur confides to me, or perhaps he is talking to himself. 'Imagine if it could be bottled and administered in tiny doses as an antidote to the madness it creates in some.'

We stroll on towards the *parking* and I wonder if he is referring to his wife.

'How much do we owe you?' I ask when we reach the vehicle where René is now helping Madame into her seat.

'Nothing at all. It has been a pleasure, and I sincerely hope that it will contribute to your enterprises here. Please come and visit my farm. I want to show you my olive trees. They are very fine. I will also show you where I found water on our land. Meanwhile, I'll draw you a plan of your underground systems. Do have it verified by another dowser, if you are in any doubt. And if I can assist you with anything else, please don't hesitate to call me.'

And then, as he steps into his car, he turns and, in impeccable English, quotes a line from Hamlet: '"There are more things in heaven and earth . . . than are dreamt of . . ." eh, Carol? *Bon nuit, et à bientôt.*'

Once I have waved them off, I pad slowly back upstairs. Inside, I pour myself a glass of wine, put Mahler's Fifth on the stereo and settle back on to the cushions, peering out through the French windows at the stars. I am ruminating on the afternoon's events, on all that has been said, when, from nowhere, I recall an episode in my twenties that until this evening I had completely forgotten.

I was a young actress following a vegetarian diet and a rather trendy, semi-Zenlike existence, meditating on a twice-daily basis, searching earnestly for Truth and Meaning in Life. I was living in a rented flat in north London and in my bedroom there was a magnificent orchid plant. I was no expert with anything botanical; I lacked green fingers alto-gether, but I had been given the plant with its several blossoming sprays as a present, a first-night gift, and I had placed it in an antique porcelain pot in my attic room. I watered it regularly and it seemed to thrive there, if the flow-ering of extra, waxy cream blossoms was evidence of health. It was extremely beautiful, very graceful. Still, the plant excited no particular interest in me until something utterly fantastical happened. I was reading in bed the first time I became aware of it: a faint but clear, high-pitched intonation, like a barely audible single note of a chant. At first I took it to be a problem with the flat's antiquated electricity circuit. I switched off the power at the mains, but the sonar-like sound continued. I was completely clueless as to what it was or where it was coming from. It was more than a week before I finally came to the conclusion that it was the plant, laden with blossoms, that was emitting the sound. This cannot be true, I said to myself. I am going mad.

The next time I had chums over to dinner I told them

about the plant. 'I think it's *singing*,' I said. They stared at me incredulously and so I trooped everyone up to my bedroom to listen. It was late in the evening, the hour of its 'song', and we all plumped ourselves down on the floor (I had no chairs: cushions spread out in hillocks was where I and my guests lolled about in those days). Everybody listened politely but with lighthearted scepticism. No one heard a dicky-bird, not even me. Frankly, I felt pretty stupid and wished that I had never mentioned the phenomenon, even to close friends such as these actor pals. Like myself, they were sometimes given to way-out beliefs or leanings, but not this one. They simply roared with laughter and accused me teasingly of hallucinating, of having consumed drugs or magic mushrooms. No amount of protestation on my part would convince them otherwise, and so I shut up about it.

Yet, when I was alone, I continued to 'hear' the plant. Occasionally, when another lay at my side, the orchid would begin its song, but I never remarked upon it, never mentioned it again. I chose to appreciate it silently, leaving my partner to fall asleep in peace and ignorance.

It was around this time, the early to mid-seventies, that I learned of a book that was causing a mild sensation. It was written by a South African anthropologist, ethologist and marine biologist called Dr Lyall Watson. He was a recluse, someone told me back then, living on some windy bluff in the west of Ireland, and a bit of a boundary-breaker as far as conventional scientific circles were concerned. The book, *Supernature*, became a bestseller and cult reading for millions. Naturally, I hurried off to buy it. The text was a revelation to me. Anyone who has read it will know that there are chapters in which Dr Watson recounts experiments carried out on plants to measure electrically their responses to human behaviour. I was astounded. Plants 'screaming' at the sight of a human being who had just cut a lawn? Plants responding favourably to beings who had a recent history of plant nurturing?

The point, for me, was that not only were plants living entities, but it seemed as though they might possess memories, be capable of recognising other living forces and reacting negatively or positively towards them.

I had no electric meter or graph by which to measure the responses of my orchid, but I began to silently propose the possibility that the plant was at peace in the space it inhabited, and recognised me as an ally. Was this going too far, being too subjective? Might the plant have simply been expanding to its environment, responding favourably to the lack of threat? Could it have been sufficiently unthreatened to emit contentment?

If you quizzed me tonight about whether I still believe the orchid was singing, I would answer in the negative. My interpretation was doubtless born of the world of hip romanticism I floated about in. Even so, I cannot dismiss the experience entirely. So, what did I hear? Dr Desmond Morris, when discussing the early stages of human sexual courtship in his book *The Naked Ape*, talks of the 'highly specialised and symbolised sound signals of speech' courting couples use with one another. 'A courting couple is often referred to as "murmuring sweet nothings" and this phrase sums up clearly the significance of the tone of voice as opposed to what is being spoken.' Might such a form of contact exist, on occasion, between man and plant? Might my plant have been emitting electrical impulses, electromagnetic signals? And if so, is it possible that I picked up those impulses, as one might be aware of another's heartbeat or a loved one's sweet murmurings? I was not plugged into *singing* exactly, but is it conceivable that I was 'in tune' with the only other living energy force in the flat? I do not have answers, and these are probably far-fetched notions, but listening to Monsieur praising his beloved olive trees, to

his claim of being in tune with them, has recalled this unfath-
omed incident.

Beyond the valley, in front of our olive farm and to the right,
there is a hill wooded with arcane and venerable pine trees.
Each stands a good twenty metres high and has been growing
on that hill for many decades. There are no buildings, no
constructions of any sort over there, and from our upper terrace it is a green and bosky sight, a round shoulder of
greenery. I have always understood the hill to be, as our land
is, a designated *zone verte*, written into the council records.
After all, it is an extension of the conservation area in which
our farm is situated. So it comes as a shock to me when I am
disturbed in my work by the sound of chainsaws. Not one,
but several. I rise from my table and walk out on to the terrace to see who is creating the noise. To my horror I see one
of those ancient pines being felled, then another and another;
decades-old trees falling in quick succession. I run in search of
Quashia, who is repairing one of the drystone walls brought
down in the night by the wild boars.

'What's going on over there?' I ask him.

'They're cutting trees,' he replies. 'I told you a while ago.'

'You told me that they were pruning the trees, not cutting
them.'

'The trees are dangerous.'

I am horrified. 'Dangerous? In what sense dangerous? To
whom?'

'The council says they can be cut down.'

'Who has the council given this permission to, and why?'

'They could fall on the *foyer* and damage the roof if these
strong winds continue. '

I cannot believe what I am hearing. This reasoning is preposterous. The trees are a perfectly reasonable distance from
the building which was constructed in the sixties to house

foreign labour on land compulsorily purchased by the local council from the previous proprietors of our farm.

I hurry back into the house and telephone the Mairie, the town hall. The young woman I speak to informs me that she knows nothing about the trees. I leap into the car and hurtle down the hill to the appropriate office, determined to find out what is going on before the entire hillside has been denuded. Eventually, after being sent from one office to the next, from pillar to post, I learn that the French *société* that owns the land on which the *foyer* is built have put forward plans to extend this housing estate. They have applied for planning permission once and were refused on the grounds that you cannot obtain planning permission to build on land that is classified as *boissé classé*, where the trees themselves are listed. On top of which, it is public land. They do not even own these plots. Their only hope, and a damned cunning ploy it is too, is to register the trees as dangerous, cut them down and then put in their request for planning permission on land now free of trees, worthless as parkland and which can be purchased for a sou.

I am incensed. Locked in my own loss, I have not been paying attention. I should have noticed what was going on weeks ago.

The felling continues. Not every day, and not at such a dramatic speed as on the day I first noticed it, but discreetly, so that the surrounding neighbourhoods are not alerted. Nevertheless, every few days one more tree disappears.

I telephone the council again. They inform me that we must put our complaints in writing. When Michel comes home on Friday, he sets to work. He writes not only to the council representative to whom I have spoken but to several different departments at their local offices, as well as their land registration people in Juan-les-Pins. These he copies to a frankly rather hopeless local organisation we subscribe to whose raison d'être is the protection of the local village and its surrounding green areas. He writes to the Department of Environment in Nice and to anyone else he can think of. All to get someone to take notice of the fact that these protected trees are being felled like sticks. I walk down the lane and glare miserably at the stacks of trunks. I behold lorries arriving to load and cart them away. I return to the council, visit some of the same individuals and then fall upon a tall, bearded man who agrees to pop by within the hour and find out what is going on.

This he does, and then he calls on us. He has warned the manager of the residence that the felling is an illegal act. He assures us that he intends to make immediate contact with the owners of the housing estate, a company operating out of Marseille, and will notify them by registered letter that they are liable to a hefty fine and that replacement trees must be planted immediately.

Le pin. Pine. Highly scented trees. Evergreen, coniferous. There are numerous species, and many grow around the Mediterranean basin. One of the most popular is the Aleppo pine. Originally from the ancient Syrian city of Aleppo? No, but it grows everywhere in the eastern Mediterranean.

Its tiered, oval cones are the pine's means of reproduction. The female cones are the larger of the two. The egg cells in the female are fertilised by the pollen from the males.

Pines are cultivated for the resin and wood.

I stand on the terrace and look out across at the hill, at the space where the pines used to grow. For the moment the felling has been halted, the damage contained. But who can say for how long? Bribes have the power to change laws down here and *escroquerie* usually wins the day. And I see no signs of replacement planting.

Arabs crouch there now, out of the heat, in the shade. Resting on their haunches, they smoke cigarettes and watch time passing, the way Bedouins do in the desert. I have no problem with those men sitting over there on their hams, idling away the hours. What I cannot get to grips with is the space itself.

I scrutinise that newly created emptiness, and it troubles me. Profoundly.

I read a while back that a scientific experiment set up by botanists in New Hampshire has found that certain trees give off pheromones, airborne hormones that are carried on the wind like alarm signals when dangers to the trees' health or survival are close at hand. Bodies of scientists are beginning to support the possibility of a level of environmental awareness being transmitted between living organisms. From tree to tree of a like kind, for example, in a forest.

I find myself, as I stand out here on our terrace, asking what if such ancient philosophies as the Provençal or Aboriginal philosophies are not entirely wacky? What if trees do possess a spirit life? If they do, what happens to that spirit when the tree dies or is chopped down? If the tree dies naturally is the spirit's departure different, more prepared perhaps, than if the end is more violent? If Dr Watson walked the hill I am staring at now and measured the responses of each of the remaining trees in the surrounding wood, what might he read on his electrical meter?

Would he be deafened by screaming? Screams of anger, outrage? Loss or pain? If we, living and going about our daily lives in the surrounding neighbourhoods, could but hear the reaction of the forest I am preoccupied by now, would we be forced to prick up our ears and listen? Would it make any difference?

The girls' school I attended was set in rolling grounds with many arcane trees and encircled by a small oak forest of its own. From the age of ten or eleven, that turbulent time, when I was caught up in the web of misery at home and had few allies I could confide in because I felt sure that all homes were normal except ours, I spent a great deal of time alone in that wooded park. Trees became my friends. I talked to them, or simply hugged them, pressed my cheeks hard against their grainy surfaces, ears glued to their trunks, musing with them as though they were people. And if I could not, for whatever reason, hide away outside, I would find wooden beams to hang on to: they were my life rafts. The material itself was reassuring. My dreams were of flying and of living in tree houses.

I remember an occasion when I had been witness to a scene at home. The words spoken, the information revealed were so distressing to me that I fled the house. I ran up the hill the mile or so to school, locked myself in the cloakroom and would not come out. No amount of rapping on the door or threats of punishment would budge me. When the afternoon classes resumed, I escaped into the grounds. I was shivering, weeping, clinging to an ancient oak. It took classmates to report me and several members of staff several hours to coax me away from – what? An object of stability, reassurance, intimacy? What did those trees offer me that I couldn't find in the human world? There must have been some communion taking place there, but I no longer know what. I have long since lost touch with whatever it might have been; 'reasons of the heart of which the reason knows nothing,' was the observation made by Pascal.

Now, sitting alone out here on the terrace, long past the gloaming light of an autumnal evening, in the stillness of the falling night, Schubert's *Quintet in C Major for Two Violins, Viola and Two Celli* playing on the stereo, I dig about for an inkling of reasoned comprehension. In the teachings of Zen, students are trained to work towards inner harmony, balance; to be so at one with themselves, so in tune with the universe, that they can *hear* a blade of grass growing. Might there have been a quintessence of life, a core energy in those trees, that I, the child, sought out and plugged into? The healing power of nature? Might those trees, along with my scribblings and play-acting, have fed me with the strength to survive?

The first side of the record has finished. I rise and walk slowly inside to flip it over, but instead make for the telephone. I am not clear what spurs me to call Rome, but I do. A desire to speak to Barbara? Not especially, but an urgent need to know how she is. I have been vaguely intending to do it for a few days but other matters have kept me occupied. It is Jacob I fall upon, blubbering and bemoaning the fractured future he is about to face.

Barbara was taken ill during the Venice Film Festival. Her jaw locked. She could not speak or swallow. When they returned to Rome, he took her to the hospital, where she was kept in for a series of tests and diagnosed with advanced leukaemia. Three weeks later, which is to say three days ago, she was dead.

I am speechless. Eventually I mutter some mindless and fairly meaningless condolences and hang up. In my thoughts, aside from the shock I am feeling, is the knowledge of those photographs. I make my way to the drawer in my den and dig them out with the intention of destroying them and then I hesitate, and don't. I sit in semi-darkness, staring hard at them. Staring *into* them. Four pictures taken by me and in every one Barbara is bleached out. For whatever reason, whatever technical cock-up or fault on my part, she is simply *not there*. I think back to those warm, early-summer gatherings, to the loneliness I picked up on, and I cannot dismiss the questions spinning in my head. Why is she not in these photographs? Is it utter madness, or even vaguely feasible, to wonder whether her spirit was already departing, moving on elsewhere? Going on ahead, to seek out her next spot? A kinder one, I pray.

Suddenly, her soft, tobacco-scratched voice replays in my mind. The Englishness of her, in spite of her bohemian manners, and the words: 'You are lucky to be having a baby.' And in our kitchen: 'I'd really love a kid.'

I wipe away a tear, slip the photos back into the drawer and wish her *bon voyage*.

I return to the telephone and call Michel. The rush in my voice must alert him. 'I have been a fool.'

'Is everything all right?' he asks.

'We must plant our trees. It is the way forward.'

'Splendid. I'd hoped you'd come to it,' he says, and kisses me, long-distance, goodnight.

Olive Finale

Days and days of deliciously golden autumn and then, from nowhere, we are pelted by a freak hailstorm. The stones are the size of golf balls and cause the loss of approximately a third of the olive crop – full and fleshy fruit ripening early after such a long dry summer; fruit that is piebald deep violet and green, falling and rolling, squashed beneath tyres, never having given of its produce.

1 November: *Toussaint*, All Saints' Day. Here, in France, it is a public holiday. In the past it was the day that marked the decanting of the new year's wines. It is also the day the Provençals regard as the beginning of winter, but this year there is not a hint of such a season. The weather is glorious, far more autumnal than wintery, and the olives that were not destroyed by the hailstones of two weeks ago have ripened way ahead of schedule. There are far fewer drupes on the

trees due to that recent shock of bad weather, but those that
remain are filled out and are first class: great damson-black
fruits, plump, luscious, oleaginous.

I stand in the dappled sunlight beneath the twisted, hanging branches of one of the older trees and gaze upwards in
admiration.

'The birds are at a feast. If we don't begin harvesting
soon, we'll have nothing left.' Quashia is at my side, head
tilted in the same direction. It is a day off for him – nobody
works on these public holidays, and he is taking a well-
deserved rest – but still he strolls up to say *bonjour* and lend
a hand with whatever essential chores need attending to, for
they are endless; work here is never done.

'But if we collect the ripe ones and leave the green, we
won't have sufficient to make our own pressing. We'll have
to share with someone else,' I reply.

It is true. The mill requires a minimum of eighty-five
kilos to press for a single estate. If we are lucky we may
gather sixty kilos of perfectly seasoned fruit. We could pick
another twenty-five of underripe olives to meet the quota,
but then we lose out on the quantity of oil the drupes will
produce: green fruit returns less oil than black. If we leave
the mature fruits on the trees and wait for the rest, or a proportion of the rest, to ripen, we will lose an extensive
percentage to the birds, who will steal the plumpest of the
pickings before they have been harvested. This is one of the
choices to be made, a part of the delicate balance to which
I would never have given a second thought before we began
to reclaim this little farm. Michel is not here, so the decision
will be mine.

'I'll telephone René and I'll leave a message at the mill; I'd
prefer to hear what they advise.'

Quashia says he'll wait. While I go indoors to make the
calls he busies himself in his newly constructed woodshed,

pulling out and dusting down our green and René's white nets ready to encircle the feet of the trees. That done, he embarks on an appraising tour of the garden to see which have branches burgeoning with ripening fruit and where the drupes have already begun to drop. We are short of netting, in spite of the thousand metres I bought. Some of it has been damaged, caught and torn during earlier harvests, other yards have been used to keep scavengers out of our vegetable gardens and the original roll was insufficient in the first place.

I am very surprised, because it is a holiday, when Christophe, the mill-owner, picks up the phone himself. He answers with a weary despondent '*Allo?*'

'How are you, Christophe?' I ask. Our paths haven't crossed since last year. His mill is located a fair distance inland of us, so we have no reason to visit that village outside the oil-pressing season.

'Ah, *bonjour*, Carol, not good, not good.' He doesn't wait for me to ask what's up but instantly embarks upon the problem every *oléiculteur* is facing this year: little if any fruit yield. 'It should have been a stupendous year with all those months of sun,' he moans. 'Yes, we began pressing this week, for those who have fruit. Come if you like, but we are only turning the mill on Wednesdays and Saturdays. Of course we'll press more frequently if there's a call for it, but I don't think there will be. It's a *catastrophe, une vrai catastrophe.*' I smile, not because I don't commiserate with the farmers' situation, but because I know Christophe sufficiently well now to understand that in his eyes life is either a *catastrophe* of monumental proportions or a veritable triumph. Today we have the downside.

I explain to him that our fruit is ripening earlier than expected, but not all of it.

'Same everywhere. It adds to the dilemma,' he interrupts.

'So I am not sure that we will have enough for a single-estate pressing.'

'I'll press for eighty kilos, as it's you, but I can't do it for less. There is the cost, you understand, of the machines, the fuel, the staff. Oh, Carol, what a *catastrophe*! How's Michel?'

'He's fine. Working hard, as usual.'

'Is he here?'

'No, he's in Paris in preproduction on an animation film.'

'He leaves you alone too frequently. You tell him that from me.'

How can this mill-owner be party to such information? René must have been gossiping. 'Come whenever you like. I'll accept eighty kilos, or why don't you find someone to share the pressing with you?'

'We'll look into it. Either way, we'll see you soon. *Merci*, Christophe. *Ciao*.'

I call René. He is sniffing and coughing. 'Only a *petit rhume*, nothing to fuss about. Too many olive trees to tend,' he explains. 'But how are you?' He does not wait to hear; he is already affirming that the olive season is a catastrophe. At Pégomas, where one of the farms he husbands is situated, there is not one single olive on any of the 120 trees. 'All lost in that hailstorm, every single drupe. Can you believe it?'

'I was about to suggest we share a pressing . . .'

He leaps at the idea. He has fifty-two kilos gathered from the lone tree in his own garden. A yield of fifty-two kilos from one tree in a year of paucity is exceptional, though still, of course, not enough for a pressing. He needs another thirty to make up his quota. He arranges to call by to collect this amount from us.

And so Quashia and I decide to begin the harvest, *la récolte*, or, in the case of olives, *la cueillette des olives*. 'We'll start tomorrow morning, then,' I tell him when I return outside.

'Why not right this very minute?' he asks, tugging off his shirt in his hurry to get to the garage to change into his work clothes. He looks happy.

'Because it's your day off,' I yell after him, but he is already out of sight.

While I have been on the phone he has started laying the nets. He prepared the ground, cutting back the grass, clearing errant stones, several days ago, anticipating my decision.

So here we are again at harvest time. *La olivaison*. The olive season.

I find a butterfly caught under one of the nets and while trying to release it I lose my entire afternoon's gathered load. With a sigh, I watch the drupes rolling down the steps and then I concentrate on the butterfly. It flaps and flutters until it is free and then flies away to alight on a terracotta pot, still, even in early November, blushed with flowering geraniums. I want to be able to identify the butterfly later so I pause to make a mental note of its markings: splashes of white with black spots, known as ocelli – they resemble dark, round eyes on its wings – and a tortoiseshell colouring which, in the sunlight, glows almost burned orange. Is this a Red Admiral? There were dozens of this species in the nectar-rich gardens of my childhood. Later, when I return to my den, I leaf through my guide and learn that I have lent a helping hand not to a Red Admiral but to another of its family: a *Vanessa cardui*, more commonly known as a Painted Lady. It is a resident of the Canary Islands and Madeira, but a migrant from North Africa – like Quashia! – where it establishes colonies along the coast. It can be found in the warmer parts of the Mediterranean until cold weather sets in.

While perusing my handbook I also discover that there is

a whole genus of butterflies, including the Red Admiral, whose Latin name includes the word *Vanessa*. Is Michel aware that one of his daughters shares her name with a species of butterfly? *Vanessid* is the adjective, I am informed by my *Oxford* dictionary. So might I say of my lovely stepdaughter that her fretting about her weight, her perennial concerns about her appearance, are, in her case, *Vanessid* behaviour? I smile. I haven't heard from her in a while and I wonder how she is getting along with her American sweetheart.

The following afternoon, I leave Quashia with the rest of this early gathering and set off for a short stay in London. Before I depart, René telephones to confirm that he must have the olives.

'Call Quashia,' I tell him. 'He'll give you all you need.'

In London, I pass delightful evenings with Clarisse. When she is not at college or at the bistro where she works as a waitress to earn her keep, or off visiting galleries, going to the movies or lectures with newly made friends, of which there seems to be a manifold and motley collection, we lounge on cushions, drinking wine, gorging on steaming great bowls of spaghetti we have rustled up together, and she shows me her artwork, her impressive portfolios, and then we talk and talk until dawn. We are like students together. Or rather, she brings an air of lightness to my heart. In her company, I revisit those late-teenage joys and revelations. When the phone rings it is usually a young voice enquiring after my stepdaughter and I gladly take messages. It is a special time, a privileged interval; we are discovering one another.

Here, in London, I am not the wife of her father – of course, I remain that too, but what bonds us here is her passion for this capital city where she is launching herself for the first time and all that it contributes to this encounter with her developing feminine self. Here she insists we speak in English. *La France* and its language are skins she has temporarily shed. Here, her pleasure is the carving of her independence within a neutral environment – a pad of her own, a city she has claimed as hers – where she can express her newly gained liberties. She speaks of Papa in a way I have never heard before and which quite takes me aback. These days he has been transformed into someone other than her father: he is a man, and I see her begin in tiny ways to look at him in a more objective light. She does not mention Serge and neither do I. Perhaps she has forgotten him among so many new discoveries. Somehow, though, I suspect not.

On the plane home, replaying my stay in London, I am reminded of a comment Michel made to me back in the summer after the eclipse. 'You say the girls are mine. They are not, Carol. I don't own them, nor does their mother. They are their own people and, if you want it, you have a part to play in their lives, too.'

Reflecting upon my days with Clarisse, I see that perhaps there might be a role for me and if she will accept me, I will gladly take it on.

I return to grey skies and a world blasted by yet another fierce wind, but this is not the *mistral* that I have grown to know. This wind is called by some the *scirocco* and by others *vent d'est*, or wind from the east, because it travels up through Spain and blows across the southern coast of France. Actually it comes from the Sahara desert bringing with it pale red sand. The cars are covered in a thick film of it and the exterior world has taken on a salmon opaqueness. From inside the house, the wind rattling through the trees sounds like a train thundering through a tunnel. I stare out of the dust-smeared windows and spy a helicopter, like a determined dragonfly, ploughing through the dense clouds. Claps of dry thunder spook the dogs. Stepping outside, I am surprised by how warm it is; such a fierce wind suggests a biting chill, but not so. A desert wind that brings desert heat.

Many of the fruits are still too green to harvest but now the wind is driving them in shoals to the ground. Traditionally, olive-gathering begins on 25 November, the feast of Ste Catherine Labouré, but it looks as though we will be forced to continue to pick up what we can and press what we have before they wither and go dry, even if we must share the pressing.

Our load turns out to be 113 kilos, more than sufficient for a rendezvous at the mill, and Christophe's assistant is happy to book it in as a single-estate pressing.

'There are dozens in your predicament,' she explains, 'forced by nature to alter their pattern.'

Michel is still in Paris, so I decide to take the six crates to the *moulin* alone, my first trip this year.

The wind has polished up the weather, leaving it clear and sharp. The landscape is a melody of yellows and tiger oranges. Startlingly beautiful. Ahead of me, beyond the road, the mauve and umbrous, snow-capped Alps. Weekend joggers in the pine-forested parks, dogs following at their heels, running and scampering.

Upon arrival I am greeted by Christophe, who is dressed in bright green, a gnome in a black woollen Noddy hat that ascends to a rather comical point. He waddles to and fro with a face as red as Christmas but he wears the desolate expression of an abandoned woman. Although it is a Saturday the place is surprisingly empty – fewer olives this year, hence fewer farmers. As always, the conversations around me are of 'four kilos to this' and 'no, olives here'.

Gravely concerned but unflustered, except for Christophe with his Noddy hat, shiny cheeks, plimsolls stained with olive paste and his air of tragedy.

He is washing out with a water spray one of his mammoth machines that clunks and gutters – the Superdecanter 1000, purchased from Firenze; a fortune forked out to align himself with European health standards. It all needs to be paid for.

A small woman less than five feet tall in a black cardigan arrives, carrying an empty plastic container which, when full, will hold fifty litres of precious oil. She nods a greeting to Christophe and his son, sits down next to me and pulls out black rosary beads. Her feet in her unpolished black slingbacks don't reach the ground; still, she has a stalwart air about her. I watch her sneakily. Eyes front, head facing forwards, tiny pearl earrings, brittle, broken nails. I try to engage her in conversation but either she does not hear me or chooses not to – the noise in here is thunderous. Now her calloused labourer's hands clutching the beads are beating her breast. Perhaps she is lost in the world of her prayers? This little woman is a very familiar figure in a disappearing Mediterranean society: the widow, the aged mother, the matriarch and backbone of any family.

We wait. The air is cold and reeks of mashed olives. The few farmers present are pacing to and fro, as though in a hospital corridor, attending the outcome of their pressing. 'This year the oil-production industry is in crisis,' I hear.

I watch the miller's son, Gérard, who is a tad plumper this year, going about his work. He is using a small iron frying pan to catch the dribbles of pressed liquid so that not a solitary drop is lost or wasted as he changes containers, manoeuvring the trolley to position the next empty canister beneath the running nozzle.

One of the machines gets clogged. Christophe calls to

Gérard and together they push and pull at the appliance. Christophe grows impatient and begins to swear, beating it with a length of wood and then, when nothing seems to make any difference, they both shrug, Provençal style, and continue with what they were previously engaged in. Seconds later, when the machine rights itself, Christophe booms triumphantly while Gérard merely nods and goes about his business.

Everyone has left, carrying off their jars of oil and their receipts. Only the Latin mother and I remain. I smile at her but she remains implacable, her short legs swinging back and forth like those of a small child.

Attending the mill, delivering the olives, seems to be becoming one of my chores, except that it is not a chore. Who would ever have thought that sitting before seven great churning machines could afford me such satisfaction? Why? It is both the beginning and the end of a process. The conclusion for nature of this year's cycle of growth and giving and, for the farmer, the beginning of the journey to the kitchens, the tables, the stomachs – meals celebrated, eaten in ignorance of the labour this oil has required. Also, there are the medicinal properties of this ancient juice. It is indeed a revered offering from the earth, blessed and warmed by the sun and irrigated by the rains. Appassionata's bottles will go as gifts, for we are not running a business.

While I am musing upon who will enjoy the receipts of our bounty, my oil has begun to drizzle through. The matriarch at my side nudges me. I thank her, leap to my feet to run my finger through the spluttering oil, green as a gooseberry, and suck on it. It is lighter, less peppery, more citrony than last year, but fresh and delicious. Smooth and scrumptious. I am delighted and turn to share my delight. The venerable Latin mama gets up and marches towards me. She is from

Italy, she tells me now, but has lived in Provence for years. Then, when my produce is bottled and ready to go, she bends and, with one sweep of the arm, deftly lifts up all the containers and asks me where my car is.

'Please, don't!' I cry.

'*Non, non*,' she insists, 'let me. This is no work for you.' Before I can stop her, this insect-sized woman singlehandedly transports my entire twenty-seven litres to the car, where she deposits them, shakes my hand formally and disappears back inside to await her own goodies.

When I return home I find Quashia in a state of great anxiety. The news from Algeria is worrying. Villages have been destroyed in this spate of blusterous weather. And worse, all telephone communication has been brought down and he cannot contact his family.

'Do you want to leave? Shall I phone for a ticket?' I realise that he must go.

But the country has been closed off. Roads are blocked everywhere. He may not even get through to his district. 'No, I'll stay. Let's wait and see. How was the pressing?' he asks.

'Not bad. Twenty-seven litres. I've left five in the garage next to your clothes.'

'*Mais, non!* That's too much!'

'Don't be ludicrous, Mr Quashia. Without you we wouldn't have any oil at all.'

He bursts out laughing.

I send an e-mail to Michel: 'See you tomorrow. *L'huile nouvelle est arrivée!*'

I write this because it is also the week of the new Beaujolais, and the tidings '*Le Beaujolais Nouveau est arrivé*' are broadcast everywhere: in bars, restaurants, supermarkets. Michel is home for Sunday. We are neither of us fans of this wine, but I buy a bottle just the same, as always, to mark the season, I suppose. It is quite frequently sold in half-litre bottles of a simple and rather lovely shape, and the empties we fill with oil for the kitchen. This year, as every other, we pour two small glasses of the wine, make a toast to the new season's produce and then put the rest in the fridge for cooking.

Michel cannot stay on to help with the olive-gathering. Paris calls, work demands his undivided attention. These pre-production periods are as critical as the timing of a farm's harvest. It has been an all too brief visit. I drive him to the airport and we kiss our heartfelt goodbyes. 'I want to ease up on all this travelling,' he says. 'And spend more time at home with you.' His words serve only to make our parting more difficult.

As I return to the *parking*, in among the huggermugger of cars, the screeching traffic and impatient taxis, I spot a rusting Cortina, a boneshaker of a jalopy with English plates, left carelessly outside a bay. There is a sticker displayed on its rear window which stops me in my tracks. It makes me smile because, before returning to the farm, I have a small errand to perform. The sticker reads:

> Practise random acts of kindness
> Senseless acts of great beauty

The little matter ahead of me might well be judged as senseless but it has been on my mind for a while and I am keen to accomplish it. I take the coast road to Cannes and then pass on through, driving towards the Esterel, with its betelnut red soil. Here the coastline is more rugged, the beaches less busy, though in this early-winter season there are few about. I sight a deserted cove, park the car and clamber down to the water's edge. It is still windy. The waves are lapping at my feet. I dig into my shoulder bag and draw out four, finger-sized excisions from the photographs I took of Barbara and her friends. These are all that remain; the four impermeable shadows that were the Englishwoman. The rest I have torn up and discarded. I set down my bag on a rock, take off my shoes and wade into the water with the four blurred images clutched tightly in my hand. The wind is against me so my original idea of throwing them out to sea won't work; they will only blow back at me. I must wade out further, which is what I do, feeling my jeans grow heavy with salt water. When I think I have shoved out far enough, I bend down and plunge the photos beneath the surface, holding them under long enough to say a silent word or two and to soak them thoroughly so that they will not fly off. Or perhaps they will, who knows? Then I release them, bequeathing my souvenirs of Barbara to the ocean, turn and, without looking back, wade out of the water, rub my feet dry and carry bag and shoes up to the car.

I am trying to contact René but he is nowhere to be found. It is now the beginning of Ramadan. Quashia is working long days gathering olives on an empty stomach. He looks tired, worrying about his children back home. I am concerned for him. Does he want me to drive him to Marseille, help him find a boat passage? He shakes his head, also refusing all offers of so much as a cup of tea, reminding me that between sun-up and sundown nothing, not even a sip of water or a puff of a cigarette, may pass his lips. Still no news from René. Quashia and I are working alone and it is backbreaking. I fall into bed exhausted but cannot sleep because the dogs won't stop barking. Nothing quietens them. If I bring them into the house, they go crazy until I get up and let them out again. They bark and, in the case of Bassett, our little hunter, howl until dawn, until I am ragged and starved of sleep. The *sangliers* are about again. The wild boars are tearing up the land, foraging for food as the autumn fades and the darker season closes in. Quashia says that he spotted a family of six roaming the land the day before yesterday. They have created hummocks of mud and grass roots everywhere in their search for fallen acorns from the oaks. They must be getting very hungry, but with their fossicking I am getting no sleep. Something needs to be done about them.

Eventually, out of the blue, René turns up.

'We haven't heard from you since you came by and took thirty kilos of olives to the mill. How did we do?' I tease, and I am both surprised and uplifted by his response.

'We are the champions,' he boasts. 'The quality is first rate and your olives, along with mine, of course, are producing excellent quantities of oil.'

'Any chance you could lend us a hand?' I ask, but he is occupied at one of his other farms.

'Everyone is gathering, fearing to lose what fruit there is. No time to waste. One of the earliest harvests I've ever experienced. I'm afraid I need my crates. Can you spare them?'

Usually he lends us half a dozen; it is part of our arrangement with him. I cannot spare them, but what can I say?

'I'll be back with them to freight your fruit to the mill,' he promises, and off he goes.

So Quashia and I continue collecting the remainder of the crop ourselves, with nothing to store it in. The fruits on the trees are improving by the day: pudgy purple and jet drupes the size of small plums. I lay them out on a plastic sheet on the floor in the summer kitchen. The cool room reeks of them and, as I turn them, to keep them free of mould, I feel their sponginess; how oliferous they are and what a fine pressing they will make for us.

I confirm with the mill that they will still press for the allotted eighty kilos. Christophe agrees. The problem is I am not sure what quantity we have. I could gauge it easily when we were storing them in René's crates because each holds twenty-five kilos, but now, while every evening our mound gets higher, I have no means of weighing it.

Eventually, I head for the Co-opérative Agricole to buy crates. René claimed that his are only available in Italy, which is why I have never troubled before and why I am not altogether hopeful of finding any, but Frédéric produces half a dozen which he assures me are for olives. They are a different shape and size, but otherwise similar. I ask about the capacity.

'My guess would be around twenty kilos, perhaps twenty-five,' he tells me.

The same as René's, then; even though these are narrower and squarer, they are deeper.

I explain to Quashia later that it should work out the same. We agree to begin the transfer in the morning. After he has left for his cottage, I set about the job myself. I love listening to that gentle rumble as the olives roll and tumble. When the first crate is full, I try to lift it but it is too heavy. So it's a good load, I am thinking.

Suddenly, behind me, at the door, is René.

'I didn't hear your car,' I puff.

'New crates?'

'I had to,' I smile.

He has dropped by to see how we are getting on and to round off a hard day in the fields with a little *apéritif*, which he knows is perenially on offer here.

I dig out a bottle of rosé and we go inside. I am exhausted but not sorry to have company and settle back, ready to hear yet another tale of bygone days in Provence. Tonight his story is of Nina, who collected the groceries.

In the days after the war, René was appointed manager of a sheep farm in the Alp mountains. He arrived to take up his position with his young family in a truck. He was the very first to take a vehicle up into those steep inclines. The shep-

herds and farmers scoffed at him, claiming that such a contraption would break down, and serve no purpose on those
serpentine uphill tracks. He begged to differ and, to show
neighbourly spirit, drove from farm to farm offering to purchase and transport everybody's provisions the next time he
was in town.

Each farmer shook his head and gave the same response,
'Nina shops for me.'

René was intrigued. 'Who is Nina?'

'The mule.'

And, sure enough, one of the locals owned a mule who set
off once a week at dawn, visiting each farm, collecting from
every household a shopping list and the cash to pay for the
goods. They just placed their orders in one of Nina's two
satchels. The mule then hoofed it all alone down the mountainside to the small town below. There she clopped from
shop to shop, where the storeholders collected the lists and
money and replaced them with the requested items. Nina
was rewarded with a sack of hay and, when the shopping
was done, she climbed slowly back up the mountainside,
stopping to eat grass wherever she fancied, but making sure
she was back by sunset. On one occasion, René's truck gave
up, marooning him in the middle of nowhere. Night was
drawing in, and he was hungry, cold and had no way of getting help – until he sighted the homebound mule. He
scribbled a note and put it into Nina's packed satchel. The
note read: 'Broken down. Need a tow.' The mule relayed the
message back to the next farmstead and René and vehicle
were retrieved, much to the merriment of the mountain
locals.

Ah, he makes me giggle, does René. But tonight, as he is
leaving, he also disturbs me with the comment: 'You know,
Carol, you should weigh those crates; they won't hold half as
much fruit as mine.'

'Surely they will, René?'

'*Mais, non.*'

The next morning Quashia and I agree that having waited ten days for an appointment at the mill – bookings are impossible to come by because everyone is harvesting at the same time – it would be a disaster if, when our load was delivered, it proved to be insufficient and I was obliged to throw in my lot with some unidentified farmer the quality of whose drupes I cannot hazard.

I run to the guest bathroom to fetch the weighing scales.

'Good idea,' laughs Quashia, and heaves the charged crate on to it. We are dismayed to discover that the entire crate-load weighs only ten kilos.

'That can't be right! The scales must be wrong.' We empty out the olives and put the empty crate on the balance. It weighs less than 200 grammes. The scales are accurate.

We have thirty-six hours left before I am due at the mill and it seems we have gathered only fifty kilos of fruit. Quashia encourages me. 'If we keep going, work until sun-down, whatever the weather, we can make our mound.'

I see that he is tired, hours without a break, or food; I send him home to eat. The rules of his faith allow that during the season of Ramadan, of diurnal fasting, he can break his fast at sunset. I continue on alone in the garden. The trees seem as laden as they were when we began, days back. And many of the olives which have fallen to the ground and are lying in the nets have been eaten; all that remains of them are the stones. It's curious that the birds are so avaricious this year, a lean year for olives, when there is plenty of food for them elsewhere. Driving through the country lanes I have noticed bushes weighed down with bright orange berries, clusters and clusters of them. Our bay trees, too, are gravid with shiny, tar-black globules.

After the recent tempestuous winds and dramatic overnight storms, the evening has turned still. The sky is almost cloudless and there is – one of my favourite perfumes – nuttiness, woodsmoke in the air. It turns the light a mulberry-blue. I work alone, collecting errant drupes hidden beneath stones or plants, until it is too dark to see and I realise that I am gathering fallen acorns by mistake. An olive branch whips against my eye and it begins to smart and weep. Time to stop, time for a glass of wine, I tell myself, and climb back up to the summer kitchen with my laden pails. As I empty my freshly gathered fruit into the crate it dawns on me that I feel deep satisfaction; I am at peace. The pain, the loss and the sense of failure which have been tearing at me are easing.

For me the gathering of olives is a therapy. Some knit or embroider; I grow, gather and press olives. I enjoy the air on my cheeks, the earth beneath my destroyed fingernails, the rich aromas of the damp soil, the birdsong all around me; the simplicity and authenticity of life in the garden. It makes sense; adds up; doesn't demand comprehension, though it does demand commitment and can be physically backbreaking. But even that I enjoy: working until I am dead beat.

All the next day we toil. The blustering wind is up again, the sky slate-coloured. By lunchtime we have another ten kilos, which means we are still at least twenty short. I go upstairs to my office, using the interlude to catch up on my messages. Afterwards, I go back outside and find Quashia climbing among the silvery branches of one of the older trees.

'Did you eat?' he calls out to me as I descend the drive with my empty buckets.

'No time.' I am bending to gather the fallen fruit concealed within the windblown nets.

'You'll never get fat on the slithers of food you consume,' he shouts from his neighbouring tree.

'I don't think that's a problem I'll ever have to worry about,' I jape in return.

'How much do you think I weigh?'

'No idea.'

'Ten kilos!' And he roars with laughter. 'I just stepped on your scales. Ten kilos! Then I put one of the flowerpots on. Ten kilos. Everything weighs ten kilos!'

'No!'

We return to the summer kitchen and conduct several tests, weighing everything in sight. The scales are accurate up to ten kilos but above that the machine is blocked. We have been pushing ourselves needlessly; we have more than the quota stipulated by the mill.

We continue gathering but now the pressure is off. Our mood grows lighthearted and there are great cries when Quashia discovers a robin trapped beneath one of the nets. He brings it to show me, clutched between his work-scarred hands, and at first I think the little creature is dead or wounded. Bassett and Lucky lope along beside him, alert to possible prey.

'Please don't squash him!'

The tiny bird with its downy pumpkin-orange breast trembles, turning its minute head with terrified eyes this way and that, pinned in the warm, earthy clutch of this new and unfamiliar threat.

'He looks so fragile. Is he injured?' I ask.

'No, but he was panicking and flapping, tangled up in all that netting.'

'He's probably freaked. Release your grip a little and see what happens, but watch out for these two.' The dogs are panting at our heels. 'If the bird is injured we'll have to nurse him indoors or these hounds of ours will nab him,' I say, but the moment Quashia unclenches his grip, the tiny thing zips from the muddy cave of fingers and flees to its arboreal refuge in the sprucy pine forest up behind the house.

Later, having harvested all that there is time for, Quashia and I settle in the summer kitchen. Our crates are filled to bursting and on the floor, laid out on the plastic sheet, is our most recently gathered pile. Because we have worked under such constraint there has been no time to sort through, *trier*, these fruits; they are mixed with leaves, bits of twig, blades of grass and the remains of bird-eaten fruits. I am not allowed to deliver such unwinnowed pickings; we need to sift them, this hillock of what must be another forty kilos. Seated cross-legged on cushions on the tiled floor, either side of the laden sheet, we begin to work. Outside it is dark; in here it is cold and our breath rises like smoke because I have turned off the radiator to preserve the oil in the drupes. The heat would dry them out. Thelonius Monk plays on the old stereo system in the corner. We work in concentrated silence until I ask Quashia about his first wife, the mother of all those children I saw on the wedding video, who died so young.

He smiles and says nothing, staring into the speckled quilt of fruits at his fingertips.

'Sorry, I didn't mean to intrude.'

He shrugs. 'You ask many questions. What do you want to know?'

'How did you meet her? Who chose her for you?'

He shakes his head. 'My father died when I was twelve or thirteen. I've told you all that.'

'Yes.'

'I chose my wife. I was sixteen, she was fifteen. In those days, before the war with France, the system was less strict and we could marry younger, which is better. Look at me now: sixty-seven years old, all my children grown up and married and I have twenty-eight grandchildren with plenty more to come. That's how it should be. These days people wait too long, women don't have children. My present wife, she never had children. It's not good.' He pauses and I don't know if it has crossed his mind that I am one of those women. It certainly crosses mine.

'Tell me about your first wife, what was her name?'

'Nadia. Oh, she was beautiful! *Comme elle était belle!* There never was a woman as beautiful who walked this earth. Aside from you, of course, Carol.' He glances up shyly and we both grin. I clench my fists and press them to my lips to blow on them. My fingers are stiff with cold. I shift position on the cushions; one of my legs has cramp.

'We had nine children but two died, both at seventeen months. A boy and a girl, both walking and talking. We never knew why. In those days the hospitals and medical conditions in Algeria were very bad. It broke Nadia's heart. She never got over the loss of them, even though there were seven others to keep house for. She was living with my mother. I came here to France when I was seventeen to join my brother who, as you know, was run over and killed by an American Jeep. I went home whenever I could and I sent money every month. Fortunately, the bond she formed with my mother was very special. My mother looked on her as a daughter; she nursed Nadia at the end. The cancer was everywhere. She was forty-four and our youngest son, the one you saw on the video getting married, was only two.'

We continue for a while in silence. He is in his past with his beautiful Nadia.

'It took me ten years to find another wife. This woman is also kind and gentle, but she's very thin, fragile, like that robin I found. You'll see when you come to Algeria and meet her. Nadia was robust and strong, muscular and hefty, like you, Carol. Built like an ox.'

I hope I'm *not*, I am thinking.

'Yet she was the one to die. My mother survived till ninety. She returns, visits and talks to me regularly, as does my father, but never Nadia. Nadia's never been back to see me.'

I am surprised by this remark. This man who labours for our land, who is of the earth, always practical, is talking to me about spirits.

'Do you see your father, Carol?' he asks. 'Does he come to visit you?'

'I think so. Certainly, I am aware of his presence in my life and I light a candle to him every day. Well, most days.'

'My parents come to me in the village house where we lived, where one of my boys now lives. Never in my new house. Well, these matters are private, aren't they?'

'Might Nadia be sad that you remarried?'

'Oh, no! She would have wanted it. I don't know where she is or why she doesn't talk to me. We grew up together. I chose her, gave her my word that she would always be mine and she knows that I would never break that word. She will always be my sweetheart.'

The record has finished and I don't get up to change it. While Quashia dreams of Nadia, I consider our relationship and what a curious but special one it is. Who would have thought it? This creased-faced Arab, in his Persian wool hat and socks with the toes worn through, cross-legged on my floor, me opposite him. As he so often claims, we are family. I know and believe it now. And I thank whoever is out there, listening to us, watching over us, that he and we have been brought together. Quashia is the guardian angel of this farm.

I wake stiff as a board, back aching, to whiffs of last night's log fire still smouldering in the hearth. Outside, the day is warm and bright. I swim in the pool in the late November sunshine, splashing fast, to and fro, in the icy-cold water like a plump otter, and hurry to get dressed, ready for my second visit to the mill.

The hills are cloudy green and rusty oak. Low clouds hang around the mountains. An incongruous sight on the way through Grasse is a falcon perched atop a set of traffic lights. I weigh in our olive load at 124 kilos. Hurrah!

Once the forms have been dealt with, I am greeted below, at mill level, by a handful of men staring at a whacking great basin of olives and shaking their heads despondently. *'Trop vieilles, trop vertes,'* they are moaning. Moving alongside them, I glance at the harvest about to be pressed and must agree that the drupes do look rather sorry for themselves: skins peeling, flesh disintegrating, old yet still green.

I ask the worker who shovels and carts, always a cigarette glued to his lips: 'What variety of olive is this?'

'Fuck knows,' he answers, and slouches away.

My questions and constant interest bemuse these *oléicul-teurs.* They are not fussed about the pressing process; they grow animated only when the oil begins to drip through. Passionate or despairing, they wear their emotions on their leathered faces. Arms folded, aimlessly pacing, they await the results, knowing the yield will be mean. They watch in silence, hoping for the best. Like the weather, this process carries with it a combination of unpredictable factors. I observe five men bent like storks staring silently at a pipe, and then the oil begins to arrive, to drip and now gush.

'Pas mal, pas mal,' they are saying. 'Considering the weather.'

'Bah, the weather,' one bleats, but their mood is softening. They chatter and begin to laugh, hands dancing, extrovert once more.

Gérard, the *fils* of Christophe, pays them no heed. He is cleaning, shunting bottles, stainless-steel containers, washing with jet sprays. A gush here, another there. He is careful never to mix one client's produce with another's. A sacrosanct affair.

Our turn next.

Christophe bustles in, a ladder rather too large for this confined space on his shoulders. He is shouting and waving, shaking hands with everyone. Due to the weight of his paunch, he waddles like a duck.

'What news of your AOC?' he bawls at me.

I sigh. 'We are still waiting.'

'*Ah, oui*,' he shrugs, as though life is nothing but a business of waiting.

Our pressing begins. I pass the time talking to a retired mason who has thirty trees. He bought his plot as a hobby for his retirement. He moans about how hard it is to maintain the price of oil. 'I tried to sell for sixty francs a litre but nobody would buy. Now I sell at fifty and they buy, but they are not happy. They moan: "*Trop cher*."'

'Perhaps because they can drive across the border into Italy and pick up oil at thirty francs a litre,' I suggest.

'*Mais oui*, but the Italians are like the Moroccans. They mix their olive oil with cashew and pistachio oils to be more competitive on the international market.'

I try to protest that this cannot possibly be so, but he will not have it.

During a lull in the proceedings I jot down what the mason has told me. He crosses over to me. 'Are you writing about me?' he demands.

'No,' I lie.

'What, then? What are you writing?'

'Ideas,' I stammer, feeling embarrassed, wishing I had left my notebook where it was in my bag. 'A thought here and there, strung together.'

'Stories,' he continues. 'You're like the Italians. Mix a bit of this and that and call it extra virgin. There's no such thing as *extra* virgin. Either she's a virgin or she's not!' He roars with lascivious laughter.

And now the moment for our oil. I rush to the spout and watch those first drips plopping into the steel dish. Others gather around me. All is silent. I cast my gaze across the intent faces, peering from face to weatherworn face, and then I return to the deep sea-green liquid. I am apprehensive. Though I know the yield will be less than last year, I long for it to be excellent. Suddenly, I catch myself as these others might see me. My expression is sombre, concentrated, just like theirs. I am no different. This transformation from drupe to oil is as sacred and as important to me as it is to any of these farmers. I burst into a broad smile. Would I rather be learning lines or drinking champagne at the Ivy? No, not today. For this moment in time, this olive season, I feel content, I am complete. I have melded with the old order. I have become one of them.

Upstairs, as I approach the cash desk to pay for our pressing, I spy Christophe slumped on a trolley. 'How did you do?' he calls out to me as one gambler might ask of another.

'Catastrophic!' I cry, feigning despair.

He takes me seriously and clambers to his feet, huffing and puffing. '*Mon Dieu*. How many litres?'

'Sixteen.'

'That's better than most. Look at this morning's yields. And it's the quality. You have the quality. What would you do with thirty litres of dishwater? And wait till you've planted those two hundred young trees. You'll get your AOC, have no fear. It takes time. Life takes time.'

We all shake hands as Gérard, the *fils,* interrupts his work to hump my *bidons* of oil to the boot of my car.

'I wouldn't do this for anyone else,' he mutters shyly.

'Thank you,' I tell him, genuinely touched by his kindness.

Everyone shakes hands again and the frightful mason attempts to kiss me while the rest of us are merrily waving and calling, 'See you soon!'

'Four kilos to the litre next time!'

A curious band we make, I am thinking, as I trundle off down the hill in a happy frame of mind.

200 New Possibilities

Spring. The weather is delicious. Blossoms have spread like confetti across the garden. Blue-black hornets in the wistaria. Scurrying lizards everywhere, exposing nutmeg stomachs as they flip and slither into stone cracks. The air is dusty with yellow pollen from the fir trees and cedars. When the wind gets up, it carries the powder like a carpet of egg yolk.

Michel and I are out in the garden, occupied with stakes for the planting of the 200 olive saplings that were delivered two days ago.

This planting requires strategic planning: the aspects of the sun, the growth rates of the olive trees, avoidance of the shadows of the towering pines and, in accordance with Michel's perennial preoccupation, *überblick,* or the overview – the overall pattern of the groves. Michel rooted around in the garage for paint and found a pot of a lime-green colour which has barely been touched. It had been destined for the kitchen but, after one wall was painted, it was quickly rejected. He handed it, with brush and stirring stick, to me. In order that we do not forget where each tree is to be planted, he decided that we should make a tour of the entire land, place a small mound of stones or a stick at each planting spot and, in case the dogs or wild boars knock them about, mark them. Hence the paint. My job is to paint the stones.

We have been at this work for two days. Today is the last and we are dressed for guests and celebration but shod in wellies. As ever, the dogs are trailing at our heels. In the distance a backdrop of foxglove-mauve mountains, the spring Alps. There are birds everywhere. I spot one I have never seen before. He is large and lime green – the colour of my paint. His head is holly-berry red and he has sooty markings on his face. His beak is hammering powerfully at the grassed earth. I ditch my can and dig into my pockets in search of pen and thick, spiral notebook curled with use and crammed tight with ideas and daily sightings. I begin to scribble: 'Tree Planting, morning one: I see a hell of a big Green Woodpecker; he is whacking his beak at the ground, foraging for insects. They are known to plunder anthills.'

Michel is calling to me. '*Chérie*, we have a hundred and seventy positions marked, but thirty to go. It will soon be lunchtime. We have dozens of people arriving, and, I don't know about you, but I am looking forward to a glass of champagne in the sun on the terrace. *Depêche-toi!*'

I lift my head and laugh. 'You're right,' I call. 'Friends are coming. Let's finish our work and crack open that champagne.'

We walk back up to the house, hand in hand, passing on our way the 200 six-year-old trees standing in tight lines at the top of the garden. A lake of silver vitality raring to get going. Trees that, when they reach a hundred years old, will be smiled upon by Provençals and called toddlers. Trees that are the signature tune of Provence. Today we will begin the business of putting these saplings in the earth, where they will stay for centuries, long beyond our fleeting lifetimes, and to celebrate this occasion we have invited friends and colleagues to Come and Plant a Tree, drink champagne, stay for lunch, come for the weekend or just pop by.

Each tree will bear the name of its planter. René is coming; the water diviner and his Corsican wife; Lord Harry, whose wife has returned to him and we have yet to meet; Christophe and Gérard; our vet, who always arrives with flowers for his favourite actress. The gentle beemaster will drop by too to meet Michel and, I hope, finalise the arrangements for our hives; friends are convening from England, Germany and locally.

I want to mark these days of planting. To celebrate them joyously. And when these junior trees, this rip-roaring chorus of olive trees, are in the ground, growing splendidly, we can be classified as genuine farmers by the bodies who count. We are now affiliated to, have been contacted by, been sent information about, among others, the following organisations: ONIOL, La Chambre d'Agriculture, FDGEDA, FOPO, FSPAOC, FNPHP, FCO, SNM, FEDICO, AFIDOL, CEAO, ONIDOL, COPEXO – and the list will not end there. We have been registered as one of 20,000 olive-growers in France. Between us, we produce three and a half million tons of olives over 20,000 hectares. Our handsome young chief from the Chambre d'Agriculture, who will also call in tomorrow, has written a booklet, *A Practical Guide to Organic Olive Farming in the Alpes-Maritimes*, and has very generously sent us a copy, along with a promise to assist us make this step in earnest.

Our tables are groaning with food. The fridges are

crammed with chilled bottles. And the sun is shining. To any farmer, to Lord Harry with his apricots or a longstanding olive or fruit farmer, this step is a humble one, but to us, who started out with a newly discovered love and a crumbling house by the sea, who never in our wildest dreams saw ourselves in the role of farmers, this is an exciting, challenging decision. We are striking root – digging deeper, nurturing our discoveries, expanding and enriching our love affair with the Midi, with the ancient ways of this mythical land known since Roman times as Provincia: Provence.

There is an Arab proverb that Quashia – I hear him digging holes and preparing the soil for the trees up behind the villa – sometimes quotes. 'When the house is finished, death walks in the door.' This house, this smallholding, has a long way to go yet before its crumbling walls and unmade kitchens and unconstructed bedrooms and dusty stables are plastered, painted and furnished and, please God, death is and will remain occupied elsewhere.

Quashia spies us approaching and waves us up. Lucky bounds on ahead.

'Who's planting the first one?' he calls.

'You should,' returns Michel. 'Quashia's tree.'

'I'll get your camera.' I hurry on inside and hike up the hill with the Nikon.

Quashia has sent Michel off to fill two buckets with water. 'You go first,' he tells me.

'No, you.'

But he insists, and begins unpotting one of the half a dozen saplings standing in black plastic pots at his side. I take the baby from him and settle it gently into the earth, straightening it, welcoming it to the farm, as Quashia hands me a shovel. 'Pack the earth in tightly around it,' he orders.

I start shovelling. Michel returns with the water, picks up the camera from beside my feet and snaps. 'Carol's tree!'

And then another as I pour the water, and another with Quashia at my side, and then another and another. 'Who's next?'

Three six-year-old trees are planted and numerous photographs taken to record the occasion. Our new, extended grove is finally underway. I hear a car purring up the drive. The first of our visitors. It's party time.

The olive tree is a symbol of peace, of wisdom, eternity and continual rebirth. The births that I will know will not be my own children, children seeded by Michel and born of my loins. My children will not take form in the physical sense. They will be born of my passion, of my creativity, such as it is. There will be stories to hear, to narrate and pass on, there will be harvests to gather and the fruits of that labour to share, there will be friends to meet and make films with, there is the love of a man who is remarkable and who stands like an oak at my side, and there is the continuous but nonetheless inspiring discovery that pain and loss recoup life and regeneration.

I am learning, slowly, and not without heartache, to take what there is, to accept it gratefully, to *celebrate* it, treasure it, to seed it and work with it, before time passes. But as time passes there will always be new damage and renovation to address, the swings and roundabouts, the helterskelters of our lives and our damaged hearts. That's it, that is the moulding of my life. It's not a profound philosophy or a secret. It is quite simply the loudly joyous choice of paths at the crossroads. But it has taken me time to see it through the fogs of my own making. Still, as Christophe at the mill so succinctly remarked: 'Life takes time.'

And I would add to that, healing also takes time.

I never took the time to grieve the loss of my little girl, and to heal myself.

Carrot.

Only when I began to write about her did I unfold fragile memories; memories returning to be cried over and released. Perhaps the most extraordinary miracle has been that, as I wept for her and let her go, she returned. She bounced back smiling and full of life. These days her spirit is here with me everywhere. I see her now. She soars and laughs through the breeze or the still heat in the olive trees; she weeps with the rain at my shortsightedness and her smile radiates the day no less than the sun. She *is* this book. My child. My gift to Michel.